THE WORKS OF
LUCIAN OF SAMOSATA

TRANSLATED BY

H. W. FOWLER AND F. G. FOWLER

What work nobler than transplanting foreign thought into the barren domestic soil? except indeed planting thought of your own, which the fewest are privileged to do.

—Sarlor Resarlus.

At each flaw, be this your first thought:
the author doubtless said something quite different, and much more to the point. And then you may hiss *me* off, if you will.

—LUCIAN, *Nigrinus, 9.*

(LUCIAN) The last great master of Attic eloquence and Attic wit.

— Lord Macaulay.

I

CONTENTS

INTRODUCTION

1. LIFE.
2. PROBABLE ORDER OF WRITINGS.
3. CIRCUMSTANCES OF THE TIME.
4. LUCIAN AS A WRITER.

It is not to be understood that all statements here made are either ascertained facts or universally admitted conjectures. The introduction is intended merely to put those who are not scholars, and probably have not books of reference at hand, in a position to approach the translation at as little disadvantage as may be. Accordingly, we give the account that commends itself to us, without discussion or reference to authorities. Those who would like a more complete idea of Lucian should read Croiset's *Essai sur la vie et les oeuvres de Lucien*, on which the first two sections of this introduction are very largely based. The only objections to the book (if they are objections) are that it is in French, and of 400 octavo pages. It is eminently readable.

1. LIFE

With the exception of a very small number of statements, of which the truth is by no means certain, all that we know of Lucian is derived from his own writings. And any reader who prefers to have his facts at first rather than at second hand can consequently get them by reading certain of his pieces, and making the natural deductions from them. Those that contain biographical matter are, in the order corresponding to the periods of his life on which they throw light, *The Vision, Demosthenes, Nigrinus, The Portrait-study* and *Defence* (in which Lucian is *Lycinus*), *The Way to write History, The double ndictment* (in which he is *The Syrian*), *The Fisher* (*Parrhesiades*), *Swans and Amber, Alexander*, Hermotimus_ (*Lycinus*), *Menippus and Icaromenippus* (in which *Menippus* represents him), *A literary Prometheus, Herodotus, Zeuxis, Harmonides, The Scythian*, The Death of Peregrine, The Book-fancier, Demonax, The Rhetorician's Vade mecum, Dionysus, Heracles, A Slip of the Tongue, Apology for 'The dependent Scholar.'_ Of these *The Vision* is a direct piece of autobiography; there is intentional but veiled autobiography in several of the other pieces; in others again conclusions can be drawn from comparison of his statements with facts known from external sources.

Lucian lived from about 125 to about 200 A.D., under the Roman Emperors Antoninus Pius, M. Aurelius and Lucius Verus, Commodus, and perhaps Pertinax. He was a Syrian, born at Samosata on the Euphrates, of parents to whom it was of importance that he should earn his living without spending much time or money on education. His maternal uncle being a statuary, he was apprenticed to him, having shown an aptitude for modelling in the wax that he surreptitiously scraped from his school writing-tablets. The apprenticeship lasted one day. It is clear that he was impulsive all through life; and when his uncle corrected him with a stick for breaking a piece of marble, he ran off home, disposed already to think he had had enough of statuary. His mother took his part, and he made up his mind by the aid of a vision that came to him the same night.

It was the age of the rhetoricians. If war was not a thing of the past, the shadow of the *pax Romana* was over all the small states, and the aspiring provincial's readiest road to fame was through words rather than deeds. The arrival of a famous rhetorician to lecture was one of the important events in any great city's annals; and Lucian's works are full of references to the impression these men produced, and the envy they enjoyed. He himself was evidently consumed, during his youth and early manhood, with desire for a position like theirs. To him, sleeping with memories of the stick, appeared two women, corresponding to *Virtue* and *Pleasure* in Prodicus's *Choice of Heracles*—the working woman *Statuary*, and the lady *Culture*. They advanced their claims to him in turn; but before *Culture* had completed her reply, the choice was made: he was to be a rhetorician. From her reminding him that she was even now not all unknown to him, we may perhaps assume that he spoke some sort of Greek, or was being taught it; but he assures us that after leaving Syria he was still a barbarian; we have also a casual mention of his offering a lock of his hair to the Syrian goddess in his youth.

He was allowed to follow his bent and go to Ionia. Great Ionian cities like Smyrna and Ephesus were full of admired sophists or teachers of rhetoric. But it is unlikely that Lucian's means would have enabled him to become the pupil of these. He probably acquired his skill to a great extent by the laborious method, which he ironically deprecates in *The Rhetorician's Vade mecum*, of studying exhaustively the old Attic orators, poets, and historians.

He was at any rate successful. The different branches that a rhetorician might choose between or combine were: (1) Speaking in court on behalf of a client; (2) Writing speeches for a client to deliver; (3) Teaching pupils; (4) Giving public displays of his skill. There is a doubtful statement that Lucian failed in (1), and took to (2) in default. His surviving rhetorical pieces (*The Tyrannicide, The Disinherited, Phalaris*) are declamations on hypothetical cases which might serve either for (3) or (4); and *The Hall, The Fly, Dipsas*, and perhaps *Demosthenes*, suggest (4). A common form of exhibition was for a sophist to appear before an audience and let them propose subjects, of which he must choose one and deliver an impromptu oration upon it.

Whatever his exact line was, he earned an income in Ionia, then in Greece, had still greater success in Italy, and appears to have settled for some time in Gaul, perhaps occupying a professorial chair there. The intimate knowledge of Roman life in some aspects which appears in *The dependent Scholar* suggests that he also lived some time in Rome. He seems to have known some Latin, since he could converse with boatmen on the Po; but his only clear reference (A Slip of the Tongue,) implies an imperfect knowledge of it; and there is not a single mention in all his works, which are crammed with literary allusions, of any Latin author. He claims to have been during his time in Gaul one of the rhetoricians who could command high fees; and his descriptions of himself as resigning his place close about his lady's (i.e. Rhetoric's) person, and as casting off his wife Rhetoric because she did not keep herself exclusively to him, show that he regarded himself, or wished to be regarded, as having been at the head of his profession.

This brings us to about the year 160 A.D. We may conceive Lucian now to have had some of that yearning for home which he ascribes in the *Patriotism* even to the successful exile. He returned home, we suppose, a distinguished man at thirty-five, and enjoyed impressing the fact on his fellow citizens in *The Vision*. He may then have lived at Antioch as a rhetorician for some years, of which we have a memorial in *The Portrait-study*. Lucius Verus, M. Aurelius's colleague, was at Antioch in 162 or 163 A.D. on his way to the Parthian war, and *The Portrait-study* is a panegyric on Verus's mistress Panthea, whom Lucian saw there.

A year or two later we find him migrating to Athens, taking his father with him, and at Athens he settled and remained many years. It was on this journey that the incident occurred, which he relates with such a curious absence of shame in the *Alexander*, of his biting that charlatan's hand.

This change in his manner of life corresponds nearly with the change in habit of mind and use of his powers that earned him his immortality. His fortieth year is the date given by himself for his abandonment of Rhetoric and, as he calls it, taking up with Dialogue, or, as we might say, becoming a man of letters. Between Rhetoric and Dialogue there was a feud, which had begun when Socrates five centuries before had fought his battles with the sophists. Rhetoric appeals to the emotions and obscures the issues (such had been Socrates's position); the way to elicit truth is by short question and answer. The Socratic method, illustrated by Plato, had become, if not the only, the accredited instrument of philosophers, who, so far as they are genuine, are truth-seekers; Rhetoric had been left to the legal persons whose object is not truth but victory. Lucian's abandonment of Rhetoric was accordingly in some sort his change from a lawyer to a philosopher. As it turned out, however, philosophy was itself only a transitional stage with him.

Already during his career as a rhetorician, which we may put at 145-164 A.D., he seems both to have had leanings to philosophy, and to have toyed with dialogue. There is reason to suppose that the Nigrinus_, with its strong contrast between the noise and vulgarity of Rome and the peace and culture of Athens, its enthusiastic picture of the charm of philosophy for a sensitive and intelligent spirit, was written in 150 A.D., or at any rate described an incident that occurred in that year; and the *Portrait-study* and its *Defence*, dialogues written with great care, whatever their other merits, belong to 162 or 163 A.D. But these had been excursions out of his own province. After settling at Athens he seems to have adopted the writing of dialogues as his regular work. The

Toxaris, a collection of stories on friendship, strung together by dialogue, the *Anacharsis*, a discussion on the value of physical training, and the *Pantomime*, a description slightly relieved by the dialogue form, may be regarded as experiments with his new instrument. There is no trace in them of the characteristic use that he afterwards made of dialogue, for the purposes of satire.

That was an idea that we may suppose to have occurred to him after the composition of the *Hermotimus*. This is in form the most philosophic of his dialogues; it might indeed be a dialogue of Plato, of the merely destructive kind; but it is at the same time, in matter, his farewell to philosophy, establishing that the pursuit of it is hopeless for mortal man. From this time onward, though he always professes himself a lover of true philosophy, he concerns himself no more with it, except to expose its false professors. The dialogue that perhaps comes next, *The Parasite*, is still Platonic in form, but only as a parody; its main interest (for a modern reader is outraged, as in a few other pieces of Lucian's, by the disproportion between subject and treatment) is in the combination for the first time of satire with dialogue.

One more step remained to be taken. In the piece called *A literary Prometheus*, we are told what Lucian himself regarded as his claim to the title of an original writer. It was the fusing of Comedy and Dialogue—the latter being the prose conversation hat had hitherto been confined to philosophical discussion. The new literary form, then, was conversation, frankly for purposes of entertainment, as in Comedy, but to be read and not acted. In this kind of writing he remains, though he has been often imitated, first in merit as clearly as in time; and nearly all his great masterpieces took this form. They followed in rapid succession, being all written, perhaps, between 165 and 175 A.D. And we make here no further comment upon them, except to remark that they fall roughly into three groups as he drew inspiration successively from the writers of the New Comedy (or Comedy of ordinary life) like Menander, from the satires of Menippus, and from writers of the Old Comedy (or Comedy of fantastic imagination) like Aristophanes. The best specimens of the first group are *The Liar* and the *Dialogues of the Hetaerae;* of the second, the *Dialogues of the Dead* and *of the Gods, Menippus* and *Icaromenippus, Zeus cross-examined;* of the third, *Timon, Charon, A Voyage to the lower World, The Sale of Creeds, The Fisher, Zeus Tragoedus, The Cock, The double Indictment, The Ship.*

During these ten or more years, though he lived at Athens, he is to be imagined travelling occasionally, to read his dialogues to audiences in various cities, or to see the Olympic Games. And these excursions gave occasion to some works not of the dialogue kind; the *Zeuxis* and several similar pieces are introductions to series of readings away from Athens; The *Way to write History*, a piece of literary criticism still very readable, if out of date for practical purposes, resulted from a visit to Ionia, where all the literary men were producing histories of the Parthian war, then in progress (165 A.D.). An attendance at the Olympic Games of 169 A.D. suggested *The Death of Peregrine*, which in its turn, through the offence given to Cynics, had to be supplemented by the dialogue of *The Runaways*. *The True History*, most famous, but, admirable as it is, far from best of his works, presumably belongs to this period also, but cannot be definitely placed. The *Book-fancier* and *The Rhetorician's Vade mecum* are unpleasant records of bitter personal quarrels.

After some ten years of this intense literary activity, producing, reading, and publishing, Lucian seems to have given up both the writing of dialogues and the presenting of them to audiences, and to have lived quietly for many years. The only pieces that belong here are the *Life of Demonax*, the man whom he held the best of all philosophers, and with whom he had been long intimate at Athens, and that of Alexander, the Asiatic charlatan, who was the prince of impostors as Demonax of philosophers. When quite old, Lucian was appointed by the Emperor Commodus to a well-paid legal post in Egypt. We also learn, from the new introductory lectures called *Dionysus* and *Heracles*, that he resumed the practice of reading his dialogues; but he wrote nothing more of importance. It is stated in Suidas that he was torn to pieces by dogs; but, as other statements in the article are discredited, it is supposed that this is the Christian revenge for Lucian's imaginary hostility to Christianity. We have it from himself that he suffered from gout in his old age. He solaced himself characteristically by writing a play on the subject; but whether the goddess Gout, who gave it its name, was appeased by it, or carried him off, we cannot tell.

2. PROBABLE ORDER OF WRITINGS

The received order in which Lucian's works stand is admitted to be entirely haphazard. The following arrangement in groups is roughly chronological, though it is quite possible that they overlap each other. It is M. Croiset's, put into tabular form. Many details in it are open to question; but to read in this order would at least be more satisfactory to any one who wishes to study Lucian seriously than to take the pieces as they come. The table will also serve as a rough guide to the first-class and the inferior pieces. The names italicized are those of pieces rejected as spurious by M. Croiset, and therefore not placed by him; we have inserted them where they seem to belong; as to their genuineness, it is our opinion that the objections made (not by M. Croiset, who does not discuss authenticity) to the *Demosthenes* and *The Cynic* at least are, in view of the merits of these, unconvincing.

(i) About 145 to 160 A.D. Lucian a rhetorician in Ionia, Greece, Italy, and Gaul.

The Tyrannicide, a rhetorical exercise.

The Disinherited.

Phalaris I & II.

Demosthenes, a panegyric.

Patriotism, an essay.

The Fly, an essay.

Swans and Amber, an introductory lecture.

Dipsas, an introductory lecture.

The Hall, an introductory lecture.

Nigrinus, a dialogue on philosophy, 150 A.D.

(ii) About 160 to 164 A.D. After Lucian's return to Asia.

The Portrait-study, a panegyric in dialogue, 162 A.D.

Defence of The Portrait-study, in dialogue.

A Trial in the Court of Vowels, a *jeu d'esprit*.

Hesiod, a short dialogue.

The Vision, an autobiographical address.

(iii) About 165 A.D. At Athens.

Pantomime, art criticism in dialogue.

Anacharsis, a dialogue on physical training.

Toxaris, stories of friendship in dialogue.

Slander, a moral essay.

The Way to write History, an essay in literary criticism.

The next eight groups, iv-xi, belong to the years from about 165 A.D. to about 175 A.D., when Lucian was at his best and busiest; iv-ix are to be regarded roughly as succeeding each other in time; x and xi being independent in this respect. Pieces are assigned to groups mainly according to their subjects; but some are placed in groups that do not seem at first sight the most appropriate, owing to specialties in their treatment; e.g. *The Ship* might seem more in place with vii than with ix; but M. Croiset finds in it a maturity that induces him to put it later.

(iv) About 165 A.D.

Hermotimus, a philosophic dialogue.

The Parasite, a parody of a philosophic dialogue.

(v) Influence of the New Comedy writers.

The Liar, a dialogue satirizing superstition.

A Feast of Lapithae, a dialogue satirizing the manners of philosophers.

Dialogues of the Hetaerae, a series of short dialogues.

(vi) Influence of the Menippean satire.

Dialogues of the Dead, a series of short dialogues.

Dialogues of the Gods, a series of short dialogues.

Dialogues of the Sea-Gods, a series of short dialogues.

Menippus, a dialogue satirizing philosophy.

Icaromenippus, a dialogue satirizing philosophy and religion.

Zeus cross-examined, a dialogue satirizing religion.

The Cynic, a dialogue against luxury.

Of Sacrifice, an essay satirizing religion.

Saturnalia, dialogue and letters on the relation of rich and poor.

The True History, a parody of the old Greek historians,

12

(vii) Influence of the Old Comedy writers:
vanity of human wishes.
A Voyage to the Lower World, a dialogue on the vanity of power.
Charon, a dialogue on the vanity of all things.
Timon, a dialogue on the vanity of riches.
The Cock, a dialogue on the vanity of riches and power,
(viii) Influence of the Old Comedy writers:
dialogues satirizing religion.
Prometheus on Caucasus.
Zeus Tragoedus.
The Gods in Council.
(ix) Influence of the Old Comedy writers:
satire on philosophers.
The Ship, a dialogue on foolish aspirations.
The Life of Peregrine, a narrative satirizing the Cynics, 169 A.D.
The Runaways, a dialogue satirizing the Cynics.
The double Indictment, an autobiographic dialogue.
The Sale of Creeds, a dialogue satirizing philosophers.
The Fisher, an autobiographic dialogue satirizing philosophers.
(x) 165-175 A.D. Introductory lectures.
Herodotus.
Zeuxis.
Harmonides.
The Scythian.
A literary Prometheus.
(xi) 165-175 A.D. Scattered pieces standing apart from the great dialogue series, but written during the same period.
The Book-fancier, an invective. About 170 A.D.
The Purist purized, a literary satire in dialogue.
Lexiphanes, a literary satire in dialogue.
The Rhetorician's Vade-mecum, a personal satire. About 178 A.D.
(xii) After 180 A.D.
Demonax, a biography.
Alexander, a satirical biography,
(xiii) In old age.
Mourning, an essay.
Dionysus, an introductory lecture.
Heracles, an introductory lecture.
Apology for 'The dependent Scholar.'
A Slip of the Tongue.

In conclusion, we have to say that this arrangement of M. Croiset's, which we have merely tabulated without intentionally departing from it in any particular, seems to us well considered in its broad lines; there are a few modifications which we should have been disposed to make in it; but we

13

thought it better to take it entire than to exercise our own judgment in a matter where we felt very little confidence.

3. CIRCUMSTANCES OF THE TIME

M. Aurelius has for us moderns this great superiority in interest over Saint Louis or Alfred, that he lived and acted in a state of society modern by its essential characteristics, in an epoch akin to our own, in a brilliant centre of civilization. Trajan talks of "our enlightened age" just as glibly as *The Times* talks of it.' M. Arnold, *Essays in Criticism, M. Aurelius.*

The age of M. Aurelius is also the age of Lucian, and with any man of that age who has, like these two, left us a still legible message we can enter into quite different relations from those which are possible with what M. Arnold calls in the same essay 'classical-dictionary heroes.' A twentieth-century Englishman, a second-century Greek or Roman, would be much more at home in each other's century, if they had the gift of tongues, than in most of those which have intervened. It is neither necessary nor possible to go deeply into the resemblance here[1]; all that need be done is to pass in review those points of it, some important, and some trifling, which are sure to occur in a detached way to readers of Lucian.

---

[1] Some words of Sir Leslie Stephen's may be given, however, describing the welter of religious opinions that prevailed at both epochs:
'The analogy between the present age and that which witnessed the introduction of Christianity is too striking to have been missed by very many observers. The most superficial acquaintance with the general facts shows how close a parallel might be drawn by a competent historian. There are none of the striking manifestations of the present day to which it would not be easy to produce an analogy, though in some respects on a smaller scale. Now, as then, we can find mystical philosophers trying to evolve a satisfactory creed by some process of logical legerdemain out of theosophical moonshine; and amiable and intelligent persons labouring hard to prove that the old mythology could be forced to accept a rationalistic interpretation— whether in regard to the inspection of entrails or prayers for fine weather; and philosophers framing systems of morality entirely apart from the ancient creeds, and sufficiently satisfactory to themselves, while hopelessly incapable of impressing the popular mind; and politicians, conscious that the basis of social order was being sapped by the decay of the faith in which it had arisen, and therefore attempting the impossible task of galvanizing dead creeds into a semblance of vitality; and strange superstitions creeping out of their lurking-places, and gaining influence in a luxurious society whose intelligence was an ineffectual safeguard against the most grovelling errors; and a dogged adherence of formalists and conservatives to ancient ways, and much empty profession of barren orthodoxy; and, beneath all, a vague disquiet, a breaking up of ancient social and natural bonds, and a blind groping toward some more cosmopolitan creed and some deeper satisfaction for the emotional needs of mankind.'— *The Religion of all Sensible Men* in *An Agnostic's Apology*, 1893.

The Graeco-Roman world was as settled and peaceful, as conscious of its imperial responsibilities, as susceptible to boredom, as greedy of amusement, could show as numerous a leisured class, and believed as firmly in money, as our own. What is more important for our purpose, it was questioning the truth of its religion as we are to-day questioning the truth of ours. Lucian was the most vehement of the questioners. Of what played the part then that the Christian religion plays now, the pagan religion was only one half; the other half was philosophy. The gods of Olympus had long lost their hold upon the educated, but not perhaps upon the masses; the educated, ill content to be without any guide through the maze of life, had taken to philosophy instead. Stoicism was the prevalent creed, and how noble a form this could take in a cultivated and virtuous mind is to be seen in the *Thoughts* of M. Aurelius. The test of a religion, however, is not what form it takes in a virtuous mind, but what effects it produces on those of another sort. Lucian applies the test of results alike to the religion usually so called, and to its philosophic substitute. He finds both wanting; the test is not a satisfactory one, but it is being applied by all sorts and conditions of men to Christianity in our own time; so is the second test, that of inherent probability, which he uses as well as the other upon the pagan theology; and it is this that gives his writings, even apart from their wit and fancy, a special interest for our own time. Our attention seems to be concentrated more and more on the ethical, as opposed to the speculative or dogmatic aspect of religion; just such was Lucian's attitude towards philosophy.

Some minor points of similarity may be briefly noted. As we read the *Anacharsis*, we are reminded of the modern prominence of athletics; the question of football *versus* drill is settled for us; light is thrown upon the question of conscription; we think of our Commissions on national deterioration, and the schoolmaster's wail over the athletic *Frankenstein's* monster which, like *Eucrates* in *The Liar*, he has created but cannot control. The 'horsy talk in every street' of the *Nigrinus* calls up the London newsboy with his 'All the winners.' We think of palmists and spiritualists in the police-courts as we read of Rutilianus and the Roman nobles consulting the impostor Alexander. This sentence reads like the description of a modern man of science confronted with the supernatural:

'It was an occasion for a man whose intelligence was steeled against such assaults by scepticism and insight, one who, if he could not detect the precise imposture, would at any rate have been perfectly certain that, though this escaped him, the whole thing was a lie and an impossibility.' The upper-class audiences who listened to Lucian's readings, taking his points with quiet smiles instead of the loud applause given to the rhetorician, must have been something like that which listens decorously to an Extension lecturer. When Lucian bids us mark 'how many there are who once were but cyphers, but whom words have raised to fame and opulence, ay, and to noble lineage too,' we remember not only Gibbon's remark about the very Herodes Atticus of whom Lucian may have been thinking ('The family of Herod, at least after it had been favoured by fortune, was lineally descended from Cimon and Miltiades'), but also the modern *carriere ouverte aux talents*, and the fact that Tennyson was a lord. There are the elements of a socialist question in the feelings between rich and poor described in the *Saturnalia*; while, on the other hand, the fact of there being an audience for the *Dialogues of the Hetaerae* is an illustration of that spirit of *humani nihil a me alienum puto* which is again prevalent today. We care now to realize the thoughts of other classes besides our own; so did they in Lucian's time; but it is significant that Francklin in 1780, refusing to translate this series, says:

'These dialogues exhibit to us only such kind of conversation as we may hear in the purlieus of Covent Garden—lewd, dull, and insipid.' The lewdness hardly goes beyond the title; they are full of humour and insight; and we make no apology for translating most of them. Lastly, a generation that is always complaining of the modern over-production of books feels that it would be at home in a state of society in which our author found that, not to be too singular, he must at least write about writing history, if he declined writing it himself, even as Diogenes took to rolling his tub, lest he should be the only idle man when Corinth was bustling about its defences.

As Lucian is so fond of saying, 'this is but a small selection of the facts which might have been quoted' to illustrate the likeness between our age and his. It may be well to allude, on the other hand, to a few peculiarities of the time that appear conspicuously in his writings.

The Roman Empire was rather Graeco-Roman than Roman; this is now a commonplace. It is interesting to observe that for Lucian 'we' is on occasion the Romans; 'we' is also everywhere the Greeks; while at the same time 'I' is a barbarian and a Syrian. Roughly speaking, the Roman element stands for energy, material progress, authority, and the Greek for thought; the Roman is the British Philistine, the Greek the man of culture. Lucian is conscious enough of the distinction, and there is no doubt where his own preference lies. He may be a materialist, so far as he is anything, in philosophy; but in practice he puts the things of the mind before the things of the body.

If our own age supplies parallels for most of what we meet with in the second century, there are two phenomena which are to be matched rather in an England that has passed away. The first is the Cynics, who swarm in Lucian's pages like the begging friars in those of a historical novelist painting the middle ages. Like the friars, they began nobly in the desire for plain living and high thinking; in both cases the thinking became plain, the living not perhaps high, but the best that circumstances admitted of, and the class—with its numbers hugely swelled by persons as little like their supposed teachers as a Marian or Elizabethan persecutor was like the founder of Christianity—a pest to society. Lucian's sympathy with the best Cynics, and detestation of the worst, make Cynicism one of his most familiar themes. The second is the class so vividly presented in *The dependent Scholar*—the indigent learned Greek who looks

16

about for a rich vulgar Roman to buy his company, and finds he has the worst of the bargain. His successors, the 'trencher chaplains' who 'from grasshoppers turn bumble-bees and wasps, plain parasites, and make the Muses mules, to satisfy their hunger-starved panches, and get a meal's meat,' were commoner in Burton's days than in our own, and are to be met in Fielding, and Macaulay, and Thackeray.

Two others of Lucian's favourite figures, the parasite and the legacy-hunter, exist still, no doubt, as they are sure to in every complex civilization; but their operations are now conducted with more regard to the decencies. This is worth remembering when we are occasionally offended by his frankness on subjects to which we are not accustomed to allude; he is not an unclean or a sensual writer, but the waters of decency have risen since his time and submerged some things which were then visible.

A slight prejudice, again, may sometimes be aroused by Lucian's trick of constant and trivial quotation; he would rather put the simplest statement, or even make his transition from one subject to another, in words of Homer than in his own; we have modern writers too who show the same tendency, and perhaps we like or dislike them for it in proportion as their allusions recall memories or merely puzzle us; we cannot all be expected to have agreeable memories stirred by insignificant Homer tags; and it is well to bear in mind by way of palliation that in Greek education Homer played as great a part as the Bible in ours. He might be taken simply or taken allegorically; but one way or the other he was the staple of education, and it might be assumed that every one[2] would like the mere sound of him.

We may end by remarking that the public readings of his own works, to which the author makes frequent reference, were what served to a great extent the purpose of our printing-press. We know that his pieces were also published; but the public that could be reached by hand-written copies would bear a very small proportion to that which heard them from the writer's own lips; and though the modern system may have the advantage on the whole, it is hard to believe that the unapproached life and naturalness of Lucian's dialogue does not owe something to this necessity.

---

[2] *Wahrheit und Dichtung,* book iv.

17

4. LUCIAN AS A WRITER

With all the sincerity of Lucian in *The True History*, 'soliciting his reader's incredulity,' we solicit our reader's neglect of this appreciation. We have no pretensions whatever to the critical faculty; the following remarks are to be taken as made with diffidence, and offered to those only who prefer being told what to like, and why, to settling the matter for themselves.

Goethe, aged fourteen, with seven languages on hand, devised the plan of a correspondence kept up by seven imaginary brothers scattered over the globe, each writing in the language of his adopted land. The stay-at-home in Frankfort was to write Jew-German, for which purpose some Hebrew must be acquired. His father sent him to Rector Albrecht. The rector was always found with one book open before him—a well-thumbed Lucian. But the Hebrew vowel-points were perplexing, and the boy found better amusement in putting shrewd questions on what struck him as impossibilities or inconsistencies in the Old-Testament narrative they were reading. The old gentleman was infinitely amused, had fits of mingled coughing and laughter, but made little attempt at solving his pupil's difficulties, beyond ejaculating *Er narrischer Kerl! Er narrischer Junge!* He let him dig for solutions, however, in an English commentary on the shelves, and occupied the time with turning the familiar pages of his Lucia. The wicked old rector perhaps chuckled to think that here was one who bade fair to love Lucian one day as well as he did himself.

For Lucian too was one who asked questions—spent his life doing little else; if one were invited to draw him with the least possible expenditure of ink, one's pen would trace a mark of interrogation. That picture is easily drawn; to put life into it is a more difficult matter. However, his is not a complex character, for all the irony in which he sometimes chooses to clothe his thought; and materials are at least abundant; he is one of the self-revealing fraternity; his own personal presence is to be detected more often than not in his work. He may give us the assistance, or he may not, of labelling a character *Lucian* or *Lycinus*; we can detect him, *volentes volentem*, under the thin disguise of *Menippus* or *Tychiades* or *Cyniscus* as well. And the essence of him as he reveals himself is the questioning spirit. He has no respect for authority. Burke describes the majority of mankind, who do not form their own opinions, as 'those whom Providence has doomed to live on trust'; Lucian entirely refuses to live on trust; he 'wants to know.' It was the wish of *Arthur Clennam*, who had in consequence a very bad name among the *Tite Barnacles* and other persons in authority. Lucian has not escaped the same fate; 'the scoffer Lucian' has become as much a commonplace as '*fidus Achates*,' or 'the well-greaved Achaeans,' the reading of him has been discountenanced, and, if he has not actually lost his place at the table of Immortals, promised him when he temporarily left the Island of the Blest, it has not been so 'distinguished' a place as it was to have been and should have been. And all because he 'wanted to know.'

His questions, of course, are not all put in the same manner. In the *Dialogues of the Gods*, for instance, the mark of interrogation is not writ large; they have almost the air at first of little stories in dialogue form, which might serve to instruct schoolboys in the attributes and legends of the gods—a manual charmingly done, yet a manual only. But we soon see that he has said to himself:

Let us put the thing into plain natural prose, and see what it looks like with its glamour of poetry and reverence stripped off; the Gods do human things; why not represent them as human persons, and see what results? What did result was that henceforth any one who still believed in the pagan deities might at the cost of an hour's light reading satisfy himself that his gods were not gods, or, if they were, had no business to be. Whether many or few did so read and so satisfy themselves, we have no means of knowing; it is easy to over-estimate the effect such writing may have had, and to forget that those who were capable of being convinced by exposition of this sort would mostly be those who were already convinced without; still, so far as Lucian had any effect on the religious position, it must have been in discrediting paganism and increasing the readiness to accept the new faith beginning to make its way. Which being so, it was ungrateful of the Christian church to turn and rend him. It did so, partly in error. Lucian had referred in the *Life of Peregrine* to the Christians, in words which might seem irreverent to Christians at a time when they were no longer an obscure sect; he had described and ridiculed in *The Liar* certain 'Syrian' miracles which have a remarkable likeness to the casting out of spirits by Christ and the apostles; and worse still, the *Philopatris* passed under his name. This dialogue, unlike what Lucian had written in the *Peregrine* and *The Liar*, is a deliberate attack on Christianity. It is clear to us now that it was written two hundred years after his time, under Julian the Apostate; but there can be no more doubt of its being an imitation of Lucian than of its not being his; it consequently passed for his, the story gained currency that he was an apostate himself, and his name was anathema for the church. It was only partly in error, however. Though Lucian might be useful on occasion ('When Tertullian or Lactantius employ their labours in exposing the falsehood and extravagance of Paganism, they are obliged to transcribe the eloquence of Cicero or the wit of Lucian'[3]), the very word heretic is enough to remind us that the Church could not show much favour to one who insisted always on thinking for himself. His works survived, but he was not read, through the Middle Ages. With the Renaissance he partly came into his own again, but still laboured under the imputations of scoffing and atheism, which confined the reading of him to the few.

The method followed in the *Dialogues of the Gods* and similar pieces is a very indirect way of putting questions. It is done much more directly in others, the *Zeus cross-examined*, for instance.

---

[3] Gibbon, *Decline and Fall*, cap. xv.

Since the fallen angels reasoned high
Of Providence, Foreknowledge, Will, and Fate—
Fixed fate, free will, foreknowledge absolute—
And found no end, in wandering mazes lost,

these subjects have had their share of attention; but the questions can hardly be put more directly, or more neatly, than in the *Zeus cross-examined*, and the thirtieth *Dialogue of the Dead*.

He has many other interrogative methods besides these, which may be left to reveal themselves in the course of reading. As for answering questions, that is another matter. The answer is sometimes apparent, sometimes not; he will not refrain from asking a question just because he does not know the answer; his *role* is asking, not answering. Nor when he gives an answer is it always certain whether it is to be taken in earnest. Was he a cynic? one would say so after reading *The Cynic*; was he an Epicurean? one would say so after reading the *Alexander*; was he a philosopher? one would say Yes at a certain point of the *Hermotimus*, No at another. He doubtless had his moods, and he was quite unhampered by desire for any consistency except consistent independence of judgement. Moreover, the difficulty of getting at his real opinions is increased by the fact that he was an ironist. We have called him a self-revealer; but you never quite know where to have an ironical self-revealer. Goethe has the useful phrase, 'direct irony'; a certain German writer 'makes too free a use of direct irony, praising the blameworthy and blaming the praiseworthy—a rhetorical device which should be very sparingly employed. In the long run it disgusts the sensible and misleads the dull, pleasing only the great intermediate class to whom it offers the satisfaction of being able to think themselves more shrewd than other people, without expending much thought of their own' (*Wahrheit und Dichtung*, book vii). Fielding gives us in *Jonathan Wild* a sustained piece of 'direct irony'; you have only to reverse everything said, and you get the author's meaning. Lucian's irony is not of that sort; you cannot tell when you are to reverse him, only that you will have sometimes to do so. He does use the direct kind; *The Rhetorician's Vade mecum* and *The Parasite* are examples; the latter is also an example (unless a translator, who is condemned not to skip or skim, is an unfair judge) of how tiresome it may become. But who shall say how much of irony and how much of genuine feeling there is in the fine description of the philosophic State given in the *Hermotimus* (with its suggestions of *Christian* in *The Pilgrim's Progress*, and of the 'not many wise men after the flesh, not many mighty, not many noble'), or in the whimsical extravagance (as it strikes a modern) of the *Pantomime*, or in the triumph permitted to the Cynic (against 'Lycinus' too) in the dialogue called after him? In one of his own introductory lectures he compares his pieces aptly enough to the bacchante's thyrsus with its steel point concealed.

With his questions and his irony and his inconsistencies, it is no wonder that Lucian is accused of being purely negative and destructive. But we need not think he is disposed of in that way, any more than our old-fashioned literary education is disposed of when it has been pointed out that it does not equip its *alumni* with knowledge of electricity or of a commercially useful modern language; it may have equipped them with something less paying, but more worth paying for. Lucian, it is certain, will supply no one with a religion or a philosophy; but it may be doubted whether any writer will supply more fully both example and precept in favour of doing one's thinking for oneself; and it may be doubted also whether any other intellectual lesson is more necessary. He is *nullius addictus iurare in verba magistri*, if ever man was; he is individualist to the core. No religion or philosophy, he seems to say, will save you; the thing is to think for yourself, and be a man of sense. 'It was but small consolation,' says *Menippus*, 'to reflect that I was in numerous and wise and eminently sensible company, if I was a fool still, all astray in my quest for truth.' *Vox populi* is no *vox dei* for him; he is quite proof against majorities; *Athanasius contra mundum* is more to his taste. "What is this I hear?" asked Arignotus, scowling upon me; "you deny the existence of the supernatural, when there is scarcely a man who has not seen some evidence of it?" "Therein lies my exculpation," I replied; "I do not believe in the supernatural, because, unlike the rest of mankind, I do not see it; if I saw, I should doubtless believe, just as you all do."' That British schoolboys should have been brought up for centuries on Ovid, and Lucian have been tabooed, is, in view of their comparative efficacy in stimulating thought, an interesting example of *habent sua fata libelli*.

It need not be denied that there is in him a certain lack of feeling, not surprising in one of his analytic temper, but not agreeable either. He is a hard bright intelligence, with no bowels; he applies the knife without the least compunction—indeed with something of savage enjoyment. The veil is relentlessly torn from family affection in the *Mourning. Solon* in the *Charon* pursues his victory so far as to make us pity instead of scorning *Croesus. Menippus* and his kind, in the shades, do their lashing of dead horses with a disagreeable gusto, which tempts us to raise a society for the prevention of cruelty to the Damned. A voyage through Lucian in search of pathos will yield as little result as one in search of interest in nature. There is a touch of it here and there (which has probably evaporated in translation) in the *Hermotimus*, the *Demonax*, and the *Demosthenes*; but that is all. He was perhaps not unconscious of all this himself. 'But what is your profession?' asks *Philosophy.* 'I profess hatred of imposture and pretension, lying and pride... However, I do not neglect the complementary branch, in which love takes the place of hate; it includes love of truth and beauty and simplicity, and all that is akin to love. *But the subjects for this branch of the profession are sadly few.*'

Before going on to his purely literary qualities, we may collect here a few detached remarks affecting rather his character than his skill as an artist. And first of his relations to philosophy. The statements in the *Menippus* and the *Icaromenippus*, as well as in *The Fisher* and *The double Indictment*, have all the air of autobiography (especially as they are in the nature of digressions), and give us to understand that he had spent much time and energy on philosophic study. He claims *Philosophy* as his mistress in *The Fisher*, and in a case where he is in fact judge as well as party, has no difficulty in getting his claim established. He is for ever reminding us that he loves philosophy and only satirizes the degenerate philosophers of his day. But it *will* occur to us after reading him through that he has dissembled his love, then, very well. There is not a passage from beginning to end of his works that indicates any real comprehension of any philosophic system. The external characteristics of the philosophers, the absurd stories current about them, and the popular misrepresentations of their doctrines—it is in these that philosophy consists for him. That he had read some of them there is no doubt; but one has an uneasy suspicion that he read Plato because he liked his humour and his style, and did not trouble himself about anything further. Gibbon speaks of 'the philosophic maze of the writings of Plato, of which the dramatic is perhaps more interesting than the argumentative part.' That is quite a legitimate opinion, provided you do not undertake to judge philosophy in the light of it. The apparently serious rejection of geometrical truth in the *Hermotimus* may fairly suggest that Lucian was as unphilosophic as he was unmathematical. Twice, and perhaps twice only, does he express hearty admiration for a philosopher. Demonax is 'the best of all philosophers'; but then he admired him just because he was so little of a philosopher and so much a man of ordinary common sense. And Epicurus is 'the thinker who had grasped the nature of things and been in solitary possession of truth'; but then that is in the *Alexander*, and any stick was good enough to beat that dog with. The fact is, Lucian was much too well satisfied with his own judgement to think that he could possibly require guidance, and the commonplace test of results was enough to assure him that philosophy was worthless:

'It is no use having all theory at your fingers' ends, if you do not conform your conduct to the right.' There is a description in the *Pantomime* that is perhaps truer than it is meant to pass for. 'Lycinus' is called 'an educated man, and *in some sort* a student of philosophy.'

If he is not a philosopher, he is very much a moralist; it is because philosophy deals partly with morals that he thinks he cares for it. But here too his conclusions are of a very commonsense order. The Stoic notion that 'Virtue consists in being uncomfortable' strikes him as merely absurd; no asceticism for him; on the other hand, no lavish extravagance and *Persici apparatus*; a dinner of herbs with the righteous—that is, the cultivated Athenian—, a neat repast of Attic taste, is honestly his idea of good living; it is probable that he really did sacrifice both money and fame to live in Athens rather than in Rome, according to his own ideal. That ideal is a very modest one; when *Menippus* took all the trouble to get down to Tiresias in Hades via

22

Babylon, his reward was the information that 'the life of the ordinary man is the best and the most prudent choice.' So thought Lucian; and it is to be counted to him for righteousness that he decided to abandon 'the odious practices that his profession imposes on the advocate—deceit, falsehood, bluster, clamour, pushing,' for the quiet life of a literary man (especially as we should probably never have heard his name had he done otherwise). Not that the life was so quiet as it might have been. He could not keep his satire impersonal enough to avoid incurring enmities. He boasts in the *Peregrine* of the unfeeling way in which he commented on that enthusiast to his followers, and we may believe his assurance that his writings brought general dislike and danger upon him. His moralizing (of which we are happy to say there is a great deal) is based on Tiresias's pronouncement. Moralizing has a bad name; but than good moralizing there is, when one has reached a certain age perhaps, no better reading. Some of us like it even in our novels, feel more at home with Fielding and Thackeray for it, and regretfully confess ourselves unequal to the artistic aloofness of a Flaubert. Well, Lucian's moralizings are, for those who like such things, of the right quality; they are never dull, and the touch is extremely light. We may perhaps be pardoned for alluding to half a dozen conceptions that have a specially modern air about them. The use that Rome may serve as a school of resistance to temptation (*Nigrinus*, 19) recalls Milton's 'fugitive and cloistered virtue, unexercised and unbreathed, that never sallies out and seeks her adversary.' 'Old age is wisdom's youth, the day of her glorious flower' (*Heracles*, 8) might have stood as a text for Browning's *Rabbi ben Ezra*. The brands visible on the tyrant's soul, and the refusal of Lethe as a sufficient punishment (*Voyage to the lower World*, 24 and 28), have their parallels in our new eschatology. The decision of *Zeus* that *Heraclitus* and *Democritus* are to be one lot that laughter and tears will go together (*Sale of Creeds*, 13)—accords with our views of the emotional temperament. *Chiron* is impressive on the vanity of fruition (*Dialogues of the Dead*, 26). And the figuring of *Truth* as 'the shadowy creature with the indefinite complexion' (*The Fisher*, 16) is only one example of Lucian's felicity in allegory.

Another weak point, for which many people will have no more inclination to condemn him than for his moralizing, is his absolute indifference to the beauties of nature. Having already given him credit for regarding nothing that is human as beyond his province, it is our duty to record the corresponding limitation; of everything that was not human he was simply unconscious; with him it was not so much that the *proper* as that the *only* study of mankind is man. The apparent exceptions are not real ones. If he is interested in the gods, it is as the creatures of human folly that he takes them to be. If he writes a toy essay with much parade of close observation on the fly, it is to show how amusing human ingenuity can be on an unlikely subject. But it is worth notice that 'the first of the moderns,' though he shows himself in many descriptions of pictures quite awake to the beauty manufactured by man, has in no way anticipated the modern discovery that nature is beautiful. To readers who have had enough of the pathetic fallacy, and of the second-rate novelist's local colour, Lucian's tacit assumption that there is nothing but man is refreshing. That he was a close enough observer of human nature, any one can satisfy himself by glancing at the *Feast of Lapithae*, the *Dialogues of the Hetaerae*, some of the *Dialogues of the Gods*, and perhaps best of all, *The Liar*.

As it occurs to himself to repel the imputation of plagiarism in *A literary Prometheus*, the point must be briefly touched upon. There is no doubt that Homer preceded him in making the gods extremely, even comically, human, that Plato showed him an example of prose dialogue, that Aristophanes inspired his constructive fancy, that Menippus provided him with some ideas, how far developed on the same lines we cannot now tell, that Menander's comedies and Herodas's mimes contributed to the absolute naturalness of his conversation. If any, or almost any, of these had never existed, Lucian would have been more or less different from what he is. His originality is not in the least affected by that; we may resolve him theoretically into his elements; but he too had the gift, that out of three sounds he framed, not a fourth sound, but a star. The question of his originality is no more important—indeed much less so—than that of Sterne's.

When we pass to purely literary matters, the first thing to be remarked upon is the linguistic miracle presented to us. It is useless to dwell upon it in detail, since this is an introduction not to Lucian, but to a translation of Lucian; it exists, none the less. A Syrian writes in Greek, and not in the Greek of his own time, but in that of five or six centuries before, and he does it, if not with absolute correctness, yet with the easy mastery that we expect only from one in a million of those who write in their mother tongue, and takes his place as an immortal classic. The miracle may be repeated; an English-educated Hindu may produce masterpieces of Elizabethan English that will rank him with Bacon and Ben Jonson; but it will surprise us, when it does happen. That Lucian was himself aware of the awful dangers besetting the writer who would revive an obsolete fashion of speech is shown in the *Lexiphanes*.

Some faults of style he undoubtedly has, of which a word or two should perhaps be said. The first is the general taint of rhetoric, which is sometimes positively intolerable, and is liable to spoil enjoyment even of the best pieces occasionally. Were it not that 'Rhetoric made a Greek of me,' we should wish heartily that he had never been a rhetorician. It is the practice of talking on unreal cases, doubtless habitual with him up to forty, that must be responsible for the self- satisfied fluency, the too great length, and the perverse ingenuity, that sometimes excite our impatience. Naturally, it is in the pieces of inferior subject or design that this taint is most perceptible; and it must be forgiven in consideration of the fact that without the toilsome study of rhetoric he would not have been the master of Greek that he was.

The second is perhaps only a special case of the first. Julius Pollux, a sophist whom Lucian is supposed to have attacked in *The Rhetorician's Vade mecum*, is best known as author of an *Onomasticon*, or word-list, containing the most important words relating to certain subjects. One would be reluctant to believe that Lucian condescended to use his enemy's manual; but it is hard to think that he had not one of his own, of which he made much too good use. The conviction is constantly forced on a translator that when Lucian has said a thing sufficiently once, he has looked at his Onomasticon, found that there are some words he has not yet got in, and forthwith said the thing again with some of them, and yet again with the rest.

The third concerns his use of illustrative anecdotes, comparisons, and phrases. It is true that, if his pieces are taken each separately, he is most happy with all these (though it is hard to forgive Alexander's bathe in the Cydnus with which *The Hall* opens); but when they are read continuously, the repeated appearances of the tragic actor disrobed, the dancing apes and their nuts, of Zeus's golden cord, and of the 'two octaves apart,' produce an impression of poverty that makes us momentarily forget his real wealth.

We have spoken of the annoying tendency to pleonasm in Lucian's style, which must be laid at the door of rhetoric. On the other hand let it have part of the credit for a thing of vastly more importance, his choice of dialogue as a form when he took to letters. It is quite obvious that he was naturally a man of detached mind, with an inclination for looking at both sides of a question. This was no doubt strengthened by the common practice among professional rhetoricians of writing speeches on both sides of imaginary cases. The level-headedness produced by this combination of nature and training naturally led to the selection of dialogue. In one of the preliminary trials of *The double Indictment, Drink*, being one of the parties, and consciously incapable at the moment of doing herself justice, employs her opponent, *The Academy*, to plead for as well as against her. There are a good many pieces in which Lucian follows the same method. In *The Hall* the legal form is actually kept; in the *Peregrine* speeches are delivered by an admirer and a scorner of the hero; in *The Rhetorician's Vade mecum* half the piece is an imaginary statement of the writer's enemy; in the *Apology for 'The dependent Scholar'* there is a long imaginary objection set up to be afterwards disposed of; the *Saturnalian Letters* are the cases of rich and poor put from opposite sides. None of these are dialogues; but they are all less perfect devices to secure the same object, the putting of the two views that the man of detached mind recognizes on every question. Not that justice is always the object; these devices, and dialogue still more, offer the further advantage of economy; no ideas need be wasted, if the subject is treated from more than one aspect. The choice of dialogue may be accounted for thus; it is true that it would not have availed much if the chooser had not possessed the nimble wit and the endless power of varying the formula which is so astonishing in Lucian; but that it was a matter of importance is proved at once by comparing the *Alexander* with *The Liar*, or *The dependent Scholar* with the *Feast of Lapithae*. Lucian's non-dialogue pieces (with the exception of *The True History*) might have been written by other people; the dialogues are all his own.

About five-and-thirty of his pieces (or sets of pieces) are in dialogue, and perhaps the greatest proof of his artistic skill is that the form never palls; so great is the variety of treatment that no one of them is like another. The point may be worth dwelling on a little. The main differences between dialogues, apart from the particular writer's characteristics, are these: the persons may be two only, or more; they may be well or ill-matched; the proportions and relations between conversation and narrative vary; and the objects in view are not always the same. It is natural for a writer to fall into a groove with some or all of these, and produce an effect of sameness. Lucian, on the contrary, so rings the changes by permutations and combinations of them that each dialogue is approached with a delightful uncertainty of what form it may take. As to number of persons, it is a long step from the *Menippus* to the crowded *dramatis personae* of *The Fisher* or the *Zeus Tragoedus*, in the latter of which there are two independent sets, one overhearing and commenting upon the other. It is not much less, though of another kind, from *The Parasite*, where the interlocutor is merely a man of straw, to the *Hermotimus*, where he has life enough to give us ever fresh hopes of a change in fortune, or to the *Anacharsis*, where we are not quite sure, even when all is over, which has had the best. Then if we consider conversation and narrative, there are all kinds. *Nigrinus* has narrative in a setting of dialogue, *Demosthenes* vice versa, *The Liar* reported dialogue inside dialogue; *Icaromenippus* is almost a narrative, while *The Runaways* is almost a play. Lastly, the form serves in the *Toxaris* as a vehicle for stories, in the *Hermotimus* for real discussion, in *Menippus* as relief for narrative, in the *Portrait-study* for description, in *The Cock* to convey moralizing, in *The double Indictment* autobiography, in the *Lexiphanes* satire, and in the short series it enshrines prose idylls.

These are considerations of a mechanical order, perhaps; it may be admitted that technical skill of this sort is only valuable in giving a proper chance to more essential gifts; but when those exist, it is of the highest value. And Lucian's versatility in technique is only a symbol of his versatile powers in general. He is equally at home in heaven and earth and hell, with philosophers and cobblers, telling a story, criticizing a book, describing a picture, elaborating an allegory, personifying an abstraction, parodying a poet or a historian, flattering an emperor's mistress, putting an audience into good temper with him and itself, unveiling an imposture, destroying a religion or a reputation, drawing a character. The last is perhaps the most disputable of the catalogue. How many of his personages are realities to us when we have read, and not mere labels for certain modes of thought or conduct? Well, characterization is not the first, but only the second thing with him; what is said matters rather more than who says it; he is more desirous that the argument should advance than that the person should reveal himself; nevertheless, nothing is ever said that is out of character; while nothing can be better of the kind than some of his professed personifications, his *Plutus* or his *Philosophy*, we do retain distinct impressions of at least an irresponsible *Zeus* and a decorously spiteful *Hera*, a well-meaning, incapable *Helius*, a bluff *Posidon*, a gallant *Prometheus*, a one- idea'd *Charon*; *Timon* is more than misanthropy, *Eucrates* than superstition, *Anacharsis* than intelligent curiosity, *Micyllus* than ignorant poverty, poor *Hermotimus* than blind faith, and Lucian than a scoffer.

THE VISION

A CHAPTER OF AUTOBIOGRAPHY

When my childhood was over, and I had just left school, my father called a council to decide upon my profession. Most of his friends considered that the life of culture was very exacting in toil, time, and money: a life only for fortune's favourites; whereas our resources were quite narrow, and urgently called for relief. If I were to take up some ordinary handicraft, I should be making my own living straight off, instead of eating my father's meat at my age; and before long my earnings would be a welcome contribution.

So the next step was to select the most satisfactory of the handicrafts; it must be one quite easy to acquire, respectable, inexpensive as regards plant, and fairly profitable. Various suggestions were made, according to the taste and knowledge of the councillors; but my father turned to my mother's brother, supposed to be an excellent statuary, and said to him:

'With you here, it would be a sin to prefer any other craft; take the lad, regard him as your charge, teach him to handle, match, and grave your marble; he will do well enough; you know he has the ability.' This he had inferred from certain tricks I used to play with wax. When I got out of school, I used to scrape off the wax from my tablets and work it into cows, horses, or even men and women, and he thought I did it creditably; my masters used to cane me for it, but on this occasion it was taken as evidence of a natural faculty, and my modelling gave them good hopes of my picking up the art quickly.

As soon as it seemed convenient for me to begin, I was handed over to my uncle, and by no means reluctantly; I thought I should find it amusing, and be in a position to impress my companions; they should see me chiselling gods and making little images for myself and my favourites. The usual first experience of beginners followed: my uncle gave me a chisel, and told me to give a gentle touch to a plaque lying on the bench:

'Well begun is half done,' said he, not very originally. In my inexperience I brought down the tool too hard, and the plaque broke; he flew into a rage, picked up a stick which lay handy, and gave me an introduction to art which might have been gentler and more encouraging; so I paid my footing with tears.

I ran off, and reached home still howling and tearful, told the story of the stick, and showed my bruises. I said a great deal about his brutality, and added that it was all envy: he was afraid of my being a better sculptor than he. My mother was very angry, and abused her brother roundly; as for me, I fell asleep that night with my eyes still wet, and sorrow was with me till the morning.

So much of my tale is ridiculous and childish. What you have now to hear, gentlemen, is not so contemptible, but deserves an attentive hearing; in the words of Homer,

To me in slumber wrapt a dream divine
  Ambrosial night conveyed,

a dream so vivid as to be indistinguishable from reality; after all these years, I have still the figures of its persons in my eyes, the vibration of their words in my ears; so clear it all was.

Two women had hold of my hands, and were trying vehemently and persistently to draw me each her way; I was nearly pulled in two with their contention; now one would prevail and all but get entire possession of me, now I would fall to the other again, All the time they were exchanging loud protests:

'He is mine, and I mean to keep him;' 'Not yours at all, and it is no use your saying he is.' One of them seemed to be a working woman, masculine looking, with untidy hair, horny hands, and dress kilted up; she was all powdered with plaster, like my uncle when he was chipping marble. The other had a beautiful face, a comely figure, and neat attire. At last they invited me to decide which of them I would live with; the rough manly one made her speech first.

'Dear youth, I am Statuary—the art which you yesterday began to learn, and which has a natural and a family claim upon you. Your grandfather' (naming my mother's father) 'and both your uncles practised it, and it brought them credit. If you will turn a deaf ear to this person's foolish cajolery, and come and live with me, I promise you wholesome food and good strong muscles; you shall never fear envy, never leave your country and your people to go wandering abroad, and you shall be commended not for your words, but for your works.

'Let not a slovenly person or dirty clothes repel you; such were the conditions of that Phidias who produced the Zeus, of Polyclitus who created the Hera, of the much-lauded Myron, of the admired Praxiteles; and all these are worshipped with the Gods. If you should come to be counted among them, you will surely have fame enough for yourself through all the world, you will make your father the envy of all fathers, and bring your country to all men's notice.' This and more said Statuary, stumbling along in a strange jargon, stringing her arguments together in a very earnest manner, and quite intent on persuading me. But I can remember no more; the greater part of it has faded from my memory. When she stopped, the other's turn came.

'And I, child, am Culture, no stranger to you even now, though you have yet to make my closer acquaintance. The advantages that the profession of a sculptor will bring with it you have just been told; they amount to no more than being a worker with your hands, your whole prospects in life limited to that; you will be obscure, poorly and illiberally paid, mean-spirited, of no account outside your doors; your influence will never help a friend, silence an enemy, nor impress your countrymen; you will be just a worker, one of the masses, cowering before the distinguished, truckling to the eloquent, living the life of a hare, a prey to your betters. You may turn out a Phidias or a Polyclitus, to be sure, and create a number of wonderful works; but even so, though your art will be generally commended, no sensible observer will be found to wish himself like you; whatever your real qualities, you will always rank as a common craftsman who makes his living with his hands.

'Be governed by me, on the other hand, and your first reward shall be a view of the many wondrous deeds and doings of the men of old; you shall hear their words and know them all, what manner of men they were; and your soul, which is your very self, I will adorn with many fair adornments, with self-mastery and justice and reverence and mildness, with consideration and understanding and fortitude, with love of what is beautiful, and yearning for what is great; these things it is that are the true and pure ornaments of the soul. Naught shall escape you either of ancient wisdom or of present avail; nay, the future too, with me to aid, you shall foresee; in a word, I will instill into you, and that in no long time, all knowledge human and divine.

'This penniless son of who knows whom, contemplating but II now a vocation so ignoble, shall soon be admired and envied of all, with honour and praise and the fame of high achievement, respected by the high-born and the affluent, clothed as I am clothed' (and here she pointed to her own bright raiment), 'held worthy of place and precedence; and if you leave your native land, you will be no unknown nameless wanderer; you shall wear my marks upon you, and every man beholding you shall touch his neighbour's arm and say, That is he.

'And if some great moment come to try your friends or country, then shall all look to you. And to your lightest word the many shall listen open-mouthed, and marvel, and count you happy in your eloquence, and your father in his son. 'Tis said that some from mortal men become immortal; and I will make it truth in you; for though you depart from life yourself, you shall keep touch with the learned and hold communion with the best. Consider the mighty Demosthenes, whose son he was, and whither I exalted him; consider Aeschines; how came a Philip to pay court to the cymbal-woman's brat? how but for my sake? Dame Statuary here had the breeding of Socrates himself; but no sooner could he discern the better part, than he deserted her and enlisted with me; since when, his name is on every tongue.

'You may dismiss all these great men, and with them all glorious deeds, majestic words, and seemly looks, all honour, repute, praise, precedence, power, and office, all lauded eloquence and envied wisdom; these you may put from you, to gird on a filthy apron and assume a servile guise; then will you handle crowbars and graving tools, mallets and chisels; you will be bowed over your work, with eyes and thoughts bent earthwards, abject as abject can be, with never a free and manly upward look or aspiration; all your care will be to proportion and fairly drape your works; to proportioning and adorning yourself you will give little heed enough, making yourself of less account than your marble.'

I waited not for her to bring her words to an end, but rose up and spoke my mind; I turned from that clumsy mechanic woman, and went rejoicing to lady Culture, the more when I thought upon the stick, and all the blows my yesterday's apprenticeship had brought me. For a time the deserted one was wroth, with clenched fists and grinding teeth; but at last she stiffened, like another Niobe, into marble. A strange fate, but I must request your belief; dreams are great magicians, are they not?

Then the other looked upon me and spoke:

—'For this justice done me,' said she, 'you shall now be recompensed; come, mount this car'—and lo, one stood ready, drawn by winged steeds like Pegasus—, 'that you may learn what fair sights another choice would have cost you.' We mounted, she took the reins and drove, and I was carried aloft and beheld towns and nations and peoples from the East to the West; and methought I was sowing like Triptolemus; but the nature of the seed I cannot call to mind—only this, that men on earth when they saw it gave praise, and all whom I reached in my flight sent me on my way with blessings.

When she had presented these things to my eyes, and me to my admirers, she brought me back, no more clad as when my flight began; I returned, methought, in glorious raiment. And finding my father where he stood waiting, she showed him my raiment, and the guise in which I came, and said a word to him upon the lot which they had come so near appointing for me. All this I saw when scarce out of my childhood; the confusion and terror of the stick, it may be, stamped it on my memory.

'Good gracious,' says some one, before I have done, 'what a longwinded lawyer's vision!' 'This,' interrupts another, 'must be a winter dream, to judge by the length of night required; or perhaps it took three nights, like the making of Heracles. What has come over him, that he babbles such puerilities? memorable things indeed, a child in bed, and a very ancient, worn-out dream! what stale frigid stuff! does he take us for interpreters of dreams?' Sir, I do not. When Xenophon related that vision of his which you all know, of his father's house on fire and the rest, was it just by way of a riddle? was it in deliberate ineptitude that he reproduced it? a likely thing in their desperate military situation, with the enemy surrounding them! no, the relation was to serve a useful purpose.

Similarly I have had an object in telling you my dream. It is that the young may be guided to the better way and set themselves to Culture, especially any among them who is recreant for fear of poverty, and minded to enter the wrong path, to the ruin of a nature not all ignoble. Such an one will be strengthened by my tale, I am well assured; in me he will find an apt example; let him only compare the boy of those days, who started in pursuit of the best and devoted himself to Culture regardless of immediate poverty, with the man who has now come back to you, as high in fame, to put it at the lowest, as any stonecutter of them all.

31

A LITERARY PROMETHEUS

So you will have me a Prometheus? If your meaning is, my good sir, that my works, like his, are of clay, I accept the comparison and hail my prototype; potter me to your heart's content, though *my* clay is poor common stuff, trampled by common feet till it is little better than mud. But perhaps it is in exaggerated compliment to my ingenuity that you father my books upon the subtlest of the Titans; in that case I fear men will find a hidden meaning, and detect an Attic curl on your laudatory lips. Where do you find my ingenuity? in what consists the great subtlety, the Prometheanism, of my writings? enough for me if you have not found them sheer earth, all unworthy of Caucasian clay-pits. How much better a claim to kinship with Prometheus have you gentlemen who win fame in the courts, engaged in real contests; *your* works have true life and breath, ay, and the warmth of fire. That is Promethean indeed, though with the difference, it may be, that you do not work in clay; your creations are oftenest of gold; we on the other hand who come before popular audiences and offer mere lectures are exhibitors of imitations only. However, I have the general resemblance to Prometheus, as I said before—a resemblance which I share with the dollmakers—, that my modelling is in clay; but then there is no motion, as with him, not a sign of life; entertainment and pastime is the beginning and the end of my work. So I must look for light elsewhere; possibly the title is a sort of *lucus a non lucendo*, applied to me as to Cleon in the comedy:

Full well Prometheus-Cleon plans—the past.

Or again, the Athenians used to call Prometheuses the makers of jars and stoves and other, clay-workers, with playful reference to the material, and perhaps to the use of fire in baking the ware. If that is all your 'Prometheus' means, you have aimed your shaft well enough, and flavoured your jest with the right Attic tartness; my productions are as brittle as their pottery; fling a stone, and you may smash them all to pieces.

But here some one offers me a crumb of comfort:
'That was not the likeness he found between you and Prometheus;
he meant to commend your innovating originality:
at a time when human beings did not exist, Prometheus conceived and fashioned them; he moulded and elaborated certain living things into agility and beauty; he was practically their creator, though Athene assisted by putting breath into the clay and bringing the models to life.' So says my some one, giving your remark its politest possible turn. Perhaps he has hit the true meaning; not that I can rest content, however, with the mere credit of innovation, and the absence of any original to which my work can be referred; if it is not good as well as original, I assure you I shall be ashamed of it, bring down my foot and crush it out of existence; its novelty shall not avail (with me at least) to save its ugliness from annihilation. If I thought otherwise, I admit

that a round dozen of vultures would be none too many for the liver of a dunce who could not see that ugliness was only aggravated by strangeness.

Ptolemy, son of Lagus, imported two novelties into Egypt; one was a pure black Bactrian camel, the other a piebald man, half absolutely black and half unusually white, the two colours evenly distributed; he invited the Egyptians to the theatre, and concluded a varied show with these two, expecting to bring down the house. The audience, however, was terrified by the camel and almost stampeded; still, it *was* decked all over with gold, had purple housings and a richly jewelled bridle, the spoil of Darius' or Cambyses' treasury, if not of Cyrus' own. As for the man, a few laughed at him, but most shrank as from a monster. Ptolemy realized that the show was a failure, and the Egyptians proof against mere novelty, preferring harmony and beauty. So he withdrew and ceased to prize them; the camel died forgotten, and the parti-coloured man became the reward of Thespis the fluteplayer for a successful after-dinner performance.

I am afraid my work is a camel in Egypt, and men's admiration limited to the bridle and purple housings; as to combinations, though the components may be of the most beautiful (as Comedy and Dialogue in the present case), that will not ensure a good effect, unless the mixture is harmonious and well-proportioned; it is possible that the resultant of two beauties may be bizarre. The readiest instance to hand is the centaur: not a lovely creature, you will admit, but a savage, if the paintings of its drunken bouts and murders go for anything. Well, but on the other hand is it not possible for two such components to result in beauty, as the combination of wine and honey in superlative sweetness? That is my belief; but I am not prepared to maintain that *my* components have that property; I fear the mixture may only have obscured their separate beauties.

For one thing, there was no great original connexion or friendship between Dialogue and Comedy; the former was a stay-at-home, spending his time in solitude, or at most taking a stroll with a few intimates; whereas Comedy put herself in the hands of Dionysus, haunted the theatre, frolicked in company, laughed and mocked and tripped it to the flute when she saw good; nay, she would mount her anapaests, as likely as not, and pelt the friends of Dialogue with nicknames— doctrinaires, airy metaphysicians, and the like. The thing she loved of all else was to chaff them and drench them in holiday impertinence, exhibit them treading on air and arguing with the clouds, or measuring the jump of a flea, as a type of their ethereal refinements. But Dialogue continued his deep speculations upon Nature and Virtue, till, as the musicians say, the interval between them was two full octaves, from the highest to the lowest note. This ill-assorted pair it is that we have dared to unite and harmonize-reluctant and ill—disposed for reconciliation.

And here comes in the apprehension of yet another Promethean analogy: have I confounded male and female, and incurred the penalty? Or no— when will resemblances end?—have I, rather, cheated my hearers by serving them up bones wrapped in fat, comic laughter in philosophic solemnity? As for stealing—for Prometheus is the thief's patron too— I defy you there; that is the one fault you cannot find with me:

from whom should I have stolen? if any one has dealt before me in such forced unions and hybrids, I have never made his acquaintance. But after all, what am I to do? I have made my bed, and I must lie in it; Epimetheus may change his mind, but Prometheus, never.

NIGRINUS

Lucian to Nigrinus. Health.

There is a proverb about carrying 'owls to Athens'—an absurd undertaking, considering the excellent supply already on the spot. Had it been my intention, in presenting Nigrinus with a volume of my composition, to indulge him of all people with a display of literary skill, I should indeed have been an arrant 'owl-fancier in Athens.' As however my object is merely to communicate to you my present sentiments, and the profound impression produced upon me by your eloquence, I may fairly plead Not Guilty, even to the charge of Thucydides, that 'Men are bold from ignorance, where mature consideration would render them cautious.' For I need not say that devotion to my subject is partly responsible for my present hardihood; it is not *all* the work of ignorance. Farewell.

NIGRINUS
A DIALOGUE

Lucian. A Friend

Fr. What a haughty and dignified Lucian returns to us from his journey! He will not vouchsafe us a glance; he stands aloof, and will hold no further communion with us. Altogether a supercilious Lucian! The change is sudden. Might one inquire the cause of this altered demeanour?

Luc. 'Tis the work of Fortune.

Fr. Of Fortune!

Luc. As an incidental result of my journey, you see in me a happy man; 'thrice-blest,' as the tragedians have it.

Fr. Dear me. What, in this short time?

Luc. Even so.

Fr. But what does it all mean? What is the secret of your elation? I decline to rejoice with you in this abridged fashion; I must have details. Tell me all about it.

Luc. What should you think, if I told you that I had exchanged servitude for freedom; poverty for true wealth; folly and presumption for good sense?

Fr. Extraordinary! But I am not quite clear of your meaning yet.

Luc. Why, I went off to Rome to see an oculist—my eyes had been getting worse—

Fr. Yes, I know about that. I have been hoping that you would light on a good man.

Luc. Well, I got up early one morning with the intention of paying a long-deferred visit to Nigrinus, the Platonic philosopher. On reaching his house, I knocked, and was duly announced and admitted to his presence. I found him with a book in his hand, surrounded by various statues of the ancient philosophers. Before him lay a tablet, with geometrical figures described on it, and a globe of reeds, designed apparently to represent the universe. He greeted me cordially, and asked after my welfare. I satisfied his inquiries, and demanded, in my turn, how he did, and whether he had decided on another trip to Greece. Once on that subject, he gave free expression to his sentiments; and, I assure you, 'twas a veritable feast of ambrosia to me. The spells of the Sirens (if ever there were Sirens), of the Pindaric 'Charmers,' of the Homeric lotus, are things to be forgotten, after his truly divine eloquence. Led on by his theme, he spoke the praises of philosophy, and of the freedom which philosophy confers; and expressed his contempt for the vulgar error which sets a value upon wealth and renown and dominion and power, upon gold and purple, and all that dazzles the eyes of the world,—and once attracted my own! I listened with rapt attention, and with a swelling heart. At the time, I knew not what had come over me; my feelings were indescribable. My dearest idols, riches and renown, lay shattered; one moment I was ready to shed bitter tears over the disillusionment, the next, I could have laughed for scorn of these very things, and was exulting in my escape from the murky atmosphere of my past life into the brightness of the upper air. The result was curious:

I forgot all about my ophthalmic troubles, in the gradual improvement of my spiritual vision; for till that day I had grovelled in spiritual blindness. Little by little I came into the condition with which you were twitting me just now. Nigrinus's words have raised in me a joyous exaltation of spirit which precludes every meaner thought. Philosophy seems to have produced the same effect on me as wine is said to have produced on the Indians the first time they drank it. The mere taste of such potent liquor threw them into a state of absolute frenzy, the intoxicating power of the wine being doubled in men so warm-blooded by nature. This is my case. I go about like one possessed; I am drunk with the words of wisdom.

Fr. This is not drunkenness, but sobriety and temperance. But I should like to hear what Nigrinus actually said, if that may be. It is only right that you should take that trouble for me; I am your friend, and share your interests.

Luc. Enough! You urge a willing steed. I was about to bespeak your attention. You must be my witness to the world, that there is reason in my madness. Indeed, apart from this, the work of recollection is a pleasure, and has become a constant practice with me; twice, thrice in a day I repeat over his words, though there is none to hear. A lover, in the absence of his mistress, remembers some word, some act of hers, dwells on it, and beguiles hours of sickness with her feigned presence. Sometimes he thinks he is face to face with her; words, heard long since, come again from her lips; he rejoices; his soul cleaves to the memory of the past, and has no time for present vexations. It is so with me. Philosophy is far away, but I have heard a philosopher's words. I piece them together, and revolve them in my heart, and am comforted. Nigrinus is the beacon-fire on which, far out in mid-ocean, in the darkness of night, I fix my gaze; I fancy him present with me in all my doings; I hear ever the same words. At times, in moments of concentration, I see his very face, his voice rings in my ears. Of him it may truly be said, as of Pericles,

In every heart he left his sting.

Fr. Stay, gentle enthusiast. Take a good breath, and start again; I am waiting to hear what Nigrinus said. You beat about the bush in a manner truly exasperating.

Luc. True, I must make a start, as you say. And yet... Tell me, did you never see a tragedy (nay, the comedies fare no better) murdered by bad acting, and the culprits finally hissed off the stage for their pains? As often as not the play is a perfectly good one, and has scored a success.

Fr. I know the sort of thing; and what about it?

Luc. I am afraid that before I have done you will find that I make as sad work of it as they do,—jumbling things together pell-mell, spoiling the whole point sometimes by inadequate expression; and you will end by damning the play instead of the actor. I could put up with my own share of the disgrace; but it would vex me indeed, that my subject should be involved in my downfall; I cannot have *it* discredited for my shortcomings. Remember, then:

whatever the imperfections in my speech, the author is not to be called to account; he sits far aloof from the stage, and knows nothing of what is going forward. The memory of the actor is all that you are invited to criticize; I am neither more nor less than the 'Messenger' in a tragedy. At each flaw in the argument, be this your first thought, that the author probably said something quite different, and much more to the point;—and then you may hiss me off if you will.

Fr. Bless me; here is quite a professional exordium! You are about to add, I think, that 'your consultation with your client has been but brief'; that you 'come into court imperfectly instructed'; that 'it were to be desired that your client were here to plead his own cause; as it is, you are reduced to such a meagre and inadequate statement of the case, as memory will supply.' Am I right? Well then, spare yourself the trouble, as far as I am concerned. Imagine all these preliminaries settled. I stand prepared to applaud:

but if you keep me waiting, I shall harbour resentment all through the case, and hiss you accordingly.

Luc. I should, indeed, have been glad to avail myself of the arguments you mention, and of others too. I might have said, that mine would be no set speech, no orderly statement such as that I heard; that is wholly beyond me. Nor can I speak in the person of Nigrinus. There again I should be like a bad actor, taking the part of Agamemnon, or Creon, or Heracles' self; he is arrayed in cloth of gold, and looks very formidable, and his mouth opens tremendously wide; and what comes out of it? A little, shrill, womanish pipe of a voice that would disgrace Polyxena or Hecuba! I for my part have no intention of exposing myself in a mask several sizes too large for me, or of wearing a robe to which I cannot do credit. Rather than play the hero's part, and involve him in my discomfiture, I will speak in my own person.

Fr. Will the man never have done with his masks and his stages?

Luc. Nay, that is all. And now to my subject. Nigrinus's first words were in praise of Greece, and in particular of the Athenians. They are brought up, he said, to poverty and to philosophy. The endeavours, whether of foreigners or of their own countrymen, to introduce luxury into their midst, find no favour with them. When a man comes among them with this view, they quietly set about to correct his tendency, and by gentle degrees to bring him to a better course of life. He mentioned the case of a wealthy man who arrived at Athens in all the vulgar pomp of retinue and gold and gorgeous raiment, expecting that every eye would be turned upon him in envy of his lot; instead of which, they heartily pitied the poor worm, and proceeded to take his education in hand. Not an ill-natured word, not an attempt at direct interference:

it was a free city; he was at liberty to live in it as he thought fit. But when he made a public nuisance of himself in the baths or gymnasiums, crowding in with his attendants, and taking up all the room, someone would whisper, in a sly aside, as if the words were not meant to reach his ears: 'He is afraid he will never come out from here alive; yet all is peace; there is no need of such an army.' The remark would be overheard, and would have its educational effect. They soon eased him of his embroidery and purple, by playful allusions to flower and colour. 'Spring is early.'—'How did that peacock get here?'—'His mother must have lent him that shawl,'—and so on. The same with the rest, his rings, his elaborate coiffure, and his table excesses. Little by little he came to his senses, and left Athens very much the better for the public education he had received.

Nor do they scruple to confess their poverty. He mentioned a sentence which he heard pronounced unanimously by the assembled people at the Panathenaic festival. A citizen had been arrested and brought before the Steward for making his appearance in coloured clothes. The onlookers felt for him, and took his part; and when the herald declared that he had violated the law by attending the festival in that attire, they all exclaimed with one voice, as if they had been in consultation, 'that he must be pardoned for wearing those clothes, as he had no others.'

He further commended the Athenian liberty, and unpretentious style of living; the peace and learned leisure which they so abundantly enjoy. To dwell among such men, he declared, is to dwell with philosophy; a single-hearted man, who has been taught to despise wealth, may here preserve a pure morality; no life could be more in harmony with the determined pursuit of all that is truly beautiful. But the man over whom gold has cast its spell, who is in love with riches, and measures happiness by purple raiment and dominion, who, living his life among flatterers and slaves, knows not the sweets of freedom, the blessings of candour, the beauty of truth; he who has given up his soul to Pleasure, and will serve no other mistress, whose heart is set on gluttony and wine and women, on whose tongue are deceit and hypocrisy; he again whose ears must be tickled with lascivious songs, and the voluptuous notes of flute and lyre;—let all such (he cried) dwell here in Rome; the life will suit them. Our streets and market-places are filled with the things they love best. They may take in pleasure through every aperture, through eye and ear, nostril and palate; nor are the claims of Aphrodite forgotten. The turbid stream surges everlastingly through our streets; avarice, perjury, adultery,—all tastes are represented. Under that rush of waters, modesty, virtue, uprightness, are torn from the soul; and in their stead grows the tree of perpetual thirst, whose flowers are many strange desires.

Such was Rome; such were the blessings she taught men to enjoy. 'As for me,' he continued, 'on returning from my first voyage to Greece, I stopped short a little way from the city, and called myself to account, in the words of Homer, for my return.

Ah, wretch! and leav'st thou then the light of day— the joyous
freedom of Greece, And wouldst behold—

the turmoil of Rome? slander and insolence and gluttony, flatterers and false friends, legacy-hunters and murderers? And what wilt thou do here? thou canst not endure these things, neither canst thou escape them! Thus reasoning, I withdrew myself out of range, as Zeus did Hector,

Far from the scene of slaughter, blood and strife,

and resolved henceforth to keep my house. I lead the life you see—a spiritless, womanish life, most men would account it—holding converse with Philosophy, with Plato, with Truth. From my high seat in this vast theatre, I look down on the scene beneath me; a scene calculated to afford much entertainment; calculated also to try a man's resolution to the utmost. For, to give evil its due, believe me, there is no better school for virtue, no truer test of moral strength, than life in this same city of Rome. It is no easy thing, to withstand so many temptations, so many allurements and distractions of sight and sound. There is no help for it:

like Odysseus, we must sail past them all; and there must be no binding of hands, no stopping of our ears with wax; that would be but sorry courage:

our ears must hear, our hands must be free,—and our contempt must be genuine. Well may that man conceive an admiration of philosophy, who is a spectator of so much folly; well may he despise the gifts of Fortune, who views this stage, and its multitudinous actors. The slave grows to be master, the rich man is poor, the pauper becomes a prince, a king; and one is His Majesty's friend, and another is his enemy, and a third he banishes. And here is the strangest thing of all:

the affairs of mankind are confessedly the playthings of Fortune, they have no pretence to security; yet, with instances of this daily before their eyes, men will reach after wealth and power;—not one of them but carries his load of hopes unrealized.

'But I said that there was entertainment also to be derived from the scene; and I will maintain it. Our rich men are an entertainment in themselves, with their purple and their rings always in evidence, and their thousand vulgarities. The latest development is the *salutation by proxy;* [4]they favour us with a

---

[4] The *spoken* salutation being performed by a servant.

glance, and that must be happiness enough. By the more ambitious spirits, an obeisance is expected; this is not performed at a distance, after the Persian fashion—you go right up, and make a profound bow, testifying with the angle of your body to the self-abasement of your soul; you then kiss his hand or breast—and happy and enviable is he who may do so much! And there stands the great man, protracting the illusion as long as may be. (I heartily acquiesce, by the way, in the churlish sentence which excludes us from a nearer acquaintance with their *lips*.)

'But if these men are amusing, their courtiers and flatterers are doubly so. They rise in the small hours of the night, to go their round of the city, to have doors slammed in their faces by slaves, to swallow as best they may the compliments of "Dog," "Toadeater," and the like. And the guerdon of their painful circumambulations? A vulgarly magnificent dinner, the source of many woes! They eat too much, they drink more than they want, they talk more than they should; and then they go away, angry and disappointed, grumbling at their fare, and protesting against the scant courtesy shown them by their insolent patron. You may see them vomiting in every alley, squabbling at every brothel. The daylight most of them spend in bed, furnishing employment for the doctors. Most of them, I say; for with some it has come to this, that they actually have no time to be ill. My own opinion is that, of the two parties, the toadies are more to blame, and have only themselves to thank for their patron's insolence. What can they expect him to think, after their commendations of his wealth, their panegyrics on money, their early attendance at his doors, their servile salutations? If by common consent they would abstain, were it only for a few days, from this voluntary servitude, the tables must surely be turned, and the rich come to the doors of the paupers, imploring them not to leave such blessedness as theirs without a witness, their fine houses and elegant furniture lying idle for want of some one to use them. Not wealth, but the envy that waits on wealth, is the object of their desire. The truth is, gold and ivory and noble mansions are of little avail to their owner, if there is no one to admire them. If we would break the power of the rich, and bring down their pretensions, we must raise up within their borders a stronghold of Indifference. As it is, their vanity is fostered by the court that is paid to them. In ordinary men, who have no pretence to education, this conduct, no doubt, is less to be blamed. But that men who call themselves philosophers should actually outdo the rest in degradation,—this, indeed, is the climax. Imagine my feelings, when I see a brother philosopher, an old man, perhaps, mingling in the herd of sycophants; dancing attendance on some great man; adapting himself to the conversational level of a possible host! One thing, indeed, serves to distinguish him from his company, and to accentuate his disgrace;—he wears the garb of philosophy. It is much to be regretted that actors of uniform excellence in other respects will not dress conformably to their part. For in the achievements of the table, what toadeater besides can be compared with them? There is an artlessness in their manner of stuffing themselves, a frankness in their tippling, which defy competition; they sponge with more spirit than other men, and sit on with greater persistency. It is not an uncommon thing for the more courtly sages to oblige the company with a song.'

All this he treated as a jest. But he had much to say on the subject of those paid philosophers, who hawk about virtue like any other marketable commodity. 'Hucksters' and 'petty traders' were his words for them. A man who proposes to teach the contempt of wealth, should begin (he maintained) by showing a soul above fees. And certainly he has always acted on this principle himself. He is not content with giving his services gratis to all comers, but lends a helping hand to all who are in difficulties, and shows an absolute disregard for riches. So far is he from grasping at other men's goods, that he could anticipate without concern the deterioration of his own property. He possessed an estate at no great distance from the city, on which for many years he had never even set foot. Nay, he disclaimed all right of property in it; meaning, I suppose, that we have no natural claim to such things; law, and the rights of inheritance, give us the use of them for an indefinite period, and for that time we are styled 'owners'; presently our term lapses, and another succeeds to the enjoyment of a name.

There are other points in which he sets an admirable example to the serious followers of philosophy:

his frugal life, his systematic habits of bodily exercise, his modest bearing, his simplicity of dress, but above all, gentle manners and a constant mind. He urges his followers not to postpone the pursuit of good, as so many do, who allow themselves a period of grace till the next great festival, after which they propose to eschew deceit and lead a righteous life; there must be no shilly-shallying, when virtue is the goal for which we start. On the other hand, there are philosophers whose idea of inculcating virtue in their youthful disciples is to subject them to various tests of physical endurance; whose favourite prescription is the strait waistcoat, varied with flagellations, or the enlightened process of scarification. Of these Nigrinus evidently had no opinion. According to him, our first care should be to inure the *soul* to pain and hardship; he who aspired to educate men aright must reckon with soul as well as body, with the age of his pupils, and with their previous training; he would then escape the palpable blunder of overtasking them. Many a one (he affirmed) had succumbed under the unreasonable strain put upon him; and I met with an instance myself, of a man who had tasted the hardships of those schools, but no sooner heard the words of true wisdom, than he fled incontinently to Nigrinus, and was manifestly the better for the change.

Leaving the philosophers to themselves, he reverted to more general subjects:

the din and bustle of the city, the theatres, the race-course, the statues of charioteers, the nomenclature of horses, the horse-talk in every side-street. The rage for horses has become a positive epidemic; many persons are infected with it whom one would have credited with more sense.

41

Then the scene changed to the pomp and circumstance attendant upon funerals and testamentary dispositions. 'Only once in his life' (he observed) 'does your thoroughbred Roman say what he means; and then,' meaning, in his will, 'it comes too late for him to enjoy the credit of it.' I could not help laughing when he told me how they thought it necessary to carry their follies with them to the grave, and to leave the record of their inanity behind them in black and white; some stipulating that their clothes or other treasures should be burnt with them, others that their graves should be watched by particular servants, or their monuments crowned with flowers;—sapient end to a life of sapience! 'Of their doings in this world,' said he, 'you may form some idea from their injunctions with reference to the next. These are they who will pay a long price for an entree; whose floors are sprinkled with wine and saffron and spices; who in midwinter smother themselves in roses, ay, for roses are scarce, and out of season, and altogether desirable; but let a thing come in its due course, and oh, 'tis vile, 'tis contemptible. These are they whose drink is of costly essences.' He had no mercy on them here. 'Very bunglers in sensuality, who know not her laws, and confound her ordinances, flinging down their souls to be trampled beneath the heels of luxury! As the play has it, Door or window, all is one to them. Such pleasures are rank solecism.' One observation of his in the same spirit fairly caps the famous censure of Momus. Momus found fault with the divine artificer for not putting his bull's horns in front of the eyes. Similarly, Nigrinus complained that when these men crown themselves in their banquets, they put the garlands in the wrong place; if they are so fond of the smell of violets and roses, they should tie on their garlands as close as may be under their nostrils; they could then snuff up the smell to their hearts' content.

Proceeding to the gentlemen who make such a serious work of their dinner, he was exceedingly merry over their painful elaborations of sauce and seasoning. 'Here again,' he cried, 'these men are sore put to it, to procure the most fleeting of enjoyments. Grant them four inches of palate apiece—'tis the utmost we can allow any man—and I will prove to you that they have four inches of gratification for their trouble. Thus:

there is no satisfaction to be got out of the costliest viands before consumption; and after it a full stomach is none the better for the price it has cost to fill it. *Ergo*, the money is paid for the pleasure snatched *in transitu*. But what are we to expect? These men are too grossly ignorant to discern those truer pleasures with which Philosophy rewards our resolute endeavours.'

The Baths proved a fertile topic, what with the insolence of the masters and the jostlings of their men;—'they will not stand without the support of a slave; it is much that they retain enough vitality to get away on their own legs at all.' One practice which obtains in the streets and Baths of Rome seemed to arouse his particular resentment. Slaves have to walk on ahead of their masters, and call out to them to 'look to their feet,' whenever there is a hole or a lump in their way; it has come to this, that men must be *reminded that they are walking*. 'It is too much,' he cried; 'these men can get through their dinner with the help of their own teeth and fingers; they can hear with their own ears:

yet they must have other men's eyes to see for them! They are in possession of all their faculties:

yet they are content to be spoken to in language which should only be addressed to poor maimed wretches! And this goes on in broad daylight, in our public places; and among the sufferers are men who are responsible for the welfare of cities!'

This he said, and much more to the same effect. At length he was silent. All the time I had listened in awestruck attention, dreading the moment when he should cease. And when it was all over, my condition was like that of the Phaeacians. For a long time I gazed upon him, spellbound; then I was seized with a violent attack of giddiness; I was bathed in perspiration, and when I attempted to speak, I broke down; my voice failed, my tongue stammered, and at last I was reduced to tears. Mine was no surface wound from a random shaft. The words had sunk deep into a vital part; had come with true aim, and cleft my soul asunder. For (if I may venture to philosophize on my own account) I conceive the case thus:

-A well-conditioned human soul is like a target of some soft material. As life goes on, many archers take aim thereat; and every man's quiver is full of subtle and varied arguments, but not every man shoots aright. Some draw the bow too tight, and let fly with undue violence. These hit the true direction, but their shafts do not lodge in the mark; their impetus carries them right through the soul, and they pass on their way, leaving only a gaping wound behind them. Others make the contrary mistake:

their bows are too slack, and their shafts never reach their destination; as often as not their force is spent at half distance, and they drop to earth. Or if they reach the mark, they do but graze its surface; there can be no deep wound, where the archer lacks strength. But a good marksman, a Nigrinus, begins with a careful examination of the mark, in case it should be particularly soft,—or again too hard; for there are marks which will take no impression from an arrow. Satisfied on this point, he dips his shaft, not in the poisons of Scythia or Crete, but in a certain ointment of his own, which is sweet in flavour and gentle in operation; then, without more ado, he lets fly. The shaft speeds with well-judged swiftness, cleaves the mark right through, and remains lodged in it; and the drug works its way through every part. Thus it is that men hear his words with mingled joy and grief; and this was my own case, while the drug was gently diffusing itself through my soul. Hence I was moved to apostrophize him in the words of Homer:

So aim; and thou shalt bring (to some) salvation.

For as it is not every man that is maddened by the sound of the Phrygian flute, but only those who are inspired of Cybele, and by those strains are recalled to their frenzy,—so too not every man who hears the words of the philosophers will go away possessed, and stricken at heart, but only those in whose nature is something akin to philosophy.

Fr. These are fearful and wonderful words; nay, they are divine. All that you said of ambrosia and lotus is true; I little knew how sumptuous had been your feast. I have listened to you with strange emotion, and now that you have ceased, I feel oppressed, nay, in your own language, 'sore stricken.' This need not surprise you. A person who has been bitten by a mad dog not only goes mad himself, you know, but communicates his madness to any one whom he bites whilst he is in that state, so that the infection may be carried on by this means through a long succession of persons.

Luc. Ah, then you confess to a tenderness?

Fr. I do; and beg that you will think upon some medicine for both our wounded breasts.

Luc. We must take a hint from Telephus.

Fr. What is that?

Luc. We want a hair of the dog that bit us.

TRIAL IN THE COURT OF VOWELS

Archon, Aristarchus of Phalerum. Seventh Pyanepsion. Court of the Seven Vowels. Action for assault with robbery. Sigma *v.* Tau. Plaintiff's case—that the words in-pp-are wrongfully withheld from him.

Vowels of the jury.—For some time this Mr. Tau's trespasses and encroachments on my property were of minor importance; I made no claim for damages, and affected unconsciousness of what I heard; my conciliatory temper both you and the other letters have reason to know. His covetousness and folly, however, have now so puffed him up, that he is no longer content with my habitual concessions, but insists on more; I accordingly find myself compelled to get the matter settled by you who know both sides of it. The fact is, I am in bodily fear, owing to the crushing to which I am subjected. This evergrowing aggression will end by ousting me completely from my own; I shall be almost dumb, lose my rank as a letter, and be degraded to a mere noise.

Justice requires then that not merely you, the jury in this case, but the other letters also, should be on your guard against such attempts. If any one who chooses is to be licensed to leave his own place and usurp that of others, with no objection on your part (whose concurrence is an indispensable condition of all writing), I fail to see how combinations are to have their ancient constitutional rights secured to them. But my first reliance is upon you, who will surely never be guilty of the negligence and indifference which permits injustice; and even if you decline the contest, I have no intention of sitting down under that injustice myself.

It is much to be regretted that the assaults of other letters were not repelled when they first began their lawless practices; then we should not be watching the still pending dispute between Lambda and Rho for possession of *kephalalgia* or *kephalargia*, *kishlis* or *kishris*.

Gamma would not have had to defend its rights over *gyaphalla*, constantly almost at blows with Kappa in the debatable land, and *per contra* it would itself have dropped its campaign against Lambda (if indeed it is more dignified than petty larceny) for converting *molis* to *mogis*.

in fact lawless confusion generally would have been nipped in the bud. And it is well to abide by the established order; such trespasses betray a revolutionary spirit.

Now our first legislators—Cadmus the islander, Palamedes, son of Nauplius, or Simonides, whom some authorities credit with the measure—were not satisfied with determining merely our order of precedence in the alphabet; they also had an eye to our individual qualities and faculties. You, Vowels of the jury, constitute the first Estate, because you can be uttered independently; the semi-vowels, requiring support before they can be distinctly heard, are the second; and the lowest Estate they declared to consist of those

45

nine which cannot be sounded at all by themselves. The vowels are accordingly the natural guardians of our laws.

But this—this Tau—I would give him a worse designation, but that is a manifest impossibility; for without the assistance of two good presentable members of your Estate, Alpha and Upsilon, he would be a mere nonentity—he it is that has dared to outdo all injuries that I have ever known, expelling me from the nouns and verbs of my inheritance, and hunting me out of my conjunctions and prepositions, till his rapacity has become quite unbearable. I am now to trace proceedings from the beginning.

I was once staying at Cybelus, a pleasant little town, said to be an Athenian colony; my travelling companion was the excellent Rho, best of neighbours. My host was a writer of comedies, called Lysimachus; he seems to have been a Boeotian by descent, though he represented himself as coming from the interior of Attica. It was while with him that I first detected Tau's depredations[5]. For some earlier occasional attempts (as when he took to tettaroakonta for tessarakonta, taemeron for saemeron, with little pilferings of that sort) I had explained as a trick and peculiarity of pronunciation; I had tolerated the sound without letting it annoy me seriously.

But impunity emboldened him; kassiteros became kattiteros, kassuma and pissa shared its fate; and then he cast off all shame and assaulted basigissa. I found myself losing the society in which I had been born and bred[6]; at such a time equanimity is out of place; I am tortured with apprehension; how long will it be before *suka* is *tuka*? Bear with me, I beseech you; I despair and have none to help me; do I not well to be angry? It is no petty everyday peril, this threatened separation from my long-tried familiars. My *kissa*, my talking bird that nestled in my breast, he has torn away and named anew; my *phassa*, my *nhssai*, my *khossuphoi*—all gone; and I had Aristarchus's own word that they were mine; half my *melissai* he has lured to strange hives; Attica itself he has

---

[5] For the probably corrupt passage Section 7 fin.—Section 8 init. I accept Dindorf's rearrangement as follows:

mechr men gar oligois epecheirei, tettarakonta legein axioun, eti de taemeron kai ta homoia epispomenon, sunaetheian thmaen idia tauti legein, kai oiston aen moi to akousma kai ou panu ti edaknomaen ep autois. 8. hupote d ek touton arxamenon etolmaese kattiteron eipein kai kattuma kai pittan, eita aperuthriasan kai basilitgan onomazein, aposteroun me ton suggegenaemenun moi kai suntethrammenun grammatun, ou metrius ipi toutois aganaktu.

[6] For the probably corrupt passage Section 7 fin.— Section 8 init. I accept Dindorf's rearrangement as follows:

mechr men gar oligois epecheirei, tettarakonta legein axioun, eti de taemeron kai ta homoia epispomenon, sunaetheian thmaen idia tauti legein, kai oiston aen moi to akousma kai ou panu ti edaknomaen ep autois. 8. _hupote d ek touton arxamenon etolmaese kattiteron eipein kai kattuma kai pittan, eita aperuthriasan kai basilitgan onomazein, aposteroun me ton suggegenaemenun moi kai suntethrammenun grammatun, ou metrius ipi toutois aganaktu.

invaded, and wrongfully annexed its Hymettus (as he calls it); and you and the rest looked on at the seizure.

But why dwell on such trifles? I am driven from all Thessaly (Thettaly, forsooth!), *thalassa* is now *mare clausum* to me; he will not leave me a poor garden-herb like *seutlion*, I have never a *passalos* to hang myself upon. What a long-suffering letter I am myself, your own knowledge is witness enough. When Zeta stole my *smaragdos*, and robbed me of all Smyrna, I never took proceedings against him; Xi might break all *sunthhkai*, and appeal to Thucydides (who ought to know) as xympathizing with his xystem; I let them alone. My neighbour Rho I made no difficulty about pardoning as an invalid, when he transplanted my *mursinai* into his garden, or, in a fit of the spleen, took liberties with my *khopsh*. So much for my temper.

Tau's, on the other hand, is naturally violent; its manifestations are not confined to me. In proof that he has not spared other letters, but assaulted Delta, Theta, Zeta, and almost the whole alphabet, I wish his various victims to be put in the box. Now, Vowels of the jury, mark the evidence of Delta:

—'He robbed me of *endelecheia*, which he claimed, quite illegally, as *entelecheia*.' Mark Theta beating his breast and plucking out his hair in grief for the loss of *kolokunthh*. And Zeta mourns for *surizein* and *salpizein*—nay, *cannot* mourn, for lack of his gryzein. What tolerance is possible, what penalty adequate, for this criminal letter's iniquities?

But his wrongs are not even limited to us, his own species; he has now extended his operations to mankind, as I shall show. He does not permit their tongues to work straight. (But that mention of mankind calls me back for a moment, reminding me how he turns glossa into glotta, half robbing me of the tongue itself. Ay, you are a disease of the tongue in every sense, Tau.) But I return from that digression, to plead the cause of mankind and its wrongs. The prisoner's designs include the constraint, racking, and mutilation of their utterance. A man sees a beautiful thing, and wishes to describe it as kalon, but in comes Tau, and forces the man to say talon he must have precedence everywhere, of course. Another man has something to say about a vine, and lo, before it is out, it is metamorphosed by this miserable creature into misery; he has changed slaema to tlaema, with a suggestive hint of tlaemon. And, not content with middle-class victims, he aims at the Persian king himself, the one for whom land and sea are said to have made way and changed their nature:

Cyrus comes out at his bidding as Tyrus.

Such are his verbal offences against man; his offences in deed remain. Men weep, and bewail their lot, and curse Cadmus with many curses for introducing Tau into the family of letters; they say it was his body that tyrants took for a model, his shape that they imitated, when they set up the erections on which men are crucified. Stayros the vile engine is called, and it derives its vile name from him. Now, with all these crimes upon him, does he not deserve death, nay, many deaths? For my part I know none bad enough but that supplied by his own shape —that shape which he gave to the gibbet named Stayros after him by men.

TIMON THE MISANTHROPE

Timon. Zeus. Hermes. Plutus. Poverty. Gnathonides. Philiades. Demeas.
Thrasycles. Blepsias.

Tim. O Zeus, thou arbiter of friendship, protector of the guest, preserver
of fellowship, lord of the hearth, launcher of the lightning, avenger of oaths,
compeller of clouds, utterer of thunder (and pray add any other epithets; those
cracked poets have plenty ready, especially when they are in difficulties with
their scansion; then it is that a string of your names saves the situation and fills
up the metrical gaps), O Zeus, where is now your resplendent lightning, where
your deep-toned thunder, where the glowing, white- hot, direful bolt? we know
now 'tis all fudge and poetic moonshine— barring what value may attach to
the rattle of the names. That renowned projectile of yours, which ranged so far
and was so ready to your hand, has gone dead and cold, it seems; never a spark
left in it to scorch iniquity.

If men are meditating perjury, a smouldering lamp-wick is as likely to
frighten them off it as the omnipotent's levin-bolt; the brand you hold over
them is one from which they see neither flame nor smoke can come; a little
soot-grime is the worst that need be apprehended from a touch of it. No
wonder if Salmoneus challenged you to a thundering-match; he was reasonable
enough when he backed his artificial heat against so cool-tempered a Zeus. Of
course he was; there are you in your opiate-trance, never hearing the perjurers
nor casting a glance at criminals, your glazed eyes dull to all that happens, and
your ears as deaf as a dotard's.

When you were young and keen, and your temper had some life in it,
you used to bestir yourself against crime and violence; there were no armistices
in those days; the thunderbolt was always hard at it, the aegis quivering, the
thunder rattling, the lightning engaged in a perpetual skirmish. Earth was
shaken like a sieve, buried in snow, bombarded with hail. It rained cats and
dogs (if you will pardon my familiarity), and every shower was a waterspout.
Why, in Deucalion's time, hey presto, everything was swamped, mankind went
under, and just one little ark was saved, stranding on the top of Lycoreus and
preserving a remnant of human seed for the generation of greater wickedness.

Mankind pays you the natural wages of your laziness; if any one offers
you a victim or a garland nowadays, it is only at Olympia as a perfunctory
accompaniment of the games; he does it not because he thinks it is any good,
but because he may as well keep up an old custom. It will not be long, most
glorious of deities, before they serve you as you served Cronus, and depose you.
I will not rehearse all the robberies of your temple—those are trifles; but they
have laid hands on your person at Olympia, my lord High-Thunderer, and you
had not the energy to wake the dogs or call in the neighbours; surely they
might have come to the rescue and caught the fellows before they had finished
packing up the swag. But there sat the bold Giant-slayer and Titan-conqueror

letting them cut his hair, with a fifteen-foot thunderbolt in his hand all the time! My good sir, when is this careless indifference to cease? how long before you will punish such wickedness? Phaethon-falls and Deucalion-deluges—a good many of them will be required to suppress this swelling human insolence.

To leave generalities and illustrate from my own case—I have raised any number of Athenians to high position, I have turned poor men into rich, I have assisted every one that was in want, nay, flung my wealth broadcast in the service of my friends, and now that profusion has brought me to beggary, they do not so much as know me; I cannot get a glance from the men who once cringed and worshipped and hung upon my nod. If I meet one of them in the street, he passes me by as he might pass the tombstone of one long dead; it has fallen face upwards, loosened by time, but he wastes no moment deciphering it. Another will take the next turning when he sees me in the distance; I am a sight of ill omen, to be shunned by the man whose saviour and benefactor I had been not so long ago.

Thus in disgrace with fortune, I have betaken me to this corner of the earth, where I wear the smock-frock and dig for sixpence a day, with solitude and my spade to assist meditation. So much gain I reckon upon here—to be exempt from contemplating unmerited prosperity; no sight that so offends the eye as that. And now, Son of Cronus and Rhea, may I ask you to shake off that deep sound sleep of yours—why, Epimenides's was a mere nap to it—, put the bellows to your thunderbolt or warm it up in Etna, get it into a good blaze, and give a display of spirit, like a manly vigorous Zeus? or are we to believe the Cretans, who show your grave among their sights?

Zeus. Hermes, who is that calling out from Attica? there, on the lower slopes of Hymettus—a grimy squalid fellow in a smock-frock; he is bending over a spade or something; but he has a tongue in his head, and is not afraid to use it. He must be a philosopher, to judge from his fluent blasphemy.

Her. What, father! have you forgotten Timon—son of Echecratides, of Collytus? many is the time he has feasted us on unexceptionable victims; the rich *parvenu* of the whole hecatombs, you know, who used to do us so well at the Diasia.

Zeus. Dear, dear, *quantum mutatus!* is this the admired, the rich, the popular? What has brought him to this pass? There he is in filth and misery, digging for hire, labouring at that ponderous spade.

Her. Why, if you like to put it so, it was kindness and generosity and universal compassion that ruined him; but it would be nearer the truth to call him a fool and a simpleton and a blunderer; he did not realize that his proteges were carrion crows and wolves; vultures were feeding on his unfortunate liver, and he took them for friends and good comrades, showing a fine appetite just to please him. So they gnawed his bones perfectly clean, sucked out with great precision any marrow there might be in them, and went off, leaving him as dry as a tree whose roots have been severed; and now they do not know him or vouchsafe him a nod—no such fools—, nor ever think of showing him charity or repaying his gifts. That is how the spade and smock-frock are accounted for; he is ashamed to show his face in town; so he hires himself out to dig, and broods over his wrongs—the rich men he has made passing him contemptuously by, apparently quite unaware that his name is Timon.

Zeus. This is a case we must take up and see to. No wonder he is down on his luck. We should be putting ourselves on the level of his despicable sycophants, if we forgot all the fat ox and goat thighs he has burnt on our altars; the savour of them is yet in my nostrils. But I have been so busy, there is such a din of perjury, assault, and burglary; I am so frightened of the temple-robbers—they swarm now, you cannot keep them out, nor take a nap with any safety; and, with one thing and another, it is an age since I had a look at Attica. I have hardly been there since philosophy and argument came into fashion; indeed, with their shouting-matches going on, prayers are quite inaudible. One must sit with one's ears plugged, if one does not want the drums of them cracked; such long vociferous rigmaroles about Incorporeal Things, or something they call Virtue! That is how we came to neglect this man—who really deserved better.

However, go to him now without wasting any more time, Hermes, and take Plutus with you. Thesaurus is to accompany Plutus, and they are both to stay with Timon, and not leave him so lightly this time, even though the generous fellow does his best to find other hosts for them. As to those parasites, and the ingratitude they showed him, I will attend to them before long; they shall have their deserts as soon as I have got the thunderbolt in order again. Its two best spikes are broken and blunted; my zeal outran my discretion the other day when I took that shot at Anaxagoras the sophist; the Gods non-existent, indeed! that was what he was telling his disciples. However, I missed him (Pericles had held up his hand to shield him), and the bolt glanced off on to the Anaceum, set it on fire, and was itself nearly pulverized on the rock. But meanwhile it will be quite sufficient punishment for them to see Timon rolling in money.

Her. Nothing like lifting up your voice, making yourself a nuisance, and showing a bold front; it is equally effective whether you are pleading with juries or deities. Here is Timon developing from pauper to millionaire, just because his prayer was loud and free enough to startle Zeus; if he had dug quietly with his face to his work, he might have dug to all eternity, for any notice he would have got.

Pl. Well, Zeus, I am not going to him.

Zeus. Your reason, good Plutus; have I not told you to go?

Pl. Good God! why, he insulted me, threw me about, dismembered me—me, his old family friend—and practically pitchforked me out of the house; he could not have been in a greater hurry to be rid of me if I had been a live coal in his hand. What, go there again, to be transferred to toadies and flatterers and harlots? No, no, Zeus; send me to people who will appreciate the gift, take care of me, value and cherish me. Let these gulls consort with the poverty which they prefer to me; she will find them a smock-frock and a spade, and they can be thankful for a miserable pittance of sixpence a day, these reckless squanderers of 1,000 pound presents.

Zeus. Ah, Timon will not treat you that way again. If his loins are not of cast iron, his spade-work will have taught him a thing or two about your superiority to poverty. You are so particular, you know; now, you are finding fault with Timon for opening the door to you and letting you wander at your own sweet will, instead of keeping you in jealous seclusion. Yesterday it was another story:

you were imprisoned by rich men under bolts and locks and seals, and never allowed a glimpse of sunlight. That was the burden of your complaint—you were stifled in deep darkness. We saw you pale and careworn, your fingers hooked with coin-counting, and heard how you would like to run away, if only you could get the chance. It was monstrous, then, that you should be kept in a bronze or iron chamber, like a Danae condemned to virginity, and brought up by those stern unscrupulous tutors, Interest, Debit and Credit.

They were perfectly ridiculous, you know, loving you to distraction, but not daring to enjoy you when they might; you were in their power, yet they could not give the reins to their passion; they kept awake watching you with their eyes glued to bolt and seal; the enjoyment that satisfied them was not to enjoy you themselves, but to prevent others' enjoying you—true dogs in the manger. Yes, and then how absurd it was that they should scrape and hoard, and end by being jealous of their own selves! Ah, if they could but see that rascally slave—steward—trainer—sneaking in bent on carouse! little enough *he* troubles his head about the luckless unamiable owner at his nightly accounts by a dim little half-fed lamp. How, pray, do you reconcile your old strictures of this sort with your contrary denunciation of Timon?

Pl. Oh, if you consider the thing candidly, you will find both attitudes reasonable. It is clear enough that Timon's utter negligence comes from slackness, and not from any consideration for me. As for the other sort, who keep me shut up in the obscurity of strong-boxes, intent on making me heavy and fat and unwieldy, never touching me themselves, and never letting me see the light, lest some one else should catch sight of me, I always thought of them as fools and tyrants; what harm had I done that they should let me rot in close confinement? and did not they know that in a little while they would pass away and have to resign me to some other lucky man?

No, give me neither these nor the off-hand gentry; my beau ideal is the man who steers a middle course, as far from complete abstention as from utter profusion. Consider, Zeus, by your own great name; suppose a man were to take a fair young wife, and then absolutely decline all jealous precautions, to the point of letting her wander where she would by day or night, keeping company with any one who had a mind to her—or put it a little stronger, and let him be procurer, janitor, pander, and advertiser of her charms in his own person—well, what sort of love is his? come, Zeus, you have a good deal of experience, you know what love is.

On the other hand, let a man make a suitable match for the express purpose of raising heirs, and then let him neither himself have anything to do with her ripe, yet modest, beauty, nor allow any other to set eyes on it, but shut her up in barren, fruitless virginity; let him say all the while that he is in love with her, and let his pallid hue, his wasting flesh and his sunken eyes confirm the statement;—is he a madman, or is he not? he should be raising a family and enjoying matrimony; but he lets this fair-faced lovely girl wither away; he might as well be bringing up a perpetual priestess of Demeter. And now you understand my feelings when one set of people kick me about or waste me by the bucketful, and the others clap irons on me like a runaway convict.

Zeus. However, indignation is superfluous; both sets have just what they deserve—one as hungry and thirsty and dry-mouthed as Tantalus, getting no further than gaping at the gold; and the other finding its food swept away from its very gullet, as the Harpies served Phineus. Come, be off with you; you will find Timon has much more sense nowadays.

Pl. Oh, of course! he will not do his best to let me run out of a leaky vessel before I have done running in! oh no, he will not be consumed with apprehensions of the inflow's gaining on the waste and flooding him! I shall be supplying a cask of the Danaids; no matter how fast I pour in, the thing will not hold water; every gallon will be out almost before it is in; the bore of the waste-pipe is so large, and never a plug.

Zeus. Well, if he does not stop the hole—if the leak is more than temporary—you will run out in no time, and he can find his smock-frock and spade again in the dregs of the cask. Now go along, both of you, and make the man rich. And, Hermes, on your way back, remember to bring the Cyclopes with you from Etna; my thunderbolt wants the grindstone; and I have work for it as soon as it is sharp.

Her. Come along, Plutus. Hullo! limping? My good man, I did not know you were lame as well as blind.

Pl. No, it is intermittent. As sure as Zeus sends me *to* any one, a sort of lethargy comes over me, my legs are like lead, and I can hardly get to my journey's end; my destined host is sometimes an old man before I reach him. As a parting guest, on the other hand, you may see me wing my way swifter than any dream. 'Are you ready?' and almost before 'Go' has sounded, up goes my name as winner; I have flashed round the course absolutely unseen sometimes.

Her. You are not quite keeping to the truth; I could name you plenty of people who yesterday had not the price of a halter to hang themselves with, and to-day have developed into lavish men of fortune; they drive their pair of high-steppers, whereas a donkey would have been beyond their means before. They go about in purple raiment with jewelled fingers, hardly convinced yet that their wealth is not all a dream.

Pl. Ah, those are special cases, Hermes. I do not go on my own feet on those occasions, and it is not Zeus who sends me, but Pluto, who has his own ways of conferring wealth and making presents; Pluto and Plutus are not unconnected, you see. When I am to flit from one house to another, they lay me on parchment, seal me up carefully, make a parcel of me and take me round. The dead man lies in some dark corner, shrouded from the knees upward in an old sheet, with the cats fighting for possession of him, while those who have expectations wait for me in the public place, gaping as wide as young swallows that scream for their mother's return.

Then the seal is taken off, the string cut, the parchment opened, and my new owner's name made known. It is a relation, or a parasite, or perhaps a domestic minion, whose value lay in his vices and his smooth cheeks; he has continued to supply his master with all sorts of unnatural pleasures beyond the years which might excuse such service, and now the fine fellow is richly rewarded. But whoever it is, he snatches me up, parchment included, and is off with me in a flash; he used to be called Pyrrhias or Dromo or Tibius, but now he is Megacles, Megabyzus, or Protarchus; off he goes, leaving the disappointed ones staring at each other in very genuine mourning-over the fine fish which has jumped out of the landing-net after swallowing their good bait.

The fellow who *has* pounced on me has neither taste nor feeling; the sight of fetters still gives him a start; crack a whip in his neighbourhood, and his ears tingle; the treadmill is an abode of awe to him. He is now insufferable—insults his new equals, and whips his old fellows to see what that side of the transaction feels like. He ends by finding a mistress, or taking to the turf, or being cajoled by parasites; these have only to swear he is handsomer than Nireus, nobler than Cecrops or Codrus, wiser than Odysseus, richer than a dozen Croesuses rolled into one; and so the poor wretch disperses in a moment what cost so many perjuries, robberies, and swindles to amass.

Her. A very fair picture. But when you go on your own feet, how can a blind man like you find the way? Zeus sends you to people who he thinks deserve riches; but how do you distinguish them?

Pl. Do you suppose I do find them? not much. I should scarcely have passed Aristides by, and gone to Hipponicus, Callias, and any number of other Athenians whose merits could have been valued in copper.

Her. Well, but what do you do when he sends you?

Pl. I just wander up and down till I come across some one; the first comer takes me off home with him, and thanks—whom but the God of windfalls, yourself?

Her. So Zeus is in error, and you do not enrich deserving persons according to his pleasure?

Pl. My dear fellow, how can he expect it? He knows I am blind, and he sends me groping about for a thing so hard to detect, and so nearly extinct this long time, that a Lynceus would have his work cut out spying for its dubious remains. So you see, as the good are few, and cities are crowded with multitudes of the bad, I am much more likely to come upon the latter in my rambles, and they keep me in their nets.

Her. But when you are leaving them, how do you find escape so easy? you do not know the way.

Pl. Ah, there is just one occasion which brings me quickness of eye and foot; and that is flight.

Her. Yet another question. You are not only blind (excuse my frankness), but pallid and decrepit; how comes it, then, that you have so many lovers? All men's looks are for you; if they get possession of you, they count themselves happy men; if they miss you, life is not worth living. Why, I have known not a few so sick for love of you that they have scaled some sky-pointing crag, and thence hurled themselves to unplumbed ocean depths[7], when they thought they were scorned by you, because you would not acknowledge their first salute. I am sure you know yourself well enough to confess that they must be lunatics, to rave about such charms as yours.

Pl. Why, you do not suppose they see me in my true shape, lame, blind, and so forth?

Her. How else, unless they are all as blind themselves?

Pl. They are not blind, my dear boy; but the ignorant misconceptions now so prevalent obscure their vision. And then I contribute; not to be an absolute fright when they see me, I put on a charming mask, all gilt and jewels, and dress myself up. They take the mask for my face, fall in love with its beauty, and are dying to possess it. If any one were to strip and show me to them naked, they would doubtless reproach themselves for their blindness in being captivated by such an ugly misshapen creature,

Her. How about fruition, then? When they are rich, and have put the mask on themselves, they are still deluded; if any one tries to take it off, they would sooner part with their heads than with it; and it is not likely they do not know by that time that the beauty is adventitious, now that they have an inside view. *Pl.* There too I have powerful allies.

Her. Namely—?

Pl. When a man makes my acquaintance, and opens the door to let me in, there enter unseen by my side Arrogance, Folly, Vainglory, Effeminacy, Insolence, Deceit, and a goodly company more. These possess his soul; he begins to admire mean things, pursues what he should abhor, reveres me amid my bodyguard of the insinuating vices which I have begotten, and would consent to anything sooner than part with me.

Her. What a smooth, slippery, unstable, evasive fellow you are, Plutus! there is no getting a firm hold of you; you wriggle through one's fingers somehow, like an eel or a snake. Poverty is so different—sticky, clinging, all over hooks; any one who comes near her is caught directly, and finds it no simple matter to get clear. But all this gossip has put business out of our heads.

---

[7] See Apology for 'The Dependent Scholar,'

55

Pl. Business? What business?

Her. We have forgotten to bring Thesaurus, and we cannot do without him.

Pl. Oh, never mind him. When I come up to see you, I leave him on earth, with strict orders to stay indoors, and open to no one unless he hears my voice.

Her. Then we may make our way into Attica; hold on to my cloak till I find Timon's retreat.

Pl. It is just as well to keep touch; if you let me drop behind, I am as likely as not to be snapped up by Hyperbolus or Cleon. But what is that noise? it sounds like iron on stone.

Her. Ah, here is Timon close to us; what a steep stony little plot he has got to dig! Good gracious, I see Poverty and Toil in attendance, Endurance, Wisdom, Courage, and Hunger's whole company in full force—much more efficient than your guards, Plutus.

Pl. Oh dear, let us make the best of our way home, Hermes. We shall never produce any impression on a man surrounded by such troops.

Her. Zeus thought otherwise; so no cowardice.

Pov. Slayer of Argus, whither away, you two hand in hand?

Her. Zeus has sent us to Timon here.

Pov. Now? What has Plutus to do with Timon now? I found him suffering under Luxury's treatment, put him in the charge of Wisdom and Toil (whom you see here), and made a good worthy man of him. Do you take me for such a contemptible helpless creature that you can rob me of my little all? have I perfected him in virtue, only to see Plutus take him, trust him to Insolence and Arrogance, make him as soft and limp and silly as before, and return him to me a worn-out rag again?

Her. It is Zeus's will.

Pov. I am off, then. Toil, Wisdom, and the rest of you, quick march! Well, he will realize his loss before long; he had a good help meet in me, and a true teacher; with me he was healthy in body and vigorous in spirit; he lived the life of a man, and could be independent, and see the thousand and one needless refinements in all their absurdity.

Her. There they go, Plutus; let us come to him.

Tim. Who are you, villains? What do you want here, interrupting a hired labourer? You shall have something to take with you, confound you all! These clods and stones shall provide you with a broken head or two.

Her. Stop, Timon, don't throw. We are not men; I am Hermes, and this is Plutus; Zeus has sent us in answer to your prayers. So knock off work, take your fortune, and much good may it do you!

Tim. I dare say you *are* Gods; that shall not save you. I hate every one, man or God; and as for this blind fellow, whoever he may be, I am going to give him one over the head with my spade.

Pl. For God's sake, Hermes, let us get out of this! the man is melancholy-mad, I believe; he will do me a mischief before I get off.

Her. Now don't be foolish, Timon; cease overdoing the ill-tempered boor, hold out your hands, take your luck, and be a rich man again. Have Athens at your feet, and from your solitary eminence you can forget ingratitude.

Tim. I have no use for you; leave me in peace; my spade is riches enough for me; for the rest, I am perfectly happy if people will let me alone.

Her. My dear sir—so unsociable?

So stiff and stubborn a reply to Zeus?

A misanthrope you may well be, after the way men have treated you; but with the Gods so thoughtful for you, you need not be a misotheist.

Tim. Very well, Hermes; I am extremely obliged to you and Zeus for your thoughtfulness—there; but I will not have Plutus.

Her. Why, pray?

Tim. He brought me countless troubles long ago—put me in the power of flatterers, set designing persons on me, stirred up ill-feeling, corrupted me with indulgence, exposed me to envy, and wound up with treacherously deserting me at a moment's notice. Then the excellent Poverty gave me a drilling in manly labour, conversed with me in all frankness and sincerity, rewarded my exertions with a sufficiency, and taught me to despise superfluities; all hopes of a livelihood were to depend on myself, and I was to know my true wealth, unassailable by parasites' flattery or informers' threats, hasty legislatures or decree-mongering legislators, and which even the tyrant's machinations cannot touch.

So, toil-hardened, working with a will at this bit of ground, my eyes rid of city offences, I get bread enough and to spare out of my spade. Go your ways, then, Hermes, and take Plutus back to Zeus. I am quite content to let every man of them go hang.

Her. Oh, that would be a pity; they are not all hanging-ripe. Don't make a passionate child of yourself, but admit Plutus. Zeus's gifts are too good to be thrown away.

Pl. Will you condescend to argue with me, Timon? or does my voice provoke you?

Tim. Oh, talk away; but be brief; no rascally lawyer's 'opening the case.' I can put up with a few words from you, for Hermes' sake.

Pl. A speech of some length might seem to be needed, considering the number of your charges; however, just examine your imputations of injustice. It was I that gave you those great objects of desire— consideration, precedence, honours, and every delight; all eyes and tongues and attentions were yours— my gifts; and if flatterers abused you, I am not responsible for that. It is I who should rather complain; you prostituted me vilely to scoundrels, whose laudations and cajolery of you were only samples of their designs upon me. As to your saying that I wound up by betraying you, you have things topsy-turvy again; *I* may complain; you took every method to estrange me, and finally kicked me out neck and crop. That is why your revered Dame Poverty has supplied you with a smock-frock to replace your soft raiment. Why, I begged and prayed Zeus (and Hermes heard me) that I might be excused from revisiting a person who had been so unfriendly to me as you.

Her. But you see how he is changed, Plutus; you need not be afraid to live with him now. Just go on digging, Timon; and you, Plutus, put Thesaurus in position; he will come at your call.

Tim. I must obey, and be a rich man again, Hermes; what can one do, when Gods insist? But reflect what troubles you are bringing on my luckless head; I have had a blissful life of late, and now for no fault of my own I am to have my hands full of gold and care again.

Her. Hard, intolerable fate! yet endure for my sake, if only that the flatterers may burst themselves with envy. And now for heaven, via Etna.

Pl. He is off, I suppose, from the beating of his wings. Now, you stay where you are, while I go and fetch Thesaurus to you; or rather, dig hard. Here, Gold! Thesaurus I say! answer Timon's summons and let him unearth you. Now, Timon, with a will; a deep stroke or two. I will leave you together.

Tim. Come, spade, show your mettle; stick to it; invite Thesaurus to step up from his retreat.... O God of Wonders! O mystic priests! O lucky Hermes! whence this flood of gold? Sure, 'tis all a dream; methinks 'twill be ashes when I wake. And yet—coined gold, ruddy and heavy, a feast of delight!

O gold, the fairest gift to mortal eyes!
be it night, or be it day,
Thou dost outshine all else like living fire.

Come to me, my own, my beloved. I doubt the tale no longer; well might Zeus take the shape of gold; where is the maid that would not open her bosom to receive so fair a lover gliding through the roof?

Talk of Midas, Croesus, Delphic treasures! they were all nothing to Timon and his wealth; why, the Persian King could not match it. My spade, my dearest smock-frock, you must hang, a votive offering to Pan. And now I will buy up this desert corner, and build a tiny castle for my treasure, big enough for me to live in all alone, and, when I am dead, to lie in. And be the rule and law of my remaining days to shun all men, be blind to all men, scorn all men. Friendship, hospitality, society, compassion—vain words all. To be moved by another's tears, to assist another's need—be such things illegal and immoral. Let me live apart like a wolf; be Timon's one friend—Timon.

All others are my foes and ill-wishers; to hold communion with them is pollution; to set eyes upon one of them marks the day unholy; let them be to me even as images of bronze or stone. I will receive no herald from them, keep with them no truce; the bounds of my desert are the line they may not cross. Cousin and kinsman, neighbour and countryman—these are dead useless names, wherein fools may find a meaning. Let Timon keep his wealth to himself, scorn all men, and live in solitary luxury, quit of flattery and vulgar

58

praise; let him sacrifice and feast alone, his own associate and neighbour, far from[8] the world. Yea, when his last day comes, let there be none to close his eyes and lay him out, but himself alone.

Be the name he loves Misanthropus, and the marks whereby he may be known peevishness and spleen, wrath and rudeness and abhorrence. If ever one burning to death should call for help against the flames, let me help—with pitch and oil. If another be swept past me by a winter torrent, and stretch out his hands for aid, then let mine press him down head under, that he never rise again. So shall they receive as they have given. Mover of this resolution— Timon, son of Echecratides of Collytus. Presiding officer—the same Timon. The ayes have it. Let it be law, and duly observed.

All the same, I would give a good deal to have the fact of my enormous wealth generally known; they would all be fit to hang themselves over it.... Why, what is this? Well, that is quick work. Here they come running from every point of the compass, all dusty and panting; they have smelt out the gold somehow or other. Now, shall I get on top of this knoll, keep up a galling fire of stones from my point of vantage, and get rid of them that way? Or shall I make an exception to my law by parleying with them for once? contempt might hit harder than stones. Yes, I think that is better; I will stay where I am, and receive them. Let us see, who is this in front? Ah, Gnathonides the flatterer; when I asked an alms of him the other day, he offered me a halter; many a cask of my wine has he made a beast of himself over. I congratulate him on his speed; first come, first served.

Gna. What did I tell them?—Timon was too good a man to be abandoned by Providence. How are you, Timon? as good-looking and good-tempered, as good a fellow, as ever?

Tim. And you, Gnathonides, still teaching vultures rapacity, and men cunning?

Gna. Ah, he always liked his little joke. But where do you dine? I have brought a new song with me, a march out of the last musical thing on.

Tim. It will be a funeral march, then, and a very touching one, with spade *obbligato*.

Gna. What means this? This is assault, Timon; just let me find a witness! ... Oh, my God, my God! ... I'll have you before the Areopagus for assault and battery.

Tim. You'd better not wait much longer, or you'll have to make it murder.

Gna. Mercy, mercy! ... Now, a little gold ointment to heal the wound; it is a first-rate styptic.

Tim. What! you *won't* go, won't you?

Gna. Oh, I am going. But you shall repent this. Alas, so genial once, and now so rude!

---

[8] Reading, with Dindorf, *hekas o 'n* for *ekseio 'n.*

Tim. Now who is this with the bald crown? Why, it is Philiades; if there is a loathsome flatterer, it is he. When I sang that song that nobody else would applaud, he lauded me to the skies, and swore no dying swan could be more tuneful; his reward was one of my farms, and a 500 pounds portion for his daughter. And then when he found I was ill, and had come to him for assistance, his generous aid took the form of blows.

Phil. You shameless creatures! yes, yes, *now* you know Timon's merits! *now* Gnathonides would be his friend and boon-companion! well, he has the right reward of ingratitude. Some of us were his familiars and playmates and neighbours; but *we* hold back a little; we would not seem to thrust ourselves upon him. Greeting, lord Timon; pray let me warn you against these abominable flatterers; they are your humble servants during meal-times, and else about as useful as carrion crows. Perfidy is the order of the day; everywhere ingratitude and vileness. I was just bringing a couple of hundred pounds, for your immediate necessities, and was nearly here before I heard of your splendid fortune. So I just came on to give you this word of caution; though indeed you are wise enough (I would take your advice before Nestor's myself) to need none of my counsel.

Tim. Quite so, Philiades. But come near, will you not, and receive my— spade!

Phil. Help, help! this thankless brute has broken my head, for giving him good counsel.

Tim. Now for number three. Lawyer Demeas—my cousin, as he calls himself, with a decree in his hand. Between three and four thousand it was that I paid in to the Treasury in ready money for him; he had been fined that amount and imprisoned in default, and I took pity on him. Well, the other day he was distributing-officer of the festival money[9]; when I applied for my share, he pretended I was not a citizen.

Dem. Hail, Timon, ornament of our race, pillar of Athens, shield of Hellas! The Assembly and both Councils are met, and expect your appearance. But first hear the decree which I have proposed in your honour. 'WHEREAS Timon son of Echecratides of Collytus who adds to high position and character a sagacity unmatched in Greece is a consistent and indefatigable promoter of his country's good and Whereas he has been victorious at Olympia on one day in boxing wrestling and running as well as in the two and the four-horse chariot races—'

Tim. Why, I was never so much as a spectator at Olympia.

Dem. What does that matter? you will be some day. It looks better to have a good deal of that sort in—'and Whereas he fought with distinction last year at Acharnae cutting two Peloponnesian companies to pieces—'

---

[9] Every citizen had the right to receive from the State the small sum which would pay for his admission to theatrical or other festival entertainments.

Tim. Good work that, considering that my name was not on the muster-rolls, because I could not afford a suit of armour.

Dem. Ah, you are modest; but it would be ingratitude in us to forget your services—'and Whereas by political measures and responsible advice and military action he has conferred great benefits on his country Now for all these reasons it is the pleasure of the Assembly and the Council the ten divisions of the High Court and the Borough Councils individually and collectively THAT a golden statue of the said Timon be placed on the Acropolis alongside of Athene with a thunderbolt in the hand and a seven-rayed aureole on the head Further that golden garlands be conferred on him and proclaimed this day at the New Tragedies[10] the said day being kept in his honour as the Dionysia. Mover of the Decree Demeas the pleader the said Timon's near relation and disciple the said Timon being as distinguished in pleading as in all else wherein it pleases him to excel.'

So runs the decree. I had designed also to present to you my son, whom I have named Timon after you.

Tim. Why, I thought you were a bachelor, Demeas.

Dem. Ah, but I intend to marry next year; my child—which is to be a boy—I hereby name Timon.

Tim. I doubt whether you will feel like marrying, my man, when I have given you—this!

Dem. Oh Lord! what is that for? ... You are plotting a *coup d'etat*, you Timon; you assault free men, and you are neither a free man nor a citizen yourself. You shall soon be called to account for your crimes; it was you set fire to the Acropolis, for one thing.

Tim. Why, you scoundrel, the Acropolis has not been set on fire; you are a common blackmailer.

Dem. You got your gold by breaking into the Treasury.

Tim. It has not been broken into, either; you are not even plausible.

Dem. There is time for the burglary yet; meantime, you are in possession of the treasures.

Tim. Well, here is another for you, anyhow.

Dem. Oh! oh! my back!

Tim. Don't make such a noise, if you don't want a third. It would be too absurd, you know, if I could cut two companies of Spartans to pieces without my armour, and not be able to give a single little scoundrel his deserts. My Olympic boxing and wrestling victories would be thrown away.

Whom have we now? is this Thrasycles the philosopher? sure enough it is. A halo of beard, eyebrows an inch above their place, superiority in his air, a look that might storm heaven, locks waving to the wind— 'tis a very Boreas or Triton from Zeuxis' pencil. This hero of the careful get-up, the solemn gait, the plain attire—in the morning he will utter a thousand maxims, expounding

---

[10] See *Dionysia* in Notes

Virtue, arraigning self- indulgence, lauding simplicity; and then, when he gets to dinner after his bath, his servant fills him a bumper (he prefers it neat), and draining this Lethe-draught he proceeds to turn his morning maxima inside out; he swoops like a hawk on dainty dishes, elbows his neighbour aside, fouls his beard with trickling sauce, laps like a dog, with his nose in his plate, as if he expected to find Virtue there, and runs his finger all round the bowl, not to lose a drop of the gravy. Let him monopolize pastry or joint, he will still criticize the carving—that is all the satisfaction his ravenous greed brings him—; when the wine is in, singing and dancing are delights not fierce enough; he must brawl and rave. He has plenty to say in his cups—he is then at his best in that kind—upon temperance and decorum; he is full of these when his potations have reduced him to ridiculous stuttering. Next the wine disagrees with him, and at last he is carried out of the room, holding on with all his might to the flute-girl. Take him sober, for that matter, and you will hardly find his match at lying, effrontery or avarice. He is *facile princeps* of flatterers, perjury sits on his tongue-tip, imposture goes before him, and shamelessness is his good comrade; oh, he is a most ingenious piece of work, finished at all points, a *multum in parvo*. I am afraid his kind heart will be grieved presently. Why, how is this, Thrasycles? I must say, you have taken your time about coming.

Thr. Ah, Timon, I am not come like the rest of the crowd; *they* are dazzled by your wealth; they are gathered together with an eye to gold and silver and high living; they will soon be showing their servile tricks before your unsuspicious, generous self. As for me, you know a crust is all the dinner I care for; the relish I like best is a bit of thyme or cress; on festal days I may go as far as a sprinkling of salt. My drink is the crystal spring; and this threadbare cloak is better than your gay robes. Gold—I value it no higher than pebbles on the beach. What brought *me* was concern for you; I would not have you ruined by this same pestilent wealth, this temptation for plunderers; many is the man it has sunk in helpless misery. Take my advice, and fling it bodily into the sea; a good man, to whom the wealth of philosophy is revealed, has no need of the other. It does not matter about deep water, my good sir; wade in up to your waist when the tide is near flood, and *let no one see you but me*. Or if that is not satisfactory, here is another plan even better. Get it all out of the house as quick as you can, not reserving a penny for yourself, and distribute it to the poor five shillings to one, five pounds to another, a hundred to a third; philosophy might constitute a claim to a double or triple share. For my part— and I do not ask for myself, only to divide it among my needy friends—I should be quite content with as much as my scrip would hold; it is something short of two standard bushels; if one professes philosophy, one must be moderate and have few needs—none that go beyond the capacity of a scrip.

Tim. Very right, Thrasycles. But instead of a mere scripful, pray take a whole headful of clouts, standard measure by the spade.

Thr. Land of liberty, equality, legality! protect me against this ruffian!

Tim. What is your grievance, my good man? is the measure short? here is a pint or two extra, then, to put it right.

Why, what now? here comes a crowd; friend Blepsias, Laches, Gniphon; their name is legion; they shall howl soon. I had better get up on the rock; my poor tired spade wants a little rest; I will collect all the stones I can lay hands on, and pepper them at long range.

Bl. Don't throw, Timon; we are going.

Tim. Whether the retreat will be bloodless, however, is another question.

PROMETHEUS ON CAUCASUS

Hermes. Hephaestus. Prometheus.

Her. This, Hephaestus, is the Caucasus, to which it is our painful duty to nail our companion. We have now to select a suitable crag, free from snow, on which the chains will have a good hold, and the prisoner will hang in all publicity.

Heph. True. It will not do to fix him too low down, or these *men* of his might come to their maker's assistance; nor at the top, where he would be invisible from the earth. What do you say to a middle course? Let him hang over this precipice, with his arms stretched across from crag to crag.

Her. The very thing. Steep rocks, slightly overhanging, inaccessible on every side; no foothold but a mere ledge, with scarcely room for the tips of one's toes; altogether a sweet spot for a crucifixion. Now, Prometheus, come and be nailed up; there is no time to lose.

Prom. Nay, hear me; Hephaestus! Hermes! I suffer injustice:

have compassion on my woes!

Her. In other words, disobey orders, and promptly be gibbeted in your stead! Do you suppose there is not room on the Caucasus to peg out a couple of us? Come, your right hand! clamp it down, Hephaestus, and in with the nails; bring down the hammer with a will. Now the left; make sure work of that too.—So!—The eagle will shortly be here, to trim your liver; so ingenious an artist is entitled to every attention.

Prom. O Cronus, and Iapetus, and Mother Earth! Behold the sufferings of the innocent!

Her. Why, as to innocence,—to begin with, there was that business of the sacrificial meats, your manner of distributing which was most unfair, most disingenuous:

you got all the choice parts for yourself, and put Zeus off with bones 'wrapped up in shining fat'; I remember the passage in Hesiod; those are his very words. Then you made these human beings; creatures of unparalleled wickedness, the women especially. And to crown all, you stole fire, the most precious possession of the Gods, and gave it to them. And with all this on your conscience, you protest that you have done nothing to deserve captivity.

Prom. Ah, Hermes; you are as bad as Hector; you 'blame the blameless.' For such crimes as these, I deserve a round pension, if justice were done. And by the way, I should like, if you can spare the time, to answer to these charges, and satisfy you of the injustice of my sentence. You can employ your practised eloquence on behalf of Zeus, and justify his conduct in nailing me up here at the Gates of the Caspian, for all Scythia to behold and pity.

Her. There is nothing to be gained now by an appeal to another court; it is too late. Proceed, however. We have to wait in any case till the eagle comes to look after that liver of yours; and the time might be worse spent than in listening to the subtleties of such a master in impudence as yourself.

Prom. You begin then, Hermes. Exert all your powers of invective; leave no stone unturned to establish the righteousness of papa's judgements.—You, Hephaestus, shall compose the jury.

Heph. The jury! Not a bit of it; I am a party in this case. My furnace has been cold, ever since you stole that fire.

Prom. Well, at this rate you had better divide the prosecution between you. You conduct the case of larceny, and Hermes can handle the man-making, and the misappropriation of meat. I shall expect a great deal of you; you are both artists.

Heph. Hermes shall speak for me. The law is not in my line; my forge takes up most of my time. But Hermes is an orator; he has made a study of these things.

Prom. Well! I should never have thought that Hermes would have the heart to reproach me with larceny; he ought to have a fellow-feeling for me there. However, with this further responsibility on your shoulders, there is no time to be lost, son of Maia; out with your accusation, and have done with it.

Her. To deal adequately with your crimes, Prometheus, would require many words and much preparation. It is not enough to mention the several counts of the accusation; how, entrusted with the distribution of meats, you defrauded the crown by retaining the choicer portions for your own use; how you created the race of men, with absolutely no justification for so doing; how you stole fire and conveyed it to these same men. You seem not to realize, my friend, that, all-things considered, Zeus has dealt very handsomely by you. Now, if you deny the charges, I shall be compelled to establish your guilt at some length, and to set the facts in the clearest possible light. But if you admit the distribution of meat in the manner described, the introduction of men, and the theft of fire,—then my case is complete, and there is no more to be said. To expatiate further would be to talk nonsense.

Prom. Perhaps there has been some nonsense talked already; that remains to be seen. But as you say your case is now complete, I will see what I can do in the way of refutation. And first about that meat. Though, upon my word, I blush for Zeus when I name it:

to think that he should be so touchy about trifles, as to send off a God of my quality to crucifixion, just because he found a little bit of bone in his share! Does he forget the services I have rendered him? And does he think what it is that he is so angry about, and how childish it is to show temper about a little thing like that? What if he did miss getting the better share? Why, Hermes, these tricks that are played over the wine-cups are not worth thinking twice about. A joke, perhaps, is carried a little too far, in the warmth of the feast; still, it is a joke, and resentment should be left behind in the dregs of the bowl. I have no patience with your long memories; this nursing of grievances, this raking up of last night's squabbles, is unworthy of a king, let alone a king of Gods. Once take away from our feasts the little elegancies of quip and crank and wile, and what is left? Muzziness; repletion; silence;—cheerful accompaniments these to the wine-bowl! For my part, I never supposed that Zeus would give the matter a thought the next morning; much less that he would make such a stir about it, and think himself so mightily injured; my little manoeuvre with the meat was merely a playful experiment, to see which he would choose. It might have been worse. Instead of giving him the inferior half, I might have defrauded him of the whole. And what if I had? Would that have been a case for putting heaven and earth in commotion, for deep designs of chain and cross and Caucasus, dispatchings of eagles, rendings of livers? These things tell a sad tale, do they not, of the puny soul, the little mind, the touchy temper of the aggrieved party? How would he take the loss of a whole ox, who storms to such purpose over a few pounds of meat? How much more reasonable is the conduct of mortals, though one would have expected them to be more irritable than Gods! A mortal would never want his cook crucified for dipping a finger into the stew-pan, or filching a mouthful from the roast; they overlook these things. At the worst their resentment is satisfied with a box on the ears or a rap on the head. I find no precedent among them for crucifixion in such cases. So much for the affair of the meat; there is little credit to be got in the refutation of such a charge, and still less in the bringing of it.

I am next to speak of my creation of mankind. And here the terms of your accusation are ambiguous. I have to choose between two distinct possibilities. Do you maintain that I had no right to create men at all, that I ought to have left the senseless clay alone? Or do you only complain of the form in which I designed them? However, I shall have something to say on both points. I shall first endeavour to show that no harm has accrued to the Gods from my bringing mankind into existence; and shall then proceed to the positive advantages and improvements which have resulted to them from the peopling of the earth. The question as to the harm done by my innovation is best answered by an appeal to the past, to those days when the race of heaven-born Gods stood alone, and earth was a hideous shapeless mass, a tangle of rude vegetation. The Gods had no altars then, nor temples (for who should raise them?), no images of wood or stone, such as now abound in every corner of the earth, and are honoured with all observance. It was to me that the idea occurred—amid my ceaseless meditations on the common welfare, on the aggrandizement of the Gods and the promotion of order and beauty in the universe—of setting all to rights with a handful of clay; of creating living things, and moulding them after our own likeness. I saw what was lacking to our godhead:

some counterpart, some foil wherein to set off its blessedness. And that counterpart must be mortal; but in all else exquisitely contrived, perfect in intelligence, keen to appreciate our superiority. Thereupon, I moulded my material,

With water mingling clay,

and created man, calling in Athene to aid me in the task. And this is my rank offence against the Gods. Destructive work,—to reduce inanimate clay to life and motion! The Gods, it seems, are Gods no longer, now that there are mortal creatures on the earth. To judge at least by Zeus's indignation, one would suppose that the Gods suffered some loss of prestige from the creation of mankind; unless it is that he is afraid of another revolt, of their waging war with heaven, like the Giants.

That the cause of the Gods suffered nothing at my hands is evident; show me the slightest instance to the contrary, and I will say no more; I have but my deserts. But for the positive benefits I have conferred, use the evidence of your eyes. The earth, no longer barren and untilled, is decked with cities and farms and the fruits of cultivation; the sea has its ships, the islands their inhabitants. Everywhere are altars and temples, everywhere festivals and sacrifices:

Zeus with his presence fills their gatherings,

He fills their streets.

Had I created mankind for my own private convenience, it might perhaps have denoted a grasping spirit:

but I made them common property; they are at the service of every God of you. Nay more:

temples of Zeus, and Apollo, and Hera, temples of Hermes, are everywhere to be seen; but who ever saw a temple of Prometheus? You may judge from this, how far I have sacrificed the common cause to my private ambition.

And further. Consider, Hermes:

can any good thing whatsoever, be it gift of Nature or work of our hands, give the full measure of enjoyment to its possessor, when there is none to see, none to admire? You see whither my question tends? But for mankind, the glories of the universe must have been without a witness; and there was little satisfaction to be derived from a wealth which was doomed to excite no envy in others. We should have lacked a standard for comparison; and should never have known the extent of our happiness, while all were as happy as ourselves. The great is not great, till it is compared with the small. Yet instead of honouring me for my political insight, you crucify me; such are the wages of wisdom!

Ah, but (you will say) there is so much wickedness among them; adultery, war, incest, parricide. Well, I fancy these are not unknown among ourselves? And I am sure no one would think that a reason for saying that Uranus and Ge made a mistake in creating us. Or again, you will complain that we have so much trouble in looking after them. At that rate, a shepherd ought to object to the possession of a flock, because he has to look after it. Besides, a certain show of occupation is rather gratifying than otherwise; the responsibility is not unwelcome,—it helps to pass the time. What should we do, if we had not mankind to think of? There would be nothing to live for; we should sit about drinking nectar and gorging ourselves with ambrosia. But what fairly takes away my breath is, your assurance in finding fault with my *women* in particular, when all the time you are in love with them:

our bulls and satyrs and swans are never tired of making descents upon the Earth; women, they find, are good enough to be made the mothers of Gods!

Yes, yes (you will say), it was quite right that men should be created, but they should not have been made in our likeness. And what better model could I have taken than this, whose perfection I knew? Was I to make them brute beasts without understanding? Had they been other than they are, how should they have paid you due honour and sacrifice? When the hecatombs are getting ready, you think nothing of a journey to the ends of the earth to see the 'blameless Ethiopians'; and my reward for procuring you these advantages is— crucifixion! But on this subject I have said enough.

And now, with your permission, I will approach the subject of that stolen fire, of which we hear so much. I have a question to ask, which I beg you will answer frankly. Has there been one spark less fire in Heaven, since men shared it with us? Of course not. It is the nature of fire, that it does not become less by being imparted to others. A fire is not put out by kindling another from it. No, this is sheer envy:

you cannot bear that men should have a share of this necessary, though you have suffered no harm thereby. For shame! Gods should be beneficent, 'givers of good'; they should be above all envy. Had I taken away fire altogether, and left not a spark behind, it would have been no great loss. You have no use for it. You are never cold; you need no artificial light; nor is ambrosia improved by boiling. To man, on the other hand, fire is indispensable for many purposes, particularly for those of sacrifice; how else are they to fill their streets with the savour of burnt-offerings, and the fumes of frankincense I how else to burn fat thigh-pieces upon your altars? I observe that you take a particular pleasure in the steam arising therefrom, and think no feast more delicious than the smell of roast meat, as it mounts heavenwards

In eddying clouds of smoke.

Your present complaint, you see, is sadly at variance with this taste. I wonder you do not forbid the Sun to shine on mankind. He too is of fire, and fire of a purer and diviner quality. Has anything been said to *him* about his lavish expenditure of your property?

And now I have done. If there is any flaw in my defence, it is for you two to refute me. I shall answer your objections in due course.

Her. Nay, you are too hard for us, Prometheus; we will not attempt a sophist of your mettle. Well for you that Zeus is not within earshot, or you would have had a round dozen of hungry vultures to reckon with, for certain; in clearing your own character, you have grievously mishandled his. But one thing puzzles me:

you are a prophet; you ought to have foreseen your sentence.

Prom. All this I knew, and more than this; for I shall be released; nay, even now the day is not far off when one of your blood shall come from Thebes, and shoot this eagle with which you threaten me[11].

Her. With all my heart! I shall be delighted to see you free again, and feasting in our midst; but not, my friend, not carving for us!

Prom. You may take my word for it; I shall be with you again. I have the wherewithal to pay abundantly for my ransom.

Her. Oh, indeed? Come, tell us all about it.

Prom. You know Thetis—But no; the secret is best kept. Ransom and reward depend upon it.

Her. Well, you know best. Now, Hephaestus, we must be going; see, here comes the eagle.—Bear a brave heart, Prometheus; and all speed to your Theban archer, who is to set a term to this creature's activity.

---

[11] See *Prometheus* in Notes.

DIALOGUES OF THE GODS

I

Prometheus. Zeus

Prom. Release me, Zeus; I have suffered enough.

Zeus. Release you? you? Why, by rights your irons should be heavier, you should have the whole weight of Caucasus upon you, and instead of one, a dozen vultures, not just pecking at your liver, but scratching out your eyes. You made these abominable human creatures to vex us, you stole our fire, you invented women. I need not remind you how you overreached me about the meat-offerings; my portion, bones disguised in fat:

yours, all the good.

Prom. And have I not been punished enough—riveted to the Caucasus all these years, feeding your bird (on which all worst curses light!) with my liver?

Zeus. 'Tis not a tithe of your deserts.

Prom. Consider, I do not ask you to release me for nothing. I offer you information which is invaluable.

Zeus. Promethean wiles!

Prom. Wiles? to what end? you can find the Caucasus another time; and there are chains to be had, if you catch me cheating.

Zeus. Tell me first the nature of your 'invaluable' offer.

Prom. If I tell you your present errand right, will that convince you that I can prophesy too?

Zeus. Of course it will.

Prom. You are bound on a little visit to Thetis.

Zeus. Right so far. And the sequel? I trust you now.

Prom. Have no dealings with her, Zeus. As sure as Nereus's daughter conceives by you, your child shall mete you the measure you meted to—

Zeus. I shall lose my kingdom, you would say?

Prom. Avert it, Fate! I say only, that union portends this issue.

Zeus. Thetis, farewell! and for this Hephaestus shall set you free.

II

Eros. Zeus

Eros. You might let me off, Zeus! I suppose it *was* rather too bad of me; but there!—I am but a child; a wayward child.

Zeus. A child, and born before Iapetus was ever thought of? You bad old man! Just because you have no beard, and no white hairs, are you going to pass yourself off for a child?

Eros. Well, and what such mighty harm has the old man ever done you, that you should talk of chains?

Zeus. Ask your own guilty conscience, what harm. The pranks you have played me! Satyr, bull, swan, eagle, shower of gold,—I have been everything in my time; and I have you to thank for it. You never by any chance make the women in love with *me*; no one is ever smitten with *my* charms, that I have noticed. No, there must be magic in it always; I must be kept well out of sight. They like the bull or the swan well enough:

but once let them set eyes on *me*, and they are frightened out of their lives.

Eros. Well, of course. They are but mortals; the sight of Zeus is too much for them.

Zeus. Then why are Branchus and Hyacinth so fond of Apollo?

Eros. Daphne ran away from him, anyhow; in spite of his beautiful hair and his smooth chin. Now, shall I tell you the way to win hearts? Keep that aegis of yours quiet, and leave the thunderbolt at home; make yourself as smart as you can; curl your hair and tie it up with a bit of ribbon, get a purple cloak, and gold-bespangled shoes, and march forth to the music of flute and drum;—and see if you don't get a finer following than Dionysus, for all his Maenads.

Zeus. Pooh! I'll win no hearts on such terms.

Eros. Oh, in that case, don't fall in love. Nothing could be simpler.

Zeus. I dare say; but I like being in love, only I don't like all this fuss. Now mind; if I let you off, it is on this understanding.

III

Zeus. Hermes

Zeus. Hermes, you know Inachus's beautiful daughter?

Her. I do. Io, you mean?

Zeus. Yes; she is not a girl now, but a heifer.

Her. Magic at work! how did that come about?

Zeus. Hera had a jealous fit, and transformed her. But that is not all; she has thought of a new punishment for the poor thing. She has put a cowherd in charge, who is all over eyes; this Argus, as he is called, pastures the heifer, and never goes to sleep.

Her. Well, what am I to do?

Zeus. Fly down to Nemea, where the pasture is, kill Argus, take Io across the sea to Egypt, and convert her into Isis. She shall be henceforth an Egyptian Goddess, flood the Nile, regulate the winds, and rescue mariners.

VI

*Hera. Zeus_*

Hera. Zeus! What is your opinion of this man Ixion?

Zeus. Why, my dear, I think he is a very good sort of man; and the best of company. Indeed, if he were unworthy of our company, he would not be here.

Hera. He *is* unworthy! He is a villain! Discard him!

Zeus. Eh? What has he been after? I must know about this.

Hera. Certainly you must; though I scarce know how to tell you. The wretch!

Zeus. Oh, oh; if he is a 'wretch,' you must certainly tell me all about it. I know what 'wretch' means, on your discreet tongue. What, he has been making love?

Hera. And to me! to me of all people! It has been going on for a long time. At first, when he would keep looking at me, I had no idea——. And then he would sigh and groan; and when I handed my cup to Ganymede after drinking, he would insist on having it, and would stop drinking to kiss it, and lift it up to his eyes; and then he would look at me again. And then of course I knew. For a long time I didn't like to say anything to you; I thought his mad fit would pass. But when he actually dared to *speak* to me, I left him weeping and groveling about, and stopped my ears, so that I might not hear his impertinences, and came to tell you. It is for you to consider what steps you will take.

Zeus. Whew! I have a rival, I find; and with my own lawful wife. Here is a rascal who has tippled nectar to some purpose. Well, we have no one but ourselves to blame for it:

we make too much of these mortals, admitting them to our table like this. When they drink of our nectar, and behold the beauties of Heaven (so different from those of Earth!), 'tis no wonder if they fall in love, and form ambitious schemes! Yes, Love is all-powerful; and not with mortals only:

we Gods have sometimes fallen beneath his sway.

Hera. He has made himself master of *you*; no doubt of that. He does what he likes with you;—leads you by the nose. You follow him whither he chooses, and assume every shape at his command; you are his chattel, his toy. I know how it will be:

you are going to let Ixion off, because you have had relations with his wife; she is the mother of Pirithous.

Zeus. Why, what a memory you have for these little outings of mine! —— Now, my idea about Ixion is this. It would never do to punish him, or to exclude him from our table; that would not look well. No; as he is so fond of you, so hard hit—even to weeping point, you tell me,——

Hera. Zeus! What *are* you going to say?

Zeus. Don't be alarmed. Let us make a cloud-phantom in your likeness, and after dinner, as he lies awake (which of course he will do, being in love), let us take it and lay it by his side. 'Twill put him out of his pain:

he will fancy he has attained his desire.

Hera. Never! The presumptuous villain!

72

Zeus. Yes, I know. But what harm can it do to you, if Ixion makes a conquest of a cloud?

Hera. But he will think that *I* am the cloud; he will be working his wicked will upon *me* for all he can tell.

Zeus. Now you are talking nonsense. The cloud is not Hera, and Hera is not the cloud. Ixion will be deceived; that is all.

Hera. Yes, but these men are all alike—they have no delicacy. I suppose, when he goes home, he will boast to every one of how he has enjoyed the embraces of Hera, the wife of Zeus! Why, he may tell them that *I* am in love with *him*! And they will believe it; *they* will know nothing about the cloud.

Zeus. If he says anything of the kind he shall soon find himself in Hades, spinning round on a wheel for all eternity. That will keep him busy! And serve him right; not for falling in love—I see no great harm in that—but for letting his tongue wag.

VII

Hephaestus. Apollo

Heph. Have you seen Maia's baby, Apollo? such a pretty little thing, with a smile for everybody; you can see it is going to be a treasure.

Ap. That baby a treasure? well, in mischief, Iapetus is young beside it.

Heph. Why, what harm can it do, only just born?

Ap. Ask Posidon; it stole his trident. Ask Ares; he was surprised to find his sword gone out of the scabbard. Not to mention myself, disarmed of bow and arrows.

Heph. Never! that infant? he has hardly found his legs yet; he is not out of his baby-linen.

Ap. Ah, you will find out, Hephaestus, if he gets within reach of you.

Heph. He has been.

Ap. Well? all your tools safe? none missing?

Heph. Of course not.

Ap. I advise you to make sure.

Heph. Zeus! where are my pincers?

Ap. Ah, you will find them among the baby-linen.

Heph. So light-fingered? one would swear he had practised petty larceny in the womb.

Ap. Ah, and you don't know what a glib young chatterbox he is; and, if he has his way, he is to be our errand-boy! Yesterday he challenged Eros—tripped up his heels somehow, and had him on his back in a twinkling; before the applause was over, he had taken the opportunity of a congratulatory hug from Aphrodite to steal her girdle; Zeus had not done laughing before—the sceptre was gone. If the thunderbolt had not been too heavy, and very hot, he would have made away with that too.

Heph. The child has some spirit in him, by your account.

73

Ap. Spirit, yes—and some music, moreover, young as he is.

Heph. How can you tell that?

Ap. He picked up a dead tortoise somewhere or other, and contrived an instrument with it. He fitted horns to it, with a cross-bar, stuck in pegs, inserted a bridge, and played a sweet tuneful thing that made an old harper like me quite envious. Even at night, Maia was saying, he does not stay in Heaven; he goes down poking his nose into Hades— on a thieves' errand, no doubt. Then he has a pair of wings, and he has made himself a magic wand, which he uses for marshalling souls— convoying the dead to their place.

Heph. Ah, I gave him that, for a toy.

Ap. And by way of payment he stole—

Heph. Well thought on; I must go and get them; you may be right about the baby-linen.

VIII

Hephaestus. Zeus

Heph. What are your orders, Zeus? You sent for me, and here I am; with such an edge to my axe as would cleave a stone at one blow.

Zeus. Ah; that's right, Hephaestus. Just split my head in half, will you?

Heph. You think I am mad, perhaps?—Seriously, now, what can I do for you?

Zeus. What I say:

crack my skull. Any insubordination, now, and you shall taste my resentment; it will not be the first time. Come, a good lusty stroke, and quick about it. I am in the pangs of travail; my brain is in a whirl.

Heph. Mind you, the consequences may be serious:

the axe is sharp, and will prove but a rough midwife.

Zeus. Hew away, and fear nothing. I know what I am about.

Heph. H'm. I don't like it:

however, one must obey orders…. Why, what have we here? A maiden in full armour! This is no joke, Zeus. You might well be waspish, with this great girl growing up beneath your *pia mater*, in armour, too! You have been carrying a regular barracks on your shoulders all this time. So active too! See, she is dancing a war-dance, with shield and spear in full swing. She is like one inspired; and (what is more to the point) she is extremely pretty, and has come to marriageable years in these few minutes; those grey eyes, even, look well beneath a helmet. Zeus, I claim her as the fee for my midwifery.

Zeus. Impossible! She is determined to remain a maid for ever. Not that *I* have any objection, personally.

Heph. That is all I want. You can leave the rest to me. I'll carry her off this moment.

Zeus. Well, if you think it so easy. But I am sure it is a hopeless case.

74

XI

Aphrodite. Selene

Aph. What is this I hear about you, Selene? When your car is over Caria, you stop it to gaze at Endymion sleeping hunter-fashion in the open; sometimes, they tell me, you actually get out and go down to him.

Sel. Ah, Aphrodite, ask that son of yours; it is he must answer for it all.

Aph. Well now, what a naughty boy! he gets his own mother into all sorts of scrapes; I must go down, now to Ida for Anchises of Troy, now to Lebanon for my Assyrian stripling;—mine? no, he put Persephone in love with him too, and so robbed me of half my darling. I have told him many a time that if he would not behave himself I would break his artillery for him, and clip his wings; and before now I have smacked his little behind with my slipper. It is no use; he is frightened and cries for a minute or two, and then forgets all about it. But tell me, is Endymion handsome? That is always a comfort in our humiliation.

Sel. Most handsome, *I* think, my dear; you should see him when he has spread out his cloak on the rock and is asleep; his javelins in his left hand, just slipping from his grasp, the right arm bent upwards, making a bright frame to the face, and he breathing softly in helpless slumber. Then I come noiselessly down, treading on tiptoe not to wake and startle him—but there, you know all about it; why tell you the rest? I am dying of love, that is all.

XII

Aphrodite. Eros

Aph. Child, child, you must think what you are doing. It is bad enough on earth,—you are always inciting men to do some mischief, to themselves or to one another;—but I am speaking of the Gods. You change Zeus into shape after shape as the fancy takes you; you make Selene come down from the sky; you keep Helius loitering about with Clymene, till he sometimes forgets to drive out at all. As for the naughty tricks you play on your own mother, you know you are safe there. But Rhea! how could you *dare* to set her on thinking of that young fellow in Phrygia, an old lady like her, the mother of so many Gods? Why, you have made her quite mad:

she harnesses those lions of hers, and drives about all over Ida with the Corybantes, who are as mad as herself, shrieking high and low for Attis; and there they are, slashing their arms with swords, rushing about over the hills, like wild things, with dishevelled hair, blowing horns, beating drums, clashing cymbals; all Ida is one mad tumult. I am quite uneasy about it; yes, you wicked boy, your poor mother is quite uneasy:

some day when Rhea is in one of her mad fits (or when she is in her senses, more likely), she will send the Corybantes after you, with orders to tear you to pieces, or throw you to the lions. You are so venturesome!

Eros. Be under no alarm, mother; I understand lions perfectly by this time. I get on to their backs every now and then, and take hold of their manes, and ride them about; and when I put my hand into their mouths, they only lick it, and let me take it out again. Besides, how is Rhea going to have time to attend to me? She is too busy with Attis. And I see no harm in just pointing out beautiful things to people; they can leave them alone;—it is nothing to do with me. And how would you like it if Ares were not in love with you, or you with him?

Aph. Masterful boy! always the last word! But you will remember this some day.

XIII

Zeus. Asclefius. Heracles

Zeus. Now, Asclepius and Heracles, stop that quarrelling; you might as well be men; such behaviour is very improper and out of place at the table of the Gods.

Her. Is this druggist fellow to have a place above me, Zeus?

Asc. Of course I am; I am your better.

Her. Why, you numskull? because it was Zeus's bolt that cracked your skull, for your unholy doings, and now you have been allowed your immortality again out of sheer pity?

Asc. You twit me with my fiery end; you seem to have forgotten that you too were burnt to death, on Oeta.

Her. Was there no difference between your life and mine, then? I am Zeus's son, and it is well known how I toiled, cleansing the earth, conquering monsters, and chastising men of violence. Whereas you are a root-grubber and a quack; I dare say you have your use for doctoring sick men, but you never did a bold deed in your life.

Asc. That comes well from you, whose burns I healed, when you came up all singed not so long ago; between the tunic and the flames, your body was half consumed. Anyhow, it would be enough to mention that I was never a slave like you, never combed wool in Lydia, masquerading in a purple shawl and being slippered by an Omphale, never killed my wife and children in a fit of the spleen. Her. If you don't stop being rude, I shall soon show you that immortality is not much good. I will take you up and pitch you head over heels out of Heaven, and Apollo himself shall never mend your broken crown. Zeus. Cease, I say, and let us hear ourselves speak, or I will send you both away from table. Heracles, Asclepius died before you, and has the right to a better place.

XIV

Hermes. Apollo

Her. Why so sad, Apollo?

Ap. Alas, Hermes,—my love!

Her. Oh; that's bad. What, are you still brooding over that affair of Daphne?

Ap. No. I grieve for my beloved; the Laconian, the son of Oebalus.

Her. Hyacinth? he is not dead?

Ap. Dead.

Her. Who killed him? Who could have the heart? That lovely boy!

Ap. It was the work of my own hand.

Her. You must have been mad!

Ap. Not mad; it was an accident.

Her. Oh? and how did it happen?

Ap. He was learning to throw the quoit, and I was throwing with him. I had just sent my quoit up into the air as usual, when jealous Zephyr (damned be he above all winds! he had long been in love with Hyacinth, though Hyacinth would have nothing to say to him)—Zephyr came blustering down from Taygetus, and dashed the quoit upon the child's head; blood flowed from the wound in streams, and in one moment all was over. My first thought was of revenge; I lodged an arrow in Zephyr, and pursued his flight to the mountain. As for the child, I buried him at Amyclae, on the fatal spot; and from his blood I have caused a flower to spring up, sweetest, fairest of flowers, inscribed with letters of woe.—Is my grief unreasonable?

Her. It is, Apollo. You knew that you had set your heart upon a mortal: grieve not then for his mortality.

XV

Hermes. Apollo

Her. To think that a cripple and a blacksmith like him should marry two such queens of beauty as Aphrodite and Charis!

Ap. Luck, Hermes—that is all. But I do wonder at their putting up with his company; they see him running with sweat, bent over the forge, all sooty-faced; and yet they cuddle and kiss him, and sleep with him!

Her. Yes, it makes me angry too; how I envy him! Ah, Apollo, you may let your locks grow, and play your harp, and be proud of your looks; I am a healthy fellow, and can touch the lyre; but, when it comes to bedtime, we lie alone.

Ap. Well, my loves never prosper; Daphne and Hyacinth were my great passions; she so detested me that being turned to a tree was more attractive than I; and him I killed with a quoit. Nothing is left me of them but wreaths of their leaves and flowers.

Her. Ah, once, once, I and Aphrodite—but no; no boasting.

Ap. I know; that is how Hermaphroditus is accounted for. But perhaps you can tell me how it is that Aphrodite and Charis are not jealous of one another.

Her. Because one is his wife in Lemnus and the other in Heaven. Besides, Aphrodite cares most about Ares; he is her real love; so she does not trouble her head about the blacksmith.

Ap. Do you think Hephaestus sees?

Her. Oh, he sees, yes; but what can he do? he knows what a martial young fellow it is; so he holds his tongue. He talks of inventing a net, though, to take them in the act with.

Ap. Ah, all I know is, I would not mind being taken in that act.

XVI

Hera. Leto

Hera. I must congratulate you, madam, on the children with whom you have presented Zeus.

Leto. Ah, madam; we cannot all be the proud mothers of Hephaestuses.

Hera. My boy may be a cripple, but at least he is of some use. He is a wonderful smith, and has made Heaven look another place; and Aphrodite thought him worth marrying, and dotes on him still. But those two of yours !—that girl is wild and mannish to a degree; and now she has gone off to Scythia, and her doings *there* are no secret; she is as bad as any Scythian herself,—butchering strangers and eating them! Apollo, too, who pretends to be so clever, with his bow and his lyre and his medicine and his prophecies; those oracle-shops that he has opened at Delphi, and Clarus, and Dindyma, are a cheat; he takes good care to be on the safe side by giving ambiguous answers that no one can understand, and makes money out of it, for there are plenty of fools who like being imposed upon,—but sensible people know well enough that most of it is clap-trap. The prophet did not know that he was to kill his favourite with a quoit; he never foresaw that Daphne would run away from him, so handsome as he is, too, such beautiful hair! I am not sure, after all, that there is much to choose between your children and Niobe's.

Leto. Oh, of course; my children are butchers and impostors. I know how you hate the sight of them. You cannot bear to hear my girl complimented on her looks, or my boy's playing admired by the company.

Hera. His playing, madam!—excuse a smile;—why, if the Muses had not favoured him, his contest with Marsyas would have cost him his skin; poor Marsyas was shamefully used on that occasion; 'twas a judicial murder.—As for your charming daughter, when Actaeon once caught sight of her charms, she had to set the dogs upon him, for fear he should tell all he knew:

I forbear to ask where the innocent child picked up her knowledge of obstetrics.

Leto. You set no small value on yourself, madam, because you are the wife of Zeus, and share his throne; you may insult whom you please. But there will be tears presently, when the next bull or swan sets out on his travels, and you are left neglected.

XVIII

Hera. Zeus

Hera. Well, Zeus, I should be ashamed if *I* had such a son; so effeminate, and so given to drinking; tying up his hair in a ribbon, indeed! and spending most of his time among mad women, himself as much a woman as any of them; dancing to flute and drum and cymbal! He resembles any one rather than his father.

Zeus. Anyhow, my dear, this wearer of ribbons, this woman among women, not content with conquering Lydia, subduing Thrace, and enthralling the people of Tmolus, has been on an expedition all the way to India with his womanish host, captured elephants, taken possession of the country, and led their king captive after a brief resistance. And he never stopped dancing all the time, never relinquished the thyrsus and the ivy; always drunk (as you say) and always inspired! If any scoffer presumes to make light of his ceremonial, he does not go unpunished; he is bound with vine-twigs; or his own mother mistakes him for a fawn, and tears him limb from limb. Are not these manful doings, worthy of a son of Zeus? No doubt he is fond of his comforts, too, and his amusements; we need not complain of that:

you may judge from his drunken achievements, what a handful the fellow would be if he were sober.

Hera. I suppose you will tell me next, that the invention of wine is very much to his credit; though you see for yourself how drunken men stagger about and misbehave themselves; one would think the liquor had made them mad. Look at Icarius, the first to whom he gave the vine:

beaten to death with mattocks by his own boon companions!

Zeus. Pooh, nonsense. That is not Dionysus's fault, nor the wine's fault; it comes of the immoderate use of it. Men *will* drink their wine neat, and drink too much of it. Taken in moderation, it engenders cheerfulness and benevolence. Dionysus is not likely to treat any of his guests as Icarius was treated.—No; I see what it is:

—you are jealous, my love; you can't forget about Semele, and so you must disparage the noble achievements of her son.

XIX

Aphrodite. Eros

Aph. Eros, dear, you have had your victories over most of the Gods— Zeus, Posidon, Rhea, Apollo, nay, your own mother; how is it you make an exception for Athene? against her your torch has no fire, your quiver no arrows, your right hand no cunning.

Eros. I am afraid of her, mother; those awful flashing eyes! she is like a man, only worse. When I go against her with my arrow on the string, a toss of her plume frightens me; my hand shakes so that it drops the bow.

Aph. I should have thought Ares was more terrible still; but you disarmed and conquered him.

Eros. Ah, he is only too glad to have me; he calls me to him. Athene always eyes me so! once when I flew close past her, quite by accident, with my torch, 'If you come near me,' she called out, 'I swear by my father, I will run you through with my spear, or take you by the foot and drop you into Tartarus, or tear you in pieces with my own hands'— and more such dreadful things. And she has such a sour look; and then on her breast she wears that horrid face with the snaky hair; that frightens me worst of all; the nasty bogy—I run away directly I see it.

Aph. Well, well, you are afraid of Athene and the Gorgon; at least so you say, though you do not mind Zeus's thunderbolt a bit. But why do you let the Muses go scot free? do *they* toss their plumes and hold out Gorgons' heads?

Eros. Ah, mother, they make me bashful; they are so grand, always studying and composing; I love to stand there listening to their music.

Aph. Let them pass too, because they are grand. And why do you never take a shot at Artemis?

Eros. Why, the great thing is that I cannot catch her; she is always over the hills and far away. But besides that, her heart is engaged already.

Aph. Where, child?

Eros. In hunting stags and fawns; she is so fleet, she catches them up, or else shoots them; she can think of nothing else. Her brother, now, though he is an archer too, and draws a good arrow—

Aph. I know, child, you have hit *him* often enough.

XX.

THE JUDGEMENT OF PARIS

Zeus. Hermes. Hera. Athene. Aphrodite. Paris

Zeus. Hermes, take this apple, and go with it to Phrygia; on the Gargaran peak of Ida you will find Priam's son, the herdsman. Give him this message:

'Paris, because you are handsome, and wise in the things of love, Zeus commands you to judge between the Goddesses, and say which is the most beautiful. And the prize shall be this apple.'—Now, you three, there is no time to be lost:

away with you to your judge. I will have nothing to do with the matter:

I love you all exactly alike, and I only wish you could all three win. If I were to give the prize to one of you, the other two would hate me, of course. In these circumstances, I am ill qualified to be your judge. But this young Phrygian to whom you are going is of the royal blood—a relation of Ganymede's,—and at the same time a simple countryman; so that we need have no hesitation in trusting his eyes.

Aph. As far as I am concerned, Zeus, Momus himself might be our judge; *I* should not be afraid to show myself. What fault could he find with *me*? But the others must agree too.

Hera. Oh, we are under no alarm, thank you,—though your admirer Ares should be appointed. But Paris will do; whoever Paris is.

Zeus. And my little Athene; have we her approval? Nay, never blush, nor hide your face. Well, well, maidens will be coy; 'tis a delicate subject. But there, she nods consent. Now, off with you; and mind, the beaten ones must not be cross with the judge; I will not have the poor lad harmed. The prize of beauty can be but one.

Herm. Now for Phrygia. I will show the way; keep close behind me, ladies, and don't be nervous. I know Paris well:

he is a charming young man; a great gallant, and an admirable judge of beauty. Depend on it, he will make a good award.

Aph. I am glad to hear that; I ask for nothing better than a just judge.— Has he a wife, Hermes, or is he a bachelor?

Herm. Not exactly a bachelor.

Aph. What do you mean?

Herm. I believe there is a wife, as it were; a good enough sort of girl—a native of those parts—but sadly countrified! I fancy he does not care very much about her.—Why do you ask?

Aph. I just wanted to know.

Ath. Now, Hermes, that is not fair. No whispering with Aphrodite.

Herm. It was nothing, Athene; nothing about you. She only asked me whether Paris was a bachelor.

Ath. What business is that of hers?

Herm. None that I know of. She meant nothing by the question; she just wanted to know.

Ath. Well, and is he?

Herm. Why, no.

Ath. And does he care for military glory? has he ambition? Or is he a *mere* neatherd?

Herm. I couldn't say for certain. But he is a young man, so it is to be presumed that distinction on the field of battle is among his desires.

Aph. There, you see; *I* don't complain; I say nothing when you whisper with *her.* Aphrodite is not so particular as some people.

Herm. Athene asked me almost exactly the same as you did; so don't be cross. It will do you no harm, my answering a plain question.— Meanwhile, we have left the stars far behind us, and are almost over Phrygia. There is Ida: I can make out the peak of Gargarum quite plainly; and if I am not mistaken, there is Paris himself.

Hera. Where is he? I don't see him.

Herm. Look over there to the left, Hera: not on the top, but down the side, by that cave where you see the herd.

Hera. But I *don't* see the herd.

Herm. What, don't you see them coming out from between the rocks,— where I am pointing, look—and the man running down from the crag, and keeping them together with his staff?

Hera. I see him now; if he it is.

Herm. Oh, that is Paris. But we are getting near; it is time to alight and walk. He might be frightened, if we were to descend upon him so suddenly.

Hera. Yes; very well. And now that we are on the earth, you might go on ahead, Aphrodite, and show us the way. You know the country, of course, having been here so often to see Anchises; or so I have heard.

Aph. Your sneers are thrown away on me, Hera.

Herm. Come; I'll lead the way myself. I spent some time on Ida, while Zeus was courting Ganymede. Many is the time that I have been sent here to keep watch over the boy; and when at last the eagle came, I flew by his side, and helped him with his lovely burden. This is the very rock, if I remember; yes, Ganymede was piping to his sheep, when down swooped the eagle behind him, and tenderly, oh, so tenderly, caught him up in those talons, and with the turban in his beak bore him off, the frightened boy straining his neck the while to see his captor. I picked up his pipes—he had dropped them in his fright and —ah! here is our umpire, close at hand. Let us accost him.— Good-morrow, herdsman!

Par. Good-morrow, youngster. And who may you be, who come thus far afield? And these dames? They are over comely, to be wandering on the mountain-side.

Herm. 'These dames,' good Paris, are Hera, Athene, and Aphrodite; and I am Hermes, with a message from Zeus. Why so pale and tremulous? Compose yourself; there is nothing the matter. Zeus appoints you the judge of their beauty. 'Because you are handsome, and wise in the things of love' (so runs the message), 'I leave the decision to you; and for the prize,—read the inscription on the apple.'

Par. Let me see what it is about. FOR THE FAIR, it says. But, my lord Hermes, how shall a mortal and a rustic like myself be judge of such unparalleled beauty? This is no sight for a herdsman's eyes; let the fine city folk decide on such matters. As for me, I can tell you which of two goats is the fairer beast; or I can judge betwixt heifer and heifer;—'tis my trade. But here, where all are beautiful alike, I know not how a man may leave looking at one, to look upon another. Where my eyes fall, there they fasten,—for there is beauty:

I move them, and what do I find? more loveliness! I am fixed again, yet distracted by neighbouring charms. I bathe in beauty:

I am enthralled:

ah, why am I not *all* eyes like Argus? Methinks it were a fair award, to give the apple to all three. Then again:

one is the wife and sister of Zeus; the others are his daughters. Take it where you will, 'tis a hard matter to judge.

Herm. So it is, Paris. At the same time—Zeus's orders! There is no way out of it.

Par. Well, please point out to them, Hermes, that the losers must not be angry with me; the fault will be in my eyes only.

Herm. That is quite understood. And now to work.

Par. I must do what I can; there is no help for it. But first let me ask,—am I just to look at them as they are, or must I go into the matter thoroughly?

Herm. That is for you to decide, in virtue of your office. You have only to give your orders; it is as you think best.

Par. As I think best? Then I will be thorough.

Herm. Get ready, ladies. Now, Mr. Umpire.—I will look the other way.

Hera. I approve your decision, Paris. I will be the first to submit myself to your inspection. You shall see that I have more to boast of than white arms and large eyes:

nought of me but is beautiful.

Par. Aphrodite, will you also prepare?

Ath. Oh, Paris,—make her take off that girdle, first; there is magic in it; she will bewitch you. For that matter, she has no right to come thus tricked out and painted,—just like a courtesan! She ought to show herself unadorned.

Par. They are right about the girdle, madam; it must go.

Aph. Oh, very well, Athene:

then take off that helmet, and show your head bare, instead of trying to intimidate the judge with that waving plume. I suppose you are afraid the colour of your eyes may be noticed, without their formidable surroundings.

Ath. Oh, here is my helmet.

Aph. And here is my girdle.

Hera. Now then.

Par. God of wonders! What loveliness is here! Oh, rapture! How exquisite these maiden charms! How dazzling the majesty of Heaven's true queen! And oh, how sweet, how enthralling is Aphrodite's smile! 'Tis too much, too much of happiness.—But perhaps it would be well for me to view each in detail; for as yet I doubt, and know not where to look; my eyes are drawn all ways at once.

Aph. Yes, that will be best.

Par. Withdraw then, you and Athene; and let Hera remain.

Hera. So be it; and when you have finished your scrutiny, you have next to consider, how you would like the present which I offer you. Paris, give me the prize of beauty, and you shall be lord of all Asia.

Par. I will take no presents. Withdraw. I shall judge as I think right. Approach, Athene.

Ath. Behold. And, Paris, if you will say that I am the fairest, I will make you a great warrior and conqueror, and you shall always win, in every one of your battles.

Par. But I have nothing to do with fighting, Athene. As you see, there is peace throughout all Lydia and Phrygia, and my father's dominion is uncontested. But never mind; I am not going to take your present, but you shall have fair play. You can robe again and put on your helmet; I have seen. And now for Aphrodite.

Aph. Here I am; take your time, and examine carefully; let nothing escape your vigilance. And I have something else to say to you, handsome Paris. Yes, you handsome boy, I have long had an eye on you; I think you must be the handsomest young fellow in all Phrygia. But it is such a pity that you don't leave these rocks and crags, and live in a town; you will lose all your beauty in this desert. What have you to do with mountains? What satisfaction can your beauty give to a lot of cows? You ought to have been married long ago; not to any of these dowdy women hereabouts, but to some Greek girl; an Argive, perhaps, or a Corinthian, or a Spartan; Helen, now, is a Spartan, and such a pretty girl—quite as pretty as I am—and so susceptible! Why, if she once caught sight of *you*, she would give up everything, I am sure, to go with you, and a most devoted wife she would be. But you have heard of Helen, of course?

Par. No, ma'am; but I should like to hear all about her now.

Aph. Well, she is the daughter of Leda, the beautiful woman, you know, whom Zeus visited in the disguise of a swan.

Par. And what is she like?

Aph. She is fair, as might be expected from the swan, soft as down (she was hatched from an egg, you know), and such a lithe, graceful figure; and only think, she is so much admired, that there was a war because Theseus ran away with her; and she was a mere child then. And when she grew up, the very first men in Greece were suitors for her hand, and she was given to Menelaus, who is descended from Pelops.— Now, if you like, she shall be your wife.

Par. What, when she is married already?

Aph. Tut, child, you are a simpleton:
I understand these things.

Par. I should like to understand them too.

Aph. You will set out for Greece on a tour of inspection:

84

and when you get to Sparta, Helen will see you; and for the rest—her falling in love, and going back with you—that will be my affair.

Par. But that is what I cannot believe,—that she will forsake her husband to cross the seas with a stranger, a barbarian.

Aph. Trust me for that. I have two beautiful children, Love and Desire. They shall be your guides. Love will assail her in all his might, and compel her to love you:

Desire will encompass you about, and make you desirable and lovely as himself; and I will be there to help. I can get the Graces to come too, and between us we shall prevail.

Par. How this will end, I know not. All I do know is, that I am in love with Helen already. I see her before me—I sail for Greece I am in Sparta—I am on my homeward journey, with her at my side! Ah, why is none of it true?

Aph. Wait. Do not fall in love yet. You have first to secure my interest with the bride, by your award. The union must be graced with my victorious presence:

your marriage-feast shall be my feast of victory. Love, beauty, wedlock; all these you may purchase at the price of yonder apple.

Par. But perhaps after the award you will forget all about *me?*

Aph. Shall I swear?

Par. No; but promise once more.

Aph. I promise that you shall have Helen to wife; that she shall follow you, and make Troy her home; and I will be present with you, and help you in all.

Par. And bring Love, and Desire, and the Graces?

_Aph Assuredly; and Passion and Hymen as well.

Par. Take the apple:

it is yours.

XXI

Ares. Hermes

Ar. Did you hear Zeus's threat, Hermes? most complimentary, wasn't it, and most practicable? 'If I choose,' says he, 'I could let down a cord from Heaven, and all of you might hang on to it and do your very best to pull me down; it would be waste labour; you would never move me. On the other hand, if I chose to haul up, I should have you all dangling in mid air, with earth and sea into the bargain and so on; you heard? Well, I dare say he *is* too much for any of us individually, but I will never believe he outweighs the whole of us in a body, or that, even with the makeweight of earth and sea, we should not get the better of him.

Her. Mind what you say, Ares; it is not safe to talk like that; we might get paid out for chattering.

Ar. You don't suppose I should say this to every one; I am not afraid of you; I know you can keep a quiet tongue. I *must* tell you what made me laugh most while he stormed:

I remember not so long ago, when Posidon and Hera and Athene rebelled and made a plot for his capture and imprisonment, he was frightened out of his wits; well, there were only three of them, and if Thetis had not taken pity on him and called in the hundred-handed Briareus to the rescue, he would actually have been put in chains, with his thunder and his bolt beside him. When I worked out the sum, I could not help laughing.

Her. Oh, do be quiet; such things are too risky for you to say or me to listen to.

XXIV

Hermes. Maia

Her. Mother, I am the most miserable god in Heaven.

Ma. Don't say such things, child.

Her. Am I to do all the work of Heaven with my own hands, to be hurried from one piece of drudgery to another, and never say a word? I have to get up early, sweep the dining-room, lay the cushions and put all to rights; then I have to wait on Zeus, and take his messages, up and down, all day long; and I am no sooner back again (no time for a wash) than I have to lay the table; and there was the nectar to pour out, too, till this new cup-bearer was bought. And it really is too bad, that when every one else is in bed, I should have to go off to Pluto with the Shades, and play the usher in Rhadamanthus's court. It is not enough that I must be busy all day in the wrestling-ground and the Assembly and the schools of rhetoric, the dead must have their share in me too. Leda's sons take turn and turn about betwixt Heaven and Hades—*I* have to be in both every day. And why should the sons of Alemena and Semele, paltry women, why should they feast at their ease, and I—the son of Maia, the grandson of Atlas—wait upon them? And now here am I only just back from Sidon, where he sent me to see after Europa, and before I am in breath again-off I must go to Argos, in quest of Danae, 'and you can take Boeotia on your way,' says father, 'and see Antiope.' I am half dead with it all. Mortal slaves are better off than I am:

they have the chance of being sold to a new master; I wish I had the same!

Ma. Come, come, child. You must do as your father bids you, like a good boy. Run along now to Argos and Boeotia; don't loiter, or you will get a whipping. Lovers are apt to be hasty.

XXV

Zeus. Helius

Zeus. What have you been about, you villainous Titan? You have utterly done for the earth, trusting your car to a silly boy like that; he has got too near and scorched it in one place, and in another killed everything with frost by withdrawing the heat too far; there is not a single thing he has not turned upside down; if I had not seen what was happening and upset him with the thunderbolt, there would not have been a remnant of mankind left. A pretty deputy driver!

Hel. I was wrong, Zeus; but do not be angry with me; my boy pressed me so; how could I tell it would turn out so badly?

Zeus. Oh, of course you didn't know what a delicate business it is, and how the slightest divergence ruins everything! it never occurred to you that the horses are spirited, and want a tight hand! oh no! why, give them their heads a moment, and they are out of control; just what happened:

they carried him now left, now right, now clean round backwards, and up or down, just at their own sweet will; he was utterly helpless.

Hel. I knew it all; I held out for a long time and told him he mustn't drive. But he wept and entreated, and his mother Clymene joined in, and at last I put him up. I showed him how to stand, and how far he was to mount upwards, and where to begin descending, and how to hold the reins, and keep the spirited beasts under control; and I told him how dangerous it was, if he did not keep the track. But, poor boy, when he found himself in charge of all that fire, and looking down into yawning space, he was frightened, and no wonder; and the horses soon knew I was not behind them, took the child's measure, left the track, and wrought all this havoc; he let go the reins—I suppose he was afraid of being thrown out—and held on to the rail. But he has suffered for it, and my grief is punishment enough for me, Zeus.

Zeus. Punishment enough, indeed! after daring to do such a thing as that!—Well, I forgive you this time. But if ever you transgress again, or send another substitute like him, I will show you how much hotter the thunderbolt is than your fire. Let his sisters bury him by the Eridanus, where he was upset. They shall weep amber tears and be changed by their grief into poplars. As for you, repair the car—the pole is broken, and one of the wheels crushed—, put the horses to and drive yourself. And let this be a lesson to you.

XXVI

Apollo. Hermes

Ap. Hermes, have you any idea which of those two is Castor, and which is Pollux? I never can make out.

Her. It was Castor yesterday, and Pollux to-day.

Ap. How do you tell? They are exactly alike.

Her. Why, Pollux's face is scarred with the wounds he got in boxing; those that Amycus, the Bebrycian, gave him, when he was on that expedition with Jason, are particularly noticeable. Castor has no marks; his face is all right.

Ap. Good; I am glad I know that. Everything else is the same for both. Each has his half egg-shell, with the star on top, each his javelin and his white horse. I am always calling Pollux Castor, and Castor Pollux. And, by the way, why are they never both here together? Why should they be alternately gods and shades?

Her. That is their brotherly way. You see, it was decreed that one of the sons of Leda must die, and the other be immortal; and by this arrangement they split the immortality between them.

Ap. Rather a stupid way of doing it:

if one of them is to be in Heaven, whilst the other is underground, they will never see one another at all; and I suppose that is just what they wanted to do. Then again:

all the other gods practise some useful profession, either here or on earth; for instance, I am a prophet, Asclepius is a doctor, you are a first-rate gymnast and trainer, Artemis ushers children into the world; now what are these two going to do? surely two such great fellows are not to have a lazy time of it?

Her. Oh no. Their business is to wait upon Posidon, and ride the waves; and if they see a ship in distress, they go aboard of her, and save the crew.

Ap. A most humane profession.

DIALOGUES OF THE SEA-GODS

I

Doris. Galatea.

Dor. A handsome lover, Galatea, this Sicilian shepherd who they say is so mad for you!

Gal. Don't be sarcastic, Doris; he is Posidon's son, after all.

Dor. Well, and if he were Zeus's, and still such a wild shaggy creature, with only one eye (there is nothing uglier than to have only one eye), do you think his birth would improve his beauty?

Gal. Shagginess and wildness, as you call them, are not ugly in a man; and his eye looks very well in the middle of his forehead, and sees just as well as if it were two.

Dor. Why, my dear, from your raptures about him one would think it was you that were in love, not he.

Gal. Oh no, I am not in love; but it is too bad, your all running him down as you do. It is my belief you are jealous, Do you remember? we were playing on the shore at the foot of Etna, where the long strip of beach comes between the mountain and the sea; he was feeding his sheep, and spied us from above; yes, but he never so much as glanced at the rest of you; I was the pretty one; he was all eyes—eye, I mean—for me. That is what makes you spiteful, because it showed I was better than you, good enough to be loved, while you were taken no notice of.

Dor. Hoity-toity! jealous indeed! because a one-eyed shepherd thinks you pretty! Why, what could he see in you but your white skin? and he only cared for that because it reminded him of cheese and milk; he thinks everything pretty that is like them. If you want to know any more than that about your looks, sit on a rock when it is calm, and lean over the water; just a bit of white skin, that is all; and who cares for that, if it is not picked out with some red?

Gal. Well, if I *am* all white, I have got a lover of some sort; there is not a shepherd or a sailor or a boatman to care for any of you. Besides, Polyphemus is very musical.

Dor. Take care, dear; we heard him singing the other day when he serenaded you. Heavens! one would have taken him for an ass braying. And his lyre! what a thing! A stag's skull, with its horns for the uprights; he put a bar across, and fastened on the strings without any tuning-pegs! then came the performance, all harsh and out of tune; he shouted something himself, and the lyre played something else, and the love ditty sent us into fits of laughter. Why, Echo, chatterbox that she is, would not answer him; she was ashamed to be caught mimicking such a rough ridiculous song. Oh, and the pet that your beau brought you in his arms!—a bear cub nearly as shaggy as himself. Now then, Galatea, do you still think we envy you your lover?

89

Gal. Well, Doris, only show us your own; no doubt he is much handsomer, and sings and plays far better.

Dor. Oh, I have not got one; *I* do not set up to be lovely. But one like the Cyclops—faugh, he might be one of his own goats!—he eats raw meat, they say, and feeds on travellers—one like him, dear, you may keep; I wish you nothing worse than to return his love.

II

Cyclops. Posidon

Cy. Only look, father, what that cursed stranger has been doing to me! He made me drunk, and set upon me whilst I was asleep, and blinded me.

Po. Who has dared to do this?

Cy. He called himself 'Noman' at first:

but when he had got safely out of range, he said his name was Odysseus.

Po. I know—the Ithacan; on his way back from Troy. But how did he come to do such a thing? He is not distinguished for courage.

Cy. When I got back from the pasture, I caught a lot of the fellows in my cave. Evidently they had designs upon the sheep:

because when I had blocked up my doorway (I have a great big stone for that), and kindled a fire, with a tree that I had brought home from the mountain,—there they were trying to hide themselves. I saw they were robbers, so I caught a few of them, and ate them of course, and then that scoundrel of a Noman, or Odysseus, whichever it is, gave me something to drink, with a drug in it; it tasted and smelt very good, but it was villanously heady stuff; it made everything spin round; even the cave seemed to be turning upside down, and I simply didn't know where I was; and finally I fell off to sleep. And then he sharpened that stake, and made it hot in the fire, and blinded me in my sleep; and blind I have been ever since, father.

Po. You must have slept pretty soundly, my boy, or you would have jumped up in the middle of it. Well, and how did Odysseus get off? He couldn't move that stone away, *I* know.

Cy. I took that away myself, so as to catch him as he went out. I sat down in the doorway, and felt about for him with my hands. I just let the sheep go out to pasture, and told the ram everything I wanted done.

Po. Ah! and they slipped out under the sheep? But you should have set the other Cyclopes on to him.

Cy. I did call them, and they came:

but when they asked me who it was that was playing tricks with me, I said 'Noman'; and then they thought I was mad, and went off home again. The villain! that name of his was just a trick! And what I minded most was the way in which he made game of my misfortune:

'Not even Papa can put this right,' he said.

Po. Never mind, my boy; I will be even with him. I may not be able to cure blindness, but he shall know that I have something to say to mariners. He is not home yet.

III

Posidon. Alpheus

Pos. What is the meaning of this, Alpheus? unlike others, when you take your plunge you do not mingle with the brine as a river should; you do not put an end to your labours by dispersing; you hold together through the sea, keep your current fresh, and hurry along in all your original purity; you dive down to strange depths like a gull or a heron; I suppose you will come to the top again and show yourself somewhere or other.

Al. Do not press me, Posidon; a love affair; and many is the time you have been in love yourself.

Pos. Woman, nymph, or Nereid?

Al. All wrong; she is a fountain.

Pos. A fountain? and where does she flow?

Al. She is an islander—in Sicily. Her name is Arethusa.

Pos. Ah, I commend your taste. She is pellucid, and bubbles up in perfect purity; the water as bright over her pebbles as if it were a mass of silver.

Al. You know my fountain, Posidon, and no mistake. It is to her that I go.

Pos. Go, then; and may the course of love run smooth! But pray where did you meet her? Arcadia and Syracuse, you know!

Al. I am in a hurry; you are detaining me, with these superfluous questions.

Pos. Ah, so I am. Be off to your beloved, rise from the sea, mingle your channels and be one water.

IV

Menelaus. Proteus

Me. I can understand your turning into *water*, you know, Proteus, because you *are* a sea-god. I can even pass the tree; and the lion is not wholly beyond the bounds of belief. But the idea of your being able to turn into *fire*, living under water as you do,—this excites my surprise, not to say my incredulity.

Pro. Don't let it; because I can.

Me. I have seen you do it. But (to be frank with you) I think there must be some deception; you play tricks with one's eyes; you don't really turn into anything of the kind?

Pro. Deception? What deception can there possibly be? Everything is above-board. Your eyes were open, I suppose, and you saw me change into all these things? If that is not enough for you, if you think it is a fraud, an optical illusion, I will turn into fire again, and you can touch me with your hand, my sagacious friend. You will then be able to conclude whether I am only visible fire, or have the additional property of burning.

Me. That would be rash.

Pro. I suppose you have never seen such a thing as a polypus, nor observed the proceedings of that fish?

Me. I have seen them; as to their proceedings, I shall be glad of your information.

Pro. The polypus, having selected his rock, and attached himself by means of his suckers, assimilates himself to it, changing his colour to match that of the rock. By this means he hopes to escape the observation of fishermen:

there is no contrast of colour to betray his presence; he looks just like stone.

Me. So I have heard. But yours is quite another matter, Proteus.

Pro. I don't know what evidence would satisfy you, if you reject that of your own eyes.

Me. I have seen it done, but it is an extraordinary business; fire and water, one and the same person!

V

Panope. Galene

Pa. Galene, did you see what Eris did yesterday at the Thessalian banquet, because she had not had an invitation?

Ga. No, I was not with you; Posidon had told me to keep the sea quiet for the occasion. What did Eris do, then, if she was not there?

Pa. Thetis and Peleus had just gone off to the bridal chamber, conducted by Amphitrite and Posidon, when Eris came in unnoticed— which was easy enough; some were drinking, some dancing, or attending to Apollo's lyre or the Muses' songs—Well, she threw down a lovely apple, solid gold, my dear; and there was written on it, FOR THE FAIR. It rolled along as if it knew what it was about, till it came in front of Hera, Aphrodite, and Athene. Hermes picked it up and read out the inscription; of course we Nereids kept quiet; what should *we* do in such company? But they all made for it, each insisting that it was hers; and if Zeus had not parted them, there would have been a battle. He would not decide the matter himself, though they asked him to. 'Go, all of you, to Ida,' he said, 'to the son of Priam; he is a man of taste, quite capable of picking out the beauty; he will be no bad judge.'

Ga. Yes. and the Goddesses, Panope?

Pa. They are going to Ida to-day, I believe; we shall soon have news of the result.

Ga. Oh, I can tell you that now; if the umpire is not a blind man, no one else can win, with Aphrodite in for it.

Triton. Posidon. Amymone

Tri. Posidon, there is such a pretty girl coming to Lerna for water every day; I don't know that I ever saw a prettier.

Pos. What is she, a lady? or a mere water-carrier?

Tri. Oh no; she is one of the fifty daughters of that Egyptian king. Her name is Amymone; I asked about that and her family. Danaus understands discipline; he is bringing them up to do everything for themselves; they have to fetch water, and make themselves generally useful.

Pos. And does she come all that way by herself, from Argos to Lerna?

Tri. Yes; and Argos, you know, is a thirsty place; she is always having to get water.

Pos. Triton, this is most exciting. We must go and see her.

Tri. Very well. It is just her time now; I reckon she will be about half-way to Lerna.

Pos. Bring out the chariot, then. Or no; it takes such a time getting it ready, and putting the horses to. Just fetch me out a good fast dolphin; that will be quickest.

Tri. Here is a racer for you.

Pos. Good; now let us be off. You swim alongside.—Here we are at Lerna. I'll lie in ambush hereabouts; and you keep a look-out. When you see her coming—

Tri. Here she comes.

Pos. A charming child; the dawn of loveliness. We must carry her off.

Am. Villain! where are you taking me to? You are a kidnapper. I know who sent you—my uncle Aegyptus. I shall call my father.

Tri. Hush, Amymone; it is Posidon.

Am. Posidon? What do you mean? Unhand me, villain! would you drag me into the sea? Help, help, I shall sink and be drowned.

Pos. Don't be frightened; no harm shall be done to you. Come, you shall have a fountain called after you; it shall spring up in this very place, near the waves; I will strike the rock with my trident.— Think how nice it will be being dead, and not having to carry water any more, like all your sisters.

VII

South Wind. West Wind

S. Zephyr, is it true about Zeus and the heifer that Hermes is convoying across the sea to Egypt?—that he fell in love with it?

W. Certainly. She was not a heifer then, though, but a daughter of the river Inachus. Hera made her what she is now; Zeus was so deep in love that Hera was jealous.

S. And is he still in love, now that she is a cow?

W. Oh, yes; that is why he has sent her to Egypt, and told us not to stir up the sea till she has swum across; she is to be delivered there of her child, and both of them are to be Gods.

S. The heifer a God?

W. Yes, I tell you. And Hermes said she was to be the patroness of sailors and our mistress, and send out or confine any of us that she chooses.

S. So we must regard ourselves as her servants at once?

W. Why, yes; she will be the kinder if we do. Ah, she has got across and landed. Do you see? she does not go on four legs now; Hermes has made her stand erect, and turned her back into a beautiful woman.

S. This is most remarkable, Zephyr; no horns, no tail, no cloven hoofs; instead, a lovely maid. But what is the matter with Hermes? he has changed his handsome face into a dog's.

W. We had better not meddle; he knows his own business best.

VIII

Posidon. Dolphins

Pos. Well done, Dolphins!—humane as ever. Not content with your former exploit, when Ino leapt with Melicertes from the Scironian cliff, and you picked the boy up and conveyed him to the Isthmus, one of you swims from Methymna to Taenarum with this musician on his back, mantle and lyre and all. Those sailors had almost had their wicked will of him; but you were not going to stand that.

Dol. You need not be surprised to find us doing a good turn to a man, Posidon; we were men before we were fishes.

Pos. Yes; I think it was too bad of Dionysus to celebrate his victory by such a transformation scene; he might have been content with adding you to the roll of his subjects.—Well, Dolphin, tell me all about Arion.

Dol. From what I can gather, Periander was very fond of him, and was always sending for him to perform; till Arion grew quite rich at his expense, and thought he would take a trip to Methymna, and show off his wealth at home. He took ship accordingly; but it was with a crew of rogues. He had made no secret of the gold and silver he had with him; and when they were in mid Aegean, the sailors rose against him. As I was swimming alongside, I heard all that went on. 'Since your minds are made up,' says Arion, 'at least let me get my mantle on, and sing my own dirge; and then I will throw myself into the sea of my own accord.'—The sailors agreed. He threw his minstrel's cloak about him, and sang a most sweet melody; and then he let himself drop into the water, never doubting but that his last moment had come. But I caught him up on my back, and swam to shore with him at Taenarum.

Pos. I am glad to find you a patron of the arts. This was handsome pay for a song.

94

Posidon. Amphitrite and other Nereids

Pos. The strait where the child fell shall be called Hellespont after her. And as for her body, you Nereids shall take it to the Troad to be buried by the inhabitants.

Amph. Oh no, Posidon. Let her grave be the sea which bears her name. We are so sorry for her; that step-mother's treatment of her was shocking.

Pos. No, my dear, that may not be. And indeed it is not desirable that she should lie here under the sand; her grave shall be in the Troad, as I said, or in the Chersonese. It will be no small consolation to her that Ino will have the same fate before long. She will be chased by Athamas from the top of Cithaeron down the ridge which runs into the sea, and there plunge in with her son in her arms. But her we must rescue, to please Dionysus; Ino was his nurse and suckled him, you know.

Amph. Rescue a wicked creature like her?

Pos. Well, we do not want to disoblige Dionysus.

Nereid. I wonder what made the poor child fall off the ram; her brother Phrixus held on all right.

Pos. Of course he did; a lusty youth equal to the flight; but it was all too strange for her; sitting on that queer mount, looking down on yawning space, terrified, overpowered by the heat, giddy with the speed, she lost her hold on the ram's horns, and down she came into the sea.

Nereid. Surely her mother Nephele should have broken her fall.

Pos. I dare say; but Fate is a great deal too strong for Nephele.

<h2 style="text-align:center">X</h2>

Iris. Posidon

Ir. Posidon:

you know that floating island, that was torn away from Sicily, and is still drifting about under water; you are to bring it to the surface, Zeus says, and fix it well in view in the middle of the Aegean; and mind it is properly secured; he has a use for it.

Pos. Very good. And when I have got it up, and anchored it, what is he going to do with it?

Ir. Leto is to lie in there; her time is near.

Pos. And is there no room in Heaven? Or is Earth too small to hold her children?

Ir. Ah, you see, Hera has bound the Earth by a great oath not to give shelter to Leto in her travail. This island, however, being out of sight, has not committed itself.

Pos. I see.—Island, be still! Rise once more from the depths; and this time there must be no sinking. Henceforth you are *terra firma*; it will be your happiness to receive my brother's twin children, fairest of the Gods.—Tritons, you will have to convey Leto across. Let all be calm.—As to that serpent who is frightening her out of her senses, wait till these children are born; they will soon avenge their mother.—You can tell Zeus that all is ready. Delos stands firm:

Leto has only to come.

XI

The Xanthus. The Sea

Xan. O Sea, take me to you; see how horribly I have been treated; cool my wounds for me.

Sea. What is this, Xanthus? who has burned you?

Xan. Hephaestus. Oh, I am burned to cinders! oh, oh, oh, I boil!

Sea. What made him use his fire upon you?

Xan. Why, it was all that son of your Thetis. He was slaughtering the Phrygians; I tried entreaties, but he went raging on, damming my stream with their bodies; I was so sorry for the poor wretches, I poured down to see if I could make a flood and frighten him off them. But Hephaestus happened to be about, and he must have collected every particle of fire he had in Etna or anywhere else; on he came at me, scorched my elms and tamarisks, baked the poor fishes and eels, made me boil over, and very nearly dried me up altogether. You see what a state I am in with the burns.

Sea. Indeed you are thick and hot, Xanthus, and no wonder; the dead men's blood accounts for one, and the fire for the other, according to your story. Well, and serve you right; assaulting my grandson, indeed! paying no more respect to the son of a Nereid than that!

Xan. Was I not to take compassion on the Phrygians? they are my neighbours.

Sea. And was Hephaestus not to take compassion on Achilles? He is the son of Thetis.

XII

Doris. Thetis

Dor. Crying, dear?

The. Oh, Doris, I have just seen a lovely girl thrown into a chest by her father, and her little baby with her; and he gave the chest to some sailors, and told them, as soon as they were far enough from the shore, to drop it into the water; he meant them to be drowned, poor things.

Dor. Oh, sister, but why? What was it all about? Did you hear?

The. Her father, Acrisius, wanted to keep her from marrying. And, as she was so pretty, he shut her up in an iron room. And—I don't know whether it's true—but they say that Zeus turned himself into gold, and came showering down through the roof, and she caught the gold in her lap,—and it was Zeus all the time. And then her father found out about it—he is a horrid, jealous old man—and he was furious, and thought she had been receiving a lover; and he put her into the chest, the moment the child was born.

Dor. And what did she do then?

The. She never said a word against her own sentence; *she* was ready to submit:

but she pleaded hard for the child's life, and cried, and held him up for his grandfather to see; and there was the sweet babe, that thought no harm, smiling at the waves. I am beginning again, at the mere remembrance of it.

Dor. You make me cry, too. And is it all over?

The. No; the chest has carried them safely so far; it is by Seriphus.

Dor. Then why should we not save them? We can put the chest into those fishermen's nets, look; and then of course they will be hauled in, and come safe to shore.

The. The very thing. She shall not die; nor the child, sweet treasure!

XIV

Triton. Iphianassa. Doris. Nereids

Tri. Well, ladies:

so the monster you sent against the daughter of Cepheus has got killed himself, and never done Andromeda any harm at all!

Nereid. Who did it? I suppose Cepheus was just using his daughter as a bait, and had a whole army waiting in ambush to kill him?

Tri. No, no.—Iphianassa, you remember Perseus, Danae's boy?—they were both thrown into the sea by the boy's grandfather, in that chest, you know, and you took pity on them.

Iph. I know; why, I suppose he is a fine handsome young fellow by now?

Tri. It was he who killed your monster.

Iph. But why? This was not the way to show his gratitude.

Tri. I'll tell you all about it. The king had sent him on this expedition against the Gorgons, and when he got to Libya—

Iph. How did he get there? all by himself? he must have had some one to help him?—it is a dangerous journey otherwise.

Tri. He flew,—Athene gave him wings.—Well, so when he got to where the Gorgons were living, he caught them napping, I suppose, cut off Medusa's head, and flew away.

Iph. How could he see them? The Gorgons are a forbidden sight. Whoever looks at them will never look at any one else again.

Tri. Athene held up her shield—I heard him telling Andromeda and Cepheus about it afterwards—Athene showed him the reflection of the Gorgon in her shield, which is as bright as any mirror; so he took hold of her hair in his left hand, grasped his scimetar with the right, still looking at the reflection, cut off her head, and was off before her sisters woke up. Lowering his flight as he reached the Ethiopian coast yonder, he caught sight of Andromeda, fettered to a jutting rock, her hair hanging loose about her shoulders; ye Gods, what loveliness was there exposed to view! And first pity of her hard fate prompted him to ask the cause of her doom:

but Fate had decreed the maiden's deliverance, and presently Love stole upon him, and he resolved to save her. The hideous monster now drew near, and would have swallowed her:

but the youth, hovering above, smote him with the drawn scimetar in his right hand, and with his left uncovered the petrifying Gorgon's head:

in one moment the monster was lifeless; all of him that had met that gaze was turned to stone. Then Perseus released the maiden from her fetters, and supported her, as with timid steps she descended from the slippery rock.— And now he is to marry her in Cepheus's palace, and take her home to Argos; so that where she looked for death, she has found an uncommonly good match.

Iph. I am not sorry to hear it. It is no fault of hers, if her mother has the vanity to set up for our rival.

Dor. Still, she *is* Andromeda's mother; and we should have had our revenge on her through the daughter.

Iph. My dear, let bygones be bygones. What matter if a barbarian queen's tongue runs away with her? She is sufficiently punished by the fright. So let us take this marriage in good part.

XV

West Wind. South Wind

W. Such a splendid pageant I never saw on the waves, since the day I first blew. You were not there, Notus? *S.* Pageant, Zephyr? what pageant? and whose?

W. You missed a most ravishing spectacle; such another chance you are not likely to have.

S. I was busy with the Red Sea; and I gave the Indian coasts a little airing too. So I don't know what you are talking about.

W. Well, you know Agenor the Sidonian?

S. Europa's father? what of him?

W. Europa it is that I am going to tell you about.

S. You need not tell me that Zeus has been in love with her this long while; that is stale news.

W. We can pass the love, then, and get on to the sequel.

Europa had come down for a frolic on the beach with her playfellows. Zeus transformed himself into a bull, and joined the game. A fine sight he was—spotless white skin, crumpled horns, and gentle eyes. He gambolled on the shore with them, bellowing most musically, till Europa took heart of grace and mounted him. No sooner had she done it than, with her on his back, Zeus made off at a run for the sea, plunged in, and began swimming; she was dreadfully frightened, but kept her seat by clinging to one of his horns with her left hand, while the right held her skirt down against the puffs of wind.

S. A lovely sight indeed, Zephyr, in every sense—Zeus swimming with his darling on his back.

W. Ay, but what followed was lovelier far.

Every wave fell; the sea donned her robe of peace to speed them on their way; we winds made holiday and joined the train, all eyes; fluttering Loves skimmed the waves, just dipping now and again a heedless toe—in their hands lighted torches, on their lips the nuptial song; up floated Nereids—few but were prodigal of naked charms—and clapped their hands, and kept pace on dolphin steeds; the Triton company, with every sea-creature that frights not the eye, tripped it around the maid; for Posidon on his car, with Amphitrite by him, led them in festal mood, ushering his brother through the waves. But, crowning all, a Triton pair bore Aphrodite, reclined on a shell, heaping the bride with all flowers that blow.

So went it from Phoenice even to Crete. But, when he set foot on the isle, behold, the bull was no more; 'twas Zeus that took Europa's hand and led her to the Dictaean Cave—blushing and downward-eyed; for she knew now the end of her bringing.

But we plunged this way and that, and roused the still seas anew.

S. Ah me, what sights of bliss! and I was looking at griffins, and elephants, and blackamoors!

DIALOGUES OF THE DEAD

I

Diogenes. Pollux

Diog. Pollux, I have a commission for you; next time you go up—and I think it is your turn for earth to-morrow—if you come across Menippus the Cynic—you will find him about the Craneum at Corinth, or in the Lyceum, laughing at the philosophers' disputes—well, give him this message:

—Menippus, Diogenes advises you, if mortal subjects for laughter begin to pall, to come down below, and find much richer material; where you are now, there is always a dash of uncertainty in it; the question will always intrude—who can be quite sure about the hereafter? Here, you can have your laugh out in security, like me; it is the best of sport to see millionaires, governors, despots, now mean and insignificant; you can only tell them by their lamentations, and the spiritless despondency which is the legacy of better days. Tell him this, and mention that he had better stuff his wallet with plenty of lupines, and any un-considered trifles he can snap up in the way of pauper doles[12] or lustral eggs.[13]

Pol. I will tell him, Diogenes. But give me some idea of his appearance.

Diog. Old, bald, with a cloak that allows him plenty of light and ventilation, and is patched all colours of the rainbow; always laughing, and usually gibing at pretentious philosophers.

Pol. Ah, I cannot mistake him now.

Diog. May I give you another message to those same philosophers?

Pol. Oh, I don't mind; go on.

Diog. Charge them generally to give up playing the fool, quarrelling over metaphysics, tricking each other with horn and crocodile puzzles [14] and teaching people to waste wit on such absurdities.

Pol. Oh, but if I say anything against their wisdom, they will call me an ignorant blockhead.

Diog. Then tell them from me to go to the devil.

Pol. Very well; rely upon me.

Diog. And then, my most obliging of Polluxes, there is this for the rich:

---

[12] In the Greek, 'a Hecate's repast lying at a street corner.' 'Rich men used to make offerings to Hecate on the 30th of every month as Goddess of roads at street corners; and these offerings were at once pounced upon by the poor, or, as here, the Cynics.' *Jacobitz.*

[13] 'Eggs were often used as purificatory offerings and set out in front of the house purified.' *Id.*

[14] See *Puzzles* in Notes.

—O vain fools, why hoard gold? why all these pains over interest sums and the adding of hundred to hundred, when you must shortly come to us with nothing beyond the dead-penny?

Pol. They shall have their message too.

Diog. Ah, and a word to the handsome and strong; Megillus of Corinth, and Damoxenus the wrestler will do. Inform them that auburn locks, eyes bright or black, rosy cheeks, are as little in fashion here as tense muscles or mighty shoulders; man and man are as like as two peas, tell them, when it comes to bare skull and no beauty.

Pol. That is to the handsome and strong; yes, I can manage that.

Diog. Yes, my Spartan, and here is for the poor. There are a great many of them, very sorry for themselves and resentful of their helplessness. Tell them to dry their tears and cease their cries; explain to them that here one man is as good as another, and they will find those who were rich on earth no better than themselves. As for your Spartans, you will not mind scolding them, from me, upon their present degeneracy?

Pol. No, no, Diogenes; leave Sparta alone; that is going too far; your other commissions I will execute.

Diog. Oh, well, let them off, if you care about it; but tell all the others what I said.

II

Before Pluto:
Croesus, Midas, and Sardanapalus v. Menippus

Cr. Pluto, we can stand this snarling Cynic no longer in our neighbourhood; either you must transfer him to other quarters, or we are going to migrate.

Pl. Why, what harm does he do to your ghostly community?

Cr. Midas here, and Sardanapalus and I, can never get in a good cry over the old days of gold and luxury and treasure, but he must be laughing at us, and calling us rude names; 'slaves' and 'garbage,' he says we are. And then he sings; and that throws us out.—In short, he is a nuisance.

Pl. Menippus, what's this I hear?

Me. All perfectly true, Pluto. I detest these abject rascals! Not content with having lived the abominable lives they did, they keep on talking about it now they are dead, and harping on the good old days. I take a positive pleasure in annoying them.

Pl. Yes, but you mustn't. They have had terrible losses; they feel it deeply.

Me. Pluto! you are not going to lend *your* countenance to these whimpering fools?

Pl. It isn't that:
but I won't have you quarrelling.

Me. Well, you scum of your respective nations, let there be no misunderstanding; I am going on just the same. Wherever you are, there shall I be also; worrying, jeering, singing you down.

Cr. Presumption!

Me. Not a bit of it. Yours was the presumption, when you expected men to fall down before you, when you trampled on men's liberty, and forgot there was such a thing as death. Now comes the weeping and gnashing of teeth:
for all is lost!

Cr. Lost! Ah God! My treasure-heaps—

Mid. My gold—

Sar. My little comforts—

Me. That's right:
stick to it! You do the whining, and I'll chime in with a string of GNOTHI-SAUTONS, best of accompaniments.

III

Menippus. Amphilochus. Trophonius

Me. Now I wonder how it is that you two dead men have been honoured with temples and taken for prophets; those silly mortals imagine you are Gods.

Amp. How can we help it, if they are fools enough to have such fancies about the dead?

Me. Ah, they would never have had them, though, if you had not been charlatans in your lifetime, and pretended to know the future and be able to foretell it to your clients.

Tro. Well, Menippus, Amphilochus can take his own line, if he likes; as for me, I *am* a Hero, and *do* give oracles to any one who comes down to me. It is pretty clear you were never at Lebadea, or you would not be so incredulous.

Me. What do you mean? I must go to Lebadea, swaddle myself up in absurd linen, take a cake in my hand, and crawl through a narrow passage into a cave, before I could tell that you are a dead man, with nothing but knavery to differentiate you from the rest of us? Now, on your seer-ship, what *is* a Hero? I am sure *I* don't know.

Tro. He is half God, and half man.

Me. So what is neither man (as you imply) nor God, is both at once? Well, at present what has become of your diviner half?

Tro. He gives oracles in Boeotia.

Me. What you may mean is quite beyond me; the one thing I know for certain is that you are dead—the whole of you.

IV

Hermes. Charon

Her. Ferryman, what do you say to settling up accounts? It will prevent any unpleasantness later on.

Ch. Very good. It does save trouble to get these things straight.

Her. One anchor, to your order, five shillings.

Ch. That is a lot of money.

Her. So help me Pluto, it is what I had to pay. One rowlock-strap, fourpence.

Ch. Five and four; put that down.

Her. Then there was a needle, for mending the sail; ten-pence.

Ch. Down with it.

Her. Caulking-wax; nails; and cord for the brace. Two shillings the lot.

Ch. They were worth the money.

Her. That's all; unless I have forgotten anything. When will you pay it?

Ch. I can't just now, Hermes; we shall have a war or a plague presently, and then the passengers will come shoaling in, and I shall be able to make a little by jobbing the fares.

Her. So for the present I have nothing to do but sit down, and pray for the worst, as my only chance of getting paid?

Ch. There is nothing else for it;—very little business doing just now, as you see, owing to the peace.

Her. That is just as well, though it does keep me waiting for my money. After all, though, Charon, in old days men were men; you remember the state they used to come down in,—all blood and wounds generally. Nowadays, a man is poisoned by his slave or his wife; or gets dropsy from overfeeding; a pale, spiritless lot, nothing like the men of old. Most of them seem to meet their end in some plot that has money for its object.

Ch. Ah; money is in great request.

Her. Yes; you can't blame me if I am somewhat urgent for payment.

V

Pluto. Hermes

Pl. You know that old, old fellow, Eucrates the millionaire—no children, but a few thousand would-be heirs?

Her. Yes—lives at Sicyon. Well?

Pl. Well, Hermes, he is ninety now; let him live as much longer, please; I should like it to be more still, if possible; and bring me down his toadies one by one, that young Charinus, Damon, and the rest of them.

Her. It would seem so strange, wouldn't it?

Pl. On the contrary, it would be ideal justice. What business have they to pray for his death, or pretend to his money? they are no relations. The most abominable thing about it is that they vary these prayers with every public attention; when he is ill, every one knows what they are after, and yet they vow offerings if he recovers; talk of versatility! So let him be immortal, and bring them away before him with their mouths still open for the fruit that never drops.

Her. Well, they *are* rascals, and it would be a comic ending. He leads them a pretty life too, on hope gruel; he always looks more dead than alive, but he is tougher than a young man. They have divided up the inheritance among them, and feed on imaginary bliss.

Pl. Just so; now he is to throw off his years like Iolaus, and rejuvenate, while they in the middle of their hopes find themselves here with their dream-wealth left behind them. Nothing like making the punishment fit the crime.

Her. Say no more, Pluto; I will fetch you them one after another; seven of them, is it?

Pl. Down with them; and he shall change from an old man to a blooming youth, and attend their funerals.

VI

Terpsion. Pluto

Ter. Now is this fair, Pluto,—that I should die at the age of thirty, and that old Thucritus go on living past ninety?

Pl. Nothing could be fairer. Thucritus lives and is in no hurry for his neighbours to die; whereas you always had some design against him; you were waiting to step into his shoes.

Ter. Well, an old man like that is past getting any enjoyment out of his money; he ought to die, and make room for younger men.

Pl. This is a novel principle:

the man who can no longer derive pleasure from his money is to die!— Fate and Nature have ordered it otherwise.

Ter. Then they have ordered it wrongly. There ought to be a proper sequence according to seniority. Things are turned upside down, if an old man is to go on living with only three teeth in his head, half blind, tottering about with a pair of slaves on each side to hold him up, drivelling and rheumy-eyed, having no joy of life, a living tomb, the derision of his juniors,—and young men are to die in the prime of their strength and beauty. 'Tis contrary to nature. At any rate the young men have a right to know when the old are going to die, so that they may not throw away their attentions on them for nothing, as is sometimes the case. The present arrangement is a putting of the cart before the horse.

Pl. There is a great deal more sound sense in it than you suppose, Terpsion. Besides, what right have you young fellows got to be prying after other men's goods, and thrusting yourselves upon your childless elders? You look rather foolish, when you get buried first; it tickles people immensely; the

105

more fervent your prayers for the death of your aged friend, the greater is the general exultation when you precede him. It has become quite a profession lately, this amorous devotion to old men and women,—childless, of course; children destroy the illusion. By the way though, some of the beloved objects see through your dirty motives well enough by now; they have children, but they pretend to hate them, and so have lovers all the same. When their wills come to be read, their faithful bodyguard is not included:

nature asserts itself, the children get their rights, and the lovers realize, with gnashings of teeth, that they have been taken in.

Ter. Too true! The luxuries that Thucritus has enjoyed at my expense! He always looked as if he were at the point of death. I never went to see him, but he would groan and squeak like a chicken barely out of the shell:

I considered that he might step into his coffin at any moment, and heaped gift upon gift, for fear of being outdone in generosity by my rivals; I passed anxious, sleepless nights, reckoning and arranging all; 'twas this, the sleeplessness and the anxiety, that brought me to my death. And he swallows my bait whole, and attends my funeral chuckling.

Pl. Well done, Thucritus! Long may you live to enjoy your wealth,— and your joke at the youngsters' expense; many a toady may you send hither before your own time comes!

Ter. Now I think of it, it *would* be a satisfaction if Charoeades were to die before him.

Pl. Charoeades! My dear Terpsion, Phido, Melanthus,—every one of them will be here before Thucritus,—all victims of this same anxiety!

Ter. That is as it should be. Hold on, Thucritus!

VII

Zenophantus. Callidemides

Ze. Ah, Callidemides, and how did *you* come by your end? As for me, I was free of Dinias's table, and there died of a surfeit; but that is stale news; you were there, of course.

Cal. Yes, I was. Now there was an element of surprise about *my* fate. I suppose you know that old Ptoeodorus?

Ze. The rich man with no children, to whom you gave most of your company?

Cal. That is the man; he had promised to leave me his heir, and I used to show my appreciation. However, it went on such a time; Tithonus was a juvenile to him; so I found a short cut to my property. I bought a potion, and agreed with the butler that next time his master called for wine (he is a pretty stiff drinker) he should have this ready in a cup and present it; and I was pledged to reward the man with his freedom.

Ze. And what happened? this is interesting.

Cal. When we came from bath, the young fellow had two cups ready, one with the poison for Ptoeodorus, and the other for me; but by some blunder he handed me the poisoned cup, and Ptoeodorus the plain; and behold, before he had done drinking, there was I sprawling on the ground, a vicarious corpse! Why are you laughing so, Zenophantus? I am your friend; such mirth is unseemly.

Ze. Well, it was such a humorous exit. And how did the old man behave?

Cal. He was dreadfully distressed for the moment; then he saw, I suppose, and laughed as much as you over the butler's trick.

Ze. Ah, short cuts are no better for you than for other people, you see; the high road would have been safer, if not quite so quick.

VIII

Cnemon. Damnippus

Cne. Why, 'tis the proverb fulfilled! The fawn hath taken the lion.

Dam. What's the matter, Cnemon?

Cne. The matter! I have been fooled, miserably fooled. I have passed over all whom I should have liked to make my heirs, and left my money to the wrong man.

Dam. How was that?

Cne. I had been speculating on the death of Hermolaus, the millionaire. He had no children, and my attentions had been well received by him. I thought it would be a good idea to let him know that I had made my will in his favour, on the chance of its exciting his emulation.

Dam. Yes; and Hermolaus?

Cne. What *his* will was, I don't know. I died suddenly,—the roof came down about my ears; and now Hermolaus is my heir. The pike has swallowed hook and bait.

Dam. And your anglership into the bargain. The pit that you digged for other....

Cue. That's about the truth of the matter, confound it.

IX

Simylus. Polystratus

Si. So here you are at last, Polystratus; you must be something very like a centenarian.

Pol. Ninety-eight.

Si. And what sort of a life have you had of it, these thirty years? you were about seventy when I died.

Pol. Delightful, though you may find it hard to believe.

Si. It is surprising that you could have any joy of your life—old, weak, and childless, moreover.

107

Pol. In the first place, I could do just what I liked; there were still plenty of handsome boys and dainty women; perfumes were sweet, wine kept its bouquet, Sicilian feasts were nothing to mine.

Si. This *is* a change, to be sure; you were very economical in my day.

Pol. Ah, but, my simple friend, these good things were presents— came in streams. From dawn my doors were thronged with visitors, and in the day it was a procession of the fairest gifts of earth.

Si. Why, you must have seized the crown after my death.

Pol. Oh no, it was only that I inspired a number of tender passions.

Si. Tender passions, indeed! what, you, an old man with hardly a tooth left in your head!

Pol. Certainly; the first of our townsmen were in love with me. Such as you see me, old, bald, blear-eyed, rheumy, they delighted to do me honour; happy was the man on whom my glance rested a moment.

Si. Well, then, you had some adventure like Phaon's, when he rowed Aphrodite across from Chios; your God granted your prayer and made you young and fair and lovely again.

Pol. No, no; I was as you see me, and I was the object of all desire.

Si. Oh, I give it up.

Pol. Why, I should have thought you knew the violent passion for old men who have plenty of money and no children.

Si. Ah, now I comprehend your beauty, old fellow; it was the *Golden* Aphrodite bestowed it.

Pol. I assure you, Simylus, I had a good deal of satisfaction out of my lovers; they idolized me, almost. Often I would be coy and shut some of them out. Such rivalries! such jealous emulations!

Si. And how did you dispose of your fortune in the end?

Pol. I gave each an express promise to make him my heir; he believed, and treated me to more attentions than ever; meanwhile I had another genuine will, which was the one I left, with a message to them all to go hang.

Si. Who was the heir by this one? one of your relations, I suppose.

Pol. Not likely; it was a handsome young Phrygian I had lately bought.

Si. Age?

Pol. About twenty.

Si. Ah, I can guess his office.

Pol. Well, you know, he deserved the inheritance much better than they did; he was a barbarian and a rascal; but by this time he has the best of society at his beck. So he inherited; and now he is one of the aristocracy; his smooth chin and his foreign accent are no bars to his being called nobler than Codrus, handsomer than Nireus, wiser than Odysseus.

Si. Well, *I* don't mind; let him be Emperor of Greece, if he likes, so long as he keeps the property away from that other crew.

X

Charon. Hermes. Various Shades

Ch. I'll tell you how things stand. Our craft, as you see, is small, and leaky, and three-parts rotten; a single lurch, and she will capsize without more ado. And here are all you passengers, each with his luggage. If you come on board like that, I am afraid you may have cause to repent it; especially those who have not learnt to swim.

Her. Then how are we to make a trip of it?

Ch. I'll tell you. They must leave all this nonsense behind them on shore, and come aboard in their skins. As it is, there will be no room to spare. And in future, Hermes, mind you admit no one till he has cleared himself of encumbrances, as I say. Stand by the gangway, and keep an eye on them, and make them strip before you let them pass.

Her. Very good. Well, Number One, who are you?

Men. Menippus. Here are my wallet and staff; overboard with them. I had the sense not to bring my cloak.

Her. Pass on, Menippus; you're a good fellow; you shall have the seat of honour, up by the pilot, where you can see every one.—Here is a handsome person; who is he?

Char. Charmoleos of Megara; the irresistible, whose kiss was worth a thousand pounds.

Her. That beauty must come off,—lips, kisses, and all; the flowing locks, the blushing cheeks, the skin entire. That's right. Now we're in better trim;—you may pass on.—And who is the stunning gentleman in the purple and the diadem?

Lam. I am Lampichus, tyrant of Gela.

Her. And what is all this splendour doing here, Lampichus?

Lam. How! would you have a tyrant come hither stripped?

Her. A tyrant! That would be too much to expect. But with a shade we must insist. Off with these things.

Lam. There, then:
  away goes my wealth.

Her. Pomp must go too, and pride; we shall be overfreighted else.

Lam. At least let me keep my diadem and robes.

Her. No, no; off they come!

Lam. Well? That is all, as you see for yourself.

Her. There is something more yet:
  cruelty, folly, insolence, hatred.

Lam. There then:
  I am bare.

Her. Pass on.—And who may you be, my bulky friend?

Dam. Damasias the athlete.

Her. To be sure; many is the time I have seen you in the gymnasium.

Dam. You have. Well, I have peeled; let me pass.

Her. Peeled! my dear sir, what, with all this fleshy encumbrance? Come, off with it; we should go to the bottom if you put one foot aboard. And those crowns, those victories, remove them.

Dam. There; no mistake about it this time; I am as light as any shade among them.

Her. That's more the kind of thing. On with you.—Crato, you can take off that wealth and luxury and effeminacy; and we can't have that funeral pomp here, nor those ancestral glories either; down with your rank and reputation, and any votes of thanks or inscriptions you have about you; and you need not tell us what size your tomb was; remarks of that kind come heavy.

Cra. Well, if I must, I must; there's no help for it.

Her. Hullo! in full armour? What does this mean? and why this trophy?

A General. I am a great conqueror; a valiant warrior; my country's pride.

Her. The trophy may stop behind; we are at peace; there is no demand for arms.—Whom have we here? whose is this knitted brow, this flowing beard? 'Tis some reverend sage, if outside goes for anything; he mutters; he is wrapped in meditation.

Men. That's a philosopher, Hermes; and an impudent quack not the bargain. Have him out of that cloak; you will find something to amuse you underneath it.

Her. Off with your clothes first; and then we will see to the rest. My goodness, what a bundle:

quackery, ignorance, quarrelsomeness, vainglory; idle questionings, prickly arguments, intricate conceptions; humbug and gammon and wishy-washy hair-splittings without end; and hullo! why here's avarice, and self-indulgence, and impudence! luxury, effeminacy and peevishness!—Yes, I see them all; you need not try to hide them. Away with falsehood and swagger and superciliousness; why, the three-decker is not built that would hold you with all this luggage.

A Philosopher. I resign them all, since such is your bidding.

Men. Have his beard off too, Hermes; only look what a ponderous bush of a thing! There's a good five pounds' weight there.

Her. Yes; the beard must go.

Phil. And who shall shave me?

Her. Menippus here shall take it off with the carpenter's axe; the gangway will serve for a block.

Men. Oh, can't I have a saw, Hermes? It would be much better fun.

Her. The axe must serve.—Shrewdly chopped!—Why, you look more like a man and less like a goat already.

Men. A little off the eyebrows?

Her. Why, certainly; he has trained them up all over his forehead, for reasons best known to himself.—Worm! what, snivelling? afraid of death? Oh, get on board with you.

Men. He has still got the biggest thumper of all under his arm.

Her. What's that?

Men. Flattery; many is the good turn that has done him.

Phil. Oh, all right, Menippus; suppose you leave your independence behind you, and your plain—speaking, and your indifference, and your high spirit, and your jests!—No one else here has a jest about him.

Her. Don't you, Menippus! you stick to them; useful commodities, these, on shipboard; light and handy.—You rhetorician there, with your verbosities and your barbarisms, your antitheses and balances and periods, off with the whole pack of them.

Rhet. Away they go.

Her. All's ready. Loose the cable, and pull in the gangway; haul up the anchor; spread all sail; and, pilot, look to your helm. Good luck to our voyage!—What are you all whining about, you fools? You philosopher, late of the beard,—you're as bad as any of them.

Phil. Ah, Hermes:

I had thought that the soul was immortal.

Men. He lies:

that is not the cause of his distress.

Her. What is it, then?

Men. He knows that he will never have a good dinner again; never sneak about at night with his cloak over his head, going the round of the brothels; never spend his mornings in fooling boys out of their money, under the pretext of teaching them wisdom.

Phil. And pray are *you* content to be dead?

Men. It may be presumed so, as I sought death of my own accord.—By the way, I surely heard a noise, as if people were shouting on the earth?

Her. You did; and from more than one quarter.—There are people running in a body to the Town-hall, exulting over the death of Lampichus; the women have got hold of his wife; his infant children fare no better,—the boys are giving them handsome pelting. Then again you hear the applause that greets the orator Diophantus, as he pronounces the funeral oration of our friend Crato. Ah yes, and that's Damasias's mother, with her women, striking up a dirge. No one has tear for you, Menippus; your remains are left in peace. Privileged person!

Men. Wait a bit:

before long you will hear the mournful howl of dogs, and the beating of crows' wings, as they gather to perform my funeral rites.

Her. I like your spirit.—However, here we are in port. Away with you all to the judgement-seat; it is straight ahead. The ferryman and I must go back for a fresh load.

Men. Good voyage to you, Hermes.—Let us be getting on; what are you all waiting for? We have got to face the judge, sooner or later; and by all accounts his sentences are no joke; wheels, rocks, vultures are mentioned. Every detail of our lives will now come to light!

XI

Crates. Diogenes

Cra. Did you know Moerichus of Corinth, Diogenes? A shipowner, rolling in money, with a cousin called Aristeas, nearly as rich. He had a Homeric quotation:

—Wilt thou heave me? shall I heave thee?[15]

Diog. What was the point of it?

Cra. Why, the cousins were of equal age, expected to succeed to each other's wealth, and behaved accordingly. They published their wills, each naming the other sole heir in case of his own prior decease. So it stood in black and white, and they vied with each other in showing that deference which the relation demands. All the prophets, astrologers, and Chaldean dream-interpreters alike, and Apollo himself for that matter, held different views at different times about the winner; the thousands seemed to incline now to Aristeas's side, now to Moerichus's.

Diog. And how did it end? I am quite curious.

Cra. They both died on the same day, and the properties passed to Eunomius and Thrasycles, two relations who had never had a presentiment of it. They had been crossing from Sicyon to Cirrha, when they were taken aback by a squall from the north-west, and capsized in mid-channel.

Diog. Cleverly done. Now, when we were alive, we never had such designs on one another. I never prayed for Antisthenes's death, with a view to inheriting his staff—though it was an extremely serviceable one, which he had cut himself from a wild olive; and I do not credit you, Crates, with ever having had an eye to my succession; it included the tub, and a wallet with two pints of lupines in it.

Cra. Why, no; these things were superfluities to me—and to yourself, indeed. The real necessities you inherited from Antisthenes, and I from you; and in those necessities was more grandeur and majesty than in the Persian Empire.

Diog. You allude to——

Cra. Wisdom, independence, truth, frankness, freedom.

Diog. To be sure; now I think of it, I did inherit all this from Antisthenes, and left it to you with some addition.

---

[15] Homer, Il. xxiii. 724. When Ajax and Odysseus have wrestled for some time without either's producing any impression, and the spectators are getting tired of it, the former proposes a change in tactics. "Let us hoist—try you with me or I with you." The idea evidently is that each in turn is to offer only a passive resistance, and let his adversary try to fling him thus.' *Leaf.*

Cra. Others, however, were not interested in such property; no one paid us the attentions of an expectant heir; they all lad their eyes on gold, instead.

Diog. Of course; they had no receptacle for such things as we could give; luxury had made them so leaky—as full of holes as a worn-out purse. Put wisdom, frankness, or truth into them, and it would have dropped out; the bottom of the bag would have let them through, like the perforated cask into which those poor Danaids are always pouring. Gold, on the other hand, they could grip with tooth or nail or somehow.

Cra. Result:

our wealth will still be ours down here; while they will arrive with no more than one penny, and even that must be left with the ferryman.

XII

Alexander. Hannibal. Minos. Scipio

Alex. Libyan, I claim precedence of you. I am the better man.

Han. Pardon me.

Alex. Then let Minos decide.

Mi. Who are you both?

Alex. This is Hannibal, the Carthaginian:

I am Alexander, the son of Philip.

Mi. Bless me, a distinguished pair! And what is the quarrel about?

Alex. It is a question of precedence. He says he is the better general:

and I maintain that neither Hannibal nor (I might almost add) any of my predecessors was my equal in strategy; all the world knows that.

Mi. Well, you shall each have your say in turn:

the Libyan first.

Han. Fortunately for me, Minos, I have mastered Greek since I have been here; so that my adversary will not have even that advantage of me. Now I hold that the highest praise is due to those who have won their way to greatness from obscurity; who have clothed themselves in power, and shown themselves fit for dominion. I myself entered Spain with a handful of men, took service under my brother, and was found worthy of the supreme command. I conquered the Celtiberians, subdued Western Gaul, crossed the Alps, overran the valley of the Po, sacked town after town, made myself master of the plains, approached the bulwarks of the capital, and in one day slew such a host, that their finger-rings were measured by bushels, and the rivers were bridged by their bodies. And this I did, though I had never been called a son of Ammon; I never pretended to be a god, never related visions of my mother; I made no secret of the fact that I was mere flesh and blood. My rivals were the ablest generals in the world, commanding the best soldiers in the world; I warred not with Medes or Assyrians, who fly before they are pursued, and yield the victory to him that dares take it.

Alexander, on the other hand, in increasing and extending as he did the dominion which he had inherited from his father, was but following the impetus given to him by Fortune. And this conqueror had no sooner crushed his puny adversary by the victories of Issus and Arbela, than he forsook the traditions of his country, and lived the life of a Persian; accepting the prostrations of his subjects, assassinating his friends at his own table, or handing them over to the executioner. I in my command respected the freedom of my country, delayed not to obey her summons, when the enemy with their huge armament invaded Libya, laid aside the privileges of my office, and submitted to my sentence without a murmur. Yet I was a barbarian all unskilled in Greek culture; I could not recite Homer, nor had I enjoyed the advantages of Aristotle's instruction; I had to make a shift with such qualities as were mine by nature.—It is on these grounds that I claim the pre-eminence. My rival has indeed all the lustre that attaches to the wearing of a diadem, and—I know not—for Macedonians such things may have charms:

but I cannot think that this circumstance constitutes a higher claim than the courage and genius of one who owed nothing to Fortune, and everything to his own resolution.

Mi. Not bad, for a Libyan.—Well, Alexander, what do you say to that?

Alex. Silence, Minos, would be the best answer to such confident self-assertion. The tongue of Fame will suffice of itself to convince you that I was a great prince, and my opponent a petty adventurer. But I would have you consider the distance between us. Called to the throne while I was yet a boy, I quelled the disorders of my kingdom, and avenged my father's murder. By the destruction of Thebes, I inspired the Greeks with such awe, that they appointed me their commander-in-chief; and from that moment, scorning to confine myself to the kingdom that I inherited from my father, I extended my gaze over the entire face of the earth, and thought it shame if I should govern less than the whole. With a small force I invaded Asia, gained a great victory on the Granicus, took Lydia, Ionia, Phrygia,—in short, subdued all that was within my reach, before I commenced my march for Issus, where Darius was waiting for me at the head of his myriads. You know the sequel:

yourselves can best say what was the number of the dead whom on one day I dispatched hither. The ferryman tells me that his boat would not hold them; most of them had to come across on rafts of their own construction. In these enterprises, I was ever at the head of my troops, ever courted danger. To say nothing of Tyre and Arbela, I penetrated into India, and carried my empire to the shores of Ocean; I captured elephants; I conquered Porus; I crossed the Tanais, and worsted the Scythians—no mean enemies—in a tremendous cavalry engagement. I heaped benefits upon my friends:

I made my enemies taste my resentment. If men took me for a god, I cannot blame them; the vastness of my undertakings might excuse such a belief. But to conclude. I died a king:

Hannibal, a fugitive at the court of the Bithynian Prusias—fitting end for villany and cruelty. Of his Italian victories I say nothing; they were the fruit not of honest legitimate warfare, but of treachery, craft, and dissimulation. He taunts me with self-indulgence:

my illustrious friend has surely forgotten the pleasant time he spent in Capua among the ladies, while the precious moments fleeted by. Had I not scorned the Western world, and turned my attention to the East, what would it have cost me to make the bloodless conquest of Italy, and Libya, and all, as far West as Gades? But nations that already cowered beneath a master were unworthy of my sword.—I have finished, Minos, and await your decision; of the many arguments I might have used, these shall suffice.

Sci. First, Minos, let me speak.

Mi. And who are you, friend? and where do you come from?

Sci. I am Scipio, the Roman general, who destroyed Carthage, and gained great victories over the Libyans.

Mi. Well, and what have you to say?

Sci. That Alexander is my superior, and I am Hannibal's, having defeated him, and driven him to ignominious flight. What impudence is this, to contend with Alexander, to whom I, your conqueror, would not presume to compare myself!

Mi. Honestly spoken, Scipio, on my word! Very well, then:

Alexander comes first, and you next; and I think we must say Hannibal third. And a very creditable third, too.

XIII

Diogenes. Alexander

Diog. Dear me, Alexander, *you* dead like the rest of us?

Alex. As you see, sir; is there anything extraordinary in a mortal's dying?

Diog. So Ammon lied when he said you were his son; you were Philip's after all.

Alex. Apparently; if I had been Ammon's, I should not have died.

Diog. Strange! there were tales of the same order about Olympias too. A serpent visited her, and was seen in her bed; we were given to understand that that was how you came into the world, and Philip made a mistake when he took you for his.

Alex. Yes, I was told all that myself; however, I know now that my mother's and the Ammon stories were all moonshine.

Diog. Their lies were of some practical value to you, though; your divinity brought a good many people to their knees. But now, whom did you leave your great empire to?

Alex. Diogenes, I cannot tell you. I had no time to leave any directions about it, beyond just giving Perdiccas my ring as I died. Why are you laughing?

Diog. Oh, I was only thinking of the Greeks' behaviour; directly you succeeded, how they flattered you! their elected patron, generalissimo against the barbarian; one of the twelve Gods according to some; temples built and sacrifices offered to the Serpent's son! If I may ask, where did your Macedonians bury you?

Alex. I have lain in Babylon a full month to-day; and Ptolemy of the Guards is pledged, as soon as he can get a moment's respite from present disturbances, to take and bury me in Egypt, there to be reckoned among the Gods.

Diog. I have some reason to laugh, you see; still nursing vain hopes of developing into an Osiris or Anubis! Pray, your Godhead, put these expectations from you; none may re-ascend who has once sailed the lake and penetrated our entrance; Aeacus is watchful, and Cerberus an awkward customer. But there is one thing I wish you would tell me:

how do you like thinking over all the earthly bliss you left to come here—your guards and armour-bearers and lieutenant-governors, your heaps of gold and adoring peoples, Babylon and Bactria, your huge elephants, your honour and glory, those conspicuous drives with white-cinctured locks and clasped purple cloak? does the thought of them *hurt*? What, crying? silly fellow! did not your wise Aristotle include in his instructions any hint of the insecurity of fortune's favours?

Alex. Wise? call him the craftiest of all flatterers. Allow me to know a little more than other people about Aristotle; his requests and his letters came to *my* address; *I* know how he profited by my passion for culture; how he would toady and compliment me, to be sure! now it was my beauty—that too is included under The Good; now it was my deeds and my money; for money too he called a Good—he meant that he was not going to be ashamed of taking it. Ah, Diogenes, an impostor; and a past master at it too. For me, the result of his wisdom is that I am distressed for the things you catalogued just now, as if I had lost in them the chief Goods.

Diog. Wouldst know thy course? I will prescribe for your distress. Our flora, unfortunately, does not include hellebore; but you take plenty of Lethe-water—good, deep, repeated draughts; that will relieve your distress over the Aristotelian Goods. Quick; here are Clitus, Callisthenes, and a lot of others making for you; they mean to tear you in pieces and pay you out. Here, go the opposite way; and remember, repeated draughts.

Philip. Alexander

Phil. You cannot deny that you are my son this time, Alexander; you would not have died if you had been Ammon's.

Alex. I knew all the time that you, Philip, son of Amyntas, were my father. I only accepted the statement of the oracle because I thought it was good policy.

Phil. What, to suffer yourself to be fooled by lying priests?

Alex. No, but it had an awe-inspiring effect upon the barbarians. When they thought they had a God to deal with, they gave up the struggle; which made their conquest a simple matter.

Phil. And whom did *you* ever conquer that was worth conquering? Your adversaries were ever timid creatures, with their bows and their targets and their wicker shields. It was other work conquering the Greeks:

Boeotians, Phocians, Athenians; Arcadian hoplites, Thessalian cavalry, javelin-men from Elis, peltasts of Mantinea; Thracians, Illyrians, Paeonians; to subdue these was something. But for gold-laced womanish Medes and Persians and Chaldaeans,—why, it had been done before:

did you never hear of the expedition of the Ten Thousand under Clearchus? and how the enemy would not even come to blows with them, but ran away before they were within bow-shot?

Alex. Still, there were the Scythians, father, and the Indian elephants; they were no joke. And *my* conquests were not gained by dissension or treachery; I broke no oath, no promise, nor ever purchased victory at the expense of honour. As to the Greeks, most of them joined me without a struggle; and I dare say you have heard how I handled Thebes.

Phil. I know all about that; I had it from Clitus, whom you ran through the body, in the middle of dinner, because he presumed to mention my achievements in the same breath with yours. They tell me too that you took to aping the manners of your conquered Medes; abandoned the Macedonian cloak in favour of the *candies*, assumed the upright tiara, and exacted oriental prostrations from Macedonian freemen! This is delicious. As to your brilliant matches, and your beloved Hephaestion, and your scholars in lions' cages,—the less said the better. I have only heard one thing to your credit:

you respected the person of Darius's beautiful wife, and you provided for his mother and daughters; there you acted like a king.

Alex. And have you nothing to say of my adventurous spirit, father, when I was the first to leap down within the ramparts of Oxydracae, and was covered with wounds?

Phil. Not a word. Not that it is a bad thing, in my opinion, for a king to get wounded occasionally, and to face danger at the head of his troops:

but this was the last thing that you were called upon to do. You were passing for a God; and your being wounded, and carried off the field on a litter, bleeding and groaning, could only excite the ridicule of the spectators:

Ammon stood convicted of quackery, his oracle of falsehood, his priests of flattery. The son of Zeus in a swoon, requiring medical assistance! who could help laughing at the sight? And now that you have died, can you doubt that many a jest is being cracked on the subject of your divinity, as men contemplate the God's corpse laid out for burial, and already going the way of all flesh? Besides, your achievements lose half their credit from this very circumstance which you say was so useful in facilitating your conquests:

nothing you did could come up to your divine reputation.

Alex. The world thinks otherwise. I am ranked with Heracles and Dionysus; and, for that matter, I took Aornos, which was more than either of them could do.

Phil. There spoke the son of Ammon. Heracles and Dionysus, indeed! You ought to be ashamed of yourself, Alexander; when will you learn to drop that bombast, and know yourself for the shade that you are?

XV

Antilochus. Achilles

Ant. Achilles, what you were saying to Odysseus the other day about death was very poor-spirited; I should have expected better things from a pupil of Chiron and Phoenix. I was listening; you said you would rather be a servant on earth to some poor hind 'of scanty livelihood possessed,' than king of all the dead. Such sentiments might have been very well in the mouth of a poor-spirited cowardly Phrygian, dishonourably in love with life:

for the son of Peleus, boldest of all Heroes, so to vilify himself, is a disgrace; it gives the lie to all your life; you might have had a long inglorious reign in Phthia, and your own choice was death and glory.

Ach. In those days, son of Nestor, I knew not this place; ignorant whether of those two was the better, I esteemed that flicker of fame more than life; now I see that it is worthless, let folk up there make what verses of it they will. 'Tis dead level among the dead, Antilochus; strength and beauty are no more; we welter all in the same gloom, one no better than another; the shades of Trojans fear me not, Achaeans pay me no reverence; each may say what he will; a man is a ghost, 'or be he churl, or be he peer.' It irks me; I would fain be a servant, and alive.

Ant. But what help, Achilles? 'tis Nature's decree that by all means all die. We must abide by her law, and not fret at her commands. Consider too how many of us are with you here; Odysseus comes ere long; how else? Is there not comfort in the common fate? 'tis something not to suffer alone. See Heracles,

Meleager, and many another great one; they, methinks, would not choose return, if one would send them up to serve poor destitute men.

Ach. Ay, your intent is friendly; but I know not, the thought of the past life irks me—and each of you too, if I mistake not. And if you confess it not, the worse for you, smothering your pain.

Ant. Not the worse, Achilles; the better; for we see that speech is unavailing. Be silent, bear, endure—that is our resolve, lest such longings bring mockery on us, as on you.

XVI

Diogenes. Heracles

Diog. Surely this is Heracles I see? By his godhead, 'tis no other! The bow, the club, the lion's-skin, the giant frame; 'tis Heracles complete. Yet how should this be?—a son of Zeus, and mortal? I say, Mighty Conqueror, are you dead? I used to sacrifice to you in the other world; I understood you were a God!

Her. Thou didst well. Heracles is with the Gods in Heaven,
And hath white-ankled Hebe there to wife.
I am his phantom.

Diog. His phantom! What then, can one half of any one be a God, and the other half mortal?

Her. Even so. The God still lives. 'Tis I, his counterpart, am dead.

Diog. I see. You're a dummy; he palms you off upon Pluto, instead of coming himself. And here are you, enjoying *his* mortality!

Her. 'Tis somewhat as thou hast said.

Diog. Well, but where were Aeacus's keen eyes, that he let a counterfeit Heracles pass under his very nose, and never knew the difference?

Her. I was made very like to him.

Diog. I believe you! Very like indeed, no difference at all! Why, we may find it's the other way round, that you are Heracles, and the phantom is in Heaven, married to Hebe!

Her. Prating knave, no more of thy gibes; else thou shalt presently learn how great a God calls me phantom.

Diog. H'm. That bow looks as if it meant business. And yet,—what have I to fear now? A man can die but once. Tell me, phantom,—by your great Substance I adjure you—did you serve him in your present capacity in the upper world? Perhaps you were one individual during your lives, the separation taking place only at your deaths, when he, the God, soared heavenwards, and you, the phantom, very properly made your appearance here?

Her. Thy ribald questions were best unanswered. Yet thus much thou shalt know.—All that was Amphitryon in Heracles, is dead; I am that mortal part. The Zeus in him lives, and is with the Gods in Heaven.

119

Diog. Ah, now I see! Alcmena had twins, you mean,—Heracles the son of Zeus, and Heracles the son of Amphitryon? You were really half-bothers all the time?

Her. Fool! not so. We twain were one Heracles.

Diog. It's a little difficult to grasp, the two Heracleses packed into one. I suppose you must have been like a sort of Centaur, man and God all mixed together?

Her. And are not all thus composed of two elements,—the body and the soul? What then should hinder the soul from being in Heaven, with Zeus who gave it, and the mortal part—myself—among the dead?

Diog. Yes, yes, my esteemed son of Amphitryon,—that would be all very well if you were a body; but you see you are a phantom, you have no body. At this rate we shall get three Heracleses.

Her. Three?

Diog. Yes; look here. One in Heaven:

one in Hades, that's you, the phantom:

and lastly the body, which by this time has returned to dust. That makes three. Can you think of a good father for number Three?

Her. Impudent quibbler! And who art *thou?*

Diog. I am Diogenes's phantom, late of Sinope. But my original, I assure you, is not 'among th' immortal Gods,' but here among dead men; where he enjoys the best of company, and snaps my ringers at Homer and all hair-splitting.

XVII

Menippus. Tantalus

Me. What are you crying out about, Tantalus? standing at the edge and whining like that!

Tan. Ah, Menippus, I thirst, I perish!

Me. What, not enterprise enough to bend down to it, or scoop up some in your palm?

Tan. It is no use bending down; the water shrinks away as soon as it sees me coming. And if I do scoop it up and get it to my mouth, the outside of my lips is hardly moist before it has managed to run through my fingers, and my hand is as dry as ever.

Me. A very odd experience, that. But by the way, why do you want to drink? you have no body—the part of you that was liable to hunger and thirst is buried in Lydia somewhere; how can you, the spirit, hunger or thirst any more?

Tan. Therein lies my punishment—soul thirsts as if it were body.

120

Me. Well, let that pass, as you say thirst is your punishment. But why do you mind it? are you afraid of *dying*, for want of drink? I do not know of any second Hades; can you die to this one, and go further?

Tan. No, that is quite true. But you see this is part of the sentence: I must long for drink, though I have no need of it.

Me. There is no meaning in that. There *is* a draught you need, though; some neat hellebore is what *you* want; you are suffering from a converse hydrophobia; you are not afraid of water, but you are of thirst.

Tan. I would as life drink hellebore as anything, if I could but drink.

Me. Never fear, Tantalus; neither you nor any other ghost will ever do that; it is impossible, you see; just as well we have not all got a penal thirst like you, with the water running away from us.

XVIII

Menippus. Hermes

Me. Where are all the beauties, Hermes? Show me round; I am a new-comer.

Her. I am busy, Menippus. But look over there to your right, and you will see Hyacinth, Narcissus, Nireus, Achilles, Tyro, Helen, Leda,— all the beauties of old.

Me. I can only see bones, and bare skulls; most of them are exactly alike.

Her. Those bones, of which you seem to think so lightly, have been the theme of admiring poets.

Me. Well, but show me Helen; I shall never be able to make her out by myself.

Her. This skull is Helen.

Me. And for this a thousand ships carried warriors from every part of Greece; Greeks and barbarians were slain, and cities made desolate.

Her. Ah, Menippus, you never saw the living Helen; or you would have said with Homer,

> Well might they suffer grievous years of toil
> Who strove for such a prize.

We look at withered flowers, whose dye is gone from them, and what can we call them but unlovely things? Yet in the hour of their bloom these unlovely things were things of beauty.

Me. Strange, that the Greeks could not realize what it was for which they laboured; how short-lived, how soon to fade.

Her. I have no time for moralizing. Choose your spot, where you will, and lie down. I must go to fetch new dead.

XIX

Aeacus. Protesilaus. Menelaus. Paris

Aea. Now then, Protesilaus, what do you mean by assaulting and throttling Helen?

Pro. Why, it was all her fault that I died, leaving my house half built, and my bride a widow.

Aea. You should blame Menelaus, for taking you all to Troy after such a light-o'-love.

Pro. That is true; he shall answer it.

Me. No, no, my dear sir; Paris surely is the man; he outraged all rights in carrying off his host's wife with him. *He* deserves throttling, if you like, and not from you only, but from Greeks and barbarians as well, for all the deaths he brought upon them.

Pro. Ah, now I have it. Here, you—you *Paris! you* shall not escape my clutches.

Pa. Oh, come, sir, you will never wrong one of the same gentle craft as yourself. Am I not a lover too, and a subject of your deity? against love you know (with the best will in the world) how vain it is to strive; 'tis a spirit that draws us whither it will.

Pro. There is reason in that. Oh, would that I had Love himself here in these hands!

Aea. Permit me to charge myself with his defence. He does not absolutely deny his responsibility for Paris's love; but that for your death he refers to yourself, Protesilaus. You forgot all about your bride, fell in love with fame, and, directly the fleet touched the Troad, took that rash senseless leap, which brought you first to shore and to death.

Pro. Now it is my turn to correct, Aeacus. The blame does not rest with me, but with Fate; so was my thread spun from the beginning.

Aea. Exactly so; then why blame our good friends here?

Menippus. Aeacus. Various Shades

Me. In Pluto's name, Aeacus, show me all the sights of Hades.

Aea. That would be rather an undertaking, Menippus. However, you shall see the principal things. Cerberus here you know already, and the ferryman who brought you over. And you saw the Styx on your way, and Pyriphlegethon.

Me. Yes, and you are the gate-keeper; I know all that; and I have seen the King and the Furies. But show me the men of ancient days, especially the celebrities.

Aea. This is Agamemnon; this is Achilles; near him, Idomeneus; next comes Odysseus; then Ajax, Diomede, and all the great Greeks.

Me. Why, Homer, Homer, what is this? All your great heroes flung down upon the earth, shapeless, undistinguishable; mere meaningless dust; 'strengthless heads,' and no mistake.—Who is this one, Aeacus?

Aea. That is Cyrus; and here is Croesus; beyond him Sardanapalus, and beyond him again Midas. And yonder is Xerxes.

Me. Ha! and it was before this creature that Greece trembled? this is our yoker of Hellesponts, our designer of Athos-canals?—Croesus too! a sad spectacle! As to Sardanapalus, I will lend him a box on the ear, with your permission.

Aea. And crack his skull, poor dear! Certainly not.

Me. Then I must content myself with spitting in his ladyship's face.

Aea. Would you like to see the philosophers?

Me. I should like it of all things.

Aea. First comes Pythagoras.

Me. Good-day, Euphorbus, *alias* Apollo, *alias* what you will.

Py. Good-day, Menippus.

Me. What, no golden thigh nowadays?

Py. Why, no. I wonder if there is anything to eat in that wallet of yours?

Me. Beans, friend; you don't like beans.

Py. Try me. My principles have changed with my quarters. I find that down here our parents' heads are in no way connected with beans.

Aea. Here is Solon, the son of Execestides, and there is Thales. By them are Pittacus, and the rest of the sages, seven in all, as you see. *Me.* The only resigned and cheerful countenances yet. Who is the one covered with ashes, like a loaf baked in the embers? He is all over blisters.

Aea. That is Empedocles. He was half-roasted when he got here from Etna.

Me. Tell me, my brazen-slippered friend, what induced you to jump into the crater?

Em. I did it in a fit of melancholy.

Me. Not you. Vanity, pride, folly; these were what burnt you up, slippers and all; and serve you right. All that ingenuity was thrown away, too:

your death was detected.—Aeacus, where is Socrates?

Aea. He is generally talking nonsense with Nestor and Palamedes.

Me. But I should like to see him, if he is anywhere about.

Aea. You see the bald one? *Me.* They are all bald; that is a distinction without a difference.

Aea. The snub-nosed one.

Me. There again:

they are all snub-nosed.

Soc. Do you want me, Menippus?

Me. The very man I am looking for.

Soc. How goes it in Athens?

Me. There are a great many young men there professing philosophy; and to judge from their dress and their walk, they should be perfect in it.

Soc. I have seen many such.

Me. For that matter, I suppose you saw Aristippus arrive, reeking with scent; and Plato, the polished flatterer from Sicilian courts?

Soc. And what do they think about *me* in Athens?

Me. Ah, you are fortunate in that respect. You pass for a most remarkable man, omniscient in fact. And all the time—if the truth must out—you know absolutely nothing.

Soc. I told them that myself:

but they would have it that that was my irony.

Me. And who are your friends?

Soc. Charmides; Phaedrus; the son of Clinias.

Me. Ha, ha! still at your old trade; still an admirer of beauty.

Soc. How could I be better occupied? Will you join us?

Me. No, thank you; I am off, to take up my quarters by Croesus and Sardanapalus. I expect huge entertainment from their outcries.

Aea. I must be off, too; or some one may escape. You shall see the rest another day, Menippus.

Me. I need not detain you. I have seen enough.

XXI

Menippus. Cerberus

Me. My dear coz—for Cerberus and Cynic are surely related through the dog—I adjure you by the Styx, tell me how Socrates behaved during the descent. A God like you can doubtless articulate instead of barking, if he chooses.

Cer. Well, while he was some way off, he seemed quite unshaken; and I thought he was bent on letting the people outside realize the fact too. Then he passed into the opening and saw the gloom; I at the same time gave him a touch of the hemlock, and a pull by the leg, as he was rather slow. Then he squalled like a baby, whimpered about his children, and, oh, I don't know what he didn't do.

Me. So *he* was one of the theorists, was he? His indifference was a sham?

Cer. Yes; it was only that he accepted the inevitable, and put a bold face on it, pretending to welcome the universal fate, by way of impressing the bystanders. All that sort are the same, I tell you— bold resolute fellows as far as the entrance; it is inside that the real test comes.

Me. What did you think of *my* performance?

Cer. Ah, Menippus, you were the exception; you are a credit to the breed, and so was Diogenes before you. You two came in without any compulsion or pushing, of your own free will, with a laugh for yourselves and a curse for the rest.

XXII

Charon. Menippus. Hermes

Ch. Your fare, you rascal.

Me. Bawl away, Charon, if it gives you any pleasure.

Ch. I brought you across:
give me my fare.

Me. I can't, if I haven't got it.

Ch. And who is so poor that he has not got a penny?

Me. I for one; I don't know who else.

Ch. Pay:
or, by Pluto, I'll strangle you.

Me. And I'll crack your skull with this stick.

Ch. So you are to come all that way for nothing?

Me. Let Hermes pay for me:
he put me on board.

Her. I dare say! A fine time I shall have of it, if I am to pay for the shades.

Ch. I'm not going to let you off.

Me. You can haul up your ship and wait, for all I care. If I have not got the money, I can't pay you, can I?

Ch. You knew you ought to bring it?

Me. I knew that:

but I hadn't got it. What would you have? I ought not to have died, I suppose?

Ch. So you are to have the distinction of being the only passenger that ever crossed gratis?

Me. Oh, come now:

gratis! I took an oar, and I baled; and I didn't cry, which is more than can be said for any of the others.

Ch. That's neither here nor there. I must have my penny; it's only right.

Me. Well, you had better take me back again to life.

Ch. Yes, and get a thrashing from Aeacus for my pains! I like that.

Me. Well, don't bother me.

Ch. Let me see what you have got in that wallet.

Me. Beans:

have some?—and a Hecate's supper.

Ch. Where did you pick up this Cynic, Hermes? The noise he made on the crossing, too! laughing and jeering at all the rest, and singing, when every one else was at his lamentations.

Her. Ah, Charon, you little know your passenger! Independence, every inch of him:

he cares for no one. 'Tis Menippus.

Ch. Wait till I catch you——

Me. Precisely; I'll wait—till you catch me again.

XXIII

Protesilaus. Pluto. Persephone

Pro. Lord, King, our Zeus! and thou, daughter of Demeter! Grant a lover's boon!

Pl. What do you want? who are you?

Pro. Protesilaus, son of Iphiclus, of Phylace, one of the Achaean host, the first that died at Troy. And the boon I ask is release and one day's life.

Pl. Ah, friend, that is the love that all these dead men love, and none shall ever win.

Pro. Nay, dread lord, 'tis not life I love, but the bride that I left new wedded in my chamber that day I sailed away—ah me, to be slain by Hector as my foot touched land! My lord, that yearning gives me no peace. I return content, if she might look on me but for an hour.

Pl. Did you miss your dose of Lethe, man?

Pro. Nay, lord; but this prevailed against it.

Pl. Oh, well, wait a little; she will come to you one day; it is so simple; no need for you to be going up.

Pro. My heart is sick with hope deferred; thou too, O Pluto, hast loved; thou knowest what love is.

Pl. What good will it do you to come to life for a day, and then renew your pains?

Pro. I think to win her to come with me, and bring two dead for one.

Pl. It may not be; it never has been.

Pro. Bethink thee, Pluto. 'Twas for this same cause that ye gave Orpheus his Eurydice; and Heracles had interest enough to be granted Alcestis; she was of my kin.

Pl. Would you like to present that bare ugly skull to your fair bride? will she admit you, when she cannot tell you from another man? I know well enough; she will be frightened and run from you, and you will have gone all that way for nothing.

Per. Husband, doctor that disease yourself:

tell Hermes, as soon as Protesilaus reaches the light, to touch him with his wand, and make him young and fair as when he left the bridal chamber.

Pl. Well, I cannot refuse a lady. Hermes, take him up and turn him into a bridegroom. But mind, you sir, a strictly temporary one.

XXIV

Diogenes. Mausolus

Diog. Why so proud, Carian? How are you better than the rest of us?

Man. Sinopean, to begin with, I was a king; king of all Caria, ruler of many Lydians, subduer of islands, conqueror of well-nigh the whole of Ionia, even to the borders of Miletus. Further, I was comely, and of noble stature, and a mighty warrior. Finally, a vast tomb lies over me in Halicarnassus, of such dimensions, of such exquisite beauty as no other shade can boast. Thereon are the perfect semblances of man and horse, carved in the fairest marble; scarcely may a temple be found to match it. These are the grounds of my pride:

are they inadequate?

Diog. Kingship—beauty—heavy tomb; is that it?

Mau. It is as you say.

Diog. But, my handsome Mausolus, the power and the beauty are no longer there. If we were to appoint an umpire now on the question of comeliness, I see no reason why he should prefer your skull to mine. Both are bald, and bare of flesh; our teeth are equally in evidence; each of us has lost his eyes, and each is snub-nosed. Then as to the tomb and the costly marbles, I dare say such a fine erection gives the Halicarnassians something to brag about and show off to strangers:

but I don't see, friend, that you are the better for it, unless it is that you claim to carry more weight than the rest of us, with all that marble on the top of you.

Mau. Then all is to go for nothing? Mausolus and Diogenes are to rank as equals?

Diog. Equals! My dear sir, no; I don't say that. While Mausolus is groaning over the memories of earth, and the felicity which he supposed to be his, Diogenes will be chuckling. While Mausolus boasts of the tomb raised to him by Artemisia, his wife and sister, Diogenes knows not whether he has a tomb or no—the question never having occurred to him; he knows only that his name is on the tongues of the wise, as one who lived the life of a man; a higher monument than yours, vile Carian slave, and set on firmer foundations.

XXV

Nireus. Thersites. Menippus

Ni. Here we are; Menippus shall award the palm of beauty. Menippus, am I not better-looking than he?

Me. Well, who are you? I must know that first, mustn't I?

Ni. Nireus and Thersites.

Me. Which is which? I cannot tell that yet.

Ther. One to me; I am like you; you have no such superiority as Homer (blind, by the way) gave you when he called you the handsomest of men; he might peak my head and thin my hair, our judge finds me none the worse. Now, Menippus, make up your mind which is handsomer.

Ni. I, of course, I, the son of Aglaia and Charopus,
Comeliest of all that came 'neath Trojan walls.

Me. But not comeliest of all that come 'neath the earth, as far as I know. Your bones are much like other people's; and the only difference between your two skulls is that yours would not take much to stove it in. It is a tender article, something short of masculine.

Ni. Ask Homer what I was, when I sailed with the Achaeans.

Me. Dreams, dreams. I am looking at what you are; what you were is ancient history.

Ni. Am I not handsomer here, Menippus?

Me. You are not handsome at all, nor any one else either. Hades is a democracy; one man is as good as another here.

Ther. And a very tolerable arrangement too, if you ask me.

XXVI

Menippus. Chiron

Me. I have heard that you were a god, Chiron, and that you died of your own choice?

Chi. You were rightly informed. I am dead, as you see, and might have been immortal.

Me. And what should possess you, to be in love with Death? He has no charm for most people.

Chi. You are a sensible fellow; I will tell you. There was no further satisfaction to be had from immortality.

Me. Was it not a pleasure merely to live and see the light?

Chi. No; it is variety, as I take it, and not monotony, that constitutes pleasure. Living on and on, everything always the same; sun, light, food, spring, summer, autumn, winter, one thing following another in unending sequence,— I sickened of it all. I found that enjoyment lay not in continual possession; that deprivation had its share therein.

Me. Very true, Chiron. And how have you got on since you made Hades your home?

Chi. Not unpleasantly. I like the truly republican equality that prevails; and as to whether one is in light or darkness, that makes no difference at all. Then again there is no hunger or thirst here; one is independent of such things.

Me. Take care, Chiron! You may be caught in the snare of your own reasonings.

Chi. How should that be?

Me. Why, if the monotony of the other world brought on satiety, the monotony here may do the same. You will have to look about for a further change, and I fancy there is no third life procurable.

Chi. Then what is to be done, Menippus?

Me. Take things as you find them, I suppose, like a sensible fellow, and make the best of everything.

XXVII

Diogenes. Antisthenes. Crates

Diog. Now, friends, we have plenty of time; what say you to a stroll? we might go to the entrance and have a look at the new-comers —what they are and how they behave.

Ant. The very thing. It will be an amusing sight—some weeping, some imploring to be let go, some resisting; when Hermes collars them, they will stick their heels in and throw their weight back; and all to no purpose.

Cra. Very well; and meanwhile, let me give you my experiences on the way down.

Diog. Yes, go on, Crates; I dare say you saw some entertaining sights.

Cra. We were a large party, of which the most distinguished were Ismenodorus, a rich townsman of ours, Arsaces, ruler of Media, and Oroetes the Armenian. Ismenodorus had been murdered by robbers going to Eleusis over Cithaeron, I believe. He was moaning, nursing his wound, apostrophizing the young children he had left, and cursing his foolhardiness. He knew

Cithaeron and the Eleutherae district were all devastated by the wars, and yet he must take only two servants with him—with five bowls and four cups of solid gold in his baggage, too. Arsaces was an old man of rather imposing aspect; he expressed his feelings in true barbaric fashion, was exceedingly angry at being expected to walk, and kept calling for his horse. In point of fact it had died with him, it and he having been simultaneously transfixed by a Thracian pikeman in the fight with the Cappadocians on the Araxes. Arsaces described to us how he had charged far in advance of his men, and the Thracian, standing his ground and sheltering himself with his buckler, warded off the lance, and then, planting his pike, transfixed man and horse together.

Ant. How could it possibly be done simultaneously?

Cra. Oh, quite simple. The Median was charging with his thirty-foot lance in front of him; the Thracian knocked it aside with his buckler; the point glanced by; then he knelt, received the charge on his pike, pierced the horse's chest—the spirited beast impaling itself by its own impetus—, and finally ran Arsaces through groin and buttock. You see what happened; it was the horse's doing rather than the man's. However, Arsaces did not at all appreciate equality, and wanted to come down on horseback. As for Oroetes, he was so tender-footed that he could not stand, far less walk. That is the way with all the Medes —once they are off their horses, they go delicately on tiptoe as if they were treading on thorns. He threw himself down, and there he lay; nothing would induce him to get up; so the excellent Hermes had to pick him up and carry him to the ferry; how I laughed!

Ant. When *I* came down, I did not keep with the crowd; I left them to their blubberings, ran on to the ferry, and secured a comfortable seat for the passage. Then as we crossed, they were divided between tears and sea-sickness, and gave me a merry time of it.

Diog. You two have described your fellow passengers; now for mine. There came down with me Blepsias, the Pisatan usurer, Lampis, an Acarnanian freelance, and the Corinthian millionaire Damis. The last had been poisoned by his son, Lampis had cut his throat for love of the courtesan Myrtium, and the wretched Blepsias is supposed to have died of starvation; his awful pallor and extreme emaciation looked like it. I inquired into the manner of their deaths, though I knew very well. When Damis exclaimed upon his son, 'You only have your deserts,' I remarked,—'an old man of ninety living in luxury yourself with your million of money, and fobbing off your eighteen-year son with a few pence! As for you, sir Acarnanian'—he was groaning and cursing Myrtium—, 'why put the blame on Love? it belongs to yourself; you were never afraid of an enemy—took all sorts of risks in other people's service—and then let yourself be caught, my hero, by the artificial tears and sighs of the first wench you came across.' Blepsias uttered his own condemnation, without giving me time to do it for him:

he had hoarded his money for heirs who were nothing to him, and been fool enough to reckon on immortality. I assure you it was no common satisfaction I derived from their whinings.

But here we are at the gate; we must keep our eyes open, and get the earliest view. Lord, lord, what a mixed crowd! and all in tears except these babes and sucklings. Why, the hoary seniors are all lamentation too; strange! has madam Life given them a love-potion? I must interrogate this most reverend senior of them all.—Sir, why weep, seeing that you have died full of years? has your excellency any complaint to make, after so long a term? Ah, but you were doubtless a king.

Pauper. Not so.

Diog. A provincial governor, then?

Pauper. No, nor that.

Diog. I see; you were wealthy, and do not like leaving your boundless luxury to die.

Pauper. You are quite mistaken; I was near ninety, made a miserable livelihood out of my line and rod, was excessively poor, childless, a cripple, and had nearly lost my sight.

Diog. And you still wished to live?

Pauper. Ay, sweet is the light, and dread is death; would that one might escape it!

Diog. You are beside yourself, old man; you are like a child kicking at the pricks, you contemporary of the ferryman. Well, we need wonder no more at youth, when age is still in love with life; one would have thought it should court death as the cure for its proper ills.—And now let us go our way, before our loitering here brings suspicion on us:

they may think we are planning an escape.

XXVIII

Menippus. Tiresias

Me. Whether you are blind or not, Tiresias, would be a difficult question. Eyeless sockets are the rule among us; there is no telling Phineus from Lynceus nowadays. However, I know that you were a seer, and that you enjoy the unique distinction of having been both man and woman; I have it from the poets. Pray tell me which you found the more pleasant life, the man's or the woman's?

Ti. The woman's, by a long way; it was much less trouble. Women have the mastery of men; and there is no fighting for them, no manning of walls, no squabbling in the assembly, no cross-examination in the law-courts.

Me. Well, but you have heard how Medea, in Euripides, compassionates her sex on their hard lot—on the intolerable pangs they endure in travail? And by the way—Medea's words remind me did you ever have a child, when you were a woman, or were you barren?

Ti. What do you mean by that question, Menippus?

Me. Oh, nothing; but I should like to know, if it is no trouble to you.

Ti. I was not barren:

but I did not have a child, exactly.

Me. No; but you might have had. That's all I wanted to know.

Ti. Certainly.

Me. And your feminine characteristics gradually vanished, and you developed a beard, and became a man? Or did the change take place in a moment?

Ti. Whither does your question tend? One would think you doubted the fact.

Me. And what should I do but doubt such a story? Am I to take it in, like a nincompoop, without asking myself whether it is possible or not?

Ti. At that rate, I suppose you are equally incredulous when you hear of women being turned into birds or trees or beasts,—Aedon for instance, or Daphne, or Callisto?

Me. If I fall in with any of these ladies, I will see what they have to say about it. But to return, friend, to your own case:

were you a prophet even in the days of your femininity? or did manhood and prophecy come together?

Ti. Pooh, you know nothing of the matter. I once settled a dispute among the Gods, and was blinded by Hera for my pains; whereupon Zeus consoled me with the gift of prophecy.

Me. Ah, you love a lie still, Tiresias. But there, 'tis your trade. You prophets! There is no truth in you.

XXIX

Agamemnon. Ajax

Ag. If you went mad and wrought your own destruction, Ajax, in default of that you designed for us all, why put the blame on Odysseus? Why would you not vouchsafe him a look or a word, when he came to consult Tiresias that day? you stalked past your old comrade in arms as if he was beneath your notice.

Aj. Had I not good reason? My madness lies at the door of my solitary rival for the arms.

Ag. Did you expect to be unopposed, and carry it over us all without a contest?

Aj. Surely, in such a matter. The armour was mine by natural right, seeing I was Achilles's cousin. The rest of you, his undoubted superiors, refused to compete, recognizing my claim. It was the son of Laertes, he that I had rescued scores of times when he would have been cut to pieces by the Phrygians, who set up for a better man and a stronger claimant than I.

132

Ag. Blame Thetis, then, my good sir; it was she who, instead of delivering the inheritance to the next of kin, brought the arms and left the ownership an open question.

Aj. No, no; the guilt was in claiming them—alone, I mean.

Ag. Surely, Ajax, a mere man may be forgiven the sin of coveting honour—that sweetest bait for which each one of us adventured; nay, and he outdid you there, if a Trojan verdict counts.

Aj. Who inspired that verdict[16]? I know, but about the Gods we may not speak. Let that pass; but cease to hate Odysseus? 'tis not in my power, Agamemnon, though Athene's self should require it of me.

XXX

Minos. Sostratus

Mi. Sostratus, the pirate here, can be dropped into Pyriphlegethon, Hermes; the temple-robber shall be clawed by the Chimera; and lay out the tyrant alongside of Tityus, there to have his liver torn by the vultures. And you honest fellows can make the best of your way to Elysium and the Isles of the Blest; this it is to lead righteous lives.

Sos. A word with you, Minos. See if there is not some justice in my plea.

Mi. What, more pleadings? Have you not been convicted of villany and murder without end?

Sos. I have. Yet consider whether my sentence is just.

Mi. Is it just that you should have your deserts? If so, the sentence is just.

Sos. Well, answer my questions; I will not detain you long.

Mi. Say on, but be brief; I have other cases waiting for me.

Sos. The deeds of my life—were they in my own choice, or were they decreed by Fate?

Mi. Decreed, of course.

Sos. Then all of us, whether we passed for honest men or rogues, were the instruments of Fate in all that we did?

Mi. Certainly; Clotho prescribes the conduct of every man at his birth.

Sos. Now suppose a man commits a murder under compulsion of a power which he cannot resist, an executioner, for instance, at the bidding of a judge, or a bodyguard at that of a tyrant. Who is the murderer, according to you?

Mi. The judge, of course, or the tyrant. As well ask whether the sword is guilty, which is but the tool of his anger who is prime mover in the affair.

Sos. I am indebted to you for a further illustration of my argument. Again:

---

[16] Athene is meant. The allusion is to Homer, *Od. xi. 547,* a passage upon the contest for the arms of Achilles, in which Odysseus states that 'The judges were the sons of the Trojans, and Pallas Athene.'

a slave, sent by his master, brings me gold or silver; to whom am I to be grateful? who goes down on my tablets as a benefactor?

Mi. The sender; the bringer is but his minister.

Sos. Observe then your injustice! You punish us who are but the slaves of Clotho's bidding, and reward these, who do but minister to another's beneficence. For it will never be said that it was in our power to gainsay the irresistible ordinances of Fate?

Mi. Ah, Sostratus; look closely enough, and you will find plenty of inconsistencies besides these. However, I see you are no common pirate, but a philosopher in your way; so much you have gained by your questions. Let him go, Hermes; he shall not be punished after that. But mind, Sostratus, you must not put it into other people's heads to ask questions of this kind.

MENIPPUS

A NECROMANTIC EXPERIMENT

Menippus. Philonides

Me. All hail, my roof, my doors, my hearth and home! How sweet again to see the light and thee!

Phi. Menippus the cynic, surely; even so, or there are visions about. Menippus, every inch of him. What has he been getting himself up like that for? sailor's cap, lyre, and lion-skin? However, here goes.—How are you, Menippus? where do *you* spring from? You have disappeared this long time.

Me. Death's lurking-place I leave, and those dark gates Where Hades dwells, a God apart from Gods.

Phi. Good gracious! has Menippus died, all on the quiet, and come to life for a second spell?

Me. Not so; a *living* guest in Hades I.

Phi. But what induced you to take this queer original journey?

Me. Youth drew me on—too bold, too little wise.

Phi. My good man, truce to your heroics; get off those iambic stilts, and tell me in plain prose what this get-up means; what did you want with the lower regions? It is a journey that needs a motive to make it attractive.

Me. Dear friend, to Hades' realms I needs must go, To counsel with Tiresias of Thebes.

Phi. Man, you must be mad; or why string verses instead of talking like one friend with another?

Me. My dear fellow, you need not be so surprised. I have just been in Euripides's and Homer's company; I suppose I am full to the throat with verse, and the numbers come as soon as I open my mouth. But how are things going up here? what is Athens about?

Phi. Oh, nothing new; extortion, perjury, forty per cent, face-grinding.

Me. Poor misguided fools! they are not posted up in the latest lower-world legislation; the recent decrees against the rich will be too much for all their evasive ingenuity.

Phi. Do you mean to say the lower world has been making new regulations for us?

Me. Plenty of them, I assure you. But I may not publish them, nor reveal secrets; the result might be a suit for impiety in the court of Rhadamanthus.

Phi. Oh now, Menippus, in Heaven's name, no secrets between friends! you know I am no blabber; and I am initiated, if you come to that.

Me. 'Tis a hard thing you ask, and a perilous; yet for you I must venture it. It was resolved, then, that these rich who roll in money and keep their gold under lock and key like a Danae——

Phi. Oh, don't come to the decrees yet; begin at the beginning. I am particularly curious about your object in going, who showed you the way, and the whole story of what you saw and heard down there; you are a man of taste, and sure not to have missed anything worth looking at or listening to.

Me. I can refuse you nothing, you see; what is one to do, when a friend insists? Well, I will show you first the state of mind which put me on the venture. When I was a boy, and listened to Homer's and Hesiod's tales of war and civil strife—and they do not confine themselves to the Heroes, but include the Gods in their descriptions, adulterous Gods, rapacious Gods, violent, litigious, usurping, incestuous Gods—, well, I found it all quite proper, and indeed was intensely interested in it. But as I came to man's estate, I observed that the laws flatly contradicted the poets, forbidding adultery, sedition, and rapacity. So I was in a very hazy state of mind, and could not tell what to make of it. The Gods would surely never have been guilty of such behaviour if they had not considered it good; and yet law-givers would never have recommended avoiding it, if avoidance had not seemed desirable.

In this perplexity, I determined to go to the people they call philosophers, put myself in their hands, and ask them to make what they would of me and give me a plain reliable map of life. This was my idea in going to them; but the effort only shifted me from the frying-pan into the fire; it was just among these that my inquiry brought the greatest ignorance and bewilderment to light; they very soon convinced me that the real golden life is that of the man in the street. One of them would have me do nothing but seek pleasure and ensue it; according to him, Happiness was pleasure. Another recommended the exact contrary—toil and moil, bring the body under, be filthy and squalid, disgusting and abusive—concluding always with the tags from Hesiod about Virtue, or something about indefatigable pursuit of the ideal. Another bade me despise money, and reckon the acquisition of it as a thing indifferent; he too had his contrary, who declared wealth a good in itself. I will spare you their metaphysics; I was sickened with daily doses of Ideas, Incorporeal Things, Atoms, Vacua, and a multitude more. The extraordinary thing was that people maintaining the most opposite views would each of them produce convincing plausible arguments; when the same thing was called hot and cold by different persons, there was no refuting one more than the other, however well one knew that it could not be hot and cold at once. I was just like a man dropping off to sleep, with his head first nodding forward, and then jerking back.

Yet that absurdity is surpassed by another. I found by observation that the practice of these same people was diametrically opposed to their precepts. Those who preached contempt of wealth would hold on to it like grim death, dispute about interest, teach for pay, and sacrifice everything to the main chance, while the depreciators of fame directed all their words and deeds to nothing else but fame; pleasure, which had all their private devotions, they were almost unanimous in condemning.

Thus again disappointed of my hope, I was in yet worse case than before; it was slight consolation to reflect that I was in numerous and wise and eminently sensible company, if I was a fool still, all astray in my quest of Truth. One night, while these thoughts kept me sleepless, I resolved to go to Babylon and ask help from one of the Magi, Zoroaster's disciples and successors; I had been told that by incantations and other rites they could open the gates of Hades, take down any one they chose in safety, and bring him up again. I thought the best thing would be to secure the services of one of these, visit Tiresias the Boeotian, and learn from that wise seer what is the best life and the right choice for a man of sense. I got up with all speed and started straight for Babylon. When I arrived, I found a wise and wonderful Chaldean; he was white-haired, with a long imposing beard, and called Mithrobarzanes. My prayers and supplications at last induced him to name a price for conducting me down.

Taking me under his charge, he commenced with a new moon, and brought me down for twenty-nine successive mornings to the Euphrates, where he bathed me, apostrophizing the rising sun in a long formula, of which I never caught much; he gabbled indistinctly, like bad heralds at the Games; but he appeared to be invoking spirits. This charm completed, he spat thrice upon my face, and I went home, not letting my eyes meet those of any one we passed. Our food was nuts and acorns, our drink milk and hydromel and water from the Choaspes, and we slept out of doors on the grass. When he thought me sufficiently prepared, he took me at midnight to the Tigris, purified and rubbed me over, sanctified me with torches and squills and other things, muttering the charm aforesaid, then made a magic circle round me to protect me from ghosts, and finally led me home backwards just as I was; it was now time to arrange our voyage.

He himself put on a magic robe, Median in character, and fetched and gave me the cap, lion's skin, and lyre which you see, telling me if I were asked my name not to say Menippus, but Heracles, Odysseus, or Orpheus.

Phi. What was that for? I see no reason either for the get-up or for the choice of names.

Me. Oh, obvious enough; there is no mystery in that. He thought that as these three had gone down alive to Hades before us, I might easily elude Aeacus's guard by borrowing their appearance, and be passed as an *habitue*; there is good warrant in the theatre for the efficiency of disguise.

Dawn was approaching when we went down to the river to embark; he had provided a boat, victims, hydromel, and all necessaries for our mystic enterprise. We put all aboard, and then,

Troubled at heart, with welling tears, we went.

For some distance we floated down stream, until we entered the marshy lake in which the Euphrates disappears. Beyond this we came to a desolate, wooded, sunless spot; there we landed, Mithrobarzanes leading the way, and proceeded to dig a pit, slay our sheep, and sprinkle their blood round the edge. Meanwhile the Mage, with a lighted torch in his hand, abandoning his customary whisper, shouted at the top of his voice an invocation to all spirits, particularly the Poenae and Erinyes,

Hecat's dark might, and dread Persephone,

with a string of other names, outlandish, unintelligible, and polysyllabic.

As he ended, there was a great commotion, earth was burst open by the incantation, the barking of Cerberus was heard far off, and all was overcast and lowering;

Quaked in his dark abyss the King of Shades;

for almost all was now unveiled to us, the lake, and Phlegethon, and the abode of Pluto. Undeterred, we made our way down the chasm, and came upon Rhadamanthus half dead with fear. Cerberus barked and looked like getting up; but I quickly touched my lyre, and the first note sufficed to lull him. Reaching the lake, we nearly missed our passage for that time, the ferry-boat being already full; there was incessant lamentation, and all the passengers had wounds upon them; mangled legs, mangled heads, mangled everything; no doubt there was a war going on. Nevertheless, when good Charon saw the lion's skin, taking me for Heracles, he made room, was delighted to give me a passage, and showed us our direction when we got off.

We were now in darkness; so Mithrobarzanes led the way, and I followed holding on to him, until we reached a great meadow of asphodel, where the shades of the dead, with their thin voices, came flitting round us. Working gradually on, we reached the court of Minos; he was sitting on a high throne, with the Poenae, Avengers, and Erinyes standing at the sides. From another direction was being brought a long row of persons chained together; I heard that they were adulterers, procurers, publicans, sycophants, informers, and all the filth that pollutes the stream of life. Separate from them came the rich and usurers, pale, pot-bellied, and gouty, each with a hundredweight of spiked collar upon him. There we stood looking at the proceedings and listening to the pleas they put in; their accusers were orators of a strange and novel species. *Phi.* Who, in God's name? shrink not; let me know all.

Me. It has not escaped your observation that the sun projects certain shadows of our bodies on the ground.

Phi. How should it have?

Me. These, when we die, are the prosecutors and witnesses who bring home to us our conduct on earth; their constant attendance and absolute attachment to our persons secures them high credit in the witness-box.

Well, Minos carefully examined each prisoner, and sent him off to the place of the wicked to receive punishment proportionate to his transgressions. He was especially severe upon those who, puffed up with wealth and authority, were expecting an almost reverential treatment; he could not away with their ephemeral presumption and superciliousness, their failure to realize the mortality of themselves and their fortunes. Stripped of all that made them glorious, of wealth and birth and power, there they stood naked and downcast, reconstructing their worldly blessedness in their minds like a dream that is gone; the spectacle was meat and drink to me; any that I knew by sight I would come quietly up to, and remind him of his state up here; what a spirit had his been, when morning crowds lined his hall, expectant of his coming, being jostled or thrust out by lacqueys! at last my lord Sun would dawn upon them, in purple or gold or rainbow hues, not unconscious of the bliss he shed upon those who approached, if he let them kiss his breast or his hand. These reminders seemed to annoy them.

Minos, however, did allow his decision to be influenced in one case. Dionysius of Syracuse was accused by Dion of many unholy deeds, and damning evidence was produced by his shadow; he was on the point of being chained to the Chimera, when Aristippus of Cyrene, whose name and influence are great below, got him off on the ground of his constant generosity as a patron of literature.

We left the court at last, and came to the place of punishment. Many a piteous sight and sound was there—cracking of whips, shrieks of the burning, rack and gibbet and wheel; Chimera tearing, Cerberus devouring; all tortured together, kings and slaves, governors and paupers, rich and beggars, and all repenting their sins. A few of them, the lately dead, we recognized. These would turn away and shrink from observation; or if they met our eyes, it would be with a slavish cringing glance—how different from the arrogance and contempt that had marked them in life! The poor were allowed half-time in their tortures, respite and punishment alternating. Those with whom legend is so busy I saw with my eyes—Ixion, Sisyphus, the Phrygian Tantalus in all his misery, and the giant Tityus—how vast, his bulk covering a whole field!

Leaving these, we entered the Acherusian plain, and there found the demi-gods, men and women both, and the common dead, dwelling in their nations and tribes, some of them ancient and mouldering, 'strengthless heads,' as Homer has it, others fresh, with substance yet in them, Egyptians chiefly, these—so long last their embalming drugs. But to know one from another was no easy task; all are so like when the bones are bared; yet with pains and long scrutiny we could make them out. They lay pell-mell in undistinguished heaps, with none of their earthly beauties left. With all those anatomies piled together as like as could be, eyes glaring ghastly and vacant, teeth gleaming bare, I knew not how to tell Thersites from Nireus the beauty, beggar Irus from the Phaeacian king, or cook Pyrrhias from Agamemnon's self. Their ancient marks were gone, and their bones alike—uncertain, unlabelled, indistinguishable.

When I saw all this, the life of man came before me under the likeness of a great pageant, arranged and marshalled by Chance, who distributed infinitely varied costumes to the performers. She would take one and array him like a king, with tiara, bodyguard, and crown complete; another she dressed like a slave; one was adorned with beauty, another got up as a ridiculous hunchback; there must be all kinds in the show. Often before the procession was over she made individuals exchange characters; they could not be allowed to keep the same to the end; Croesus must double parts and appear as slave and captive;

Maeandrius, starting as slave, would take over Polycrates's despotism, and be allowed to keep his new clothes for a little while. And when the procession is done, every one disrobes, gives up his character with his body, and appears, as he originally was, just like his neighbour. Some, when Chance comes round collecting the properties, are silly enough to sulk and protest, as though they were being robbed of their own instead of only returning loans. You know the kind of thing on the stage—tragic actors shifting as the play requires from Creon to Priam, from Priam to Agamemnon; the same man, very likely, whom you saw just now in all the majesty of Cecrops or Erechtheus, treads the boards next as a slave, because the author tells him to. The play over, each of them throws off his gold-spangled robe and his mask, descends from the buskin's height, and moves a mean ordinary creature; his name is not now Agamemnon son of Atreus or Creon son of Menoeceus, but Polus son of Charicles of Sunium or Satyrus son of Theogiton of Marathon. Such is the condition of mankind, or so that sight presented it to me.

Phi. Now, if a man occupies a costly towering sepulchre, or leaves monuments, statues, inscriptions behind him on earth, does not this place him in a class above the common dead?

Me. Nonsense, my good man; if you had looked on Mausolus himself—the Carian so famous for his tomb—, I assure you, you would never have stopped laughing; he was a miserable unconsidered unit among the general mass of the dead, flung aside in a dusty hole, with no profit of his sepulchre but its extra weight upon him. No, friend, when Aeacus gives a man his allowance of space—and it never exceeds a foot's breadth—, he must be content to pack himself into its limits. You might have laughed still more if you had beheld the kings and governors of earth begging in Hades, selling salt fish for a living, it might be, or giving elementary lessons, insulted by any one who met them, and cuffed like the most worthless of slaves. When I saw Philip of Macedon, I could not contain myself; some one showed him to me cobbling old shoes for money in a corner. Many others were to be seen begging—people like Xerxes, Darius, or Polycrates.

Phi. These royal downfalls are extraordinary almost incredible. But what of Socrates, Diogenes, and such wise men?

Me. Socrates still goes about proving everybody wrong, the same as ever; Palamedes, Odysseus, Nestor, and a few other conversational shades, keep him company. His legs, by the way, were still puffy and swollen from the poison. Good Diogenes pitches close to Sardanapalus, Midas, and other specimens of magnificence. The sound of their lamentations and better-day memories keeps him in laughter and spirits; he is generally stretched on his back roaring out a noisy song which drowns lamentation; it annoys them, and they are looking out for a new pitch where he may not molest them.

Phi. I am satisfied. And now for that decree which you told me had been passed against the rich.

Me. Well remembered; that was what I meant to tell you about, but I have somehow got far astray. Well, during my stay the presiding officers gave notice of an assembly on matters of general interest. So, when I saw every one flocking to it, I mingled with the shades and constituted myself a member. Various measures were decided upon, and last came this question of the rich. Many grave accusations were preferred against them, including violence, ostentation, pride, injustice; and at last a popular speaker rose and moved this decree.

DECREE

'Whereas the rich are guilty of many illegalities on earth, harrying and oppressing the poor and trampling upon all their rights, it is the pleasure of the Senate and People that after death they shall be punished in their bodies like other malefactors, but their souls shall be sent on earth to inhabit asses, until they have passed in that shape a quarter-million of years, generation after generation, bearing burdens under the tender mercies of the poor; after which they shall be permitted to die. Mover of this decree—Cranion son of Skeletion of the deme Necysia in the Alibantid[17] tribe.' The decree read, a formal vote was taken, in which the people accepted it. A snort from Brimo and a bark from Cerberus completed the proceedings according to the regular form.

So went the assembly. And now, in pursuance of my original design, I went to Tiresias, explained my case fully, and implored him to give me his views upon the best life. He is a blind little old man, pale and weak-voiced. He smiled and said:

—'My son, the cause of your perplexity, I know, is the fact that doctors differ; but I may not enlighten you; Rhadamanthus forbids.' 'Ah, say not so, father,' I exclaimed; 'speak out, and leave me not to wander through life in a blindness worse than yours.' So he drew me apart to a considerable distance, and whispered in my ear:

—'The life of the ordinary man is the best and most prudent choice; cease from the folly of metaphysical speculation and inquiry into origins and ends, utterly reject their clever logic, count all these things idle talk, and pursue one end alone—how you may do what your hand finds to do, and go your way with ever a smile and never a passion.'

So he, and sought the lawn of asphodel.

It was now late, and I told Mithrobarzanes that our work was done, and we might reascend. 'Very well, Menippus,' said he, 'I will show you an easy short cut.' And taking me to a place where the darkness was especially thick, he pointed to a dim and distant ray of light—a mere pencil admitted through a chink. 'There,' he said, 'is the shrine of Trophonius, from which the Boeotian inquirers start; go up that way, and you will be on Grecian soil without more ado.' I was delighted, took my leave of the Mage, crawled with considerable difficulty through the aperture, and found myself, sure enough, at Lebadea.

---

[17] The four names are formed from words meaning skull, skeleton, corpse, anatomy.

CHARON

Hermes. Charon

Her. So gay, Charon? What makes you leave your ferry to come up here? You are quite a stranger in the upper world.

Ch. I thought I should like to see what life is like; what men do with it, and what are these blessings of which they all lament the loss when they come down to us. Never one of them has made the passage dry-eyed. So I got leave from Pluto to take a day off, like that Thessalian lad[18], you know; and here I am, in the light of day. I am in luck, it seems, to fall in with you. You will show me round, of course, and point out all that is to be seen, as you know all about it.

Her. I have no time, good ferryman. I am bound on certain errands of the Upper Zeus, certain human matters. He is short-tempered:

any loitering on my part, and he may hand me over to you Powers of Darkness for good and all; or treat me as he did Hephaestus the other day— hurl me down headlong from the threshold of Heaven; there would be a pair of lame cupbearers then, to amuse the gods.

Ch. And you would leave an old messmate wandering at large on the face of the earth? Think of the cruises we have sailed together, the cargoes you and I have handled! You might remember one thing, son of Maia; I have never set you down to bale or row. You lie sprawling about the deck, you great strong lubber, snoring away, or chatting the whole trip through with any communicative shade you can find; and the old man plies both oars at once. Come, stand by me, like a true son of Zeus as you are, and show me all the ins and outs, there's a dear lad. I want to see something of life before I go back, and if you leave me in the lurch, I shall be no better off than a blind man:

he comes to grief because he is always in the dark, and, contrariwise, *I* can make nothing of it in the light. Do me this good turn, and I'll not forget it.

Her. Clearly this is to be a flogging matter for me. There will go some shrewd knocks to the settlement of this reckoning. However, I must give you a helping hand. What is one to do, when a friend is so pressing? Now, as to going over everything thoroughly, it is out of the question; it would take us years. Meanwhile, I should have the hue-and-cry out after me, you would be neglecting your ghostly work, Pluto would lose the shades that you ought to be shipping over all that time, and Aeacus would never take a single toll, and would be proportionately furious. We have only to think, therefore, of contriving you a general view of what is going on.

Ch. You must do the best you can for me. I know nothing of the matter, being a stranger up here.

Her. The main thing is to get an elevation from which you may see in every direction. If you could come up to Heaven, we should be saved any

---

[18] See Protesilaus in Notes.

143

further trouble; you would then have a good bird's-eye view of everything. But it would be sacrilege for one so conversant with phantoms to set foot in the courts of Zeus. Let us lose no time, therefore, in looking out a good high mountain.

Ch. You know what I sometimes say to you on the ship, Hermes.—If a sudden gust strikes the sail from a new quarter, and the waves are rising high, you landsmen know not what to make of it; you are for taking in sail, or slackening the sheet, or letting her go before the wind, and then I tell you not to trouble your heads, for *I* know what to do. Well, now it is your turn; you are sailing this ship; do as you think best, and I'll sit quiet, as a passenger should, and obey orders.

Her. Just so; leave it to me, and I will find a good look-out. How would Caucasus do? Or is Parnassus higher? Olympus, perhaps, is higher than either of them. Olympus! stay, that reminds me; I have a happy thought. But there is work for two here; I shall want your assistance.

Ch. Give your orders, I'll bear a hand, to the best of my ability.

Her. Homer tells us how the sons of Aloeus [19] (they were but two, like ourselves) took it into their heads, when they were yet children, to drag up Ossa from its foundations, and plant it on the top of Olympus, and then Pelion on the top of all; they thought that would serve as a ladder for getting into heaven. The two boys were rightly punished for their presumption. But *we* have no design against the Gods:

why should not we take the hint, and make an erection of mountains piled one on the top of another? From such a height we should get a better view.

Ch. What, shall we two be able to lift Pelion or Ossa?

Her. Why not? We are gods; I should hope we are as good as those two infants.

Ch. Yes; but I should never have thought we could do such a job as that.

Her. Ah, my dear Charon, you don't understand these things; you have no imagination. To the lofty spirit of Homer this is simplicity itself. Just a couple of lines, and the mountains are in place;—we have only to walk up. I wonder you make such a marvel of this. You know Atlas, of course? He holds up the entire heaven by himself, Gods and all. And I dare say you have heard how my brother Heracles relieved him once, and took the burden on his own shoulders for a time?

Ch. Yes, I have heard it. But you and the poets best know whether it is true.

Her. Oh, perfectly true. What should induce wise men to lie?—Come, let us get to work on Ossa first; for so the masterbuilder directs:

---

[19] See *Olus* in Notes.

Ossa first;
On Ossa leafy Pelion.

There! What think you of this? Is it suave work? is it poetry? I must run up, and see whether we shall want another storey. Oh dear, we are no way up as yet. On the East, it is all I can do to make out Ionia and Lydia; on the West is nothing but Italy and Sicily; on the North, nothing to be seen beyond the Danube; and on the South, Crete, none too clear. It looks to me as if we should want Oeta, my nautical friend; and Parnassus into the bargain.

Ch. So be it; but take care not to make the height too great for the width; or down we shall come, ladder and all, and pay our footing in the Homeric school of architecture with a cracked crown apiece.

Her. No fear; all will be safe enough. Pass Oeta along. Now trundle Parnassus up. There; I'll go up again.... That's better! A fine view. You can come now.

Ch. Give me a hand up, Hermes. This *is* an erection, and no mistake!

Her. Well, you know, you would see everything. Safety is one thing, my friend, and sight-seeing is another. Here is my hand; hang on, and keep clear of the slippery bits. There, now *you* are up. Let us sit down; here are two peaks, one for each of us. Now take a general look round at the prospect.

Ch. I see a vast stretch of land, and a huge lake surrounding it, and mountains, and rivers bigger than Cocytus and Pyriphlegethon; and men, tiny little things! and I suppose their dens.

Her. Dens? Those are cities!

Ch. I tell you what it is, Hermes; all this is no use. Here have we been shifting about Parnassus (Castalia and all complete), and Oeta, and these others, and we might have spared ourselves the trouble!

Her. How so?

Ch. Why, I can make nothing out up here. These cities and mountains look for all the world like a map. It is *men* that I am after; I want to see what they do, and hear what they say. That is what I was laughing about just now, when first you met me, and asked me what the joke was. I had heard something that tickled me hugely.

Her. And what might that be?

Ch. One of them had been asked by a friend to dinner, I think it was, the next day. 'Depend on it,' says he, 'I'll be with you.' And before the words were out of his mouth, down came a tile—started somehow from the roof—and he was a dead man! Ha, ha, thought I, *that* promise will never be kept. So I think I shall go down again; I want to see and hear.

Her. Sit where you are. I will soon put that right; you shall see with the best; Homer has a charm for this too. Now, the moment I say the lines, there must be no more dull eyes; all must be clear as daylight. Don't forget!

Ch. Say on.

Her.

See, from before thine eyes I lift the veil;
So shalt thou clearly know both God and man.

Well? Are the eyes any better?

Ch. A marvellous improvement! Lynceus is blind to me. Now, the next thing I want is information. I have some questions to ask. Will you have them couched in the Homeric style, to convince you that I am not wholly unversed in his poems?

Her. And how should you know anything of Homer? A seaman, chained to the oar!

Ch. Come, come; no abuse of my profession. The fact is, when he died, and I ferried him over, I heard a good many of his ballads, and a few of them still run in my head. There was a pretty stiff gale on at the time, too. You see, he began singing a song about Posidon, which boded no good to us mariners,—how Posidon gathered the clouds, and stirred the depths with his trident, as with a ladle, and roused the whirlwind, and a good deal more (enough to raise a storm of itself),—when suddenly there came a black squall which nearly capsized the boat. The poet was extremely ill, and disgorged such an avalanche of minstrelsy (Scylla, Charybdis, the Cyclops, all came up bodily), that I had no difficulty in preserving a few snatches. I should like to know, for instance,

Who is yon hero, stout and strong and tall,
O'ertopping all mankind by head and shoulders?

Her. That is Milo of Croton, the athlete. He has just picked up a bull, and is carrying it along the race-course; and the Greeks are applauding him.

Ch. It would be more to the point, if they were to offer their congratulations to *me.* I shall presently be picking up Milo himself, and putting him into my boat; that will be after he has had his fall from Death, that most invincible of antagonists, who will have him on his back before he knows what is happening. We shall hear a sad tale then, no doubt, of the crowns and the applause he has left behind him. Meanwhile, he is mightily elated over the bull exploit, and the distinction it has won him. What is one to think? Does it ever occur to him that he must *die* some day?

Her. How should he think of death? He is at his zenith.

Ch. Well, never mind him. We shall have sport enough with him before long; he will come aboard with no strength left to pick up a gnat, let alone a bull. But pray,

Who is yon haughty hero?
No Greek, to judge by his dress.

Her. That is Cyrus, son of Cambyses, who transferred to the Persians the ancient empire of the Medes. He has lately conquered Assyria, and reduced Babylon; and now it looks as if he meditated an invasion of Lydia, to complete his dominion by the overthrow of Croesus.

Ch. And whereabouts is Croesus?

146

Her. Look over there. You see the great city with the triple wall? That is Sardis. And there, look, is Croesus himself, reclining on a golden couch, and conversing with Solon the Athenian. Shall we listen to what they are saying?

Ch. Yes, let us.

Cr. Stranger, you have now seen my stores of treasure, my heaps of bullion, and all my riches. Tell me therefore, whom do you account the happiest of mankind?

Ch. What will Solon say, I wonder?

Her. Trust Solon; he will not disgrace himself.

So. Croesus, few men are happy. Of those whom I know, the happiest, I think, were Cleobis and Biton, the sons of the Argive priestess.

Ch. Ah, he means those two who yoked themselves to a waggon, and drew their mother to the temple, and died the moment after. It was but the other day.

Cr. Ah. So they are first on the list. And who comes next?

So. Tellus the Athenian, who lived a righteous life, and died for his country.

Cr. And where do I come, reptile?

So. That I am unable to say at present, Croesus; I must see you end your days first. Death is the sure test;—a happy end to a life of happiness.

Ch. Bravo, Solon; *you* have not forgotten us! As you say, Charon's ferry is the proper place for the decision of these questions.—But who are these men whom Croesus is sending out? And what have they got on their shoulders?

Her. Those are bars of gold; they are going to Delphi, to pay for an oracle, which oracle will presently be the ruin of Croesus. But oracles are a hobby of his.

Ch. Oh, so that is *gold*, that glittering yellow stuff, with just a tinge of red in it. I have often heard of gold, but never saw it before.

Her. Yes, that is the stuff there is so much talking and squabbling about.

Ch. Well now, I see no advantages about it, unless it is an advantage that it is heavy to carry.

Her. Ah, you do not know what it has to answer for; the wars and plots and robberies, the perjuries and murders; for this men will endure slavery and imprisonment; for this they traffic and sail the seas.

Ch. For this stuff? Why, it is not much different from copper. I know copper, of course, because I get a penny from each passenger.

Her. Yes, but copper is plentiful, and therefore not much esteemed by men. Gold is found only in small quantities, and the miners have to go to a considerable depth for it. For the rest, it comes out of the earth, just the same as lead and other metals.

Ch. What fools men must be, to be enamoured of an object of this sallow complexion; and of such a weight!

Her. Well, Solon, at any rate, seems to have no great affection for it. See, he is making merry with Croesus and his outlandish magnificence. I think he is going to ask him a question. Listen.

So. Croesus, will those bars be any use to Apollo, do you think?

Cr. Any use! Why there is nothing at Delphi to be compared to them.

So. And that is all that is wanting to complete his happiness, eh?— some bar gold?

Cr. Undoubtedly.

So. Then they must be very hard up in Heaven, if they have to send all the way to Lydia for their gold supply?

Cr. Where else is gold to be had in such abundance as with us?

So. Now is any iron found in Lydia?

Cr. Not much.

So. Ah; so you are lacking in the more valuable metal.

Cr. More valuable? Iron more valuable than gold?

So. Bear with me, while I ask you a few questions, and I will convince you it is so.

Cr. Well?

So. Of protector and protege, which is the better man?

Cr. The protector, of course.

So. Now in the event of Cyrus's invading Lydia—there is some talk of it—shall you supply your men with golden swords? or will iron be required, on the occasion?

Cr. Oh, iron.

So. Iron accordingly you must have, or your gold would be led captive into Persia?

Cr. Blasphemer!

So. Oh, we will hope for the best. But it is clear, on your own admission, that iron is better than gold.

Cr. And what would you have me do? Recall the gold, and offer the God bars of iron?

So. He has no occasion for iron either. Your offering (be the metal what it may) will fall into other hands than his. It will be snapped up by the Phocians, or the Boeotians, or the God's own priests; or by some tyrant or robber. Your goldsmiths have no interest for Apollo.

Cr. You are always having a stab at my wealth. It is all envy!

Her. This blunt sincerity is not to the Lydian's taste. Things are come to a strange pass, he thinks, if a poor man is to hold up his head, and speak his mind in this frank manner! He will remember Solon presently, when the time comes for Cyrus to conduct him in chains to the pyre. I heard Clotho, the other day, reading over the various dooms. Among other things, Croesus was to be led captive by Cyrus, and Cyrus to be murdered by the queen of the Massagetae. There she is:

that Scythian woman, riding on a white horse; do you see?

148

Ch. Yes.

Her. That is Tomyris. She will cut off Cyrus's head, and put it into a wine-skin filled with blood. And do you see his son, the boy there? That is Cambyses. He will succeed to his father's throne; and, after innumerable defeats in Libya and Ethiopia, will finally slay the god Apis, and die a raving madman.

Ch. What fun! Why, at this moment no one would presume to meet their eyes; from such a height do they look down on the rest of mankind. Who would believe that before long one of them will be a captive, and the other have his head in a bottle of blood?—But who is that in the purple robe, Hermes?—the one with the diadem? His cook has just been cleaning a fish, and is now handing him a ring,—"in yonder sea-girt isle"; "'tis, sure, some king."

Her. Ha, ha! A parody, this time.—That is Polycrates, tyrant of Samos. He is extremely well pleased with his lot:

yet that slave who now stands at his side will betray him to the satrap Oroetes, and he will be crucified. It will not take long to overturn *his* prosperity, poor man! This, too, I had from Clotho.

Ch. I like Clotho; she is a lady of spirit. Have at them, madam! Off with their heads! To the cross with them! Let them know that they are men. And let them be exalted in the meantime; the higher they mount, the heavier will be the fall. I shall have a merry time of it hereafter, identifying their naked shades, as they come aboard; no more purple robes then; no tiaras; no golden couches!

Her. So much for royalty; and now to the common herd. Do you see them, Charon;—on their ships and on the field of battle; crowding the law-courts and following the plough; usurers here, beggars there?

Ch. I see them. What a jostling life it is! What a world of ups and downs! Their cities remind me of bee-hives. Every man keeps a sting for his neighbour's service; and a few, like wasps, make spoil of their weaker brethren. But what are all these misty shapes that beset them on every side?

Her. Hopes, Fears, Follies, Pleasures, Greeds, Hates, Grudges, and such like. They differ in their habits. The Folly is a domestic creature, with vested rights of its own. The same with the Grudge, the Hate, the Envy, the Greed, the Know-not, and the What's-to-do. But the Fear and the Hope fly overhead. The Fear swoops on its prey from above; sometimes it is content with startling a man out of his wits, sometimes it frightens him in real earnest. The Hope hovers almost within reach, and just when a man thinks he is going to catch it, off it flies, and leaves him gaping—like Tantalus in the water, you know. Now look closely, and you will make out the Fates up aloft, spinning each man his spindle-full; from that spindle a man hangs by a narrow thread. Do you see what looks like a cobweb, coming down to each man from the spindles?

Ch. I see each has a very slight thread. They are mostly entangled, one with another, and that other with a third.

Her. Of course they are. Because the first man has got to be murdered by the second, and he by the third; or again, B is to be A's heir (A's thread being the shorter), and C is to be B's. That is what the entangling means. But you see what thin threads they all have to depend on. Now here is one drawn high up into the air; presently his thread will snap, when the weight becomes too much for it, and down he will come with a bang:

whereas yonder fellow hangs so low that when he does fall it makes no noise; his next-door neighbours will scarcely hear him drop.

Ch. How absurd it all is!

Her. My dear Charon, there is no word for the absurdity of it. They do take it all so seriously, that is the best of it; and then, long before they have finished scheming, up comes good old Death, and whisks them off, and all is over! You observe that he has a fine staff of assistants at his command;—agues, consumptions, fevers, inflammations, swords, robbers, hemlock, juries, tyrants,—not one of which gives them a moment's concern so long as they are prosperous; but when they come to grief, then it is Alack! and Well-a-day! and Oh dear me! If only they would start with a clear understanding that they are mortal, that after a brief sojourn on the earth they will wake from the dream of life, and leave all behind them,—they would live more sensibly, and not mind dying so much. As it is, they get it into their heads that what they possess they possess for good and all; the consequence is, that when Death's officer calls for them, and claps on a fever or a consumption, they take it amiss; the parting is so wholly unexpected. Yonder is a man building his house, urging the workmen to use all dispatch. How would he take the news, that he was just to see the roof on and all complete, when he would have to take his departure, and leave all the enjoyment to his heir?—hard fate, not once to sup beneath it! There again is one rejoicing over the birth of a son; the child is to inherit his grandfather's name, and the father is celebrating the occasion with his friends. He would not be so pleased, if he knew that the boy was to die before he was eight years old! It is natural enough:

he sees before him some happy father of an Olympian victor, and has no eyes for his neighbour there, who is burying a child; *that* thin-spun thread escapes his notice. Behold, too, the money-grubbers, whom the aforesaid Death's-officers will never permit to be money-spenders; and the noble army of litigant neighbours!

Ch. Yes! I see it all; and I ask myself, what is the satisfaction in life? What is it that men bewail the loss of? Take their kings; they seem to be best off, though, as you say, they have their happiness on a precarious tenure; but apart from that, we shall find their pleasures to be outweighed by the vexations inseparable from their position—worry and anxiety, flattery here, conspiracy there, enmity everywhere; to say nothing of the tyranny of Sorrow, Disease, and Passion, with whom there is confessedly no respect of persons. And if the king's lot is a hard one, we may make a pretty shrewd guess at that of the commoner. Come now, I will give you a similitude for the life of man. Have you ever stood at the foot of a waterfall, and marked the bubbles rising to the surface and gathering into foam? Some are quite small, and break as soon as they are born. Others last longer; new ones come to join them, and they swell up to a great size:

yet in the end they burst, as surely as the rest; it cannot be otherwise. There you have human life. All men are bubbles, great or small, inflated with the breath of life. Some are destined to last for a brief space, others perish in the very moment of birth:

but all must inevitably burst.

Her. Homer compares mankind to leaves. Your simile is full as good as his.

Ch. And being the things they are, they do—the things you see; squabbling among themselves, and contending for dominion and power and riches, all of which they will have to leave behind them, when they come down to us with their penny apiece. Now that we are up here, how would it be for me to cry out to them at the top of my voice, to abstain from their vain endeavours, and live with the prospect of Death before their eyes? 'Fools' (I might say), 'why so much in earnest? Rest from your toils. You will not live for ever. Nothing of the pomp of this world will endure; nor can any man take anything hence when he dies. He will go naked out of the world, and his house and his lands and his gold will be another's, and ever another's.' If I were to call out something of this sort, loud enough for them to hear, would it not do some good? Would not the world be the better for it?

Her. Ah, my poor friend, you know not what you say. Ignorance and deceit have done for them what Odysseus did for his crew when he was afraid of the Sirens; they have waxed men's ears up so effectually, that no drill would ever open them. How then should they hear you? You might shout till your lungs gave way. Ignorance is as potent here as the waters of Lethe are with you. There are a few, to be sure, who from a regard for Truth have refused the wax process; men whose eyes are open to discern good and evil.

Ch. Well then, we might call out to *them?*

Her. There again:

where would be the use of telling them what they know already? See, they stand aloof from the rest of mankind, and scoff at all that goes on; nothing is as they would have it. Nay, they are evidently bent on giving life the slip, and joining you. Their condemnations of folly make them unpopular here.

Ch. Well done, my brave boys! There are not many of them, though, Hermes.

Her. These must serve. And now let us go down.

Ch. There is still one thing I had a fancy to see. Show me the receptacles into which they put the corpses, and your office will have been discharged.

Her. Ah, *sepulchres,* those are called, or *tombs,* or *graves.* Well, do you see those mounds, and columns, and pyramids, outside the various city walls? Those are the store-chambers of the dead.

151

Ch. Why, they are putting flowers on the stones, and pouring costly essences upon them. And in front of some of the mounds they have piled up faggots, and dug trenches. Look:

there is a splendid banquet laid out, and they are burning it all; and pouring wine and mead, I suppose it is, into the trenches! What does it all mean?

Her. What satisfaction it affords to their friends in Hades, I am unable to say. But the idea is, that the shades come up, and get as close as they can, and feed upon the savoury steam of the meat, and drink the mead in the trench.

Ch. Eat and drink, when their skulls are dry bone? But I am wasting my breath:

you bring them down every day;—*you* can say whether they are likely ever to get up again, once they are safely underground! That would be too much of a good thing! You would have your work cut out for you and no mistake, if you had not only to bring them down, but also to take them up again when they wanted a drink. Oh, fools and blockheads! You little know how we arrange matters, or what a gulf is set betwixt the living and the dead!

The buried and unburied, both are Death's.
He ranks alike the beggar and the king;
Thersites sits by fair-haired Thetis' son.
Naked and withered roam the fleeting shades
Together through the fields of asphodel.

Her. Bless me, what a deluge of Homer! And now I think of it, I must show you Achilles's tomb. There it is on the Trojan shore, at Sigeum. And across the water is Rhoeteum, where Ajax lies buried.

Ch. Rather small tombs, considering. Now show me the great cities, those that we hear talked about in Hades; Nineveh, Babylon, Mycenae, Cleonae, and Troy itself. I shipped numbers across from there, I remember. For ten years running I had no time to haul my boat up and clean it.

Her. Why, as to Nineveh, it is gone, friend, long ago, and has left no trace behind it; there is no saying whereabouts it may have been. But there is Babylon, with its fine battlements and its enormous wall. Before long it will be as hard to find as Nineveh. As to Mycenae and Cleonae, I am ashamed to show them to you, let alone Troy. You will throttle Homer, for certain, when you get back, for puffing them so. They were prosperous cities, too, in their day; but they have gone the way of all flesh. Cities, my friend, die, just like men; stranger still, so do rivers! Inachus is gone from Argos—not a puddle left.

Ch. Oh, Homer, Homer! You and your 'holy Troy,' and your 'city of broad streets,' and your 'strong-walled Cleonae'!—By the way, what is that battle going on over there? What are they murdering one another about?

Her. It is between the Argives and the Lacedaemonians. The general who lies there half-dead, writing an inscription on the trophy with his own blood, is Othryades.

152

Ch. And what were they fighting for?

Her. For the field of battle, neither more nor less.

Ch. The fools! Not to know that though each one of them should win to himself a whole Peloponnesus, he will get but a bare foot of ground from Aeacus! As to yonder plain, one nation will till it after another, and many a time will that trophy be turned up by the plough.

Her. Even so. And now let us get down, and put these mountains to rights again. After which, I must be off on my errand, and you back to your ferry. You will see me there before long, with the day's contingent of shades.

Ch. I am much obliged to you, Hermes; the service shall be perpetuated in my records. Thanks to you, my outing has been a success. Dear, dear, what a world it is!—And never a word of Charon!

OF SACRIFICE

Methinks that man must lie sore stricken under the hand of sorrow, who has not a smile left for the folly of his superstitious brethren, when he sees them at work on sacrifice and festival and worship of the gods, hears the subject of their prayers, and marks the nature of their creed. Nor, I fancy, will a smile be all. He will first have a question to ask himself:

Is he to call them devout worshippers or very outcasts, who think so meanly of God as to suppose that he can require anything at the hand of man, can take pleasure in their flattery, or be wounded by their neglect? Thus the afflictions of the Calydonians, that long tale of misery and violence, ending with the death of Meleager—all is attributed to the resentment of Artemis, at Oeneus's neglect in not inviting her to a feast. She must have taken the disappointment very much to heart. I fancy I see her, poor Goddess, left all alone in Heaven, after the rest have set out for Calydon, brooding darkly over the fine spread at which she will not be present. Those Ethiopians, too; privileged, thrice-happy mortals! Zeus, one supposes, is not unmindful of the handsome manner in which they entertained him and all his family for twelve days running. With the Gods, clearly, nothing goes for nothing. Each blessing has its price. Health is to be had, say, for a calf; wealth, for a couple of yoke of oxen; a kingdom, for a hecatomb. A safe conduct from Troy to Pylos has fetched as much as nine bulls, and a passage from Aulis to Troy has been quoted at a princess. For six yoke of oxen and a robe, Athene sold Hecuba a reprieve for Troy; and it is to be presumed that a cock, a garland, a handful of frankincense, will each buy something.

Chryses, that experienced divine and eminent theologian, seems to have realized this principle. Returning from his fruitless visit to Agamemnon, he approaches Apollo with the air of a creditor, and demands repayment of his loan. His attitude is one of remonstrance, almost, 'Good Apollo,' he cries, 'here have I been garlanding your temple, where never garland hung before, and burning unlimited thigh- pieces of bulls and goats upon your altars:

yet when I suffer wrong, you take no heed; you count my benefactions as nothing worth.' The God is quite put out of countenance:

he seizes his bow, settles down in the harbour and smites the Achaeans with shafts of pestilence, them and their mules and their dogs.

And now that I have mentioned Apollo, I cannot refrain from an allusion to certain other passages in his life, which are recorded by the sages. With his unfortunate love affairs—the sad end of Hyacinth, and the cruelty of Daphne—we are not concerned. But when that vote of censure was passed on him for the slaughter of the Cyclopes, he was dismissed from Heaven, and condemned to share the fortunes of men upon earth. It was then that he served Admetus in Thessaly, and Laomedon in Phrygia; and in the latter service he was not alone. He and Posidon together, since better might not be, made bricks and built the walls of Troy; and did not even get their full wages;—the

Phrygian, it is said, remained their debtor for no less a sum than five-and-twenty shillings Trojan, and odd pence. These, and yet holier mysteries than these, are the high themes of our poets. They tell of Hephaestus and of Prometheus; of Cronus and Rhea, and well-nigh all the family of Zeus. And as they never commence their poems without bespeaking the assistance of the Muses, we must conclude that it is under that divine inspiration that they sing, how Cronus unmanned his father Uranus, and was king in his room; and how, like Argive Thyestes, he swallowed his own children; and how thereafter Rhea saved Zeus by the fraud of the stone, and the child was exposed in Crete, and suckled by a goat, as Telephus was by a hind, and Cyrus the Great by a bitch; and how he dethroned his father, and threw him into prison, and was king; and of his many wives, and how finally (like a Persian or an Assyrian) he married his own sister Hera; and of his love adventures, and how he peopled the Heaven with gods, ay, and with demi-gods, the rogued for he wooed the daughters of earth, appearing to them now in a shower of gold, now in the form of a bull or a swan or an eagle; a very Proteus for versatility. Once, and only once, he conceived within his own brain, and gave birth to Athene. For Dionysus, they say, he tore from the womb of Semele before the fire had yet consumed her, and hid the child within his thigh, till the time of travail was come.

Similarly, we find Hera conceiving without external assistance, and giving birth to Hephaestus; no child of fortune he, but a base mechanic, living all his life at the forge, soot-begrimed as any stoker. He is not even sound of limb; he has been lame ever since Zeus threw him down from Heaven. Fortunately for us the Lemnians broke his fall, or there would have been an end of him, as surely as there was of Astyanax when he was flung from the battlements. But Hephaestus is nothing to Prometheus. Who knows not the sorrows of that officious philanthropist? How he too fell a victim to the wrath of Zeus, and was carried into Scythia, and nailed up on Caucasus, with an eagle to keep him company and make daily havoc of his liver? However, *there* was a reckoning settled, at any rate. But Rhea, now! We cannot, I think, pass over her conduct unnoticed. It is surely most discreditable;—a lady of her venerable years, the mother of such a family, still feeling the pangs of love and jealousy, and carrying her beloved Attis about with her in the lion-drawn car,—and he so ill qualified to play the lover's part! After that, we can but wink, if we find Aphrodite making a slip, or Selene time after time pulling up in mid-career to pay a visit to Endymion.

But enough of scandal. Borne on the wings of poesy, let us take flight for Heaven itself, as Homer and Hesiod have done before us, and see how all is disposed up there. The vault is of brass on the under side, as we know from Homer. But climb over the edge, and take a peep up. You are now actually in Heaven. Observe the increase of light; here is a purer Sun, and brighter stars; daylight is everywhere, and the floor is of gold. We arrive first at the abode of the Seasons; they are the fortresses of Heaven. Then we have Iris and Hermes, the servants and messengers of Zeus; and next Hephaestus's smithy, which is stocked with all manner of cunning contrivances. Last come the dwellings of the Gods, and the palace of Zeus. All are the work of Hephaestus; and noble work it is.

Hard by the throne of Zeus
(I suppose we must adapt our language to our altitude)
sit all the gods.

Their eyes are turned downwards; intently they search every corner of the earth; is there nowhere a fire to be seen, or the steam of burnt- offerings

... in eddying clouds upborne?

If a sacrifice is going forward, all mouths are open to feast upon the smoke; like flies they settle on the altar to drink up the trickling streams of blood. If they are dining at home, nectar and ambrosia is the bill of fare. In ancient days, mortals have eaten and drunk at their table. Such were Ixion and Tantalus; but they forgot their manners, and talked too much. They are paying the penalty for it to this day; and since then mortals have been excluded from Heaven.

The life of the Gods being such as I have described, our religious ordinances are in admirable harmony with the divine requirements. Our first care has been to supply each God with his sacred grove, his holy hill, and his own peculiar bird or plant. The next step was to assign them their various sacred cities. Apollo has the freedom of Delphi and Delos, Athene that of Athens (there is no disputing *her* nationality); Hera is an Argive, Rhea a Mygdonian, Aphrodite a Paphian. As for Zeus, he is a Cretan born and bred— and buried, as any native of that island will show you. It was a mistake of ours to suppose that Zeus was dispensing the thunder and the rain and the rest of it;—he has been lying snugly underground in Crete all this time. As it would never have done to leave the Gods without a hearth and home, temples were now erected, and the services of Phidias, Polyclitus, and Praxiteles were called in to create images in their likeness. Chance glimpses of their originals (but where obtained I know not) enabled these artists to do justice to the beard of Zeus, the perpetual youth of Apollo, the down on Hermes's cheek, Posidon's sea-green hair, and Athene's flashing eyes; with the result that on entering the temple of Zeus men believe that they see before them, not Indian ivory, nor gold from a Thracian mine, but the veritable son of Cronus and Rhea, translated to earth by the hand of Phidias, with instructions to keep watch over the deserted plains of Pisa, and content with his lot, if, once in four years, a spectator of the games can snatch a moment to pay him sacrifice.

And now the altars stand ready; proclamation has been made, and lustration duly performed. The victims are accordingly brought forward—an ox from the plough, a ram or a goat, according as the worshipper is a farmer, a shepherd, or a goatherd; sometimes it is only frankincense or a honey cake; nay, a poor man may conciliate the God by merely kissing his hand. But it is with the priests that we are concerned. They first make sure that the victim is without blemish, and worthy of the sacrificial knife; then they crown him with garlands and lead him to the altar, where he is slaughtered before the God's eyes, to the broken accompaniment of his own sanctimonious bellowings, most musical, most melancholy. The delight of the Gods at such a spectacle, who can doubt?

According to the proclamation, no man shall approach the holy ground with *unclean hands*. Yet there stands the priest himself, wallowing in gore; handling his knife like a very Cyclops, drawing out entrails and heart, sprinkling the altar with blood,—in short, omitting no detail of his holy office. Finally, he kindles fire, and sets the victim bodily thereon, sheep or goat, unfleeced, unflayed. A godly steam, and fit for godly nostrils, rises heavenwards, and drifts to each quarter of the sky. The Scythian, by the way, will have nothing to do with paltry cattle:

he offers *men* to Artemis; and the offering is appreciated.

But all this, and all that Assyria, Phrygia, and Lydia can show, amounts to nothing much. If you would see the Gods in their glory, fit denizens of Heaven, you must go to Egypt. There you will find that Zeus has sprouted ram's horns, our old friend Hermes has the muzzle of a dog, and Pan is perfect goat; ibis, crocodile, ape,—each is a God in disguise.

And wouldst thou know the truth that lurks herein?

If so, you will find no lack of sages and scribes and shaven priests to inform you (after expulsion of the *profanum vulgus*) how, when the Giants and their other enemies rose against them, the Gods fled to Egypt to hide themselves, and there took the form of goat and ram, of bird and reptile, which forms they preserve to this day. Of all this they have documentary evidence, dating from thousands of years back, stored up in their temples. Their sacrifices differ from others only in this respect, that they go into mourning for the victim, slaying him first, and beating their breasts for grief afterwards, and (in some parts) burying him as soon as he is killed. When their great god Apis dies, off comes every man's hair, however much he values himself on it; though he had the purple lock of Nisus, it would make no difference:

he must show a sad crown on the occasion, if he die for it. It is as the result of an election that each succeeding Apis leaves his pasture for the temple; his superior beauty and majestic bearing prove that he is something more than bull.

On such absurdities as these, such vulgar credulity, remonstrance would be thrown away; a Heraclitus would best meet the case, or a Democritus; for the ignorance of these men is as laughable as their folly is deplorable.

157

SALE OF CREEDS[20]

Zeus. Hermes. Several Dealers. Creeds.

Zeus. Now get those benches straight there, and make the place fit to be seen. Bring up the lots, one of you, and put them in line. Give them a rub up first, though; we must have them looking their best, to attract bidders. Hermes, you can declare the sale-room open, and a welcome to all comers.—*For Sale! A varied assortment of Live Creeds. Tenets of every description.—Cash on delivery; or credit allowed on suitable security.*

Hermes. Here they come, swarming in. No time to lose; we must not keep them waiting.

Zeus. Well, let us begin.

Her. What are we to put up first?

Zeus. The Ionic fellow, with the long hair. He seems a showy piece of goods.

Her. Step up, Pythagoreanism, and show yourself.

Zeus. Go ahead.

Her. Now here is a creed of the first water. Who bids for this handsome article? What gentleman says Superhumanity? Harmony of the Universe! Transmigration of souls! Who bids?

First Dealer. He looks all right. And what can he do?

Her. Magic, music, arithmetic, geometry, astronomy, jugglery. Prophecy in all its branches.

First D. Can I ask him some questions?

Her. Ask away, and welcome.

First D. Where do you come from?

Py. Samos.

First D. Where did you get your schooling?

Py. From the sophists in Egypt.

First D. If I buy you, what will you teach me?

Py. Nothing. I will remind you.

First D. Remind me?

Py. But first I shall have to cleanse your soul of its filth.

First D. Well, suppose the cleansing process complete. How is the reminding done?

Py. We shall begin with a long course of silent contemplation. Not a word to be spoken for five years.

First D. You would have been just the creed for Croesus's son! But *I* have a tongue in my head; I have no ambition to be a statue. And after the five years' silence?

---

[20] The distinction between the personified creeds or philosophies here offered for sale, and their various founders or principal exponents, is but loosely kept up. Not only do most of the creeds bear the names of their founders, but some are even credited with their physical peculiarities and their personal experiences.

Py. You will study music and geometry.

First D. A charming recipe! The way to be wise:
learn the guitar.

Py. Next you will learn to count.

First D. I can do that already.

Py. Let me hear you.

First D. One, two, three, four,—

Py. There you are, you see. *Four* (as you call it) is *ten*. Four the perfect triangle. Four the oath of our school.

First D. Now by Four, most potent Four!—higher and holier mysteries than these I never heard.

Py. Then you will learn of Earth, Air, Fire, and Water; their action, their movement, their shapes.

First D. Have Fire and Air and Water *shapes?*

Py. Clearly. That cannot move which lacks shape and form You will also find that God is a number; an intelligence; a harmony.

First D. You surprise me.

Py. More than this, you have to learn that you yourself are not the person you appear to be.

First D. What, I am some one else, not the I who am speaking to you?

Py. You are that you now:
but you have formerly inhabited another body, and borne another name. And in course of time you will change once more.

First D. Why then I shall be immortal, and take one shape after another? But enough of this. And now what is your diet?

Py. Of living things I eat none. All else I eat, except beans.

First D. And why no beans? Do you dislike them?

Py. No. But they are sacred things. Their nature is a mystery. Consider them first in their generative aspect; take a green one and peel it, and you will see what I mean. Again, boil one and expose it to moonlight for a proper number of nights, and you have—blood. What is more, the Athenians use beans to vote with.

First D. Admirable! A very feast of reason. Now just strip, and let me see what you are like. Bless me, here is a creed with a golden thigh! He is no mortal, he is a God. I must have him at any price. What do you start him at?

Her. Forty pounds.

First D. He is mine for forty pounds.

Zeus. Take the gentleman's name and address.

Her. He must come from Italy, I should think; Croton or Tarentum, or one of the Greek towns in those parts. But he is not the only buyer. Some three hundred of them have clubbed together.

Zeus. They are welcome to him. Now up with the next.

Her. What about yonder grubby Pontian?[21]

Zeus. Yes, he will do.

Her. You there with the wallet and cloak; come along, walk round the room. Lot No. 2. A most sturdy and valiant creed, free-born. What offers?

Second D. Hullo, Mr. Auctioneer, are you going to sell a free man?

Her. That was the idea.

Second D. Take care, he may have you up for kidnapping. This might be matter for the Areopagus.

Her. Oh, he would as soon be sold as not. He feels just as free as ever.

Second D. But what is one to do with such a dirty fellow? He is a pitiable sight. One might put him to dig perhaps, or to carry water.

Her. That he can do and more. Set him to guard your house, and you will find him better than any watch-dog.—They call him Dog for short.

Second D. Where does he come from? and what is his method?

Her. He can best tell you that himself.

Second D. I don't like his looks. He will probably snarl if I go near him, or take a snap at me, for all I know. See how he lifts his stick, and scowls; an awkward-looking customer!

Her. Don't be afraid. He is quite tame.

Second D. Tell me, good fellow, where do you come from?

Dio. Everywhere. *Second D.* What does that mean?

Dio. It means that I am a citizen of the world.

Second D. And your model?

Dio. Heracles.

Second D. Then why no lion's-skin? You have the orthodox club.

Dio. My cloak is my lion's-skin. Like Heracles, I live in a state of warfare, and my enemy is Pleasure; but unlike him I am a volunteer. My purpose is to purify humanity.

Second D. A noble purpose. Now what do I understand to be your strong subject? What is your profession?

Dio. The liberation of humanity, and the treatment of the passions. In short, I am the prophet of Truth and Candour.

Second D. Well, prophet; and if I buy you, how shall you handle my case?

Dio. I shall commence operations by stripping off yours superfluities, putting you into fustian, and leaving you closeted with Necessity. Then I shall give you a course of hard labour. You will sleep on the ground, drink water, and fill your belly as best you can. Have you money? Take my advice and throw it into the sea. With wife and children and country you will not concern yourself; there will be no more of that nonsense. You will exchange your present home for a sepulchre, a ruin, or a tub. What with lupines and close-written tomes, your knapsack will never be empty; and you will vote yourself

---

[21] See *Diogenes* in Notes.

160

happier than any king. Nor will you esteem it any inconvenience, if a flogging or a turn of the rack should fall to your lot.

Second D. How! Am I a tortoise, a lobster, that I should be flogged and feel it not?

Dio. You will take your cue from Hippolytus; *mutates mutandis.*

Second D. How so?

Dio. 'The heart may burn, the tongue knows nought thereof'.[22] Above all, be bold, be impudent; distribute your abuse impartially to king and commoner. They will admire your spirit. You will talk the Cynic jargon with the true Cynic snarl, scowling as you walk, and walking as one should who scowls; an epitome of brutality. Away with modesty, good-nature, and forbearance. Wipe the blush from your cheek for ever. Your hunting-ground will be the crowded city. You will live alone in its midst, holding communion with none, admitting neither friend nor guest; for such would undermine your power. Scruple not to perform the deeds of darkness in broad daylight:

select your love-adventures with a view to the public entertainment:

and finally, when the fancy takes you, swallow a raw cuttle-fish, and die. Such are the delights of Cynicism.

Second D. Oh, vile creed! Monstrous creed! Avaunt!

Dio. But look you, it is all so easy; it is within every man's reach. No education is necessary, no nonsensical argumentation. I offer you a short cut to Glory. You may be the merest clown—cobbler, fishmonger, carpenter, money-changer; yet there is nothing to prevent your becoming famous. Given brass and boldness, you have only to learn to wag your tongue with dexterity.

Second D. All this is of no use to me. But I might make a sailor or a gardener of you at a pinch; that is, if you are to be had cheap. Three-pence is the most I can give.

Her. He is yours, to have and to hold. And good riddance to the brawling foul-mouthed bully. He is a slanderer by wholesale.

Zeus. Now for the Cyrenaic, the crowned and purple-robed.

Her. Attend please, gentlemen all. A most valuable article, this, and calls for a long purse. Look at him. A sweet thing in creeds. A creed for a king. Has any gentleman a use for the Lap of Luxury? Who bids?

Third D. Come and tell me what you know. If you are a practical creed, I will have you.

Her. Please not to worry him with questions, sir. He is drunk, and cannot answer; his tongue plays him tricks, as you see.

---

[22] Hippolytus (in Euripides's play of that name) is reproached with having broken an oath, and thus defends himself:

'The tongue hath sworn:
the heart knew nought thereof.'

Third D. And who in his senses would buy such an abandoned reprobate? How he smells of scent! And how he slips and staggers about! Well, you must speak for him, Hermes. What can he do? What is his line?

Her. Well, for any gentleman who is not strait-laced, who loves a pretty girl, a bottle, and a jolly companion, he is the very thing. He is also a past master in gastronomy, and a connoisseur in voluptuousness generally. He was educated at Athens, and has served royalty in Sicily[23], where he had a very good character. Here are his principles in a nutshell:

Think the worst of things:

make the most of things:

get all possible pleasure out of things.

Third D. You must look for wealthier purchasers. My purse is not equal to such a festive creed.

Her. Zeus, this lot seems likely to remain on our hands.

Zeus. Put it aside, and up with another. Stay, take the pair from Abdera and Ephesus; the creeds of Smiles and Tears. They shall make one lot.

Her. Come forward, you two. Lot No. 4. A superlative pair. The smartest brace of creeds on our catalogue.

Fourth D. Zeus! What a difference is here! One of them does nothing but laugh, and the other might be at a funeral; he is all tears.—You there! what is the joke?

Democr. You ask? You and your affairs are all one vast joke.

Fourth D. So! You laugh at us? Our business is a toy?

Democr. It is. There is no taking it seriously. All is vanity. Mere interchange of atoms in an infinite void.

Fourth D. Your vanity is infinite, if you like. Stop that laughing, you rascal.—And you, my poor fellow, what are you crying for? I must see what I can make of you.

Heracl. I am thinking, friend, upon human affairs; and well may I weep and lament, for the doom of all is sealed. Hence my compassion and my sorrow. For the present, I think not of it; but the future!— the future is all bitterness. Conflagration and destruction of the world. I weep to think that nothing abides. All things are whirled together in confusion. Pleasure and pain, knowledge and ignorance, great and small; up and down they go, the playthings of Time.

Fourth D. And what is Time?

Heracl. A child; and plays at draughts and blindman's-bluff.

Fourth D. And men?

Heracl. Are mortal Gods.

Fourth D. And Gods?

Heracl. Immortal men.

---

[23] See *Aristippus* in Notes.

Fourth D. So! Conundrums, fellow? Nuts to crack? You are a very oracle for obscurity.

Heracl. Your affairs do not interest me.

Fourth D. No one will be fool enough to bid for you at that rate.

Heracl. Young and old, him that bids and him that bids not, a murrain seize you all!

Fourth D. A sad case. He will be melancholy mad before long. Neither of these is the creed for my money.

Her. No one bids.

Zeus. Next lot.

Her. The Athenian there? Old Chatterbox?

Zeus. By all means.

Her. Come forward!—A good sensible creed this. Who buys Holiness?

Fifth D. Let me see. What are you good for?

Soc. I teach the art of love.

Fifth D. A likely bargain for me! I want a tutor for my young Adonis.

Soc. And could he have a better? The love I teach is of, the spirit, not of the flesh. Under my roof, be sure, a boy will come to no harm.

Fifth D. Very unconvincing that. A teacher of the art of love, and never meddle with anything but the spirit? Never use the opportunities your office gives you?

Soc. Now by Dog and Plane-tree, it is as I say!

Fifth D. Heracles! What strange Gods are these?

Soc. Why, the Dog is a God, I suppose? Is not Anubis made much of in Egypt? Is there not a Dog-star in Heaven, and a Cerberus in the lower world?

Fifth D. Quite so. My mistake. Now what is your manner of life?

Soc. I live in a city of my own building; I make my own laws, and have a novel constitution of my own.

__*Fifth D.* I should like to hear some of your statutes.

Soc. You shall hear the greatest of them all. No woman shall be restricted to one husband. Every man who likes is her husband.

Fifth D. What! Then the laws of adultery are clean swept away?

Soc. I should think they were! and a world of hair-splitting with them.

Fifth D. And what do you do with the handsome boys?

Soc. Their kisses are the reward of merit, of noble and spirited actions.

Fifth D. Unparalleled generosity!—And now, what are the main features of your philosophy?

Soc. Ideas and types of things. All things that you see, the earth and all that is upon it, the sea, the sky,—each has its counterpart in the invisible world.

Fifth D. And where are they?

Soc. Nowhere. Were they anywhere, they were not what they are.

Fifth D. I see no signs of these 'types' of yours.

Soc. Of course not; because you are spiritually blind. *I* see the counterparts of all things; an invisible you, an invisible me; everything is in duplicate.

Fifth D. Come, such a shrewd and lynx-eyed creed is worth a bid. Let me see. What do you want for him?

Her. Five hundred.

Fifth D. Done with you. Only I must settle the bill another day.

Her. What name?

Fifth D. Dion; of Syracuse.

Her. Take him, and much good may he do you. Now I want Epicureanism. Who offers for Epicureanism? He is a disciple of the laughing creed and the drunken creed, whom we were offering just now. But he has one extra accomplishment—impiety. For the rest, a dainty, lickerish creed.

Sixth D. What price?

Her. Eight pounds.

Sixth D. Here you are. By the way, you might let me know what he likes to eat.

Her. Anything sweet. Anything with honey in it. Dried figs are his favourite dish.

Sixth D. That is all right. We will get in a supply of Carian fig-cakes.

Zeus. Call the next lot. Stoicism; the creed of the sorrowful countenance, the close-cropped creed.

Her. Ah yes, several customers, I fancy, are on the look-out for him. Virtue incarnate! The very quintessence of creeds! Who is for universal monopoly?

Seventh D. How are we to understand that?

Her. Why, here is monopoly of wisdom, monopoly of beauty, monopoly of courage, monopoly of justice. Sole king, sole orator, sole legislator, sole millionaire.

Seventh D. And I suppose sole cook, sole tanner, sole carpenter, and all that?

Her. Presumably.

Seventh D. Regard me as your purchaser, good fellow, and tell me all about yourself. I dare say you think it rather hard to be sold for a slave?

Chrys. Not at all. These things are beyond our control. And what is beyond our control is indifferent.

Seventh D. I don't see how you make that out.

Chrys. What! Have you yet to learn that of *indifferentia* some are *praeposita* and others *rejecta?*

Seventh D. Still I don't quite see.

Chrys. No; how should you? You are not familiar with our terms. You lack the *comprehensio visi.* The earnest student of logic knows this and more than this. He understands the nature of subject, predicate, and contingent, and the distinctions between them.

164

Seventh D. Now in Wisdom's name, tell me, pray, what is a predicate? what is a contingent? There is a ring about those words that takes my fancy.

Chrys. With all my heart. A man lame in one foot knocks that foot accidentally against a stone, and gets a cut. Now the man is *subject* to lameness; which is the *predicate*. And the cut is a *contingency*.

Seventh D. Oh, subtle! What else can you tell me?

Chrys. I have verbal involutions, for the better hampering, crippling, and muzzling of my antagonists. This is performed by the use of the far-famed syllogism.

Seventh D. Syllogism! I warrant him a tough customer.

Chrys. Take a case. You have a child?

Seventh D. Well, and what if I have?

Chrys. A crocodile catches him as he wanders along the bank of a river, and promises to restore him to you, if you will first guess correctly whether he means to restore him or not. Which are you going to say?

Seventh D. A difficult question. I don't know which way I should get him back soonest. In Heaven's name, answer for me, and save the child before he is eaten up.

Chrys. Ha, ha. I will teach you far other things than that.

Seventh D. For instance?

Chrys. There is the 'Reaper.' There is the 'Rightful Owner.' Better still, there is the 'Electra' and the 'Man in the Hood.'

Seventh D. Who was he? and who was Electra?

Chrys. She was *the* Electra, the daughter of Agamemnon, to whom the same thing was known and unknown at the same time. She knew that Orestes was her brother:

yet when he stood before her she did not know (until he revealed himself) that her brother was Orestes. As to the Man in the Hood, he will surprise you considerably. Answer me now:

do you know your own father?

Seventh D. Yes.

Chrys. Well now, if I present to you a man in a hood, shall you know him? eh?

Seventh D. Of course not.

Chrys. Well, but the Man in the Hood is your father. You don't know the Man in the Hood. Therefore you don't know your own father.

Seventh D. Why, no. But if I take his hood off, I shall get at the facts. Now tell me, what is the end of your philosophy? What happens when you reach the goal of virtue?

Chrys. In regard to things external, health, wealth, and the like, I am then all that Nature intended me to be. But there is much previous toil to be undergone. You will first sharpen your eyes on minute manuscripts, amass commentaries, and get your bellyful of outlandish terms. Last but not least, it is forbidden to be wise without repeated doses of hellebore.

Seventh D. All this is exalted and magnanimous to a degree. But what am I to think when I find that you are also the creed of cent-per-cent, the creed of the usurer? Has *he* swallowed his hellebore? is *he* made perfect in virtue?

Chrys. Assuredly. On none but the wise man does usury sit well. Consider. His is the art of putting two and two together, and usury is the art of putting interest together. The two are evidently connected, and one as much as the other is the prerogative of the true believer; who, not content, like common men, with simple interest, will also take interest *upon* interest. For interest, as you are probably aware, is of two kinds. There is simple interest, and there is its offspring, compound interest. Hear Syllogism on the subject. 'If I take simple interest, I shall also take compound. But I *shall* take simple interest:

therefore I shall take compound.'

Seventh D. And the same applies to the fees you take from your youthful pupils? None but the true believer sells virtue for a fee?

Chrys. Quite right. I take the fee in my pupil's interest, not because I want it. The world is made up of diffusion and accumulation. I accordingly practise my pupil in the former, and myself in the latter.

Seventh D. But it ought to be the other way. The pupil ought to accumulate, and you, 'sole millionaire,' ought to diffuse.

Chrys. Ha! you jest with me? Beware of the shaft of insoluble syllogism.

Seventh D. What harm can that do?

Chrys. It cripples; it ties the tongue, and turns the brain. Nay, I have but to will it, and you are stone this instant.

Seventh D. Stone! You are no Perseus, friend?

Chrys. See here. A stone is a body?

Seventh D. Yes.

Chrys. Well, and an animal is a body?

Seventh D. Yes.

Chrys. And you are an animal?

Seventh D. I suppose I am.

Chrys. Therefore you are a body. Therefore a stone.

Seventh D. Mercy, in Heaven's name! Unstone me, and let me be flesh as heretofore.

Chrys. That is soon done. Back with you into flesh! Thus:

Is every body animate?

Seventh D. No.

Chrys. Is a stone animate?

Seventh D. No.

Chrys. Now, you are a body?

Seventh D. Yes.

Chrys. And an animate body?

Seventh D. Yes.

Chrys. Then being animate, you cannot be a stone.

Seventh D. Ah! thank you, thank you. I was beginning to feel my limbs growing numb and solidifying like Niobe's. Oh, I must have you. What's to pay?

Her. Fifty pounds.

Seventh D. Here it is.

Her. Are you sole purchaser?

Seventh D. Not I. All these gentlemen here are going shares.

Her. A fine strapping lot of fellows, and will do the 'Reaper' credit.

Zeus. Don't waste time. Next lot,—the Peripatetic!

Her. Now, my beauty, now, Affluence! Gentlemen, if you want Wisdom for your money, here is a creed that comprises all knowledge.

Eighth D. What is he like?

Her. He is temperate, good-natured, easy to get on with; and his strong point is, that he is twins.

Eighth D. How can that be?

Her. Why, he is one creed outside, and another inside. So remember, if you buy him, one of him is called Esoteric, and the other Exoteric.

Eighth D. And what has he to say for himself?

Her. He has to say that there are three kinds of good:
spiritual, corporeal, circumstantial.

Eighth D. *There's* something a man can understand. How much is he?

Her. Eighty pounds.

Eighth D. Eighty pounds is a long price.

Her. Not at all, my dear sir, not at all. You see, there is some money with him, to all appearance. Snap him up before it is too late. Why, from him you will find out in no time how long a gnat lives, to how many fathoms' depth the sunlight penetrates the sea, and what an oyster's soul is like.

Eighth D. Heracles! Nothing escapes him.

Her. Ah, these are trifles. You should hear some of his more abstruse speculations, concerning generation and birth and the development of the embryo; and his distinction between man, the laughing creature, and the ass, which is neither a laughing nor a carpentering nor a shipping creature.

Eighth D. Such knowledge is as useful as it is ornamental. Eighty pounds be it, then.

Her. He is yours.

Zeus. What have we left?

Her. There is Scepticism. Come along, Pyrrhias, and be put up. Quick's the word. The attendance is dwindling; there will be small competition. Well, who buys Lot 9?

Ninth D. I. Tell me first, though, what do you know?

Sc. Nothing.

Ninth D. But how's that?

Sc. There does not appear to me to *be* anything.

Ninth D. Are not *we* something?

Sc. How do I know that?

Ninth D. And you yourself?

Sc. Of that I am still more doubtful.

Ninth D. Well, you *are* in a fix! And what have you got those scales for?

Sc. I use them to weigh arguments in, and get them evenly balanced, They must be absolutely equal—not a feather-weight to choose between them; then, and not till then, can I make uncertain which is right. *Ninth D.* What else can you turn your hand to?

Sc. Anything; except catching a runaway.

Ninth D. And why not that?

Sc. Because, friend, everything eludes my grasp.

Ninth D. I believe you. A slow, lumpish fellow you seem to be. And what is the end of your knowledge?

Sc. Ignorance. Deafness. Blindness.

Ninth D. What! sight and hearing both gone?

Sc. And with them judgement and perception, and all, in short, that distinguishes man from a worm.

Ninth D. You are worth money!—What shall we say for him?

Her. Four pounds.

Ninth D. Here it is. Well, fellow; so you are mine?

Sc. I doubt it.

Ninth D. Nay, doubt it not! You are bought and paid for.

Sc. It is a difficult case.... I reserve my decision.

Ninth D. Now, come along with me, like a good slave.

Sc. But how am I to know whether what you say is true?

Ninth D. Ask the auctioneer. Ask my money. Ask the spectators.

Sc. Spectators? But can we be sure there are any?

Ninth D. Oh, I'll send you to the treadmill. That will convince you with a vengeance that I am your master.

Sc. Reserve your decision.

Ninth D. Too late. It is given.

Her. Stop that wrangling and go with your purchaser. Gentlemen, we hope to see you here again to-morrow, when we shall be offering some lots suitable for plain men, artisans, and shopkeepers.

THE FISHER
A RESURRECTION PIECE

Lucian or *Parrhesiades. Socrates, Empedocles. Plato. Chrysippus. Diogenes. Aristotle. Other Philosophers. Platonists. Pythagoreans. Stoics. Peripatetics. Epicureans. Academics. Philosophy. Truth. Temperance. Virtue. Syllogism. Exposure. Priestess of Athene.*

Soc. Stone the miscreant; stone him with many stones; clod him with clods; pot him with pots; let the culprit feel your sticks; leave him no way out. At him, Plato! come, Chrysippus, let him have it! Shoulder to shoulder, close the ranks;

Let wallet succour wallet, staff aid staff!

We are all parties in this war; not one of us but he has assailed. You, Diogenes, now if ever is the time for that stick of yours; stand firm, all of you. Let him reap the fruits of his reveling. What, Epicurus, Aristippus, tired already? 'tis too soon; ye sages,

Be men; relume that erstwhile furious wrath!

Aristotle, one more sprint. There! the brute is caught; we have you, villain. You shall soon know a little more about the characters you have assailed. Now, what shall we do with him? it must be rather an elaborate execution, to meet all our claims upon him; he owes a separate death to every one of us.

First Phil. Impale him, say I.

Second Phil. Yes, but scourge him first.

Third Phil. Tear out his eyes.

Fourth Phil. Ah, but first out with the offending tongue.

Soc. What say you, Empedocles?

Emp. Oh, fling him into a crater; that will teach him to vilify his betters.

Pl. 'Twere best for him, Orpheus or Pentheus like, to

Find death, dashed all to pieces on the rock;

so each might have taken a piece home with him.

Lu. Forbear; spare me; I appeal to the God of suppliants.

Soc. Too late; no loophole is left you now. And you know your Homer:

'Twixt men and lions, covenants are null.'

Lu. Why, it is in Homer's name that I ask my boon. You will perhaps pay reverence to his lines, and listen to a selection from him:

Slay not; no churl is he; a ransom take
Of bronze and gold, whereof wise hearts are fain.

Pl. Why, two can play at that game; *exempli gratia,*

Reviler, babble not of gold, nor nurse

Hope of escape from these our hands that hold thee.

Lu. Ah me, ah me! my best hopes dashed, with Homer! Let me fly to Euripides; it may be he will protect me:

169

Leave him his life; the suppliant's life is sacred.

Pl. Does this happen to be Euripides too—

Evil men evil treated is no evil?

Lu. And will you slay me now for nought but words?

Pl. Most certainly; our author has something on that point too:

Unbridled   lips

And   folly's   slips

Invite Fate's whips.

Lu. Oh, very well; as you are all set on murdering me, and escape is impossible, do at least tell me who you are, and what harm I have done you; it must be something irreparable, to judge by your relentless murderous pursuit.

Pl. What harm you have done us, vile fellow? your own conscience and your fine dialogues will tell you; you have called Philosophy herself bad names, and as for us, you have subjected us to the indignity of a public auction, and put up wise men—ay, and free men, which is more— for sale. We have reason to be angry; we have got a short leave of absence from Hades, and come up against you—Chrysippus here, Epicurus and myself, Aristotle yonder, the taciturn Pythagoras, Diogenes and all of us that your dialogues have made so free with.

Lu. Ah, I breathe again. Once hear the truth about my conduct to you, and you will never put me to death. You can throw away those stones. Or, no, keep them; you shall have a better mark for them presently.

Pl. This is trifling. This day thou diest; nay, even now,

A suit of stones shalt don, thy livery due.

Lu. Believe me, good gentlemen, I have been at much pains on your behalf to slay me is to slay one who should rather be selected for commendation a kindred spirit, a well-wisher, a man after your own heart, a promoter, if I may be bold to say it, of your pursuits. See to it that you catch not the tone of our latter-day philosophers, and be thankless, petulant, and hard of heart, to him that deserves better of you.

Pl. Talk of a brazen front! So to abuse us is to oblige us. I believe you are under the delusion that you are really talking to slaves; after the insolent excesses of your tongue, do you propose to chop gratitude with us?

Lu. How or when was I ever insolent to you? I have always been an admirer of philosophy, your panegyrist, and a student of the writings you left. All that comes from my pen is but what you give me; I deflower you, like a bee, for the behoof of mankind; and then there is praise and recognition; they know the flowers, whence and whose the honey was, and the manner of my gathering; their surface feeling is for my selective art, but deeper down it is for you and your meadow, where you put forth such bright blooms and myriad dyes, if one knows but how to sort and mix and match, that one be not in discord with another. Could he that had found you such have the heart to abuse those

170

benefactors to whom his little fame was due? then he must be a Thamyris or Eurytus, defying the Muses who gave his gift of song, or challenging Apollo with the bow, forgetful from whom he had his marksmanship.

Pl. All this, good sir, is quite according to the principles of rhetoric; that is to say, it is clean contrary to the facts; your unscrupulousness is only emphasized by this adding of insult to injury; you confess that your arrows are from our quiver, and you use them against us; your one aim is to abuse us. This is our reward for showing you that meadow, letting you pluck freely, fill your bosom, and depart. For this alone you richly deserve death.

Lu. There; your ears are partial; they are deaf to the right. Why, I would never have believed that personal feeling could affect a Plato, a Chrysippus, an Aristotle; with you, of all men, I thought there was dry light. But, dear sirs, do not condemn me unheard; give me trial first. Was not the principle of your establishing—that the law of the stronger was not the law of the State, and that differences should be settled in court after due hearing of both sides? Appoint a judge, then; be you my accusers, by your own mouths or by your chosen representative; and let me defend my own case; then if I be convicted of wrong, and that be the court's decision, I shall get my deserts, and you will have no violence upon your consciences. But if examination shows me spotless and irreproachable, the court will acquit me, and then turn you your wrath upon the deceivers who have excited you against me.

Pl. Ah, every cock to his own dunghill! You think you will hoodwink the jury and get off. I hear you are a lawyer, an advocate, an old hand at a speech. Have you any judge to suggest who will be proof against such an experienced corrupter as you?

Lu. Oh, be reassured. The official I think of proposing is no suspicious, dubious character likely to sell a verdict. What say you to forming the court yourselves, with Philosophy for your President?

Pl. Who is to prosecute, if we are the jury?

Lu. Oh, you can do both; I am not in the least afraid; so much stronger is my case; the defence wins, hands down.

Pl. Pythagoras, Socrates, what do you think? perhaps the I man's appeal to law is not unreasonable.

Soc. No; come along, form the court, fetch Philosophy, and see what he has to say for himself. To condemn unheard is a sadly crude proceeding, not for us; leave that to the hasty people with whom might is right. We shall give occasion to the enemy to blaspheme if we stone a man without a hearing, professed lovers of justice as we are. We shall have to keep quiet about Anytus and Meletus, my accusers, and the jury on that occasion, if we cannot spare an hour to hear this fellow before he suffers. *Pl.* Very true, Socrates. We will go and fetch Philosophy. The decision shall be hers, and we will accept it, whatever it is.

Lu. Why, now, my masters, you are in a better and more law-abiding mood. However, keep those stones, as I said; you will need them in court. But where is Philosophy to be found? I do not know where she lives, myself. I once spent a long time wandering about in search of her house, wishing to make her acquaintance. Several times I met some long-bearded people in threadbare cloaks who professed to be fresh from her presence; I took their word for it, and asked them the way; but they knew considerably less about it than I, and either declined to answer, by way of concealing their ignorance, or else pointed to one door after another. I have never been able to find the right one to this day.

Many a time, upon some inward prompting or external offer of guidance, I have come to a door with the confident hope that this time I really was right; there was such a crowd flowing in and out, all of solemn persons decently habited and thoughtful-faced; I would insinuate myself into the press and go in too. What I found would be a woman who was not really natural, however skillfully she played at beauty unadorned; I could see at once that the apparent *neglige* of her hair was studied for effect, and the folds of her dress not so careless as they looked. One could tell that nature was a scheme of decoration with her, and artlessness an artistic device. The white lead and the rouge did not absolutely defy detection, and her talk betrayed her real vocation; she liked her lovers to appreciate her beauty, had a ready hand for presents, made room by her side for the rich, and hardly vouchsafed her poorer lovers a distant glance. Now and then, when her dress came a little open by accident, I saw that she had on a massive gold necklace heavier than a penal collar. That was enough for me; I would retrace my steps, sincerely pitying the unfortunates whom she led by the—beard, and their Ixion embracings of a phantom.

Pl. You are right there; the door is not conspicuous, nor generally known. However, we need not go to her house; we will wait for her here in the Ceramicus. I should think it is near her hour for coming back from the Academy, and taking her walk in the Poecile; she is very regular; to be sure, here she comes. Do you see the orderly, rather prim lady there, with the kindly look in her eyes, and the slow meditative walk?

Lu. I see several answering the description so far as looks and walk and clothes go. Yet among them all the real lady Philosophy can be but one.

Pl. True; but as soon as she opens her lips you will know.

Philos. Dear me, what are Plato and Chrysippus and Aristotle doing up here, and the rest of them—a living dictionary of my teachings? Alive again? how is this? have things been going wrong down there? you look angry. And who is your prisoner? a rifler of tombs? A murderer? a temple-robber?

Pl. Worse yet, Philosophy. He has dared to slander your most sacred self, and all of us who have been privileged to impart anything from you to posterity.

Philos. And did you lose your tempers over abusive words? Did you forget how Comedy handled me at the Dionysia, and how I yet counted her a friend? Did I ever sue her, or go and remonstrate? Or did I let her enjoy her holidays in the harmless old-fashioned way? I know very well that a jest spoils

172

no real beauty, but rather improves it; so gold is polished by hard rubs, and shines all the brighter for it. But you seem to have grown passionate and censorious. Come, why are you strangling him like that?

Pl. We have got this one day's leave, and come after him to give him his deserts. Rumours had reached us of the things he used to say about us in his lectures.

Philos. And are you going to kill him without a trial or a hearing? I can see he wishes to say something.

Pl. No; we decided to refer it all to you. If you will accept the task, the decision shall be yours.

Philos. Sir, what is your wish?

Lu. The same, dear Mistress; for none but you can find the truth. It cost me much entreaty to get the case reserved for you.

Pl. You call her Mistress now, scoundrel; the other day you were making out Philosophy the meanest of things, when before that great audience you let her several doctrines go for a pitiful threepence apiece.

Philos. It may be that it was not Ourself he then reviled, but some impostors who practised vile arts in our name.

Pl. The truth will soon come to light, if you will hear his defence.

Philos. Come we to the Areopagus—or better, to the Acropolis, where the panorama of Athens will be before us.

Ladies, will you stroll in the Poecile meanwhile? I will join you when I have given judgement.

Lu. Who are these, Philosophy? methinks their appearance is seemly as your own.

Philos. This with the masculine features is Virtue; then there is Temperance, and Justice by her side. In front is Culture; and this shadowy creature with the indefinite complexion is Truth.

Lu. I do not see which you mean.

Philos. Not see her? over there, all naked and unadorned, shrinking from observation, and always slipping out of sight.

Lu. Now I just discern her. But why not bring them all with you? there would be a fullness and completeness about that commission. Ah yes, and I should like to brief Truth on my behalf.

Philos. Well thought of; come, all of you; you will not mind sitting through a single case—in which we have a personal interest, too?

Truth. Go on, the rest of you; it is superfluous for me to hear what I know all about before.

Philos. But, Truth dear, your presence will be useful to us; you will show us what to think.

Truth. May I bring my two favourite maids, then?

Philos. And as many more as you like.

173

Truth. Come with me, Freedom and Frankness; this poor little adorer of ours is in trouble without any real reason; we shall be able to get him out of it. Exposure, my man, we shall not want you.

Lu. Ah yes, Mistress, let us have him, of all others; my opponents are no ordinary ruffians; they are people who make a fine show and are hard to expose; they have always some back way out of a difficulty; we must have Exposure.

Philos. Yes, we must, indeed; and you had better bring Demonstration too.

Truth. Come all of you, as you are such important legal persons.

Ar. What is this? Philosophy, he is employing Truth against us!

Philos. And are Plato and Chrysippus and Aristotle afraid of her lying on his behalf, being who she is?

Pl. Oh, well, no; only he is a sad plausible rogue; he will take her in.

Philos. Never fear; no wrong will be done, with madam Justice on the bench by us. Let us go up.

Prisoner, your name?

Lu. Parrhesiades, son of Alethion, son of Elanxicles.[24]

Philos. And your country?

Lu. I am a Syrian from the Euphrates, my lady. But is the question relevant? Some of my accusers I know to be as much barbarians by blood as myself; but character and culture do not vary as a man comes from Soli or Cyprus, Babylon or Stagira. However, even one who could not talk Greek would be none the worse in your eyes, so long as his sentiments were right and just.

Philos. True, the question was unnecessary.

But what is your profession? that at least is essential.

Lu. I profess hatred of pretension and imposture, lying, and pride; the whole loathsome tribe of them I hate; and you know how numerous they are.

Philos. Upon my word, you must have your hands full at this profession!

Lu. I have; you see what general dislike and danger it brings upon me. However, I do not neglect the complementary branch, in which love takes the place of hate; it includes love of truth and beauty and simplicity and all that is akin to love. But the subjects for this branch of the profession are sadly few; those of the other, for whom hatred is the right treatment, are reckoned by the thousand. Indeed there is some danger of the one feeling being atrophied, while the other is over-developed.

Philos. That should not be; they run in couples, you know. Do not separate your two branches; they should have unity in diversity.

Lu. You know better than I, Philosophy. My way is just to hate a villain, and love and praise the good.

---

[24] i e Free-speaker, son of Truthful, son of Exposure.

174

Philos. Well, well. Here we are at the appointed place. We will hold the trial in the forecourt of Athene Polias. Priestess, arrange our seats, while we salute the Goddess.

Lu. Polias, come to my aid against these pretenders, mindful of the daily perjuries thou hearest from them. Their deeds too are revealed to thee alone, in virtue of thy charge. Thou hast now thine hour of vengeance. If thou see me in evil case, if blacks be more than whites, then cast thou thy vote and save me!

Philos. So. Now we are seated, ready to hear your words. Choose one of your number, the best accuser you may, make your charge, and bring your proofs. Were all to speak, there would be no end. And you, Parrhesiades, shall afterwards make your defence.

Ch. Plato, none of us will conduct the prosecution better than you. Your thoughts are heaven-high, your style the perfect Attic; grace and persuasion, insight and subtlety, the cogency of well-ordered proof— all these are gathered in you. Take the spokesman's office and say what is fitting on our behalf. Call to memory and roll in one all that ever you said against Gorgias, Polus, Hippias, Prodicus; you have now to do with a worse than them. Let him taste your irony; ply him with your keen incessant questions; and if you will, perorate with the mighty Zeus charioting his winged car through Heaven, and grudging if this fellow get not his deserts.

Pl. Nay, nay; choose one of more strenuous temper—Diogenes, Antisthenes, Crates, or yourself, Chrysippus. It is no time now for beauty or literary skill; controversial and forensic resource is what we want. This Parrhesiades is an orator.

Diog. Let me be accuser; no need for long speeches here. Moreover, I was the worst treated of all; threepence was my price the other day.

Pl. Philosophy, Diogenes will speak for us. But mind, friend, you are not to represent yourself alone, but think of us all. If we have any private differences of doctrine, do not go into that; never mind now which of us is right, but keep your indignation for Philosophy's wrongs and the names he has called her. Leave alone the principles we differ about, and maintain what is common to us all. Now mark, you stand for us all; on you our whole fame depends; shall it come out majestic, or in the semblance he has given it?

Diog. Never fear; nothing shall be omitted; I speak for all. Philosophy may be softened by his words—she was ever gentle and forgiving—*she* may be minded to acquit him; but the fault shall not be mine; I will show him that our staves are more than ornaments.

Philos. Nay, take not that way; words, not bludgeons; 'tis better so. But no delay now; your time-allowance has begun; and the court is all attention.

Lu. Philosophy, let the rest take their seats and vote with you, leaving Diogenes as sole accuser.

Philos. Have you no fears of their condemning you?

Lu. None whatever; I wish to increase my majority, that is all.

175

Philos. I commend your spirit. Gentlemen, take your seats. Now, Diogenes.

Diog. With our lives on earth, Philosophy, you are acquainted; I need not dwell long upon them. Of myself I say nothing; but Pythagoras, Plato, Aristotle, Chrysippus, and the rest—who knows not the benefits that they conferred on mankind? I will come at once, then, to the insults to which we have been subjected by the thrice accursed Parrhesiades. He was, by his own account, an advocate; but he has left the courts and the fame there to be won, and has availed himself of all the verbal skill and proficiency so acquired for a campaign of abuse against us. We are impostors and deceivers; his audiences must ridicule and scorn us for nobodies. Did I say 'nobodies'? he has made us an abomination, rather, in the eyes of the vulgar, and yourself with us, Philosophy. Your teachings are balderdash and rubbish; the noblest of your precepts to us he parodies, winning for himself applause and approval, and for us humiliation. For so it is with the great public; it loves a master of flouts and jeers, and loves him in proportion to the grandeur of what he assails; you know how it delighted long ago in Aristophanes and Eupolis, when they caricatured our Socrates on the stage, and wove farcical comedies around him. But they at least confined themselves to a single victim, and they had the charter of Dionysus; a jest might pass at holiday time, and the laughing God might be well pleased.

But this fellow gets together an upper-class audience, gives long thought to his preparations, writes down his slanders in a thick notebook, and uplifts his voice in vituperation of Plato, Pythagoras, Aristotle, Chrysippus, and in short all of us; *he* cannot plead holiday time, nor yet any private grievance; he might perhaps be forgiven if he had done it in self-defence; but it was he that opened hostilities. Worst of all, Philosophy, he shelters himself under your name, entices Dialogue from our company to be his ally and mouthpiece, and induces our good comrade Menippus to collaborate constantly with him; Menippus, more by token, is the one deserter and absentee on this occasion.

Does he not then abundantly deserve his fate? What conceivable defence is open to him, after his public defamation of all that is noblest? On the public which listened to him, too, the spectacle of his condign punishment will have a healthy effect; we shall see no more ridicule of Philosophy. Tame submission to insult would naturally enough be taken, not for moderation, but for insensibility and want of spirit. Who could be expected to put up with his last performance? He brought us to market like a gang of slaves, and handed us over to the auctioneer. Some, I believe, fetched high prices; but others went for four or five pounds, and as for me—confound his impudence, threepence! And fine fun the audience had out of it! We did well to be angry; we have come from Hades; and we ask you to give us satisfaction for this abominable outrage.

Resurgents. Hear, hear! well spoken, Diogenes; well and loyally.

Philos. Silence in court! Time the defence. Parrhesiades, it is now your turn; they are timing you; so proceed.

Par. Philosophy, Diogenes has been far indeed from exhausting his material; the greater part of it, and the more strongly expressed, he has passed by, for reasons best known to himself. I refer to statements of mine which I am as far from denying that I made as from having provided myself with any elaborate defence of them. Any of these that have been omitted by him, and not previously emphasized by myself, I propose now to quote; this will be the best way to show you who were the persons that I sold by auction and inveighed against as pretenders and impostors; please to concentrate your vigilance on the truth or falsehood of my descriptions. If what I say is injurious or severe, your censure will be more fairly directed at the perpetrators than at the discoverer of such iniquities. I had no sooner realized the odious practices which his profession imposes on an advocate—the deceit, falsehood, bluster, clamour, pushing, and all the long hateful list, than I fled as a matter of course from these, betook myself to your dear service, Philosophy, and pleased myself with the thought of a remainder of life spent far from the tossing waves in a calm haven beneath your shadow.

At my first peep into your realm, how could I but admire yourself and all these your disciples? there they were, legislating for the perfect life, holding out hands of help to those that would reach it, commending all that was fairest and best; fairest and best—but a man must keep straight on for it and never slip, must set his eyes unwaveringly on the laws that you have laid down, must tune and test his life thereby; and that, Zeus be my witness, there are few enough in these days of ours to do.

So I saw how many were in love, not with Philosophy, but with the credit it brings; in the vulgar externals, so easy for any one to ape, they showed a striking resemblance to the real article, perfect in beard and walk and attire; but in life and conduct they belied their looks, read your lessons backwards, and degraded their profession. Then I was wroth; methought it was as though some soft womanish actor on the tragic stage should give us Achilles or Theseus or Heracles himself; he cannot stride nor speak out as a Hero should, but minces along under his enormous mask; Helen or Polyxena would find him too realistically feminine to pass for them; and what shall an invincible Heracles say? Will he not swiftly pound man and mask together into nothingness with his club, for womanizing and disgracing him?

Well, these people were about as fit to represent you, and the degradation of it all was too much for me. Apes daring to masquerade as heroes! emulators of the ass at Cyme! The Cymeans, you know, had never seen ass or lion; so the ass came the lion over them, with the aid of a borrowed skin and his most awe-inspiring bray; however, a stranger who had often seen both brought the truth to light with a stick. But what most distressed me, Philosophy, was this:

177

when one of these people was detected in rascality, impropriety, or immorality, every one put it down to philosophy, and to the particular philosopher whose name the delinquent took in vain without ever acting on his principles; the living rascal disgraced you, the long dead; for you were not there in the flesh to point the contrast; so, as it was clear enough that *his* life was vile and disgusting, your case was given away by association with his, and you had to share his disgrace.

This spectacle, I say, was too much for me; I began exposing them, and distinguishing between them and you; and for this good work you now arraign me. So then, if I find one of the Initiated betraying and parodying the Mysteries of the two Goddesses, and if I protest and denounce him, the transgression will be mine? There is something wrong there; why, at the Games, if an actor who has to present Athene or Posidon or Zeus plays his part badly, derogating from the divine dignity, the stewards have him whipped; well, the Gods are not angry with them for having the officers whip the man who wears their mask and their attire; I imagine they approve of the punishment. To play a slave or a messenger badly is a trifling offence, but to represent Zeus or Heracles to the spectators in an unworthy manner—that is a crime and a sacrilege.

I can indeed conceive nothing more extraordinary than that so many of them should get themselves absolutely perfect in your words, and then live precisely as if the sole object of reading and studying them had been to reverse them in practice. All their professions of despising wealth and appearances, of admiring nothing but what is noble, of superiority to passion, of being proof against splendour, and associating with its owners only on equal terms—how fair and wise and laudable they all are! But they take pay for imparting them, they are abashed in presence of the rich, their lips water at sight of coin; they are dogs for temper, hares for cowardice, apes for imitativeness, asses for lust, cats for thievery, cocks for jealousy. They are a perfect laughing-stock with their strivings after vile ends, their jostling of each other at rich men's doors, their attendance at crowded dinners, and their vulgar obsequiousness at table. They swill more than they should and would like to swill more than they do, they spoil the wine with unwelcome and untimely disquisitions, and they cannot carry their liquor. The ordinary people who are present naturally flout them, and are revolted by the philosophy which breeds such brutes.

What is so monstrous is that every man of them says he has no needs, proclaims aloud that wisdom is the only wealth, and directly afterwards comes begging and makes a fuss if he is refused; it would hardly be stranger to see one in kingly attire, with tall tiara, crown, and all the attributes of royalty, asking his inferiors for a little something more. When they want to get something, we hear a great deal, to be sure, about community of goods—how wealth is a thing indifferent—and what is gold and silver?—neither more nor less worth than pebbles on the beach. But when an old comrade and tried friend needs help and comes to them with his modest requirements, ah, then there is silence and searchings of heart, unlearning of tenets and flat renunciation of doctrines. All their fine talk of friendship, with Virtue and The Good, have vanished and flown, who knows whither? they were winged words in sad truth, empty phantoms, only meant for daily conversational use.

These men are excellent friends so long as there is no gold or silver for them to dispute the possession of; exhibit but a copper or two, and peace is broken, truce void, armistice ended; their books are blank, their Virtue fled, and they so many dogs; some one has flung a bone into the pack, and up they spring to bite each other and snarl at the one which has pounced successfully. There is a story of an Egyptian king who taught some apes the sword-dance; the imitative creatures very soon picked it up, and used to perform in purple robes and masks; for some time the show was a great success, till at last an ingenious spectator brought some nuts in with him and threw them down. The apes forgot their dancing at the sight, dropped their humanity, resumed their apehood, and, smashing masks and tearing dresses, had a free fight for the provender. Alas for the *corps de ballet* and the gravity of the audience!

These people are just those apes; it is they that I reviled; and I shall never cease exposing and ridiculing them; but about you and your like—for there *are*, in spite of all, some true lovers of philosophy and keepers of your laws—about you or them may I never be mad enough to utter an injurious or rude word! Why, what could I find to say? what is there in your lives that lends itself to such treatment? but those pretenders deserve my detestation, as they have that of heaven. Why, tell me, all of you, what have such creatures to do with you? Is there a trace in their lives of kindred and affinity? Does oil mix with water? If they grow their beards and call themselves philosophers and look solemn, do these things make them like you? I could have contained myself if there had been any touch of plausibility in their acting; but the vulture is more like the nightingale than they like philosophers. And now I have pleaded my cause to the best of my ability. Truth, I rely upon you to confirm my words.

Philos. Parrhesiades, retire to a further distance. Well, and our verdict? How think you the man has spoken?

Truth. Ah, Philosophy, while he was speaking I was ready to sink through the ground; it was all so true. As I listened, I could identify every offender, and I was fitting caps all the time—this is so-and-so, that is the other man, all over. I tell you they were all as plain as in a picture—speaking likenesses not of their bodies only, but of their very souls.

Tem. Yes, Truth, I could not help blushing at it.

Philos. What say you, gentlemen?

Res. Why, of course, that he is acquitted of the charge, and stands recorded as our friend and benefactor. Our case is just that of the Trojans, who entertained the tragic actor only to find him reciting their own calamities. Well, recite away, our tragedian, with these pests of ours for dramatis personae.

Diog. I too, Philosophy, give him my need of praise; I withdraw my charges, and count him a worthy friend.

Philos. I congratulate you, Parrhesiades; you are unanimously acquitted, and are henceforth one of us.

Par. Your humble servant. Or no, I must find more tragic words to fit the solemnity of the occasion:

Victorious   might
My   life's   path   light,
And ever strew with garlands bright!

Vir. Well, now we come to our second course; let us have in the other people and try them for their insults. Parrhesiades shall accuse them each in turn.

Par. Well said, Virtue. Syllogism, my boy, put your head out over the city and summon the philosophers.

Syl. Oyez, oyez! All philosophers to the Acropolis to make their defence before Virtue, Philosophy, and Justice.

Par. The proclamation does not bring them in flocks, does it? They have their reasons for keeping clear of Justice. And a good many of them are too busy with their rich friends. If you want them all to come, Syllogism, I will tell you what to say.

Philos. No, no; call them yourself, Parrhesiades, in your own way.

Par. Quite a simple matter. Oyez, oyez! All who profess philosophy and hold themselves entitled to the name of philosopher shall appear on the Acropolis for largesse; 8 pounds, with a sesame cake, to each. A long beard shall qualify for a square of compressed figs, in addition. Every applicant to have with him, of temperance, justice, and self-control, any that he is in possession of, it being clearly understood that these are not indispensable, and, of syllogisms, a complete set of five, these being the condition precedent of wisdom.
Two golden talents in the midst are set,
  His prize who wrangles best amongst his peers.

Just look! the ascent packed with a pushing crowd, at the very first sound of my 8 pounds. More of them along the Pelasgicum, more by the temple of Asclepius, a bigger crowd still over the Areopagus. Why, positively there are a few at the tomb of Talos; and see those putting ladders against the temple of Castor and Pollux; up they climb, buzzing and clustering like a swarm of bees. In Homeric phrase, on this side are exceeding many, and on that
  Ten thousand, thick as leaves and flowers in spring.

Noisily they settle, the Acropolis is covered with them in a trice; everywhere wallet and beard, flattery and effrontery, staves and greed, logic and avarice. The little company which came up at the first proclamation is swamped beyond recovery, swallowed up in these later crowds; it is hopeless to find them, because of the external resemblance. That is the worst of it, Philosophy; you are really open to censure for not marking and labelling them; these impostors are often more convincing than the true philosophers.

Philos. It shall be done before long; at present let us receive them.

Platon. Platonists first!

Pyth. No, no; Pythagoreans first; our master is senior.

Stoics. Rubbish! the Porch is the best.

Peri. Now, now, this is a question of money; Peripatetics first there!

Epic. Hand over those cakes and fig-squares; as to the money, Epicureans will not mind waiting till the last.

Acad. Where are the two talents? none can touch the Academy at a wrangle; we will soon show you that.

Stoics. Not if we know it.

Philos. Cease your strife. Cynics there, no more pushing! And keep those sticks quiet. You have mistaken the nature of this summons. We three, Philosophy, Virtue, and Truth, are about to decide which are the true philosophers; that done, those whose lives are found to be in accord with our pleasure will be made happy by our award; but the impostors who are not truly of our kin we shall crush as they deserve, that they may no more make vain claims to what is too high for them. Ha! you fly? In good truth they do, jumping down the crags, most of them. Why, the Acropolis is deserted, except for—yes, a few have stood their ground and are not afraid of the judgement.

Attendants, pick up the wallet which yonder flying Cynic has dropped. Let us see what it contains—beans? a book? some coarse crust?

Par. Oh dear no. Here is gold; some scent; a mirror; dice.

Philos. Ah, good honest man! such were his little necessaries for the philosophic life, such his title to indulge in general abuse and instruct his neighbours.

Par. There you have them. The problem before you is, how the general ignorance is to be dispersed, and other people enabled to discriminate between the genuine and the other sort. Find the solution, Truth; for indeed it concerns you; Falsehood must not prevail; shall Ignorance shield the base while they counterfeit the good, and you never know it?

Truth. I think we had better give Parrhesiades this commission; he has been shown an honest man, our friend and your true admirer, Philosophy. Let him take Exposure with him and have interviews with all who profess philosophy; any genuine scion that he finds let him crown with olive and entertain in the Banqueting Hall; and for the rascals—ah, how many!—who are only costume philosophers, let him pull their cloaks off them, clip their beards short with a pair of common goatshears, and mark their foreheads or brand them between the eyebrows; the design on the branding iron to be a fox or an ape.

Philos. Well planned, Truth. And, Parrhesiades, here is a test for you; you know how young eagles are supposed to be tested by the sun; well, our candidates have not got to satisfy us that they can look at light, of course; but put gold, fame, and pleasure before their eyes; when you see one remain unconscious and unattracted, there is your man for the olive; but when one looks hard that way, with a motion of his hand in the direction of the gold, first off with his beard, and then off with him to the brander.

Par. I will follow your instructions, Philosophy; you will soon find a large majority ornamented with fox or ape, and very few with olive. If you like, though, I will get some of them up here for you to see.

Philos. What do you mean? bring them back after that stampede?

Par. Oh yes, if the priestess will lend me the line I see there and the Piraean fisherman's votive hook; I will not keep them long.

Priestess. You can have them; and the rod to complete the equipment.

Par. Thanks; now quickly, please, a few dried figs and a handful of gold.

Priestess. There.

Philos. What *is* all this about?

Priestess. He has baited his hook with the figs and gold, and is sitting on the parapet dangling it over the city.

Philos. What *are* you doing, Parrhesiades? do you think you are going to fish up stones from the Pelasgicum?

Par. Hush! I wait till I get a bite. Posidon, the fisherman's friend, and you, dear Amphitrite, send me good fishing!

Ah, a fine bass; no, it is not; it is a gilthead.

Expo. A shark, you mean; there, see, he is getting near the hook, open-mouthed too. He scents the gold; now he is close—touching—he has it; up with him!

Par. Give me a hand with the line, Exposure; here he is. Now, my best of fishes, what do we make of you? *Salmo Cynicus*, that is what *you* are. Good gracious, what teeth! Aha, my brave fish, caught snapping up trifles in the rocks, where you thought you could lurk unobserved? But now you shall hang by the gills for every one to look at you. Pull out hook and bait. Why, the hook is bare; he has not been long assimilating the figs, eh? and the gold has gone down too.

Diog. Make him disgorge; we want the bait for some more.

Par. There, then. Now, Diogenes, do you know who it is? has the fellow anything to do with you?

Diog. Nothing whatever.

Par. Well, what do you put him at? threepence was the price fixed the other day.

Diog. Too much. His flavour and his looks are intolerable—a coarse worthless brute. Drop him head first over the rock, and catch another. But take care your rod does not bend to breaking point.

Par. No fear; they are quite light—about the weight of a gudgeon.

Diog. About the weight and about the wit. However, up with them.

Par. Look; what is this one? a sole? flat as a plate, thin as one of his own fillets; he gapes for the hook; down it goes; we have him; up he comes.

Diog. What is he?

Expo. His plateship would be a Platonist.

Pl. You too after the gold, villain?

Par. Well, Plato? what shall we do with him?

Pl. Off with him from the same rock.

Diog. Try again.

Par. Ah, here is a lovely one coming, as far as one can judge in deep water, all the colours of the rainbow, with gold bars across the back. Do you see, Exposure? this is the sham Aristotle. There he is; no, he has shied. He is having a good look round; here he comes again; his jaws open; caught! haul up.

Ar. You need not apply to me; I do not know him.

Par. Very well, Aristotle; over he goes.

Hullo! I see a whole school of them together, all one colour, and covered with spines and horny scales, as tempting to handle as a hedgehog. We want a net for these; but we have not got one. Well, it will do if we pull up one out of the lot. The boldest of them will no doubt try the hook.

Expo. You had better sheathe a good bit of the line before you let it down; else he will gorge the gold and then saw the line through.

Par. There it goes. Posidon grant me a quick catch! There now! they are fighting for the bait, a lot of them together nibbling at the figs, and others with their teeth well in the gold. That is right; one soundly hooked. Now let me see, what do *you* call yourself? And yet how absurd to try and make a fish speak; they are dumb. Exposure, tell us who is his master,

Expo. Chrysippus.

Par. Ah, he must have a master with gold in his name, must he? Chrysippus, tell me seriously, do you know these men? are you responsible for the way they live?

Ch. My dear Parrhesiades, I take it ill that you should suggest any connexion between me and such creatures.

Par. Quite right, and like you. Over he goes head first like the others; if one tried to eat him, those spines might stick in one's throat.

Philos. You have fished long enough, Parrhesiades; there are so many of them, one might get away with gold, hook and all, and you have the priestess to pay. Let us go for our usual stroll; and for all you it is time to be getting back to your place, if you are not to outstay your leave. Parrhesiades, you and Exposure can go the rounds now, and crown or brand as I told you.

Par. Good, Philosophy. Farewell, ye best of men. Come, Exposure, to our commission. Where shall we go first? the Academy, do you think, or the Porch?

Expo. We will begin with the Lyceum.

Par. Well, it makes no difference. I know well enough that wherever we go there will be few crowns wanted, and a good deal of branding.

VOYAGE TO THE LOWER WORLD

Charon. Clotho. Hermes. Shades. Rhadamanthus. Tisiphone. Lamp. Bed

Cha. You see how it is, Clotho; here has all been ship-shape and ready for a start this long time; the hold baled out, the mast stepped, the sail hoisted, every oar in its rowlock; it is no fault of mine that we don't weigh anchor and sail. 'Tis Hermes keeps us; he should have been here long ago. Not a passenger on board, as you may see; and we might have made the trip three times over by this. Evening is coming on now; and never a penny taken all day! I know how it will be:

Pluto will think *I* have been wanting to my work. It is not I that am to blame, but our fine gentleman of a supercargo. He is just like any mortal:

he has taken a drink of their Lethe up there, and forgotten to come back to us. He'll be wrestling with the lads, or playing on his lyre, or giving his precious gift of the gab a good airing; or he's off after plunder, the rascal, for what I know:

'tis all in the day's work with him. He is getting too independent:

he ought to remember that he belongs to us, one half of him.

Clo. Well, well, Charon; perhaps he has been busy:

Zeus may have had some particular occasion for his services in the upper world; *he* has the use of him too, remember.

Cha. That doesn't say that he should make use of him beyond what's reasonable. Hermes is common property. We have never kept him here when he was due to go. No, I know what it is. In these parts of ours all is mist and gloom and darkness, and nothing to be had but asphodel and libations and sacrificial cakes and meats. Yonder in Heaven, all's bright, with plenty of ambrosia, and no end of nectar. Small wonder that he likes to loiter there. When he leaves us, 'tis on wings; it is as though he escaped from prison. But when the time comes for return, he tramps it on foot, and has much ado to get here at all.

Clo. Well, never mind now; here he comes, look, and a fine host of passengers with him; a fine flock, rather; he hustles them along with his staff like so many goats. But what's this? One of them is bound, and another enjoying the joke; and there is one with a wallet slung beside him, and a stick in his hand; a cantankerous-looking fellow; he keeps the rest moving. And just look at Hermes! Bathed in perspiration, and his feet covered with dust! See how he pants; he is quite out of breath. What is the matter, Hermes? Tell us all about it; you seem disturbed.

Her. The matter is that this rascal ran away; I had to go after him, and had well nigh played you false for this trip, I can tell you.

Clo. Why, who is he? What did he want to run away for?

Her. His motive is sufficiently clear:

he had a preference for remaining alive. He is some king or tyrant, as I gather from his piteous allusions to blessedness no longer his.

Clo. And the fool actually tried to run away, and thought to prolong his life when the thread of Fate was exhausted?

Her. Tried! He would have got clean away, but for that capital fellow there with the club; he gave me a hand, and we caught and bound him. The whole way along, from the moment that Atropus handed him over to me, he dragged and hung back, and dug his heels into the ground:

it was no easy work getting him along. Every now and then he would take to prayers and entreaties:

Would I let him go just for a few minutes? he would make it worth my while. Of course I was not going to do that; it was out of the question.—Well, we had actually got to the very pit's mouth, when somehow or other this double-dyed knave managed to slip off, whilst I was telling over the Shades to Aeacus, as usual, and he checking them by your sister's invoice. The consequence was, we were one short of tally. Aeacus raised his eyebrows. 'Hermes,' he said, 'everything in its right place:

no larcenous work here, please. You play enough of those tricks in Heaven. We keep strict accounts here:

nothing escapes us. The invoice says 1,004; there it is in black and white. You have brought me one short, unless you say that Atropus was too clever for you.' I coloured up at that; and then all at once I remembered what had happened on the way, and when I looked round and this fellow was nowhere to be seen, I knew that he must have made off, and I set off after him along the road to the upper world, as fast as I could go. My worthy friend here volunteered for the service; so we made a race of it, and caught the runaway just as he got to Taenarum! It was a near thing.

Clo. There now, Charon! And we were beginning to accuse Hermes of neglect.

Cha. Well, and why are we waiting here, as if there had not been enough delay already?

Clo. True. Let them come aboard. I'll to my post by the gangway, with my notebook, and take their names and countries as they come up, and details of their deaths; and you can stow them away as you get them.—Hermes, let us have those babies in first; I shall get nothing out of them.

Her. Here, skipper. Three hundred of them, including those that were exposed.

Cha. A precious haul, on my word!-These are but green grapes, Hermes.

Her. Who next, Clotho? The Unwept?

Clo. Ah! I take you.—Yes, up with the old fellows. I have no time to-day for prehistoric research. All over sixty, pass on! What's the matter with them? They don't hear me; they are deaf with age. I think you will have to pick them up, like the babies, and get them along that way.

Her. Here they are; fine well-matured fruit, gathered in due season; three hundred and ninety-eight of them.

Cha. Nay, nay; these are no better than raisins.

Clo. Bring up the wounded next, Hermes. *Now* I can get to work. Tell me how you were killed. Or no; I had better look at my notes, and call you over. Eighty-four due to be killed in battle yesterday, in Mysia, These to include Gobares, son of Oxyartes.

Her. Adsunt.

Clo. The seven who killed themselves for love. Also Theagenes, the philosopher, for love of the Megarian courtesan.

Her. Here they are, look.

Clo. And the rival claimants to thrones, who slew one another?

Her. Here!

Clo. And the one murdered by his wife and her paramour?

Her. Straight in front of you.

Clo. Now the victims of the law,—the cudgelled and the crucified. And where are those sixteen who were killed by robbers?

Her. Here; you may know them by their wounds. Am I to bring the women too?

Clo. Yes, certainly; and all who were shipwrecked; it is the same kind of death. And those who died of fever, bring them too, the doctor Agathocles and all. Then there was a Cynic philosopher, who was to have succumbed to a dinner with Dame Hecate, eked out with sacrificial eggs and a raw cuttlefish; where is he?

Cy. Here I stand this long time, my good Clotho.—Now what had I done to deserve such a weary spell of life? You gave me pretty nearly a spindleful of it. I often tried to cut the thread and away; but somehow it never would give.

Clo. I left you as a censor and physician of human frailties; pass on, and good luck to you.

Cy. No, by Zeus! First let us see our captive safe on board. Your judgement might be perverted by his entreaties.

Clo. Let me see; who is he?

Her. Megapenthes, son of Lacydes; tyrant.

Clo. Come up, Megapenthes.

Me. Nay, nay, my lady Clotho; suffer me to return for a little while, and I will come of my own accord, without waiting to be summoned.

Clo. What do you want to go for?

Me. I crave permission to complete my palace; I left the building half-finished.

Clo. Pooh! Come along.

Me. Oh Fate, I ask no long reprieve. Vouchsafe me this one day, that I may inform my wife where my great treasure lies buried.

Clo. Impossible. 'Tis Fate's decree.

Me. And all that money is to be thrown away?

Clo. Not thrown away. Be under no uneasiness. Your cousin Megacles will take charge of it.

186

Me. Oh, monstrous! My enemy, whom from sheer good nature I omitted to put to death?

Clo. The same. He will survive you for rather more than forty years; in the full enjoyment of your harem, your wardrobe, and your treasure.

Me. It is too bad of you, Clotho, to hand over my property to my worst enemy.

Clo. My dear sir, it was Cydimachus's property first, surely? You only succeeded to it by murdering him, and butchering his children before his eyes.

Me. Yes, but it was mine after that.

Clo. Well, and now your term of possession expires.

Me. A word in your ear, madam; no one else must hear this.—Sirs, withdraw for a space.—Clotho, if you will let me escape, I pledge myself to give you a quarter of a million sterling this very day.

Clo. Ha, ha! So your millions are still running in your head?

Me. Shall I throw in the two mixing-bowls that I got by the murder of Cleocritus? They weigh a couple of tons apiece; refined gold!

Clo. Drag him up. We shall never get him to come on board by himself.

Me. I call you all to witness! My city-wall, my docks, remain unfinished. I only wanted five days more to complete them.

Clo. Never mind. It will be another's work now.

Me. Stay! One request I can make with a clear conscience.

Clo. Well?

Me. Suffer me only to complete the conquest of Persia; ... and to impose tribute on Lydia; ... and erect a colossal monument to myself, ... and inscribe thereon the military achievements of my life. Then let me die.

Clo. Creature, this is no single day's reprieve:
you would want something like twenty years.

Me. Oh, but I am quite prepared to give security for my expeditious return. Nay, I could provide a substitute, if preferred—my well-beloved!

Clo. Wretch! How often have you prayed that he might survive you!

Me. That was a long time ago. Now,—I see a better use for him.

Clo. But he is due to be here, shortly, let me tell you. He is to be put to death by the new sovereign.

Me. Well, Clotho, I hope you will not refuse my last request.

Clo. Which is?

Me. I should like to know how things will be, now that I am gone.

Clo. Certainly; you shall have that mortification. Your wife will pass into the hands of Midas, your slave; he has been her gallant for some time past.

Me. A curse on him! 'Twas at her request that I gave him his freedom.

Clo. Your daughter will take her place in the harem of the present monarch. Then all the old statues and portraits which the city set up in your honour will be overturned,—to the entertainment, no doubt, of the spectators.

Me. And will no friend resent these doings?

Clo. Who was your friend? Who had any reason to be? Need I explain that the cringing courtiers who lauded your every word and deed were actuated either by hope or by fear—time-servers every man of them, with a keen eye to the main chance?

Me. And these are they whose feasts rang with my name! who, as they poured their libations, invoked every blessing on my head! Not one but would have died before me, could he have had his will; nay, they swore by no other name.

Clo. Yes; and you dined with one of them yesterday, and it cost you your life. It was that last cup you drank that brought you here.

Me. Ah, I noticed a bitter taste.—But what was his object?

Clo. Oh, you want to know too much. It is high time you came on board.

Me. Clotho, I had a particular reason for desiring one more glimpse of daylight. I have a burning grievance!

Clo. And what is that? Something of vast importance, I make no doubt.

Me. It is about my slave Carion. The moment he knew of my death, he came up to the room where I lay; it was late in the evening; he had plenty of time in front of him, for not a soul was watching by me; he brought with him my concubine Glycerium (an old affair, this, I suspect), closed the door, and proceeded to take his pleasure with her, as if no third person had been in the room! Having satisfied the demands of passion, he turned his attention to me. 'You little villain,' he cried, 'many's the flogging I've had from you, for no fault of mine!' And as he spoke he plucked out my hair and smote me on the face. 'Away with you,' he cried finally, spitting on me, 'away to the place of the damned!'—and so withdrew. I burned with resentment:

but there I lay stark and cold, and could do nothing. That baggage Glycerium, too, hearing footsteps approaching, moistened her eyes and pretended she had been weeping for me; and withdrew sobbing, and repeating my name.—If I could but get hold of them—

Clo. Never mind what you would do to them, but come on board. The hour is at hand when you must appear before the tribunal.

Me. And who will presume to give his vote against a tyrant?

Clo. Against a tyrant, who indeed? Against a Shade, Rhadamanthus will take that liberty. He is strictly impartial, as you will presently observe, in adapting his sentences to the requirements of individual cases. And now, no more delay.

Me. Dread Fate, let me be some common man,—some pauper! I have been a king,—let me be a slave! Only let me live!

Clo. Where is the one with the stick? Hermes, you and he must drag him up feet foremost. He will never come up by himself.

Her. Come along, my runagate. Here you are, skipper. And I say, keep an eye—

Cha. Never fear. We'll lash him to the mast.

Me. Look you, I must have the seat of honour.

Clo. And why exactly?

Me. Can you ask? Was I not a tyrant, with a guard of ten thousand men?

Cy. Oh, dullard! And you complain of Carion's pulling your hair! Wait till you get a taste of this stick; you shall know what it is to be a tyrant.

Me. What, shall a Cynic dare to raise his staff against me? Sirrah, have you forgotten the other day, when I had all but nailed you to the cross, for letting that sharp censorious tongue of yours wag too freely?

Cynic. Well, and now it is your turn to be nailed,—to the mast.

Mi. And what of me, mistress? Am I to be left out of the reckoning? Because I am poor, must I be the last to come aboard?

Clo. Who are you?

Mi. Micyllus the cobbler.

Clo. A cobbler, and cannot wait your turn? Look at the tyrant:

see what bribes he offers us, only for a short reprieve. It is very strange that delay is not to your fancy too.

Mi. It is this way, my lady Fate. I find but cold comfort in that promise of the Cyclops:

'Outis shall be eaten last,' said he; but first or last, the same teeth are waiting. And then, it is not the same with me as with the rich. Our lives are what they call 'diametrically opposed.' This tyrant, now, was thought happy while he lived; he was feared and respected by all:

he had his gold and his silver; his fine clothes and his horses and his banquets; his smart pages and his handsome ladies,—and had to leave them all. No wonder if he was vexed, and felt the tug of parting. For I know not how it is, but these things are like birdlime:

a man's soul sticks to them, and will not easily come away; they have grown to be a part of him. Nay, 'tis as if men were bound in some chain that nothing can break; and when by sheer force they are dragged away, they cry out and beg for mercy. They are bold enough for aught else, but show them this same road to Hades, and they prove to be but cowards. They turn about, and must ever be looking back at what they have left behind them, far off though it be,—like men that are sick for love. So it was with the fool yonder:

as we came along, he was for running away; and now he tires you with his entreaties. As for me, I had no stake in life; lands and horses, money and goods, fame, statues,—I had none of them; I could not have been in better trim:

it needed but one nod from Atropus,—I was busied about a boot at the time, but down I flung knife and leather with a will, jumped up, and never waited to get my shoes, or wash the blacking from my hands, but joined the procession there and then, ay, and headed it, looking ever forward; I had left nothing behind me that called for a backward glance. And, on my word, things begin to look well already. Equal rights for all, and no man better than his neighbour; that is hugely to my liking. And from what I can learn there is no

189

collecting of debts in this country, and no taxes; better still, no shivering in winter, no sickness, no hard knocks from one's betters. All is peace. The tables are turned:

the laugh is with us poor men; it is the rich that make moan, and are ill at ease.

Clo. To be sure, I noticed that you were laughing, some time ago. What was it in particular that excited your mirth?

Mi. I'll tell you, best of Goddesses. Being next door to a tyrant up there, I was all eyes for what went on in his house; and he seemed to me neither more nor less than a God. I saw the embroidered purple, the host of courtiers, the gold, the jewelled goblets, the couches with their feet of silver:

and I thought, this is happiness. As for the sweet savour that arose when his dinner was getting ready, it was too much for me; such blessedness seemed more than human. And then his proud looks and stately walk and high carriage, striking admiration into all beholders! It seemed almost as if he must be handsomer than other men, and a good eighteen inches taller. But when he was dead, he made a queer figure, with all his finery gone; though I laughed more at myself than at him:

there had I been worshipping mere scum on no better authority than the smell of roast meat, and reckoning happiness by the blood of Lacedaemonian sea-snails! There was Gniphon the usurer, too, bitterly reproaching himself for having died without ever knowing the taste of wealth, leaving all his money to his nearest relation and heir-at-law, the spendthrift Rhodochares, when he might have had the enjoyment of it himself.

When I saw him, I laughed as if I should never stop:

to think of him as he used to be, pale, wizened, with a face full of care, his fingers the only rich part of him, for they had the talents to count,—scraping the money together bit by bit, and all to be squandered in no time by that favourite of Fortune, Rhodochares!—But what are we waiting for now? There will be time enough on the voyage to enjoy their woebegone faces, and have our laugh out.

Clo. Come on board, and then the ferryman can haul up the anchor.

Cha. Now, now! What are you doing here? The boat is full. You wait till to-morrow. We can bring you across in the morning.

Mi. What right have you to leave me behind,—a shade of twenty-four hours' standing? I tell you what it is, I shall have you up before Rhadamanthus. A plague on it, she's moving! And here I shall be left all by myself. Stay, though:

why not swim across in their wake? No matter if I get tired; a dead man will scarcely be drowned. Not to mention that I have not a penny to pay my fare.

Clo. Micyllus! Stop! You must not come across that way; Heaven forbid!

Mi. Ha, ha! I shall get there first, and I shouldn't wonder.

Clo. This will never do. We must get to him, and pick him up.... Hermes, give him a hand up.

Cha. And where is he to sit now he is here? We are full up, as you may see.

Her. What do you say to the tyrant's shoulders?

Clo. A good idea that.

Cha. Up with you then; and make the rascal's back ache. And now, good luck to our voyage!

Cy. Charon, I may as well tell you the plain truth at once. The penny for my fare is not forthcoming; I have nothing but my wallet, look, and this stick. But if you want a hand at baling, here I am; or I could take an oar; only give me a good stout one, and you shall have no fault to find with me.

Cha. To it, then; and I'll ask no other payment of you.

Cy. Shall I tip them a stave?

Cha. To be sure, if you have a sea-song about you.

Cy. I have several. Look here though, an opposition is starting: a song of lamentation. It will throw me out.

Sh. Oh, my lands, my lands!—Ah, my money, my money!—Farewell, my fine palace!—The thousands that fellow will have to squander!—Ah, my helpless children!—To think of the vines I planted last year! Who, ah who, will pluck the grapes?—

Her. Why, Micyllus, have *you* never an Oh or an Ah? It is quite improper that any shade should cross the stream, and make no moan.

Mi. Get along with you. What have I to do with Ohs and Ahs? I'm enjoying the trip!

Her. Still, just a groan or two. It's expected.

Mi. Well, if I must, here goes.—Farewell, leather, farewell! Ah, Soles, old Soles!—Oh, ancient Boots!—Woe's me! Never again shall I sit empty from morn till night; never again walk up and down, of a winter's day, naked, unshod, with chattering teeth! My knife, my awl, will be another's:
whose, ah! whose?

Her. Yes, that will do. We are nearly there.

Cha. Wait a bit! Fares first, please. Your fare, Micyllus; every one else has paid; one penny.

Mi. You don't expect to get a penny out of the poor cobbler? You're joking, Charon; or else this is what they call a 'castle in the air.' I know not whether your penny is square or round.

Cha. A fine paying trip this, I must say! However,—all ashore! I must fetch the horses, cows, dogs, and other livestock. Their turn comes now.

Clo. You can take charge of them for the rest of the way, Hermes. I am crossing again to see after the Chinamen, Indopatres and Heramithres. They have been fighting about boundaries, and have killed one another by this time.

Her. Come, shades, let us get on;—follow me, I mean, in single file.

Mi. Bless me, how dark it is! Where is handsome Megillus *now*? There would be no telling Simmiche from Phryne. All complexions are alike here, no question of beauty, greater or less. Why, the cloak I thought so shabby before passes muster here as well as royal purple; the darkness hides both alike. Cyniscus, whereabouts are you?

Cy. Use your ears; here I am. We might walk together. What do you say?

Mi. Very good; give me your hand.——I suppose you have been admitted to the mysteries at Eleusis? That must have been something like this, I should think?

Cy. Pretty much. Look, here comes a torch-bearer; a grim, forbidding dame. A Fury, perhaps?

Mi. She looks like it, certainly.

Her. Here they are, Tisiphone. One thousand and four.

Ti. It is time we had them. Rhadamanthus has been waiting.

Rhad. Bring them up, Tisiphone. Hermes, you call out their names as they are wanted.

Cy. Rhadamanthus, as you love your father Zeus, have me up first for examination.

Rhad. Why?

Cy. There is a certain shade whose misdeeds on earth I am anxious to denounce. And if my evidence is to be worth anything, you must first be satisfied of my own character and conduct.

Rhad. Who are you?

Cy. Cyniscus, your worship; a student of philosophy.

Rhad. Come up for judgement; I will take you first. Hermes, summon the accusers.

Her. If any one has an accusation to bring against Cyniscus here present, let him come forward.

Cy. No one stirs!

Rhad. Ah, but that is not enough, my friend. Off with your clothes; I must have a look at your brands.

Cy. Brands? Where will you find them?

Rhad. Never yet did mortal man sin, but he carried about the secret record thereof, branded on his soul.

Cy. Well, here I am stripped. Now for the 'brands.'

Rhad. Clean from head to heel, except three or four very faint marks, scarcely to be made out. Ah! what does this mean? Here is place after place that tells of the iron; all rubbed out apparently, or cut out. How do you explain this, Cyniscus? How did you get such a clean skin again?

Cy. Why, in old days, when I knew no better, I lived an evil life, and acquired thereby a number of brands. But from the day that I began to practise philosophy, little by little I washed out all the scars from my soul,-thanks to the efficiency of that admirable lotion.

Rhad. Off with you then to the Isles of the Blest, and the excellent company you will find there. But we must have your impeachment of the tyrant before you go. Next shade, Hermes!

Mi. Mine is a very small affair, too, Rhadamanthus; I shall not keep you long. I have been stripped all this time; so do take me next.

Rhad. And who may you be?

Mi. Micyllus the cobbler.

Rhad. Very well, Micyllus. As clean as clean could be; not a mark anywhere. You may join Cyniscus. Now the Tyrant.

Her. Megapenthes, son of Lacydes, wanted! Where are you off to? This way! You there, the Tyrant! Up with him, Tisiphone, neck and crop.

Rhad. Now, Cyniscus, your accusation and your proofs. Here is the party.

Cy. There is in fact no need of an accusation. You will very soon know the man by the marks upon him. My words however may serve to unveil him, and to show his character in a clearer light. With the conduct of this monster as a private citizen, I need not detain you. Surrounded with a bodyguard, and aided by unscrupulous accomplices, he rose against his native city, and established a lawless rule. The persons put to death by him without trial are to be counted by thousands, and it was the confiscation of their property that gave him his enormous wealth. Since then, there is no conceivable iniquity which he has not perpetrated. His hapless fellow-citizens have been subjected to every form of cruelty and insult. Virgins have been seduced, boys corrupted, the feelings of his subjects outraged in every possible way. His overweening pride, his insolent bearing towards all who had to do with him, were such as no doom of yours can adequately requite. A man might with more security have fixed his gaze upon the blazing sun, than upon yonder tyrant. As for the refined cruelty of his punishments, it baffles description; and not even his familiars were exempt. That this accusation has not been brought without sufficient grounds, you may easily satisfy yourself, by summoning the murderer's victims.—Nay, they need no summons; see, they are here; they press round as though they would stifle him. Every man there, Rhadamanthus, fell a prey to his iniquitous designs. Some had attracted his attention by the beauty of their wives; others by their resentment at the forcible abduction of their children; others by their wealth; others again by their understanding, their moderation, and their unvarying disapproval of his conduct.

Rhad. Villain, what have you to say to this?

Me. I committed the murders referred to. As for the rest, the adulteries and corruptions and seductions, it is all a pack of lies.

Cy. I can bring witnesses to these points too, Rhadamanthus.

Rhad. Witnesses, eh?

Cy. Hermes, kindly summon his Lamp and Bed. They will appear in evidence, and state what they know of his conduct.

Her. Lamp and Bed of Megapenthes, come into court. Good, they respond to the summons.

Rhad. Now, tell us all you know about Megapenthes. Bed, you speak first.

Bed. All that Cyniscus said is true. But really, Mr. Rhadamanthus, I don't quite like to speak about it; such strange things used to happen overhead.

Rhad. Why, your unwillingness to speak is the most telling evidence of all!—Lamp, now let us have yours.

Lamp. What went on in the daytime I never saw, not being there. As for his doings at night, the less said the better. I saw some very queer things, though, monstrous queer. Many is the time I have stopped taking oil on purpose, and tried to go out. But then he used to bring me close up. It was enough to give any lamp a bad character.

Rhad. Enough of verbal evidence. Now, just divest yourself of that purple, and we will see what you have in the way of brands. Goodness gracious, the man's a positive network! Black and blue with them! Now, what punishment can we give him? A bath in Pyriphlegethon? The tender mercies of Cerberus, perhaps?

Cy. No, no. Allow me,—I have a novel idea; something that will just suit him.

Rhad. Yes? I shall be obliged to you for a suggestion.

Cy. I fancy it is usual for departed spirits to take a draught of the water of Lethe?

Rhad. Just so.

Cy. Let him be the sole exception.

Rhad. What is the idea in that?

Cy. His earthly pomp and power for ever in his mind; his fingers ever busy on the tale of blissful items;—'tis a heavy sentence!

Rhad. True. Be this the tyrant's doom. Place him in fetters at Tantalus's side,—never to forget the things of earth.

THE DEPENDENT SCHOLAR

The dependent scholar! The great man's licensed friend!—if friend, not slave, is to be the word. Believe me, Timocles, amid the humiliation and drudgery of his lot, I know not where to turn for a beginning. Many, if not most, of his hardships are familiar to me; not, heaven knows, from personal experience, for I have never been reduced to such extremity, and pray that I never may be; but from the lips of numerous victims; from the bitter outcries of those who were yet in the snare, and the complacent recollections of others who, like escaped prisoners, found a pleasure in detailing all that they had been through. The evidence of the latter was particularly valuable. Mystics, as it were, of the highest grade, Dependency had no secrets for them. Accordingly, it was with keen interest that I listened to their stories of miraculous deliverance from moral shipwreck. They reminded me of the mariners who, duly cropped, gather at the doors of a temple, with their tale of stormy seas and monster waves and promontories, castings out of cargoes, snappings of masts, shatterings of rudders; ending with the appearance of those twin brethren [25] so indispensable to nautical story, or of some other *deus ex machina*, who, seated at the masthead or standing at the helm, guides the vessel to some sandy shore, there to break up at her leisure—not before her crew (so benevolent is the God!) have effected a safe landing. The mariner, however, is liberal in embellishment, being prompted thereto by the exigencies of his situation; for by his appearance as a favourite of heaven, not merely a victim of fortune, the number of the charitable is increased. It is otherwise with those whose narrative is of domestic storms, of billows rising mountain high (if so I may phrase it) within four walls. They tell us of the seductive calm that first lured them on to those waters, of the sufferings they endured throughout the voyage, the thirst, the sea-sickness, the briny drenchings; and how at last their luckless craft went to pieces upon some hidden reef or at the foot of some steep crag, leaving them to swim for it, and to land naked and utterly destitute. All this they tell us:

but I have ever suspected them of having convenient lapses of memory, and omitting the worst part for very shame. For myself, I shall have no such scruple. All that I have heard, or can reasonably infer, of the evils of dependence, I shall place before you. For either, friend, my penetration is at fault, or you have long had a hankering for this profession.

Yes, I have seen it from the first, whenever the conversation has fallen on this subject of salaried intellects. 'Happy men!' some enthusiast has cried. 'The *elite* of Rome are their friends. They dine sumptuously, and call for no reckoning. They are lodged splendidly, and travel comfortably—nay, luxuriously—with cushions at their backs, and as often as not a fine pair of

---

[25] The Dioscuri, Castor and Pollux, who were supposed to appear to sailors in distress.

creams in front of them. And, as if this were not enough, the friendship they enjoy and the handsome treatment they receive is made good to them with a substantial salary. They sow not, they plough not; yet all things grow for their use.' How I have seen you prick up your ears at such words as these! How wide your mouth has opened to the bait!

Now I will have a clear conscience in this matter. I will not be told hereafter that I saw you swallowing this palpable bait, and never stirred a finger to snatch it from you, and show you the hook while there was yet time; that I watched you nibbling, saw the hook well in and the fish hauled up, and then stood by shedding useless tears. A grave charge, indeed, were I to leave it in your power to bring it; such neglect would admit of no palliation. You shall therefore hear the whole truth. Now, in leisurely fashion, from without, not hereafter from within, shall you examine this weel from which no fish escapes. You shall take in hand this hook of subtle barb. You shall try the prongs of this eel-spear against your inflated cheek; and if you decide that they are not sharp, that they would be easily evaded, that a wound from them would be no great matter, that they are deficient in power and grasp—then write me among those who have cowardice to thank for their empty bellies; and for yourself, take heart of grace, and swoop upon your prey, and cormorant-wise, if you will, swallow all at a gulp.

But however much the present treatise is indebted to you for its existence, its application is not confined to you who are philosophers, whose ambition it is to form your conduct upon serious principles; it extends to the teachers of literature, of rhetoric, of music,—to all, in short, whose intellectual attainments can command a maintenance and a wage. And where the life, from beginning to end, is one and the same for all, the philosopher (I need not say), so far from being a privileged person, has but the additional ignominy of being levelled with the rest, and treated by his paymaster with as scant ceremony as the rest. In conclusion, whatever disclosures I may be led to make, the blame must fall in the first instance on the aggressors, and in the second instance on those who suffer the aggression. For me, unless truth and candour be crimes, I am blameless.

As to the vulgar rabble of trainers and toadies, illiterate, mean-souled creatures, born to obscurity, should we attempt to dissuade *them* from such pursuits, our labour would be wasted. Nor can we fairly blame them, for putting up any affront, rather than part with their employers. The life suits them; they are in their element. And what other channel is there, into which their energies could be directed? Take away this, their sole vocation, and they are idle cumberers of the earth. They have nothing, then, to complain of; nor are their employers unreasonable in turning these humble vessels to the use for which they were designed. They come into a house prepared for such treatment from the first; it is their profession to endure and suffer wrong.

But the case of educated men, such as I have mentioned above, is another matter; it calls for our indignation, and for our utmost endeavours to restore

196

them to liberty. I think it will not be amiss, if I first examine into the provocations under which they turn to a life of dependence. By showing how trivial, how inadequate these provocations are, I shall forestall the main argument used by the defenders of voluntary servitude. Most of them are content to cloak their desertion under the names of Poverty and Necessity. It is enough, they think, to plead in extenuation, that they sought to flee from this greatest of human ills, Poverty. Theognis comes pat to their purpose. His

Poverty, soul-subduing Poverty,

is in continual requisition, together with other fearful utterances of our most degenerate poets to the same effect. Now if I could see that they really found an escape from poverty in the lives they lead, I would not be too nice on the point of absolute freedom. But when we find them (to use the expression of a famous orator) 'faring like men that are sick,' what conclusion is then left to us to draw? What but this, that here again they have been misled, the very evil which they sold their liberty to escape remaining as it was? Poverty unending is their lot. From the bare pittance they receive nothing can be set apart. Suppose it paid, and paid in full:

the whole sum is swallowed up to the last farthing, before their necessities are supplied. I would advise them to think upon better expedients; not such as are merely the protectors and accomplices of Poverty, but such as will make an end of her altogether. What say you, Theognis? Might this be a case for,

Steep plunge from crags into the teeming deep?

For when a pauper, a needy hireling, persuades himself that by being what he is he has escaped poverty, one cannot avoid the conclusion that he labours under some mistake.

Others tell a different tale. For them, mere poverty would have had no terrors, had they been able, like other men, to earn their bread by their labours. But, stricken as they were by age or infirmity, they turned to this as the easiest way of making a living. Now let us consider whether they are right. This 'easy' way may be found to involve much labour before it yields any return; more labour perhaps than any other. To find money ready to one's hand, without toil or trouble on one's own part, would indeed be a dream of happiness. But the facts are otherwise. The toils and troubles of their situation are such as no words can adequately describe. Health, as it turns out, is nowhere more essential than in this vocation, in which a thousand daily labours combine to grind the victim down, and reduce him to utter exhaustion. These I shall describe in due course, when I come to speak of their other grievances. For the present let it suffice to have shown that this excuse for the sale of one's liberty is as untenable as the former.

And now for the true reason, which you will never hear from their lips. Voluptuousness and a whole pack of desires are what induce them to force their way into great houses. The dazzling spectacle of abundant gold and silver, the joys of high feeding and luxurious living, the immediate prospect of wallowing in riches, with no man to say them nay,—these are the temptations that lure them on, and make slaves of free men; not lack of the necessaries of life, as they pretend, but lust of its superfluities, greed of its costly refinements. And their employers, like finished coquettes, exercise their rigours upon these hapless slaves of love, and keep them for ever dangling in amorous attendance; but for fruition, no! never so much as a kiss may they snatch. To grant that would be to give the lover his release, a conclusion against which they are jealously on their guard. But upon hopes he is abundantly fed. Despair might else cure his ardent passion, and the lover be lover no more. So there are smiles for him, and promises; always something shall be done, some favour shall be granted, a handsome provision shall be made for him,—some day. Meanwhile, old age steals upon the pair; the superannuated lover ceases from desire, and his mistress has nothing left to give. Life has gone by, and all they have to show for it is *hope*.

Well now, that a man for the sake of pleasure should put up with every hardship is perhaps no great matter. Devoted to this one object, he can think of nothing, but how to procure it. Let that pass. Though it seems but a scurvy bargain, a bargain for a slave; to sell one's liberty for pleasures far less pleasant than liberty itself. Still, as I say, let that pass, provided the price is paid. But to endure unlimited pain, merely in the hope that pleasure may come of it, this surely is carrying folly to the height of absurdity. And men do it with their eyes open. The hardships, they know, are certain, unmistakable, inevitable. As to the pleasure, that vague, hypothetic pleasure, they have never had it in all these years, and in all reasonable probability they never will. The comrades of Odysseus forgot all else in the Lotus:

but it was while they were tasting its sweets. They esteemed lightly of Honour:

but it was in the immediate presence of Pleasure. In men so occupied, such forgetfulness was not wholly unnatural. But to dwell a prisoner, with Famine for company, to watch one's neighbour fattening on the Lotus, and keeping it all to himself, and to forget Honour and Virtue in the bare prospect of a possible mouthful,—by Heaven, it is too absurd, and calls in good truth for Homeric scourgings.

Such, as nearly as I can describe them, are men's motives for taking service with the rich, for handing themselves over bodily, to be used as their employers think fit. There is one class, however, of which I ought perhaps to make mention—those whose vanity is gratified by the mere fact of being seen in the company of well-born and well-dressed men. For there are those who consider this a distinguished privilege; though for my own part I would not give a fig to enjoy and to be seen enjoying the company of the King of Persia, if I was to get nothing by it.

And now, since we understand what it is that these men would be at, let us mentally review their whole career;—the difficulties that beset the applicant before he gains acceptance; his condition when he is duly installed in his office;

and the closing scene of his life's drama. You may perhaps suppose that his situation, whatever its drawbacks, is at least attainable without much trouble; that you have but to will it, and the thing is done in a trice. Far from it. Much tramping about is in store for you, much kicking of heels. You will rise early, and stand long before your patron's closed door; you will be jostled; you will hear occasional comments on your impudence. You will be exposed to the vile gabble of a Syrian porter, and to the extortions of a Libyan nomenclator, whose memory must be fee'd, if he is not to forget your name. You must dress beyond your means, or you will be a discredit to your patron; and select his favourite colours, or you will be out of harmony with your surroundings. Finally, you will be indefatigable in following his steps, or rather in preceding them, for you will be thrust forward by his slaves, to swell his triumphal progress. And for days together you will not be favoured with a glance.

But one day the best befalls you. You catch his eye; he beckons you to him, and puts a random question. In that supreme moment what cold sweats, what palpitations, what untimely tremors are yours! and what mirth is theirs who witness your confusion! 'Who was the king of the Achaeans?' is the question:

and your answer, as likely as not, 'A thousand sail.' With the charitable this passes for bashfulness; but to the impudent you are a craven, and to the ill-natured a yokel. This first experience teaches you that the condescensions of the great are not unattended with danger; and as you depart you pronounce upon yourself a sentence of utter despair. Thereafter,

many a sleepless night, Many a day of strife shall be thy lot—

not for the sake of Helen, not for the towers of Troy, but for the sevenpence halfpenny of your desire. At length some heaven-sent protector gives you an introduction:

the scholar is brought up for examination. For the great man, who has but to receive your flatteries and compliments, this is an agreeable pastime:

for you, it is a life-and-death struggle; all is hazarded on the one throw. For it will of course occur to you, that if you are rejected at the first trial, you will never pass current with any one else. A thousand different feelings now distract you. You are jealous of your rivals (for we will assume that there is competition for the post); you are dissatisfied with your own replies; you hope; you fear; you cannot remove your eye from the countenance of your judge. Does he pooh-pooh your efforts? You are a lost man. Was that a smile? You rejoice, and hope rises high. It is only to be expected, that many of the company are your enemies, and others your rivals, and each has his secret shaft to let fly at you from his lurking-place. What a picture! The venerable grey-beard being put through his paces. Is he any use? Some say yes, others no. Time is taken for consideration. Your antecedents are industriously overhauled. Some envious compatriot, some neighbour with a trivial grievance, is asked his opinion; he has but to drop a word of 'loose morality,' and your

199

business is done; 'the man speaks God's truth!' Every one else may testify to your character:

their evidence proves nothing; they are suspected; they are venal. The fact is, you must gain every point; there must be no hitch anywhere. That is your only chance of success.

And now, take it that you *have* succeeded—beyond all expectation. Your words have found favour with the great man. Those friends, by whose judgement in such matters he sets most store, have made no attempt to alter his decision. His wife approves his choice; the steward and the major-domo have neither of them anything against you. No aspersions have been cast on your character; all is propitious, every omen is in your favour. Hail, mighty conqueror, wreathed in the Olympian garland! Babylon is yours, Sardis falls before you. The horn of plenty is within your grasp; pigeons shall yield you milk.

Now, if your crown is to be of anything better than leaves, there must be some solid benefits to compensate you for the labours you have undergone. A considerable salary will be placed at your disposal, and you will draw upon it without ceremony, whenever you have occasion. You will be a privileged person in every respect. As for toils, and muddy tramps, and wakeful nights, the time for those have gone by. Your prayers have been heard:

you will take your ease, and sleep your fill. You will do the work you were engaged to do, and not a stroke besides. This, indeed, is what you have a right to expect. There would be no great hardship in bowing one's neck to a yoke so light, so easy—and so superbly gilded. But alas, Timocles, many, nay all of these requirements are unsatisfied. Your office, now that you have got it, is attended with a thousand details insufferable to all but slaves. Let me rehearse them to you; you shall judge for yourself whether any man with the slightest pretence to culture would endure such treatment.

Let me begin with your first invitation to dinner, which may reasonably be expected to follow, as an earnest of the patronage to come. It is brought to you by a most communicative slave, whose goodwill it must be your first care to secure. Five shillings is the least you can slip into his palm, if you would do the thing properly. He has scruples. 'Really, sir—couldn't think of it; no, indeed, sir.' But he is prevailed upon at last, and goes off, grinning from ear to ear. You then look out your best clothes, have your bath, make yourself as presentable as possible, and arrive—in fear and trembling lest you should be the first, which would wear an awkward air, just as it savours of ostentation to arrive last. Accordingly you contrive to hit on the right moment, are received with every attention, and shown to your place, a little above the host, separated from him only by a couple of his intimates. And now you feel as if you were in heaven. You are all admiration; everything you see done throws you into ecstasies. It is all so new and strange! The waiters stare at you, the company watch your movements. Nor is the host without curiosity. Some of his servants have instructions to observe you narrowly, lest your glance should fall too often on his wife or children. The other guests' men perceive your amazement at the novel scene, and exchange jesting asides. From the fact that you do not know what to make of your napkin, they conclude that this is your first experience of dining-out. You perspire with embarrassment; not unnaturally. You are thirsty, but you dare not ask for wine, lest you should be thought a tippler. The due connexion between the various dishes which make their appearance is beyond you:

which ought you to take first? which next? There is nothing for it but to snatch a side glance at your neighbour, do as he does, and learn to dine in sequence. On the whole, your feelings are mingled, your spirit perturbed, and stricken with awe. One moment you are envying your host his gold, his ivory, and all his magnificence; the next, you are pitying yourself,—that miserable nonentity which calls its existence life; and then at intervals comes the thought, 'how happy shall I be, sharing in these splendours, enjoying them as if they were my own!' For you conceive of your future life as one continual feast; and the smiling attendance of gracious Ganymedes gives a charming finish to the picture. That line of Homer keeps coming to your lips:

Small blame to Trojan or to greaved Achaean, if such happiness as this was to be the reward of their toils and sufferings. Presently healths are drunk. The host calls for a large beaker, and drinks to 'the Professor,' or whatever your title is to be. You, in your innocence, do not know that you ought to say something in reply; you receive the cup in silence, and are set down as a boor.

Apart from this, your host's pledge has secured you the enmity of many of his old friends, with some of whom it was already a grievance, that an acquaintance of a few hours' standing should sit above men who have been drinking the cup of slavery for years. Tongues are busy with you at once. Listen to some of them. 'So! We are to give place to new-comers! It wanted but this. The gates of Rome are open to none but these Greeks. Now what is their claim to be set over our heads? I suppose they think they are conferring a favour on us with their wordy stuff?' 'How he did drink, to be sure!' says another. 'And did you see how he shovelled his food down, hand over hand? Mannerless starveling! He has never so much as dreamt of white bread before. 'Twas the same with the capon and pheasant; much if he left us the bones to pick!' 'My dear sirs' (cries number three), 'I give him five days at the outside; after which you will see him at our end of the table, making like moan with ourselves. He is a new pair of shoes just now, and is treated with all ceremony. Wait till he has been worn a few times, and the mud has done its work; he will be flung under the bed, poor wretch, like the rest of us, to be a receptacle for bugs.' Such are some among the many comments you excite; and, for all we know, mischief may be brewing at this moment.

Meanwhile, you are the guest of the evening, and the principal theme of conversation. Your unwonted situation has led you on to drink more than was advisable. For some time you have been feeling uncomfortable effects from your host's light, eager wine. To get up before the rest would be bad manners:

to remain is perilous. The drinking is prolonged; subject upon subject is started, spectacle after spectacle is produced; for your host is determined that you shall see all he has to show. You suffer the torments of the damned. You see nothing of what is going forward:

some favourite singer or musician is performing—you hear him not; and while you force out some complimentary phrase, you are praying that an earthquake may swallow up all, or that the news of a fire may break up the party.

Such, my friend, is your first dinner, the best you will ever get. For my part, give me a dinner of herbs, with liberty to eat when I will and as much as I will. I shall spare you the recital of the nocturnal woes that follow your excess. The next morning, you have to come to terms as to the amount of your salary, and the times of payment. Appearing in answer to his summons, you find two or three friends with him. He bids you be seated, and begins to speak. 'You have now seen the sort of way in which we live—no ostentation, no fuss; everything quite plain and ordinary. Now you will consider everything here as your own. It would be a strange thing, indeed, were I to entrust you with the highest responsibility of all, the moral guidance of myself and my children'—if there are children to be taught—'and yet hesitate to place the rest at your disposal. Something, however, must be settled. I know your moderate, independent spirit. I quite realize that you come to us from no mercenary motive, that you are influenced only by the regard and uniform respect which will be assured to you in this house. Still, as I say, something must be settled. Now, my dear sir, tell me yourself, what you think right; remembering that there is something to be expected at the great festivals; for you will not find me remiss in that respect, though I say nothing definite at present; and these occasions, as you know, come pretty frequently in the course of the year. This consideration will no doubt influence you in settling the amount of your salary; and apart from that, it sits well on men of culture like yourself, to be above the thought of money.' Your hopes are blasted at the words, and your proud spirit is tamed. The dream of the millionaire and landed proprietor fades away, as you gradually catch his parsimonious drift. Yet you smirk appreciation of the promise. You are to 'consider everything as your own'; there, surely, is something solid? 'Tis a draught (did you but know it)

That wets the lips, but leaves the palate dry. After an interval of embarrassment, you leave the matter to his decision. He declines the responsibility, and calls for the intervention of one of the company:

let him name a sum, at once worthy of your acceptance, and not burdensome to his purse, which has so many more urgent calls upon it. 'Sir,' says this officious old gentleman, who has been a toady from his youth, 'Sir, you are the luckiest man in Rome. Deny it if you can! You have gained a privilege which many a man has longed for, and is not like to obtain at Fortune's hands. You have been admitted to enjoy the company and share the hearth and home of the first citizen of our empire. Used aright, such a privilege will be more to you than the wealth of a Croesus or a Midas. Knowing as I do how many there are—persons of high standing —who would be glad to pay money down, merely for the honour and glory of the acquaintanceship, of being seen in his company, and ranking as his friends and intimates,—knowing this, I am at a loss for words in which to express my sense of your good fortune. You are not only to enjoy this happiness, but to be paid for enjoying it! Under the circumstances, I think we shall satisfy your most extravagant expectations, if we say'— and he names a sum which in itself is of the smallest, quite apart from all reference to your brilliant hopes. However, there is nothing for it but to submit with a good grace. It is too late now for escape; you are in the toils. So you open your mouth for the bit, and are very manageable from the first. You give your rider no occasion to keep a tight rein, or to use the spur; and at last by imperceptible degrees you are quite broken in to him.

The outside world from that time watches you with envy. You dwell within his courts; you have free access; you are become a person of consequence. Yet it is now incomprehensible to you how they can suppose you to be happy. At the same time, you are not without a certain exultation:

you cheat yourself from day to day with the thought that there are better things to come. Quite the contrary turns out to be the case. Your prospects, like the proverbial sacrifice of Mandrobulus, dwindle and contract from day to day. Gradually you get some faint glimmerings of the truth. It begins to dawn upon you at last, that those golden hopes were neither more nor less than gilded bubbles:

the vexations, on the other hand, are realities; solid, abiding, uncompromising realities. 'And what are these vexations?' you will perhaps exclaim; 'I see nothing so vexatious about the matter; I know not what are the hardships and the drudgery alluded to.' Then listen. And do not confine yourself to the article of drudgery, but keep a sharp look-out for ignominy, for degradation, for everything, in short, that is unworthy of a free man.

Let me remind you then, to begin with, that you are no longer free-born, no longer a man of family. Birth, freedom, ancestry, all these you will leave on the other side of the door, when you enter upon the fulfilment of your servile contract; for Freedom will never bear you company in that ignoble station. You are a slave, wince as you may at the word; and, be assured, a slave of many masters; a downward-looking drudge, from morning till night

serving for sorry wage.

Then again, you are a backward pupil:

Servitude was not the nurse of your childhood; you are getting on in years when she takes you in hand; accordingly, you will do her little credit, and give little satisfaction to your lord. Recollections of Freedom will exercise their demoralizing influence upon you, causing you to jib at times, and you will make villanous work of your new profession. Or will your aspirations after Freedom be satisfied, perhaps, with the thought, that you are no son of a Pyrrhias or a Zopyrion, no Bithynian, to be knocked down under the hammer of a bawling auctioneer? My dear sir, when pay-day comes round each month, and you mingle in the herd of Pyrrhiases and Zopyrions, and hold out your hand for the wage that is due to you, what is that but a sale? No need of an auctioneer, for the man who can cry his own wares, and hawks his liberty about from day to day. Wretch! (one is prompted to exclaim, and particularly when the culprit is a professed philosopher) Wretch! Were you captured and sold by a pirate or a brigand, you would bewail your lot, and think that Fortune had dealt hardly with you. Were a man to lay violent hands on you, and claim a master's rights in you, loud and bitter would be your outcry:

'By heaven and earth, 'tis monstrous! I appeal to the laws!' And now, at an age at which a born slave may begin to look towards Freedom, *now* for a few pence do you sell yourself, your virtue and wisdom, in one parcel? And could Plato's noble words, could all that Chrysippus and Aristotle have said, of the blessings of freedom and the curse of slavery, raise no compunction in you? Do you count it no shame to be pitted against toadies and vulgar parasites? no shame to sit at the noisy banquets of a promiscuous, and for the most part a disreputable company, a Greek among Romans, wearing the foreign garb of philosophy, and stammering their tongue with a foreign accent? How fulsome are your flatteries on these occasions! how indecent your tipplings! And next morning the bell rings, and up you must get, losing the best of your sleep, to trudge up and down with yesterday's mud still on your shoes. Were lupines and wild herbs so scarce with you? had the springs ceased to give their wonted supply, that you were brought to such a pass? No, the cause of your captivity is too clear. Not water, not lupines were the object of your desire, but dainty viands and fragrant wines; and your sin has found you out:

you are hooked like a pike by your greedy jaws. We have not far to look for the reward of gluttony. Like a monkey with a collar about its neck, you are kept to make amusement for the company; fancying yourself supremely happy, because you are unstinted in the matter of dried figs. As to freedom and generosity, they are fled, with the memories of Greece, and have left no trace behind them. And would that that were all, the disgrace of falling from freedom to servitude! Would that your employments were not those of a very menial! Consider:

are your duties any lighter than those of a Dromo or a Tibius? As to the studies in which your employer professed an interest when he engaged you, they are nothing to him. Shall an ass affect the lyre? Remove from these men's minds the gold and the silver, with the cares that these involve, and what remains? Pride, luxury, sensuality, insolence, wantonness, ignorance. Consuming must be their desire, doubt it not, for the wisdom of Homer, the eloquence of Demosthenes, the sublimity of Plato!

No, your employer has no need of your services in this direction. On the other hand, you have a long beard and a venerable countenance; the Grecian cloak hangs admirably upon your shoulders, and you are known to be a professor of rhetoric, or literature, or philosophy; it will not be amiss, he thinks, to have such pursuits represented in the numerous retinue that marches before him. It will give him an air of Grecian culture, of liberal curiosity in fact. Friend, friend! your stock-in-trade would seem to be not words of wisdom, but a cloak and a beard. If you would do your duty, therefore, be always well in evidence; begin your unfailing attendance from the early hours of the morning, and never quit his side. Now and again he places a hand upon your shoulder, and mutters some nonsense for the benefit of the passers-by, who are to understand that though he walk abroad the Muses are not forgotten, that in all his comings and goings he can find elegant employment for his mind. Breathless and perspiring, you trot, a pitiable spectacle, at the litter's side; or if he walks—you know what Rome is—, up hill and down dale after him you tramp. While he is paying a call on a friend, you are left outside, where, for lack of a seat, you are fain to take out your book and read standing.

Night finds you hungry and thirsty. You snatch an apology for a bath; and it is midnight or near it before you get to dinner. You are no longer an honoured guest; no longer do you engage the attention of the company. You have retired to make room for some newer capture. Thrust into the most obscure corner, you sit watching the progress of dinner, gnawing in canine sort any bones that come down to you and regaling yourself with hungry zest on such tough mallow-leaves—the wrappers of daintier fare— as may escape the vigilance of those who sit above you. No slight is wanting. You have not so much as an egg to call your own; for there is no reason why you should expect to be treated in the same way as a stranger; that would be absurd. The birds that fall to your lot are not like other birds. Your neighbour gets some plump, luscious affair; you, a poor half-chicken, or lean pigeon, an insult, a positive outrage in poultry. As often as not, an extra guest appears unexpectedly, and the waiter solves the difficulty by removing your share (with the whispered consolation that you are 'one of the family'), and placing it before the new-comer. When the joint, be it pork or venison, is brought in to be carved, let us hope that you stand well with the carver, or you will receive a Promethean helping of 'bones wrapped up in fat.' And the way in which a dish is whisked past you, after remaining with your neighbour till he can eat no more!—what free man would endure it, though he were as innocent of gall as any stag? And I have said nothing yet of the wine. While the other guests are drinking of some rare old vintage, you have vile thick stuff, whose colour you must industriously conceal with the help of a gold or silver cup, lest it should betray the estimation in which the drinker is held. It would be something if you could get enough even of this. Alas! you may call and call:

the waiter is
as one that marketh not.

Many are your grievances; nay, all is one huge grievance. And the climax is reached, when you find yourself eclipsed by some minion, some dancing-master, some vile Alexandrian patterer of Ionic lays. How should you hope to rank with the minister of Love's pleasures, with the stealthy conveyer of billets-doux? You cower shamefaced in your corner, and bewail your hard lot, as well you may; cursing your luck that you have never a smattering of such graceful accomplishments yourself. I believe you wish that *you* could turn love-songs, or sing other men's with a good grace; perceiving as you do what a thing it is to be in request. Nay, you could find it in you to play the wizard's, the fortune-teller's part; to deal in thrones and in millions of money. For these, too, you observe, make their way in the world, and are high in favour. Gladly would you enter on any one of these vocations, rather than be a useless castaway. Alas, even these are beyond you; you lack plausibility. It remains for you to give place to others; to endure neglect, and keep your complaints to yourself.

Nay, more. Should some slave whisper that you alone withheld your praise, when his mistress's favourite danced or played, the neglect may cost you dear. Then let your dry throat be as busy as any thirsty frog's. See to it, that your voice is heard leading the chorus of applause; and time after time, when all else are silent, throw in some studied servile compliment. The situation is not without humour. Hungry as you are, ay, and thirsty into the bargain, you must anoint yourself with oil of gladness, and crown your head with garlands. It reminds one of the offerings made by recent mourners at a tomb. The tomb gets the ointment and the garlands, while the mourners drink and enjoy the feast.

If your patron is of a jealous disposition, and has a young wife or handsome children, and you are not wholly without personal attractions, then beware! you are on dangerous ground. Many are the ears of a king, and many the eyes, that see not the truth only, but ever something over and above the truth, lest they should seem to fail of their office. Imagine yourself, therefore, at a Persian banquet. Keep your eyes downwards, lest a eunuch should catch them resting on one of the concubines. For see, there stands another with his bow ever on the stretch:

one glance at the forbidden object as you raise your cup, and his arrow is through your jaw before you can put it down.

And now dinner is over; you retire, and snatch a little sleep. But at cock-crow you are aroused. 'Wretch! Worm that I am!' you exclaim. 'To sacrifice the pursuits, the society of former days, the placid life wherein sleep was measured by inclination, and my comings and goings were unfettered, and all to precipitate myself bodily into this hideous gulf! And why? What, in God's name, is my glorious recompense? Was there no other way? Could I not have provided for myself better than this, and preserved liberty and free-will into the bargain? Alas! the lion is fast bound in the net. I am haled hither and thither. Pitiable is my lot, where no honour is to be won, no favour to be hoped for. Untaught, unpractised in the arts of flattery, I am pitted against professionals. I am no choice spirit, no jolly companion; to raise a laugh is beyond me. My presence (well do I know it) is a vexation to my patron, and then most when he is in his most gracious mood. He finds me sullen; and how to attune myself to him I know not. If I wear a grim face, I am a sour fellow, scarcely to be endured. If I assume my most cheerful expression, my smiles arouse his contempt and disgust. As well attempt to act a comic part in the mask of tragedy! And what is the end of it all? My present life has been another's:

do I look to have a new life which shall be my own?'

Your soliloquy is interrupted by the bell. The old routine awaits you:

you must trudge, and you must stand; and first anoint your limbs, if you would hold out to the end. Dinner will be the same as ever, and go on as late as ever. The change from all your former habits, the wakeful night, the violent exercise, the exhaustion, are slowly undermining your health at this moment, and preparing you for consumption or colic, for asthma or the delights of gout. However, you hold out in spite of all, though many a time your right place would be in bed. But that would never do:

that looks like shamming, like shirking your work. The result is that you grow as pallid as a man at the point of death.

So much for your city life. And now for an excursion into the country. I will content myself with a single detail. As likely as not it is a wet day. Your turn for the carriage (as might be expected) comes last. You wait and wait, till at last its return is out of the question, and you are squeezed into some vehicle with the cook, or with my lady's *friseur*, without even a proper allowance of straw. I shall make no scruple of relating to you an experience of Thesmopolis the Stoic, which I had from his own mouth; a most amusing incident, and just the sort of thing one might expect to find happening again. He was in the service of a certain wealthy and luxurious lady of quality, whom on one occasion he had to accompany on a journey from Rome. The fun began at once. The philosopher received as his travelling companion a beardless exquisite of the pitch-plastering persuasion, by whom, you may be certain, my lady set great store; his name, she informed the philosopher, was 'Robinetta.' Is not this a promising start?—the grave and reverend Thesmopolis, with his hoary beard (you know what a long, venerable affair it is), side by side with this rouged and painted ogler, whose drooping neck and plucked throat suggested the vulture rather than the robin! 'Twas all that Thesmopolis could do to persuade him not to wear his hair-net; and as it was he had a sad journey of it, with the fellow singing and whistling all the time—I daresay he would have danced there and then, if Thesmopolis had not prevented him. But there was more to come, as you will see. 'Thesmopolis,' cries my lady, calling him to her, 'I have a great favour to ask of you; now please don't say no, and don't wait to be asked twice, there's a good creature.' Of course, he said he would do anything she wished. 'I only ask you, because I know you are to be trusted; you are so good-natured and affectionate! I want you to take my little dog Myrrhina in with you, and see that she wants for nothing. Poor little lady! she is soon to become a mother. These hateful, inattentive servants take no notice of *me* when we are travelling, much less of her. You will be doing me a great kindness, I assure you, in taking charge of her; I am so fond of the sweet little pet!' She prayed and almost wept; and Thesmopolis promised. Imagine the ludicrous picture. The little beast peeping out from beneath the philosophic cloak; within licking distance of that beard, which perhaps still held traces of the thick soup of yesterday; yapping away with its shrill pipe of a voice, as Maltese terriers will; and no doubt taking other liberties, which Thesmopolis did not think worth mentioning. That night at dinner, the exquisite, his fellow traveller, after cracking a passable joke here and there at the expense of the other guests, came to Thesmopolis. 'Of him,' he remarked, 'I have only this to say, that our Stoic has turned Cynic.' According to what I heard, the little animal actually littered in his mantle!

Such are the caprices, nay, the insults, let me rather say, with which the patron gradually breaks the spirit of his dependants. I know myself of an orator, a very free speaker, who was actually ordered to stand up and deliver a speech at table; and a masterly speech it was, trenchant and terse. He received the congratulations of the company on being timed by a *wine*—instead of a *water*-clock; and this affront, it is said, he was content to put up, for the consideration of 8 pounds. But what of that? Wait till you get a patron who has poetical or historical tendencies, and spouts passages of his own works all through dinner:

you must praise, you must flatter, you must devise original compliments for him,—or die in the attempt. Then there are the beaux, the Adonises and Hyacinths, as you must be careful to call them, undeterred by the eighteen inches or so of nose that some of them carry on their faces. Do your praises halt? 'Tis envy, 'tis treason! Away with you, Philoxenus that you are, to Syracusan quarries!—Let them be orators, let them be philosophers, if they will:

what matter for a solecism here and there? Find Attic elegance, find honey of Hymettus in every word; and pronounce it law henceforth, to speak as they speak.

If we had only men to deal with, it would be something:

but there are the women too. For among the objects of feminine ambition is this, of having a scholar or two in their pay, to dance attendance at the litter's side; it adds one more to the list of their adornments, if they can get the reputation of culture and philosophy, of turning a song which will bear comparison with Sappho's. So they too keep their philosopher, their orator, or their *litterateur*; and give him audience—when, think you? Why, at the toilet, by all that is ridiculous, among the rouge-pots and hair-brushes; or else at the dinner-table. They have no leisure at other times. As it is, the philosopher is often interrupted by the entrance of a maid with a billet-doux. Virtue has then to bide her time; for the audience will not be resumed till the gallant has his answer.

At rare intervals, at the Saturnalia or the Feast of Minerva, you will be presented with a sorry cloak, or a worn-out tunic; and a world of ceremony will go to the presentation. The first who gets wind of the great man's intention flies to you with the news of what is in store for you; and the bringer of glad tidings does not go away empty-handed. The next morning a dozen of them arrive, conveying the present, each with his tale of how he spoke up for you, or the hints he threw out, or how he was entrusted with the choice, and chose the best. Not a man of them but departs with your money in his pocket, grumbling that it is no more.

As to that salary, it will be paid to you sixpence at a time, and there will be black looks when you ask for it. Still, you must get it somehow. Ply your patron therefore with flatteries and entreaties, and pay due observance to his steward, and let it be the kind of observance that stewards like best; nor must you forget your kind introducer. You do get something at last; but it all goes to pay the tailor, the doctor, or the shoemaker, and you are left the proud possessor of nothing at all.

Meanwhile, jealousy is rife, and some slander is perhaps working its stealthy way to ears which are predisposed to hear anything to your discredit. For your employer perceives that by this time incessant fatigues have worn you out; you are crippled, you are good for nothing more, and gout is coming on. All the profit that was to be had of you, he has effectually sucked out. Your prime has gone by, your bodily vigour is exhausted, you are a tattered remnant. He begins to look about for a convenient dunghill whereon to deposit you, and for an able-bodied substitute to do your work. You have attempted the honour of one of his minions:

you have been trying to corrupt his wife's maid, venerable sinner that you are!—any accusation will serve. You are gagged and turned out neck and crop into the darkness. Away you go, helpless and destitute, with gout for the cheering companion of your old age. Whatever you once knew, you have unlearnt in all these years:

on the other hand, you have developed a paunch like a balloon; a monster insatiable, inexorable, which has acquired a habit of asking for more, and likes not at all the unlearning process. It is not to be supposed that any one else will give you employment, at your age; you are like an old horse, whose very hide has deteriorated in value. Not to mention that the worst interpretation will be put upon your late dismissal; you will be credited with adultery, or poisoning, or something of that kind. Your accuser, you see, is convincing even in silence; whereas you—you are a loose- principled, unscrupulous *Greek*. That is the character we Greeks bear; and it serves us right; I see excellent grounds for the opinion they have of us. Greek after Greek who enters their service sets up (in default of any other practical knowledge) for wizard or poisoner, and deals in love-charms and evil spells; and these are they who talk of culture, who wear grey beards and philosophic cloaks! When these, who are accounted the best of us, stand thus exposed, when men observe their interested servility, their gross flatteries at table and elsewhere, it is not to be wondered at that we have all fallen under suspicion. Those whom they have cast off, they hate, and seek to make an end of them altogether; arguing, naturally enough, that men who know their secrets, and have seen them in all their nakedness, may divulge many a foible which will not bear the light; and the thought is torment to them. The fact is, that these great men are for all the world like handsomely bound books. Outside are the gilt edges and the purple cover:

and within? a Thyestes feasts upon his own children; an Oedipus commits incest with his mother; a Tereus woos two sisters at once. Such are these human books:

their brilliancy attracts all eyes, but between the purple covers lurks many a horrid tale. Turn over the pages of any one of them, and you find a drama worthy the pen of Sophocles or Euripides:

close the volume—all is gilt edge and exquisite tooling. Well may they hate the confidants of such crimes, and plot their destruction! What if the outcast should take to rehearsing in public the tragedy that he has got by heart?

I am minded to give you, after the manner of Cebes, a life-picture of Dependence; with this before your eyes, you may judge for yourself, whether it is the life for you. I would gladly call in the aid of an Apelles or a Parrhasius, an Aetion or a Euphranor, but no such perfect painters are to be found in these days; I must sketch you the picture in outline as best I can. I begin then with tall golden gates, not set in the plain, but high upon a hill. Long and steep and slippery is the ascent; and many a time when a man looks to reach the top, his foot slips, and he is plunged headlong. Within the gates sits Wealth, a figure all of gold (so at least she seems); most fair, most lovely. Her lover painfully scales the height, and draws near to the door; and that golden sight fills him with amazement. The beautiful woman in gorgeous raiment who now takes him by the hand is Hope. As she leads him in, his spirit is stricken with awe. Hope still shows the way; but two others, Despair and Servitude, now take charge of him, and conduct him to Toil, who grinds the poor wretch down with labour, and at last hands him over to Age. He looks sickly now, and all his colour is gone. Last comes Contempt, and laying violent hands on him drags him into the presence of Despair; it is now time for Hope to take wing and vanish. Naked, potbellied, pale and old, he is thrust forth, not by those golden gates by which he entered, but by some obscure back-passage. One hand covers his nakedness; with the other he would fain strangle himself. Now let Regret meet him without, dropping vain tears and heaping misery on misery,—and my picture is complete.

Examine it narrowly in all its details, and see whether you like the idea of going in at my golden front door, to be expelled ignominiously at the back. And whichever way you decide, remember the words of the wise man:

'Blame not Heaven, but your own choice.'

APOLOGY FOR
'THE DEPENDENT SCHOLAR'

DEAR SABINUS,

I have been guessing how you are likely to have expressed yourself upon reading my essay about dependants. I feel pretty sure you read it all and had a laugh over it; but it is your running and general comment in words that I am trying to piece on to it. If I am any good at divination, this is the sort of thing:

To think that a man can set down such a scathing indictment of the life, and then forget it all, get hold of the other end of the stick, and plunge headlong into such manifest conspicuous slavery! Take Midas, Croesus, golden Pactolus, roll them into one, multiply them, and could they induce him to relinquish the freedom which he has loved and consorted with from a child? He is nearly in the clutches of Aeacus, one foot is on the ferryman's boat, and it is now that he lets himself be dragged submissively about by a golden collar.[26] There is some slight inconsistency between his life and his treatise; the rivers are running up-hill; topsy-turvydom prevails; our recantations are new-fashioned; the first palinodist[27] mended words with words for Helen of Troy; but we spoil words (those words we thought so wise) with deeds.

Such, I imagine, were your inward remarks. And I dare say you will give me some overt advice to the same effect; well, it will not be ill-timed; it will illustrate your friendship, and do you credit as a good man and a philosopher. If I render your part respectably for you, that will do, and we will pay our homage to the God of words;[28] if I fail, you will fill in the deficiency for yourself. There, the stage is ready; I am to hold my tongue, and submit to any necessary carving and cauterizing for my good, and you are to plaster me, and have your scalpel handy, and your iron red-hot. Sabinus takes the word, and thus addresses me:

_My dear friend, this treatise of yours has quite rightly been earning you a fine reputation, from its first delivery before the great audience I had described to me, to its private use by the educated who have consulted and thumbed it since. For indeed it presents the case meritoriously; there is study of detail and experience of life in abundance; your views are the reverse of vague; and above all the book is practically useful, chiefly but not exclusively to the educated whom it might save from an unforeseen slavery. However, your mind is changed; the life you described is now the better; good-bye to freedom; your motto is that contemptible line:

Give me but gain, I'll turn from free to slave.

---

[26] Omitting as a scholium, with Dindorf and Fritzsche, the words:
hoia esti ton tryphonton plousion ta sphingia kai ta kourallia
[27] See *Stesichorus* in Notes.
[28] i.e. Hermes.

Let none hear the lecture from you again, then; see to it that no copy of it comes under the eyes of any one aware of your present life; ask Hermes to bring Lethe-water from below, enough to drug your former hearers; else you will remind us of the Corinthian tale, and your writing, like Bellerophon's, be your own condemnation. I assure you I see no decent defence you can make, at least if your detractors have the humour to commend the independence of the writings while the writer is a slave and a voluntary beast of burden before their eyes.

They will say with some plausibility:

Either the book is some other good man's work, and you a jackdaw strutting in borrowed, plumes; or, if it is really yours, you are a second Salaethus; the Crotoniate legislator made most severe laws against adultery, was much looked up to on the strength of it, and was shortly after taken in adultery with his brother's wife. You are an exact reproduction of Salaethus, they will say; or rather he was not half so bad as you, seeing that he was mastered by passion, as he pleaded in court, and moreover preferred to leap into the flames, like a brave man, when the Crotoniates were moved to compassion and gave him the alternative of exile. The difference between *your* precept and practice is infinitely more ridiculous; you draw a realistic word-picture of that servile life; you pour contempt on the man who runs into the trap of a rich man's house, where a thousand degradations, half of them self-inflicted, await him; and then in extreme old age, when you are on the border between life and death, you take this miserable servitude upon you and make a sort of circus exhibition of your chains. The conspicuousness of your position will only make the more ridiculous that contrast between your book and your life.

But I need not beat my brains for phrases of reprobation; there is one good enough in a noble tragedy:

Wisdom begins at home; no wisdom, else.

And your censors will find no lack of illustrations against you; some will compare you to the tragic actor; on the stage he is Agamemnon or Creon or great Heracles; but off it, stripped of his mask, he is just Polus or Aristodemus, a hireling liable to be hissed off, or even whipped on occasion, at the pleasure of the audience. Others will say you have had the experience of Queen Cleopatra's monkey:

the docile creature used to dance in perfect form and time, and was much admired for the regularity and decorum of its movements, adapted to the voices and instruments of a bridal chorus; alas, one day it spied a fig or almond a little way off on the ground; flutes and measures and steps were all forgotten, the mask was far off in several pieces, and there was he chewing his find.

You, they will say, are the author (for 'actor' would understate the case) who has laid down the laws of noble conduct; and no sooner is the lump of figs presented than the monkey is revealed; your lips are the lips of a philosopher, and your heart is quite other; it is no injustice to say that those sentiments for which you claim admiration have 'wetted your lips, and left your palate dry.' You have not had to wait long for retribution; you spoke unadvisedly in scorn of human needs; and, this little while after, behold you making public renunciation of your freedom! Surely Nemesis was standing behind your back as you drank in the flattering tributes to your superiority; did she not smile in her divine fore-knowledge of the impending change, and mark how you forgot to propitiate her before you assailed the victims whom fortune's mutability had reduced to such courses?

Now I want you to imagine a rhetorician writing on the theme that Aeschines, after his indictment of Timarchus, was himself proved guilty by eyewitnesses of similar iniquity; would, or would not, the amusement of the audience be heightened by the fact that he had got Timarchus punished for offences excused by youth, whereas he was himself an old man at the time of his own guilt? Why, you are like the quack who offered a cough-mixture which was to cure instantaneously, and could hardly get the promise out for coughing._

Yes, Sabinus, and there is plenty more of the same sort for an accuser like you to urge; the subject is all handles; you can take hold of it anywhere. I have been looking about for my best line of defence. Had I better turn craven, face right-about, confess my sin, and have recourse to the regular plea of Chance, Fate, Necessity? Shall I humbly beseech my critics to pardon me, remembering that nothing is in a man's own choice— we are led by some stronger power, one of the three I mentioned, probably, and are not true agents but guiltless altogether, whatever we say or do? Or will you tell me this might do well enough for one of the common herd, but you cannot have *me* sheltering myself so? *I* must not brief Homer; it will not serve me to plead:

No mortal man e'er yet escaped his fate;
nor again,
His thread was spun, then when his mother bare him.

On the other hand, I might avoid that plea as wanting in plausibility, and say that I did not accept this association under the temptation of money or any prospects of that kind, but in pure admiration of the wisdom, strength, and magnanimity of my patron's character, which inspired the wish to partake his activity. But I fear I should only have brought on myself the additional imputation of flattery. It would be a case of 'one nail drives out one nail,' and this time the one left in would be the bigger; for flattery is the most servile, and consequently reckoned the worst, of all vices.

Both these pleas, then, being excluded, what is left me but to confess that I have no sound defence to make? I have indeed one anchor yet aboard:

I may whine over age and ill health, and their attendant poverty, from which a man will purchase escape at any cost. The situation tempts me to send an invitation to Euripides's *Medea*:

213

will she come and recite certain lines of hers on my behalf, kindly making the slight changes needed?—

Too well I know how monstrous is the deed;
My poverty, but not my will, consents.

And every one knows the place in Theognis, whether I quote it or not, where he approves of people's flinging themselves to the unplumbed deep from sky-pointing crags, if one may be quit of poverty that way.

That about exhausts the obvious lines of defence; and none of them is very promising. But never fear, my friend, I am not going to try any of them. May never Argos be so hard put to it that Cyllarabis must be sown! nor ever I be in such straits for a tolerable defence as to be driven upon these evasions! No, I only ask you to consider the vast difference between being a hireling in a rich man's house, where one is a slave, and must put up with all that is described in my book—between that and entering the public service, doing one's best as an administrator, and taking the Emperor's pay for it. Go fully into the matter; take the two things separately and have a good look at them; you will find that they are two octaves apart, as the musical people say; the two lives are about as like each other as lead is to silver, bronze to gold, an anemone to a rose, a monkey to a man; there is pay, and there is subordination, in each case; but the essence of the two things is utterly different. In one we have manifest slavery; the new-comers who accept the terms are barely distinguishable from the human chattels a man has bought or bred; but persons who have the management of public business, and give their services to states and nations, are not to have insinuations aimed at them just because they are paid; that single point of resemblance is not to level them down to the others. If that is to be the principle, we had better do away with all such offices at once; governors of whole provinces, prefects of cities, commanders of legions and armies, will all fall under the same condemnation; for they are paid. But of course everything is not to be upset to suit a single case; all who receive pay are not to be lumped together.

It is all a mistake; I never said that all drawers of salaries lived a degraded life; I only pitied those domestic slaves who have been caught by compliments on their culture. My position, you see, is entirely different; my private relations are as they were before, though in a public capacity I am now an active part of the great Imperial machine. If you care to inquire, you will find that my charge is not the least important in the government of Egypt. I control the cause-list, see that trials are properly conducted, keep a record of all proceedings and pleas, exercise censorship over forensic oratory, and edit the Emperor's rescripts with a view to their official and permanent preservation in the most lucid, accurate, and genuine form. My salary comes from no private person, but from the Emperor; and it is considerable, amounting to many hundreds. In the future too there is before *me* the brilliant prospect of attaining in due course to a governorship or other distinguished employment.

214

Accordingly I am now going to throw off reserve, come to grips with the charge against me, and prove my case *a fortiori*. I tell you that nobody does anything for nothing; you may point to people in high places—as high as you like; the Emperor himself is paid. I am not referring to the taxes and tribute which flow in annually from subjects; the chief item in the Emperor's pay is panegyrics, world-wide fame, and grateful devotion; the statues, temples, and consecrated ground which their subjects bestow upon them, what are these but pay for the care and forethought which they apply to public policy and improvements? To compare small things with great, if you will begin at the top of the heap and work down through the grains of which it is composed, you will find that we inferior ones differ from the superior in point of size, but all are wage-earners together.

If the law I laid down had been that no one should do anything, I might fairly have been accused of transgressing it; but as my book contains nothing of the sort, and as goodness consists in doing good, what better use can you make of yourself than if you join forces with your friends in the cause of progress, come out into the open, and let men see that you are loyal and zealous and careful of your trust, not what Homer calls a vain cumberer of the earth?

But before all, my critics are to remember that in me they will be criticizing not a wise man (if indeed there is such a person on earth), but one of the common people, one who has indeed practised rhetoric and won some little reputation therein, but has never been trained up to the perfect virtue of the really great. Well, I may surely be forgiven for that; if any one ever did come up to the ideal of the wise man, it has not been my fortune to meet him. And I confess further that I should be disappointed if I found you criticizing my present life; you knew me long ago when I was making a handsome income out of the public profession of rhetoric; for on that Atlantic tour of yours which included Gaul, you found me numbered among those teachers who could command high fees. Now, my friend, you have my defence; I am exceedingly busy, but could not be indifferent to securing *your* vote of acquittal; as for others, let them all denounce me with one voice if they will; on them I shall waste no more words than, What cares Hippoclides?

A SLIP OF THE TONGUE IN SALUTATION [29]

If a poor mortal has some difficulty in guarding against that spirit of mischief which dwells aloft, he has still more in clearing himself of the absurd

---

[29] This piece, which even in the Greek fails to convince us that Asclepius heard the prayer with which it concludes, is still flatter in English, because we have no words of salutation which correspond at once in etymological meaning and in conventional usage to the Greek. The English reader who cares to understand a piece so little worth his attention, will obligingly bear in mind that the Greek word represented here by Joy and Rejoice roughly answered in Lucian's time to our Good- morning and How do you do, as well as to the epistolary My dear———; while that represented by Hail or Health did the work of Good-night, Good-bye, Farewell, and (in letters) Yours truly.

consequences when that spirit trips him up. I am in both predicaments at once; coming to make you my morning salutation, which should have taken the orthodox form of Rejoice, I bade you, in a very choice fit of absent-mindedness, Be healthy—a good enough wish in its way, but a little untimely and unconnected with that early hour. I at once went moist and red, not quite aware whether I was on my head or my heels; some of the company took me for a lunatic, no doubt, some thought I was in my second childhood, some that I had not quite got over my last night's wine—though you yourself were the pink of good manners, not showing your consciousness of the slip by any ghost of a smile. It occurred to me to write to myself a little something in the way of comfort, and so modify the distress my blunder gave me—prove to myself that it was not absolutely unpardonable for an old man to transgress etiquette so flagrantly before so many witnesses. As to apology, there could be no occasion for that, when one's slip had resulted in so well- omened a wish.

I began to write expecting my task to be very difficult, but found plenty of material as I went on. I will defer it, however, till I have cleared the way with a few necessary remarks on the three forms—Rejoice or Joy, Prosper or Prosperity, Hail or Health. Joy is a very ancient greeting; but it was not confined to the morning, or the first meeting. They did use it when they first saw one another:

Joy to thee, Lord of this Tirynthian land!
But again at the moment when the wine succeeded to the meal:

Achilles, Joy! We lack not fair repast—
so says Odysseus discharging his embassy. And even at parting:

Joy be with you! And henceforth know me God,
No longer mortal man.
In fact the apostrophe was not limited to any particular season, as now to the morning alone; indeed they used it on gloomy, nay, on the most lamentable occasions; in Euripides, Polynices ends his life with the words,
Joy with you! for the darkness closes on me.

Nor was it necessarily significative of friendliness; it could express hatred and the determination to see no more of another. To wish much joy to, was a regular form for ceasing to care about.

The modern use of the word dates back to Philippides the dispatch-runner. Bringing the news of Marathon, he found the archons seated, in suspense regarding the issue of the battle. 'Joy, we win!' he said, and died upon his message, breathing his last in the word Joy. The earliest letter beginning with it is that in which Cleon the Athenian demagogue, writing from Sphacteria, sends the good news of his victory and capture of Spartans at that place. However, later than that we find Nicias writing from Sicily and keeping to the older custom of coming to business at once with no such introduction.

216

Now the admirable Plato, no bad authority on such matters, would have us reject the salutation Joy altogether; it is a mean wish, wanting in seriousness, according to him; his substitute is Prosperity, which stands for a satisfactory condition both of body and soul; in a letter to Dionysius, he reproves him for commencing a hymn to Apollo with Joy, which he maintains is unworthy of the Pythian, and not fit even for men of any discretion, not to mention Gods.

Pythagoras the mystic has vouchsafed us no writings of his own; but we may infer from his disciples, Ocellus the Lucanian and Archytas, for instance, that he headed his letters neither with Joy nor Prosperity, but recommended beginning with Hail. At any rate all the Pythagoreans in writing to one another (when their tone is serious, that is) started with wishing Health, which they took to be the prime need of soul and body alike, and to include all human blessings. The Pentagram[30], that interlaced triple triangle which served them as a sort of password, they called by the name Health. They argued that Health included Joy and Prosperity, but that neither of those two was coextensive with Health. Some of them gave to the Quaternion, which is their most solemn oath, and sums their perfect number, the name of Beginning of Health. Philolaus might be quoted.

But I need hardly go so far back. Epicurus assuredly rejoiced in joy— pleasure was the chief Good in his eyes; yet in his most earnest letters (which are not very numerous), and in those to his most intimate friends, he starts with Hail. And in tragedy and the old comedy you will constantly find it used quite at the beginning. You remember,

Hail to thee, joy be thine—

which puts health before rejoicing clearly enough. And says Alexis:

All hail, my lord; after long time thou comest.
Again Achaeus:

I come in sorry plight, yet wish thee health.
And Philemon:

   Health first I ask, and next prosperity,
Joy thirdly, and to owe not any man.

As for the writer of the drinking-song mentioned in Plato, what says he?—'Best is health, and second beauty, and third wealth'; joy he never so much as names. I need hardly adduce the trite saw:

   Chief of them that blessings give,
Health, with thee I mean to live.

But, if Health is chief, her gift, which is the enjoyment of health, should rank before other Goods.

---

[30] See *Pythagoras* in Notes.

I could multiply these examples by the thousand from poets, historians, philosophers, who give Health the place of honour; but you will not require any such childish pedantry of me, wiping out my original offence by another; I shall do better to add a historical anecdote or two which occur to me as relevant.

Eumenes of Cardia, writing to Antipater, states that just before the battle of Issus, Hephaestion came at dawn into Alexander's tent. Either in absence of mind and confusion like mine, or else under a divine impulse, he gave the evening salutation like me—'Hail, sire; 'tis time we were at our posts.' All present were confounded at the irregularity, and Hephaestion himself was like to die of shame, when Alexander said, 'I take the omen; it is a promise that we shall come back safe from battle.'

Antiochus Soter, about to engage the Galatians, dreamed that Alexander stood over him and told him to give his men the password Health; and with this word it was that he won that marvellous victory.

Ptolemy, the son of Lagus, in a letter to Seleucus, just reversed the usual order, bidding him Hail at the beginning, and adding Rejoice at the end instead of wishing him Health; this is recorded by Dionysodorus, the collector of his letters.

The case of Pyrrhus the Epirot is well worth mention; as a general he was only second to Alexander, and he experienced a thousand vicissitudes of fortune. In all his prayers, sacrifices, and offerings, he never asked for victory or increase of his royal dignity, for fame or excessive wealth; his whole prayer was always in one word, Health; as long as he had that, he thought all else would come of itself. And it was true wisdom, in my opinion; he remembered that all other good things are worthless, if health is wanting.

Oh, certainly (says some one); but we have assigned each form to its proper place by this time; and if you disregard that—even though there was no bad meaning in what you did say—you cannot fairly claim to have made no mistake; it is as though one should put a helmet on the shins, or greaves on the head. My dear sir (I reply), your simile would go on all fours if there were any season at all which did not require health; but in point of fact it is needed in the morning and at noonday and at night —especially by busy rulers like you Romans, to whom physical condition is so important. And again, the man who gives you Joy is only beginning auspiciously; it is no more than a prayer; whereas he who bids you Hail is doing you a practical service in reminding you of the means to health; his is more than a prayer, it is a precept.

Why, in that book of instructions which you all receive from the Emperor, is not the first recommendation to take care of your health? Quite rightly; that is the condition precedent of efficiency. Moreover, if I know any Latin, you yourselves, in *returning* a salutation, constantly use the equivalent of Health.

However, all this does not mean that I have deliberately abandoned Rejoice and substituted Hail for it. I admit that it was quite unintentional; I am not so foolish as to innovate like that, and exchange the regular formulae.

No, I only thank Heaven that my stumble had such very fortunate results, landing me in a better position than I had designed; may it not be that Health itself, or Asclepius, inspired me to give you this promise of health? How else should it have befallen me? In the course of a long life I have never been guilty of such a confusion before.

Or, if I may not have recourse to the supernatural, it is no wonder that my extreme desire to be known to you for good should so confuse me as to work the contrary effect. Possibly, too, one might be robbed of one's presence of mind by the crowd of military persons pushing for precedence, or treating the salutation ceremony in their cavalier fashion.

As to yourself, I feel sure that, however others may have referred it to stupidity, ignorance, or lunacy, you took it as the sign of a modest, simple, unspoiled, unsophisticated soul. Absolute confidence in such matters comes dangerously near audacity and impudence. My first wish would be to make no such blunder; my second that, if I did, the resulting omen should be good.

There is a story told of the first Augustus. He had given a correct legal decision, which acquitted a maligned person of a most serious charge. The latter expressed his gratitude in a loud voice, thus:

—'I thank your majesty for this bad and inequitable verdict.' Augustus's attendants raged, and were ready to tear the man to pieces. But the Emperor restrained them; 'Never mind what he said; it is what he meant that matters.' That was Augustus's view. Well, take my meaning, and it was good; or take my word, and it was auspicious.

And now that I have got to this point, I have reason to fear that I may be suspected of having made the slip on purpose, leading up to this apology. O God of health, only grant me that the quality of my piece may justify the notion that I wanted no more than a peg whereon to hang an essay!

HERMOTIMUS, OR THE RIVAL PHILOSOPHIES

Lycinus. Hermotimus

Ly. Good morning, Hermotimus; I guess by your book and the pace you are going at that you are on your way to lecture, and a little late. You were conning over something as you walked, your lips working and muttering, your hand flung out this way and that as you got a speech into order in your mind; you were doubtless inventing one of your crooked questions, or pondering some tricky problem; never a vacant mind, even in the streets; always on the stretch and in earnest, bent on advancing in your studies.

Her. I admit the impeachment; I was running over the details of what he said in yesterday's lecture. One must lose no chance, you know; the Coan doctor[31] spoke so truly:

ars longa, vita brevis. And what be referred to was only physic—a simpler matter. As to philosophy, not only will you never attain it, however long you study, unless you are wide awake all the time, contemplating it with intense eager gaze; the stake is so tremendous, too,—whether you shall rot miserably with the vulgar herd, or be counted among philosophers and reach Happiness.

Ly. A glorious prize, indeed! however, you cannot be far off it now, if one may judge by the time you have given to philosophy, and the extraordinary vigour of your long pursuit. For twenty years now, I should say, I have watched you perpetually going to your professors, generally bent over a book taking notes of past lectures, pale with thought and emaciated in body. I suspect you find no release even in your dreams, you are so wrapped up in the thing. With all this you must surely get hold of Happiness soon, if indeed you have not found it long ago without telling us.

Her. Alas, Lycinus, I am only just beginning to get an inkling of the right way. Very far off dwells Virtue, as Hesiod says, and long and steep and rough is the way thither, and travellers must bedew it with sweat.

Ly. And you have not yet sweated and travelled enough?

Her. Surely not; else should I have been on the summit, with nothing left between me and bliss; but I am only starting yet, Lycinus.

Ly. Ah, but Hesiod, your own authority, tells us, Well begun is half done; so we may safely call you half-way by this time.

Her. Not even there yet; that would indeed have been much.

Ly. Where *shall* we put you, then?

Her. Still on the lower slopes, just making an effort to get on; but it is slippery and rough, and needs a helping hand.

Ly. Well, your master can give you that; from his station on the summit, like Zeus in Homer with his golden cord, he can let you down his discourse,

---

[31] Hippocrates

and therewith haul and heave you up to himself and to the Virtue which he has himself attained this long time.

Her. The very picture of what he is doing; if it depended on him alone, I should have been hauled up long ago; it is my part that is still wanting.

Ly. You must be of good cheer and keep a stout heart; gaze at the end of your climb and the Happiness at the top, and remember that he is working with you. What prospect does he hold out? when are you to be up? does he think you will be on the top next year—by the Great Mysteries, or the Panathenaea, say?

Her. Too soon, Lycinus.

Ly. By next Olympiad, then?

Her. All too short a time, even that, for habituation to Virtue and attainment of Happiness.

Ly. Say two Olympiads, then, for an outside estimate. You may fairly be found guilty of laziness, if you cannot get it done by then; the time would allow you three return trips from the Pillars of Heracles to India, with a margin for exploring the tribes on the way instead of sailing straight and never stopping. How much higher and more slippery, pray, is the peak on which your Virtue dwells than that Aornos crag which Alexander stormed in a few days?

Her. There is no resemblance, Lycinus; this is not a thing, as you conceive it, to be compassed and captured quickly, though ten thousand Alexanders were to assault it; in that case, the sealers would have been legion. As it is, a good number begin the climb with great confidence, and do make progress, some very little indeed, others more; but when they get half-way, they find endless difficulties and discomforts, lose heart, and turn back, panting, dripping, and exhausted. But those who endure to the end reach the top, to be blessed thenceforth with wondrous days, looking down from their height upon the ants which are the rest of mankind.

Ly. Dear me, what tiny things you make us out—not so big as the Pygmies even, but positively grovelling on the face of the earth. I quite understand it; your thoughts are up aloft already. And we, the common men that walk the earth, shall mingle you with the Gods in our prayers; for you are translated above the clouds, and gone up whither you have so long striven.

Her. If but that ascent might be, Lycinus! but it is far yet.

Ly. But you have never told me *how* far, in terms of time.

Her. No; for I know not precisely myself. My guess is that it will not be more than twenty years; by that time I shall surely be on the summit.

Ly. Mercy upon us, you take long views!

Her. Ay; but, as the toil, so is the reward.

Ly. That may be; but about these twenty years—have you your master's promise that you will live so long? is he prophet as well as philosopher? or is it a soothsayer or Chaldean expert that you trust? such things are known to them, I understand. You would never, of course, if there were any uncertainty of your life's lasting to the Virtue-point, slave and toil night and day like this; why, just as you were close to the top, your fate might come upon you, lay hold of you by the heel, and lug you down with your hopes unfulfilled.

Her. God forbid! these are words of ill omen, Lycinus; may life be granted me, that I may grow wise, and have if it be but one day of Happiness!

Ly. For all these toils will you be content with your one day?

Her. Content? yes, or with the briefest moment of it.

Ly. But is there indeed Happiness up there—and worth all the pains? How can you tell? You have never been up yourself.

Her. I trust my master's word; and he knows well; is he not on the topmost height?

Ly. Oh, do tell me what he says about it; what is Happiness like? wealth, glory, pleasures incomparable?

Her. Hush, friend! all these have nought to do with the Virtuous life.

Ly. Well, if these will not do, what *are* the good things he offers to those who carry their course right through?

Her. Wisdom, courage, true beauty, justice, full and firm knowledge of all things as they are; but wealth and glory and pleasure and all bodily things— these a man strips off and abandons before he mounts up, like Heracles burning on Mount Oeta before deification; he too cast off whatever of the human he had from his mother, and soared up to the Gods with his divine part pure and unalloyed, sifted by the fire. Even so those I speak of are purged by the philosophic fire of all that deluded men count admirable, and reaching the summit have Happiness with never a thought of wealth and glory and pleasure—except to smile at any who count them more than phantoms.

Ly. By Heracles (and his death on Oeta), they quit themselves like men, and have their reward, it seems. But there is one thing I should like to know:

are they allowed to come down from their elevation sometimes, and have a taste of what they left behind them? or when they have once got up, must they stay there, conversing with Virtue, and smiling at wealth and glory and pleasure?

Her. The latter, assuredly; more than that, a man once admitted of Virtue's company will never be subject to wrath or fear or desire any more; no, nor can he feel pain, nor any such sensation.

Ly. Well, but—if one might dare to say what one thinks—but no—let me keep a good tongue in my head—it were irreverent to pry into what wise men do.

Her. Nay, nay; let me know your meaning.

Ly. Dear friend, I have not the courage.

Her. Out with it, my good fellow; we are alone.

Ly. Well, then—most of your account I followed and accepted—how they grow wise and brave and just, and the rest—indeed I was quite fascinated by it; but then you went on to say they despised wealth and glory and pleasure; well, just there (quite between ourselves, you know) I was pulled up; I thought

222

of a scene t'other day with—shall I tell you whom? Perhaps we can do without a name?

Her. No, no; we must have that too.

Ly. Your own professor himself, then,—a person to whom all respect is due, surely, not to mention his years.

Her. Well?

Ly. You know the Heracleot, quite an old pupil of his in philosophy by this time—red-haired—likes an argument?

Her. Yes; Dion, he is called.

Ly. Well, I suppose he had not paid up punctually; anyhow the other day the old man haled him before the magistrate, with a halter made of his own coat; he was shouting and fuming, and if some friends had not come up and got the young man out of his hands, he would have bitten off his nose, he was in such a temper.

Her. Ah, *he* is a bad character, always an unconscionable time paying his debts. There are plenty of others who owe the professor money, and he has never treated any of them so; they pay him his interest punctually.

Ly. Not so fast; what in the world does it matter to him, if they do not pay up? he is purified by philosophy, and has no further need of the cast clothes of Oeta.

Her. Do you suppose his interest in such things is selfish? no, but he has little ones; his care is to save them from indigence.

Ly. Whereas he ought to have brought them up to Virtue too, and let them share his inexpensive Happiness.

Her. Well, I have no time to argue it, Lycinus; I must not be late for lecture, lest in the end I find myself left behind.

Ly. Don't be afraid, my duteous one; to-day is a holiday; I can save you the rest of your walk.

Her. What do you mean?

Ly. You will not find him just now, if the notice is to be trusted; there was a tablet over the door announcing in large print, No meeting this day. I hear he dined yesterday with the great Eucrates, who was keeping his daughter's birthday. He talked a good deal of philosophy over the wine, and lost his temper a little with Euthydemus the Peripatetic; they were debating the old Peripatetic objections to the Porch. His long vocal exertions (for it was midnight before they broke up) gave him a bad headache, with violent perspiration. I fancy he had also drunk a little too much, toasts being the order of the day, and eaten more than an old man should. When he got home, he was very ill, they said, just managed to check and lock up carefully the slices of meat which he had conveyed to his servant at table, and then, giving orders that he was not at home, went to sleep, and has not waked since. I overheard Midas his man telling this to some of his pupils; there were a number of them coming away.

Her. Which had the victory, though, he or Euthydemus—if Midas said anything about that?

Ly. Why, at first, I gathered, it was very even between them; but you Stoics had it in the end, and your master was much too hard for him. Euthydemus did not even get off whole; he had a great cut on his head. He was pretentious, insisted on proving his point, would not give in, and proved a hard nut to crack; so your excellent professor, who had a goblet as big as Nestor's in his hand, brought this down on him as he lay within easy reach, and the victory was his.

Her. Good; so perish all who will not yield to their betters!

Ly. Very reasonable, Hermotimus; what was Euthydemus thinking of, to irritate an old man who is purged of wrath and master of his passions, when he had such a heavy goblet in his hand?

But we have time to spare—you might tell a friend like me the story of your start in philosophy; then I might perhaps, if it is not too late, begin now and join your school; you are my friends; you will not be exclusive?

Her. If only you would, Lycinus! you will soon find out how much you are superior to the rest of men. I do assure you, you will think them all children, you will be so much wiser.

Ly. Enough for me, if after twenty years of it I am where you are now.

Her. Oh, I was about your age when I started on philosophy; I was forty; and you must be about that.

Ly. Just that; so take and lead me on the same way; that is but right. And first tell me—do you allow learners to criticize, if they find difficulties in your doctrines, or must juniors abstain from that?

Her. Why, yes, they must; but *you* shall have leave to ask questions and criticize; you will learn easier that way.

Ly. I thank you for it, Hermotimus, by your name-God Hermes.

Now, is there only one road to philosophy—the Stoic way? they tell me there are a great many other philosophers; is that so?

Her. Certainly—Peripatetics, Epicureans, Platonists, followers of Diogenes, Antisthenes, Pythagoras, and more yet.

Ly. Quite so; numbers of them. Now, are their doctrines the same, or different?

Her. Entirely different.

Ly. But the truth, I presume, is bound to be in one of them, and not in all, as they differ?

Her. Certainly.

Ly. Then, as you love me, answer this:

when you first went in pursuit of philosophy, you found many gates wide open; what induced you to pass the others by, and go in at the Stoic gate? Why did you assume that that was the only true one, which would set you on the straight road to Virtue, while the rest all opened on blind alleys? What was the test you applied *then*? Please abolish your present self, the self which is now instructed, or half-instructed, and better able to distinguish between good and bad than we outsiders, and answer in your then character of a layman, with no advantage over me as I am now.

Her. I cannot tell what you are driving at.

Ly. Oh, there is nothing recondite about it. There are a great many philosophers—let us say Plato, Aristotle, Antisthenes, and your spiritual fathers, Chrysippus, Zeno, and all the rest of them; what was it that induced you, leaving the rest alone, to pick out the school you did from among them all, and pin your philosophic faith to it? Were you favoured like Chaerephon with a revelation from Apollo? Did he tell you the Stoics were the best of men, and send you to their school? I dare say he recommends different philosophers to different persons, according to their individual needs?

Her. Nothing of the kind, Lycinus; I never consulted him upon it.

Ly. Why? was it not a *dignus vindice nodus?* or were you confident in your own unaided discrimination?

Her. Why, yes; I was.

Ly. Then this must be my first lesson from you—how one can decide out of hand which is the best and the true philosophy to be taken, and the others left.

Her. I will tell you:

I observed that it attracted most disciples, and thence inferred that it was superior.

Ly. Give me figures; how many more of them than of Epicureans, Platonists, Peripatetics? Of course you took a sort of show of hands.

Her. Well, no; I didn't count; I just guessed.

Ly. Now, now! you are not teaching, but hoaxing me; judge by guess work and impression, indeed, on a thing of this importance! You are hiding the truth.

Her. Well, that was not my only way; every one told me the Epicureans were sensual and self-indulgent, the Peripatetics avaricious and contentious, the Platonists conceited and vain; about the Stoics, on the contrary, many said they had fortitude and an open mind; he who goes their way, I heard, was the true king and millionaire and wise man, alone and all in one.

Ly. And, of course, it was other people who so described them; you would not have taken their own word for their excellences.

Her. Certainly not; it was others who said it.

Ly. Not their rivals, I suppose?

Her. Oh, no.

Ly. Laymen, then?

Her. Just so.

Ly. There you are again, cheating me with your irony; you take me for a blockhead, who will believe that an intelligent person like Hermotimus, at the age of forty, would accept the word of laymen about philosophy and philosophers, and make his own selection on the strength of what they said.

Her. But you see, Lycinus, I did not depend on their judgement entirely, but on my own too. I saw the Stoics going about with dignity, decently dressed and groomed, ever with a thoughtful air and a manly countenance, as far from effeminacy as from the utter repulsive negligence of the Cynics, bearing themselves, in fact, like moderate men; and every one admits that moderation is right.

Ly. Did you ever see them behaving like your master, as I described him to you just now? Lending money and clamouring for payment, losing their tempers in philosophic debates, and making other exhibitions of themselves? Or perhaps these are trifles, so long as the dress is decent, the beard long, and the hair close-cropped? We are provided for the future, then, with an infallible rule and balance, guaranteed by Hermotimus? It is by appearance and walk and haircutting that the best men are to be distinguished; and whosoever has not these marks, and is not solemn and thoughtful, shall be condemned and rejected?

Nay, do not play with me like this; you want to see whether I shall catch you at it.

Her. Why do you say that?

Ly. Because, my dear sir, this appearance test is one for statues; *their* decent orderly attire has it easily over the Stoics, because Phidias or Alcamenes or Myron designed them to be graceful. However, granting as much as you like that these are the right tests, what is a blind man to do, if he wants to take up philosophy? how is he to find the man whose principles are right, when he cannot see his appearance or gait?

Her. I am not teaching the blind, Lycinus; I have nothing to do with them.

Ly. Ah, but, my good sir, there ought to have been some universal criterion, in a matter of such great and general use. Still, if you will have it so, let the blind be excluded from philosophy, as they cannot see—though, by the way, they are just the people who most need philosophy to console them for their misfortune; but now, the people who *can* see—give them the utmost possible acuity of vision, and what can they detect of the spiritual qualities from this external shell?

What I mean is this:

was it not from admiration of their *spirit* that you joined them, expecting to have your own spirit purified?

Her. Assuredly.

Ly. How could you possibly discern the true philosopher from the false, then, by the marks you mentioned? It is not the way of such qualities to come out like that; they are hidden and secret; they are revealed only under long and patient observation, in talk and debate and the conduct they inspire. You have probably heard of Momus's indictment of Hephaestus; if not, you shall have it now. According to the myth, Athene, Posidon, and Hephaestus had a match in inventiveness. Posidon made a bull, Athene planned a house, Hephaestus

226

constructed a man; when they came before Momus, who was to judge, he examined their productions; I need not trouble you with his criticisms of the other two; but his objection to the man, and the fault he found with Hephaestus, was this:

he should have made a window in his chest, so that, when it was opened, his thoughts and designs, his truth or falsehood, might have been apparent. Momus must have been blear-eyed, to have such ideas about men; but you have sharper eyes than Lynceus, and pierce through the chest to what is inside; all is patent to you, not merely any man's wishes and sentiments, but the comparative merits of any pair.

Her. You trifle, Lycinus. I made a pious choice, and do not repent it; that is enough for me.

Ly. And will you yet make a mystery of it to your friend, and let him be lost with the vulgar herd?

Her. Why, you will not accept anything I say.

Ly. On the contrary, my good sir, it is you who will not say anything I can accept. Well, as you refuse me your confidence, and are so jealous of my becoming a philosopher and your equal, I must even do my best to find out the infallible test and learn to choose safely for myself. And you may listen, if you like.

Her. That I will, Lycinus; you will very likely hit on some good idea.

Ly. Then attend, and do not mock me, if my inquiry is quite unscientific; it is all I can do, as you, who know better, will not give me any clearer light.

I conceive Virtue, then, under the figure of a State whose citizens are happy—as your professor, who is one of them, phrases it,—absolutely wise, all of them brave, just, and self-controlled, hardly distinguishable, in fact, from Gods. All sorts of things that go on here, such as robbery, assault, unfair gain, you will never find attempted there, I believe; their relations are all peace and unity; and this is quite natural, seeing that none of the things which elsewhere occasion strife and rivalry, and prompt men to plot against their neighbours, so much as come in their way at all. Gold, pleasures, distinctions, they never regard as objects of dispute; they have banished them long ago as undesirable elements. Their life is serene and blissful, in the enjoyment of legality, equality, liberty, and all other good things.

Her. Well, Lycinus? Must not all men yearn to belong to a State like that, and never count the toil of getting there, nor lose heart over the time it takes? Enough that one day they will arrive, and be naturalized, and given the franchise.

Ly. In good truth, Hermotimus, we should devote all our efforts to this, and neglect everything else; we need pay little heed to any claims of our earthly country; we should steel our hearts against the clingings and cryings of children or parents, if we have them; it is well if we can induce them to go with us; but, if they will not or cannot, shake them off and march straight for the city of bliss, leaving your coat in their hands, if they lay hold of it to keep you back, in your hurry to get there; what matter for a coat? You will be admitted there without one.

I remember hearing a description of it all once before from an old man, who urged me to go there with him. He would show me the way, enroll me when I got there, introduce me to his own circles, and promise me a share in the universal Happiness. But I was stiff-necked, in my youthful folly (it was some fifteen years ago); else might I have been in the outskirts, nay, haply at the very gates, by now. Among the noteworthy things he told me, I seem to remember these:

all the citizens are aliens and foreigners, not a native among them; they include numbers of barbarians, slaves, cripples, dwarfs, and poor; in fact any one is admitted; for their law does not associate the franchise with income, with shape, size, or beauty, with old or brilliant ancestry; these things are not considered at all; any one who would be a citizen needs only understanding, zeal for the right, energy, perseverance, fortitude and resolution in facing all the trials of the road; whoever proves his possession of these by persisting till he reaches the city is *ipso facto* a full citizen, regardless of his antecedents. Such distinctions as superior and inferior, noble and common, bond and free, simply do not exist there, even in name.

Her. There, now; you see I am not wasting my pains on trifles; I yearn to be counted among the citizens of that fair and happy State.

Ly. Why, your yearning is mine too; there is nothing I would sooner pray for. If the city had been near at hand and plain for all to see, be assured I would never have doubted, nor needed prompting; I would have gone thither and had my franchise long ago; but as you tell me—you and your bard Hesiod—that it is set exceeding far off, one must find out the way to it, and the best guide. You agree?

Her. Of course that is the only thing to do.

Ly. Now, so far as promises and professions go, there is no lack of guides; there are numbers of them waiting about, all representing themselves as from there. But instead of one single road there seem to be many different and inconsistent ones. North and South, East and West, they go; one leads through meadows and vegetation and shade, and is well watered and pleasant, with never a stumbling-block or inequality; another is rough and rocky, threatening heat and drought and toil. Yet all these are supposed to lead to the one city, though they take such different directions.

That is where my difficulty lies; whichever of them I try, there is sure to be a most respectable person stationed just at the entrance, with a welcoming hand and an exhortation to go his way; each of them says he is the only one who knows the straight road; his rivals are all mistaken, have never been themselves, nor learnt the way from competent guides. I go to his neighbour, and he gives the same assurances about *his* way, abusing the other respectable persons; and so the next, and the next, and the next. This multiplicity and dissimilarity of the roads gives me searchings of heart, and still more the assertiveness and self- satisfaction of the guides; I really cannot tell which turning or whose directions are most likely to bring me to the city.

Her. Oh, but I can solve that puzzle for you; you cannot go wrong, if you trust those who have been already.

Ly. Which do you mean? those who have been by which road, and under whose guidance? It is the old puzzle in a new form; you have only substituted men for measures.

Her. How do you mean?

Ly. Why, the man who has taken Plato's road and travelled with him will recommend that road; so with Epicurus and the rest; and *you* will recommend your own. How else, Hermotimus? it must be so.

Her. Well, of course.

Ly. So you have not solved my puzzle; I know just as little as before which traveller to trust; I find that each of them, as well as his guide, has tried one only, which he now recommends and will have to be the only one leading to the city. Whether he tells the truth I have no means of knowing; that he has attained *some* end, and seen *some* city, I may perhaps allow; but whether he saw the right one, or whether, Corinth being the real goal, he got to Babylon and thought he had seen Corinth—that is still undecided; for surely every one who has seen a city has not seen Corinth, unless Corinth is the only city there is. But my greatest difficulty of all is the absolute certainty that the true road is one; for Corinth is one, and the other roads lead anywhere but to Corinth, though there may be people deluded enough to suppose that the North road and the South road lead equally to Corinth.

Her. But that is absurd, Lycinus; they go opposite ways, you see.

Ly. Then, my dear good man, this choice of roads and guides is quite a serious matter; we can by no means just follow our noses; we shall be discovering that we are well on the way to Babylon or Bactria instead of to Corinth. Nor is it advisable to toss up, either, on the chance that we may hit upon the right way if we start upon any one at a venture. That is no impossibility; it may have come off once and again in a cycle; but I cannot think we ought to gamble recklessly with such high stakes, nor commit our hopes to a frail craft, like the wise men who went to sea in a bowl; we should have no fair complaint against Fortune, if her arrow or dart did not precisely hit the centre; the odds are ten thousand to one against her; just so the archer in Homer—Teucer, I suppose it was—when he meant to hit the dove, only cut the string, which held it; of course it is infinitely more likely that the point of the arrow will find its billet in one of the numberless other places, than just in that particular central one. And as to the perils of blundering into one of the wrong roads instead of the right one, misled by a belief in the discretion of Fortune, here is an illustration:

—it is no easy matter to turn back and get safe into port when you have once cast loose your moorings and committed yourself to the breeze; you are at the mercy of the sea, frightened, sick and sorry with your tossing about, most likely. Your mistake was at the beginning:

before leaving, you should have gone up to some high point, and observed whether the wind was in the right quarter, and of the right strength for a crossing to Corinth, not neglecting, by the way, to secure the very best pilot obtainable, and a seaworthy craft equal to so high a sea.

Her. Much better so, Lycinus. However, I know that, if you go the whole round, you will find no better guides or more expert pilots than the Stoics; if you mean ever to get to Corinth, you will follow them, in the tracks of Chrysippus and Zeno. It is the only way to do it.

Ly. Ah, many can play at the game of assertion. Plato's fellow traveller, Epicurus's follower, and all the rest, will tell me just what you do, that I shall never get to Corinth except with whichever of them it is. So I must either believe them all, or disbelieve impartially. The latter is much the safest, until we have found out the truth.

Put a case, now:

just as I am, as uncertain as ever which of the whole number has the truth, I choose your school; I rely on you, who are my friend, but who still know only the Stoic doctrine, and have not travelled any way but that. Now some God brings Plato, Pythagoras, Aristotle, and the rest to life again; they gather round and cross- examine me, or actually sue me in court for constructive defamation; *Good Lycinus*, they say, *what possessed or who induced you to exalt Chrysippus and Zeno at our expense? we are far older established; they are mere creatures of yesterday; yet you never gave us a hearing, nor inquired into our statements at all.* Well, what am I to plead? will it avail me to say I trusted my friend Hermotimus? I feel sure they will say, *We know not this Hermotimus, who he is, nor he us; you had no right to condemn us all, and give judgement by default against us, on the authority of a man who knew only one of the philosophic roads, and even that, perhaps, imperfectly. These are not the instructions issued to juries, Lycinus; they are not to hear one party, and, refuse the other permission to say what he deems advisable; they are to hear both sides alike, with a view to the better sifting of truth from falsehood by comparison of the arguments; if they fail in these duties, the law allows an appeal to another court.* That is what we may expect them to say.

Then one of them might proceed to question me like this:

Suppose, Lycinus, that an Ethiopian who had never been abroad in his life, nor seen other men like us, were to state categorically in an Ethiopian assembly that there did not exist on earth any white or yellow men— nothing but blacks—, would his statement be accepted? or would some Ethiopian elder remark, How do you know, my confident friend? you have never been in foreign parts, nor had any experience of other nations. Shall I tell him the old man's question was justified? what do you advise, my counsel?

Her. Say that, certainly; I consider the old man's rebuke quite reasonable.

Ly. So do I. But I am not so sure you will approve what comes next; as for me, I have as little doubt of that as of the other.

Her. What is it?

Ly. The next step will be the application; my questioner will say, *Now Lycinus, let us suppose an analogue, in a person acquainted only with the Stoic doctrine, like your friend Hermotimus; he has never travelled in Plato's country, or to Epicurus, or any other land; now, if he were to state that there was no such beauty or truth in those many countries as there is in the Porch and its teaching, would you not be justified in considering it bold of him to give you his opinion about them all, whereas he knew only one, having never set foot outside the bounds of Ethiopia?* What reply do you advise to that?

Her. The perfectly true one, of course, that it is indeed the Stoic doctrine that we study fully, being minded to sink or swim with that, but still we do know what the others say also; our teacher rehearses the articles of their beliefs to us incidentally, and demolishes them with his comments.

Ly. Do you suppose the Platonists, Pythagoreans, Epicureans, and other schools, will let that pass? or will they laugh out loud and say, _What remarkable methods your friend has, Lycinus! he accepts our adversaries' character of us, and gathers our doctrines from the description of people who do not know, or deliberately misrepresent them. If he were to see an athlete getting his muscles in trim by kicking high, or hitting out at empty space as though he were getting a real blow home, would he (in the capacity of umpire) at once proclaim him victor, because he *could not help winning?* No; _he would reflect that these displays are easy and safe, when there is no defence to be reckoned with, and that the real decision must wait till he has beaten and mastered his opponent, and the latter 'has had enough'. Well then, do not let Hermotimus suppose from his teachers' sparrings with our shadows (for *we* are not there) that they have the victory, or that our doctrines are so easily upset; tell him the business is too like the sand houses which children, having built them weak, have no difficulty in overturning, or, to change the figure, like people practising archery; they make a straw target, hang it to a post, plant it a little way off, and then let fly at it; if they hit and get through the straw, they burst into a shout, as if it were a great triumph to have driven through the dry stuff. That is not the way the Persians take, or those Scythian tribes which use the bow. Generally, when *they* shoot, in the first place they are themselves mounted and in motion, and secondly, they like the mark to be moving too; it is not to be stationary, waiting for the arrival of the arrow, but passing at full speed; they can usually kill beasts, and their marksmen hit birds. If it ever happens that they want to test the actual impact on a target, they set up one of stout wood, or a shield of raw hide; piercing that, they reckon that their shafts will go through armour too. So, Lycinus, tell Hermotimus from us that his teachers fierce straw targets, and then say they have disposed of armed men; or paint up figures of us, spar at them, and, after a not surprising success, think

231

they have beaten us. But we shall severally quote against them Achilles's words against Hector:

They dare not face the nodding of my plume._
So say all of them, one after the other.

I suspect that Plato, with his intimate knowledge of Sicily, will add an anecdote from there. Gelo of Syracuse had disagreeable breath, but did not find it out himself for a long time, no one venturing to mention such a circumstance to a tyrant. At last a foreign woman who had a connexion with him dared to tell him; whereupon he went to his wife and scolded her for never having, with all her opportunities of knowing, warned him of it; she put in the defence that, as she had never been familiar or at close quarters with any other man, she had supposed all men were like that. So Hermotinus (Plato will say) after his exclusive association with Stoics, cannot be expected to know the savour of other people's mouths. Chrysippus, on the other hand, might say as much or more if I were to put *him* out of court and betake myself to Platonism, in reliance upon some one who had conversed with Plato alone. And in a word, as long as it is uncertain which is the true philosophic school, I choose none; choice of one is insult to the rest.

Her. For Heaven's sake, Lycinus, let us leave Plato, Aristotle, Epicurus, and the rest of them alone; to argue with them is not for me. Why not just hold a private inquiry, you and I, whether philosophy is what I say it is? As for the Ethiopians and Gelo's wife, what a long way you have brought them on none of their business!

Ly. Away with them, then, if you find their company superfluous. And now do you proceed; my expectations are high.

Her. Well, it seems to me perfectly possible, Lycinus, after studying the Stoic doctrines alone, to get at the truth from them, without going through a course of all the others too. Look at it this way:

if any one tells you simply, Twice two is four, need you go round all the mathematicians to find out whether there is one who makes it five, or seven; or would you know at once that the man was right?

Ly. Certainly I should.

Her. Then why should you think it impossible for a man who finds, without going further, that the Stoics make true statements, to believe them and dispense with further witness? He knows that four can never be five, though ten thousand Platos or Pythagorases said it was.

Ly. Not to the point. You compare accepted with disputed facts, whereas they are completely different. Tell me, did you ever meet a man who said twice two was seven or eleven?

Her. Not I; any one who did not make four of it must be mad.

Ly. But on the other hand—try to tell the truth, I adjure you—, did you ever meet a Stoic and an Epicurean who did *not* differ about principles or ends?

Her. No.

Ly. You are an honest man; now ask yourself whether you are trapping a friend with false logic. We are trying to find out with whom philosophic truth lies; and you beg the question and make a present of that same truth to the Stoics; for you say (what is quite unproved) that they are the people who make twice two four; the Epicureans or Platonists would say that *they* bring out that result, whereas you get five or seven. Does it not amount to that, when your school reckon goodness the only end, and the Epicureans pleasure? or again when you say everything is material, and Plato recognizes an immaterial element also in all that exists? As I said, you lay hold of the thing in dispute, as though it were the admitted property of the Stoics, and put it into their hands, though the others claim it and maintain that it is theirs; why, it is the very point at issue. If it is once established that Stoics have the monopoly of making four out of twice two, it is time for the rest to hold their tongues; but as long as they refuse to yield that point, we must hear all alike, or be prepared for people's calling us partial judges.

Her. It seems to me, Lycinus, you do not understand what I mean.

Ly. Very well, put it plainer, if it is something different from that.

Her. You will see in a minute. Let us suppose two people have gone into the temple of Asclepius or Dionysus, and subsequently one of the sacred cups is missing. Both of them will have to be searched, to see which has it about him.

Ly. Clearly.

Her. Of course one of them has it.

Ly. Necessarily, if it is missing.

Her. Then, if you find it on the first, you will not strip the other; it is clear he has not got it.

Ly. Quite.

Her. And if we fail to find it on the first, the other certainly has it; it is unnecessary to search him that way either.

Ly. Yes, he has it.

Her. So with us; if we find the cup in the possession of the Stoics, we shall not care to go on and search the others; we have what we were looking for; why trouble further?

Ly. There is no why, if you really find it, and can be certain it is the missing article, the sacred object being unmistakable. But there are some differences in this case, friend, the temple-visitors are not two, so that if one has not got the booty the other has, but many; and the identity of the missing object is also uncertain; it may be cup, or bowl, or garland; every priest gives a different description of it; they do not agree even about the material; bronze, say these, silver, say those—anything from gold to tin. So there is nothing for it but to strip the visitors, if you want to find it; even if you discover a gold cup on the first man, you must go on to the others.

Her. What for?

Ly. Because it is not certain that the thing was a cup. And even if that is generally admitted, they do not all agree that it was gold; and if it is well known that a gold cup is missing, and you find a gold cup on your first man, even so you are not quit of searching the others; it is not clear that this is *the* sacred cup; do you suppose there is only one gold cup in the world?

Her. No, indeed.

Ly. So you will have to go the round, and then collect all your finds together and decide which of them is most likely to be divine property.

For the source of all the difficulty is this:

every one who is stripped has something or other on him, one a bowl, one a cup, one a garland, which again may be bronze, gold, or silver; but whether the one he has is the sacred one, is not yet clear. It is absolutely impossible to know which man to accuse of sacrilege; even if all the objects were similar, it would be uncertain who had robbed the God; for such things may be private property too. Our perplexity, of course, is simply due to the fact that the missing cup—assume it to be a cup—has no inscription; if either the God's or the donor's name had been on it, we should not have had all this trouble; when we found the inscribed one, we should have stopped stripping and inconveniencing other visitors. I suppose, Hermotimus, you have often been at athletic meetings?

Her. You suppose right; and in many places too.

Ly. Did you ever have a seat close by the judges?

Her. Dear me, yes; last Olympia, I was on the left of the stewards; Euandridas of Elis had got me a place in the Elean enclosure; I particularly wanted to have a near view of how things are done there.

Ly. So you know how they arrange ties for the wrestling or the pancratium?

Her. Yes.

Ly. Then you will describe it better than I, as you have seen it so close.

Her. In old days, when Heracles presided, bay leaves—

Ly. No old days, thank you; tell me what you saw with your own eyes.

Her. A consecrated silver urn is produced, and into it are thrown little lots about the size of a bean, with letters on them. Two are marked alpha[32], two beta, two more gamma, and so on, if the competitors run to more than that—two lots always to each letter. A competitor comes up, makes a prayer to Zeus, dips his hand into the urn, and pulls out one lot; then another does the same; there is a policeman to each drawer, who holds his hand so that he cannot see what letter he has drawn. When all have drawn, the chief police officer, I think it is, or one of the stewards themselves—I cannot quite remember this detail—, goes round and examines the lots while they stand in a

---

[32] The Greek alphabet runs:

alpha, beta, gamma, delta, epsilon, zeta, eta, theta, iota, kappa, lambda, mu, nu, xi, omicron, pi, rho, sigma, tau, upsilon, phi, chi, psi, omega.

circle, and puts together the two alphas for the wrestling or pancratium, and so for the two betas, and the rest. That is the procedure when the number of competitors is even, as eight, four, or twelve. If it is five, seven, nine, or other odd number, an odd letter is marked on one lot, which is put in with the others, not having a duplicate. Whoever draws this is a bye, and waits till the rest have finished their ties; no duplicate turns up for him, you see; and it is a considerable advantage to an athlete, to know that he will come fresh against tired competitors.

Ly. Stop there; that is just what I wanted. There are nine of them, we will say, and they have all drawn, and the lots are in their hands. You go round— for I promote you from spectator to steward—examining the letters; and I suppose you will not know who is the bye till you have been to them all and paired them.

Her. How do you mean?

Ly. It is impossible for you to hit straight upon the letter which indicates the bye; at least, you may hit upon the letter, but you will not know about the bye; it was not announced beforehand that kappa or mu or iota had the appointment in its gift; when you find alpha, you look for the holder of the other alpha, whom finding, you pair the two. Again finding beta, you inquire into the whereabouts of the second beta which matches it; and so all through, till there is no one left but the holder of the single unpaired letter.

Her. But suppose you come upon it first or second, what will you do then?

Ly. Never mind me; I want to know what *you* will do, Mr. Steward. Will you say at once, Here is the bye? or will you have to go round to all, and see whether there is a duplicate to be found, it being impossible to know the bye till you have seen all the lots?

Her. Why, Lycinus, I shall know quite easily; nine being the number, if I find the epsilon first or second, I know the holder of it for the bye.

Ly. But how?

Her. How? Why, two of them must have alpha, two beta, and of the next two pairs one has certainly drawn gammas and the other deltas, so that four letters have been used up over eight competitors. Obviously, then, the next letter, which is epsilon, is the only one that can be odd, and the drawer of it is the bye.

Ly. Shall I extol your intelligence, or would you rather I explained to you my own poor idea, which differs?

Her. The latter, of course, though I cannot conceive how you can reasonably differ.

Ly. You have gone on the assumption that the letters are taken in alphabetical order, until at a particular one the number of competitors runs short; and I grant you it may be done so at Olympia. But suppose we were to pick out five letters at random, say chi, sigma, zeta, kappa, theta, and duplicate the other four on the lots for eight competitors, but put a single zeta on the

235

ninth, which we meant to indicate the bye—what then would you do if you came on the zeta first? How can you tell that its holder is the bye till you have been all round and found no counterpart to it? for you could not tell by the alphabetical order, as at Olympia.

Her. A difficult question.

Ly. Look at the same thing another way. Suppose we put no letters at all on the lots, but, instead of them, signs and marks such as the Egyptians use for letters, men with dogs' or lions' heads. Or no, those are rather too strange; let us avoid hybrids, and put down simple forms, as well as our draughtsmanship will allow—men on two lots, horses on two, a pair of cocks, a pair of dogs, and let a lion be the mark of the ninth. Now, if you hit upon the lion at the first try, how can you tell that this is the bye-maker, until you have gone all round and seen whether any one else has a lion to match?

Her. Your question is too much for me.

Ly. No wonder; there is no plausible answer. Consequently if we mean to find either the man who has the sacred cup, or the bye, or our best guide to the famous city of Corinth, we must absolutely go to and examine them all, trying them carefully, stripping and comparing them; the truth will be hard enough to find, even so. If I am to take any one's advice upon the right philosophy to choose, I insist upon his knowing what they all say; every one else I disqualify; I will not trust him while there is one philosophy he is unacquainted with; that one may possibly be the best of all. If some one were to produce a handsome man, and state that he was the handsomest of mankind, we should not accept that, unless we knew he had seen all men; very likely his man is handsome, but whether the handsomest, he has no means of knowing without seeing all. Now we are looking not simply for beauty, but for the greatest beauty, and if we miss that, we shall account ourselves no further than we were; we shall not be content with chancing upon some sort of beauty; we are in search of a definite thing, the supreme beauty, which must necessarily be *one.*

Her. True.

Ly. Well then, can you name me a man who has tried every road in philosophy? one who, knowing the doctrine of Pythagoras, Plato, Aristotle, Chrysippus, Epicurus, and the rest, has ended by selecting one out of all these roads, because he has proved it genuine, and had found it by experience to be the only one that led straight to Happiness? If we can meet with such a man, we are at the end of our troubles.

Her. Alas, that is no easy matter.

Ly. What shall we do, then? I do not think we ought to despair, in the momentary absence of such a guide. Perhaps the best and safest plan of all is to set to work oneself, go through every system, and carefully examine the various doctrines.

Her. That is what seems to be indicated. I am afraid, though, there is an obstacle in what you said just now:

236

it is not easy, when you have committed yourself with a spread of canvas to the wind, to get home again. How can a man try all the roads, when, as you said, he will be unable to escape from the first of them?

Ly. My notion is to copy Theseus, get dame Ariadne to give us a skein, and go into one labyrinth after another, with the certainty of getting out by winding it up.

Her. Who is to be our Ariadne? Where shall we find the skein?

Ly. Never despair; I fancy I have found something to hold on to and escape.

Her. And what is that?

Ly. It is not original; I borrow it from one of the wise men:

'Be sober and doubt all things,' says he. If we do not believe everything we are told, but behave like jurymen who suspend judgement till they have heard the other side, we may have no difficulty in getting out of the labyrinths.

Her. A good plan; let us try it.

Ly. Very well, which shall we start with? However, that will make no difference; we may begin with whomsoever we fancy, Pythagoras, say; how long shall we allow for learning the whole of Pythagoreanism? and do not omit the five years of silence; including those, I suppose thirty altogether will do; or, if you do not like that, still we cannot put it lower than twenty.

Her. Put it at that.

Ly. Plato will come next with as many more, and then Aristotle cannot do with less.

Her. No.

Ly. As to Chrysippus, I need not ask you; you have told me already that forty is barely enough.

Her. That is so.

Ly. And we have still Epicurus and the others. I am not taking high figures, either, as you will see if you reflect upon the number of octogenarian Stoics, Epicureans, and Platonists who confess that they have not yet completely mastered their own systems. Or, if they did not confess it, at any rate Chrysippus, Aristotle, and Plato would for them; still more Socrates, who is as good as they; he used to proclaim to all comers that, so far from knowing all, he knew nothing whatever, except the one fact of his own ignorance. Well, let us add up. Twenty years we gave Pythagoras, the same to Plato, and so to the others. What will the total come to, if we assume only ten schools?

Her. Over two hundred years.

Ly. Shall we deduct a quarter of that, and say a hundred and fifty will do? or can we halve it?

Her. You must decide about that; but I see that, at the best, it will be but few who will get through the course, though they begin philosophy and life together.

Ly. In that case, what are we to do? Must we withdraw our previous admission, that no one can choose the best out of many without trying all? We thought selection without experiment a method of inquiry savouring more of divination than of judgement, did we not?

Her. Yes.

Ly. Without such longevity, then, it is absolutely impossible for us to complete the series—experiment, selection, philosophy, Happiness. Yet anything short of that is a mere game of blindman's-buff; whatever we knock against and get hold of we shall be taking for the thing we want, because the truth is hidden from us. Even if a mere piece of luck brings us straight to it, we shall have no grounded conviction of our success; there are so many similar objects, all claiming to be the real thing.

Her. Ah, Lycinus, your arguments seem to me more or less logical, but—but—to be frank with you—I hate to hear you going through them and wasting your acuteness. I suspect it was in an evil hour that I came out to-day and met you; my hopes were almost in my grasp; and now here are you plunging me into a slough of despond with your demonstrations; truth is undiscoverable, if the search needs so many years.

Ly. My dear friend, it would be much fairer to blame your parents, Menecrates and whatever your mother's name may have been—or indeed to go still further back to human nature. Why did not they make you a Tithonus for years and durability? instead of which, they limited you like other men to a century at the outside. As for me, I have only been helping you to deduce results.

Her. No, no; it is just your way; you want to crow over me; you detest philosophy—I cannot tell why—and poke fun at philosophers.

Ly. Hermotimus, I cannot show what truth is, so well as wise people like you and your professor; but one thing I do know about it, and that is that it is not pleasant to the ear; falsehood is far more esteemed; it is prettier, and therefore pleasanter; while Truth, conscious of its purity, blurts out downright remarks, and offends people. Here is a case of it:

even you are offended with me for having discovered (with your assistance) how this matter really stands, and shown that our common object is hard of attainment. Suppose you had been in love with a statue and hoped to win it, under the impression that it was human, and I had realized that it was only bronze or marble, and given you a friendly warning that your passion was hopeless—you might just as well have thought I was your enemy then, because I would not leave you a prey to extravagant and impracticable delusions.

Her. Well, well; are we to give up philosophy, then, and idle our lives away like the common herd?

Ly. What have I said to justify that? My point is not that we are to give up philosophy, but this:

whereas we are to pursue philosophy, and whereas there are many roads, each professing to lead to philosophy and Virtue, and whereas it is uncertain which of these is the true road, therefore the selection shall be made with care. Now we resolved that it was impossible out of many offers to choose the best, unless a man should try all in turn; and then the process of trial was found to be long. What do *you* propose?—It is the old question again. To follow and join philosophic forces with whomsoever you first fall in with, and let him thank Fortune for his proselyte?

Her. What is the good of answering your questions? You say no one can judge for himself, unless he can devote the life of a phoenix to going round experimenting; and on the other hand you refuse to trust either previous experience or the multitude of favourable testimony.

Ly. Where is your multitude, with knowledge and experience *of all*? Never mind the multitude; one man who answers the description will do for me. But if you mean the people who do not know, their mere numbers will never persuade me, as long as they pronounce upon all from knowledge of, at the most, one.

Her. Are you the only man who has found the truth, and are all the people who go in for philosophy fools?

Ly. You wrong me, Hermotimus, when you imply that I put myself above other people, or rank myself at all with those who know; you forget what I said; I never claimed to know the truth better than others, only confessed that I was as ignorant of it as every one else.

Her. Well, but, Lycinus, it may be all very well to insist on going the round, testing the various statements, and eschewing any other method of choice; but it is ridiculous to spend so many years on each experiment, as though there were no such thing as judging from samples. That device seems to me quite simple, and economical of time. There is a story that some sculptor, Phidias, I think, seeing a single claw, calculated from it the size of the lion, if it were modelled proportionally. So, if some one were to let you see a man's hand, keeping the rest of his body concealed, you would know at once that what was behind was a man, without seeing his whole body. Well, it is easy to find out in a few hours the essential points of the various doctrines, and, for selecting the best, these will suffice, without any of your scrupulous exacting investigation.

Ly. Upon my word, how confident you are in your faculty of divining the whole from the parts! and yet I remember being told just the opposite— that knowledge of the whole includes that of the parts, but not vice versa. Well, but tell me; when Phidias saw the claw, would he ever have known it for a lion's, if he had never seen a lion? Could you have said the hand was a man's, if you had never known or seen a man? Why are you dumb? Let me make the only possible answer for you—that you could *not*; I am afraid Phidias has modelled his lion all for nothing; for it proves to be neither here nor there. What resemblance is there? What enabled you and Phidias to recognize the parts was just your knowledge of the wholes—the lion and the man. But in philosophy—the Stoic, for instance—how will the part reveal the other parts to you, or how can you conclude that they are beautiful? You do not know the whole to which the parts belong.

239

Then you say it is easy to hear in a few hours the essentials of all philosophy—meaning, I suppose, their principles and ends, their accounts of God and the soul, their views on the material and the immaterial, their respective identification of pleasure or goodness with the desirable and the Happy; well, it is easy—it is quite a trifle—to deliver an opinion after such a hearing; but really to *know* where the truth lies will be work, I suspect, not for a few hours, but for a good many days. If not, what can have induced them to enlarge on these rudiments to the tune of a hundred or a thousand volumes apiece? I imagine they only wanted to establish the truth of those few points which you thought so easy and intelligible. If you refuse to spend your time on a conscientious selection, after personal examination of each and all, in sum and in detail, it seems to me you will still want your soothsayer to choose the best for you. It would be a fine short cut, with no meanderings or wastings of time, if you sent for him, listened to the summaries, and killed a victim at the end of each; by indicating in its liver which is the philosophy for you, the God would save you a pack of troubles.

Or, if you like, I can suggest a still simpler way; you need not shed all this blood in sacrifice to any God, nor employ an expensive priest; put into an urn a set of tablets, each marked with a philosopher's name, and tell a boy (he must be quite young, and his parents both be living) to go to the urn and pick out whichever tablet his hand first touches; and live a philosopher ever after, of the school which then comes out triumphant.

Her. This is buffoonery, Lycinus; I should not have expected it of you. Now tell me, did you ever buy wine? in person, I mean.

Ly. Many a time.

Her. Well, did you go to every wine vault in town, one after another, tasting and comparing?

Ly. Certainly not.

Her. No; as soon as you find good sound stuff, you have only to get it sent home.

Ly. To be sure.

Her. And from that little taste you could have answered for the quality of the whole?

Ly. Yes.

Her. Now suppose you had gone to all the wine-merchants and said:

I want to buy a pint of wine; I must ask you, gentlemen, to let me drink the whole of the cask which each of you has on tap; after that exhaustive sampling, I shall know which of you keeps the best wine, and is the man for my money. If you had talked like that, they might have laughed at you, and, if you persisted in worrying them, have tried how you liked water.

Ly. Yes; it would be no more than my deserts.

Her. Apply this to philosophy. What need to drink the whole cask, when you can judge the quality of the whole from one little taste?

240

Ly. What an adept at evasion you are, Hermotimus! How you slip through one's fingers! However, it is all the better this time; you fancied yourself out, but you have flopped into the net again.

Her. What do you mean?

Ly. You take a thing whose nature is self-evident and universally admitted, like wine, and argue from it to perfectly unlike things, whose nature is obscure and generally debated. In fact I cannot tell what analogy you find between philosophy and wine; there is just one, indeed:

philosophers and wine-merchants both sell their wares, mostly resorting to adulteration, fraud, and false measures, in the process. But let us look into your real meaning. You say all the wine in a cask is of the same quality—which is perfectly reasonable; further, that any one who draws and tastes quite a small quantity will know at once the quality of the whole—of which the same may be said; I should never have thought of objecting. But mark what comes now:

do philosophy and its professors (your own, for instance) give you every day the same remarks on the same subjects, or do they vary them? They vary them a great deal, friend; you would never have stuck to your master through your twenty years' wandering—quite a philosophic Odyssey—if he had always said the same thing; one hearing would have been enough.

Her. So it would.

Ly. How could you have known the whole of his doctrines from the first taste, then? They were not homogeneous, like the wine; novelty to-day, and novelty to-morrow on the top of it. Consequently, dear friend, short of drinking the whole cask, you might soak to no purpose; Providence seems to me to have hidden the philosophic Good right at the bottom, underneath the lees. So you will have to drain it dry, or you will never get to that nectar for which I know you have so long thirsted. According to your idea, it has such virtue that, could you once taste it and swallow the very least drop, you would straightway have perfect wisdom; so they say the Delphian prophetess is inspired by one draught of the sacred spring with answers for those who consult the oracle. But it seems not to be so; you have drunk more than half the cask; yet you told me you were only beginning yet.

Now see whether this is not a better analogy. You shall keep your merchant, and your cask; but the contents of the latter are not to be wine, but assorted seeds. On the top is wheat, next beans, then barley, below that lentils, then peas—and other kinds yet. You go to buy seeds, and he takes some wheat out of that layer, and puts it in your hand as a sample; now, could you tell by looking at that whether the peas were Sound, the lentils tender, and the beans full?

Her. Impossible.

Ly. No more can you tell the quality of a philosophy from the first statements of its professor; it is not uniform, like the wine to which you compared it, claiming that it must resemble the sample glass; it is heterogeneous, and it had better not be cursorily tested. If you buy bad wine,

241

the loss is limited to a few pence; but to rot with the common herd (in your own words) is not so light a loss. Moreover, your man who wants to drink up the cask as a preliminary to buying a pint will injure the merchant, with his dubious sampling; but philosophy knows no such danger; you may drink your fill, but this cask grows no emptier, and its owner suffers no loss. It is cut and come again here; we have the converse of the Danaids' cask; that would not hold what was put into it; it ran straight through; but here, the more you take away, the more remains.

And I have another similar remark to make about these specimen drops of philosophy. Do not fancy I am libelling it, if I say it is like hemlock, aconite, or other deadly poison. Those too, though they have death in them, will not kill if a man scrapes off the tiniest particle with the edge of his nail and tastes it; if they are not taken in the right quantity, the right manner, and the right vehicle, the taker will not die; you were wrong in claiming that the least possible quantity is enough to base a generalization on.

Her. Oh, have it your own way, Lycinus. Well then, we have got to live a hundred years, and go through all this trouble? There is no other road to philosophy?

Ly. No, none; and we need not complain; as you very truly said, *ars longa, vita brevis*. But I do not know what has come over you; you now make a grievance of it, if you cannot before set of sun develop into a Chrysippus, a Plato, a Pythagoras.

Her. You trap me, and drive me into a corner, Lycinus; yet I never provoked you; it is all envy, I know, because I have made some progress in my studies, whereas you have neglected yourself, when you were old enough to know better.

Ly. Seest, then, thy true course? never mind me, but leave me as a lunatic to my follies, and you go on your way and accomplish what you have intended all this time.

Her. But you are so masterful, you will not let me make a choice, till I have proved all.

Ly. Why, I confess, you will never get me to budge from that. But when you call me masterful, it seems to me you blame the blameless, as the poet says; for I am myself being dragged along by reason, until you bring up some other reason to release me from durance. And here is reason about to talk more masterfully still, you will see; but I suppose you will exonerate it, and blame me.

Her. What can it be? I am surprised to hear it still has anything in reserve.

Ly. It says that seeing and going through all philosophies will not suffice, if you want to choose the best of them; the most important qualification is still missing.

Her. Indeed? Which?

Ly. Why (bear with me), a critical investigating faculty, mental acumen, intellectual precision and independence equal to the occasion; without this, the completest inspection will be useless. Reason insists that the owner of it must further be allowed ample time; he will collect the rival candidates together, and make his choice with long, lingering, repeated deliberation; he will give no heed to the candidate's age, appearance, or repute for wisdom, but perform his functions like the Areopagites, who judge in the darkness of night, so that they must regard not the pleaders, but the pleadings. Then and not till then will you be able to make a sound choice and live a philosopher.

Her. Live? an after life, then. No mortal span will meet your demands; let me see:

go the whole round, examine each with care, on that examination form a judgement, on that judgement make a choice, on that choice be a philosopher; so and no otherwise you say the truth may be found.

Ly. I hardly dare tell you—even that is not exhaustive; I am afraid, after all, the solid basis we thought we had found was imaginary. You know how fishermen often let down their nets, feel a weight, and pull them up expecting a great haul; when they have got them up with much toil, behold, a stone, or an old pot full of sand. I fear our catch is one of those.

Her. I don't know what this particular net may be; your nets are all round me, anyhow.

Ly. Well, try and get through; providentially, you are as good a swimmer as can be. Now, this is it:

granted that we go all round experimenting, and get it done at last, too, I do not believe we shall have solved the elementary question, whether *any* of them has the much-desired; perhaps they are all wrong together.

Her. Oh, come now! not one of *them* right either?

Ly. I cannot tell. Do you think it impossible they may all be deluded, and the truth be something which none of them has yet found?

Her. How can it possibly be?

Ly. This way:

take a correct number, twenty; suppose, I mean, a man has twenty beans in his closed hand, and asks ten different persons to guess the number; they guess seven, five, thirty, ten, fifteen—various numbers, in short. It is possible, I suppose, that one may be right?

Her. Yes.

Ly. It is not impossible, however, that they may all guess different incorrect numbers, and not one of them suggest twenty beans. What say you?

Her. It is not impossible.

Ly. In the same way, all philosophers are investigating the nature of Happiness; they get different answers one Pleasure, another Goodness, and so through the list. It is probable that Happiness *is* one of these; but it is also not improbable that it is something else altogether. We seem to have reversed the proper procedure, and hurried on to the end before we had found the

243

beginning I suppose we ought first to have ascertained that the truth has actually been discovered, and that some philosopher or other has it, and only then to have gone on to the next question, *which* of them is to be believed.

Her. So that, even if we go all through all philosophy, we shall have no certainty of finding the truth even then; that is what you say.

Ly. Please, please do not ask *me*; once more, apply to reason itself. Its answer will perhaps be that there can be no certainty yet—as long as we cannot be sure that it is one or other of the things they say it is.

Her. Then, according to you, we shall never finish our quest nor be philosophers, but have to give it up and live the life of laymen. What you say amounts to that:

philosophy is impossible and inaccessible to a mere mortal; for you expect the aspirant first to choose the best philosophy; and you considered that the only guarantee of such choice's being correct was to go through all philosophy before choosing the truest. Then in reckoning the number of years required by each you spurned all limits, extended the thing to several generations, and made out the quest of truth too long for the individual life; and now you crown all by proving success doubtful even apart from all that; you say it is uncertain whether the philosophers have ever found truth at all.

Ly. Could you state on oath that they have?

Her. Not on oath, no.

Ly. And yet there is much that I have intentionally spared you, though it merits careful examination too.

Her. For instance?

Ly. Is it not said that, among the professed Stoics, Platonists, and Epicureans, some do know their respective doctrines, and some do not (without prejudice to their general respectability)?

Her. That is true.

Ly. Well, don't you think it will be a troublesome business to distinguish the first, and know them from the ignorant professors?

Her. Very.

Ly. So, if you are to recognize the best of the Stoics, you will have to go to most, if not all, of them, make trial, and appoint the best your teacher, first going through a course of training to provide you with the appropriate critical faculty; otherwise you might mistakenly prefer the wrong one. Now reflect on the additional time this will mean; I purposely left it out of account, because I was afraid you might be angry; all the same, it is the most important and necessary thing of all in questions like this—so uncertain and dubious, I mean. For the discovery of truth, your one and only sure or well-founded hope is the possession of this power:

you *must* be able to judge and sift truth from falsehood; you must have the assayer's sense for sound and true or forged coin; if you could have come to your examination of doctrines equipped with a technical skill like that, I should have nothing to say; but without it there is nothing to prevent their severally leading you by the nose; you will follow a dangled bunch of carrots like a donkey; or, better still, you will be water spilt on a table, trained whichever way one chooses with a finger-tip; or again, a reed growing on a river's bank, bending to every breath, however gentle the breeze that shakes it in its passage.

If you could find a teacher, now, who understood demonstration and controversial method, and would impart his knowledge to you, you would be quit of your troubles; the best and the true would straightway be revealed to you, at the bidding of this art of demonstration, while falsehood would stand convicted; you would make your choice with confidence; judgement would be followed by philosophy; you would reach your long-desired Happiness, and live in its company, which sums up all good things.

Her. Thank you, Lycinus; that is a much better hearing; there is more than a glimpse of hope in that. We must surely look for a man of that sort, to give us discernment, judgement, and, above all, the power of demonstration; then all will be easy and clear, and not too long. I am grateful to you already for thinking of this short and excellent plan.

Ly. Ah, no, I cannot fairly claim gratitude yet. I have not discovered or revealed anything that will bring you nearer your hope; on the contrary, we are further off than ever; it is a case of much cry and little wool.

Her. Bird of ill omen, pessimist, explain yourself.

Ly. Why, my friend, even if we find some one who claims to know this art of demonstration, and is willing to impart it, we shall surely not take his word for it straight off; we shall look about for another man to resolve us whether the first is telling the truth. Finding number two, we shall still be uncertain whether our guarantor really knows the difference between a good judge and a bad, and shall need a number three to guarantee number two; for how can we possibly know ourselves how to select the best judge? You see how far this must go; the thing is unending; its nature does not allow us to draw the line and put a stop to it; for you will observe that all the demonstrations that can possibly be thought of are themselves unfounded and open to dispute; most of them struggle to establish their certainty by appealing to facts as questionable as themselves; and the rest produce certain truisms with which they compare, quite illegitimately, the most speculative theories, and then say they have demonstrated the latter:

our eyes tell us there are altars to the Gods; therefore there must be Gods; that is the sort of thing.

Her. How unkindly you treat me, Lycinus, turning my treasure into ashes; I suppose all these years are to have been lost labour.

Ly. At least your chagrin will be considerably lessened by the thought that you are not alone in your disappointment; practically all who pursue philosophy do no more than disquiet themselves in vain. Who could conceivably go through all the stages I have rehearsed? you admit the impossibility yourself. As to your present mood, it is that of the man who cries and curses his luck because he cannot climb the sky, or plunge into the depths of the sea at Sicily and come up at Cyprus, or soar on wings and fly within the day from Greece to India; what is responsible for his discontent is his basing of hopes on a dream-vision or his own wild fancy, without ever asking whether his aspirations were realizable or consistent with humanity. You too, my friend, have been having a long and marvellous dream; and now reason has stuck a pin into you and startled you out of your sleep; your eyes are only half open yet, you are reluctant to shake off a sleep which has shown you such fair visions, and so you scold. It is just the condition of the day-dreamer; he is rolling in gold, digging up treasure, sitting on his throne, or somehow at the summit of bliss; for dame *How-I-wish* is a lavish facile Goddess, that will never turn a deaf ear to her votary, though he have a mind to fly, or change statures with Colossus, or strike a gold- reef; well, in the middle of all this, in comes his servant with some every-day question, wanting to know where he is to get bread, or what he shall say to the landlord, tired of waiting for his rent; and then he flies into a temper, as though the intrusive questioner had robbed him of all his bliss, and is ready to bite the poor fellow's nose off.

As you love me, do not treat me like that. I see you digging up treasure, spreading your wings, nursing extravagant ideas, indulging impossible hopes; and I love you too well to leave you to the company of a life-long dream—a pleasant one, if you will, but yet a dream; I beseech you to get up and take to some every-day business, such as may direct the rest of your life's course by common sense. Your acts and your thoughts up to now have been no more than Centaurs, Chimeras, Gorgons, or what else is figured by dreams and poets and painters, chartered libertines all, who reek not of what has been or may be. Yet the common folk believe them, bewitched by tale and picture just because they are strange and monstrous.

I fancy you hearing from some teller of tales how there is a certain lady of perfect beauty, beyond the Graces themselves or the Heavenly Aphrodite, and then, without ever an inquiry whether his tale is true, and such a person to be found on earth, falling straight in love with her, like Medea in the story enamoured of a dream-Jason. And what most drew you on to love, you and the others who worship the same phantom, was, if I am not mistaken, the consistent way in which the inventor of the lady added to his picture, when once he had got your ear. That was the only thing you all looked to, with that he turned you about as he would, having got his first hold upon you, averring that he was leading you the straight way to your beloved. After the first step, you see, all was easy; none of you ever looked round when he came to the entrance, and inquired whether it was the right one, or whether he had accidentally taken the wrong; no, you all followed in your predecessors' footsteps, like sheep after the bell-wether, whereas the right thing was to decide at the entrance whether you should go in.

Perhaps an illustration will make my meaning clearer:

when one of those audacious poets affirms that there was once a three-headed and six-handed man, if you accept that quietly without questioning its possibility, he will proceed to fill in the picture consistently—six eyes and ears, three voices talking at once, three mouths eating, and thirty fingers instead of our poor ten all told; if he has to fight, three of his hands will have a buckler, wicker targe, or shield apiece, while of the other three one swings an axe, another hurls a spear, and the third wields a sword. It is too late to carp at these details, when they come; they are consistent with the beginning; it was about that that the question ought to have been raised whether it was to be accepted and passed as true. Once grant that, and the rest comes flooding in, irresistible, hardly now susceptible of doubt, because it is consistent and accordant with your initial admissions. That is just your case; your love-yearning would not allow you to look into the facts at each entrance, and so you are dragged on by consistency; it never occurs to you that a thing may be self- consistent and yet false; if a man says twice five is seven, and you take his word for it without checking the sum, he will naturally deduce that four times five is fourteen, and so on *ad libitum*. This is the way that weird geometry proceeds:

it sets before beginners certain strange assumptions, and insists on their granting the existence of inconceivable things, such as points having no parts, lines without breadth, and so on, builds on these rotten foundations a superstructure equally rotten, and pretends to go on to a demonstration which is true, though it starts from premisses which are false.

Just so you, when you have granted the principles of any school, believe in the deductions from them, and take their consistency, false as it is, for a guarantee of truth. Then with some of you, hope travels through, and you die before you have seen the truth and detected your deceivers, while the rest, disillusioned too late, will not turn back for shame:

what, confess at their years that they have been abused with toys all this time? so they hold on desperately, putting the best face upon it and making all the converts they can, to have the consolation of good company in their deception; they are well aware that to speak out is to sacrifice the respect and superiority and honour they are accustomed to; so they will not do it if it may be helped, knowing the height from which they will fall to the common level. Just a few are found with the courage to say they were deluded, and warn other aspirants. Meeting such a one, call him a good man, a true and an honest; nay, call him philosopher, if you will; to my mind, the name is his or no one's; the rest either have no knowledge of the truth, though they think they have, or else have knowledge and hide it, shamefaced cowards clinging to reputation.

But now for goodness' sake let us drop all this, cover it up with an amnesty, and let it be as if it had not been said; let us, assume that the Stoic philosophy, and no other, is correct; then we can examine whether it is practicable and possible, or its disciples wasting their pains; it makes wonderful promises, I am told, about the Happiness in store for those who reach the summit; for none but they shall enter into full possession of the true Good. The next point you must help me with— whether you have ever met such a Stoic, such a pattern of Stoicism, as to be unconscious of pain, untempted by pleasure, free from wrath, superior to envy, contemptuous of wealth, and, in one word, Happy; such should the example and model of the Virtuous life be; for any one who falls short in the slightest degree, even though he is better than other men at all points, is not complete, and in that case not yet Happy.

Her. I never saw such a man.

Ly. I am glad you do not palter with the truth. But what are your hopes in pursuing philosophy, then? You see that neither your own teacher, nor his, nor his again, and so on to the tenth generation, has been absolutely wise and so attained Happiness. It will not serve you to say that it is enough to get near Happiness; that is no good; a person on the doorstep is just as much outside and in the air as another a long way off, though with the difference that the former is tantalized by a nearer view. So it is to get into the neighbourhood of Happiness—I will grant you so much—that you toil like this, wearing yourself away, letting this great portion of your life slip from you, while you are sunk in dullness and wakeful weariness; and you are to go on with it for twenty more years at the least, you tell me, to take your place when you are eighty—always assuming some one to assure you that length of days—in the ranks of the not yet Happy. Or perhaps you reckon on being the exception; you are to crown your pursuit by attaining what many a good man before you, swifter far, has pursued and never overtaken.

Well, overtake it, if that is your plan, grasp it and have it whole, this something, mysterious to me, of which the possession is sufficient reward for such toils; this something which I wonder how long you will have the enjoyment of, old man that you will be, past all pleasure, with one foot in the grave; ah, but perhaps, like a brave soul, you are getting ready for another life, that you may spend it the better when you come to it, having learned how to live:

as though one should take so long preparing and elaborating a superlative dinner that he fainted with hunger and exhaustion!

However, there is another thing I do not think you have observed:

Virtue is manifested, of course, in action, in doing what is just and wise and manly; but you—and when I say you, I mean the most advanced philosophers—you do not seek these things and ensue them, but spend the greater part of your life conning over miserable sentences and demonstrations and problems; it is the man who does best at these that you hail a glorious victor. And I believe that is why you admire this experienced old professor of yours:

he nonplusses his associates, knows how to put crafty questions and inveigle you into pitfalls; so you pay no attention to the fruit—which consists in action—, but are extremely busy with the husks, and smother each other with the leaves in your debates; come now, Hermotimus, what else are you about from morning to night?

Her. Nothing; that is what it comes to.

Ly. Is it wronging you to say that you hunt the shadow or the snake's dead slough, and neglect the solid body or the creeping thing itself? You are no better than a man pouring water into a mortar and braying it with an iron pestle; he thinks he is doing a necessary useful job, whereas, let him bray till all's blue (excuse the slang), the water is as much water as ever it was.

And here let me ask you whether, putting aside his discourse, you would choose to resemble your master, and be as passionate, as sordid, as quarrelsome, ay, and as addicted to pleasure (though that trait of his is not generally known). Why no answer, Hermotimus? Shall I tell you a plea for philosophy which I lately heard? It was from the mouth of an old, old man, who has quite a company of young disciples. He was angrily demanding his fees from one of these; they were long overdue, he said; the day stated in the agreement was the first of the month, and it was now the fifteenth.

The youth's uncle was there, a rustic person without any notion of your refinements; and by way of stilling the storm, *Come, come, sir,* says he, _you need not make such a fuss because we have bought words of you and not yet settled the bill. As to what you have sold us, you have got it still; your stock of learning is none the less; and in what I really sent the boy to you for, you have not improved him a bit; he has carried off and seduced neighbour Echecrates's daughter, and there would have been an action for assault, only Echecrates is a poor man; but the prank cost me a couple of hundred. And the other day he struck his mother; she had tried to stop him when he was smuggling wine out of the house, for one of his club-dinners, I suppose. As to temper and conceit and impudence and brass and lying, he was not half so bad twelve months ago as he is now. That is where I should have liked him to profit by your teaching; and we could have done, without his knowing the stuff he reels of at table every day:

'a crocodile [33] seized hold of a baby,' says he, 'and promised to give it back if its father could answer'—the Lord knows what; or how, 'day being, night cannot be'; and sometimes his worship twists round what we say somehow or other, till there we are with horns on our heads! We just laugh at it—most of all when he stuffs up his ears and repeats to himself what he calls temperaments and conditions and conceptions and impressions, and a lot more like that. And he tells us God is not in heaven, but goes about in everything, wood and stone and animals—the meanest of them, too; and if his mother asks him why he talks such stuff, he laughs at her and says if once he gets the 'stuff' pat off, there will be nothing to prevent him from being the only rich man, the only king, and counting every one else slaves and offscourings._

---

[33] See *Puzzles* in Notes.

When he had finished, mark the reverend philosopher's answer. *You should consider, he said, that if he had never come to me, he would have behaved far worse—very possibly have come to the gallows. As it is, philosophy and the respect he has for it have been a check upon him, so that you find he keeps within bounds and is not quite unbearable; the philosophic system and name tutor him with their presence, and the thought of disgracing them shames him. I should be quite justified in taking your money, if not for any positive improvement I have effected, yet for the abstentions due to his respect for philosophy; the very nurses will tell you as much:*

children should go to school, because, even if they are not old enough to learn, they will at least be out of mischief there. My conscience is quite easy about him; if you like to select any of your friends who is acquainted with Stoicism and bring him here to-morrow, you shall see how the boy can question and answer, how much he has learnt, how many books he has read on axioms, syllogisms, conceptions, duty, and all sorts of subjects. As for his hitting his mother or seducing girls, what have I to do with that? am I his keeper?

A dignified defence of philosophy for an old man! Perhaps *you* will say too that it is a good enough reason for pursuing it, if it will keep us from worse employments. Were our original expectations from philosophy at all of a different nature, by the way? did they contemplate anything beyond a more decent behaviour than the average? Why this obstinate silence?

Her. Oh, why but that I could cry like a baby? It cuts me to the heart, it is all so true; it is too much for me, when I think of my wretched, wasted years—paying all that money for my own labour, too! I am sober again after a debauch, I see what the object of my maudlin affection is like, and what it has brought upon me.

Ly. No need for tears, dear fellow; that is a very sensible fable of Aesop's. A man sat on the shore and counted the waves breaking; missing count, he was excessively annoyed. But the fox came up and said to him:

'Why vex yourself, good sir, over the past ones? you should let them go, and begin counting afresh.' So you, since this is your mind, had better reconcile yourself now to living like an ordinary man; you will give up your extravagant haughty hopes and put yourself on a level with the commonalty; if you are sensible, you will not be ashamed to unlearn in your old age, and change your course for a better.

Now I beg you not to fancy that I have said all this as an anti-Stoic, moved by any special dislike of your school; my arguments hold against all schools. I should have said just the same if you had chosen Plato or Aristotle, and condemned the others unheard. But, as Stoicism was your choice, the argument has seemed to be aimed at that, though it had no such special application.

Her. You are quite right. And now I will be off to metamorphose myself. When we next meet, there will be no long, shaggy beard, no artificial composure; I shall be natural, as a gentleman should. I may go as far as a fashionable coat, by way of publishing my renunciation of nonsense. I only wish there were an emetic that would purge out every doctrine they have instilled into me; I assure you, if I could reverse Chrysippus's plan with the hellebore, and drink forgetfulness, not of the world but of Stoicism, I would not think twice about it. Well, Lycinus, I owe you a debt indeed; I was being swept along in a rough turbid torrent, unresisting, drifting with the stream; when lo, you stood there and fished me out, a true *deus ex machina*. I have good enough reason, I think, to shave my head like the people who get clear off from a wreck; for I am to make votive offerings to-day for the dispersion of that thick cloud which was over my eyes. Henceforth, if I meet a philosopher on my walks (and it will not be with my will), I shall turn aside and avoid him as I would a mad dog.

HERODOTUS AND AETION

I devoutly wish that Herodotus's other characteristics were imitable; not all of them, of course—that is past praying for—, but any one of them:

the agreeable style, the constructive skill, the native charm of his Ionic, the sententious wealth, or any of a thousand beauties which he combined into one whole, to the despair of imitators. But there is one thing—the use he made of his writings, and the speed with which he attained the respect of all Greece; from that you, or I, or any one else, might take a hint. As soon as he had sailed from his Carian home for Greece, he concentrated his thoughts on the quickest and easiest method of winning a brilliant reputation for himself and his works. He might have gone the round, and read them successively at Athens, Corinth, Argos, and Sparta; but that would be a long toilsome business, he thought, with no end to it; so he would not do it in detail, collecting his recognition by degrees, and scraping it together little by little; his idea was, if possible, to catch all Greece together. The great Olympic Games were at hand, and Herodotus bethought him that here was the very occasion on which his heart was set. He seized the moment when the gathering was at its fullest, and every city had sent the flower of its citizens; then he appeared in the temple hall, bent not on sight-seeing, but on bidding for an Olympic victory of his own; he recited his *Histories*, and bewitched his hearers; nothing would do but each book must be named after one of the Muses, to whose number they corresponded.

He was straightway known to all, better far than the Olympic winners. There was no man who had not heard his name; they had listened to him at Olympia, or they were told of him by those who had been there; he had only to appear, and fingers were pointing at him:

'There is the great Herodotus, who wrote the Persian War in Ionic, and celebrated our victories.' That was what he made out of his *Histories*; a single meeting sufficed, and he had the general unanimous acclamation of all Greece; his name was proclaimed, not by a single herald; every spectator did that for him, each in his own city.

The royal road to fame was now discovered; it was the regular practice of many afterwards to deliver their discourses at the festival; Hippias the rhetorician was on his own ground there; but Prodicus came from Ceos, Anaximenes from Chios, Polus from Agrigentum; and a rapid fame it brought, to them and many others.

However, I need not have cited ancient rhetoricians, historians, and chroniclers like these; in quite recent times the painter Aetion is said to have brought his picture, *Nuptials of Roxana and Alexander*, to exhibit at Olympia; and Proxenides, High Steward of the Games on the occasion, was so delighted with his genius that he gave him his daughter.

It must have been a very wonderful picture, I think I hear some one say, to make the High Steward give his daughter to a stranger. Well, I have seen it—it is now in Italy—, so I can tell you. A fair chamber, with the bridal bed in it; Roxana seated—and a great beauty she is—with downcast eyes, troubled by the presence of Alexander, who is standing. Several smiling Loves; one stands behind Roxana, pulling away the veil on her head to show her to Alexander; another obsequiously draws off her sandal, suggesting bed-time; a third has hold of Alexander's mantle, and is dragging him with all his might towards Roxana. The King is offering her a garland, and by him as supporter and groom's-man is Hephaestion, holding a lighted torch and leaning on a very lovely boy; this is Hymenaeus, I conjecture, for there are no letters to show. On the other side of the picture, more Loves playing among Alexander's armour; two are carrying his spear, as porters do a heavy beam; two more grasp the handles of the shield, tugging it along with another reclining on it, playing king, I suppose; and then another has got into the breast-plate, which lies hollow part upwards; he is in ambush, and will give the royal equipage a good fright when it comes within reach.

All this is not idle fancy, on which the painter has been lavishing needless pains; he is hinting that Alexander has also another love, in War; though he loves Roxana, he does not forget his armour. And, by the way, there was some extra nuptial virtue in the picture itself, outside the realm of fancy; for it did Aetion's wooing for him. He departed with a wedding of his own as a sort of pendant to that of Alexander; *his* groom's-man was the King; and the price of his marriage-piece was a marriage.

Herodotus, then (to return to him), thought that the Olympic festival would serve a second purpose very well—that of revealing to the Greeks a wonderful historian who had related their victories as he had done. As for me—and in Heaven's name do not suppose me so beside myself as to intend any comparison between my works and his; I desire his favour too much for that—but one experience I have in common with him. On my first visit to Macedonia, *my* thoughts too were busy with my best policy. My darling wish was to be known to you all, and to exhibit my writings to as many Macedonians as might be; I decided that it would be too great an undertaking at such a time of year to go round in person visiting city by city; but if I seized the occasion of this your meeting, appeared before you all, and delivered my discourse, my aspirations, I thought, might be realized that way.

And now here are you met together, the *elite* of every city, the true soul of Macedonia; the town which lodges you is the chief of all, little enough resembling Pisa, with its crowding, its tents and hovels and stifling heat; there is as great a difference between this audience and that promiscuous crowd, mainly intent upon mere athletics, and thinking of Herodotus only as a stop-gap; here we have orators, historians, professors, the first in each kind—that is much in itself; my arena, it seems, need not suffer from comparison with Olympia. And though, if you insist on matching me with the Polydamases, Glaucuses, and Milos of literature, you must think me a very presumptuous person, it is open to you on the other hand to put them out of your thoughts altogether; and if you strip and examine me independently, you may decide that at least I need not be whipped.[34] Considering the nature of the contest, I may well be satisfied with that measure of success.

[34] Cf. *Remarks addressed to an Illiterate Book-fancier*, 9.

ZEUXIS AND ANTIOCHUS

I was lately walking home after lecturing, when a number of my audience (you are now my friends, gentlemen, and there can be no objection to my telling you this)—these persons, then, came to me and introduced themselves, with the air of admiring hearers. They accompanied me a considerable way, with such laudatory exclamations that I was reduced to blushing at the discrepancy between praise and thing praised. Their chief point, which they were absolutely unanimous in emphasizing, was that the substance of my work was so fresh, so crammed with novelty. I had better give you their actual phrases:

'How new! What paradoxes, to be sure! What invention the man has! His ideas are quite unequalled for originality.' They said a great deal of this sort about my fascinating lecture, as they called it; they could have had no motive for pretending, or addressing such flatteries to a stranger who had no independent claims on their attention.

These commendations, to be quite frank, were very far from gratifying to me; when at length they left me to myself, my reflections took this course:

—*So the only attraction in my work is that it is unusual, and does not follow the beaten track; good vocabulary, orthodox composition, insight, subtlety, Attic grace, general constructive skill—these may for aught I know be completely wanting; else indeed they would hardly have left them unnoticed, and approved my method only as new and startling. Fool that I was, I did indeed guess, when they jumped up to applaud, that novelty was part of the attraction; I knew that Homer spoke truly when he said there is favour for the new song; but I did not see that novelty was to have so vast a share—the whole, indeed—of the credit; I thought it gave a sort of adventitious charm, and contributed, its part to the success, but that the real object of commendation—what extracted the cheers—was those other qualities. Why, I have been absurdly self- satisfied, and come very near believing them when they called me the one and only real Greek, and such nonsense. But behold, my gold is turned to ashes; my fame, after all, is little different from that enjoyed by a conjuror.*

Now I should like to give you an illustration from painting. The great Zeuxis, after he had established his artistic supremacy, seldom or never painted such common popular subjects as Heroes, Gods, and battle-pieces; he was always intent on novelty; he would hit upon some extravagant and strange design, and then use it to show his mastery of the art. One of these daring pieces of his represented a female Centaur, nursing a pair of infant Centaur twins. There is a copy of the picture now at Athens, taken exactly from the original. The latter is said to have been put on ship—board for Italy with the rest of Sulla's art treasures, and to have been lost with them by the sinking of the ship, off Malea, I think it was. The picture of the picture I have seen, and the best word-picture I can manage of that I am now to give you; I am no connoisseur, you must understand, but I have a vivid recollection of it as I saw it in an Athenian studio not long ago; and my warm admiration of it as a work of art may perhaps inspire me with a clear description.

On fresh green-sward appears the mother Centaur, the whole equine part of her stretched on the ground, her hoofs extended backwards; the human part is slightly raised on the elbows; the fore feet are not extended like the others, for she is only partially on her side; one of them is bent as in the act of kneeling, with the hoof tucked in, while the other is beginning to straighten and take a hold on the ground—the action of a horse rising. Of the cubs she is holding one in her arms suckling it in the human fashion, while the other is drawing at the mare's dug like a foal. In the upper part of the picture, as on higher ground, is a Centaur who is clearly the husband of the nursing mother; he leans over laughing, visible only down to the middle of his horse body; he holds a lion whelp aloft in his right hand, terrifying the youngsters with it in sport.

There are no doubt qualities in the painting which evade analysis by a mere amateur, and yet involve supreme craftsmanship—such things as precision of line, perfect mastery of the palette, clever brush-work, management of shadow, perspective, proportion, and relation of the parts to the whole; but I leave all that to the professionals whose business it is to appreciate it; what strikes *me* especially about Zeuxis is the manifold scope which he has found for his extraordinary skill, in a single subject. You have in the husband a truly terrible savage creature; his locks toss about, he is almost covered with hair, human part as well as equine; the shoulders high to monstrosity; the look, even in his merry mood, brutal, uncivilized, wild.

In contrast with him, the animal half of the female is lovely; a Thessalian filly, yet unbroken and unbacked, might come nearest; and the human upper half is also most beautiful, with the one exception of the ears, which are pointed as in a satyr. At the point of junction which blends the two natures, there is no sharp line of division, but the most gradual of transitions; a touch here, a trait there, and you are surprised to find the change complete. It was perfectly wonderful, again, to see the combination of wildness and infancy, of terrible and tender, in the young ones, looking up in baby curiosity at the lion-cub, while they held on to breast and dug, and cuddled close to their dam.

Zeuxis imagined that when the picture was shown the technique of it would take visitors by storm. Well, they did acclaim him; they could hardly help that, with such a masterpiece before them; but their commendations were all in the style of those given to me the other night; it was the strangeness of the idea, the fresh unhackneyed sentiment of the picture, and so on. Zeuxis saw that they were preoccupied with the novelty of his subject, art was at a discount, and truth of rendering quite a minor matter. 'Oh, pack it up, Miccio,' he said to his pupil, 'and you and the others take it home; these people are delighted with the earthy part of the work; the questions of its aim, its beauty, its artistic merit, are of no importance whatever; novelty of subject goes for much more than truth of rendering.'

So said Zeuxis, not in the best of tempers. Antiochus Soter had a somewhat similar experience about his battle with the Galatians. If you will allow me, I propose to give you an account of that event also. These people were good fighters, and on this occasion in great force; they were drawn up in a serried phalanx, the first rank, which consisted of steel- clad warriors, being supported by men of the ordinary heavy-armed type to the depth of four-and-twenty; twenty thousand cavalry held the flanks; and there were eighty scythed, and twice that number of ordinary war chariots ready to burst forth from the centre. These dispositions filled Antiochus with apprehension, and he thought the task was too hard for him. His own preparations had been hurried, on no great scale, and inadequate to the occasion; he had brought quite a small force, mostly of skirmishers and light-armed troops; more than half his men were without defensive armour. He was disposed to negotiate and find some honourable composition.

Theodotas of Rhodes, however, a brave and skilful officer, put him in heart again. Antiochus had sixteen elephants; Theodotas advised him to conceal these as well as he could for the present, not letting their superior height betray them; when the signal for battle was given, the shock just at hand, the enemy's cavalry charging, and their phalanx opening to give free passage to the chariots, then would be the time for the elephants. A section of four was to meet the cavalry on each flank, and the remaining eight to engage the chariot squadron. 'By this means,' he concluded, 'the horses will be frightened, and there will be a stampede into the Galatian infantry.' His anticipations were realized, thus:

Neither the Galatians nor their horses had ever seen an elephant, and they were so taken aback by the strange sight that, long before the beasts came to close quarters, the mere sound of their trumpeting, the sight of their gleaming tusks relieved against dark bodies, and minatory waving trunks, was enough; before they were within bow-shot, the enemy broke and ran in utter disorder; the infantry were spitted on each other's spears, and trampled by the cavalry who came scurrying on to them. The chariots, turning in like manner upon their own friends, whirled about among them by no means harmlessly; it was a Homeric scene of 'rumbling tumbling cars'; when once the horses shied at those formidable elephants, off went the drivers, and 'the lordless chariots rattled on,' their scythes maiming and carving any of their late masters whom they came within reach of; and, in that chaos, many were the victims. Next came the elephants, trampling, tossing, tearing, goring; and a very complete victory they had made of it for Antiochus.

The carnage was great, and all the Galatians were either killed or captured, with the exception of a quite small band which got off to the mountains; Antiochus's Macedonians sang the Paean, gathered round, and garlanded him with acclamations on the glorious victory. But the King—so the story goes—was in tears; 'My men,' he said, 'we have more reason for shame; saved by those sixteen brutes! if their strangeness had not produced the panic, where should we have been?' And on the trophy he would have nothing carved except just an elephant.

Gentlemen, *de me fabula*; are my resources like those of Antiochus— quite unfit for battle on the whole, but including some elephants, some queer impositions, some jugglery, in fact? That is what all the praise I hear points at. The things I really relied upon seem to be of little account; the mere fact that my picture is of a female Centaur exercises fascination; it passes for a novelty and a marvel, as indeed it is. The rest of Zeuxis's pains is thrown away, I suppose. But ah, no, not thrown away—; *you* are connoisseurs, and judge by the rules of art. I only hope the show may be worthy of the spectators.

HARMONIDES

'Tell me, Timotheus,' said Harmonides the flute-player one day to his teacher, 'tell me how I may win distinction in my art. What can I do to make myself known all over Greece? Everything but this you have taught me. I have a correct ear, thanks to you, and a smooth, even delivery, and have acquired the light touch so essential to the rendering of rapid measures; rhythmical effect, the adaptation of music to dance, the true character of the different moods— exalted Phrygian, joyous Lydian, majestic Dorian, voluptuous Ionic—all these I have mastered with your assistance. But the prime object of my musical aspirations seems out of my reach:

I mean popular esteem, distinction, and notoriety; I would have all eyes turn in my direction, all tongues repeat my name:

"There goes Harmonides, the great flute-player." Now when *you* first came from your home in Boeotia, and performed in the *Procne*, and won the prize for your rendering of the *Ajax Furens*, composed by your namesake, there was not a man who did not know the name of Timotheus of Thebes; and in these days you have only to show yourself, and people flock together as birds do at the sight of an owl in daylight. It is for this that I sought to become a flute-player; this was to be the reward of all my toil. The skill without the glory I would not take at a gift, not though I should prove to be a Marsyas or an Olympus in disguise. What is the use of a light that is to be hidden under a bushel? Show me then, Timotheus, how I may avail myself of my powers and of my art. I shall be doubly your debtor:

not for my skill alone, but for the glory that skill confers.'

'Why, really,' says Timotheus, 'it is no such easy matter, Harmonides, to become a public character, or to gain the prestige and distinction to which you aspire; and if you propose to set about it by performing in public, you will find it a long business, and at the best will never achieve a universal reputation. Where will you find a theatre or circus large enough to admit the whole nation as your audience? But if you would attain your object and become known, take this hint. By all means perform occasionally in the theatres, but do not concern yourself with the public. Here is the royal road to fame:

get together a small and select audience of connoisseurs, real experts, whose praise, whose blame are equally to be relied upon; display your skill to these; and if you can win *their* approval, you may rest content that in a single hour you have gained a national reputation. I argue thus. If you are known to be an admirable performer by persons who are themselves universally known and admired, what have you to do with public opinion? Public opinion must inevitably follow the opinion of the best judges. The public after all is mainly composed of untutored minds, that know not good from bad themselves; but when they hear a man praised by the great authorities, they take it for granted that he is not undeserving of praise, and praise him accordingly. It is the same at the games:

most of the spectators know enough to clap or hiss, but the judging is done by some five or six persons.'

Harmonides had no time to put this policy into practice. The story goes that in his first public competition he worked so energetically at his flute, that he breathed his last into it, and expired then and there, before he could be crowned. His first Dionysiac performance was also his last.

But Timotheus's remarks need not be confined to Harmonides, nor to his profession:

they seem applicable to all whose ambition prompts them to exhibit their talents and to aim at the approbation of the public. Accordingly, when I, like Harmonides, was debating within myself the speediest means of becoming known, I took Timotheus's advice:

'Who,' I asked myself, 'is the foremost man in all this city? Whose credit is highest with his neighbours? Who shall be my *multum in parvo*?' Only one name could reasonably suggest itself—your own; which stands for the perfection of every excellence, the glass of culture and the mould of wit. To submit my works to you, to win *your* approbation—if such a thing might be!—were to reach the goal of my desire; for your suffrage carries the rest with it. Whom, indeed, could I substitute in your place, and hope to preserve a reputation for sanity? In a sense, no doubt, I shall be hazarding all on one cast of the die:

yet with more truth I might be said to have summoned the whole population into one audience- chamber; for your single judgement must assuredly outweigh the rest, taken individually or collectively. The Spartan kings had two votes each to the ordinary man's one:

but you are a whole Privy Council and Senate in yourself. Your influence is unequalled in the Court of Literature, and, above all, yours is the casting-vote of acquittal; an encouraging thought for me, who might well be uneasy otherwise at the extent of my hardihood. Moreover, I am not wholly without a claim on your interest, as belonging to that city which has so often enjoyed peculiar benefits at your hand, in addition to those which it has shared with the nation at large; and this encourages me to hope that in the present instance, if judgement is going against me, and the votes of acquittal are in a minority, you will use your prerogative, and make all right with that casting-vote of yours. I may have had successes, I may have made a name, my lectures may have been well received:

—all this amounts to nothing; it is visionary; it is a mere bubble. The truth must come to light now; I am put to a final test; there will be no room for doubt or hesitation after this. It rests with you, whether my literary rank shall be assured, or my pretensions—but no! with such a contest before me, I will abstain from words of evil omen.

Ye Gods, give me approval *here*, and set the seal upon my reputation! I may then face the world with a light heart:

he who has carried the prize at Olympia need fear no other course.

THE SCYTHIAN

Anacharsis was not the first Scythian who was induced by the love of Greek culture to leave his native country and visit Athens:

he had been preceded by Toxaris, a man of high ability and noble sentiments, and an eager student of manners and customs; but of low origin, not like Anacharsis a member of the royal family or of the aristocracy of his country, but what they call *'an eight-hoof man,'* a term which implies the possession of a waggon and two oxen. Toxaris never returned to Scythia, but died at Athens, where he presently came to be ranked among the Heroes; and sacrifice is still paid to 'the Foreign Physician,' as he was styled after his deification. Some account of the significance of this name, the origin of his worship, and his connexion with the sons of Asclepius, will not, I think, be out of place:

for it will be seen from this that the Scythians, in conferring immortality on mortals, and sending them to keep company with Zamolxis, do not stand alone; since the Athenians permit themselves to make Gods of Scythians upon Greek soil.

At the time of the great plague, the wife of Architeles the Areopagite had a vision:

the Scythian Toxaris stood over her and commanded her to tell the Athenians that the plague would cease if they would sprinkle their back-streets with wine. The Athenians attended to his instructions, and after several sprinklings had been performed, the plague troubled them no more; whether it was that the perfume of the wine neutralized certain noxious vapours, or that the hero, being a medical hero, had some other motive for his advice. However that may be, he continues to this day to draw a fee for his professional services, in the shape of a white horse, which is sacrificed on his tomb. This tomb was pointed out by Dimaenete as the place from which he issued with his instructions about the wine; and beneath it Toxaris was found buried, his identity being established not merely by the inscription, of which only a part remained legible, but also by the figure engraved on the monument, which was that of a Scythian, with a bow, ready strung, in his left hand, and in the right what appeared to be a book. You may still make out more than half the figure, with the bow and book complete:

but the upper portion of the stone, including the face, has suffered from the ravages of time. It is situated not far from the Dipylus, on your left as you leave the Dipylus for the Academy. The mound is of no great size, and the pillar lies prostrate:

yet it never lacks a garland, and there are statements to the effect that fever-patients have been known to be cured by the hero; which indeed is not surprising, considering that he once healed an entire city.

However, my reason for mentioning Toxaris was this. He was still alive, when Anacharsis landed at Piraeus and made his way up to Athens, in no small perturbation of spirit; a foreigner and a barbarian, everything was strange to him, and many things caused him uneasiness; he knew not what to do with himself; he saw that every one was laughing at his attire; he could find no one to speak his native tongue;—in short he was heartily sick of his travels, and made up his mind that he would just see Athens, and then retreat to his ship without loss of time, get on board, and so back to the Bosphorus; once there he had no great journey to perform before he would be home again. In this frame of mind he had already reached the Ceramicus, when his good genius appeared to him in the guise of Toxaris. The attention of the latter was immediately arrested by the dress of his native country, nor was it likely that he would have any difficulty in recognizing Anacharsis, who was of noble birth and of the highest rank in Scythia. Anacharsis, on the other hand, could not be expected to see a compatriot in Toxaris, who was dressed in the Greek fashion, without sword or belt, wore no beard, and from his fluent speech might have been an Athenian born; so completely had time transformed him. 'You are surely Anacharsis, the son of Daucetas?' he said, addressing him in the Scythian language. Anacharsis wept tears of joy; he not only heard his mother-tongue, but heard it from one who had known him in Scythia. 'How comes it, sir, that you know me?' he asked.

'I too am of that country; my name is Toxaris; but it is probably not known to you, for I am a man of no family.'

'Are you that Toxaris,' exclaimed the other, 'of whom I heard that for love of Greece he had left wife and children in Scythia, and gone to Athens, and was there dwelling in high honour?'

'What, is my name still remembered among you?—Yes, I am Toxaris.'

'Then,' said Anacharsis, 'you see before you a disciple, who has caught your enthusiasm for Greece; it was with no other object than this that I set out on my travels. The hardships I have endured in the countries through which I passed on my way hither are infinite; and I had already decided, when I met you, that before the sun set I would return to my ship; so much was I disturbed at the strange and outlandish sights that I have seen. And now, Toxaris, I adjure you by Scimetar and Zamolxis, our country's Gods,—take me by the hand, be my guide, and make me acquainted with all that is best in Athens and in the rest of Greece; their great men, their wise laws, their customs, their assemblies, their constitution, their everyday life. You and I have both travelled far to see these things:

you will not suffer me to depart without seeing them?'

'What! come to the very door, and then turn back? This is not the language of enthusiasm. However, there is no fear of that—you will not go back, Athens will not let you off so easily. She is not so much at a loss for charms wherewith to detain the stranger:

she will take such a hold on you, that you will forget your own wife and children—if you have any. Now I will put you into the readiest way of seeing Athens, ay, and Greece, and the glories of Greece. There is a certain philosopher living here; he is an Athenian, but has travelled a great deal in Asia and Egypt, and held intercourse with the most eminent men. For the rest, he is none of your moneyed men:

indeed, he is quite poor; be prepared for an old man, dressed as plainly as could be. Yet his virtue and wisdom are held in such esteem, that he was employed by them to draw up a constitution, and his ordinances form their rule of life. Make this man your friend, study him, and rest assured that in knowing him you know Greece; for he is an epitome of all that is excellent in the Greek character. I can do you no greater service than to introduce you to him.'

'Let us lose no time, then, Toxaris. Take me to him. But perhaps that is not so easily done? He may slight your intercessions on my behalf?'

'You know not what you say. Nothing gives him greater pleasure than to have an opportunity of showing his hospitality to strangers. Only follow me, and you shall see how courteous and benevolent he is, and how devout a worshipper of the God of Hospitality. But stay:

how fortunate! here he comes towards us. See, he is wrapped in thought, and mutters to himself. —Solon!' he cried; 'I bring you the best of gifts—a stranger who craves your friendship. He is a Scythian of noble family; but has left all and come here to enjoy the society of Greeks, and to view the wonders of their country. I have hit upon a simple expedient which will enable him to do both, to see all that is to be seen, and to form the most desirable acquaintances:

in other words, I have brought him to Solon, who, if I know anything of his character, will not refuse to take him under his protection, and to make him a Greek among Greeks.—It is as I told you, Anacharsis:

having seen Solon, you have seen all; behold Athens; behold Greece. You are a stranger no longer:

all men know you, all men are your friends; this it is to possess the friendship of the venerable Solon. Conversing with him, you will forget Scythia and all that is in it. Your toils are rewarded, your desire is fulfilled. In him you have the mainspring of Greek civilization, in him the ideals of Athenian philosophers are realized. Happy man—if you know your happiness—to be the friend and intimate of Solon!'

It would take too long to describe the pleasure of Solon at Toxaris's 'gift,' his words on the occasion, and his subsequent intercourse with Anacharsis—how he gave him the most valuable instruction, procured him the friendship of all Athens, showed him the sights of Greece, and took every trouble to make his stay in the country a pleasant one; and how Anacharsis for his part regarded the sage with such reverence, that he was never willingly absent from his side. Suffice it to say, that the promise of Toxaris was fulfilled:

thanks to Solon's good offices, Anacharsis speedily became familiar with Greece and with Greek society, in which he was treated with the consideration due to one who came thus strongly recommended; for here too Solon was a lawgiver:

those whom he esteemed were loved and admired by all. Finally, if we may believe the statement of Theoxenus, Anacharsis was presented with the freedom of the city, and initiated into the mysteries; nor does it seem likely that he would ever have returned to Scythia, had not Solon died.

And now perhaps I had better put the moral to my tale, if it is not to wander about in a headless condition. What are Anacharsis and Toxaris doing here to-day in Macedonia, bringing Solon with them too, poor old gentleman, all the way from Athens? It is time for me to explain. The fact is, my situation is pretty much that of Anacharsis. I crave your indulgence, in venturing to compare myself with royalty. Anacharsis, after all, was a barbarian; and I should hope that we Syrians are as good as Scythians. And I am not comparing myself with Anacharsis the king, but Anacharsis the barbarian. When first I set foot in your city, I was filled with amazement at its size, its beauty, its population, its resources and splendour generally. For a time I was dumb with admiration; the sight was too much for me. I felt like the island lad Telemachus, in the palace of Menelaus; and well I might, as I viewed this city in all her pride;

A garden she, whose flowers are ev'ry blessing.

Thus affected, I had to bethink me what course I should adopt. For as to lecturing here, my mind had long been made up about *that*; what other audience could I have in view, that I should pass by this great city in silence? To make a clean breast of it, then, I set about inquiring who were your great men; for it was my design to approach them, and secure their patronage and support in facing the public. Unlike Anacharsis, who had but one informant, and a barbarian at that, I had many; and all told me the same tale, in almost the same words. 'Sir,' they said, 'we have many excellent and able men in this city—nowhere will you find more:

but two there are who stand pre-eminent; who in birth and in prestige are without a rival, and in learning and eloquence might be matched with the Ten Orators of Athens. They are regarded by the public with feelings of absolute devotion:

their will is law; for they will nothing but the highest interests of the city. Their courtesy, their hospitality towards strangers, their unassuming benevolence, their modesty in the midst of greatness, their gentleness, their affability,— all these you will presently experience, and will have something to say on the subject yourself. But—wonder of wonders!—these two are of one house, father and son. For the father, conceive to yourself a Solon, a Pericles, an Aristides:

as to the son, his manly comeliness and noble stature will attract you at the first glance; and if he do but say two words, your ears will be taken captive by the charm that sits upon his tongue. When he speaks in public, the city listens like one man, open- mouthed; 'tis Athens listening to Alcibiades; yet the Athenians presently repented of their infatuation for the son of Clinias, but here love grows to reverence; the welfare of this city, the happiness of her citizens, are all bound up in one man. Once let the father and son admit you to their friendship, and the city is yours; they have but to raise a finger, to put your success beyond a doubt.'—Such, by Heaven (if Heaven must be invoked for the purpose), such was the unvarying report I heard; and I now know from experience that it fell far short of the truth.

Then up, nor waste thy days In indolent delays,

as the Cean poet cries; I must strain every nerve, work body and soul, to gain these friends. That once achieved, fair weather and calm seas are before me, and my haven is near at hand.

THE WAY TO WRITE HISTORY

MY DEAR PHILO,

There is a story of a curious epidemic at Abdera, just after the accession of King Lysimachus. It began with the whole population's exhibiting feverish symptoms, strongly marked and unintermittent from the very first attack. About the seventh day, the fever was relieved, in some cases by a violent flow of blood from the nose, in others by perspiration not less violent. The mental effects, however, were most ridiculous; they were all stage-struck, mouthing blank verse and ranting at the top of their voices. Their favourite recitation was the *Andromeda* of Euripides; one after another would go through the great speech of Perseus; the whole place was full of pale ghosts, who were our seventh- day tragedians vociferating,

O Love, who lord'st it over Gods and men,

and the rest of it. This continued for some time, till the coming of winter put an end to their madness with a sharp frost. I find the explanation of the form it took in this fact:

Archelaus was then the great tragic actor, and in the middle of the summer, during some very hot weather, he had played the *Andromeda* there; most of them took the fever in the theatre, and convalescence was followed by a relapse—into tragedy, the *Andromeda* haunting their memories, and Perseus hovering, Gorgon's head in hand, before the mind's eye.

Well, to compare like with like, the majority of our educated class is now suffering from an Abderite epidemic. They are not stage-struck, indeed; that would have been a minor infatuation—to be possessed with other people's verses, not bad ones either; no; but from the beginning of the present excitements—the barbarian war, the Armenian disaster, the succession of victories—you cannot find a man but is writing history; nay, every one you meet is a Thucydides, a Herodotus, a Xenophon. The old saying must be true, and war be the father of all things[35], seeing what a litter of historians it has now teemed forth at a birth.

Such sights and sounds, my Philo, brought into my head that old anecdote about the Sinopean. A report that Philip was marching on the town had thrown all Corinth into a bustle; one was furbishing his arms, another wheeling stones, a third patching the wall, a fourth strengthening a battlement, every one making himself useful somehow or other. Diogenes having nothing to do—of course no one thought of giving *him* a job—was moved by the sight to gird up his philosopher's cloak and begin rolling his tub-dwelling energetically up and down the Craneum; an acquaintance asked, and got, the explanation:

'I do not want to be thought the only idler in such a busy multitude; I am rolling my tub to be like the rest.'

---

[35] See note on *Icaromenippus*, 8.

I too am reluctant to be the only dumb man at so vociferous a season; I do not like walking across the stage, like a 'super', in gaping silence; so I decided to roll *my* cask as best I could. I do not intend to write a history, or attempt actual narrative; I am not courageous enough for that; have no apprehensions on my account; I realize the danger of rolling the thing over the rocks, especially if it is only a poor little jar of brittle earthenware like mine; I should very soon knock against some pebble and find myself picking up the pieces. Come, I will tell you my idea for campaigning in safety, and keeping well out of range.

Give a wide berth to all that foam and spray, and to the anxieties which vex the historian—that I shall be wise enough to do; but I propose to give a little advice, and lay down a few principles for the benefit of those who do venture. I shall have a share in their building, if not in the dedicatory inscription; my finger-tips will at least have touched their wet mortar.

However, most of them see no need for advice here:

there might as well be an art of talking, seeing, or eating; history-writing is perfectly easy, comes natural, is a universal gift; all that is necessary is the faculty of translating your thoughts into words. But the truth is—you know it without my telling, old friend—, it is *not* a task to be lightly undertaken, or carried through without effort; no, it needs as much care as any sort of composition whatever, if one means to create 'a possession for ever,' as Thucydides calls it. Well, I know I shall not get a hearing from many of them, and some will be seriously offended—especially any who have finished and produced their work; in cases where its first reception was favourable, it would be folly to expect the authors to recast or correct; has it not the stamp of finality? is it not almost a State document? Yet even they may profit by my words; *we* are not likely to be attacked again; we have disposed of all our enemies; but there might be a Celto-Gothic or an Indo-Bactrian war; then our friends' composition might be improved by the application of my measuring-rod—always supposing that they recognize its correctness; failing that, let them do their own mensuration with the old foot-rule; the doctor will not particularly mind, though all Abdera insists on spouting the *Andromeda.*

Advice has two provinces—one of choice, the other of avoidance; let us first decide what the historian is to avoid—of what faults he must purge himself—, and then proceed to the measures he must take for putting himself on the straight high road. This will include the manner of his beginning, the order in which he should marshal his facts, the questions of proportion, of discreet silence, of full or cursory narration, of comment and connexion. Of all that, however, later on; for the present we deal with the vices to which bad writers are liable. As to those faults of diction, construction, meaning, and general amateurishness, which are common to every kind of composition, to discuss them is neither compatible with my space nor relevant to my purpose.

But there are mistakes peculiar to history; your own observation will show you just those which a constant attendance at authors' readings [36] has impressed on me; you have only to keep your ears open at every opportunity. It will be convenient, however, to refer by the way to a few illustrations in recent histories. Here is a serious fault to begin with. It is the fashion to neglect the examination of facts, and give the space gained to eulogies of generals and commanders; those of their own side they exalt to the skies, the other side they disparage intemperately. They forget that between history and panegyric there is a great gulf fixed, barring communication; in musical phrase, the two things are a couple of octaves apart. The panegyrist has only one concern—to commend and gratify his living theme some way or other; if misrepresentation will serve his purpose, he has no objection to that. History, on the other hand, abhors the intrusion of any least scruple of falsehood; it is like the windpipe, which the doctors tell us will not tolerate a morsel of stray food.

Another thing these gentlemen seem not to know is that poetry and history offer different wares, and have their separate rules. Poetry enjoys unrestricted freedom; it has but one law—the poet's fancy. He is inspired and possessed by the Muses; if he chooses to horse his car with winged steeds, or set others a-galloping over the sea, or standing corn, none challenges his right; his Zeus, with a single cord, may haul up earth and sea, and hold them dangling together—there is no fear the cord may break, the load come tumbling down and be smashed to atoms. In a complimentary picture of Agamemnon, there is nothing against his having Zeus's head and eyes, his brother Posidon's chest, Ares's belt—in fact, the son of Atreus and Aerope will naturally be an epitome of all Divinity; Zeus or Posidon or Ares could not singly or severally provide the requisite perfections. But, if history adopts such servile arts, it is nothing but poetry without the wings; the exalted tones are missing; and imposition of other kinds without the assistance of metre is only the more easily detected. It is surely a great, a superlative weakness, this inability to distinguish history from poetry; what, bedizen history, like her sister, with tale and eulogy and their attendant exaggerations? as well take some mighty athlete with muscles of steel, rig him up with purple drapery and meretricious ornament, rouge and powder his cheeks; faugh, what an object would one make of him with such defilements!

I would not be understood to exclude eulogy from history altogether; it is to be kept to its place and used with moderation, is not to tax the reader's patience; I shall presently show, indeed, that in all such matters an eye is to be had to posterity. It is true, there is a school which makes a pretty division of

---

[36] These were very common in Roman Imperial times, for purposes of advertisement, of eliciting criticism, &c. 'The audience at recitations may be compared with the modern literary reviews, discharging the functions of a preventive and emendatory, not merely of a correctional tribunal. Before publication a work might thus be known to more hearers than it would now find readers' Mayor, *Juvenal*, iii. 9.

history into the agreeable and the useful, and defends the introduction of panegyric on the ground that it is agreeable, and pleases the general reader. But nothing could be further from the truth. In the first place the division is quite a false one; history has only one concern and aim, and that is the useful; which again has one single source, and that is truth. The agreeable is no doubt an addition, if it is present; so is beauty to an athlete; but a Nicostratus, who is a fine fellow and proves himself a better man than either of his opponents, gets his recognition as a Heracles, however ugly his face may be; and if one opponent is the handsome Alcaeus himself— handsome enough to make Nicostratus in love with him, says the story—, that does not affect the issue. History too, if it can deal incidentally in the agreeable, will attract a multitude of lovers; but so long as it does its proper business efficiently—and that is the establishment of truth—, it may be indifferent to beauty.

It is further to be remarked, that in history sheer extravagance has not even the merit of being agreeable; and the extravagance of eulogy is doubly repulsive, as extravagance, and as eulogy; at least it is only welcome to the vulgar majority, not to that critical, that perhaps hypercritical audience, whom no slip can escape, who are all eyes like Argus, but keener than he, who test every word as a moneychanger might his coins, rejecting the false on the spot, but accepting the good and heavy and true; it is they that we should have in mind as we write history, and never heed the others, though they applaud till they crack their voices. If you neglect the critics, and indulge in the cloying sweetness of tales and eulogies and such baits, you will soon find your history a 'Heracles in Lydia.' No doubt you have seen some picture of him:

he is Omphale's slave, dressed up in an absurd costume, his lion- skin and club transferred to her, as though she were the true Heracles, while he, in saffron robe and purple jacket, is combing wool and wincing under Omphale's slipper. A degrading spectacle it is—the dress loose and flapping open, and all that was man in him turned to woman.

The vulgar may very likely extend their favour to this; but the select (whose judgement you disregard) will get a good deal of entertainment out of your heterogeneous, disjointed, fragmentary stuff. There is nothing which has not a beauty of its own; but take it out of its proper sphere, and the misuse turns its beauty to ugliness. Eulogy, I need hardly say, may possibly please one person, the eulogized, but will disgust every one else; this is particularly so with the monstrous exaggerations which are in fashion; the authors are so intent on the patron-hunt that they cannot relinquish it without a full exhibition of servility; they have no idea of finesse, never mask their flattery, but blurt out their unconvincing bald tale anyhow.

The consequence is, they miss even their immediate end; the objects of their praise are more inclined (and quite right too) to dislike and discard them for toadies—if they are men of spirit, at any rate. Aristobulus inserted in his history an account of a single combat between Alexander and Porus, and selected this passage to read aloud to the former; he reckoned that his best chance of pleasing was to invent heroic deeds for the king, and heighten his achievements. Well, they were on board ship in the Hydaspes; Alexander took hold of the book, and tossed it overboard; 'the author should have been treated the same way, by rights,' he added, 'for presuming to fight duels for me like that, and shoot down elephants single-handed.' A very natural indignation in Alexander, of a piece with his treatment of the intrusive architect; this person offered to convert the whole of Mount Athos into a colossal statue of the king—who however decided that he was a toady, and actually gave him less employment in ordinary than before.

The fact is, there is nothing agreeable in these things, except to any one who is fool enough to enjoy commendations which the slightest inquiry will prove to be unfounded; of course there *are* ugly persons—women more especially—who ask artists to paint them as beautiful as they can; they think they will be really better-looking if the painter heightens the rose a little and distributes a good deal of the lily. There you have the origin of the present crowd of historians, intent only upon the passing day, the selfish interest, the profit which they reckon to make out of their work; execration is their desert—in the present for their undisguised clumsy flattery, in the future for the stigma which their exaggerations bring upon history in general. If any one takes some admixture of the agreeable to be an absolute necessity, let him be content with the independent beauties of style; these are agreeable without being false; but they are usually neglected now, for the better foisting upon us of irrelevant substitutes.

Passing from that point, I wish to put on record some fresh recollections of Ionian histories—supported, now I think of it, by Greek analogies also of recent date—both concerned with the war already alluded to. You may trust my report, the Graces be my witness; I would take oath to its truth, if it were polite to swear on paper. One writer started with invoking the Muses to lend a hand. What a tasteful exordium! How suited to the historic spirit! How appropriate to the style! When he had got a little way on, he compared our ruler to Achilles, and the Parthian king to Thersites; he forgot that Achilles would have done better if he had had Hector instead of Thersites to beat, if there had been a man of might fleeing in front,

But at his heels a mightier far than he.

He next proceeded to say something handsome about himself, as a fit chronicler of such brilliant deeds. As he got near his point of departure, he threw in a word for his native town of Miletus, adding that he was thus improving on Homer, who never so much as mentioned his birthplace. And he concluded his preface with a plain express promise to advance our cause and personally wage war against the barbarians, to the best of his ability. The actual history, and recital of the causes of hostilities, began with these words:

—'The detestable Vologesus (whom Heaven confound!) commenced war on the following pretext.'

270

Enough of him. Another is a keen emulator of Thucydides, and by way of close approximation to his model starts with his own name—most graceful of beginnings, redolent of Attic thyme! Look at it:

'Crepereius Calpurnianus of Pompeiopolis wrote the history of the war between Parthia and Rome, how they warred one upon the other, beginning with the commencement of the war.' After that exordium, what need to describe the rest—what harangues he delivers in Armenia, resuscitating our old friend the Corcyrean envoy—what a plague he inflicts on Nisibis (which would not espouse the Roman cause), lifting the whole thing bodily from Thucydides—except the Pelasgicum and the Long Walls, where the victims of the earlier plague found shelter; there the difference ends; like the other, 'it began in Ethiopia, whence it descended to Egypt,' and to most of the Parthian empire, where it very discreetly remained. I left him engaged in burying the poor Athenians in Nisibis, and knew quite well how he would continue after my exit. Indeed it is a pretty common belief at present that you are writing like Thucydides, if you just use his actual words, *mutatis mutandis*.[37] Ah, and I almost forgot to mention one thing:

this same writer gives many names of weapons and military engines in Latin—*phossa* for trench, *pons* for bridge, and so forth. Just think of the dignity of history, and the Thucydidean style—the Attic embroidered with these Latin words, like a toga relieved and picked out with the purple stripe—so harmonious!

Another puts down a bald list of events, as prosy and commonplace as a private's or a carpenter's or a sutler's diary. However, there is more sense in this poor man's performance; he flies his true colours from the first; he has cleared the ground for some educated person who knows how to deal with history. The only fault I have to find with him is that he inscribes his volumes with a solemnity rather disproportioned to the rank of their contents—'Parthian History, by Callimorphus, Surgeon of the 6th Pikemen, volume so-and-so.' Ah, yes, and there is a lamentable preface, which closes with the remark that, since Asclepius is the son of Apollo, and Apollo director of the Muses and patron of all culture, it is very proper for a doctor to write history. Also, he starts in Ionic, but very soon, for no apparent reason, abandons it for every-day Greek, still keeping the Ionic *es* and *ks* and *ous*, but otherwise writing like ordinary people—rather too ordinary, indeed.

Perhaps I should balance him with a philosophic historian; this gentleman's name I will conceal, and merely indicate his attitude, as revealed in a recent publication at Corinth. Much had been expected of him, but not enough; starting straight off with the first sentence of the preface, he subjects his readers to a dialectic catechism, his thesis being the highly philosophic one,

---

[37] Omitting, with Dindorf, the words which appear in the Teubner text, after emendation, as:
mikra rakia, opos kai autos au phaiaes, on di autaen.

that no one but a philosopher should write history. Very shortly there follows a second logical process, itself followed by a third; in fact the whole preface is one mass of dialectic figures. There is flattery, indeed, *ad nauseam*, eulogy vulgar to the point of farce; but never without the logical trimmings; always that dialectical catechism. I confess it strikes me as a vulgarity also, hardly worthy of a philosopher with so long and white a beard, when he gives it in his preface as our ruler's special good fortune that philosophers should consent to record his actions; he had better have left us to reach that conclusion for ourselves—if at all.

Again, it would be a sinful neglect to omit the man who begins like this:

—'I devise to tell of Romans and Persians'; then a little later, 'For 'twas Heaven's decree that the Persians should suffer evils'; and again, 'One Osroes there was, whom Hellenes name Oxyroes'—and much more in that style. He corresponds, you see, to one of my previous examples; only he is a second Herodotus, and the other a second Thucydides.

There is another distinguished artist in words—again rather more Thucydidean than Thucydides—, who gives, according to his own idea, the clearest, most convincing descriptions of every town, mountain, plain, or river. I wish my bitterest foe no worse fate than the reading of them. Frigid? Caspian snows, Celtic ice, are warm in comparison. A whole book hardly suffices him for the Emperor's shield—the Gorgon on its boss, with eyes of blue and white and black, rainbow girdle, and snakes twined and knotted. Why, Vologesus's breeches or his bridle, God bless me, they take up several thousand lines apiece; the same for the look of Osroes's hair as he swims the Tigris—or what the cave was like that sheltered him, ivy and myrtle and bay clustered all together to shut out every ray of light. You observe how indispensable it all is to the history; without the scene, how could we have comprehended the action?

It is helplessness about the real essentials, or ignorance of what should be given, that makes them take refuge in word-painting—landscapes, caves, and the like; and when they do come upon a series of important matters, they are just like a slave whose master has left him his money and made him a rich man; he does not know how to put on his clothes or take his food properly; partridges or sweetbreads or hare are served; but he rushes in, and fills himself up with pea soup or salt fish, till he is fit to burst. Well, the man I spoke of gives the most unconvincing wounds and singular deaths:

some one has his big toe injured, and dies on the spot; the general Priscus calls out, and seven-and-twenty of the enemy fall dead at the sound. As to the numbers killed, he actually falsifies dispatches; at Europus he slaughters 70,236 of the enemy, while the Romans lose two, and have seven wounded! How any man of sense can tolerate such stuff, I do not know.

Here is another point quite worth mention. This writer has such a passion for unadulterated Attic, and for refining speech to the last degree of purity, that he metamorphoses the Latin names and translates them into Greek; Saturninus figures as Cronius, Fronto must be Phrontis, Titianus Titanius, with queerer transmogrifications yet. Further, on the subject of Severian's death, he accuses all other writers of a blunder in putting him to the sword; he is really to have starved himself to death, as the most painless method; the fact, however, is that it was all over in three days, whereas seven days is the regular time for starvation; are we perhaps to conceive an Osroes waiting about for Severian to complete the process, and putting off his assault till after the seventh day?

Then, Philo, how shall we class the historians who indulge in poetical phraseology? 'The catapult rocked responsive,' they say; 'Loud thundered the breach'; or, somewhere else in this delectable history, 'Thus Edessa was girdled with clash of arms, and all was din and turmoil,' or, 'The general pondered in his heart how to attack the wall.' Only he fills up the interstices with such wretched common lower-class phrases as 'The military prefect wrote His Majesty,' 'The troops were procuring the needful,' 'They got a wash [38] and put in an appearance,' and so on. It is like an actor with one foot raised on a high buskin, and the other in a slipper.

You will find others writing brilliant high-sounding prefaces of outrageous length, raising great expectations of the wonders to follow— and then comes a poor little appendix of a—history; it is like nothing in the world but a child—say the Eros you must have seen in a picture playing in an enormous mask of Heracles or a Titan; *parturiunt montes*, cries the audience, very naturally. That is not the way to do things; the whole should be homogeneous and uniform, and the body in proportion to the head—not a helmet of gold, a ridiculous breastplate patched up out of rags or rotten leather, shield of wicker, and pig-skin greaves. You will find plenty of historians prepared to set the Rhodian Colossus's head on the body of a dwarf; others on the contrary show us headless bodies, and plunge into the facts without exordium. These plead the example of Xenophon, who starts with 'Darius and Parysatis had two children'; if they only knew it, there is such a thing as a *virtual* exordium, not realized as such by everybody; but of that hereafter.

However, any mistake in mere expression or arrangement is excusable; but when you come to fancy geography, differing from the other not by miles or leagues, but by whole days' journeys, where is the classical model for that? One writer has taken so little trouble with his facts—never met a Syrian, I suppose, nor listened to the stray information you may pick up at the barber's—, that he thus locates Europus:

---

[38] It was suggested in the Introduction that Lucian's criticism is for practical purposes out of date; but Prescott writes:

'He was surrounded by a party of friends, who had *dropped in*, it seems, after mass, to inquire after the state of his health, some of whom had remained to partake of his repast.'

—'Europus lies in Mesopotamia, two days' journey from the Euphrates, and is a colony from Edessa.' Not content with that, this enterprising person has in the same book taken up my native Samosata and shifted it, citadel, walls, and all, into Mesopotamia, giving it the two rivers for boundaries, and making them shave past it, all but touching the walls on either side. I suspect you would laugh at me, Philo, if I were to set about convincing you that I am neither Parthian nor Mesopotamian, as this whimsical colony-planter makes me.

By the way, he has also a very attractive tale of Severian, learnt, he assures us on oath, from one of the actual fugitives. According to this, he would not die by the sword, the rope, or poison, but contrived a death which should be tragic and impressive. He was the owner of some large goblets of the most precious glass; having made up his mind to die, he broke the largest of these, and used a splinter of it for the purpose, cutting his throat with the glass. A dagger or a lancet, good enough instruments for a manly and heroic death, he could not come at, forsooth!

Then, as Thucydides composed a funeral oration over the first victims of that old war, our author feels it incumbent on him to do the same for Severian; they all challenge Thucydides, you see, little as he can be held responsible for the Armenian troubles. So he buries Severian, and then solemnly ushers up to the grave, as Pericles's rival, one Afranius Silo, a centurion; the flood of rhetoric which follows is so copious and remarkable that it drew tears from me—ye Graces!—tears of laughter; most of all where the eloquent Afranius, drawing to a close, makes mention, with weeping and distressful moans, of all those costly dinners and toasts. But he is a very Ajax in his conclusion. He draws his sword, gallantly as an Afranius should, and in sight of all cuts his throat over the grave—and God knows it was high time for an execution, if oratory can be felony. The historian states that all the spectators admired and lauded Afranius; as for me, I was inclined to condemn him on general grounds—he had all but given a catalogue of sauces and dishes, and shed tears over the memory of departed cakes—, but his capital offence was that he had not cut the historian-tragedian's throat before he left this life himself.

I assure you, my friend, I could largely increase my list of such offenders; but one or two more will suffice, before proceeding to the second part of my undertaking, the suggestions for improvement. There are some, then, who leave alone, or deal very cursorily with, all that is great and memorable; amateurs and not artists, they have no selective faculty, and loiter over copious laboured descriptions of the veriest trifles; it is as if a visitor to Olympia, instead of examining, commending or describing to his stay-at-home friends the general greatness and beauty of the Zeus, were to be struck with the exact symmetry and polish of its footstool, or the proportions of its shoe, and give all his attention to these minor points.

For instance, I have known a man get through the battle of Europus in less than seven whole lines, and then spend twenty mortal hours on a dull and perfectly irrelevant tale about a Moorish trooper. The trooper's name was Mausacas; he wandered up the hills in search of water, and came upon some Syrian yokels getting their lunch; at first they were afraid of him, but when they found he was on the right side, they invited him to share the meal; for one of them had travelled in the Moorish country, having a brother serving in the army. Then come long stories and descriptions of how he hunted there, and saw a great herd of elephants at pasture, and was nearly eaten up by a lion, and what huge fish he had bought at Caesarea. So this quaint historian leaves the terrible carnage to go on at Europus, and lets the pursuit, the forced armistice, the settling of outposts, shift for themselves, while he lingers far into the evening watching Malchion the Syrian cheapen big mackarel at Caesarea; if night had not come all too soon, I dare say he would have dined with him when the fish was cooked. If all this had not been accurately set down in the history, what sad ignorance we should have been left in! The loss to the Romans would have been irreparable, if Mausacas the Moor had got nothing to quench his thirst, and come back fasting to camp. Yet I am wilfully omitting innumerable details of yet greater importance—the arrival of a flute-girl from the next village, the exchange of gifts (Mausacas's was a spear, Malchion's a brooch), and other incidents most essential to the battle of Europus. It is no exaggeration to say that such writers never give the rose a glance, but devote all their curiosity to the thorns on its stem.

Another entertaining person, who has never set foot outside Corinth, nor travelled as far as its harbour—not to mention seeing Syria or Armenia —, starts with words which impressed themselves on my memory:

—'Seeing is believing:

I therefore write what I have seen, not what I have been told.' His personal observation has been so close that he describes the Parthian 'Dragons' (they use this ensign as a numerical formula—a thousand men to the Dragon, I believe):

they are huge live dragons, he says, breeding in Persian territory beyond Iberia; these are first fastened to great poles and hoisted up aloft, striking terror at a distance while the advance is going on; then, when the battle begins, they are released and set on the enemy; numbers of our men, it seems, were actually swallowed by them, and others strangled or crushed in their coils; of all this he was an eye-witness, taking his observations, however, from a safe perch up a tree. Thank goodness he did not come to close quarters with the brutes! we should have lost a very remarkable historian, and one who did doughty deeds in this war with his own right hand; for he had many adventures, and was wounded at Sura (in the course of a stroll from the Craneum to Lerna, apparently). All this he used to read to a Corinthian audience, which was perfectly aware that he had never so much as seen a battle-picture. Why, he did not know one weapon or engine from another; the names of manoeuvres and formations had no meaning for him; flank or front, line or column, it was all one.

275

Then there is a splendid fellow, who has boiled down into the compass of five hundred lines (or less, to be accurate) the whole business from beginning to end—campaigns in Armenia, in Syria, in Mesopotamia, on the Tigris, and in Media; and having done it, he calls it a history. His title very narrowly misses being longer than his book:

'An account of the late campaigns of the Romans in Armenia, Mesopotamia, and Media, by Antiochianus, victor at the festival of Apollo'; he had probably won some junior flat race.

I have known one writer compile a history of the future, including the capture of Vologesus, the execution of Osroes (he is to be thrown to the lions), and, crowning all, our long-deferred triumph. In this prophetic vein, he sweeps hastily on to the end of his work; yet he finds time for the foundation in Mesopotamia of a city, greatest of the great, and fairest of the fair; he is still debating, however, whether the most appropriate name will be Victoria, Concord, or Peacetown; that is yet unsettled; we must leave the fair city unnamed for the present; but it is already thickly populated—with empty dreams and literary drivellings. He has also pledged himself to an account of coming events in India, and a circumnavigation of the Atlantic; nay, the pledge is half redeemed; the preface to the *India* is complete; the third legion, the Celtic contingent, and a small Moorish division, have crossed the Indus in full force under Cassius; our most original historian will soon be posting us up in their doings—their method of 'receiving elephants,' for instance— in letters dated Muziris or Oxydracae.

These people's uneducated antics are infinite; they have no eyes for the noteworthy, nor, if they had eyes, any adequate faculty of expression; invention and fiction provide their matter, and belief in the first word that comes their style; they pride themselves on the number of books they run to, and yet more on their titles; for these again are quite absurd:

—*So-and-so's so many books of Parthian victories; The Parthis*, book I; *The Parthis*, book II—quite a rival to the *Atthis*, eh? Another does it (I have read the book) still more neatly—'*The Parthonicy of Demetrius of Sagalassus.*' I do not wish to ridicule or make a jest of these pretty histories; I write for a practical purpose:

any one who avoids these and similar errors is already well on the road to historical success; nay, he is almost there, if the logical axiom is correct, that, with incompatibles, denial of the one amounts to affirmation of the other.

Well, I may be told, *you have now a clear field; the thorns and brambles have all been extirpated, the debris of others' buildings has been carted of, the rough places have been made smooth; come, do a little construction yourself, and show that you are not only good at destroying, but capable of yourself planning a model, in which criticism itself shall find nothing to criticize.*

Well then, my perfect historian must start with two indispensable qualifications; the one is political insight, the other the faculty of expression; the first is a gift of nature, which can never be learnt; the second should have been acquired by long practice, unremitting toil, and loving study of the classics. There is nothing technical here, and no room for any advice of mine; this essay does not profess to bestow insight and acumen on those who are not endowed with them by nature; valuable, or invaluable rather, would it have been, if it could recast and modify like that, transmute lead into gold, tin into silver, magnify a Conon or Leotrophides into Titormus or Milo.

But what is the function of professional advice? not the creation of qualities which should be already there, but the indication of their proper use. No trainer, of course,—let him be Iccus, Herodicus, Theon, or who he may— will suggest that he can take a Perdiccas[39] and make an Olympic victor of him, fit to face Theagenes of Thasos or Polydamas of Scotussa; what he *will* tell you is that, given a constitution that will stand training, his system will considerably improve it. So with us—we are not to have every failure cast in our teeth, if we claim to have invented a system for so great and difficult a subject. We do not offer to take the first comer and make a historian of him— only to point out to any one who has natural insight and acquired literary skill certain straight roads (they may or may not be so in reality) which will bring him with less waste of time and effort to his goal.

I do not suppose you will object that the man with insight has no need of system and instruction upon the things he is ignorant of; in that case he might have played the harp or flute untaught, and in fact have been omniscient. But, as things are at present, he cannot perform in these ways untaught, though with some assistance he will learn very easily, and soon be able to get along by himself.

You now know what sort of a pupil I (like the trainer) insist upon. He must not be weak either at understanding or at making himself understood, but a man of penetration, a capable administrator—potentially, that is, —with a soldierly spirit (which does not however exclude the civil spirit), and some military experience; at the least he must have been in camp, seen troops drilled or manoeuvred, know a little about weapons and military engines, the differences between line and column, cavalry and infantry tactics (with the reasons for them), frontal and flank attacks; in a word, none of your armchair strategists relying wholly on hearsay.

But first and foremost, let him be a man of independent spirit, with nothing to fear or hope from anybody; else he will be a corrupt judge open to undue influences. If Philip's eye is knocked out at Olynthus by Aster the Amphipolite archer, it is not his business to exclaim, but just to show him as he is; he is not to think whether Alexander will be annoyed by a circumstantial account of the cruel murder of Clitus at table. If a Cleon has the ear of the assembly, and a monopoly of the tribune, he will not shrink on that account

---

[39] Omitting, with Dindorf, a note on Perdiccas which runs thus:
'if Perdiccas it was, and not rather Seleucus's son Antiochus, who was wasted to a shadow by his passion for his step-mother.'

from describing him as a pestilent madman; all Athens will not stop him from dwelling on the Sicilian disaster, the capture of Demosthenes, the death of Nicias, the thirst, the foul water, and the shooting down of the drinkers. He will consider very rightly that no man of sense will blame him for recounting the effects of misfortune or folly in their entirety; he is not the author, but only the reporter of them. If a fleet is destroyed, it is not he who sinks it; if there is a rout, he is not in pursuit—unless perhaps he ought to have prayed for better things, and omitted to do so. Of course, if silence or contradiction would have put matters right, Thucydides might with a stroke of the pen have knocked down the counterwall on Epipolae, sent Hermocrates's trireme to the bottom, let daylight through the accursed Gylippus before he had done blocking the roads with wall and trench, and, finally, have cast the Syracusans into their own quarries and sent the Athenians cruising round Sicily and Italy with Alcibiades's first high hopes still on board. Alas, not Fate itself may undo the work of Fate.

The historian's one task is to tell the thing as it happened. This he cannot do, if he is Artaxerxes's physician[40] trembling before him, or hoping to get a purple cloak, a golden chain, a horse of the Nisaean breed, in payment for his laudations. A fair historian, a Xenophon, a Thucydides, will not accept that position. He may nurse some private dislikes, but he will attach far more importance to the public good, and set the truth high above his hate; he may have his favourites, but he will not spare their errors. For history, I say again, has this and this only for its own; if a man will start upon it, he must sacrifice to no God but Truth; he must neglect all else; his sole rule and unerring guide is this—to think not of those who are listening to him now, but of the yet unborn who shall seek his converse.

Any one who is intent only upon the immediate effect may reasonably be classed among the flatterers; and History has long ago realized that flattery is as little congenial to her as the arts of personal adornment to an athlete's training. An anecdote of Alexander is to the point. 'Ah, Onesicritus,' said he, 'how I should like to come to life again for a little while, and see how your stuff strikes people by that time; at present they have good enough reason to praise and welcome it; that is their way of angling for a share of my favour.' On the same principle some people actually accept Homer's history of Achilles, full of exaggerations as it is; the one great guarantee which they recognize of his truth is the fact that his subject was not living; that leaves him no motive for lying.

There stands my model, then:

fearless, incorruptible, independent, a believer in frankness and veracity; one that will call a spade a spade, make no concession to likes and dislikes, nor spare any man for pity or respect or propriety; an impartial judge, kind to all, but too kind to none; a literary cosmopolite with neither suzerain nor king,

---

[40] See Ctesias in Notes

never heeding what this or that man may think, but setting down the thing that befell.

Thucydides is our noble legislator; he marked the admiration that met Herodotus and gave the Muses' names to his nine books; and thereupon he drew the line which parts a good historian from a bad:

our work is to be a possession for ever, not a bid for present reputation; we are not to seize upon the sensational, but bequeath the truth to them that come after; he applies the test of use, and defines the end which a wise historian will set before himself:

it is that, should history ever repeat itself, the records of the past may give present guidance.

Such are to be my historian's principles. As for diction and style, he is not to set about his work armed to the teeth from the rhetorician's arsenal of impetuosity and incisiveness, rolling periods, close-packed arguments, and the rest; for him a serener mood. His matter should be homogeneous and compact, his vocabulary fit to be understood of the people, for the clearest possible setting forth of his subject.

For to those marks which we set up for the historic spirit—frankness and truth—corresponds one at which the historic style should first of all aim, namely, a lucidity which leaves nothing obscure, impartially avoiding abstruse out-of-the-way expressions, and the illiberal jargon of the market; we wish the vulgar to comprehend, the cultivated to commend us. Ornament should be unobtrusive, and never smack of elaboration, if it is not to remind us of over-seasoned dishes.

The historian's spirit should not be without a touch of the poetical; it needs, like poetry, to employ impressive and exalted tones, especially when it finds itself in the midst of battle array and conflicts by land or sea; it is then that the poetic gale must blow to speed the vessel on, and help her ride the waves in majesty. But the diction is to be content with *terra firma*, rising a little to assimilate itself to the beauty and grandeur of the subject, but never startling the hearer, nor forgetting a due restraint; there is great risk at such times of its running wild and falling into poetic frenzy; and then it is that writers should hold themselves in with bit and bridle; with them as with horses an uncontrollable temper means disaster. At these times it is best for the spirit to go a-horseback, and the expression to run beside on foot, holding on to the saddle so as not to be outstripped.

As to the marshalling of your words, a moderate compromise is desirable between the harshness which results from separating what belongs together, and the jingling concatenations—one may almost call them— which are so common; one extreme is a definite vice, and the other repellent.

Facts are not to be collected at haphazard, but with careful, laborious, repeated investigation; when possible, a man should have been present and seen for himself; failing that, he should prefer the disinterested account, selecting the informants least likely to diminish or magnify from partiality. And here comes the occasion for exercising the judgement in weighing probabilities.

The material once complete, or nearly so, an abstract should be made of it, and a rough draught of the whole work put down, not yet distributed into its parts; the detailed arrangement should then be introduced, after which adornment may be added, the diction receive its colour, the phrasing and rhythm be perfected.

The historian's position should now be precisely that of Zeus in Homer, surveying now the Mysians', now the Thracian horsemen's land. Even so *he* will survey now his own party (telling us what we looked like to him from his post of vantage), now the Persians, and yet again both at once, if they come to blows. And when they are face to face, his eyes are not to be on one division, nor yet on one man, mounted or afoot—unless it be a Brasidas leading the forlorn hope, or a Demosthenes repelling it; his attention should be for the generals first of all; their exhortations should be recorded, the dispositions they make, and the motives and plans that prompted them. When the engagement has begun, he should give us a bird's-eye view of it, show the scales oscillating, and accompany pursuers and pursued alike.

All this, however, with moderation; a subject is not to be ridden to death; no neglect of proportion, no childish engrossment, but easy transitions. He should call a halt here, while he crosses over to another set of operations which demands attention; that settled up, he can return to the first set, now ripe for him; he must pass swiftly to each in turn, keeping his different lines of advance as nearly as possible level, fly from Armenia to Media, thence swoop straight upon Iberia, and then take wing for Italy, everywhere present at the nick of time.

He has to make of his brain a mirror, unclouded, bright, and true of surface; then he will reflect events as they presented themselves to him, neither distorted, discoloured, nor variable. Historians are not writing fancy school essays; what they have to say is before them, and will get itself said somehow, being solid fact; their task is to arrange and put it into words; they have not to consider what to say, but how to say it. The historian, we may say, should be like Phidias, Praxiteles, Alcamenes, or any great sculptor. They similarly did not create the gold, silver, ivory, or other material they used; it was ready to their hands, provided by Athens, Elis, or Argos; they only made the model, sawed, polished, cemented, proportioned the ivory, and plated it with gold; that was what their art consisted in—the right arrangement of their material. The historian's business is similar—to superinduce upon events the charm of order, and set them forth in the most lucid fashion he can manage. When subsequently a hearer feels as though he were looking at what is being told him, and expresses his approval, then our historical Phidias's work has reached perfection, and received its appropriate reward.

When all is ready, a writer will sometimes start without formal preface, if there is no pressing occasion to clear away preliminaries by that means, though even then his explanation of what he is to say constitutes a virtual preface.

When a formal preface is used, one of the three objects to which a public speaker devotes his exordium may be neglected; the historian, that is, has not to bespeak goodwill—only attention and an open mind. The way to secure the reader's attention is to show that the affairs to be narrated are great in themselves, throw light on Destiny, or come home to his business and bosom; and as to the open mind, the lucidity in the body of the work, which is to secure that, will be facilitated by a preliminary view of the causes in operation and a precise summary of events.

Prefaces of this character have been employed by the best historians—by Herodotus, 'to the end that what befell may not grow dim by lapse of time, seeing that it was great and wondrous, and showed forth withal Greeks vanquishing and barbarians vanquished'; and by Thucydides, 'believing that that war would be great and memorable beyond any previous one; for indeed great calamities took place during its course.'

After the preface, long or short in proportion to the subject, should come an easy natural transition to the narrative; for the body of the history which remains is nothing from beginning to end but a long narrative; it must therefore be graced with the narrative virtues— smooth, level, and consistent progress, neither soaring nor crawling, and the charm of lucidity—which is attained, as I remarked above, partly by the diction, and partly by the treatment of connected events. For, though all parts must be independently perfected, when the first is complete the second will be brought into essential connexion with it, and attached like one link of a chain to another; there must be no possibility of separating them; no mere bundle of parallel threads; the first is not simply to be next to the second, but part of it, their extremities intermingling.

Brevity is always desirable, and especially where matter is abundant; and the problem is less a grammatical than a substantial one; the solution, I mean, is to deal summarily with all immaterial details, and give adequate treatment to the principal events; much, indeed, is better omitted altogether. Suppose yourself giving a dinner, and extremely well provided; there is pastry, game, kickshaws without end, wild boar, hare, sweetbreads; well, you will not produce among these a pike, or a bowl of peasoup, just because they are there in the kitchen; you will dispense with such common things.

Restraint in descriptions of mountains, walls, rivers, and the like, is very important; you must not give the impression that you are making a tasteless display of word-painting, and expatiating independently while the history takes care of itself. Just a light touch—no more than meets the need of clearness—, and you should pass on, evading the snare, and denying yourself all such indulgences. You have the mighty Homer's example in such a case; poet as he is, he yet hurries past Tantalus and Ixion, Tityus and the rest of them. If

Parthenius, Euphorion, or Callimachus had been in his place, how many lines do you suppose it would have taken to get the water to Tantalus's lip; how many more to set Ixion spinning? Better still, mark how Thucydides—a very sparing dealer in description—leaves the subject at once, as soon as he has given an idea (very necessary and useful, too) of an engine or a siege-operation, of the conformation of Epipolae, or the Syracusan harbour. It may occur to you that his account of the plague is long; but you must allow for the subject; then you will appreciate his brevity; *he* is hastening on; it is only that the weight of matter holds him back in spite of himself.

When it comes in your way to introduce a speech, the first requirement is that it should suit the character both of the speaker and of the occasion; the second is (once more) lucidity; but in these cases you have the counsel's right of showing your eloquence.

Not so with praise or censure; these should be sparing, cautious, avoiding hypercriticism and producing proofs, always brief, and never intrusive; historical characters are not prisoners on trial. Without these precautions you will share the ill name of Theopompus, who delights in flinging accusations broadcast, makes a business of the thing in fact, and of himself rather a public prosecutor than a historian.

It may occasionally happen that some extraordinary story has to be introduced; it should be simply narrated, without guarantee of its truth, thrown down for any one to make what he can of it; the writer takes no risks and shows no preference.

But the general principle I would have remembered—it will ever be on my lips—is this:

do not write merely with an eye to the present, that those now living may commend and honour you; aim at eternity, compose for posterity, and from it ask your reward; and that reward?—that it be said of you, 'This was a man indeed, free and free-spoken; flattery and servility were not in him; he was truth all through.' It is a name which a man of judgement might well prefer to all the fleeting hopes of the present.

Do you know the story of the great Cnidian architect? He was the builder of that incomparable work, whether for size or beauty, the Pharus tower. Its light was to warn ships far out at sea, and save them from running on the Paraetonia, a spot so fatal to all who get among its reefs that escape is said to be hopeless. When the building was done, he inscribed on the actual masonry his own name, but covered this up with plaster, on which he then added the name of the reigning king. He knew that, as happened later, letters and plaster would fall off together, and reveal the words:

SOSTRATUS SON OF DEXIPHANES OF CNIDUS ON BEHALF OF ALL MARINERS TO THE SAVIOUR GODS

He looked not, it appears, to that time, nor to the space of his own little life, but to this time, and to all time, as long as his tower shall stand and his art abide.

So too should the historian write, consorting with Truth and not with flattery, looking to the future hope, not to the gratification of the flattered.

There is your measuring-line for just history. If any one be found to use it, well; I have not written in vain:

if none, yet have I rolled my tub on the Craneum.

THE TRUE HISTORY
INTRODUCTION

Athletes and physical trainers do not limit their attention to the questions of perfect condition and exercise; they say there is a time for relaxation also—which indeed they represent as the most important element in training. I hold it equally true for literary men that after severe study they should unbend the intellect, if it is to come perfectly efficient to its next task.

The rest they want will best be found in a course of literature which does not offer entertainment pure and simple, depending on mere wit or felicity, but is also capable of stirring an educated curiosity—in a way which I hope will be exemplified in the following pages. They are intended to have an attraction independent of any originality of subject, any happiness of general design, any verisimilitude in the piling up of fictions. This attraction is in the veiled reference underlying all the details of my narrative; they parody the cock-and-bull stories of ancient poets, historians, and philosophers; I have only refrained from adding a key because I could rely upon you to recognize as you read.

Ctesias, son of Ctesiochus of Cnidus, in his work on India and its characteristics, gives details for which he had neither the evidence of his eyes nor of hearsay. Iambulus's *Oceanica* is full of marvels; the whole thing is a manifest fiction, but at the same time pleasant reading. Many other writers have adopted the same plan, professing to relate their own travels, and describing monstrous beasts, savages, and strange ways of life. The fount and inspiration of their humour is the Homeric Odysseus, entertaining Alcinous's court with his prisoned winds, his men one-eyed or wild or cannibal, his beasts with many heads, and his metamorphosed comrades; the Phaeacians were simple folk, and he fooled them to the top of their bent.

When I come across a writer of this sort, I do not much mind his lying; the practice is much too well established for that, even with professed philosophers; I am only surprised at his expecting to escape detection. Now I am myself vain enough to cherish the hope of bequeathing something to posterity; I see no reason for resigning my right to that inventive freedom which others enjoy; and, as I have no truth to put on record, having lived a very humdrum life, I fall back on falsehood—but falsehood of a more consistent variety; for I now make the only true statement you are to expect—that I am a liar. This confession is, I consider, a full defence against all imputations. My subject is, then, what I have neither seen, experienced, nor been told, what neither exists nor could conceivably do so. I humbly solicit my readers' incredulity.

BOOK I

Starting on a certain date from the Pillars of Heracles, I sailed with a fair wind into the Atlantic. The motives of my voyage were a certain intellectual restlessness, a passion for novelty, a curiosity about the limits of the ocean and the peoples who might dwell beyond it. This being my design, I provisioned and watered my ship on a generous scale. My crew amounted to fifty, all men whose interests, as well as their years, corresponded with my own. I had further provided a good supply of arms, secured the best navigator to be had for money, and had the ship—a sloop—specially strengthened for a long and arduous voyage.

For a day and a night we were carried quietly along by the breeze, with land still in sight. But with the next day's dawn the wind rose to a gale, with a heavy sea and a dark sky; we found ourselves unable to take in sail. We surrendered ourselves to the elements, let her run, and were storm-driven for more than eleven weeks. On the eightieth day the sun came out quite suddenly, and we found ourselves close to a lofty wooded island, round which the waves were murmuring gently, the sea having almost fallen by this time. We brought her to land, disembarked, and after our long tossing lay a considerable time idle on shore; we at last made a start, however, and leaving thirty of our number to guard the ship I took the other twenty on a tour of inspection.

We had advanced half a mile inland through woods, when we came upon a brazen pillar, inscribed in Greek characters—which however were worn and dim—'Heracles and Dionysus reached this point.' Not far off were two footprints on rock; one might have been an acre in area, the other being smaller; and I conjecture that the latter was Dionysus's, and the other Heracles's; we did obeisance, and proceeded. Before we had gone far, we found ourselves on a river which ran wine; it was very like Chian; the stream full and copious, even navigable in parts. This evidence of Dionysus's sojourn was enough to convince us that the inscription on the pillar was authentic. Resolving to find the source, I followed the river up, and discovered, instead of a fountain, a number of huge vines covered with grapes; from the root of each there issued a trickle of perfectly clear wine, the joining of which made the river. It was well stocked with great fish, resembling wine both in colour and taste; catching and eating some, we at once found ourselves intoxicated; and indeed when opened the fish were full of wine-lees; presently it occurred to us to mix them with ordinary water fish, thus diluting the strength of our spirituous food.

We now crossed the river by a ford, and came to some vines of a most extraordinary kind. Out of the ground came a thick well-grown stem; but the upper part was a woman, complete from the loins upward. They were like our painters' representations of Daphne in the act of turning into a tree just as Apollo overtakes her. From the finger-tips sprang vine twigs, all loaded with grapes; the hair of their heads was tendrils, leaves, and grape-clusters. They

285

greeted us and welcomed our approach, talking Lydian, Indian, and Greek, most of them the last. They went so far as to kiss us on the mouth; and whoever was kissed staggered like a drunken man. But they would not permit us to pluck their fruit, meeting the attempt with cries of pain. Some of them made further amorous advances; and two of my comrades who yielded to these solicitations found it impossible to extricate themselves again from their embraces; the man became one plant with the vine, striking root beside it; his fingers turned to vine twigs, the tendrils were all round him, and embryo grape-clusters were already visible on him.

We left them there and hurried back to the ship, where we told our tale, including our friends' experiment in viticulture. Then after taking some casks ashore and filling them with wine and water we bivouacked near the beach, and next morning set sail before a gentle breeze. But about midday, when we were out of sight of the island, a waterspout suddenly came upon us, which swept the ship round and up to a height of some three hundred and fifty miles above the earth. She did not fall back into the sea, but was suspended aloft, and at the same time carried along by a wind which struck and filled the sails.

For a whole week we pursued our airy course, and on the eighth day descried land; it was an island with air for sea, glistening, spherical, and bathed in light. We reached it, cast anchor, and landed; inspection soon showed that it was inhabited and cultivated. In the daytime nothing could be discerned outside of it; but night revealed many neighbouring islands, some larger and some smaller than ours; there was also another land below us containing cities, rivers, seas, forests, and mountains; and this we concluded to be our Earth.

We were intending to continue our voyage, when we were discovered and detained by the Horse-vultures, as they are called. These are men mounted on huge vultures, which they ride like horses; the great birds have ordinarily three heads. It will give you some idea of their size if I state that each of their quill-feathers is longer and thicker than the mast of a large merchantman. This corps is charged with the duty of patrolling the land, and bringing any strangers it may find to the king; this was what was now done with us. The king surveyed us, and, forming his conclusions from our dress, 'Strangers,' said he, 'you are Greeks, are you not?' we assented. 'And how did you traverse this vast space of air?' In answer we gave a full account of ourselves, to which he at once replied with his own history. It seemed he too was a mortal, named Endymion, who had been conveyed up from our Earth in his sleep, and after his arrival had become king of the country; this was, he told us, what we knew on our Earth as the moon. He bade us be of good cheer and entertain no apprehensions; all our needs should be supplied.

'And if I am victorious,' he added, 'in the campaign which I am now commencing against the inhabitants of the Sun, I promise you an extremely pleasant life at my court.' We asked about the enemy, and the quarrel. 'Phaethon,' he replied, 'king of the Sun (which is inhabited, like the Moon), has long been at war with us. The occasion was this:

I wished at one time to collect the poorest of my subjects and send them as a colony to Lucifer, which is uninhabited. Phaethon took umbrage at this, met the emigrants half way with a troop of Horse-ants, and forbade them to proceed. On that occasion, being in inferior force, we were worsted and had to retreat; but I now intend to take the offensive and send my colony. I shall be glad if you will participate; I will provide your equipment and mount you on vultures from the royal coops; the expedition starts to-morrow.' I expressed our readiness to do his pleasure.

That day we were entertained by the king; in the morning we took our place in the ranks as soon as we were up, our scouts having announced the approach of the enemy. Our army numbered 100,000 (exclusive of camp-followers, engineers, infantry, and allies), the Horse-vultures amounting to 80,000, and the remaining 20,000 being mounted on Salad-wings. These latter are also enormous birds, fledged with various herbs, and with quill-feathers resembling lettuce leaves. Next these were the Millet- throwers and the Garlic-men. Endymion had also a contingent from the North of 30,000 Flea-archers and 50,000 Wind-coursers. The former have their name from the great fleas, each of the bulk of a dozen elephants, which they ride. The Wind-coursers are infantry, moving through the air without wings; they effect this by so girding their shirts, which reach to the ankle, that they hold the wind like a sail and propel their wearers ship-fashion. These troops are usually employed as skirmishers. 70,000 Ostrich-slingers and 50,000 Horse-cranes were said to be on their way from the stars over Cappadocia. But as they failed to arrive I did not actually see them; and a description from hearsay I am not prepared to give, as the marvels related of them put some strain on belief.

Such was Endymion's force. They were all armed alike; their helmets were made of beans, which grow there of great size and hardness; the breastplates were of overlapping lupine-husks sewn together, these husks being as tough as horn; as to shields and swords, they were of the Greek type.

When the time came, the array was as follows:

on the right were the Horse-vultures, and the King with the *elite* of his forces, including ourselves. The Salad-wings held the left, and in the centre were the various allies. The infantry were in round numbers 60,000,000; they were enabled to fall in thus:

there are in the Moon great numbers of gigantic spiders, considerably larger than an average Aegean island; these were instructed to stretch webs across from the Moon to Lucifer; as soon as the work was done, the King drew up his infantry on this artificial plain, entrusting the command to Nightbat, son of Fairweather, with two lieutenants.

On the enemy's side, Phaethon occupied the left with his Horse-ants; they are great winged animals resembling our ants except in size; but the largest of them would measure a couple of acres. The fighting was done not only by their riders; they used their horns also; their numbers were stated at 50,000. On their right was about an equal force of Sky-gnats— archers mounted on

287

great gnats; and next them the Sky-pirouetters, light- armed infantry only, but of some military value; they slung monstrous radishes at long range, a wound from which was almost immediately fatal, turning to gangrene at once; they were supposed to anoint their missiles with mallow juice. Next came the Stalk-fungi, 10,000 heavy-armed troops for close quarters; the explanation of their name is that their shields are mushrooms, and their spears asparagus stalks. Their neighbours were the Dog-acorns, Phaethon's contingent from Sirius. These were 5,000 in number, dog-faced men fighting on winged acorns. It was reported that Phaethon too was disappointed of the slingers whom he had summoned from the Milky Way, and of the Cloud-centaurs. These latter, however, arrived, most unfortunately for us, after the battle was decided; the slingers failed altogether, and are said to have felt the resentment of Phaethon, who wasted their territory with fire. Such was the force brought by the enemy.

As soon as the standards were raised and the asses on both sides (their trumpeters) had brayed, the engagement commenced. The Sunite left at once broke without awaiting the onset of the Horse-vultures, and we pursued, slaying them. On the other hand, their right had the better of our left, the Sky-gnats pressing on right up to our infantry. When these joined in, however, they turned and fled, chiefly owing to the moral effect of our success on the other flank. The rout became decisive, great numbers were taken and slain, and blood flowed in great quantities on to the clouds, staining them as red as we see them at sunset; much of it also dropped earthwards, and suggested to me that it was possibly some ancient event of the same kind which persuaded Homer that Zeus had rained blood at the death of Sarpedon.

Relinquishing the pursuit, we set up two trophies, one for the infantry engagement on the spiders' webs, and one on the clouds for the air- battle. It was while we were thus engaged that our scouts announced the approach of the Cloud-centaurs, whom Phaethon had expected in time for the battle. They were indeed close upon us, and a strange sight, being compounded of winged horses and men; the human part, from the middle upwards, was as tall as the Colossus of Rhodes, and the equine the size of a large merchantman. Their number I cannot bring myself to write down, for fear of exciting incredulity. They were commanded by Sagittarius. Finding their friends defeated, they sent a messenger after Phaethon to bring him back, and, themselves in perfect order, charged the disarrayed Moonites, who had left their ranks and were scattered in pursuit or pillage; they routed the whole of them, chased the King home, and killed the greater part of his birds; they tore up the trophies, and overran the woven plain; I myself was taken, with two of my comrades. Phaethon now arrived, and trophies were erected on the enemy's part. We were taken off to the Sun the same day, our hands tied behind with a piece of the cobweb.

They decided not to lay siege to the city; but after their return they constructed a wall across the intervening space, cutting off the Sun's rays from the Moon. This wall was double, and built of clouds; the consequence was total eclipse of the Moon, which experienced a continuous night. This severity forced Endymion to negotiate. He entreated that the wall might be taken down, and his kingdom released from this life of darkness; he offered to pay tribute, conclude an alliance, abstain from hostilities in future, and give hostages for these engagements. The Sunites held two assemblies on the question, in the first of which they refused all concessions; on the second day, however, they relented, and peace was concluded on the following terms.

Articles of peace between the Sunites and their allies of the one part, and the Moonites and their allies of the other part.

I. The Sunites shall demolish the party-wall, shall make no further incursion into the Moon, and shall hold their captives to ransom at a fixed rate.

2. The Moonites shall restore to the other stars their autonomy, shall not bear arms against the Sunites, and shall conclude with them a mutual defensive alliance.

3. The King of the Moonites shall pay to the King of the Sunites, annually, a tribute of ten thousand jars of dew, and give ten thousand hostages of his subjects.

4. The high contracting parties shall found the colony of Lucifer in common, and shall permit persons of any other nationality to join the same.

5. These articles shall be engraved on a pillar of electrum, which shall be set up on the border in mid-air.

Sworn to on behalf of the Sun by Firebrace, Heaton, and Flashman; and on behalf of the Moon by Nightwell, Monday, and Shimmer.

Peace concluded, the removal of the wall and restoration of captives at once followed. As we reached the Moon, we were met and welcomed by our comrades and King Endymion, all weeping for joy. The King wished us to remain and take part in founding the colony, and, women not existing in the Moon, offered me his son in marriage. I refused, asking that we might be sent down to the sea again; and finding that he could not prevail, he entertained us for a week, and then sent us on our way.

I am now to put on record the novelties and singularities which attracted my notice during our stay in the Moon.

When a man becomes old, he does not die, but dissolves in smoke into the air. There is one universal diet; they light a fire, and in the embers roast frogs, great numbers of which are always flying in the air; they then sit round as at table, snuffing up the fumes which rise and serve them for food; their drink is air compressed in a cup till it gives off a moisture resembling dew. Beauty with them consists in a bald head and hairless body; a good crop of hair is an abomination. On the comets, as I was told by some of their inhabitants who were there on a visit, this is reversed. They have beards, however, just above the knee; no toe-nails, and but one toe on each foot. They are all tailed, the tail being a large cabbage of an evergreen kind, which does not break if they fall upon it.

Their mucus is a pungent honey; and after hard work or exercise they sweat milk all over, which a drop or two of the honey curdles into cheese. The oil which they make from onions is very rich, and as fragrant as balsam. They have an abundance of water-producing vines, the stones of which resemble hailstones; and my own belief is that it is the shaking of these vines by hurricanes, and the consequent bursting of the grapes, that results in our hailstorms. They use the belly as a pouch in which to keep necessaries, being able to open and shut it. It contains no intestines or liver, only a soft hairy lining; their young, indeed, creep into it for protection from cold.

The clothing of the wealthy is soft glass, and of the poor, woven brass; the land is very rich in brass, which they work like wool after steeping it in water. It is with some hesitation that I describe their eyes, the thing being incredible enough to bring doubt upon my veracity. But the fact is that these organs are removable; any one can take out his eyes and do without till he wants them; then he has merely to put them in; I have known many cases of people losing their own and borrowing at need; and some—the rich, naturally—keep a large stock. Their ears are plane- leaves, except with the breed raised from acorns; theirs being of wood.

Another marvel I saw in the palace. There is a large mirror suspended over a well of no great depth; any one going down the well can hear every word spoken on our Earth; and if he looks at the mirror, he sees every city and nation as plainly as though he were standing close above each. The time I was there, I surveyed my own people and the whole of my native country; whether they saw me also, I cannot say for certain. Any one who doubts the truth of this statement has only to go there himself, to be assured of my veracity.

When the time came, we took our leave of King and court, got on board, and weighed anchor. Endymion's parting gifts to me were two glass shirts, five of brass, and a suit of lupine armour, all of which, however, I afterwards left in the whale's belly; he also sent, as our escort for the first fifty miles, a thousand of his Horse-vultures.

We passed on our way many countries, and actually landed on Lucifer, now in process of settlement, to water. We then entered the Zodiac and passed the Sun on the left, coasting close by it. My crew were very desirous of landing, but the wind would not allow of this. We had a good view of the country, however, and found it covered with vegetation, rich, well- watered, and full of all good things. The Cloud-centaurs, now in Phaethon's pay, espied us and pounced upon the ship, but left us alone when they learned that we were parties to the treaty.

By this time our escort had gone home. We now took a downward course, and twenty-four hours' sailing brought us to Lampton. This lies between the atmospheres of the Pleiads and the Hyads, though in point of altitude it is considerably lower than the Zodiac. When we landed, we found no human beings, but numberless lamps bustling about or spending their time in the market-place and harbour; some were small, and might represent the lower classes, while a few, the great and powerful, were exceedingly bright and conspicuous. They all had their own homes or lodgings, and their individual names, like us; we heard them speak, and they did us no harm, offering us entertainment, on the contrary; but we were under some apprehension, and none of us accepted either food or bed. There is a Government House in the middle of the city, where the Governor sits all night long calling the roll-call; any one not answering to his name is capitally punished as a deserter; that is to say, he is extinguished. We were present and witnessed the proceedings, and heard lamps defending their conduct and advancing reasons for their lateness. I there recognized our own house lamp, accosted him, and asked for news of my friends, in which he satisfied me. We stayed there that night, set sail next morning, and found ourselves sailing, now, nearly as low as the clouds. Here we were surprised to find Cloud-cuckoo-land; we were prevented from landing by the direction of the wind, but learned that the King's name was Crookbeak, son of Fitz-Ousel. I bethought me of Aristophanes, the learned and veracious poet whose statements had met with unmerited incredulity. Three days more, and we had a distinct view of the Ocean, though there was no land visible except the islands suspended in air; and these had now assumed a brilliant fiery hue. About noon on the fourth day the wind slackened and fell, and we were deposited upon the sea.

The joy and delight with which the touch of water affected us is indescribable; transported at our good fortune, we flung ourselves overboard and swam, the weather being calm and the sea smooth. Alas, how often is a change for the better no more than the beginning of disaster! We had but two days' delightful sail, and by the rising sun of the third we beheld a crowd of whales and marine monsters, and among them one far larger than the rest— some two hundred miles in length. It came on open- mouthed, agitating the sea far in front, bathed in foam, and exhibiting teeth whose length much surpassed the height of our great phallic images, all pointed like sharp stakes and white as elephants' tusks. We gave each other a last greeting, took a last embrace, and so awaited our doom. The monster was upon us; it sucked us in; it swallowed ship and crew entire. We escaped being ground by its teeth, the ship gliding in through the interstices.

Inside, all was darkness at first, in which we could distinguish nothing; but when it next opened its mouth, an enormous cavern was revealed, of great extent and height; a city of ten thousand inhabitants might have had room in it. Strewn about were small fish, the *disjecta membra* of many kinds of animal, ships' masts and anchors, human bones, and merchandise; in the centre was land with hillocks upon it, the alluvial deposit, I supposed, from what the whale swallowed. This was wooded with trees of all kinds, and vegetables were growing with all the appearance of cultivation. The coast might have measured thirty miles round. Sea- birds, such as gulls and halcyons, nested on the trees.

We spent some time weeping, but at last got our men up and had the ship made fast, while we rubbed wood to get a fire and prepared a meal out of

291

the plentiful materials around us; there were fragments of various fish, and the water we had taken in at Lucifer was unexhausted. Upon getting up next day, we caught glimpses, as often as the whale opened his mouth, of land, of mountains, it might be of the sky alone, or often of islands; we realized that he was dashing at a great rate to every part of the sea. We grew accustomed to our condition in time, and I then took seven of my comrades and entered the wood in search of information. I had scarcely gone half a mile when I came upon a shrine, which its inscription showed to have been raised to Posidon; a little further were a number of graves with pillars upon them, and close by a spring of clear water; we also heard a dog bark, saw some distant smoke, and conjectured that there must be a habitation.

We accordingly pressed on, and found ourselves in presence of an old man and a younger one, who were working hard at a plot of ground and watering it by a channel from the spring. We stood still, divided between fear and delight. They were standing speechless, no doubt with much the same feelings. At length the old man spoke:

—'What are you, strangers; are you spirits of the sea, or unfortunate mortals like ourselves? As for us, we are men, bred on land; but now we have suffered a sea change, and swim about in this containing monster, scarce knowing how to describe our state; reason tells us we are dead, but instinct that we live.' This loosed my tongue in turn. 'We too, father,' I said, 'are men, just arrived; it is but a day or two since we were swallowed with our ship. And now we have come forth to explore the forest; for we saw that it was vast and dense. Methinks some heavenly guide has brought us to the sight of you, to the knowledge that we are not prisoned all alone in this monster. I pray you, let us know your tale, who you are and how you entered.' Then he said that, before he asked or answered questions, he must give us such entertainment as he could; so saying, he brought us to his house—a sufficient dwelling furnished with beds and what else he might need—, and set before us green-stuff and nuts and fish, with wine for drink. When we had eaten our fill, he asked for our story. I told him all as it had passed, the storm, the island, the airy voyage, the war, and so to our descent into the whale.

It was very strange, he said, and then gave us his history in return. 'I am a Cyprian, gentlemen. I left my native land on a trading voyage with my son here and a number of servants. We had a fine ship, with a mixed cargo for Italy; you may have seen the wreckage in the whale's mouth. We had a fair voyage to Sicily, but on leaving it were caught in a gale, and carried in three days out to the Atlantic, where we fell in with the whale and were swallowed, ship and crew; of the latter we two alone survived. We buried our men, built a temple to Posidon, and now live this life, cultivating our garden, and feeding on fish and nuts. It is a great wood, as you see, and in it are vines in plenty, from which we get delicious wine; our spring you may have noticed; its water is of the purest and coldest. We use leaves for bedding, keep a good fire, snare the birds that fly in, and catch living fish by going out on the monster's gills; it is there also that we take our bath when we are disposed. There is moreover at no great distance a salt lake two or three miles round, producing all sorts of fish; in this we swim and sail, in a little boat of my building. It is now seven and twenty years since we were swallowed.

'Our lot might have been endurable enough, but we have bad and troublesome neighbours, unfriendly savages all.' 'What,' said I, 'are there other inhabitants?' 'A great many,' he replied, 'inhospitable and abhorrent to the sight. The western part of the wood (so to name the caudal region) is occupied by the Stockfish tribe; they have eels' eyes and lobster faces, are bold warriors, and eat their meat raw. Of the sides of the cavern, the right belongs to the Tritonomendetes, who from the waist upwards are human, and weazels below; their notions of justice are slightly less rudimentary than the others'. The left is in possession of the Crabhands and the Tunnyheads, two tribes in close alliance. The central part is inhabited by the Crays and the Flounderfoots, the latter warlike and extremely swift. As to this district near the mouth, the East, as it were, it is in great part desert, owing to the frequent inundations. I hold it of the Flounderfoots, paying an annual tribute of five hundred oysters.

'Such is the land; and now it is for you to consider how we may make head against all these tribes, and what shall be our manner of life.' 'What may their numbers be, all told?' I asked. 'More than a thousand.' 'And how armed?' 'They have no arms but fishbones.' 'Why then,' I said, 'let us fight them by all means; we are armed, and they are not; and, if we win, we shall live secure.' We agreed on this course, and returned to the ship to make our preparations. The pretext for war was to be non-payment of the tribute, which was on the point of falling due. Messengers, in fact, shortly came to demand it, but the old man sent them about their business with an insolent answer. The Flounderfoots and Crays were enraged, and commenced operations with a tumultuous inroad upon Scintharus—this was our old man's name.

Expecting this, we were awaiting the attack in full armour. We had put five and twenty men in ambush, with directions to fall on the enemy's rear as soon as they had passed; they executed their orders, and came on from behind cutting them down, while the rest of us—five and twenty also, including Scintharus and his son—met them face to face with a spirited and resolute attack. It was risky work, but in the end we routed and chased them to their dens. They left one hundred and seventy dead, while we lost only our navigating officer, stabbed in the back with a mullet rib, and one other.

We held the battlefield for the rest of that day and the night following, and erected a trophy consisting of a dolphin's backbone upright. Next day the news brought the other tribes out, with the Stockfish under a general called Slimer on the right, the Tunnyheads on the left, and the Crabhands in the centre; the Tritonomendetes stayed at home, preferring neutrality. We did not wait to be attacked, but charged them near Posidon's temple with loud shouts, which echoed as in a subterranean cave. Their want of armour gave us the victory; we pursued them to the wood, and were henceforth masters.

Soon after, they sent heralds to treat for recovery of their dead, and for peace. But we decided to make no terms with them, and marching out next day exterminated the whole, with the exception of the Tritonomendetes. These too, when they saw what was going on, made a rush for the gills, and cast themselves into the sea. We went over the country, now clear of enemies, and occupied it from that time in security. Our usual employments were exercise, hunting, vine-dressing, and fruit-gathering; we were in the position of men in a vast prison from which escape is out of the question, but within which they have luxury and freedom of movement. This manner of life lasted for a year and eight months.

It was on the fifth of the next month, about the second gape (the whale, I should say, gaped regularly once an hour, and we reckoned time that way)— about the second gape, then, a sudden shouting and tumult became audible; it sounded like boatswains giving the time and oars beating. Much excited, we crept right out into our monster's mouth, stood inside the teeth, and beheld the most extraordinary spectacle I ever looked upon—giants of a hundred yards in height rowing great islands as we do triremes. I am aware that what I am to relate must sound improbable; but I cannot help it. Very long islands they were, but of no great height; the circumference of each would be about eleven miles; and its complement of giants was some hundred and twenty. Of these some sat along each side of the island, rowing with big cypresses, from which the branches and leaves were not stripped; in the stern, so to speak, was a considerable hillock, on which stood the helmsman with his hand on a brazen steering- oar of half a mile in length; and on the deck forward were forty in armour, the combatants; they resembled men except in their hair, which was flaming fire, so that they could dispense with helmets. The work of sails was done by the abundant forest on all the islands, which so caught and held the wind that it drove them where the steersman wished; there was a boatswain timing the stroke, and the islands jumped to it like great galleys.

We had seen only two or three at first; but there appeared afterwards as many as six hundred, which formed in two lines and commenced an action. Many crashed into each other stem to stem, many were rammed and sunk, others grappled, fought an obstinate duel, and could hardly get clear after it. Great courage was shown by the troops on deck, who boarded and dealt destruction, giving no quarter. Instead of grappling-irons, they used huge captive squids, which they swung out on to the hostile island; these grappled the wood and so held the island fast. Their missiles, effective enough, were oysters the size of waggons, and sponges which might cover an acre.

Aeolocentaur and Thalassopot were the names of the rival chiefs; and the question between them was one of plunder; Thalassopot was supposed to have driven off several herds of dolphins, the other's property; we could hear them vociferating the charge and calling out their Kings' names. Aeolocentaur's fleet finally won, sinking one hundred and fifty of the enemy's islands and capturing three with their crews; the remainder backed away, turned and fled. The victors pursued some way, but, as it was now evening, returned to the disabled ones, secured most of the enemy's, and recovered their own, of which as many as eighty had been sunk. As a trophy of victory they slung one of the enemy's islands to a stake which they planted in our whale's head. They lay moored round him that night, attaching cables to him or anchoring hard by; they had vast glass anchors, very strong. Next morning they sacrificed on the whale's back, buried their dead there, and sailed off rejoicing, with something corresponding to our paean. So ended the battle of the islands.

BOOK II

I now began to find life in the whale unendurable; I was tired to death of it, and concentrated my thoughts on plans of escape. Our first idea was to excavate a passage through the beast's right side, and go out through it. We actually began boring, but gave it up when we had penetrated half a mile without getting through. We then determined to set fire to the forest, our object being the death of the whale, which would remove all difficulties. We started burning from the tail end; but for a whole week he made no sign; on the eighth and ninth days it was apparent that he was unwell; his jaws opened only languidly, and each time closed again very soon. On the tenth and eleventh days mortification had set in, evidenced by a horrible stench; on the twelfth, it occurred to us, just in time, that we must take the next occasion of the mouth's being open to insert props between the upper and lower molars, and so prevent his closing it; else we should be imprisoned and perish in the dead body. We successfully used great beams for the purpose, and then got the ship ready with all the water and provisions we could manage. Scintharus was to navigate her. Next day the whale was dead.

We hauled the vessel up, brought her through one of the gaps, slung her to the teeth, and so let her gently down to the water. We then ascended the back, where we sacrificed to Posidon by the side of the trophy, and, as there was no wind, encamped there for three days. On the fourth day we were able to start. We found and came into contact with many corpses, the relics of the sea-fight, and our wonder was heightened when we measured them. For some days we enjoyed a moderate breeze, after which a violent north wind rose, bringing hard frost; the whole sea was frozen—not merely crusted over, but solidified to four hundred fathoms' depth; we got out and walked about. The continuance of the wind making life intolerable, we adopted the plan, suggested by Scintharus, of hewing an extensive cavern in the ice, in which we stayed a month, lighting fires and feeding on fish; we had only to dig these out. In the end, however, provisions ran short, and we came out; the ship was frozen in, but we got her free; we then hoisted sail, and were carried along as well as if we had been afloat, gliding smoothly and easily over the ice. After five days more the temperature rose, a thaw set in, and all was water again.

A stretch of five and thirty miles brought us to a small desert isle, where we got water—of which we were now in want—, and shot two wild bulls before we departed. These animals had their horns not on the top of the head, but, as Momus recommended, below the eyes. Not long after this, we entered a sea of milk, in which we observed an island, white in colour, and full of vines. The island was one great cheese, quite firm, as we afterwards ascertained by eating it, and three miles round. The vines were covered with fruit, but the drink we squeezed from it was milk instead of wine. In the centre of the island was a temple to Galatea the Nereid, as the inscription informed us. During our stay there, the ground itself served us for bread and meat, and the vine-milk for drink. We learned that the queen of these regions was Tyro, daughter of Salmoneus, on whom Posidon had conferred this dignity at her decease.

After spending five days there we started again with a gentle breeze and a rippling sea. A few days later, when we had emerged from the milk into blue salt water, we saw numbers of men walking on the sea; they were like ourselves in shape and stature, with the one exception of the feet, which were of cork; whence, no doubt, their name of Corksoles. It struck us as curious that they did not sink in, but travelled quite comfortably clear of the water. Some of them came up and hailed us in Greek, saying that they were making their way to their native land of Cork. They ran alongside for some distance, and then turned off and went their own way, wishing us a pleasant voyage. A little further we saw several islands; close to us on the left was Cork, our friends' destination, consisting of a city founded on a vast round cork; at a greater distance, and a little to the right, were five others of considerable size and high out of the water, with great flames rising from them.

There was also a broad low one, as much as sixty miles in length, straight in our course. As we drew near it, a marvellous air was wafted to us, exquisitely fragrant, like the scent which Herodotus describes as coming from Arabia Felix. Its sweetness seemed compounded of rose, narcissus, hyacinth, lilies and violets, myrtle and bay and flowering vine. Ravished with the perfume, and hoping for reward of our long toils, we drew slowly near. Then were unfolded to us haven after haven, spacious and sheltered, and crystal rivers flowing placidly to the sea. There were meadows and groves and sweet birds, some singing on the shore, some on the branches; the whole bathed in limpid balmy air. Sweet zephyrs just stirred the woods with their breath, and brought whispering melody, delicious, incessant, from the swaying branches; it was like Pan-pipes heard in a desert place. And with it all there mingled a volume of human sound, a sound not of tumult, but rather of revels where some flute, and some praise the fluting, and some clap their hands commending flute or harp.

Drawn by the spell of it we came to land, moored the ship, and left her, in charge of Scintharus and two others. Taking our way through flowery meadows we came upon the guardians of the peace, who bound us with rose-garlands—their strongest fetters—and brought us to the governor. As we went they told us this was the island called of the Blest, and its governor the Cretan Rhadamanthus. When we reached the court, we found there were three cases to be taken before our turn would come.

The first was that of Ajax, son of Telamon, and the question was whether he was to be admitted to the company of Heroes; it was objected that he had been mad and taken his own life. After long pleadings Rhadamanthus gave his decision:

he was to be put under the charge of Hippocrates the physician of Cos for the hellebore treatment, and, when he had recovered his wits, to be made free of the table.

The second was a matrimonial case, the parties Theseus and Menelaus, and the issue possession of Helen. Rhadamanthus gave it in favour of Menelaus, on the ground of the great toils and dangers the match had cost him—added to the fact that Theseus was provided with other wives in the Amazon queen and the daughters of Minos.

The third was a dispute for precedence between Alexander son of Philip and Hannibal the Carthaginian; it was won by the former, who had a seat assigned him next to Cyrus the elder.

It was now our turn. The judge asked by what right we set foot on this holy ground while yet alive. In answer we related our story. He then had us removed while he held a long consultation with his numerous assessors, among whom was the Athenian Aristides the Just. He finally reached a conclusion and gave judgement:

on the charges of curiosity and travelling we were remanded till the date of our deaths; for the present we were to stay in the island, with admission to the Heroic society, for a fixed term, after which we must depart. The limit he appointed for our stay was seven months.

Our rose-chains now fell off of their own accord, we were released and taken into the city, and to the Table of the Blest. The whole of this city is built of gold, and the enclosing wall of emerald. It has seven gates, each made of a single cinnamon plank. The foundations of the houses, and all ground inside the wall, are ivory; temples are built of beryl, and each contains an altar of one amethyst block, on which they offer hecatombs. Round the city flows a river of the finest perfume, a hundred royal cubits in breadth, and fifty deep, so that there is good swimming. The baths, supplied with warm dew instead of ordinary water, are in great crystal domes heated with cinnamon wood.

Their raiment is fine cobweb, purple in colour. They have no bodies, but are intangible and unsubstantial—mere form without matter; but, though incorporeal, they stand and move, think and speak; in short, each is a naked soul, but carries about the semblance of body; one who did not touch them would never know that what he looked at was not substantial; they are shadows, but upright, and coloured. A man there does not grow old, but stays at whatever age he brought with him. There is no night, nor yet bright day; the morning twilight, just before sunrise, gives the best idea of the light that prevails. They have also but one season, perpetual spring, and the wind is always in the west.

The country abounds in every kind of flower, in shrubs and garden herbs. There are twelve vintages in the year, the grapes ripening every month; and they told us that pomegranates, apples, and other fruits were gathered thirteen times, the trees producing twice in their month Minous. Instead of grain, the corn develops loaves, shaped like mushrooms, at the top of the stalks. Round the city are 365 springs of water, the same of honey, and 500, less in volume however, of perfume. There are also seven rivers of milk and eight of wine.

The banqueting-place is arranged outside the city in the Elysian Plain. It is a fair lawn closed in with thick-grown trees of every kind, in the shadow of which the guests recline, on cushions of flowers. The waiting and handing is done by the winds, except only the filling of the wine- cup. That is a service not required; for all round stand great trees of pellucid crystal, whose fruit is drinking-cups of every shape and size. A guest arriving plucks a cup or two and sets them at his place, where they at once fill with wine. So for their drink; and instead of garlands, the nightingales and other singing birds pick flowers with their beaks from the meadows round, and fly over snowing the petals down and singing the while. Nor is perfume forgotten; thick clouds draw it up from the springs and river, and hanging overhead are gently squeezed by the winds till they spray it down in fine dew.

During the meal there is music and song. In the latter kind, Homer's verse is the favourite; he is himself a member of the festal company, reclining next above Odysseus. The choirs are of boys and girls, conducted and led by Eunomus the Locrian, Arion of Lesbos, Anacreon and Stesichorus; this last had made his peace with Helen, and I saw him there. When these have finished, a second choir succeeds, of swans and swallows and nightingales; and when their turn is done, all the trees begin to pipe, conducted by the winds.

I have still to add the most important element in their good cheer:

there are two springs hard by, called the Fountain of Laughter, and the Fountain of Delight. They all take a draught of both these before the banquet begins, after which the time goes merrily and sweetly.

I should now like to name the famous persons I saw. To begin with, all the demi-gods, and the besiegers of Troy, with the exception of Ajax the Locrian; he, they said, was undergoing punishment in the place of the wicked. Of barbarians there were the two Cyruses, Anacharsis the Scythian, Zamolxis the Thracian, and the Latin Numa; and then Lycurgus the Spartan, Phocion and Tellus of Athens, and the Wise Men, but without Periander. And I saw Socrates son of Sophroniscus in converse with Nestor and Palamedes; clustered round him were Hyacinth the Spartan, Narcissus of Thespiae, Hylas, and many another comely boy. With Hyacinth I suspected that he was in love; at least he was for ever poking questions at him. I heard that Rhadamanthus was dissatisfied with Socrates, and had several times threatened him with expulsion, if he insisted on talking nonsense, and would not drop his irony and enjoy himself. Plato was the only one I missed, but I was told that he was living in his own Utopia, working the constitution and laws which he had drawn up.

For popularity, Aristippus and Epicurus bore the palm, in virtue of their kindliness, sociability, and good-fellowship. Aesop the Phrygian was there, and held the office of jester. Diogenes of Sinope was much changed; he had married Lais the courtesan, and often in his cups would oblige the company with a dance, or other mad pranks. The Stoics were not represented at all; they were supposed to be still climbing the steep hill of Virtue; and as to Chrysippus himself, we were told that he was not to set foot on the island till he had taken a fourth course of hellebore. The Academics contemplated coming, but were taking time for consideration; they could not yet regard it as a certainty that any such island existed. There was probably the added difficulty that they were not comfortable about the judgement of Rhadamanthus, having themselves disputed the possibility of judgement. It was stated that many of them had started to follow persons travelling to the island, but, their energy failing, had abandoned the journey half-way and gone back.

I have mentioned the most noteworthy of the company, and add that the most highly respected among them are, first Achilles, and second Theseus.

Before many days had passed, I accosted the poet Homer, when we were both disengaged, and asked him, among other things, where he came from; it was still a burning question with us, I explained. He said he was aware that some brought him from Chios, others from Smyrna, and others again from Colophon; the fact was, he was a Babylonian, generally known not as Homer, but as Tigranes; but when later in life he was given as a *homer* or hostage to the Greeks, that name clung to him. Another of my questions was about the so-called spurious lines; had he written them, or not? He said they were all genuine; so I now knew what to think of the critics Zenodotus and Aristarchus, and all their lucubrations. Having got a categorical answer on that point, I tried him next on his reason for starting the Iliad at the wrath of Achilles; he said he had no exquisite reason; it had just come into his head that way. Another thing I wanted to know was whether he had composed the Odyssey before the Iliad, as generally believed. He said this was not so. As to his reported blindness, I did not need to ask; he had his sight, so there was an end of that. It became a habit of mine, whenever I saw him at leisure, to go up and ask him things, and he answered quite readily—especially after his acquittal; a libel suit had been brought against him by Thersites, on the ground of the ridicule to which he is subjected in the poem; Homer had briefed Odysseus, and been acquitted.

It was during our sojourn that Pythagoras arrived; he had undergone seven transmigrations, lived the lives of that number of animals, and completed his psychic travels. It was the entire right half of him that was gold. He was at once given the franchise, but the question was still pending whether he was to be known as Pythagoras or Euphorbus. Empedocles also came, scorched all over and baked right through; but not all his entreaties could gain him admittance.

The progress of time brought round the Games of the Dead. The umpires were Achilles, holding that office for the fifth, and Theseus for the seventh time. A full report would take too long; but I will summarize the events. The wrestling went to Carus the Heraclid, who won the garland from Odysseus. The boxing resulted in a tie; the pair being the Egyptian Areus, whose grave is in Corinth, and Epeus. For mixed boxing and wrestling they have no prize. Who won the flat race, I have forgotten. In poetry, Homer really did much the best, but the award was for Hesiod. All prizes were plaited wreaths of peacock feathers.

Just after the Games were over, news came that the Damned had broken their fetters, overpowered their guard, and were on the point of invading the island, the ringleaders being Phalaris of Agrigentum, Busiris the Egyptian, Diomedes the Thracian, Sciron, and Pityocamptes. Rhadamanthus at once drew up the Heroes on the beach, giving the command to Theseus, Achilles, and Ajax Telamonius, now in his right senses. The battle was fought, and won by the Heroes, thanks especially to Achilles. Socrates, who was in the right wing, distinguished himself still more than in his lifetime at Delium, standing firm and showing no sign of trepidation as the enemy came on; he was afterwards given as a reward of valour a large and beautiful park in the outskirts, to which he invited his friends for conversation, naming it the Post-mortem Academy.

The defeated party were seized, re-fettered, and sent back for severer torments. Homer added to his poems a description of this battle, and at my departure handed me the MS. to bring back to the living world; but it was unfortunately lost with our other property. It began with the line:

Tell now, my Muse, how fought the mighty Dead.
According to their custom after successful war, they boiled beans, held the feast of victory, and kept high holiday. From this Pythagoras alone held aloof, fasting and sitting far off, in sign of his abhorrence of bean-eating.

We were in the middle of our seventh month, when an incident happened. Scintharus's son, Cinyras, a fine figure of a man, had fallen in love with Helen some time before, and it was obvious that she was very much taken with the young fellow; there used to be nods and becks and takings of wine between them at table, and they would go off by themselves for strolls in the wood. At last love and despair inspired Cinyras with the idea of an elopement. Helen consented, and they were to fly to one of the neighbouring islands, Cork or Cheese Island. They had taken three of the boldest of my crew into their confidence; Cinyras said not a word to his father, knowing that he would put a stop to it. The plan was carried out; under cover of night, and in my absence— I had fallen asleep at table—, they got Helen away unobserved and rowed off as hard as they could.

300

About midnight Menelaus woke up, and finding his wife's place empty raised an alarm, and got his brother to go with him to King Rhadamanthus. Just before dawn the look-outs announced that they could make out the boat, far out at sea. So Rhadamanthus sent fifty of the Heroes on board a boat hollowed out of an asphodel trunk, with orders to give chase. Pulling their best, they overtook the fugitives at noon, as they were entering the milky sea near the Isle of Cheese; so nearly was the escape effected. The boat was towed back with a chain of roses. Helen shed tears, and so felt her situation as to draw a veil over her face. As to Cinyras and his associates, Rhadamanthus interrogated them to find whether they had more accomplices, and, being assured to the contrary, had them whipped with mallow twigs, bound, and dismissed to the place of the wicked.

It was further determined that we should be expelled prematurely from the island; we were allowed only one day's grace. This drew from me loud laments and tears for the bliss that I was now to exchange for renewed wanderings. They consoled me for their sentence, however, by telling me that it would not be many years before I should return to them, and assigning me my chair and my place at table—a distinguished one—in anticipation. I then went to Rhadamanthus, and was urgent with him to reveal the future to me, and give me directions for our voyage. He told me that I should come to my native land after many wanderings and perils, but as to the time of my return he would give me no certainty. He pointed, however, to the neighbouring islands, of which five were visible, besides one more distant, and informed me that the wicked inhabited these, the near ones, that is, 'from which you see the great flames rising; the sixth yonder is the City of Dreams; and beyond that again, but not visible at this distance, is Calypso's isle. When you have passed these, you will come to the great continent which is opposite your own; there you will have many adventures, traverse divers tribes, sojourn among inhospitable men, and at last reach your own continent.' That was all he would say.

But he pulled up a mallow root and handed it to me, bidding me invoke it at times of greatest danger. When I arrived in this world, he charged me to abstain from stirring fire with a knife, from lupines, and from the society of boys over eighteen; these things if I kept in mind, I might look for return to the island. That day I made ready for our voyage, and when the banquet hour came, I shared it. On the morrow I went to the poet Homer and besought him to write me a couplet for inscription; when he had done it, I carved it on a beryl pillar which I had set up close to the harbour; it ran thus:

> This   island,   ere   he   took   his   homeward   way,
> The blissful Gods gave Lucian to survey.

I stayed out that day too, and next morning started, the Heroes attending to see me off. Odysseus took the opportunity to come unobserved by Penelope and give me a letter for Calypso in the isle Ogygia. Rhadamanthus sent on board with me the ferryman Nauplius, who, in case we were driven on to the islands, might secure us from seizure by guaranteeing that our destination was different. As soon as our progress brought us out of the scented air, it was succeeded by a horrible smell as of bitumen, brimstone, and pitch all burning together; mingled with this were the disgusting and intolerable fumes of roasting human flesh; the air was dark and thick, distilling a pitchy dew upon us; we could also hear the crack of whips and the yelling of many voices.

We only touched at one island, on which we also landed. It was completely surrounded by precipitous cliffs, arid, stony, rugged, treeless, unwatered. We contrived to clamber up the rocks, and advanced along a track beset with thorns and snags—a hideous scene. When we reached the prison and the place of punishment, what first drew our wonder was the character of the whole. The very ground stood thick with a crop of knife- blades and pointed stakes; and it was ringed round with rivers, one of slime, a second of blood, and the innermost of flame. This last was very broad and quite impassable; the flame flowed like water, swelled like the sea, and teemed with fish, some resembling firebrands, and others, the small ones, live coals; these were called lamplets.

One narrow way led across all three; its gate was kept by Timon of Athens. Nauplius secured us admission, however, and then we saw the chastisement of many kings, and many common men; some were known to us; indeed there hung Cinyras, swinging in eddies of smoke. Our guides described the life and guilt of each culprit; the severest torments were reserved for those who in life had been liars and written false history; the class was numerous, and included Ctesias of Cnidus, and Herodotus. The fact was an encouragement to me, knowing that I had never told a lie.

I soon found the sight more than I could bear, and returning to the ship bade farewell to Nauplius and resumed the voyage. Very soon we seemed quite close to the Isle of Dreams, though there was a certain dimness and vagueness about its outline; but it had something dreamlike in its very nature; for as we approached it receded, and seemed to get further and further off. At last we reached it and sailed into Slumber, the port, close to the ivory gates where stands the temple of the Cock. It was evening when we landed, and upon proceeding to the city we saw many strange dreams. But I intend first to describe the city, as it has not been done before; Homer indeed mentions it, but gives no detailed description.

The whole place is embowered in wood, of which the trees are poppy and mandragora, all thronged with bats; this is the only winged thing that exists there. A river, called the Somnambule, flows close by, and there are two springs at the gates, one called Wakenot, and the other Nightlong. The rampart is lofty and of many colours, in the rainbow style. The gates are not two, as Homer says, but four, of which two look on to the plain Stupor; one of them is of iron, the other of pottery, and we were told that these are used by the grim, the murderous, and the cruel. The other pair face the sea and port, and are of horn—it was by this that we had entered—and of ivory. On the right as you enter the city stands the temple of Night, which deity divides with the Cock their chief allegiance; the temple of the latter is close to the port. On the left is the palace of Sleep. He is the governor, with two lieutenants, Nightmare, son of Whimsy, and Flittergold, son of Fantasy. A well in the middle of the market-place goes by the name of Heavyhead; beside which are the temples of Deceit and Truth. In the market also is the shrine in which oracles are given, the priest and prophet, by special appointment from Sleep, being Antiphon the dream-interpreter.

The dreams themselves differed widely in character and appearance. Some were well-grown, smooth-skinned, shapely, handsome fellows, others rough, short, and ugly; some apparently made of gold, others of common cheap stuff. Among them some were found with wings, and other strange variations; others again were like the mummers in a pageant, tricked out as kings or Gods or what not. Many of them we felt that we had seen in our world, and sure enough these came up and claimed us as old acquaintance; they took us under their charge, found us lodgings, entertained us with lavish kindness, and, not content with the magnificence of this present reception, promised us royalties and provinces. Some of them also took us to see our friends, doing the return trip all in the day.

For thirty days and nights we abode there—a very feast of sleep. Then on a sudden came a mighty clap of thunder:

we woke; jumped up; provisioned; put off. In three days we were at the Isle of Ogygia, where we landed. Before delivering the letter, I opened and read it; here are the contents:

ODYSSEUS TO CALYPSO, GREETING. Know that in the faraway days when I built my raft and sailed away from you, I suffered shipwreck; I was hard put to it, but Leucothea brought me safe to the land of the Phaeacians; they gave me passage home, and there I found a great company suing for my wife's hand and living riotously upon our goods. All them I slew, and in after years was slain by Telegonus, the son that Circe bare me. And now I am in the Island of the Blest, ruing the day when I left the life I had with you, and the everlasting life you proffered. I watch for opportunity, and meditate escape and return. Some words were added, commending us to her hospitality.

A little way from the sea I found the cave just as it is in Homer, and herself therein at her spinning. She took and read the letter, wept for a space, and then offered us entertainment; royally she feasted us, putting questions the while about Odysseus and Penelope; what were her looks? and was she as discreet as Odysseus had been used to vaunt her? To which we made such answers as we thought she would like.

Leaving her, we went on board, and spent the night at anchor just off shore; in the morning we started with a stiff breeze, which grew to a gale lasting two days; on the third day we fell in with the Pumpkin- pirates. These are savages of the neighbouring islands who prey upon passing ships. They use large boats made of pumpkins ninety feet long. The pumpkin is dried and hollowed out by removal of the pulp, and the boat is completed by the addition of cane masts and pumpkin-leaf sails. Two boatfuls of them engaged us, and we had many casualties from their pumpkin-seed missiles. The fight was long and well matched; but about noon we saw a squadron of Nut-tars coming up in rear of the enemy. It turned out that the two parties were at war; for as soon as our assailants observed the others, they left us alone and turned to engage them.

Meanwhile we hoisted sail and made the best of our way off, leaving them to fight it out. It was clear that the Nut-tars must win, as they had both superior numbers—there were five sail of them—and stronger vessels. These were made of nutshells, halved and emptied, measuring ninety feet from stem to stern. As soon as they were hull down, we attended to our wounded; and from that time we made a practice of keeping on our armour, to be in instant readiness for an attack—no vain precaution either.

Before sunset, for instance, there assailed us from a bare island some twenty men mounted on large dolphins—pirates again. Their dolphins carried them quite well, curvetting and neighing. When they got near, they divided, and subjected us to a cross fire of dry cuttlefish and crabs' eyes. But our arrows and javelins were too much for them, and they fled back to the island, few of them unwounded.

At midnight, in calm weather, we found ourselves colliding with an enormous halcyon's nest; it was full seven miles round. The halcyon was brooding, not much smaller herself than the nest. She got up, and very nearly capsized us with the fanning of her wings; however, she went off with a melancholy cry. When it was getting light, we got on to the nest, and found on examination that it was composed like a vast raft of large trees. There were five hundred eggs, larger in girth than a tun of Chian. We could make out the chicks inside and hear them croaking; we hewed open one egg with hatchets, and dug out an unfledged chick bulkier than twenty vultures.

Sailing on, we had left the nest some five and twenty miles behind, when a miracle happened. The wooden goose of our stern-post suddenly clapped its wings and started cackling; Scintharus, who was bald, recovered his hair; most striking of all, the ship's mast came to life, putting forth branches sideways, and fruit at the top; this fruit was figs, and a bunch of black grapes, not yet ripe. These sights naturally disturbed us, and we fell to praying the Gods to avert any disaster they might portend.

We had proceeded something less than fifty miles when we saw a great forest, thick with pines and cypresses. This we took for the mainland; but it was in fact deep sea, set with trees; they had no roots, but yet remained in their places, floating upright, as it were. When we came near and realized the state of the case, we could not tell what to do; it was impossible to sail between the trees, which were so close as to touch one another, and we did not like the thought of turning back. I climbed the tallest tree to get a good view, and found that the wood was five or six miles across, and was succeeded by open water. So we determined to hoist the ship on to the top of the foliage, which was very dense, and get her across to the other sea, if possible. It proved to be so. We attached a strong cable, got up on the tree-tops, and hauled her after us with some difficulty; then we laid her on the branches, hoisted sail, and floating thus were propelled by the wind. A line of Antimachus came into my head:

And as they voyaged thus the woodland through—

Well, we made our way over and reached the water, into which we let her down in the same way. We then sailed through clear transparent sea, till we found ourselves on the edge of a great gorge which divided water from water, like the land fissures which are often produced by earthquakes. We got the sails down and brought her to just in time to escape making the plunge. We could bend over and see an awful mysterious gulf perhaps a hundred miles deep, the water standing wall against wall. A glance round showed us not far off to the right a water bridge which spanned the chasm, and gave a moving surface crossing from one sea to the other. We got out the sweeps, pulled her to the bridge, and with great exertions effected that astonishing passage.

There followed a sail through smooth water, and then a small island, easy of approach, and inhabited; its occupants were the Ox-heads, savage men with horns, after the fashion of our poets' Minotaur. We landed and went in search of water and provisions, of which we were now in want. The water we found easily, but nothing else; we heard, however, not far off, a numerous lowing; supposing it to indicate a herd of cows, we went a little way towards it, and came upon these men. They gave chase as soon as they saw us, and seized three of my comrades, the rest of us getting off to sea. We then armed—for we would not leave our friends unavenged— and in full force fell on the Ox-heads as they were dividing our slaughtered men's flesh. Our combined shout put them to flight, and in the pursuit we killed about fifty, took two alive, and returned with our captives. We had found nothing to eat; the general opinion was for slaughtering the prisoners; but I refused to accede to this, and kept them in bonds till an embassy came from the Ox-heads to ransom them; so we understood the motions they made, and their tearful supplicatory lowings. The ransom consisted of a quantity of cheese, dried fish, onions, and four deer; these were three-footed, the two forefeet being joined into one. In exchange for all this we restored the prisoners, and after one day's further stay departed.

By this time we were beginning to observe fish, birds on the wing, and other signs of land not far off; and we shortly saw men, practising a mode of navigation new to us; for they were boat and crew in one. The method was this:

they float on their backs, erect a sail, and then, holding the sheets with their hands, catch the wind. These were succeeded by others who sat on corks, to which were harnessed pairs of dolphins, driven with reins. They neither attacked nor avoided us, but drove along in all confidence and peace, admiring the shape of our craft and examining it all round.

That evening we touched at an island of no great size. It was occupied by what we took for women, talking Greek. They came and greeted us with kisses, were attired like courtesans, all young and fair, and with long robes sweeping the ground. Cabbalusa was the name of the island, and Hydramardia the city's. These women paired off with us and led the way to their separate homes. I myself tarried a little, under the influence of some presentiment, and looking more closely observed quantities of human bones and skulls lying about. I did not care to raise an alarm, gather my men, and resort to arms; instead, I drew out my mallow, and prayed earnestly to it for escape from our perilous position. Shortly after, as my hostess was serving me, I saw that in place of human feet she had ass's hoofs; whereupon I drew my sword, seized, bound, and closely questioned her. Reluctantly enough she had to confess; they were sea- women called Ass-shanks, and their food was travellers. 'When we have made them drunk,' she said, 'and gone to rest with them, we overpower them in their sleep.' After this confession I left her there bound, went up on to the roof, and shouted for my comrades. When they appeared, I repeated it all to them, showed them the bones, and brought them in to see my prisoner; she at once vanished, turning to water; however, I thrust my sword into this experimentally, upon which the water became blood.

Then we marched hurriedly down to our ship and sailed away. With the first glimmering of dawn we made out a mainland, which we took for the continent that faces our own. We reverently saluted it, made prayer, and held counsel upon our best course. Some were for merely landing and turning back at once, others for leaving the ship, and going into the interior to make trial of the inhabitants. But while we were deliberating, a great storm arose, which dashed us, a complete wreck, on the shore. We managed to swim to land, each snatching up his arms and anything else he could.

Such are the adventures that befell me up to our arrival at that other continent:

our sea-voyage; our cruise among the islands and in the air; then our experiences in and after the whale; with the Heroes; with the dreams; and finally with the Ox-heads and the Ass-shanks. Our fortunes on the continent will be the subject of the following books.

THE TYRANNICIDE

A man forces his way into the stronghold of a tyrant, with the intention of killing him. Not finding the tyrant himself, he kills his son, and leaves the sword sticking in his body. The tyrant, coming, and finding his son dead, slays himself with the same sword.—The assailant now claims that the killing of the son entitles him to the reward of tyrannicide.

Two tyrants—a father advanced in years, a son in the prime of life, waiting only to step into his nefarious heritage—have fallen by my hand on a single day:

I come before this court, claiming but one reward for my twofold service. My case is unique. With one blow I have rid you of two monsters:

with my sword I slew the son; grief for the son slew the father. The misdeeds of the tyrant are sufficiently punished:

he has lived to see his son perish untimely; and—wondrous sequel!—the tyrant's own hand has freed us from tyranny. I slew the son, and used his death to slay another:

in his life he shared the iniquities of his father; in his death, so far as in him lay, he was a parricide. Mine is the hand that freed you, mine the sword that accomplished all:

as to the order and manner of procedure, there, indeed, I have deviated from the common practice of tyrannicides:

I slew the son, who had strength to resist me, and left my sword to deal with the aged father. In acting thus, I had thought to increase your obligation to me; a twofold deliverance—I had supposed—would entitle me to a twofold reward; for I have freed you not from tyranny alone, but from the fear of tyranny, and by removing the heir of iniquity have made your salvation sure. And now it seems that my services are to go for nothing; I, the preserver of the constitution, am to forgo the recompense prescribed by its laws. It is surely from no patriotic motive, as he asserts, that my adversary disputes my claim; rather it is from grief at the loss of the tyrants, and a desire to avenge their death.

Bear with me, gentlemen, for a little, while I dwell in some detail upon those evils of tyranny with which you are only too familiar; I shall thus enable you to realize the extent of my services, and to enjoy the contemplation of sufferings from which you have escaped. Ours was not the common experience:

we had not *one* tyranny, *one* servitude to endure, we were not subjected to the caprice of a single master. Other cities have had their tyrant:

it was reserved for us to have two tyrants at once, to groan beneath a double oppression. That of the old man was light by comparison, his anger mildness, his resentment long-suffering; age had blunted his passions, checked their headlong impetus, and curbed the lust of pleasure. His crimes, so it is said, were involuntary; resulting from no tyrannical disposition in himself, but from the instigations of his son. For in him paternal affection had too clearly

307

become a mania; his son was all in all to him; he did his bidding, committed every crime at his pleasure, dealt out punishment at his command, was subservient to him in all things; the minister of a tyrant's caprice, and that tyrant his son. The young man left him in possession of the name and semblance of rule; so much he conceded to his years:

but in all essentials *he* was the real tyrant. By him the power of the tyrant was upheld; by him and by him alone the fruits of tyranny were gathered. He it was who maintained the garrison, intimidated the victims of oppression, and butchered those who meditated resistance; who laid violent hands on boys and maidens, and trampled on the sanctity of marriage. Murder, banishment, confiscation, torture, brutality; all bespeak the wantonness of youth. The father followed his son's lead, and had no word of blame for the crimes in which he participated. Our situation became unbearable:

for when the promptings of passion draw support from the authority of rule, then iniquity knows no further bounds.

We knew moreover (and here was the bitterest thought of all) that our servitude must endure—ay, endure for ever; that our city was doomed to pass in unending succession from master to master, to be the heritage of the oppressor. To others it is no small consolation that they may count the days, and say in their hearts:

'The end will be soon; he will die, and we shall be free.' We had no such hope:

there stood the heir of tyranny before our eyes. There were others—men of spirit—who cherished like designs with myself; yet all lacked resolution to strike the blow; freedom was despaired of; to contend against a succession of tyrants seemed a hopeless task.

Yet I was not deterred. I had reckoned the difficulties of my undertaking, and shrank not back, but faced the danger. Alone, I issued forth to cope with tyranny in all its might. Alone, did I say? nay, not alone; I had my sword for company, my ally and partner in tyrannicide. I saw what the end was like to be:

and, seeing it, resolved to purchase your freedom with my blood. I grappled with the outer watch, with difficulty routed the guards, slew all I met, broke down all resistance, —and so to the fountain-head, the well-spring of tyranny, the source of all our calamities; within his stronghold I found him, and there slew him with many wounds, fighting valiantly for his life.

From that moment, my end was gained:

tyranny was destroyed; we were free men. There remained the aged father, alone, unarmed, desolate; his guards scattered, his strong protector slain; no adversary this for a brave man. And now I debated within myself:

'My work is done, my aim achieved, all is as I would have it. And how shall this remnant of tyranny be punished? He is unworthy of the hand that shed that other blood:

the glory of a noble enterprise shall not be so denied. No, let some other executioner be found. It were too much happiness for him to die, and never know the worst; let him see all, for his punishment, and let the sword be ready to his hand; to that sword I leave the rest.' In this design I withdrew; and the sword—as I had foreseen—did its office, slew the tyrant, and put the finishing touch to my work. And now I come to you, bringing democracy with me, and call upon all men to take heart, and hear the glad tidings of liberty. Enjoy the work of my hands! You see the citadel cleared of the oppressors; you are under no man's orders; the law holds its course; honours are awarded, judgements given, pleadings heard. And all springs from one bold stroke, from the slaying of that son whom his father might not survive. I claim from you the recompense that is my due; and that in no paltry, grasping spirit; it was not for a wage's sake that I sought to serve my country; but I would have my deed confirmed by your award; I would not be disparaged by slanderous tongues, as one who attempted and failed, and was deemed unworthy of honour.

My adversary tells me that I am unreasonable in asking for reward and distinction. I did not slay the tyrant; I have not fulfilled the requirements of the statute; there is a flaw in my claim.—And what more does he want of me? Say:

did I flinch? did I not ascend into the citadel? did I not slay? are we not free men? have we a master? do we hear a tyrant's threats? did any of the evil-doers escape me?—No; all is peace; the laws are in force; freedom is assured; democracy is established; our wives, our daughters are unmolested, our sons are safe; the city keeps festival in the general joy. And who is the cause of it all? who has wrought the change? Has any man a prior claim? Then I withdraw; be his the honour and the reward. But if not—if mine was the deed, mine the risk, mine the courage to ascend and smite and punish, dealing vengeance on the father through the son—then why depreciate my services? why seek to deprive me of a people's gratitude?

'But you did not kill the *tyrant*; the law assigns the reward to him who kills the tyrant.' And pray what is the difference between killing him and causing his death? I see none. The law-giver had but one end in view,—freedom, equality, deliverance from oppression. This was the signal service that he deemed worthy of recompense; and this service you cannot deny that I have rendered. In slaying one whom the tyrant could not survive, I myself wrought the tyrant's death. His was the hand:

the deed was mine. Let us not chop logic as to the manner and circumstances of his death, but rather ask:

has he ceased to exist, and am I the cause? Your scruples might go further, and object to some future deliverer of his country, that he struck not with the sword, but with a stick or a stone or the like. Had I blockaded the tyrant, and brought about his death by starvation, you would still, I suppose, have objected that it was not the work of my own hand? Again there would have been a flaw in my claim? The increased bitterness of such a death would have counted for nothing with you? Confine your attention to this one question:

does any of our oppressors survive? is there any ground for anxiety, any vestige of our past misery? If not, if all is peace, then none but an envious detractor would attempt to deprive me of the reward of my labours by inquiring into the means employed.

Moreover, it is laid down in our laws (unless after all these years of servitude my memory plays me false) that blood-guiltiness is of two kinds. A man may slay another with his own hand, or, without slaying him, he may put death unavoidably in his way; in the latter case the penalty is the same as in the former; and rightly, it being the intention of the law that the cause should rank with the act itself; the manner in which death is brought about is not the question. You would not acquit a man who in this sense had slain another; you would punish him as a murderer:

how then can you refuse to reward as a benefactor the man who, by parity of reasoning, has shown himself to be the liberator of his country?

Nor again can it be objected that all I did was to strike the blow, and that the resulting benefits were accidental, and formed no part of my design. What had I to fear, when once the stronger of our oppressors was slain? And why did I leave my sword in the wound, if not because I foresaw the very thing that would happen? Are you prepared to deny that the death so occasioned was that of a tyrant both in name and in fact, or that his death was an event for which the state would gladly pay an abundant reward? I think not. If then the tyrant is slain, how can you withhold the reward from him who occasioned his death? What scrupulousness is this—to concern yourself with the manner of his end, while you are enjoying the freedom that results from it? Democracy is restored:

what more can you demand from him who restored it? You refer us to the terms of the law:

well, the law looks only at the end; of the means it says nothing; it has no concern with them. Has not the reward of tyrannicide been paid before now to him who merely expelled a tyrant? And rightly so:

for he too has made free men of slaves. But I have done more:

banishment may be followed by restitution:

but here the family of tyrants is utterly annihilated and destroyed; the evil thing is exterminated, root and branch.

I implore you, gentlemen, to review my conduct from beginning to end, and see whether there has been any such omission on my part as to make my act appear less than tyrannicide in the eye of the law. The high patriotic resolve which prompts a man to face danger for the common good, and to purchase the salvation of his country at the price of his own life; this is the first requirement. Have I been wanting here? Have I lacked courage? Have I shrunk back at the prospect of the dangers through which I must pass? My enemy cannot say it of me. Now at this stage let us pause. Consider only the intention, the design, apart from its success; and suppose that I come before you to claim the reward of patriotism merely on the ground of my resolve. I have failed, and another, following in my footsteps, has slain the tyrant. Say, is it unreasonable in such a case to allow my claim? 'Gentlemen,' I might say, 'the will, the intention, was mine; I made the attempt, I did what I could; my resolve entitles me of itself to your reward.' What would my enemy say to that?

But in fact my case stands far otherwise. I mounted into the stronghold, I faced danger, I had innumerable difficulties to contend with, before I slew the son. Think not that it was a light or easy matter, to make my way past the watch, and single-handed to overcome one body of guards after another and put them to flight:

herein is perhaps the greatest difficulty with which the tyrannicide has to contend. It is no such great matter to bring the tyrant to bay, and dispatch him. Once overcome the guards that surround him, and success is ensured; little remains to be done. I could not make my way to the tyrants till I had mastered every one of their satellites and bodyguards:

each of those preliminary victories had to be won. Once more I pause, and consider my situation. I have got the better of the guards; I am master of the garrison; I present you the tyrant stripped, unarmed, defenceless. May I claim some credit for this, or do you still require his blood? Well, if blood you must have, that too is not wanting; my hands are not unstained; the glorious deed is accomplished; the youthful tyrant, the terror of all men, his father's sole security and protection, the equivalent of many bodyguards, is slain in the prime of his strength. Have I not earned my reward? Am I to have no credit for all that is done? What if I had killed one of his guards, some underling, some favourite domestic? Would it not have been thought a great thing, to go up and dispatch the tyrant's friend within his own walls, in the midst of his armed attendants? But who *was* my victim? The tyrant's son, himself a more grievous tyrant than his father, more cruel in his punishments, more violent in his excesses; a pitiless master; one, above all, whose succession to the supreme power promised a long continuance of our miseries. Shall I concede that this is the sum of my achievements? Shall we put it, that the tyrant has escaped, and lives? Still I claim my recompense. What say you, gentlemen? do you withhold it? The son, perhaps, caused you no uneasiness; he was no despot, no grievous oppressor?

And now for the final stroke. All that my adversary demands of me, I have performed; and that in the most effectual manner. I slew the tyrant when I slew his son; slew him not with a single blow—he could have asked no easier expiation of his guilt than that—but with prolonged torment. I showed him his beloved lying in the dust, in pitiable case, weltering in blood. And what if he were a villain? he was still his son, still the old man's likeness in the pride of youth. These are the wounds that fathers feel; this the tyrannicide's sword of justice; this the death, the vengeance, that befits cruelty and oppression. The tyrant who dies in a moment, and knows not his loss, and sees not such sights as these, dies unpunished. I knew—we all knew—his affection for his son;

knew that not for one day would he survive his loss. Other fathers may be devoted to their sons:

his devotion was something more than theirs. How should it be otherwise? In him, and in him alone, the father saw the zealous guardian of his lawless rule, the champion of his old age, the sole prop of tyranny. If grief did not kill him on the spot, despair, I knew, must do so; there could be no further joy in life for him when his protector was slain. Nature, grief, despair, foreboding, terror,—these were my allies; with these I hemmed him in, and drove him to his last desperate resolve. Know that your oppressor died childless, heartbroken, weeping, groaning in spirit; the time of his mourning was short, but it was a father mourning for his son; he died by his own hand, bitterest, most awful of deaths; that death comes lightly, by comparison, which is dealt by another.

Where is my sword?

Does any one else know anything of this sword? Does any one claim it? Who took it up into the citadel? The tyrant used this sword. Who had it before him? Who put it in his way?—Sword, fellow labourer, partner of my enterprise,—we have faced danger and shed blood to no purpose. We are slighted. Men say that we have not earned our reward.

Suppose that I had advanced a claim solely on my sword's behalf:

suppose that I had said to you:

'Gentlemen, the tyrant had resolved to slay himself, but was without a weapon at the moment, when this sword of mine supplied his need, and thereby played its part in our deliverance.' Should you not have considered that the owner of a weapon so public- spirited was entitled to honour and reward? Should you not have recompensed him, and inscribed his name among those of your benefactors; consecrated his sword, and worshipped it as a God?

Now consider how the tyrant may be supposed to have acted and spoken as his end approached.—His son lies mortally wounded at my hand; the wounds are many, and are exposed to view, that so the father's heart may be torn asunder at the very first sight of him. He cries out piteously to his father, not for help—he knows the old man's feebleness—, but for sympathy in his sufferings. I meanwhile am making my way home:

I have written in the last line of my tragedy, and now I leave the stage clear for the actor; there is the body, the sword, all that is necessary to complete the scene. The father enters. He beholds his son, his only son, gasping, blood-stained, weltering in gore; he sees the wounds—mortal wound upon wound—and exclaims:

'Son, we are slain, we are destroyed, we are stricken in the midst of our power. Where is the assassin? For what fate does he reserve me, who am dead already in thy death, O my son? Because I am old he fears me not, he withholds his vengeance, and would prolong my torment.' Then he looks for a sword; he has always gone unarmed himself, trusting all to his son. The sword is not wanting; it has been waiting for him all this time; I left it ready for the deed that was to follow. He draws it from the wound and speaks:

'Sword, that but a moment past hast slain me, complete thy work:

comfort the stricken father, aid his aged hand; dispatch, slay, make an end of the tyrant and his grief. Would that I had met thee first, that my blood had been shed before his! I could but have died a tyrant's death, and should have left an avenger behind me. And now I die childless:

I have not so much as a murderer at my need.' Even as he speaks, with trembling hand he plunges the sword into his breast:

he is in haste to die; but that feeble hand lacks strength to do its dread office.

Is he punished? Are these wounds? Is this death? A tyrant's death? Is there reward for this?

The closing scene you have all witnessed:

the son—no mean antagonist— prostrate in death; the father fallen upon him; blood mingling with blood, the drink-offering of Victory and Freedom; and in the midst my sword, that wrought all; judge by its presence there, whether the weapon was unworthy of its master, whether it did him faithful service. Had all been done by my hand, it had been little; the strangeness of the deed is its glory. The tyranny was overthrown by me, and no other; but many actors had their part to play in the drama. The first part was mine; the second was the son's; the third the tyrant's; and my sword was never absent from the stage.

THE DISINHERITED

A disinherited son adopts the medical profession. His father going mad, and being given up by the other physicians, he treats him successfully, and is then reinstated in his rights. Subsequently his step-mother also goes mad; he is bidden to cure her, and, declaring his inability to do so, is once more disinherited.

There is neither novelty nor strangeness, gentlemen of the jury, in my father's present proceedings. It is not the first time his passions have taken this direction; it has become an instinctive habit with him to pay a visit to this familiar court. Still, my unfortunate position has this much of novelty about it:

the charge I have to meet is not personal, but professional; I am to be punished for the inability of Medicine to do my father's bidding. A curious demand, surely, that healing should be done to order, and depend not on the limits of one's art, but on the wishes of one's father. For my part, I should be only too glad to find drugs in the pharmacopoeia which could relieve not only disordered wits, but disordered tempers; then I might be serviceable to my father. As it is, he is completely cured of madness, but is worse-tempered than ever. The bitterest part of it is, he is sane enough in all other relations, and mad only where his healer is concerned. You see what my medical fee amounts to; I am again disinherited, cut off from my family once more, as though the sole purpose of my brief reinstatement had been the accentuation of my disgrace by repetition.

When a thing is within the limits of possibility, I require no bidding; I came before I was summoned, to see what I could do in this case. But when there is absolutely no hope, I will not meddle. With this particular patient, such caution is especially incumbent upon me; how my father would treat me, if I tried and failed, I can judge by his disinheriting me when I refused to try. Gentlemen, I am sorry for my stepmother's illness—for she was an excellent woman; I am sorry for my father's distress thereat; I am most sorry of all that I should seem rebellious, and be unable to give the required service; but the disease is incurable, and my art is not omnipotent. I do not see the justice of disinheriting one who, when he cannot do a thing, refuses to undertake it.

The present case throws a clear light upon the reasons for my first disinheriting. The allegations of those days I consider to have been disposed of by my subsequent life; and the present charges I shall do my best to clear away with a short account of my proceedings. Wilful and disobedient son that I am, a disgrace to my father, unworthy of my family, I thought proper to say very little indeed in answer to his long and vehement denunciations. Banished from my home, I reflected that I should find my most convincing plea, my best acquittal, in the life I then led, in practically illustrating the difference between my father's picture and the reality, in devotion to the worthiest pursuits and association with the most reputable company. But I had also a presentiment of what actually happened; it occurred to me even then that a perfectly sane father

314

does not rage causelessly at his son, nor trump up false accusations against him. Persons were not wanting who detected incipient madness; it was the warning and precursor of a stroke which would fall before long—this unreasoning dislike, this harsh conduct, this fluent abuse, this malignant prosecution, all this violence, passion, and general ill temper. Yes, gentlemen, I saw that the time might come when Medicine would serve me well.

I went abroad, attended lectures by the most famous foreign physicians, and by hard work and perseverance mastered my craft. Upon my return, I found that my father's madness had developed, and that he had been given up by the local doctors, who are not distinguished for insight, and are much to seek in accurate diagnosis. I did no more than a son's duty when I forgot and forgave the disinheritance, and visited him without waiting to be called in; I had in fact nothing to complain of that was properly his act; his errors were not his, but, as I have implied, those of his illness. I came unsummoned, then. But I did not treat him at once; that is not our custom, nor what our art enjoins upon us. What we are taught to do is first of all to ascertain whether the disease is curable or incurable—has it passed beyond our control? After that, if it is susceptible of treatment, we treat it, and do our very best to relieve the sufferer. But if we realize that the complaint has got the entire mastery, we have nothing to do with it at all. That is the tradition that has come down to us from the fathers of our art, who direct us not to attempt hopeless cases. Well, I found that there was yet hope for my father; the complaint had not gone too far; I watched him for a long time; formed my conclusions with scrupulous care; then, I commenced operations and exhibited my drugs without hesitation—though many of his friends were suspicious of my prescription, impugned the treatment, and took notes to be used against me.

My step-mother was present, distressed and doubtful—the result not of any dislike to me, but of pure anxiety, based on her full knowledge of his sad condition; no one but her, who had lived with and nursed him, knew the worst. However, I never faltered; the symptoms would not lie to me, nor my art fail me; when the right moment came, I applied the treatment, in spite of the timidity of some of my friends, who were afraid of the scandal that might result from a failure; it would be said that the medicine was my vengeful retort to the disinheritance. To make a long story short, it was at once apparent that he had taken no harm; he was in his senses again, and aware of all that went on. The company were amazed; my step-mother thanked me, and every one could see that she was delighted both at my triumph and at her husband's recovery. He himself— to give credit where it is due—did not take time to consider, nor to ask advice, but, as soon as he heard the story, undid what he had done, made me his son again, hailed me as his preserver and benefactor, confessed that I had now given my proofs, and withdrew his previous charges. All this was delightful to the better, who were many, among his friends, but distasteful to the persons who enjoy a quarrel more than a reconciliation. I observed at the time that all were not equally pleased; there were changes of colour, uneasy glances, signs of mortification, in one quarter at least, which told of envy and hatred. With us, who had recovered each other, all was naturally affection and rejoicing.

Quite a short time after, my step-mother's disorder commenced—a very terrible and unaccountable one, gentlemen of the jury. I observed it from its very beginning; it was no slight superficial case, this; it was a long-established but hitherto latent mental disease, which now burst out and forced its way into notice. There are many signs by which we know that madness is incurable— among them a strange one which I noticed in this case. Ordinary society has a soothing, alleviating effect; the patient forgets to be mad; but if he sees a doctor, or even hears one mentioned, he at once displays acute irritation—an infallible sign that he is far gone, incurable in fact. I was distressed to notice this symptom; my step-mother was a worthy person who deserved a better fate, and I was all compassion for her.

But my father in his simplicity, knowing neither when nor how the trouble began, and quite unable to gauge its gravity, bade me cure her by the drugs that had cured him. His idea was that madness was to be nothing else but mad; the disease was the same, its effects the same, and it must admit of the same treatment. When I told him, as was perfectly true, that his wife was incurable, and confessed that the case was beyond me, he thought it an outrage, said I was refusing because I chose to, and treating the poor woman shamefully—in short, visited upon me the limitations of my art. Such ebullitions are common enough in distress; we all lose our tempers then with the people who tell us the truth. I must nevertheless defend myself and my profession, as well as I can, against his strictures.

I will begin with some remarks upon the law under which I am to be disinherited; my father will please to observe that it is not quite so much now as before a matter for his absolute discretion. You will find, sir, that the author of the law has not conferred the right of disherison upon any father against any son upon any pretext. It is true he has armed fathers with this weapon; but he has also protected sons against its illegitimate use. That is the meaning of his insisting that the procedure shall not be irresponsible and uncontrolled, but come under the legal cognizance of inspectors whose decision will be uninfluenced by passion or misrepresentation. He knew how often irritation is unreasonable, and what can be effected by a lying tale, a trusted slave, or a spiteful woman. He would not have the deed done without form of law; sons were not to be condemned unheard and out of hand; they are to have the ear of the court for so long by the clock, and there is to be adequate inquiry into the facts.

My father's competence, then, being confined to preferring his complaints, and the decision whether they are reasonable or not resting with you, I shall be within my rights in requesting you to defer consideration of the grievance on which he bases the present suit, until you have determined whether a second disinheritance is admissible in the abstract. He has cast me off, has exercised his legal rights, enforced his parental powers to the full, and then restored me to my position as his son. Now it is iniquitous, I maintain, that fathers should have these unlimited penal powers, that disgrace should be multiplied, apprehension made perpetual, the law now chastize, now relent, now resume its severity, and justice be the shuttlecock of our fathers' caprices. It is quite proper for the law to humour, encourage, give effect to, *one* punitive impulse on the part of him who has begotten us; but if, after shooting his bolt, insisting on his right, indulging his wrath, he discovers our merits and takes us back, then he should be held to his decision, and not allowed to oscillate, waver, do and undo any more. Originally, he had no means of knowing whether his offspring would turn out well or ill; that is why parents who have decided to bring up children before they knew their nature are permitted to reject such as are found unworthy of their family.

But when a man has taken his son back, not upon compulsion, but of his own motion and after inquiry, how can further chopping and changing be justified? What further occasion for the law? Its author might fairly say to you, sir:

If your son was vicious and deserved to be disinherited, what were you about to recall him? Why have him home again? Why suspend the law's operation? You were a free agent; you need not have done it. The laws are not your play-ground; you are not to put the courts in motion every time your mood varies; the laws are not to be suspended to-day and enforced to-morrow, with juries to look on at the proceedings, or rather to be the ministers of your whims, executioners or peace-makers according to your taste and fancy. The boy cost you one begetting, and one rearing; in return for which you may disinherit him, once, always provided you have reason to show for it. Disinheriting as a regular habit, a promiscuous pastime, is not included in the patria potestas.

Gentlemen of the jury, I entreat you in Heaven's name not to permit him, after voluntarily reinstating me, reversing the previous decision, and renouncing his anger, to revive the old sentence and have recourse to the same paternal rights; the period of their validity is past and gone; his own act suffices to annul and exhaust their power. You know the general rule of the courts, that a party dissatisfied with the verdict of a ballot—provided jury is allowed an appeal to another court; but that is not so when the parties have agreed upon arbitrators, and, after such selection, put the matter in their hands. They had the choice, there, of not recognizing the court *ab initio*; if they nevertheless did so, they may fairly be expected to abide by its award. Similarly you, sir, had the choice of never taking back your son, if you thought him unworthy; having decided that he was worthy, and taken him back, you cannot be permitted to disinherit him anew; the evidence of his not deserving it is your own admission of his worth. It is only right that the reinstatement and reconciliation should be definitive, after such abundant investigation; there have been two trials, observe:

the first, that in which you rejected me; the second, that in your own conscience, which reversed the decision of the other; the fact of reversal only adds force to the later result. Abide, then, by your second thoughts, and uphold your own verdict. You are to be my father; such was your determination, approved and ratified.

Suppose I were not your begotten, but only your adopted son, I hold that you could not then have disinherited me; for what it is originally open to us not to do, we have no right, having done, to undo. But where there is both the natural tie, and that of deliberate choice, how can a second rejection, a repeated deprivation of the one relationship, be justified? Or again, suppose I had been a slave, and you had seen reason to put me in irons, and afterwards, convinced of my innocence, made me a free man; could you, upon an angry impulse, have enslaved me again? Assuredly not; the law makes these acts binding and irrevocable. Upon this contention, that the voluntary annulment of a disinheritance precludes a repetition of the act, I could enlarge further, but will not labour the point.

You have next to consider the character of the man now to be disinherited. I lay no stress upon the fact that I was then nothing, and am now a physician; my art will not help me here. As little do I insist that I was then young, and am now middle-aged, with my years as a guarantee against misconduct; perhaps there is not much in that either. But, gentlemen, at the time of my previous expulsion, if I had never done my father any harm (as I should maintain), neither had I done him any good; whereas now I have recently been his preserver and benefactor; could there be worse ingratitude than so, and so soon, to requite me for saving him from that terrible fate? My care of him goes for nothing; it is lightly forgotten, and I am driven forth desolate—I, whose wrongs might have excused my rejoicing at his troubles, but who, so far from bearing malice, saved him and restored him to his senses.

For, gentlemen, it is no ordinary slight kindness that he is choosing this way of repaying. You all know (though he may not realize) what he was capable of doing, what he had to endure, what his state was, in fact, during those bad days. The doctors had given him up, his relations had cleared away and dared not come near him; but I undertook his case and restored him to the power of—accusing me and going to law. Let me help your imagination, sir. You were very nearly in the state in which your wife now is, when I gave you back your understanding. It is surely not right that my reward for that should be this—that your understanding should be used against me alone. That it is no trifling kindness I have done you is apparent from the very nature of your accusation. The ground of your hatred is that she whom I do not cure is in extremities, is terribly afflicted; then, seeing that I relieved you of just such an affliction, there is surely better reason for you to love and be grateful to me for your own release from such horrors. But you are unconscionable enough to make the first employment of your restored faculties an indictment of me; you smite your healer, the ancient hate revives, and we have you reciting the same

old law again. My art's handsome fee, the worthy payment for my drugs, is—
your present manifestation of vigour!

But you, gentlemen of the jury, will you allow him to punish his
benefactor, drive away his preserver, pay for his wits with hatred, and for his
recovery with chastisement? I hope better things of your justice. However
flagrantly I had now been misconducting myself, I had a large balance of
gratitude to draw upon. With that consideration in his memory, he need not
have been extreme to mark what is now done amiss; it might have inspired him
with ready indulgence, the more if the antecedent service was great enough to
throw anything that might follow into the shade. That fairly states my relation
to him; I preserved him; he owes his life absolutely to me; his existence, his
sanity, his understanding, are my gifts, given, moreover, when all others
despaired and confessed that the case was beyond their skill.

The service that I did was the more meritorious, it seems to me, in that I
was not at the time my father's son, nor under any obligation to undertake the
case; I was independent of him, a mere stranger; the natural bond had been
snapped. Yet I was not indifferent; I came as a volunteer, uninvited, at my own
instance. I brought help, I persevered, I effected the cure, I restored him,
thereby securing myself at once a father and an acquittal; I conquered anger
with kindness, disarmed law with affection, purchased readmission to my
family with important service, proved my filial loyalty at that critical moment,
was adopted (or adopted myself, rather) on the recommendation of my art,
while my conduct in trying circumstances proved me a son by blood also. For I
had anxiety and fatigue enough in being always on the spot, ministering to my
patient, watching for my opportunities, now humouring the disease when it
gathered strength, now availing myself of a remission to combat it. Of all a
physician's tasks the most hazardous is the care of patients like this, with the
personal attendance it involves; for in their moments of exasperation they are
apt to direct their fury upon any one they can come at. Yet I never shrank or
hesitated; I was always there; I had a life- and-death struggle with the malady,
and the final victory was with me and my drugs.

Now I can fancy a person who hears all this objecting hastily, 'What a
fuss about giving a man a dose of medicine!' But the fact is, there are many
preliminaries to be gone through; the ground has to be prepared; the body
must first be made susceptible to treatment; the patient's whole condition has
to be studied; he must be purged, reduced, dieted, properly exercised, enabled
to sleep, coaxed into tranquillity. Now other invalids will submit to all this;
but mania robs its victims of self-control; they are restive and jib; their
physicians are in danger, and treatment at a disadvantage. Constantly, when we
are on the very point of success and full of hope, some slight hitch occurs, and
a relapse takes place which undoes all in a moment, neutralizing our care and
tripping up our art.

Now, after my going through all this, after my wrestle with this
formidable disease and my triumph over so elusive an ailment, is it still your

intention to support him in disinheriting me? Shall he interpret the laws as he will against his benefactor? Will you look on while he makes war upon nature? I obey nature, gentlemen of the jury, in saving my father from death, and myself from the loss of him, unjust as he had been. He on the contrary defers to law (he calls it law) in ruining and cutting off from his kin the son who has obliged him. He is a cruel father, I a loving son. I own the authority of nature:

he spurns and flings it from him. How misplaced is this paternal hate! How worse misplaced this filial love! For I must reproach myself—my father will have it so. And the reproach? That where I should hate (for I am hated), I love, and where I should love little, I love much. Yet surely nature requires of parents that they love their children more than of children that they love their parents. But he deliberately disregards both the law, which secures children their family rights during good behaviour, and nature, which inspires parents with fervent love for their offspring. Having greater incentives to affection, you might suppose that he would confer the fruits of it upon me in larger measure, or at the least reciprocate and emulate my love. Alas, far from it! he returns hate for love, persecution for devotion, wrong for service, disinheritance for respect; the laws which guard, he converts into means of assailing, the rights of children. Ah, my father, how do you force law into your service in this battle against nature!

The facts, believe me, are not as you would have them. You are a bad exponent, sir, of good laws. In this matter of affection there is no war between law and nature; they hunt in couples, they work together for the remedying of wrongs. When you evil entreat your benefactor, you are wronging nature; now I ask, do you wrong the laws as well as nature? You do; it is their intention to be fair and just and give sons their rights; but you will not allow it; you hound them on again and again upon one child as though he were many; you keep them ever busy punishing, when their own desire is peace and goodwill between father and son. I need hardly add that, as against the innocent, they may be said to have no existence. But let me tell you, ingratitude also is an offence known to the law; an action will lie against a person who fails to recompense his benefactor. If he adds to such failure an attempt to punish, he has surely reached the uttermost limits of wrong in this sort. And now I think I have sufficiently established two points:

first, my father has not the right, after once exerting his parental privilege and availing himself of the law, to disinherit me again; and secondly, it is on general grounds inadmissible to cast off and expel from his family one who has rendered service so invaluable.

Let us next proceed to the actual reasons given for the disinheritance; let us inquire into the nature of the charge. We must first go back for a moment to the intention of the legislator. We will grant you for the sake of argument, sir, that it is open to you to disinherit as often as you please; we will further concede you this right against your benefactor; but I presume that disinheritance is not to be the beginning and the ending in itself; you will not resort to it, that is, without sufficient cause. The legislator's meaning is not that the father can disinherit, whatever his grievance may be, that nothing is required beyond the wish and a complaint; in that case, what is the court's function? No, gentlemen, it is your business to inquire whether the parental anger rests upon good and sufficient grounds. That is the question which I am now to put before you; and I will take up the story from the moment when sanity was restored.

The first-fruits of this was the withdrawal of the disinheritance; I was preserver, benefactor, everything. So far my conduct is not open to exception, I take it. Well, and later on what fault has my father to find? What attention or filial duty did I omit? Did I stay out o' nights, sir? Do you charge me with untimely drinkings and revellings? Was I extravagant? Did I get into some disreputable brawl? Did any such complaint reach you? None whatever. Yet these are just the offences for which the law contemplates disherison. Ah, but my step-mother fell ill. Indeed, and do you make that a charge against me? Do you prefer a suit for ill health? I understand you to say no.

What *is* the grievance, then?-*That you refuse to treat her at my bidding, and for such disobedience to your father deserve to be disinherited.*— Gentlemen, I will explain presently how the nature of this demand results in a seeming disobedience, but a real inability. Meanwhile, I simply remark that neither the authority which the law confers on him, nor the obedience to which I am bound, is indiscriminate. Among orders, some have no sanction, while the disregard of others justifies anger and punishment. My father may be ill, and I neglect him; he may charge me with the management of his house, and I take no notice; he may tell me to look after his country estate, and I evade the task. In all these and similar cases, the parental censure will be well deserved. But other things again are for the sons to decide, as questions of professional skill or policy—especially if the father's interests are not touched. If a painter's father says to him, 'Paint this, my boy, and do not paint that'; or a musician's, 'Strike this note, and not the other'; or a bronze-founder's, 'Cast so-and-so'; would it be tolerable that the son should be disinherited for not taking such advice? Of course not.

But the medical profession should be left still more to their own discretion than other artists, in proportion to the greater nobility of their aims and usefulness of their work; this art should have a special right of choosing its objects; this sacred occupation, taught straight from Heaven, and pursued by the wisest of men, should be secured against all compulsion, enslaved to no law, intimidated and penalized by no court, exposed to no votes or paternal threats or uninstructed passions. If I had told my father directly and expressly, 'I will not do it, I refuse the case, though I could treat it, I hold my art at no man's service but my own and yours, as far as others are concerned I am a layman'—if I had taken that position, where is the masterful despot who would have applied force and compelled me to practise against my will? The appropriate inducements are request and entreaty, not laws and browbeating and tribunals; the physician is to be persuaded, not commanded; he is to choose, not be terrorized; he is not to be haled to his patient, but to come with his consent and at his pleasure. Governments are wont to give physicians the public recognition of honours, precedence, immunities and privileges; and shall the art which has State immunities not be exempt from the *patria fotestas?*

All this I was entitled to say simply as a professional man, even on the assumption that you had had me taught, and devoted much care and expense to my training, that this particular case had been within my competence, and I had yet declined it. But in fact you have to consider also how utterly unreasonable it is that you should not let me use at my own discretion my own acquisition. It was not as your son nor under your authority that I acquired this art; and yet it was for your advantage that I acquired it—you were the first to profit by it—, though you had contributed nothing to my training. Will you mention the fees you paid? How much did the stock of my surgery cost you? Not one penny. I was a pauper, I knew not where to turn for necessaries, and I owed my instruction to my teachers' charity. The provision my father made for my education was sorrow, desolation, distress, estrangement from my friends and banishment from my family. And do you then claim to have the use of my skill, the absolute control of what was acquired independently? You should be content with the previous service rendered to yourself, not under obligation, but of free will; for even on that occasion nothing could have been demanded of me on the score of gratitude.

My kindness of the past is not to be my duty of the future; a voluntary favour is not to be turned into an obligation to take unwelcome orders; the principle is not to be established that he who once cures a man is bound to cure any number of others at his bidding ever after. That would be to appoint the patients we cure our absolute masters; *we* should be paying *them*, and the fee would be slavish submission to their commands. Could anything be more absurd? Because you were ill, and I was at such pains to restore you, does that make you the owner of my art?

All this I could have said, if the tasks he imposed upon me had been within my powers, and I had declined to accept all of them, or, on compulsion, any of them. But I now wish you to look further into their nature. 'You cured me of madness (says he); my wife is now mad and in the condition I was in (that of course is his idea); she has been given up as I was by the other doctors, but you have shown that nothing is too hard for you; very well, then, cure her too, and make an end of her illness.' Now, put like that, it sounds very reasonable, especially in the ears of a layman innocent of medical knowledge. But if you will listen to what I have to say for my art, you will find that there *are* things too hard for us, that all ailments are not alike, that the same treatment and the same drugs will not always answer; and then you will understand what a difference there is between refusing and being unable. Pray bear with me while I generalize a little, without condemning my disquisition as pedantic, irrelevant, or ill-timed.

322

To begin with, human bodies differ in nature and temperament; compounded as they admittedly are of the same elements, they are yet compounded in different proportions. I am not referring at present to sexual differences; the *male* body is not the same or alike in different individuals; it differs in temperament and constitution; and from this it results that in different men diseases also differ both in character and in intensity; one man's body has recuperative power and is susceptible to treatment; another's is utterly crazy, open to every infection, and without vigour to resist disease. To suppose, then, that all fever, all consumption, lung-disease, or mania, being generically the same, will affect every subject in the same way, is what no sensible, thoughtful, or well-informed person would do; the same disease is easily curable in one man, and not in another. Why, sow the same wheat in various soils, and the results will vary. Let the soil be level, deep, well watered, well sunned, well aired, well ploughed, and the crop will be rich, fat, plentiful. Elevated stony ground will make a difference, no sun another difference, foothills another, and so on. Just so with disease; its soil makes it thrive and spread, or starves it. Now all this quite escapes my father; he makes no inquiries of this sort, but assumes that all mania in every body is the same, and to be treated accordingly.

Besides such differences between males, it is obvious that the female body differs widely from the male both in the diseases it is subject to and in its capacity or non-capacity of recovery. The bracing effect of toil, exercise, and open air gives firmness and tone to the male; the female is soft and unstrung from its sheltered existence, and pale with anaemia, deficient caloric and excess of moisture. It is consequently, as compared with the male, open to infection, exposed to disease, unequal to vigorous treatment, and, in particular, liable to mania. With their emotional, mobile, excitable tendencies on the one hand, and their defective bodily strength on the other, women fall an easy prey to this affliction.

It is quite unfair, then, to expect the physician to cure both sexes indifferently; we must recognize how far apart they are, their whole lives, pursuits, and habits, having been distinct from infancy. Do not talk of a mad person, then, but specify the sex; do not confound distinctions and force all cases under the supposed identical title of madness; keep separate what nature separates, and then examine the respective possibilities. I began this exposition with stating that the first thing we doctors look to is the nature and temperament of our patient's body:

which of the humours predominates in it; is it full- blooded or the reverse; at, or past, its prime; big or little; fat or lean? When a man has satisfied himself upon these and other such points, his opinion, favourable or adverse, upon the prospects of recovery may be implicitly relied upon.

It must be remembered too that madness itself has a thousand forms, numberless causes, and even some distinct names. Delusion, infatuation, frenzy, lunacy—these are not the same; they all express different degrees of the affection. Again, the causes are not only different in men and women, but, in men, they are different for the old and for the young; for instance, in young men some redundant humour is the usual cause; whereas with the old a shrewdly timed slander, or very likely a fancied domestic slight, will get hold of them, first cloud their understanding, and finally drive them distracted. As for women, all sorts of things effect a lodgement and make easy prey of them, especially bitter dislike, envy of a prosperous rival, pain or anger. These feelings smoulder on, gaining strength with time, till at last they burst out in madness.

Such, sir, has been your wife's case, perhaps with the addition of some recent trouble; for she used to have no strong dislikes, yet she is now in the grasp of the malady—and that beyond hope of medical relief. For if any physician undertakes and cures the case, you have my permission to hate me for the wrong I have done you. Yet I must go so far as to say that, even had the case not been so desperate—had there been a glimmer of hope—even then I should not have lightly intervened, nor been very ready to administer drugs; I should have been afraid of what might happen, and of the sort of stories that might get about. You know the universal belief that every step-mother, whatever her general merits, hates her step-sons; it is supposed to be a feminine mania from which none of them is exempt. If the disease had taken a wrong turn, and the medicine failed of its effect, there would very likely have been suspicions of intentional malpractice.

Your wife's condition, sir—and I describe it to you after close observation—, is this:

she will never mend, though she take ten thousand doses of medicine. It is therefore undesirable to make the experiment, unless your object is merely to compel me to fail and cover me with disgrace. Pray do not enable my professional brethren to triumph over me; their jealousy is enough. If you disinherit me again, I shall be left desolate, but I shall pray for no evil upon your head. But suppose— though God forbid!—suppose your malady should return; relapses are common enough in such cases, under irritation; what is my course then to be? Doubt not, I shall restore you once more; I shall not desert the post which nature assigns to children; I for my part shall not forget my descent. And then if you recover, must I look for another restitution? You understand me? your present proceedings are calculated to awake your disease and stir it to renewed malignancy. It is but the other day that you emerged from your sad condition, and you are vehement and loud—worst of all, you are full of anger, indulging your hatred and appealing once more to the law. Alas, father, even such was the prelude to your first madness.

PHALARIS, I

We are sent to you, Priests of Delphi, by Phalaris our master, with instructions to present this bull to the God, and to speak the necessary words on behalf of the offering and its donor. Such being our errand, it remains for us to deliver his message, which is as follows:

'It is my desire above all things, men of Delphi, to appear to the Greeks as I really am, and not in that character in which Envy and Malice, availing themselves of the ignorance of their hearers, have represented me:

and if to the Greeks in general, then most of all to you, who are holy men, associates of the God, sharers (I had almost said) of his hearth and home. If I can clear myself before you, if I can convince you that I am not the cruel tyrant I am supposed to be, then I may consider myself cleared in the eyes of all the world. For the truth of my statements, I appeal to the testimony of the God himself. Methinks *he* is not likely to be deceived by lying words. It may be an easy matter to mislead men:

but to escape the penetration of a God—and that God Apollo—is impossible.

'I was a man of no mean family; in birth, in breeding, in education, the equal of any man in Agrigentum. In my political conduct I was ever public-spirited, in my private life mild and unassuming; no unseemly act, no deed of violence, oppression, or headstrong insolence was ever laid to my charge in those early days. But our city at that time was divided into factions:

I saw myself exposed to the plots of my political opponents, who sought to destroy me by every means:

if I would live in security, if I would preserve the city from destruction, there was but one course open to me—to seize upon the government, and thereby baffle my opponents, put an end to their machinations, and bring my countrymen to their senses. There were not a few who approved my design:

patriots and men of cool judgement, they understood my sentiments, and saw that I had no alternative. With their help, I succeeded without difficulty in my enterprise.

'From that moment, the disturbances ceased. My opponents, became my subjects, I their ruler; and the city was freed from dissension. From executions and banishments and confiscations I abstained, even in the case of those who had plotted against my life. Such strong measures are indeed never more necessary than at the commencement of a new rule:

but I was sanguine; I proposed to treat them as my equals, and to win their allegiance by clemency, mildness, and humanity. My first act was to reconcile myself with my enemies, most of whom I invited to my table and took into my confidence.

'I found the city in a ruinous condition, owing to the neglect of the magistrates, who had commonly been guilty of embezzlement, if not of wholesale plunder. I repaired the evil by means of aqueducts, beautified the city with noble buildings, and surrounded it with walls. The public revenues were easily increased by proper attention on the part of the fiscal authorities. I provided for the education of the young and the maintenance of the old; and for the general public I had games and spectacles, banquets and doles. As for rape and seduction, tyrannical violence or intimidation, I abhorred the very name of such things.

'I now began to think of laying down my power; and how to do so with safety was my only concern. The cares of government and public business had begun to weigh upon me; I found my position as burdensome as it was invidious. But it was still a question, how to render the city independent of such assistance for the future. And whilst I—honest man! —was busied with such thoughts, my enemies were even then combining against me, and debating the ways and means of rebellion; conspiracies were forming, arms and money were being collected, neighbour states were invited to assist, embassies were on their way to Sparta and Athens. The torments that were in store for me, had I fallen into their hands, I afterwards learnt from their public confession under torture, from which it appeared that they had vowed to tear me limb from limb with their own hands. For my escape from such a fate, I have to thank the Gods, who unmasked the conspiracy; and, in particular, the God of Delphi, who sent dreams to warn me, and dispatched messengers with detailed information.

'And now, men of Delphi, I would ask your advice. Imagine yourselves to- day in the perilous situation in which I then stood; and tell me what was my proper course. I had almost fallen unawares into the hands of my enemies, and was casting about for means of safety. Leave Delphi for a while, and transport yourselves in spirit to Agrigentum:

behold the preparations of my enemies:

listen to their threats; and say, what is your counsel? Shall I sit quietly on the brink of destruction, exercising clemency and long-suffering as heretofore? bare my throat to the sword? see my nearest and dearest slaughtered before my eyes? What would this be but sheer imbecility? Shall I not rather bear myself like a man of spirit, give the rein to my rational indignation, avenge my injuries upon the conspirators, and use my present power with a view to my future security? This, I know, would have been your advice.

'Now observe my procedure. I sent for the guilty persons, heard their defence, produced my evidence, established every point beyond a doubt; and when they themselves admitted the truth of the accusation, I punished them; for I took it ill, not that they had plotted against my life, but that on their account I was compelled to abandon my original policy. From that day to this, I have consulted my own safety by punishing conspiracy as often as it has shown itself.

'And men call me cruel! They do not stop to ask who was the aggressor; they condemn what they think the cruelty of my vengeance, but pass lightly over the provocation, and the nature of the crime. It is as if a man were to see a temple-robber hurled from the rock at Delphi, and, without reflecting how the transgressor had stolen into your temple by night, torn down the votive-offerings, and laid hands upon the graven image of the God, were to exclaim against the inhumanity of persons who, calling themselves Greeks and holy men, could yet find it in them to inflict this awful punishment upon their fellow Greek, and that within sight of the holy place;—for the rock, as I am told, is not far from the city. Surely you would laugh to scorn such an accusation as this; and your *cruel* treatment of the impious would be universally applauded.

'But so it is:

the public does not inquire into the character of a ruler, into the justice or injustice of his conduct; the mere name of tyranny ensures men's hatred; the tyrant might be an Aeacus, a Minos, a Rhadamanthus,—they would be none the less eager for his destruction; their thoughts ever run on those tyrants who have been bad rulers, and the good, because they bear the same name, are held in the like detestation. I have heard that many of your tyrants in Greece have been wise men, who, labouring under that opprobrious title, have yet given proofs of benevolence and humanity, and whose pithy maxims are even now stored up in your temple among the treasures of the God.

'Observe, moreover, the prominence given to punishment by all constitutional legislators; they know that when the fear of punishment is wanting, nothing else is of avail. And this is doubly so with us who are tyrants; whose power is based upon compulsion; who live in the midst of enmity and treachery. The bugbear terrors of the law would never serve our turn. Rebellion is a many-headed Hydra:

we cut off one guilty head, two others grow in its place. Yet we must harden our hearts, smite them off as they grow, and—like Iolaus—sear the wounds; thus only shall we hold our own. The man who has once become involved in such a strife as this must play the part that he has undertaken; to show mercy would be fatal. Do you suppose that any man was ever so brutal, so inhuman, as to rejoice in torture and groans and bloodshed for their own sake, when there was no occasion for punishment? Many is the time that I have wept while others suffered beneath the lash, and groaned in spirit over the hard fate that subjected me to a torment more fierce and more abiding than theirs. For to the man who is benevolent by nature, and harsh only by compulsion, it is more painful to inflict punishment than it would be to undergo it.

'Now I will speak my mind frankly. If I had to choose between punishing innocent men, and facing death myself, believe me, I should have no hesitation in accepting the latter alternative. But if I am asked, whether I had rather die an undeserved death than give their deserts to those who plotted against my life, I answer no; and once more, Delphians, I appeal to you:

which is better—to die when I deserve not death, or to spare my enemies who deserve not mercy?[41] No man surely can be such a fool that he would not rather live than preserve his enemies by his death. Yet in spite of this how many have I spared who were palpably convicted of conspiring against me; such were Acanthus, Timocrates, and his brother Leogoras, all of whom I saved out of regard for our former intercourse.

'If you would learn more of me, apply to any of the strangers who have visited Agrigentum; and see what account they give of the treatment they received, and of my hospitality to all who land on my coasts. My messengers are waiting for them in every port, to inquire after their names and cities, that they may not go away without receiving due honour at my hands. Some—the wisest of the Greeks—have come expressly to visit me, so far are they from avoiding intercourse with me. It was but lately that I received a visit from the sage Pythagoras. The account that he had heard of me was belied by his experience; and on taking his departure he expressed admiration of my justice, and deplored the circumstances which made severity a duty. Now is it likely that one who is so benevolent to strangers should deal unjustly with his fellow citizens? is it not to be supposed that the provocation has been unusually great?

'So much then in defence of my own conduct; I have spoken the words of truth and justice, and would persuade myself that I have merited your approbation rather than your resentment. And now I must explain to you the origin of my present offering, and the manner in which it came into my hands. For it was by no instructions of mine that the statuary made this bull:

far be it from me to aspire to the possession of such works of art! A countryman of my own, one Perilaus, an admirable artist, but a man of evil disposition, had so far mistaken my character as to think that he could win my regard by the invention of a new form of torture; the love of torture, he thought, was my ruling passion. He it was who made the bull and brought it to me. I no sooner set eyes on this beautiful and exquisite piece of workmanship, which lacked only movement and sound to complete the illusion, than I exclaimed:

"Here is an offering fit for the God of Delphi:

to him I must send it." "And what will you say," rejoined Perilaus, who stood by, "when you see the ingenious mechanism within it, and learn the purpose it is designed to serve?" He opened the back of the animal, and continued:

"When you are minded to punish any one, shut him up in this receptacle, apply these pipes to the nostrils of the bull, and order a fire to be kindled beneath. The occupant will shriek and roar in unremitting agony; and

---

[41] Apparently the speaker intended to repeat the last pair of alternatives in different words:

instead of which, he gives us one of those alternatives twice over. Lucian's tautologic genius fails him for once.

his cries will come to you through the pipes as the tenderest, most pathetic, most melodious of bellowings. Your victim will be punished, and you will enjoy the music."

'His words revolted me. I loathed the thought of such ingenious cruelty, and resolved to punish the artificer in kind. "If this is anything more than an empty boast, Perilaus," I said to him, "if your art can really produce this effect, get inside yourself, and pretend to roar; and we will see whether the pipes will make such music as you describe." He consented; and when he was inside I closed the aperture, and ordered a fire to be kindled. "Receive," I cried, "the due reward of your wondrous art:

let the music-master be the first to play." Thus did his ingenuity meet with its deserts. But lest the offering should be polluted by his death, I caused him to be removed while he was yet alive, and his body to be flung dishonoured from the cliffs. The bull, after due purification, I sent as an offering to your God, with an inscription upon it, setting forth all the circumstances; the names of the donor and of the artist, the evil design of the latter, and the righteous sentence which condemned him to illustrate by his own agonized shrieks the efficacy of his musical device.

'And now, men of Delphi, you will be doing me no more than justice, if you join my ambassadors in making sacrifice on my behalf, and set up the bull in a conspicuous part of the temple; that all men may know what is my attitude towards evil-doers, and in what manner I chastise their inordinate craving after wickedness. Herein is a sufficient indication of my character:

Perilaus punished, the bull consecrated, not reserved for the bellowings of other victims. The first and last melody that issued from those pipes was wrung from their artificer; that one experiment made, the harsh, inhuman notes are silenced for ever. So much for the present offering, which will be followed by many others, so soon as the God vouchsafes me a respite from my work of chastisement.'

Such was the message of Phalaris; and his statement is in strict accordance with the facts. You may safely accept our testimony, as we are acquainted with the circumstances, and can have no object in deceiving you on the present occasion. Must entreaty be added? Then on behalf of one whose character has been misrepresented, and whose severities were forced upon him against his will, we implore you,—we who are Agrigentines, Greeks like yourselves and of Dorian origin—to accept his offer of friendship, and not to thwart his benevolent intentions towards your community and the individuals of which it is composed. Take the bull into your keeping; consecrate it; and offer up your prayers on behalf of Agrigentum and of Phalaris. Suffer us not to have come hither in vain:

repulse not our master with scorn:

nor deprive the God of an offering whose intrinsic beauty is only equalled by its righteous associations.

PHALARIS, II

Men of Delphi:

I stand in no public relation to the city of Agrigentum, in no private relation to its ruler; I am bound to him neither by gratitude for past favours, nor by the prospect of future friendship:

but I have heard the just and temperate plea advanced by his emissaries, and I rise to advocate the claims of religion, the interests of our community, the duties of the priesthood; I charge you, thwart not the pious intention of a mighty prince, nor deprive the God of an offering which in the intention of the donor is already his, and which is destined to serve as an eternal threefold record,—of the sculptor's art, of inventive cruelty, and of righteous retribution. To me it seems that only to have raised this question, only to have halted between acceptance and rejection, is in itself an offence against Heaven; nay, a glaring impiety. For what is this but a sacrilege more heinous than that of the temple-robber, who does but plunder those sacred things to which you would even deny consecration? I implore you,—your fellow priest, your partner in good report (if so it may be), or in evil (should that now befall us), implores you:

close not the temple-doors upon the devout worshipper; suffer us not to be known to the world as men who examine jealously into the offerings that are brought, and subject the donor to the narrow scrutiny of a court, and to the hazard of a vote. For who would not be deterred at the thought that the God accepts no offering without the previous sanction of his priests?

Already Apollo has declared his true opinion. Had he hated Phalaris, or scorned his gift, it had been easy for him to sink the gift and the ship that bore it in mid-ocean; instead, we learn that he vouchsafed them a calm passage and a safe arrival at Cirrha. Clearly the monarch's piety is acceptable in his sight. It behoves you to confirm his decision, and to add this bull to the glories of the temple. Strange indeed, if the sender of so magnificent a gift is to meet with rejection at the temple-door, and his piety to be rewarded with the judgement that his offering is unclean.

My opponent tells a harrowing tale of butchery and violence, of plunder and abduction; it is much that he does not call himself an eyewitness thereof; we might suppose that he was but newly arrived from Agrigentum, did we not know that his travels have never carried him on board ship. In matters of this kind, it is not advisable to place much reliance even on the assertions of the supposed victims; there is no knowing how far they are speaking the truth;—as to bringing allegations ourselves, when we know nothing of the facts, that is out of the question. Granting even that something of the kind *did* happen, it happened in Sicily:

we are at Delphi; we are not called upon to interfere. Do we propose to abandon the temple for the law-court? Are we, whose office it is to sacrifice, and minister to the God, and receive his offerings,—are we to sit here debating whether certain cities on the other side of the Ionian sea are well or ill governed? Let other men's affairs be as they may, it is our business, as I take it, to know our own:

our past history, our present situation, our best interests. We need not wait for Homer to inform us that we inhabit a land of crags, and are tillers of a rocky soil; our eyes tell us that; if we depended on our soil, we must go hungry all our days. Apollo; his temple; his oracle; his worshippers; his sacrifices;— these are the fields of the Delphians, these their revenues, their wealth, their maintenance. I can speak the truth here. It is as the poets say:

we sow not, we plough not, yet all things grow for our use; for a God is our husbandman, and gives us not the good things of Greece only; all that Phrygia, all that Lydia, all that Persia, Assyria, Phoenicia, Italy, and the far North can yield,—all comes to Delphi. We live in prosperity and plenty; in the esteem of mankind we are second to none but the God himself. So it was in the beginning:

so it is now:

and so may it ever be!

But who has ever heard before of our putting an offering to the vote, or hindering men from paying sacrifice? No one; and herein, as I maintain, is the secret of our temple's greatness, and of the abundant wealth of its offerings. Then let us have no innovations now, no new-fangled institutions, no inquiries into the origin and nature and nationality and pedigree of a gift; let us take what is brought to us, and set it in the store-chamber without more ado. In this way we shall best serve both the God and his worshippers. I think it would be well if, before you deliberate further on the question before you, you would consider how great and how various are the issues involved. There is the God, his temple, his sacrifices and offerings, the ancient customs and ordinances, the reputation of the oracle; again, our city as a whole, our common interests, and those of every individual Delphian among us; lastly—and I know not what consideration could seem of more vital importance to a well-judging mind—, our own credit or discredit with the world at large.

I say, then, we have to deal not with Phalaris, not with a single tyrant, not with this bull, not with so much weight of bronze,—but with every king and prince who frequents our temple at this day; with gold and silver and all the precious offerings that should pour in upon the God; that God whose interests claim our first attention. Say, why should we change the old-established usage in regard to offerings? What fault have we to find with the ancient custom, that we should propose innovations? Never yet, from the day when Delphi was first inhabited, and Apollo prophesied, and the tripod gave utterance, and the priestess was inspired, never yet have the bringers of gifts been subjected to scrutiny. And shall they now? Consider how the ancient custom, which granted free access to all men, has filled the temple with treasures; how all men have brought their offerings, and how some have impoverished themselves to enrich the God. My mind misgives me that, when you have assumed the censorship of offerings, you will lack employment:

men may refuse to submit themselves to your court; they may think it is enough to spend their money, without having to undergo the risk of a rejection for their pains. Would life be worth living, to the man who should be judged unworthy to offer sacrifice?

ALEXANDER THE
ORACLE-MONGER

You, my dear Celsus, possibly suppose yourself to be laying upon me quite a trifling task:

Write me down in a book and send me the life and adventures, the tricks and frauds, of the impostor Alexander of Abonutichus. In fact, however, it would take as long to do this in full detail as to reduce to writing the achievements of Alexander of Macedon; the one is among villains what the other is among heroes. Nevertheless, if you will promise to read with indulgence, and fill up the gaps in my tale from your imagination, I will essay the task. I may not cleanse that Augean stable completely, but I will do my best, and fetch you out a few loads as samples of the unspeakable filth that three thousand oxen could produce in many years.

I confess to being a little ashamed both on your account and my own. There are you asking that the memory of an arch-scoundrel should be perpetuated in writing; here am I going seriously into an investigation of this sort—the doings of a person whose deserts entitled him not to be read about by the cultivated, but to be torn to pieces in the amphitheatre by apes or foxes, with a vast audience looking on. Well, well, if any one does cast reflections of that sort upon us, we shall at least have a precedent to plead. Arrian himself, disciple of Epictetus, distinguished Roman, and product of lifelong culture as he was, had just our experience, and shall make our defence. He condescended, that is, to put on record the life of the robber Tilliborus. The robber we propose to immortalize was of a far more pestilent kind, following his profession not in the forests and mountains, but in cities; *he* was not content to overrun a Mysia or an Ida; *his* booty came not from a few scantily populated districts of Asia; one may say that the scene of his depredations was the whole Roman Empire.

I will begin with a picture of the man himself, as lifelike (though I am not great at description) as I can make it with nothing better than words. In person—not to forget that part of him—he was a fine handsome man with a real touch of divinity about him, white-skinned, moderately bearded; he wore besides his own hair artificial additions which matched it so cunningly that they were not generally detected. His eyes were piercing, and suggested inspiration, his voice at once sweet and sonorous. In fact there was no fault to be found with him in these respects.

So much for externals. As for his mind and spirit—well, if all the kind Gods who avert disaster will grant a prayer, it shall be that they bring me not within reach of such a one as he; sooner will I face my bitterest enemies, my country's foes. In understanding, resource, acuteness, he was far above other men; curiosity, receptiveness, memory, scientific ability—all these were his in overflowing measure. But he used them for the worst purposes. Endowed with all these instruments of good, he very soon reached a proud pre-eminence

333

among all who have been famous for evil; the Cercopes, Eurybatus, Phrynondas, Aristodemus, Sostratus—all thrown into the shade. In a letter to his father-in-law Rutilianus, which puts his own pretensions in a truly modest light, he compares himself to Pythagoras. Well, I should not like to offend the wise, the divine Pythagoras; but if he had been Alexander's contemporary, I am quite sure he would have been a mere child to him. Now by all that is admirable, do not take that for an insult to Pythagoras, nor suppose I would draw a parallel between their achievements. What I mean is:

if any one would make a collection of all the vilest and most damaging slanders ever vented against Pythagoras—things whose truth I would not accept for a moment—, the sum of them would not come within measurable distance of Alexander's cleverness. You are to set your imagination to work and conceive a temperament curiously compounded of falsehood, trickery, perjury, cunning; it is versatile, audacious, adventurous, yet dogged in execution; it is plausible enough to inspire confidence; it can assume the mask of virtue, and seem to eschew what it most desires. I suppose no one ever left him after a first interview without the impression that this was the best and kindest of men, ay, and the simplest and most unsophisticated. Add to all this a certain greatness in his objects; he never made a small plan; his ideas were always large.

While in the bloom of his youthful beauty, which we may assume to have been great both from its later remains and from the report of those who saw it, he traded quite shamelessly upon it. Among his other patrons was one of the charlatans who deal in magic and mystic incantations; they will smooth your course of love, confound your enemies, find you treasure, or secure you an inheritance. This person was struck with the lad's natural qualifications for apprenticeship to his trade, and finding him as much attracted by rascality as attractive in appearance, gave him a regular training as accomplice, satellite, and attendant. His own ostensible profession was medicine, and his knowledge included, like that of Thoon the Egyptian's wife,

Many a virtuous herb, and many a bane;

to all which inheritance our friend succeeded. This teacher and lover of his was a native of Tyana, an associate of the great Apollonius, and acquainted with all his heroics. And now you know the atmosphere in which Alexander lived.

By the time his beard had come, the Tyanean was dead, and he found himself in straits; for the personal attractions which might once have been a resource were diminished. He now formed great designs, which he imparted to a Byzantine chronicler of the strolling competitive order, a man of still worse character than himself, called, I believe, Cocconas. The pair went about living on occult pretensions, shearing 'fat-heads,' as they describe ordinary people in the native Magian lingo. Among these they got hold of a rich Macedonian woman; her youth was past, but not her desire for admiration; they got sufficient supplies out of her, and accompanied her from Bithynia to

Macedonia. She came from Pella, which had been a flourishing place under the Macedonian kingdom, but has now a poor and much reduced population.

There is here a breed of large serpents, so tame and gentle that women make pets of them, children take them to bed, they will let you tread on them, have no objection to being squeezed, and will draw milk from the breast like infants. To these facts is probably to be referred the common story about Olympias when she was with child of Alexander; it was doubtless one of these that was her bed-fellow. Well, the two saw these creatures, and bought the finest they could get for a few pence.

And from this point, as Thucydides might say, the war takes its beginning. These ambitious scoundrels were quite devoid of scruples, and they had now joined forces; it could not escape their penetration that human life is under the absolute dominion of two mighty principles, fear and hope, and that any one who can make these serve his ends may be sure of a rapid fortune. They realized that, whether a man is most swayed by the one or by the other, what he must most depend upon and desire is a knowledge of futurity. So were to be explained the ancient wealth and fame of Delphi, Delos, Clarus, Branchidae; it was at the bidding of the two tyrants aforesaid that men thronged the temples, longed for fore- knowledge, and to attain it sacrificed their hecatombs or dedicated their golden ingots. All this they turned over and debated, and it issued in the resolve to establish an oracle. If it were successful, they looked for immediate wealth and prosperity; the result surpassed their most sanguine expectations.

The next things to be settled were, first the theatre of operations, and secondly the plan of campaign. Cocconas favoured Chalcedon, as a mercantile centre convenient both for Thrace and Bithynia, and accessible enough for the province of Asia, Galatia, and tribes still further east. Alexander, on the other hand, preferred his native place, urging very truly that an enterprise like theirs required congenial soil to give it a start, in the shape of 'fat-heads' and simpletons; that was a fair description, he said, of the Paphlagonians beyond Abonutichus; they were mostly superstitious and well-to-do; one had only to go there with some one to play the flute, the tambourine, or the cymbals, set the proverbial mantic sieve[42] a-spinning, and there they would all be gaping as if he were a God from heaven.

This difference of opinion did not last long, and Alexander prevailed. Discovering, however, that a use might after all be made of Chalcedon, they went there first, and in the temple of Apollo, the oldest in the place, they buried some brazen tablets, on which was the statement that very shortly

---

[42] I have no information on Coscinomancy or sieve- divination. 'This kind of divination was generally practised to discover thieves ... They tied a thread to the sieve, by which it was upheld, then prayed to the Gods to direct and assist them. After which they repeated the names of the person suspected, and he at whose name the sieve whirled round or moved was thought to have committed the fact' *Francklin's Lucian.*

Asclepius, with his father Apollo, would pay a visit to Pontus, and take up his abode at Abonutichus. The discovery of the tablets took place as arranged, and the news flew through Bithynia and Pontus, first of all, naturally, to Abonutichus. The people of that place at once resolved to raise a temple, and lost no time in digging the foundations. Cocconas was now left at Chalcedon, engaged in composing certain ambiguous crabbed oracles. He shortly afterwards died, I believe, of a viper's bite.

Alexander meanwhile went on in advance; he had now grown his hair and wore it in long curls; his doublet was white and purple striped, his cloak pure white; he carried a scimetar in imitation of Perseus, from whom he now claimed descent through his mother. The wretched Paphlagonians, who knew perfectly well that his parentage was obscure and mean on both sides, nevertheless gave credence to the oracle, which ran:

Lo, sprung from Perseus, and to Phoebus dear,
High Alexander, Podalirius' son!

Podalirius, it seems, was of so highly amorous a complexion that the distance between Tricca and Paphlagonia was no bar to his union with Alexander's mother. A Sibylline prophecy had also been found:

Hard by Sinope on the Euxine shore
Th' Italic age a fortress prophet sees.
To the first monad let thrice ten be added,
Five monads yet, and then a triple score:

Such the quaternion of th' alexic name.[43]

This heroic entry into his long-left home placed Alexander conspicuously before the public; he affected madness, and frequently foamed at the mouth—a manifestation easily produced by chewing the herb soap-wort, used by dyers; but it brought him reverence and awe. The two had long ago manufactured and fitted up a serpent's head of linen; they had given it a more or less human expression, and painted it very like the real article; by a contrivance of horsehair, the mouth could be opened and shut, and a forked black serpent tongue protruded, working on the same system. The serpent from Pella was also kept ready in the house, to be produced at the right moment and take its part in the drama—the leading part, indeed.

In the fullness of time, his plan took shape. He went one night to the temple foundations, still in process of digging, and with standing water in them which had collected from the rainfall or otherwise; here he deposited a goose

---

[43] In I. 2 of the oracle, the Italic age is the Roman Empire; the fortress prophet is one who belongs to a place ending in—tichus (fort). II>> 3-5 mean:
Take I, 30, 5, 60 (the Greek symbols for which are the letters of the alphabet A, L, E, X), and you will have four letters of the name of your coming protector (alexic).

egg, into which, after blowing it, he had inserted some new-born reptile. He made a resting-place deep down in the mud for this, and departed. Early next morning he rushed into the market-place, naked except for a gold-spangled loin-cloth; with nothing but this and his scimetar, and shaking his long loose hair, like the fanatics who collect money in the name of Cybele, he climbed on to a lofty altar and delivered a harangue, felicitating the city upon the advent of the God now to bless them with his presence. In a few minutes nearly the whole population was on the spot, women, old men, and children included; all was awe, prayer, and adoration. He uttered some unintelligible sounds, which might have been Hebrew or Phoenician, but completed his victory over his audience, who could make nothing of what he said, beyond the constant repetition of the names Apollo and Asclepius.

He then set off at a run for the future temple. Arrived at the excavation and the already completed sacred fount, he got down into the water, chanted in a loud voice hymns to Asclepius and Apollo, and invited the God to come, a welcome guest, to the city. He next demanded a bowl, and when this was handed to him, had no difficulty in putting it down at the right place and scooping up, besides water and mud, the egg in which the God had been enclosed; the edges of the aperture had been joined with wax and white lead. He took the egg in his hand and announced that here he held Asclepius. The people, who had been sufficiently astonished by the discovery of the egg in the water, were now all eyes for what was to come. He broke it, and received in his hollowed palm the hardly developed reptile; the crowd could see it stirring and winding about his fingers; they raised a shout, hailed the God, blessed the city, and every mouth was full of prayers—for treasure and wealth and health and all the other good things that he might give. Our hero now departed homewards, still running, with the new-born Asclepius in his hands—the twice-born, too, whereas ordinary men can be born but once, and born moreover not of Coronis[44] nor even of her namesake the crow, but of a goose! After him streamed the whole people, in all the madness of fanatic hopes.

He now kept the house for some days, in hopes that the Paphlagonians would soon be drawn in crowds by the news. He was not disappointed; the city was filled to overflowing with persons who had neither brains nor individuality, who bore no resemblance to men that live by bread, and had only their outward shape to distinguish them from sheep. In a small room he took his seat, very imposingly attired, upon a couch. He took into his bosom our Asclepius of Pella (a very fine and large one, as I observed), wound its body round his neck, and let its tail hang down; there was enough of this not only to fill his lap, but to trail on the ground also; the patient creature's head he kept hidden in his armpit, showing the linen head on one side of his beard exactly as if it belonged to the visible body.

---

[44] Coronis was the mother of Asclepius; 'corone' is Greek for a crow.

Picture to yourself a little chamber into which no very brilliant light was admitted, with a crowd of people from all quarters, excited, carefully worked up, all a-flutter with expectation. As they came in, they might naturally find a miracle in the development of that little crawling thing of a few days ago into this great, tame, human-looking serpent. Then they had to get on at once towards the exit, being pressed forward by the new arrivals before they could have a good look. An exit had been specially made just opposite the entrance, for all the world like the Macedonian device at Babylon when Alexander was ill; he was *in extremis*, you remember, and the crowd round the palace were eager to take their last look and give their last greeting. Our scoundrel's exhibition, though, is said to have been given not once, but many times, especially for the benefit of any wealthy new-comers.

And at this point, my dear Celsus, we may, if we will be candid, make some allowance for these Paphlagonians and Pontics; the poor uneducated 'fat-heads' might well be taken in when they handled the serpent—a privilege conceded to all who choose—and saw in that dim light its head with the mouth that opened and shut. It was an occasion for a Democritus, nay, for an Epicurus or a Metrodorus, perhaps, a man whose intelligence was steeled against such assaults by scepticism and insight, one who, if he could not detect the precise imposture, would at any rate have been perfectly certain that, though this escaped him, the whole thing was a lie and an impossibility.

By degrees Bithynia, Galatia, Thrace, came flocking in, every one who had been present doubtless reporting that he had beheld the birth of the God, and had touched him after his marvellous development in size and in expression. Next came pictures and models, bronze or silver images, and the God acquired a name. By divine command, metrically expressed, he was to be known as Glycon. For Alexander had delivered the line:

Glycon my name, man's light, son's son to Zeus.

And now at last the object to which all this had led up, the giving of oracular answers to all applicants, could be attained. The cue was taken from Amphilochus in Cilicia. After the death and disappearance at Thebes of his father Amphiaraus, Amphilochus, driven from his home, made his way to Cilicia, and there did not at all badly by prophesying to the Cilicians at the rate of threepence an oracle. After this precedent, Alexander proclaimed that on a stated day the God would give answers to all comers. Each person was to write down his wish and the object of his curiosity, fasten the packet with thread, and seal it with wax, clay, or other such substance. He would receive these, and enter the holy place (by this time the temple was complete, and the scene all ready), whither the givers should be summoned in order by a herald and an acolyte; he would learn the God's mind upon each, and return the packets with their seals intact and the answers attached, the God being ready to give a definite answer to any question that might be put.

The trick here was one which would be seen through easily enough by a person of your intelligence (or, if I may say so without violating modesty, of my own), but which to the ordinary imbecile would have the persuasiveness of what is marvellous and incredible. He contrived various methods of undoing the seals, read the questions, answered them as seemed good, and then folded, sealed, and returned them, to the great astonishment of the recipients. And then it was, 'How could he possibly know what I gave him carefully secured under a seal that defies imitation, unless he were a true God, with a God's omniscience?'

Perhaps you will ask what these contrivances were; well, then—the information may be useful another time. One of them was this. He would heat a needle, melt with it the under part of the wax, lift the seal off, and after reading warm the wax once more with the needle—both that below the thread and that which formed the actual seal—and re-unite the two without difficulty. Another method employed the substance called collyrium; this is a preparation of Bruttian pitch, bitumen, pounded glass, wax, and mastich. He kneaded the whole into collyrium, heated it, placed it on the seal, previously moistened with his tongue, and so took a mould. This soon hardened; he simply opened, read, replaced the wax, and reproduced an excellent imitation of the original seal as from an engraved stone. One more I will give you. Adding some gypsum to the glue used in book-binding he produced a sort of wax, which was applied still wet to the seal, and on being taken off solidified at once and provided a matrix harder than horn, or even iron. There are plenty of other devices for the purpose, to rehearse which would seem like airing one's knowledge. Moreover, in your excellent pamphlets against the magians (most useful and instructive reading they are) you have yourself collected enough of them—many more than those I have mentioned.

So oracles and divine utterances were the order of the day, and much shrewdness he displayed, eking out mechanical ingenuity with obscurity, his answers to some being crabbed and ambiguous, and to others absolutely unintelligible. He did however distribute warning and encouragement according to his lights, and recommend treatments and diets; for he had, as I originally stated, a wide and serviceable acquaintance with drugs; he was particularly given to prescribing 'cytmides,' which were a salve prepared from goat's fat, the name being of his own invention. For the realization of ambitions, advancement, or successions, he took care never to assign early dates; the formula was, 'All this shall come to pass when it is my will, and when my prophet Alexander shall make prayer and entreaty on your behalf.'

There was a fixed charge of a shilling the oracle. And, my friend, do not suppose that this would not come to much; he made something like L3,000 *per annum*; people were insatiable—would take from ten to fifteen oracles at a time. What he got he did not keep to himself, nor put it by for the future; what with accomplices, attendants, inquiry agents, oracle writers and keepers, amanuenses, seal-forgers, and interpreters, he had now a host of claimants to satisfy.

He had begun sending emissaries abroad to make the shrine known in foreign lands; his prophecies, discovery of runaways, conviction of thieves and robbers, revelations of hidden treasure, cures of the sick, restoration of the dead to life—all these were to be advertised. This brought them running and crowding from all points of the compass; victims bled, gifts were presented, and the prophet and disciple came off better than the God; for had not the oracle spoken?—

Give what ye give to my attendant priest;
My care is not for gifts, but for my priest.

A time came when a number of sensible people began to shake off their intoxication and combine against him, chief among them the numerous Epicureans; in the cities, the imposture with all its theatrical accessories began to be seen through. It was now that he resorted to a measure of intimidation; he proclaimed that Pontus was overrun with atheists and Christians, who presumed to spread the most scandalous reports concerning him; he exhorted Pontus, as it valued the God's favour, to stone these men. Touching Epicurus, he gave the following response. An inquirer had asked how Epicurus fared in Hades, and was told:

Of slime is his bed,
And his fetters of lead.

The prosperity of the oracle is perhaps not so wonderful, when one learns what sensible, intelligent questions were in fashion with its votaries. Well, it was war to the knife between him and Epicurus, and no wonder. What fitter enemy for a charlatan who patronized miracles and hated truth, than the thinker who had grasped the nature of things and was in solitary possession of that truth? As for the Platonists, Stoics, Pythagoreans, they were his good friends; he had no quarrel with them. But the unmitigated Epicurus, as he used to call him, could not but be hateful to him, treating all such pretensions as absurd and puerile. Alexander consequently loathed Amastris beyond all the cities of Pontus, knowing what a number of Lepidus's friends and others like-minded it contained. He would not give oracles to Amastrians; when he once did, to a senator's brother, he made himself ridiculous, neither hitting upon a presentable oracle for himself, nor finding a deputy equal to the occasion. The man had complained of colic, and what he meant to prescribe was pig's foot dressed with mallow. The shape it took was:

In basin hallowed
Be pigments mallowed.

I have mentioned that the serpent was often exhibited by request; he was not completely visible, but the tail and body were exposed, while the head was concealed under the prophet's dress. By way of impressing the people still more, he announced that he would induce the God to speak, and give his responses without an intermediary. His simple device to this end was a tube of cranes' windpipes, which he passed, with due regard to its matching, through the artificial head, and, having an assistant speaking into the end outside, whose voice issued through the linen Asclepius, thus answered questions. These oracles were called *autophones*, and were not vouchsafed casually to any one, but reserved for officials, the rich, and the lavish.

It was an autophone which was given to Severian regarding the invasion of Armenia. He encouraged him with these lines:

Armenia, Parthia, cowed by thy fierce spear,
To Rome, and Tiber's shining waves, thou com'st,
Thy brow with leaves and radiant gold encircled.

Then when the foolish Gaul took his advice and invaded, to the total destruction of himself and his army by Othryades, the adviser expunged that oracle from his archives and substituted the following:

Vex not th' Armenian land; it shall not thrive;
One in soft raiment clad shall from his bow
Launch death, and cut thee off from life and light.

For it was one of his happy thoughts to issue prophecies after the event as antidotes to those premature utterances which had not gone right. Frequently he promised recovery to a sick man before his death, and after it was at no loss for second thoughts:

No longer seek to arrest thy fell disease;
Thy fate is manifest, inevitable.

Knowing the fame of Clarus, Didymus, and Mallus for sooth-saying much like his own, he struck up an alliance with them, sending on many of his clients to those places. So

Hie thee to Clarus now, and hear my sire.

And again,

Draw near to Branchidae and counsel take.

Or

Seek Mallus; be Amphilochus thy counsellor.

So things went within the borders of Ionia, Cilicia, Paphlagonia, and Galatia. When the fame of the oracle travelled to Italy and entered Rome, the only question was, who should be first; those who did not come in person sent messages, the powerful and respected being the keenest of all. First and foremost among these was Rutilianus; he was in most respects an excellent person, and had filled many high offices in Rome; but he suffered from religious mania, holding the most extraordinary beliefs on that matter; show him a bit of stone smeared with unguents or crowned with flowers, and he would incontinently fall down and worship, and linger about it praying and asking for blessings. The reports about our oracle nearly induced him to throw up the appointment he then held, and fly to Abonutichus; he actually did send messenger upon messenger. His envoys were ignorant servants, easily taken in. They came back having really seen certain things, relating others which they probably thought they had seen and heard, and yet others which they deliberately invented to curry favour with their master. So they inflamed the poor old man and drove him into confirmed madness.

He had a wide circle of influential friends, to whom he communicated the news brought by his successive messengers, not without additional touches of his own. All Rome was full of his tales; there was quite a commotion, the gentlemen of the Court being much fluttered, and at once taking measures to learn something of their own fate. The prophet gave all who came a hearty welcome, gained their goodwill by hospitality and costly gifts, and sent them off ready not merely to report his answers, but to sing the praises of the God and invent miraculous tales of the shrine and its guardian.

This triple rogue now hit upon an idea which would have been too clever for the ordinary robber. Opening and reading the packets which reached him, whenever he came upon an equivocal, compromising question, he omitted to return the packet; the sender was to be under his thumb, bound to his service by the terrifying recollection of the question he had written down. You know the sort of things that wealthy and powerful personages would be likely to ask. This blackmail brought him in a good income.

I should like to quote you one or two of the answers given to Rutilianus. He had a son by a former wife, just old enough for advanced teaching. The father asked who should be his tutor, and was told,

Pythagoras, and the mighty battle-bard.

When the child died a few days after, the prophet was abashed, and quite unable to account for this summary confutation. However, dear good Rutilianus very soon restored the oracle's credit by discovering that this was the very thing the God had foreshown; he had not directed him to choose a living teacher; Pythagoras and Homer were long dead, and doubtless the boy was now enjoying their instructions in Hades. Small blame to Alexander if he had a taste for dealings with such specimens of humanity as this.

Another of Rutilianus's questions was, Whose soul he had succeeded to, and the answer:

First thou wast Peleus' son, and next Menander;
Then thine own self; next, a sunbeam shalt be;
And nine score annual rounds thy life shall measure.

At seventy, he died of melancholy, not waiting for the God to pay in full.

That was an autophone too. Another time Rutilianus consulted the oracle on the choice of a wife. The answer was express:

Wed Alexander's daughter and Selene's.

He had long ago spread the report that the daughter he had had was by Selene:

she had once seen him asleep, and fallen in love, as is her way with handsome sleepers. The sensible Rutilianus lost no time, but sent for the maiden at once, celebrated the nuptials, a sexagenarian bridegroom, and lived with her, propitiating his divine mother-in-law with whole hecatombs, and reckoning himself now one of the heavenly company.

His finger once in the Italian pie, Alexander devoted himself to getting further. Sacred envoys were sent all over the Roman Empire, warning the various cities to be on their guard against pestilence and conflagrations, with the prophet's offers of security against them. One oracle in particular, an autophone again, he distributed broadcast at a time of pestilence. It was a single line:

Phoebus long-tressed the plague-cloud shall dispel.

This was everywhere to be seen written up on doors as a prophylactic. Its effect was generally disappointing; for it somehow happened that the protected houses were just the ones to be desolated. Not that I would suggest for a moment that the line was their destruction; but, accidentally no doubt, it did so fall out. Possibly common people put too much confidence in the verse, and lived carelessly without troubling to help the oracle against its foe; were there not the words fighting their battle, and long-tressed Phoebus discharging his arrows at the pestilence?

In Rome itself he established an intelligence bureau well manned with his accomplices. They sent him people's characters, forecasts of their questions, and hints of their ambitions, so that he had his answers ready before the messengers reached him.

It was with his eye on this Italian propaganda, too, that he took a further step. This was the institution of mysteries, with hierophants and torch-bearers complete. The ceremonies occupied three successive days. On the first, proclamation was made on the Athenian model to this effect:

'If there be any atheist or Christian or Epicurean here spying upon our rites, let him depart in haste; and let all such as have faith in the God be initiated and all blessing attend them.' He led the litany with, 'Christians, avaunt!' and the crowd responded, 'Epicureans, avaunt!' Then was presented the child-bed of Leto and birth of Apollo, the bridal of Coronis, Asclepius born. The second day, the epiphany and nativity of the God Glycon.

On the third came the wedding of Podalirius and Alexander's mother; this was called Torch-day, and torches were used. The finale was the loves of Selene and Alexander, and the birth of Rutilianus's wife. The torch- bearer and hierophant was Endymion-Alexander. He was discovered lying asleep; to him from heaven, represented by the ceiling, enter as Selene one Rutilia, a great beauty, and wife of one of the Imperial procurators. She and Alexander were lovers off the stage too, and the wretched husband had to look on at their public kissing and embracing; if there had not been a good supply of torches, things might possibly have gone even further. Shortly after, he reappeared amidst a profound hush, attired as hierophant; in a loud voice he called, 'Hail, Glycon!', whereto the Eumolpidae and Ceryces of Paphlagonia, with their clod-hopping shoes and their garlic breath, made sonorous response, 'Hail, Alexander!'

The torch ceremony with its ritual skippings often enabled him to bestow a glimpse of his thigh, which was thus discovered to be of gold; it was presumably enveloped in cloth of gold, which glittered in the lamp-light. This gave rise to a debate between two wiseacres, whether the golden thigh meant that he had inherited Pythagoras's soul, or merely that their two souls were alike; the question was referred to Alexander himself, and King Glycon relieved their perplexity with an oracle:

Waxes and wanes Pythagoras' soul:
the seer's
Is from the mind of Zeus an emanation.
His Father sent him, virtuous men to aid,
And with his bolt one day shall call him home.

I will now give you a conversation between Glycon and one Sacerdos of Tius; the intelligence of the latter you may gauge from his questions. I read it inscribed in golden letters in Sacerdos's house at Tius. 'Tell me, lord Glycon,' said he, 'who you are.' 'The new Asclepius.' 'Another, different from the former one? Is that the meaning?' 'That it is not lawful for you to learn.' 'And how many years will you sojourn and prophesy among us?' 'A thousand and three.' 'And after that, whither will you go?' 'To Bactria; for the barbarians too must be blessed with my presence.' 'The other oracles, at Didymus and Clarus and Delphi, have they still the spirit of your grandsire Apollo, or are the answers that now come from them forgeries?' 'That, too, desire not to know; it is not lawful.' 'What shall I be after this life?' 'A camel; then a horse; then a wise man, no less a prophet than Alexander.' Such was the conversation. There was added to it an oracle in verse, inspired by the fact that Sacerdos was an associate of Lepidus:

Shun Lepidus; an evil fate awaits him.

As I have said, Alexander was much afraid of Epicurus, and the solvent action of his logic on imposture.

On one occasion, indeed, an Epicurean got himself into great trouble by daring to expose him before a great gathering. He came up and addressed him in a loud voice. 'Alexander, it was you who induced So-and-so the Paphlagonian to bring his slaves before the governor of Galatia, charged with the murder of his son who was being educated in Alexandria. Well, the young man is alive, and has come back, to find that the slaves had been cast to the beasts by your machinations.' What had happened was this. The lad had sailed up the Nile, gone on to a Red Sea port, found a vessel starting for India, and been persuaded to make the voyage. He being long overdue, the unfortunate slaves supposed that he had either perished in the Nile or fallen a victim to some of the pirates who infested it at that time; so they came home to report his disappearance. Then followed the oracle, the sentence, and finally the young man's return with the story of his absence.

All this the Epicurean recounted. Alexander was much annoyed by the exposure, and could not stomach so well deserved an affront; he directed the company to stone the man, on pain of being involved in his impiety and called Epicureans. However, when they set to work, a distinguished Pontic called Demostratus, who was staying there, rescued him by interposing his own body; the man had the narrowest possible escape from being stoned to death—as he richly deserved to be; what business had he to be the only sane man in a crowd of madmen, and needlessly make himself the butt of Paphlagonian infatuation?

This was a special case; but it was the practice for the names of applicants to be read out the day before answers were given; the herald asked whether each was to receive his oracle; and sometimes the reply came from within, To perdition! One so repulsed could get shelter, fire or water, from no man; he must be driven from land to land as a blasphemer, an atheist, and— lowest depth of all—an Epicurean.

In this connexion Alexander once made himself supremely ridiculous. Coming across Epicurus's *Accepted Maxims*, the most admirable of his books, as you know, with its terse presentment of his wise conclusions, he brought it into the middle of the market-place, there burned it on a fig-wood fire for the sins of its author, and cast its ashes into the sea. He issued an oracle on the occasion:

The dotard's maxims to the flames be given.

The fellow had no conception of the blessings conferred by that book upon its readers, of the peace, tranquillity, and independence of mind it produces, of the protection it gives against terrors, phantoms, and marvels, vain hopes and inordinate desires, of the judgement and candour that it fosters, or of its true purging of the spirit, not with torches and squills and such rubbish, but with right reason, truth, and frankness.

Perhaps the greatest example of our rogue's audacity is what I now come to. Having easy access to Palace and Court by Rutilianus's influence, he sent an oracle just at the crisis of the German war, when M. Aurelius was on the point of engaging the Marcomanni and Quadi. The oracle required that two lions should be flung alive into the Danube, with quantities of sacred herbs and magnificent sacrifices. I had better give the words:

To rolling Ister, swoln with Heaven's rain,
Of Cybelean thralls, those mountain beasts,
Fling ye a pair; therewith all flowers and herbs

345

Of savour sweet that Indian air doth breed.
Hence victory, and fame, and lovely peace.

These directions were precisely followed; the lions swam across to the enemy's bank, where they were clubbed to death by the barbarians, who took them for dogs or a new kind of wolves; and our forces immediately after met with a severe defeat, losing some twenty thousand men in one engagement. This was followed by the Aquileian incident, in the course of which that city was nearly lost. In view of these results, Alexander warmed up that stale Delphian defence of the Croesus oracle:

the God had foretold a victory, forsooth, but had not stated whether Romans or barbarians should have it.

The constant increase in the number of visitors, the inadequacy of accommodation in the city, and the difficulty of finding provisions for consultants, led to his introducing what he called *night oracles*. He received the packets, slept upon them, in his own phrase, and gave answers which the God was supposed to send him in dreams. These were generally not lucid, but ambiguous and confused, especially when he came to packets sealed with exceptional care. He did not risk tampering with these, but wrote down any words that came into his head, the results obtained corresponding well enough to his conception of the oracular. There were regular interpreters in attendance, who made considerable sums out of the recipients by expounding and unriddling these oracles. This office contributed to his revenue, the interpreters paying him L250 each.

Sometimes he stirred the wonder of the silly by answers to persons who had neither brought nor sent questions, and in fact did not exist. Here is a specimen:

Who is't, thou askst, that with Calligenia
All secretly defiles thy nuptial bed?
The slave Protogenes, whom most thou trustest.
Him thou enjoyedst:
he thy wife enjoys—
The fit return for that thine outrage done.
And know that baleful drugs for thee are brewed,
Lest thou or see or hear their evil deeds.
Close by the wall, at thy bed's head, make search.
Thy maid Calypso to their plot is privy.

The names and circumstantial details might stagger a Democritus, till a moment's thought showed him the despicable trick.

He often gave answers in Syriac or Celtic to barbarians who questioned him in their own tongue, though he had difficulty in finding compatriots of theirs in the city. In these cases there was a long interval between application and response, during which the packet might be securely opened at leisure, and somebody found capable of translating the question. The following is an answer given to a Scythian:

Morphi ebargulis for night
Chnenchicrank shall leave the light.

Another oracle to some one who neither came nor existed was in prose. 'Return the way thou earnest,' it ran; 'for he that sent thee hath this day been slain by his neighbour Diocles, with aid of the robbers Magnus, Celer, and Bubalus, who are taken and in chains.'

I must give you one or two of the answers that fell to my share. I asked whether Alexander was bald, and having sealed it publicly with great care, got a night oracle in reply:

Sabardalachu malach Attis was not he.

Another time I did up the same question—What was Homer's birthplace?—in two packets given in under different names. My servant misled him by saying, when asked what he came for, a cure for lung trouble; so the answer to one packet was:

Cytmide and foam of steed the liniment give.

As for the other packet, he got the information that the sender was inquiring whether the land or the sea route to Italy was preferable. So he answered, without much reference to Homer:

Fare not by sea; land-travel meets thy need.

I laid a good many traps of this kind for him; here is another. I asked only one question, but wrote outside the packet in the usual form, So- and-so's eight Queries, giving a fictitious name and sending the eight shillings. Satisfied with the payment of the money and the inscription on the packet, he gave me eight answers to my one question. This was, When will Alexander's imposture be detected? The answers concerned nothing in heaven or earth, but were all silly and meaningless together. He afterwards found out about this, and also that I had tried to dissuade Rutilianus both from the marriage and from putting any confidence in the oracle; so he naturally conceived a violent dislike for me. When Rutilianus once put a question to him about me, the answer was:

Night-haunts and foul debauch are all his joy.

It is true his dislike was quite justified. On a certain occasion I was passing through Abonutichus, with a spearman and a pikeman whom my friend the governor of Cappadocia had lent me as an escort on my way to the sea. Ascertaining that I was the Lucian he knew of, he sent me a very polite and hospitable invitation. I found him with a numerous company; by good luck I had brought my escort. He gave me his hand to kiss according to his usual custom. I took hold of it as if to kiss, but instead bestowed on it a sound bite that must have come near disabling it. The company, who were already offended at my calling him Alexander instead of Prophet, were inclined to throttle and beat me for sacrilege. But he endured the pain like a man, checked their violence, and assured them that he would easily tame me, and illustrate Glycon's greatness in converting his bitterest foes to friends. He then dismissed them all, and argued the matter with me:

he was perfectly aware of my advice to Rutilianus; why had I treated him so, when I might have been preferred by him to great influence in that quarter? By this time I had realized my dangerous position, and was only too glad to welcome these advances; I presently went my way in all friendship with him. The rapid change wrought in me greatly impressed the observers.

When I intended to sail, he sent me many parting gifts, and offered to find us (Xenophon and me, that is; I had sent my father and family on to Amastris) a ship and crew—which offer I accepted in all confidence. When the passage was half over, I observed the master in tears arguing with his men, which made me very uneasy. It turned out that Alexander's orders were to seize and fling us overboard; in that case his war with me would have been lightly won. But the crew were prevailed upon by the master's tears to do us no harm. 'I am sixty years old, as you can see,' he said to me; 'I have lived an honest blameless life so far, and I should not like at my time of life, with a wife and children too, to stain my hands with blood.' And with that preface he informed us what we were there for, and what Alexander had told him to do.

He landed us at Aegiali, of Homeric fame, and thence sailed home. Some Bosphoran envoys happened to be passing, on their way to Bithynia with the annual tribute from their king Eupator. They listened kindly to my account of our dangerous situation, I was taken on board, and reached Amastris safely after my narrow escape. From that time it was war between Alexander and me, and I left no stone unturned to get my revenge. Even before his plot I had hated him, revolted by his abominable practices, and I now busied myself with the attempt to expose him; I found plenty of allies, especially in the circle of Timocrates the Heracleot philosopher. But Avitus, the then governor of Bithynia and Pontus, restrained me, I may almost say with prayers and entreaties. He could not possibly spoil his relations with Rutilianus, he said, by punishing the man, even if he could get clear evidence against him. Thus arrested in my course, I did not persist in what must have been, considering the disposition of the judge, a fruitless prosecution.

Among instances of Alexander's presumption, a high place must be given to his petition to the Emperor:

the name of Abonutichus was to be changed to Ionopolis; and a new coin was to be struck, with a representation on the obverse of Glycon, and, on the reverse, Alexander bearing the garlands proper to his paternal grandfather Asclepius, and the famous scimetar of his maternal ancestor Perseus.

He had stated in an oracle that he was destined to live to a hundred and fifty, and then die by a thunderbolt; he had in fact, before he reached seventy, an end very sad for a son of Podalirius, his leg mortifying from foot to groin and being eaten of worms; it then proved that he was bald, as he was forced by pain to let the doctors make cooling applications to his head, which they could not do without removing his wig.

So ended Alexander's heroics; such was the catastrophe of his tragedy; one would like to find a special providence in it, though doubtless chance must have the credit. The funeral celebration was to be worthy of his life, taking the form of a contest—for possession of the oracle. The most prominent of the impostors his accomplices referred it to Rutilianus's arbitration which of them should be selected to succeed to the prophetic office and wear the hierophantic oracular garland. Among these was numbered the grey-haired physician Paetus, dishonouring equally his grey hairs and his profession. But Steward-of-the-Games Rutilianus sent them about their business ungarlanded, and continued the defunct in possession of his holy office.

My object, dear friend, in making this small selection from a great mass of material has been twofold. First, I was willing to oblige a friend and comrade who is for me the pattern of wisdom, sincerity, good humour, justice, tranquillity, and geniality. But secondly I was still more concerned (a preference which you will be very far from resenting) to strike a blow for Epicurus, that great man whose holiness and divinity of nature were not shams, who alone had and imparted true insight into the good, and who brought deliverance to all that consorted with him. Yet I think casual readers too may find my essay not unserviceable, since it is not only destructive, but, for men of sense, constructive also.

OF PANTOMIME[45]

Lycinus. Crato

Ly. Here are heavy charges, Crato; I suppose you have been getting up this subject for some time. You are not content with attacking the whole pantomimic art, practical and theoretic; we too, the pleased spectators thereof, come in for our share:

we have been lavishing our admiration, it seems, on effeminate triflers. And now let me show you how completely you have been mistaken; you will find that the art you have been maligning is the greatest boon of our existence. There is some excuse for your strictures:

how should you know any better, confirmed ascetic that you are, believing that virtue consists in being uncomfortable?

Cr. Now, my dear sir, can any one who calls himself a man, and an educated man, and in some sort a student of philosophy,—can such a one leave those higher pursuits, leave communing with the sages of old, to sit still and listen to the sound of a flute, and watch the antics of an effeminate creature got up in soft raiment to sing lascivious songs and mimic the passions of prehistoric strumpets, of Rhodopes and Phaedras and Parthenopes, to the accompaniment of twanging string and shrilling pipe and clattering heel? It is too absurd:

these are not amusements for a gentleman; not amusements for Lycinus. When I first heard of your spending your time in this way, I was divided betwixt shame and indignation, to think that you could so far forget Plato and Chrysippus and Aristotle, as to sit thus having your ears tickled with a feather. If you want amusements, are there not a thousand things *worth* seeing and hearing? Can you not hear classical music performed at the great festivals? Are there not lofty tragedy and brilliant comedy,—things that have been deemed worthy of state recognition? My friend, you have a long reckoning to settle with men of learning, if you would not be repudiated altogether, and expelled from the congregation of the wise. I think your best course will be a point-blank denial:

declare flatly that you never did anything of the kind. Anyhow, you must watch your conduct for the future:

---

[45] 'Pantomime' has been chosen as the most natural translation of *orchaesis*, which in this dialogue has reference for the most part to the ballet-dancer (*pantomimus*) of imperial times. On the other hand, Lycinus, in order to establish the antiquity and the universality of an art that for all practical purposes dates only from the Augustan era, and (despite the Greek artists) is Roman in origin, avails himself of the wider meaning of *orchaesis* to give us the historic and prehistoric associations of *dance* in Greece and elsewhere; and in such passages it seemed advisable to sacrifice consistency, and to translate *orchaesis* dance.

we do not want to find that our Lycinus has changed his sex, and become a Bacchante or a Lydian damsel. That would be as much to our discredit as to yours:

for ours should be Odysseus's part,—to tear you from the lotus, and bring you back to your accustomed pursuits; to save you from the clutches of these stage Sirens before it is too late. The Sirens, after all, did but plot against men's ears; it needed but a little wax, and a man might sail past them uninjured:

but yours is a captivity of ear and eye, of body and soul.

Ly. Goodness gracious! All the Cynic in you is loose, and snarls at me. At the same time, I think your Lotus-and-Siren simile is rather off the point:

you see, the people who ate the Lotus and listened to the Sirens paid for the gratification of ear and palate with their lives:

whereas I not only have a great deal more enjoyment than they had, but am all the better for it. I have experienced no oblivion of my domestic affairs, nor blindness to my own interests; in fact—if I may venture to say so—you will find my penetration and practical wisdom considerably increased by my theatrical experiences. Homer has it exactly:

the spectator

Returns a gladder and a wiser man.

Cr. Dear, dear! Yours is a sad case, Lycinus. You are not even ashamed; you seem quite pleased with yourself. That is the worst of it:

there seems no hope of your recovery, while you can actually commend the mire in which you wallow.

Ly. Now, Crato,—you talk of pantomimes and theatres,—have you seen these performances yourself, that you are so hard on them? or do you decide that they are 'foul mire' without personal experience? If you have seen them, you are just as bad as I am; and if not, are you justified in censuring them? does it not savour of over-confidence, to condemn what you know nothing about?

Cr. Truly that would be the climax:

that I should show my long beard and white hairs amid that throng of women and lunatics; and clap and yell in unseemly rapture over the vile contortions of an abandoned buffoon.

Ly. I can make allowance for you. But wait till I have prevailed on you to give it a fair trial, to accept the judgement of your own eyes:

after that you will never be happy till you have secured the best seat in the theatre, where you may hear every syllable, mark every gesture.

Cr. While this beard is yet unplucked, these limbs unshaven, God forbid that I should ever find happiness in such things. As it is, my poor friend, I see that *you* are wholly possessed.

Ly. Now suppose you were to abstain from further abuse, and hear what I have to say of the merits of Pantomime; of the manner in which it combines profit with amusement; instructing, informing, perfecting the intelligence of the beholder; training his eyes to lovely sights, filling his ears with noble sounds, revealing a beauty in which body and soul alike have their share. For

351

that music and dancing are employed to produce these results is no disparagement of the art; it is rather a recommendation.

Cr. I have not much time for listening to a madman's discourse in praise of his own madness. However—if you must deluge me with nonsense—I am prepared to do you that friendly office. My ears are at your service:

they need no wax to render them deaf to foolishness. Henceforth I will be silent:

speak on;—no one is listening.

Ly. Thank you, Crato; just what I wanted. As to 'foolishness,' that remains to be seen. Now, to begin with, you seem to be quite ignorant of the antiquity of the pantomimic art. It is not a new thing; it does not date from to-day or yesterday; not, that is to say, from our grandfathers' times, nor from *their* grandfathers' times. The best antiquarians, let me tell you, trace dancing back to the creation of the universe; it is coeval with that Eros who was the beginning of all things. In the dance of the heavenly bodies, in the complex involutions whereby the planets are brought into harmonious intercourse with the fixed stars, you have an example of that art in its infancy, which, by gradual development, by continual improvements and additions, seems at length to have reached its climax in the subtle harmonious versatility of modern Pantomime.

The first step, we learn, was taken by Rhea, who was so pleased with the art that she introduced it among the Corybantes in Phrygia and the Curetes in Crete. She was richly rewarded:

for by their dancing they saved her child Zeus, who owes it to them (nor can he with decency deny it) that he escaped the paternal teeth. The dancing was performed in full armour; sword clashed against shield, and inspired heels beat martial time upon the ground. The art was presently taken up by the leading men in Crete, who by dint of practice became admirable dancers; and this applies not only to private persons, but to men of the first eminence, and of royal blood. Thus Homer, when he calls Meriones a dancer, is not disparaging him, but paying him a compliment:

his dancing fame, it seems, had spread not only throughout the Greek world, but even into the camp of his enemies, the Trojans, who would observe, no doubt, on the field of battle that agility and grace of movement which he had acquired as a dancer. The passage runs as follows:

Meriones, great dancer though thou be,
My spear had stopped thy dancings,—

it did not, however, do so; his practice in that art enabling him, apparently, to evade without difficulty any spears that might be hurled at him.

I could mention a number of other heroes who went through a similar course of training, and made a serious study of dancing:

but I will confine myself to the case of Neoptolemus, the son of Achilles, and a most eminent dancer. He it was who invented that beautiful dance called after him the Pyrrhic; a circumstance which may be supposed to have afforded more gratification to his father than his comeliness, or his prowess in other respects. Thus Troy, impregnable till then, falls a victim to the dancer's skill, and is levelled with the dust.

The Lacedaemonians, who are reputed the bravest of the Greeks, ever since they learnt from Castor and Pollux the Caryatic (a form of dance which is taught in the Lacedaemonian town of Caryae), will do nothing without the accompaniment of the Muses:

on the field of battle their feet keep time to the flute's measured notes, and those notes are the signal for their onset. Music and rhythm ever led them on to victory. To this day you may see their young men dividing their attention between dance and drill; when wrestling and boxing are over, their exercise concludes with the dance. A flute-player sits in their midst, beating time with his foot, while they file past and perform their various movements in rhythmic sequence, the military evolutions being followed by dances, such as Dionysus and Aphrodite love. Hence the song they sing is an invitation to Aphrodite and the Loves to join in their dance and revel; while the other (I should have said that they have two songs) contains instructions to the dancers:

'Forward, lads:

foot it lightly:

reel it bravely' (i.e. dance actively). It is the same with the chain dance, which is performed by men and girls together, dancing alternately, so as to suggest the alternating beads of a necklace. A youth leads off the dance:

his active steps are such as will hereafter be of use to him on the field of battle:

a maiden follows, with the modest movements that befit her sex; manly vigour, maidenly reserve,—these are the beads of the necklace. Similarly, their Gymnopaedia is but another form of dance.

You have read your Homer; so that I need say nothing of the Shield of Achilles, with its choral dance, modelled on that which Daedalus designed for Ariadne; nor of the two dancers ('tumblers,' he calls them) there represented as leading the dance; nor again of the 'whirling dance of youth,' so beautifully wrought thereon by Hephaestus. As to the Phaeacians, living as they did in the lap of luxury, nothing is more natural than that *they* should have rejoiced in the dance. Odysseus, we find, is particularly struck with this:

he gazes with admiration on the 'twinkling of their feet.' In Thessaly, again, dancing was such a prominent feature, that their rulers and generals were called 'Dancers-in- chief,' as may be seen from the inscriptions on the statues of their great men:

'Elected Prime Dancer,' we read; and again:

'This statue was erected at the public expense to commemorate Ilation's well-danced victory.'

I need hardly observe that among the ancient mysteries not one is to be found that does not include dancing. Orpheus and Musaeus, the best dancers of their time, were the founders of these rites; and their ordinances show the value they attached to rhythm and dance as elements in religion. To illustrate this point would be to make the ceremonial known to the uninitiated:

but so much is matter of common knowledge, that persons who divulge the mysteries are popularly spoken of as 'dancing them out.' In Delos, not even sacrifice could be offered without dance and musical accompaniment. Choirs of boys gathered and performed their dance to the sound of flute and lyre, and the best of them were chosen to act characters; the songs written for these occasions were known as chorales; and the ancient lyric poetry abounded in such compositions.

But I need not confine myself to the Greeks. The Indians, when they rise to offer their morning salutation to the Sun, do not consider it enough to kiss their hands after the Greek fashion; turning to the East, they silently greet the God with movements that are designed to represent his own course through the heavens; and with this substitute for our prayers and sacrifices and choral celebrations they seek his favour at the beginning of every day and at its close. The Ethiopians go further, and dance even while they fight; the shaft an Ethiopian draws from that arrow-crown that serves him in place of a quiver will never be discharged before he has intimidated his enemy with the threatening gestures of the war-dance.

Having dealt with India and Ethiopia, let us now consider the neighbouring country of Egypt. If I am not mistaken, the Egyptian Proteus of ancient legend is no other than a dancer, whose mimetic skill enables him to adapt himself to every character:

in the activity of his movements, he is liquid as water, rapid as fire; he is the raging lion, the savage panther, the trembling bough; he is what he will. The legend takes these data, and gives them a supernatural turn,—for mimicry substituting metamorphosis. Our modern pantomimes have the same gift, and Proteus himself sometimes appears as the subject of their rapid transformations. And it may be conjectured that in that versatile lady Empusa we have but another artist of the same kind, mythologically treated.

Our attention is next claimed by the Roman dance of the Salii, a priesthood drawn from the noblest families; the dance is performed in honour of Mars, the most warlike of the Gods, and is of a particularly solemn and sacred character. According to a Bithynian legend, which agrees well with this Italian institution, Priapus, a war-like divinity (probably one of the Titans, or of the Idaean Dactyls, whose profession it was to teach the use of arms), was entrusted by Hera with the care of her son Ares, who even in childhood was remarkable for his courage and ferocity. Priapus would not put weapons into his hands till he had turned him out a perfect dancer; and he was rewarded by Hera with a tenth part of all Ares's spoils. As to the rites of Dionysus, you know, without my telling you, that they consisted in dancing from beginning to end. Of the three main types of dance, the cordax, the sicinnis, and the emmelia, each was the invention and bore the name of one of the Satyrs, his followers. Assisted by this art, and accompanied by these revellers, he conquered Tyrrhenians, Indians, Lydians, dancing those warlike tribes into submission.

Then beware, my enlightened friend, of the guilt of sacrilege. Will you attack the holy mystic art in which so many Gods delight; by which their worshippers do them honour; which affords so much pleasure, so much useful instruction? To return once more to the poets:

when I think of your affection for Homer and Hesiod, I am amazed to find you disputing the preeminence they assign to the dance. Homer, in enumerating all that is sweetest and best, mentions sleep, love, song, and dance; but of these dance alone is 'faultless.' He testifies, moreover, to the 'sweetness' of song:

now our art includes 'sweet song' as well as the 'faultless dance' which you take upon you to censure. Again, in another passage we read:

To one the God hath given warlike deeds:

But to another dance and lovely song.

And lovely indeed is the song that accompanies the dance; it is the Gods' best gift. Homer seems to divide all things under the two heads of war and peace; and among the things of peace he singles out these two as the best counterpart to the things of war. Hesiod, not speaking from hearsay, but coming fresh from the sight of the Muses' morning dance, has this high tribute to them in the beginning of his poem:

Their dainty feet round the dark waters dance,

about the altar of Zeus.—My dear sir, your onslaught upon the dance is little short of blasphemy.

Socrates—that wisest of men, if we may accept the judgement of the Pythian oracle—not only approved of dancing, but made a careful study of it; and, in his zeal for grace and elegance, for harmonious movement and carriage of the body, thought it no shame, reverend sage that he was, to rank this among the most important branches of learning. And well might he have an enthusiasm for dancing, who scrupled not to study the humblest arts; who frequented the schools of the flute-girls, and could stoop to learn wisdom from the mouth of an Aspasia. Yet in his days the art was in its infancy, its beauties undeveloped. Had Socrates seen the artists who have made modern Pantomime what it is, he would assuredly have given it his exclusive attention, and assigned it the first place in the education of youth.

I think you forget, when you advocate the claims of tragedy and comedy, that each of them has its own peculiar form of dance; tragedy its emmelia, comedy its cordax, supplemented occasionally by the sicinnis. You began by asserting the superiority of tragedy, of comedy, and of the periodic performances on flute and lyre, which you pronounce to be respectable, because they are included in public competitions. Let us take each of these and compare its merits with those of dancing. The flute and the lyre, to be sure, we might leave out of the discussion, as these have their part to play in the dance.

In forming our estimate of tragedy, let us first consider its externals—the hideous, appalling spectacle that the actor presents. His high boots raise him up out of all proportion; his head is hidden under an enormous mask; his huge mouth gapes upon the audience as if he would swallow them; to say nothing of the chest-pads and stomach-pads with which he contrives to give himself an artificial corpulence, lest his deficiency in this respect should emphasize his disproportionate height. And in the middle of it all is the actor, shouting away, now high, now low,—*chanting* his iambics as often as not; could anything be more revolting than this sing- song recitation of tragic woes? The actor is a mouthpiece:

that is his sole responsibility;—the poet has seen to the rest, ages since. From an Andromache or a Hecuba, one can endure recitative:

but when Heracles himself comes upon the stage, and so far forgets himself, and the respect due to the lion-skin and club that he carries, as to deliver a solo, no reasonable person can deny that such a performance is in execrable taste. Then again, your objection to dancing—that men act women's parts—is equally applicable to tragedy and comedy, in which indeed there are more women than men.

By comedy, the absurdity of the masks—of a Davus, for instance, or a Tibius, or a cook—is actually claimed as one of its attractions. On the other hand, I need not tell you how decent, how seemly, is the dancer's attire; any one who is not blind can see that for himself. His very mask is elegant, and well adapted to his part; there is no gaping here; the lips are closed, for the dancer has plenty of other voices at his service. In old days, dancer and singer were one:

but the violent exercise caused shortness of breath; the song suffered for it, and it was found advisable to have the singing done independently.

As to the subjects treated, they are the same for both, Pantomime differing from tragedy only in the infinite variety of its plots, and in the superior ingenuity and learning displayed in them. Dancing may not be included in our public competitions; but the reason is that the stewards regard it as a matter too high and solemn to be subjected to criticism. I forbear to add that in one Italian city—the greatest of the Chalcidian name—a special lustre has been added to the public games by the introduction of a dancing competition.

And now, before I proceed further, I wish to offer an explanation of themany omissions I have made, which might otherwise be attributed to ignorance. I am well aware that the subject has already been dealt with by a number of writers, who have chiefly occupied themselves with a description of the various forms of dance, and a catalogue of their names, their characters, and their inventors; and this they regard as a proof of erudition. Such work I leave to the ambition of dullards and pedants, as foreign to my own purpose. I would have you observe, and bear in mind, that I do not propose to make a complete history of the art of dancing; nor is it my object to enumerate the names of dances, except so far as I have already done, in handling a few of the principal types:

on the contrary, I am chiefly concerned with pointing out the profit and pleasure to be derived from modern Pantomime, which did not begin to take its present admirable form in ancient days, but only in the time of Augustus, or thereabouts. In those earlier times we have but the beginnings of the art; the tree is taking root; the flower and the fruit have reached their perfection only in our own day, and it is with these that I have to do. The tongs-dance, the crane-dance, and others I pass over because they are alien to my subject; similarly, if I have said nothing of the Phrygian dance,—that riotous convivial fling, which was performed by energetic yokels to the piping of a flute-girl, and which still prevails in country districts,—I have omitted it not from ignorance, but because it has no connexion with the Pantomime of to-day. I have the authority of Plato, in his *Laws*, for approving some forms of dance and rejecting others; he there examines the dance from the two points of view of pleasure and utility, banishes those forms that are unseemly, and selects others for his recommendation.

Of dancing then, in the strict sense of the word, I have said enough. To enlarge further upon its history would be pedantic. And now I come to the pantomime. What must be his qualifications? what his previous training? what his studies? what his subsidiary accomplishments? You will find that his is no easy profession, nor lightly to be undertaken; requiring as it does the highest standard of culture in all its branches, and involving a knowledge not of music only, but of rhythm and metre, and above all of your beloved philosophy, both natural and moral, the subtleties of dialectic alone being rejected as serving no useful purpose. Rhetoric, too, in so far as that art is concerned with the exposition of human character and human passions, claims a share of its attention. Nor can it dispense with the painter's and the sculptor's arts; in its close observance of the harmonious proportions that these teach, it is the equal of an Apelles or a Phidias. But above all Mnemosyne, and her daughter Polyhymnia, must be propitiated by an art that would remember all things. Like Calchas in Homer, the pantomime must know all 'that is, that was, that shall be'; nothing must escape his ever ready memory. Faithfully to represent his subject, adequately to express his own conceptions, to make plain all that might be obscure;—these are the first essentials for the pantomime, to whom no higher compliment could be paid than Thucydides's tribute to Pericles, who, he says, 'could not only conceive a wise policy, but render it intelligible to his hearers'; the intelligibility, in the present case, depending on clearness of gesticulation.

For his materials, he must draw continually, as I have said, upon his unfailing memory of ancient story; and memory must be backed by taste and judgement. He must know the history of the world, from the time when it first emerged from Chaos down to the days of Egyptian Cleopatra. These limitations we will concede to the pantomime's wide field of knowledge; but within them he must be familiar with every detail:

—the mutilation of Uranus, the origin of Aphrodite, the battle of Titans, the birth of Zeus, Rhea's deception, her substitution of a stone for her child, the binding of Cronus, the partition of the world between the three brothers. Again, the revolt of the Giants, Prometheus's theft of fire, his creation of mankind, and the punishment that followed; the might of Eros and of Anteros, the wanderings of the island Delos, the travail of Leto, the Python's destruction, the evil design of Tityus, the flight of eagles, whereby the earth's centre was discovered. He must know of Deucalion, in whose days the whole world suffered shipwreck, of that single chest wherein were preserved the remnants of the human race, of the new generation born of stones; of the rending of Iacchus, the guile of Hera, the fiery death of Semele, the double birth of Dionysus; of Athene and Hephaestus and Erichthonius, of the strife for the possession of Athens, of Halirrhothius and that first trial on the Areopagus, and all the legendary lore of Attica. Above all, the wanderings of Demeter, the finding of Persephone, the hospitality of Celeus; Triptolemus's plough, Icarius's vineyard, and the sad end of Erigone; the tale of Boreas and Orithyia, of Theseus, and of Aegeus; of Medea in Greece, and of her flight thereafter into Persia, and of Erechtheus's daughters and Pandion's, and all that they did and suffered in Thrace. Acamas, and Phyllis, and that first rape of Helen, and the expedition of Castor and Pollux against Athens, and the fate of Hippolytus, and the return of the Heraclids,—all these may fairly be included in the Athenian mythology, from the vast bulk of which I select only these few examples.

Then in Megara we have Nisus, his daughter Scylla, and his purple lock; the invasion of Minos, and his ingratitude towards his benefactress. Then we come to Cithaeron, and the story of the Thebans, and of the race of Labdacus; the settlement of Cadmus on the spot where the cow rested, the dragon's teeth from which the Thebans sprang up, the transformation of Cadmus into a serpent, the building of the walls of Thebes to the sound of Amphion's lyre, the subsequent madness of the builder, the boast of Niobe his wife, her silent grief; Pentheus, Actaeon, Oedipus, Heracles; his labours and slaughter of his children.

Corinth, again, abounds in legends:

of Glauce and of Creon; in earlier days, of Bellerophon and Stheneboea, and of the strife between Posidon and the Sun; and, later, of the frenzy of Athamas, of Nephele's children and their flight through the air on the ram's back, and of the deification of Ino and Melicertes. Next comes the story of Pelops's line, of all that befell in Mycenae, and before Mycenae was; of Inachus and Io and Argus her guardian; of Atreus and Thyestes and Aerope, of the golden ram and the marriage of Pelopeia, the murder of Agamemnon and the

358

punishment of Clytemnestra; and before their days, the expedition of the Seven against Thebes, the reception of the fugitives Tydeus and Polynices by their father-in-law Adrastus; the oracle that foretold their fate, the unburied slain, the death of Antigone, and that of Menoeceus.

Nor is any story more essential to the pantomime's purpose than that of Hypsipyle and Archemorus in Nemea; and, in older days, the imprisonment of Danae, the begetting of Perseus, his enterprise against the Gorgons; and connected therewith is the Ethiopian narrative of Cassiopea, and Cepheus, and Andromeda, all of whom the belief of later generations has placed among the stars. To these must be added the ancient legend of Aegyptus and Danaus, and of that guilty wedding-night.

Lacedaemon, too, supplies him with many similar subjects:

Hyacinth, and his rival lovers, Zephyr and Apollo, and the quoit that slew him, the flower that sprang up from his blood, and the inscription of woe thereon; the raising of Tyndareus from the dead, and the consequent wrath of Zeusagainst Asclepius; again, the reception of Paris by Menelaus, and the rape of Helen, the sequel to his award of the golden apple. For the Spartan mythology must be held to include that of Troy, in all its abundance and variety. Of all who fell at Troy, not one but supplies a subject for the stage; and all—from the rape of Helen to the return of the Greeks—must ever be borne in mind:

the wanderings of Aeneas, the love of Dido; and side by side with this the story of Orestes, and his daring deeds in Scythia. And there are earlier episodes which will not be out of place; they are all connected with the tale of Troy:

such are the seclusion of Achilles in Scyrus, the madness of Odysseus, the solitude of Philoctetes, with the whole story of Odysseus's wanderings, of Circe and Telegonus, of Aeolus, controller of the winds, down to the vengeance wreaked upon the suitors of Penelope; and, earlier, Odysseus's plot against Palamedes, the resentment of Nauplius, the frenzy of the one Ajax, the destruction of the other on the rocks.

Elis, too, affords many subjects for the intending pantomime:

Oenomaus, Myrtilus, Cronus, Zeus, and that first Olympian contest. Arcadia, no less rich in legendary lore, gives him the flight of Daphne, the transformation of Callisto into a bear, the drunken riot of the Centaurs, the birth of Pan, the love of Alpheus, and his submarine wanderings.

Extending our view, we find that Crete, too, may be laid under contribution:

Europa's bull, Pasiphae's, the Labyrinth, Ariadne, Phaedra, Androgeos; Daedalus and Icarus; Glaucus, and the prophecy of Polyides; and Talos, the island's brazen sentinel.

It is the same with Aetolia:

there you will find Althaea, Meleager, Atalanta, and the fatal brand; the strife of Achelous with Heracles, the birth of the Sirens, the origin of the

Echinades, those islands on which Alcmaeon dwelt after his frenzy was past; and, following these, the story of Nessus, and of Deianira's jealousy, which brought Heracles to the pyre upon Oeta. Thrace, too, has much that is indispensable to the pantomime:

of the head of murdered Orpheus, that sang while it floated down the stream upon his lyre; of Haemus and of Rhodope; and of the chastisement of Lycurgus.

Thessalian story, richer still, tells of Pelias and Jason; of Alcestis; and of the Argo with her talking keel and her crew of fifty youths; of what befell them in Lemnos; of Aeetes, Medea's dream, the rending of Absyrtus, the eventful flight from Colchis; and, in later days, of Protesilaus and Laodamia.

Cross once more to Asia, and Samos awaits you, with the fall of Polycrates, and his daughter's flight into Persia; and the ancient story of Tantalus's folly, and of the feast that he gave the Gods; of butchered Pelops, and his ivory shoulder.

In Italy, we have the Eridanus, Phaethon, and his poplar-sisters, who wept tears of amber for his loss.

The pantomime must be familiar, too, with the story of the Hesperides, and the dragon that guarded the golden fruit; with burdened Atlas, and Geryon, and the driving of the oxen from Erythea; and every tale of metamorphosis, of women turned into trees or birds or beasts, or (like Caeneus and Tiresias) into men. From Phoenicia he must learn of Myrrha and Adonis, who divides Assyria betwixt grief and joy; and in more modern times of all that Antipater[46] and Seleucus suffered for the love of Stratonice.

The Egyptian mythology is another matter:

it cannot be omitted, but on account of its mysterious character it calls for a more symbolical exposition;—the legend of Epaphus, for instance, and that of Osiris, and the conversion of the Gods into animals; and, in particular, their love adventures, including those of Zeus himself, with his various transformations.

Hades still remains to be added, with all its tragic tale of guilt and the punishment of guilt, and the loyal friendship that brought Theseus thither with Pirithous. In a word, all that Homer and Hesiod and our best poets, especially the tragedians, have sung,—all must be known to the pantomime. From the vast, nay infinite, mass of mythology, I have made this trifling selection of the more prominent legends; leaving the rest for poets to celebrate, for pantomimes to exhibit, and for your imagination to supply from the hints already given; and all this the artist must have stored up in his memory, ready to be produced when occasion demands.

Since it is his profession to imitate, and to show forth his subject by means of gesticulation, he, like the orators, must acquire lucidity; every scene

---

[46] Not Antipater, but Antiochus, is meant.

must be intelligible without the aid of an interpreter; to borrow the expression of the Pythian oracle,

Dumb though he be, and speechless, he is heard

by the spectator. According to the story, this was precisely the experience of the Cynic Demetrius. He had inveighed against Pantomime in just your own terms. The pantomime, he said, was a mere appendage to flute and pipe and beating feet; he added nothing to the action; his gesticulations were aimless nonsense; there was no meaning in them; people were hoodwinked by the silken robes and handsome mask, by the fluting and piping and the fine voices, which served to set off what in itself was nothing. The leading pantomime of the day—this was in Nero's reign—was apparently a man of no mean intelligence; unsurpassed, in fact, in wideness of range and in grace of execution. Nothing, I think, could be more reasonable than the request he made of Demetrius, which was, to reserve his decision till he had witnessed his performance, which he undertook to go through without the assistance of flute or song. He was as good as his word. The time-beaters, the flutes, even the chorus, were ordered to preserve a strict silence; and the pantomime, left to his own resources, represented the loves of Ares and Aphrodite, the tell-tale Sun, the craft of Hephaestus, his capture of the two lovers in the net, the surrounding Gods, each in his turn, the blushes of Aphrodite, the embarrassment of Ares, his entreaties,—in fact the whole story. Demetrius was ravished at the spectacle; nor could there be higher praise than that with which he rewarded the performer. 'Man,' he shrieked at the top of his voice, 'this is not seeing, but hearing and seeing, both:

'tis as if your hands were tongues!'

And before we leave Nero's times, I must tell you of the high tribute paid to the art by a foreigner of the royal family of Pontus, who was visiting the Emperor on business, and had been among the spectators of this same pantomime. So convincing were the artist's gestures, as to render the subject intelligible even to one who (being half a Greek) could not follow the vocal accompaniment. When he was about to return to his country, Nero, in taking leave of him, bade him choose what present he would have, assuring him that his request should not be refused. 'Give me,' said the Pontian, 'your great pantomime; no gift could delight me more.' 'And of what use can he be to you in Pontus?' asked the Emperor. 'I have foreign neighbours, who do not speak our language; and it is not easy to procure interpreters. Your pantomime could discharge that office perfectly, as often as required, by means of his gesticulations.' So profoundly had he been impressed with the extraordinary clearness of pantomimic representation.

The pantomime is above all things an actor:

that is his first aim, in the pursuit of which (as I have observed) he resembles the orator, and especially the composer of 'declamations,' whose success, as the pantomime knows, depends like his own upon verisimilitude, upon the adaptation of language to character:

prince or tyrannicide, pauper or farmer, each must be shown with the peculiarities that belong to him. I must give you the comment of another foreigner on this subject. Seeing five masks laid ready—that being the number of parts in the piece—and only one pantomime, he asked who were going to play the other parts. He was informed that the whole piece would be performed by a single actor. 'Your humble servant, sir,' cries our foreigner to the artist; 'I observe that you have but one body:

it had escaped me, that you possessed several souls.'

The term 'pantomime,' which was introduced by the Italian Greeks, is an apt one, and scarcely exaggerates the artist's versatility. 'Oh boy,' cries the poet, in a beautiful passage,

As that sea-beast, whose hue
With each new rock doth suffer change,
So let thy mind free range
Through ev'ry land, shaping herself anew.

Most necessary advice, this, for the pantomime, whose task it is to identify himself with his subject, and make himself part and parcel of the scene that he enacts. It is his profession to show forth human character and passion in all their variety; to depict love and anger, frenzy and grief, each in its due measure. Wondrous art!—on the same day, he is mad Athamas and shrinking Ino; he is Atreus, and again he is Thyestes, and next Aegisthus or Aerope; all one man's work.

Other entertainments of eye or ear are but manifestations of a single art:

'tis flute or lyre or song; 'tis moving tragedy or laughable comedy. The pantomime is all-embracing in the variety of his equipment:

flute and pipe, beating foot and clashing cymbal, melodious recitative, choral harmony. Other arts call out only one half of a man's powers—the bodily or the mental:

the pantomime combines the two. His performance is as much an intellectual as a physical exercise:

there is meaning in his movements; every gesture has its significance; and therein lies his chief excellence. The enlightened Lesbonax of Mytilene called pantomimes 'manual philosophers,' and used to frequent the theatre, in the conviction that he came out of it a better man than he went in. And Timocrates, his teacher, after accidentally witnessing a pantomimic performance, exclaimed:

'How much have I lost by my scrupulous devotion to philosophy!' I know not what truth there may be in Plato's analysis of the soul into the three elements of spirit, appetite, and reason:

but each of the three is admirably illustrated by the pantomime; he shows us the angry man, he shows us the lover, and he shows us every passion under the control of reason; this last—like touch among the senses—is all-pervading. Again, in his care for beauty and grace of movement, have we not an illustration of the Aristotelian principle, which makes beauty a third part of

Good? Nay, I once heard some one hazard a remark, to the effect that the philosophy of Pantomime went still further, and that in the *silence* of the characters a Pythagorean doctrine was shadowed forth.

All professions hold out some object, either of utility or of pleasure:

Pantomime is the only one that secures both these objects; now the utility that is combined with pleasure is doubled in value. Who would choose to look on at a couple of young fellows spilling their blood in a boxing-match, or wrestling in the dust, when he may see the same subject represented by the pantomime, with the additional advantages of safety and elegance, and with far greater pleasure to the spectator? The vigorous movements of the pantomime—turn and twist, bend and spring— afford at once a gratifying spectacle to the beholder and a wholesome training to the performer; I maintain that no gymnastic exercise is its equal for beauty and for the uniform development of the physical powers, —of agility, suppleness, and elasticity, as of solid strength.

Consider then the universality of this art:

it sharpens the wits, it exercises the body, it delights the spectator, it instructs him in the history of bygone days, while eye and ear are held beneath the spell of flute and cymbal and of graceful dance. Would you revel in sweet song? Nowhere can you procure that enjoyment in greater variety and perfection. Would you listen to the clear melody of flute and pipe? Again the pantomime supplies you. I say nothing of the excellent moral influence of public opinion, as exercised in the theatre, where you will find the evil-doer greeted with execration, and his victim with sympathetic tears. The pantomime's most admirable quality I have yet to mention,—his combination of strength and suppleness of limb; it is as if brawny Heracles and soft Aphrodite were presented to us in one and the same person.

I now propose to sketch out the mental and physical qualifications necessary for a first-rate pantomime. Most of the former, indeed, I have already mentioned:

he must have memory, sensibility, shrewdness, rapidity of conception, tact, and judgement; further, he must be a critic of poetry and song, capable of discerning good music and rejecting bad. For his body, I think I may take the Canon of Polyclitus as my model. He must be perfectly proportioned:

neither immoderately tall nor dwarfishly short; not too fleshy (a most unpromising quality in one of his profession) nor cadaverously thin. Let me quote you certain comments of the people of Antioch, who have a happy knack in expressing their views on such subjects. They are a most intelligent people, and devoted to Pantomime; each individual is all eyes and ears for the performance; not a word, not a gesture escapes them. Well, when a small man came on in the character of Hector, they cried out with one voice:

'Here is Astyanax; and where is Hector?' On another occasion, an exceedingly tall man was taking the part of Capaneus scaling the walls of Thebes; 'Step over' suggested the audience; 'you need no ladder.' The well-meant activity of a fat and heavy dancer was met with earnest entreaties to 'spare the platform'; while a thin performer was recommended to 'take care of his health.' I mention these criticisms, not on account of their humorous character, but as an illustration of the profound interest that whole cities have sometimes taken in Pantomime, and of their ability to discern its merits and demerits.

Another essential for the pantomime is ease of movement. His frame must be at once supple and well-knit, to meet the opposite requirements of agility and firmness. That he is no stranger to the science of the boxing—and the wrestling-ring, that he has his share of the athletic accomplishments of Hermes and Pollux and Heracles, you may convince yourself by observing his renderings of those subjects. The eyes, according to Herodotus, are more credible witnesses than the ears; though the pantomime, by the way, appeals to both kinds of evidence.

Such is the potency of his art, that the amorous spectator is cured of his infirmity by perceiving the evil effects of passion, and he who enters the theatre under a load of sorrow departs from it with a serene countenance, as though he had drunk of that draught of forgetfulness

That lulls all pain and wrath.

How natural is his treatment of his subjects, how intelligible to every one of his audience, may be judged from the emotion of the house whenever anything is represented that calls for sorrow or compassion. The Bacchic form of Pantomime, which is particularly popular in Ionia and Pontus, in spite of its being confined to satyric subjects has taken such possession of those peoples, that, when the Pantomime season comes round in each city, they leave all else and sit for whole days watching Titans and Corybantes, Satyrs and neat-herds. Men of the highest rank and position are not ashamed to take part in these performances:

indeed, they pride themselves more on their pantomimic skill than on birth and ancestry and public services.

Now that we know what are the qualities that a good pantomime ought to possess, let us next consider the faults to which he is liable. Deficiencies of person I have already handled; and the following I think is a fair statement of their mental imperfections. Pantomimes cannot all be artists; there are plenty of ignorant performers, who bungle their work terribly. Some cannot adapt themselves to their music; they are literally 'out of tune'; rhythm says one thing, their feet another. Others are free from this fault, but jumble up their chronology. I remember the case of a man who was giving the birth of Zeus, and Cronus eating his own children:

seduced by the similarity of subject, he ran off into the tale of Atreus and Thyestes. In another case, Semele was just being struck by the lightning, when she was transformed into Creusa, who was not even born at that time. Still, it seems to me that we have no right to visit the sins of the artist upon the art:

let us recognize him for the blunderer that he is, and do justice to the accuracy and skill of competent performers.

The fact is, the pantomime must be completely armed at every point. His work must be one harmonious whole, perfect in balance and proportion, self-consistent, proof against the most minute criticism; there must be no flaws, everything must be of the best; brilliant conception, profound learning, above all human sympathy. When every one of the spectators identifies himself with the scene enacted, when each sees in the pantomime as in a mirror the reflection of his own conduct and feelings, then, and not till then, is his success complete. But let him reach that point, and the enthusiasm of the spectators becomes uncontrollable, every man pouring out his whole soul in admiration of the portraiture that reveals him to himself. Such a spectacle is no less than a fulfilment of the oracular injunction KNOW THYSELF; men depart from it with increased knowledge; they have learnt something that is to be sought after, something that should be eschewed.

But in Pantomime, as in rhetoric, there can be (to use a popular phrase) too much of a good thing; a man may exceed the proper bounds of imitation; what should be great may become monstrous, softness may be exaggerated into effeminacy, and the courage of a man into the ferocity of a beast. I remember seeing this exemplified in the case of an actor of repute. In most respects a capable, nay, an admirable performer, some strange fatality ran him a-ground upon this reef of over-enthusiasm. He was acting the madness of Ajax, just after he has been worsted by Odysseus; and so lost control of himself, that one might have been excused for thinking his madness was something more than feigned. He tore the clothes from the back of one of the iron-shod time-beaters, snatched a flute from the player's hands, and brought it down in such trenchant sort upon the head of Odysseus, who was standing by enjoying his triumph, that, had not his cap held good, and borne the weight of the blow, poor Odysseus must have fallen a victim to histrionic frenzy. The whole house ran mad for company, leaping, yelling, tearing their clothes. For the illiterate riffraff, who knew not good from bad, and had no idea of decency, regarded it as a supreme piece of acting; and the more intelligent part of the audience, realizing how things stood, concealed their disgust, and instead of reproaching the actor's folly by silence, smothered it under their plaudits; they saw only too clearly that it was not Ajax but the pantomime who was mad. Nor was our spirited friend content till he had distinguished himself yet further:

descending from the stage, he seated himself in the senatorial benches between two consulars, who trembled lest he should take one of them for a ram and apply the lash. The spectators were divided between wonder and amusement; and some there were who suspected that his ultra-realism had culminated in reality. However, it seems that when he came to his senses again he bitterly repented of this exploit, and was quite ill from grief, regarding his conduct as that of a veritable madman, as is clear from his own words. For when his partisans begged him to repeat the performance, he recommended another actor for the part of Ajax, saying that 'it was enough for him to have been mad once.' His mortification was increased by the success of his rival, who, though a similar part had been written for him, played it with admirable judgement and discretion, and was complimented on his observance of decorum, and of the proper bounds of his art.

I hope, my dear Crato, that this cursory description of the Pantomime may mitigate your wrath against its devoted admirer. If you can bring yourself to bear me company to the theatre, you will be captivated; you will run Pantomime-mad. I shall have no occasion to exclaim, with Circe,

Strange, that my drugs have wrought no change in thee!

The change will come; but will not involve an ass's head, nor a pig's heart, but only an improved understanding. In your delight at the potion, you will drain it off, and leave not a drop for any one else. Homer says, of the golden wand of Hermes, that with it he

charms the eyes of men, When so he will, and rouses them that sleep.

So it is with Pantomime. It charms the eyes-to wakefulness; and quickens the mental faculties at every turn.

Cr. Enough, Lycinus:

behold your convert! My eyes and ears are opened. When next you go to the theatre, remember to take a seat for me next your own. I too would issue from those doors a wiser man.

LEXIPHANES

Lycinus. Lexiphanes. Sopolis

Ly. What, our exquisite with his essay?

Lex. Ah, Lycinus, 'tis but a fledgeling of mine; 'tis all incondite.

Ly. O ho, conduits—that is your subject, is it?

Lex. You mistake me; I said nothing of conduits; you are behind the times; incondite—'tis the word we use now when a thing lacks the finishing touches. But you are the deaf adder that stoppeth her ears.

Ly. I beg your pardon, my dear fellow; but conduit, incondite, you know. Well now, what is the idea of your piece?

Lex. A symposium, a modest challenge to the son of Ariston.

Ly. There are a good many sons of Aristons; but, from the symposium, I presume you mean Plato.

Lex. You take me; what I said could fit no other.

Ly. Well, come, read me a little of it; do not send me away thirsty; I see there is nectar in store.

Lex. Ironist, avaunt! And now open your ears to my charming; adder me no adders.

Ly. Go ahead; I am no Adam, nor Eve either.

Lex. Have an eye to my conduct of the discourse, whether it be fair in commencement, fair in speech, fair in diction, fair in nomenclature.

Ly. Oh, we know what to expect from Lexiphanes. But come, begin.

Lex. _'Then to dinner,' quoth Callicles, 'then to our post-prandial deambulation in the Lyceum; but now 'tis time for our parasolar unction, ere we bask and bathe and take our nuncheon; go we our way. Now, boy, strigil and mat, towels and soap; transport me them bathwards, and see to the bath-penny; you will find it a-ground by the chest. And thou, Lexiphanes, comest thou, or tarriest here?' 'Its a thousand years,' quoth I, 'till I bathe; for I am in no comfort, with sore posteriors from my mule-saddle. Trod the mule-man as on eggs, yet kept his beast a-moving. And when I got to the farm, still no peace for the wicked. I found the hinds shrilling the harvest-song, and there were persons burying my father, I think it was. I just gave them a hand with the grave and things, and then I left them; it was so cold, and I had prickly heat; one does, you know, in a hard frost. So I went round the plough-lands; and there I found garlic growing, delved radishes, culled chervil and all herbs, bought parched barley, and (for not yet had the meadows reached the redolency that tempts the ten toes)-so to mule-back again; whence this tenderness behind. And now I walk with pain, and the sweat runs down; my bones languish, and yearn for the longest of water-swims; 'tis ever my joy to wash me after toil.

I will speed back to my boy; 'tis like he waits for me at the pease-puddingry, or the curiosity shop; yet stay; his instructions were to meet me at the frippery. Ah, hither comes he in the nick of time:

ay, and has purchased a beesting-pudding and girdle-cakes and leeks, sausages and steak, dewlap and tripe and collops.—Good, Atticion, you have made most of my journey no thoroughfare.' 'Why, sir, I have been looking round the corner for you till I squint. Where dined you yesterday? with Onomacritus?' 'God bless me, no. I was off to the country; hey presto! and there we were. You know how I dote on the country. I suppose you all thought I was making the glasses ring. Now go in, and spice all these things, and scour the kneading-trough, ready to shred the lettuces. I shall be of for a dry rub.'

'We are with you,' cried Philinus, 'Onomarchus, Hellanicus, and I; the dial's mid point is in shadow; beware, or we shall bathe in the Carimants' water, huddled and pushed by the vulgar herd.' Then said Hellanicus:

'Ah, and my eyes are disordered; my pupils are turbid, I wink and blink, the tears come unbidden, my eyes crave the ophthalmic leech's healing drug, mortar-brayed and infused, that they may blush and blear no more, nor moistly peer.'

In such wise conversing, all our company departed. Arrived at the gymnasium, we stripped; the finger-wrench, the garotte, the standing- grip, each had its votaries; one oiled and suppled his joints; another punched the bladder; a third heaved and swung the dumb-bells. Then, when we had rubbed ourselves, and ridden pick-a-back, and had our sport of the gymnasium, we took our plunge, Philinus and I, in the warm basin, and departed. But the rest dipped frigid heads, soused in, and swam subaqueous, a wonder to behold. Then back we came, and one here, one there, did this and that. Shod, with toothed comb I combed me. For I had had a short crop, not to convict-measure, but saucer-wise, deflation having set in on crown and chin-tip. One chewed lupines, another cleared his fasting throat, a third took fish soup on radish-wafer sippets; this ate olives, that supped down barley.

When it was dinner-time, we took it reclining, both chairs and couches standing ready. A joint-stock meal it was, and the contributions many and various. Pigs' pettitoes, ribs of beef, paunch and pregnant womb of sow, fried liver lobe, garlic paste, sauce piquante, mayonnaise, and so on; pastry, ramequins, and honey-cakes. In the aquatic line, much of the cartilaginous, of the testaceous much; many a salt slice, basket-hawked, eels of Copae, fowls of the barn-door, a cock past crowing-days, and fish to keep him company; add to these a sheep roast whole, and ox's rump of toothless eld. The loaves were firsts, no common stuff, and therewithal remainders from the new moon; vegetables both radical and excrescent. For the wine, 'twas of no standing, but came from the skin; its sweetness was gone, but its roughness remained.

On the dolphin-foot table stood divers store of cups; the eye-shutter, the ladle, slender-handled, genuine Mentor; crane-neck and gurgling bombyl; and many an earth-born child of Thericlean furnace, the wide- mouthed, the kindly-lipped; Phocaean, Cnidian work, but all light as air, and thin as eggshell; bowls and pannikins and posied cups; oh, 'twas a well-stocked sideboard.

But the kettle boiled over, and sent the ashes flying about our heads. It was bumpers and no heeltaps, and we were full to the throat. Then to the nard; and enter to us guitar and light fantastic toe. Thereafter, one shinned up the ladder, on post-prandial japery intent, another beat the devil's tattoo, a third writhed cachinnatory.

At this moment broke in upon us from the bath, all uninvited, Megalonymus the attorney, Chaereas the goldsmith, striped back and all, and the bruiser Eudemus. I asked them what they were about to come so late. Quoth Chaereas; 'I was working a locket and ear-rings and bangles for my daughter; that is why I come after the fair.' 'I was otherwise engaged,' said Megalonymus; 'know you not that it was a lawless day and a dumb? So, as it was linguistice, there was truce to my calendarial clockings and plea-mensurations. But hearing the governor was giving a warm reception, I took my shiniest clothes, fresh from the tailor, and my unmatched shoes, and showed myself out.

'The first I met were a torch-bearer, a hierophant, and others of the initiated, haling Dinias before the judge, and protesting that he had called them by their names, though he well knew that, from the time of their sanctification, they were nameless, and no more to be named but by hallowed names; so then he appealed to me.' 'Dinias?' I put in; 'Who is Dinias?' 'Oh, he's a dance-for-your-supper carry-your-luggage rattle- your-patter gaming-house sort of man; eschews the barber, and takes care of his poor chest and toes.' 'Well,' said I, 'paid he the penalty in some wise, or showed a clean pair of heels?' 'Our delicate goer is now fast bound. The governor, regardless of his retiring disposition, slipped him on a pair of bracelets and a necklace, and brought him acquainted with stocks and boot. The poor worm quaked for fear, and could not contain himself, and offered money, if so he might save his soul alive.'

'As for me,' said Eudemus, 'I was sent for in the gloaming by Damasias, the athlete many-victoried of yore, now pithless from age; you know him in bronze in the market. He was busy with roast and boiled. He was this day to exdomesticate his daughter, and was decking her out for her husband, when a baleful incident occurred, which cleft the feast in twain. For Dion his son, on grievance unknown, if it were not rather the hostility of Heaven, hanged himself; and be sure he was a dead man, had I not been there, and dislocated and loosed him from his implication. Long time I squatted a-knee, pricking and rocking, and sounding him, to see whether his throat was still whole. What profited most was compressure of the extremities with both my hands.'

'What, Dion the effeminate, the libertine, the debauchee, the mastich-chewer, the too susceptible to amorous sights?' 'Yes; the lecher and whore-master. Well, Damasias fell down and worshipped the Goddess (they have an Artemis by Scopas in the middle of the court), he and his old white-headed wife, and implored her compassion. The Goddess straightway nodded assent, and he was well; and now he is their Theodorus, or indeed their manifest Artemidorus. So they made offerings to her, among them darts and bows and

369

arrows; for these are acceptable in her sight; bow- woman she, far-dartress, telepolemic'

'Let us drink, then' said Megalonymus; 'here have I brought you a flagon of antiquated wine, with cream cheese and windfall olives—I keep them under seal, and the seals are worm-eaten—and others brine-steeped, and these fictile cups, thin-edged, firm-based, that we might drink therefrom, and a pasty of tripe rolled like a top-knot.—Now, you sir, pour me in some more water; if my head begins to ache, I shall be sending for your master to talk to you.—You know, gentlemen, what megrims I get, and what a numskull mine is. After drinking, we will chirp a little as is our wont; 'tis not amiss to prate in one's cups'

'So be it,' quoth I; 'we are the very pink and perfection of the true Attic' 'Done with you!' says Callicles, 'frequent quizzings are a whetstone of conversation' 'For my part,' cries Eudemus, '—it grows chill—I like my liquor stronger, and more of it; I am deathly cold; if I could get some warmth into me, I had rather listen to these light- fingered gentry of flute and lyre.' 'What is this you say, Eudemus?' says I; 'You would exact mutation from us? are we so hard-mouthed, so untongued? For my tongue, 'tis garriturient. I was just getting under way, and making ready to hail you with a fine old Attic shower. 'Tis as if a three-master were sailing before the breeze, with stay-sails wind-bellied, scudding along wave-skimming, and you should throw out two-tongued anchorage and iron stoppers and ship-fetters, and block her foaming course, in envy of her fair-windedness.' 'Why then, if you will, splash and dash and crash through the waves; and I upsoaring, and drinking the while, will watch like Homer's Zeus from some bald-crowned hill or from Heaven-top, while you and your ship are swept along with the wind behind you.'_

Ly. Thanks, Lexiphanes; enough of drink and reading. I assure you I am full beyond my capacity as it is; if I do not succeed in quickly unloading my stomach of what you have put into it, there is not a doubt I shall go raving mad under the intoxication of your exuberant verbosity. At first I was inclined to be amused; but there is such a lot of it, and all just alike; I pity you now, poor misguided one, trapped in your endless maze, sick unto death, a prey to melancholia.

Where in the world can you have raked up all this rubbish from? How long has it taken you? Or what sort of a hive could ever keep together such a swarm of lop-sided monstrosities? Of some you are the proud creator, the rest you have dug up from dark lurking-places, till 'tis

Curse on you, piling woe on mortal woe!

How have you gathered all the minor sewers into one cloaca maxima, and discharged the whole upon my innocent head! Have you never a friend or relation or well-wisher? Did you never meet a plain-dealer to give you a dose of candour? That would have cured you. You are dropsical, man; you are like to burst with it; and you take it for muscular healthy stoutness; you are congratulated only by the fools who do not see what is the matter; the instructed cannot help being sorry for you.

But here in good time comes Sopolis; we will put you in the good doctor's hands, tell him all about it, and see if anything can be done for you. He is a clever man; he has taken many a helpless semi-lunatic like you in hand and dosed him into sanity.—Good day, Sopolis. Lexiphanes here is a friend of mine, you know. Now I want you to undertake his case; he is afflicted with a delirious affection of the vocal organs, and I fear a complete breakdown. Pray take measures to cure him.

Lex. Heal him, not me, Sopolis; he is manifestly moon-struck; persons duly pia-matered he accounts beside their five wits; he might come from Samos and call Mnesarchus father; for he enjoins silence and linguinanity. But by the unabashed Athene, by Heracles the beast-killer, no jot or tittle of notice shall he have from me. 'Tis my foreboding that I fall not in with him again. For his censures, I void my rheum upon them.

Sop. What is the matter with him, Lycinus?

Ly. Why, *this* is the matter; don't you hear? He leaves us his contemporaries, and goes a thousand years off to talk to us, which he does by aid of these tongue-gymnastics and extraordinary compounds— prides himself upon it, too, as if it were a great thing to disguise yourself, and mutilate the conversational currency.

Sop. Well, to be sure, this is a serious case; we must do all we can for him. Providentially, here is an emetic I had just mixed for a bilious patient; here, Lexiphanes, drink it off; the other man can wait; let us purge you of this vocal derangement, and get you a clean bill of health. Come along, down with it; you will feel much easier.

Lex. I know not what you would be at, you and Lycinus, with your drenches; I fear me you are more like to end than mend my speech.

Ly. Drink, quick; it will make a man of you in thought and word.

Lex. Well, if I must. Lord, what is this? How it rumbles! I must have swallowed a ventriloquist.

Sop. Now, let it come. Look, look! Here comes *in sooth, anon* follows, close upon them *quoth he, withal, sirrah, I trow,* and a general sprinkling of *sundry.* But try again; tickle your throat; that will help. *Hard, by* has not come up yet, nor *a-weary,* nor *rehearse,* nor *quandary.* Oh, there are lots of them lurking yet, a whole stomachful. It would be well to get rid of some of them by purging; there should be an impressive explosion when *orotundity* makes its windy exit. However, he is pretty well cleaned out, except for what may be left in the lower bowels. Lycinus, I shall now leave him in your charge; teach him better ways, and tell him what are the right words to use.

Ly. I will, Sopolis; and thank you for clearing the way. Now, Lexiphanes, listen to me. If you want sincere commendations upon your style, and success with popular audiences, give a wide berth to that sort of stuff. Make a beginning with the great poets, read them with some one to help you, then go

371

on to the orators, and when you have assimilated their vocabulary, proceed in due time to Thucydides and Plato, not forgetting a thorough course also of pleasant Comedy and grave Tragedy. When you have culled the best that all these can show, you may reckon that you have a style. You have not realized it, but at present you are like the toymen's dolls, all gaudy colouring outside, and inside, fragile clay.

If you will take this advice, put up for a little while with being called uneducated, and not be ashamed to mend your ways, you may face an audience without a tremor; you will not then be a laughing-stock any more; the cultivated will no longer exercise their irony upon you and nickname you the Hellene and the Attic just because you are less intelligible than many barbarians. But above all things, do bear in mind not to ape the worst tricks of the last generation's professors; you are always nibbling at their wares; put your foot upon them once for all, and take the ancients for your model. And no dallying with unsubstantial flowers of speech; accustom yourself, like the athletes, to solid food. And let your devotions be paid to the Graces and to Lucidity, whom you have so neglected.

Further, put a stopper on bombast and grandiloquence and mannerism; be neither supercilious nor overbearing; cease to carp at other people's performances and to count their loss your gain. And then, perhaps the greatest of all your errors is this:

instead of arranging your matter first, and then elaborating the diction, you find some out-of-the-way word, or are captivated by one of your own invention, and try to build up your meaning round it; if you cannot get it in somehow or other, though it may have nothing to do with the matter, you are inconsolable; do you remember the *mobled queen* you let off the other day? It was quite off the point, and you did not know what it meant yourself; however, its oddness tickled the ears of the ignorant many; as for the cultivated, they were equally amused at you and at your admirers.

Again, could anything be more ludicrous than for one who claims to be a purist, drawing from the undefiled fountain of antiquity, to mix in (though indeed that reverses the proportion) expressions that would be impossible to the merest schoolboy? I felt as if I should like the earth to swallow me up, when I heard you talk of a man's *chemise*, and use *valet* of a woman; who does not know that a man wears a shirt, and that a valet is male? But you abound in far more flagrant blunders than these:

I have *chidden*, not *chode* you; we do not *write* a friend, we *write to* him; we say *'onest*, not *honest*; these usages of yours cannot claim even alien rights among us. Moreover, we do not like even poetry to read like the dictionary. But the sort of poetry to which your prose corresponds would be Dosiadas's *Altar*, Lycophron's *Alexandra*, or any more pestilent pedantry that may happen to exist. If you take the pains to unlearn all this, you will have done the best you can for yourself. If you let yourself be seduced by your sweet baits again, I have at least put in my word of warning, and you will have only yourself to blame when you find yourself on the downward path.

LIFE OF DEMONAX

It was in the book of Fate that even this age of ours should not be destitute entirely of noteworthy and memorable men, but produce a body of extraordinary power, and a mind of surpassing wisdom. My allusions are to Sostratus the Boeotian, whom the Greeks called, and believed to be, Heracles; and more particularly to the philosopher Demonax. I saw and marvelled at both of them, and with the latter I long consorted. I have written of Sostratus elsewhere[47], and described his stature and enormous strength, his open-air life on Parnassus, sleeping on the grass and eating what the mountain afforded, the exploits that bore out his surname—robbers exterminated, rough places made smooth, and deep waters bridged.

This time I am to write of Demonax, with two sufficient ends in view:

first, to keep his memory green among good men, as far as in me lies; and secondly, to provide the most earnest of our rising generation, who aspire to philosophy, with a contemporary pattern, that they may not be forced back upon the ancients for worthy models, but imitate this best—if I am any judge—of all philosophers.

He came of a Cyprian family which enjoyed considerable property and political influence. But his views soared above such things as these; he claimed nothing less than the highest, and devoted himself to philosophy. This was not due to any exhortations of Agathobulus, his predecessor Demetrius, or Epictetus. He did indeed enjoy the converse of all these, as well as of Timocrates of Heraclea, that wise man whose gifts of expression and of understanding were equal. It was not, however, to the exhortations of any of these, but to a natural impulse towards the good, an innate yearning for philosophy which manifested itself in childish years, that he owed his superiority to all the things that ordinary men pursue. He took independence and candour for his guiding principles, lived himself an upright, wholesome, irreproachable life, and exhibited to all who saw or heard him the model of his own disposition and philosophic sincerity.

He was no half-baked enthusiast either; he had lived with the poets, and knew most of them by heart; he was a practised speaker; he had a knowledge of philosophic principles not of the superficial skin-deep order; he had developed and hardened his body by exercise and toil, and, in short, had been at the pains to make himself every man's equal at every point. He was consistent enough, when he found that he could no longer suffice to himself, to depart voluntarily from life, leaving a great reputation behind him among the true nobility of Greece.

Instead of confining himself to a single philosophic school, he laid them all under contribution, without showing clearly which of them he preferred; but perhaps he was nearest akin to Socrates; for, though he had leanings as regards externals and plain living to Diogenes, he never studied effect or lived

---

[47] The life of Sostratus is not extant.

for the applause and admiration of the multitude; his ways were like other people's; he mounted no high horse; he was just a man and a citizen. He indulged in no Socratic irony; but his discourse was full of Attic grace; those who heard it went away neither disgusted by servility nor repelled by ill-tempered censure, but on the contrary lifted out of themselves by charity, and encouraged to more orderly, contented, hopeful lives.

He was never known to shout or be over vehement or angry, even when he had to correct; he touched offences, but pardoned offenders, saying that the doctors' was the right model, who treat sickness but are not angry with the sick. It is human, he thought, to err, but divine (whether in God or man) to put the error right.

A life of this sort left him without wants of his own; but he was always ready to render any proper service to his friends—including reminders to those among them who passed for fortunate, how brief was their tenure of what they so prided themselves upon. To all, on the other hand, who repined at poverty, resented exile, or complained of old age or bad health, he administered laughing consolation, and bade them not forget how soon their troubles would be over, the distinction between good and bad be obsolete, and long freedom succeed to short-lived distress.

He was fond of playing peace-maker between brothers at variance, or presiding over the restoration of marital harmony. He could say a word in season, too, before an agitated political assembly, which would turn the scale in favour of patriotic duty. Such was the temper that philosophy produced in him, kindly, mild, and cheerful.

Nothing ever grieved him except the illness or death of a friend, friendship being the one among blessings that he put highest; and indeed he was every man's friend, counting among his kindred whatever had human shape. Not that there were no degrees in the pleasure different people's society gave him; but he avoided none, except those who seemed so far astray that they could get no good from him. And every word or act in which these principles took shape might have been dictated by the Graces and Aphrodite; for 'on his lips Persuasion sat,' as the play has it.

Accordingly he was regarded with reverence at Athens, both by the collective assembly and by the officials; he always continued to be a person of great consequence in their eyes. And this though most of them had been at first offended with him, and hated him as heartily as their ancestors had Socrates. Besides his candour and independence, there had been found Anytuses and Meletuses to repeat the historic charges:

he had never been known to sacrifice, and he made himself singular by avoiding initiation at Eleusis. On this occasion he showed his courage by appearing in a garland and festal attire, and then pleading his cause before the people with a dash of unwonted asperity infused into his ordinary moderate tone. On the count of never having sacrificed to Athene, 'Men of Athens,' he said, 'there is nothing wonderful in this; it was only that I gave the Goddess credit for being able to do very well without sacrifices from me.' And in the matter of the Mysteries, his reason for not following the usual practice was this:

if the Mysteries turned out to be bad, he would never be able to keep quiet about it to the uninitiated, but must dissuade them from the ceremony; while, if they were good, humanity would tempt him to divulge them. The Athenians, stone in hand already, were at once disarmed, and from that time onwards paid him honour and respect, which ultimately rose to reverence. Yet he had opened his case with a bitter enough reproof:

'Men of Athens, you see me ready garlanded; proceed to sacrifice me, then; your former offering[48] was deficient in this formality.'

I will now give some specimens of his pointed and witty sayings, which may begin with his answers to Favorinus. The latter had heard that he made fun of his lectures, and in particular of the sentimental verses with which they were garnished, and which Demonax thought contemptible, womanish, and quite unsuited to philosophy. So he came and asked him:

'Who, pray, are you, that you should pour scorn upon me?' 'I am the possessor of a critical pair of ears,' was the answer. The sophist had not had enough; '*You* are no infant,' he went on, 'but a philosopher, it seems; may one ask what marks the transformation?' 'The marks of manhood,' said Demonax.

Another time the same person came up and asked him what school of philosophy he belonged to. 'Who told you I was a philosopher?' was all he said. But as he left him, he had a good laugh to himself, which Favorinus observing, demanded what he was laughing at; 'I was only amused by your taking a man for a philosopher because he wears a beard, when you have none yourself.'

When Sidonius, who had a great reputation at Athens as a teacher, was boasting that he was conversant with all the philosophic systems—but I had better quote his words. 'Let Aristotle call, and I follow to the Lyceum; Plato, and I hurry to the Academy; Zeno, and I make my home in the Porch; Pythagoras, and I keep the rule of silence.' Then rose Demonax from among the audience:

'Sidonius, Pythagoras calls.'

A pretty girlish young man called Python, son of some Macedonian grandee, once by way of quizzing him asked a riddling question and invited him to show his acumen over it. 'I only see one thing, dear child,' he said, 'and that is, that you are a *fair* logician.' The other lost his temper at this equivoque, and threatened him:

'You shall see in a minute what a man can do.' 'Oh, you keep a man, do you?' was Demonax's smiling retort.

He once, for daring to laugh at an athlete who displayed himself in gay clothes because he had won an Olympic victory, received a blow on the head

---

[48] i.e., Socrates.

with a stone, which drew blood. The bystanders were all as angry as if they had themselves been the victims, and set up a shout—'The Proconsul! the Proconsul!' 'Thank you, gentlemen,' said Demonax, 'but I should prefer the doctor.'

He once picked up a little gold charm in the road as he walked, and posted a notice in the market-place stating that the loser could recover his property, if he would call upon Demonax and give particulars of the weight, material, and workmanship. A handsome young exquisite came, professing to have lost it. The philosopher soon saw that it was a got-up story; 'Ah, my boy,' he said, 'you will do very well, if you lose your other charms as little as you have lost this one.'

A Roman senator at Athens once presented his son, who had great beauty of a soft womanish type. 'My son salutes you, sir,' he said. To which Demonax answered, 'A pretty lad, worthy of his father, and extremely like his mother.'

A cynic who emphasized his principles by wearing a bear's skin he insisted on addressing not by his name of Honoratus, but as Bruin.

Asked for a definition of Happiness, he said that only the free was happy. 'Well,' said the questioner, 'there is no lack of free men.'—'I count no man free who is subject to hopes and fears.'— 'You ask impossibilities; of these two we are all very much the slaves.' 'Once grasp the nature of human affairs,' said Demonax, 'and you will find that they justify neither hope nor fear, since both pain and pleasure are to have an end.'

Peregrine Proteus was shocked at his taking things so lightly, and treating mankind as a subject for humour:

'You have no teeth, Demonax.' 'And you, Peregrine, have no bowels.'

A physical philosopher was discoursing about the antipodes; Demonax took his hand, and led him to a well, in which he showed him his own reflection:

'Do you want us to believe that the antipodes are like *that?*'

A man once boasted that he was a wizard, and possessed of mighty charms whereby he could get what he chose out of anybody. 'Will it surprise you to learn that I am a fellow-craftsman?' asked Demonax; 'pray come with me to the baker's, and you shall see a single charm, just one wave of my magic wand, induce him to bestow several loaves upon me.' Current coin, he meant, is as good a magician as most.

The great Herodes, mourning the untimely death of Pollux, used to have the carriage and horses got ready, and the place laid at table, as though the dead were going to drive and eat. To him came Demonax, saying that he brought a message from Pollux. Herodes, delighted with the idea that Demonax was humouring his whim like other people, asked what it was that Pollux required of him. 'He cannot think why you are so long coming to him.'

When another person kept himself shut up in the dark, mourning his son, Demonax represented himself to him as a magician:

377

he would call up the son's ghost, the only condition being that he should be given the names of three people who had never had to mourn. The father hum'd and ha'd, unable, doubtless, to produce any such person, till Demonax broke in:

'And have you, then, a monopoly of the unendurable, when you cannot name a man who has not some grief to endure?'

He often ridiculed the people who use obsolete and uncommon words in their lectures. One of these produced a bit of Attic purism in answer to some question he had put. 'My dear sir,' he said, 'the date of my question is to-day; that of your answer is *temp. Bell. Troj.*'

A friend asking him to come to the temple of Asclepius, there to make prayer for his son, 'Poor deaf Asclepius!' he exclaimed; 'can he not hear at this distance?'

He once saw two philosophers engaged in a very unedifying game of cross questions and crooked answers. 'Gentlemen,' said he, 'here is one man milking a billy-goat, and another catching the proceeds in a sieve.'

When Agathocles the Peripatetic vaunted himself as the first and only dialectician, he asked him how he could be the first, if he was the only, or the only, if he was the first.

The consular Cethegus, on his way to serve under his father in Asia, said and did many foolish things. A friend describing him as a great ass, 'Not even a *great* ass,' said Demonax.

When Apollonius was appointed professor of philosophy in the Imperial household, Demonax witnessed his departure, attended by a great number of his pupils. 'Why, here is Apollonius with all his Argonauts,' he cried.

Asked whether he held the soul to be immortal, 'Dear me, yes,' he said; 'everything is.'

He remarked a propos of Herodes that Plato was quite right about our having more than one soul; the same soul could not possibly compose those splendid declamations, and have places laid for Regilla and Pollux after their death.

He was once bold enough to ask the assembled people, when he heard the sacred proclamation, why they excluded barbarians from the Mysteries, seeing that Eumolpus, the founder of them, was a barbarian from Thrace.

When he once had a winter voyage to make, a friend asked how he liked the thought of being capsized and becoming food for fishes. 'I should be very unreasonable to mind giving them a meal, considering how many they have given me.'

To a rhetorician who had given a very poor declamation he recommended constant practice. 'Why, I am always practising to myself,' says the man. 'Ah, that accounts for it; you are accustomed to such a foolish audience.'

Observing a soothsayer one day officiating for pay, he said:

'I cannot see how you can ask pay. If it is because you can change the course of Fate, you cannot possibly put the figure high enough:

if everything is settled by Heaven, and not by you, what is the good of your soothsaying?'

A hale old Roman once gave him a little exhibition of his skill in fence, taking a clothes-peg for his mark. 'What do you think of my play, Demonax?' he said. 'Excellent, so long as you have a wooden man to play with.'

Even for questions meant to be insoluble he generally had a shrewd answer at command. Some one tried to make a fool of him by asking, If I burn a hundred pounds of wood, how many pounds of smoke shall I get? 'Weigh the ashes; the difference is all smoke.'

One Polybius, an uneducated man whose grammar was very defective, once informed him that he had received Roman citizenship from the Emperor. 'Why did he not make you a Greek instead?' asked Demonax.

Seeing a decorated person very proud of his broad stripe, he whispered in his ear, while he took hold of and drew attention to the cloth, 'This attire did not make its original wearer anything but a sheep.'

Once at the bath the water was at boiling point, and some one called him a coward for hesitating to get in. 'What,' said he, 'is my country expecting me to do my duty?'

Some one asked him what he took the next world to be like. 'Wait a bit, and I will send you the information.'

A minor poet called Admetus told him he had inserted a clause in his will for the inscribing on his tomb of a monostich, which I will give:

Admetus' husk earth holds, and Heaven himself.

'What a beautiful epitaph, Admetus!' said Demonax, 'and what a pity it is not up yet!'

The shrunk shanks of old age are a commonplace; but when his reached this state, some one asked him what was the matter with them. 'Ah,' he said with a smile, 'Charon has been having a bite at them.'

He interrupted a Spartan who was scourging his servant with, 'Why confer on your slave the privilege of Spartans[49] like yourself?' He observed to one Danae, who was bringing a suit against her brother, 'Have the law of him by all means; it was another Danae whose father was called the Lawless.[50]

He waged constant warfare against all whose philosophy was not practical, but for show. So when he saw a cynic, with threadbare cloak and wallet, but a braying-pestle instead of a staff, proclaiming himself loudly as a follower of Antisthenes, Crates, and Diogenes, he said:

'Tell us no lies; your master is the professor of braying.'

---

[49] See *Spartans* in Notes.
[50] See *Danae* in Notes.

Noticing how foul play was growing among the athletes, who often supplemented the resources of boxing and wrestling with their teeth, he said it was no wonder that the champions' partisans had taken to describing them as lions.

There was both wit and sting in what he said to the proconsul. The latter was one of the people who take all the hair off their bodies with pitch-plaster. A cynic mounted a block of stone and cast this practice in his teeth, suggesting that it was for immoral purposes. The proconsul in a rage had the man pulled down, and was on the point of condemning him to be beaten or banished, when Demonax, who was present, pleaded for him on the ground that he was only exercising the traditional cynic licence. 'Well,' said the proconsul, 'I pardon him this time at your request; but if he offends again, what shall I do to him?' 'Have him depilated,' said Demonax.

Another person, entrusted by the Emperor with the command of legions and the charge of a great province, asked him what was the way to govern well. 'Keep your temper, say little, and hear much.'

Asked whether he ate honey-cakes, 'Do you suppose,' he said, 'that bees only make honey for fools?'

Noticing near the Poecile a statue minus a hand, he said it had taken Athens a long time to get up a bronze to Cynaegirus.

Alluding to the lame Cyprian Rufinus, who was a Peripatetic and spent much time in the Lyceum walks, 'What presumption,' he exclaimed, 'for a cripple to call himself a Walking Philosopher!'

Epictetus once urged him, with a touch of reproof, to take a wife and raise a family—for it beseemed a philosopher to leave some one to represent him after the flesh. But he received the home thrust:

'Very well, Epictetus; give me one of your daughters.'

His remark to Herminus the Aristotelian is equally worth recording. He was aware that this man's character was vile and his misdeeds innumerable, and yet his mouth was always full of Aristotle and his ten predicaments. 'Certainly, Herminus,' he said, 'no predicament is too bad for you.'

When the Athenians were thinking, in their rivalry with Corinth, of starting gladiatorial shows, he came forward and said:

'Men of Athens, before you pass this motion, do not forget to destroy the altar of Pity.'

On the occasion of his visiting Olympia, the Eleans voted a bronze statue to him. But he remonstrated:

'It will imply a reproach to your ancestors, men of Elis, who set up no statue to Socrates or Diogenes.'

I once heard him observe to a learned lawyer that laws were not of much use, whether meant for the good or for the bad; the first do not need them, and upon the second they have no effect.

There was one line of Homer always on his tongue:

Idle or busy, death takes all alike.

He had a good word for Thersites, as a cynic and a leveller.

Asked which of the philosophers was most to his taste, he said:

'I admire them all; Socrates I revere, Diogenes I admire, Aristippus I love.'

He lived to nearly a hundred, free from disease and pain, burdening no man, asking no man's favour, serving his friends, and having no enemies. Not Athens only, but all Greece was so in love with him that as he passed the great would give him place and there would be a general hush. Towards the end of his long life he would go uninvited into the first house that offered, and there get his dinner and his bed, the household regarding it as the visit of some heavenly being which brought them a blessing. When they saw him go by, the baker-wives would contend for the honour of supplying him, and a happy woman was the actual donor. Children too used to call him father, and bring him offerings of fruit.

Party spirit was once running high at Athens; he came into the assembly, and his mere appearance was enough to still the storm. When he saw that they were ashamed, he departed again without having uttered a word.

When he found that he was no longer able to take care of himself, he repeated to his friends the tag with which the heralds close the festival:

The games are done,
The crowns all won;
No more delay,
But haste away,

and from that moment abstaining from food, left life as cheerfully as he had lived it.

When the end was near, he was asked his wishes about burial. 'Oh, do not trouble; scent will summon my undertakers.' Well, but it would be indecent for the body of so great a man to feed birds and dogs. 'Oh, no harm in making oneself useful in death to anything that lives.'

However, the Athenians gave him a magnificent public funeral, long lamented him, worshipped and garlanded the stone seat on which he had been wont to rest when tired, accounting the mere stone sanctified by him who had sat upon it. No one would miss the funeral ceremony, least of all any of the philosophers. It was these who bore him to the grave.

I have made but a small selection of the material available; but it may serve to give readers some idea of this great man's character.

A PORTRAIT-STUDY

Lycinus. Polystratus

Ly. Polystratus, I know now what men must have felt like when they saw the Gorgon's head. I have just experienced the same sensation, at the sight of a most lovely woman. A little more, and I should have realized the legend, by being turned to stone; I am benumbed with admiration.

Poly. Wonderful indeed must have been the beauty, and terrible the power of the woman who could produce such an impression on Lycinus. Tell me of this petrifying Medusa. Who is she, and whence? I would see her myself. You will not grudge me that privilege? Your jealousy will not take alarm at the prospect of a rival petrifaction at your side?

Ly. Well, I give you fair warning:

one distant glimpse of her, and you are speechless, motionless as any statue. Nay, that is a light affliction:

the mortal wound is not dealt till *her* glance has fallen on *you*. What can save you then? She will lead you in chains, hither and thither, as the magnet draws the steel.

Poly. Enough! You would make her more than human. And now tell me who she is.

Ly. You think I am exaggerating:

I fear you will have but a poor opinion of my eloquence when you see her as she is—so far above my praise. *Who* she is, I cannot say:

but to judge from the splendour of her surroundings, her retinue, her host of eunuchs and maids, she must be of no ordinary rank.

Poly. And you never even asked her name?

Ly. Why no; but she is from Ionia; because, as she passed, I heard one of the bystanders speak aside to his neighbour:

'See, he exclaimed, 'what Smyrna can produce! And what wonder, if the fairest of Ionian cities has given birth to the fairest of women?' I thought he must come from Smyrna himself, he was so proud of her.

Poly. There you acted your stony part to perfection. As you could neither follow her, nor make inquiries of the Smyrnaean, it only remains for you to describe her as best you can, on the chance of my recognizing her.

Ly. You know not what you ask. It is not in the power of words—certainly not of *my* words—to portray such wondrous beauty; scarcely could an Apelles, a Zeuxis, a Parrhasius,—a Phidias or an Alcamenes, do justice to it; as for my flimsy workmanship, it will but insult the original.

Poly. Well, never mind; what was she like? There can be no harm in trying your hand. What if the portrait be somewhat out of drawing?—the critic is your good friend.

Ly. I think my best way out of it will be to call in the aid of some of the old masters I have named:

let them fashion the likeness for me.

Poly. Well, but—will they come? They have been dead so long.

Ly. That is easily managed:

 but you must not mind answering me a few questions.

Poly. You have but to ask.

Ly. Were you ever at Cnidus?

Poly. I was.

Ly. Then you have seen the *Aphrodite*, of course?

Poly. That masterpiece of Praxiteles's art! I have.

Ly. And heard the story they tell there,—of the man who fell in love with the statue, and contrived to get shut into the temple alone, and there enjoyed such favours as a statue is able to bestow.—But that is neither here nor there.—You have seen the Cnidian *Aphrodite*, anyhow; now I want to know whether you have also seen our own *Aphrodite of the Gardens*,—the Alcamenes.

Poly. I must be a dullard of dullards, if that most exquisite of Alcamenes's works had escaped my notice.

Ly. I forbear to ask whether in the course of your many visits to the Acropolis you ever observed the *Sosandra* of Calamis.[51]

Poly. Frequently.

Ly. That is really enough for my purpose. But I should just like to know what you consider to be Phidias's best work.

Poly. Can you ask?—The Lemnian *Athene*, which bears the artist's own signature; oh, and of course the *Amazon* leaning on her spear.

Ly. I approve your judgement. We shall have no need of other artists:

 I am now to cull from each of these its own peculiar beauty, and combine all in a single portrait.

Poly. And how are you going to do that?

Ly. It is quite simple. All we have to do is to hand over our several types to Reason, whose care it must be to unite them in the most harmonious fashion, with due regard to the consistency, as to the variety, of the result.

Poly. To be sure; let Reason take her materials and begin. What will she make of it, I wonder? Will she contrive to put all these different types together without their clashing?

Ly. Well, look; she is at work already. Observe her procedure. She begins with our Cnidian importation, from which she takes only the head; with the rest she is not concerned, as the statue is nude. The hair, the forehead, the exquisite eyebrows, she will keep as Praxiteles has rendered them; the eyes, too, those soft, yet bright-glancing eyes, she leaves unaltered. But the cheeks and the

---

[51] This statue is usually identified with one of Aphrodite by the same sculptor, mentioned in Pausanias. Soteira ('saviour') is known as an epithet of Aphrodite:
 but Sosandra ('man-saving') is explained as a nickname of the particular statue, in playful allusion to Callias, the donor, who was apparently indebted to Aphrodite for his success with a certain Elpinice.

front of the face are taken from the 'Garden' Goddess; and so are the lines of the hands, the shapely wrists, the delicately-tapering fingers. Phidias and the Lemnian *Athene* will give the outline of the face, and the well-proportioned nose, and lend new softness to the cheeks; and the same artist may shape her neck and closed lips, to resemble those of his *Amazon*. Calamis adorns her with Sosandra's modesty, Sosandra's grave half- smile; the decent seemly dress is Sosandra's too, save that the head must not be veiled. For her stature, let it be that of Cnidian *Aphrodite*; once more we have recourse to Praxiteles.—What think you, Polystratus? Is it a lovely portrait?

Poly. Assuredly it will be, when it is perfected. At present, my paragon of sculptors, one element of loveliness has escaped your comprehensive grasp.

Ly. What is that?

Poly. A most important one. You will agree with me that colour and tone have a good deal to do with beauty? that black should *be* black, white be white, and red play its blushing part? It looks to me as if the most important thing of all were still lacking.

Ly. Well, how shall we manage? Call in the painters, perhaps, selecting those who were noted for their skill in mixing and laying on their colours? Be it so:

we will have Polygnotus, Euphranor of course, Apelles and Aetion; they can divide the work between them. Euphranor shall colour the hair like his *Hera's*; Polygnotus the comely brow and faintly blushing cheek, after his *Cassandra* in the Assembly-room at Delphi. Polygnotus shall also paint her robe,—of the finest texture, part duly gathered in, but most of it floating in the breeze. For the flesh-tints, which must be neither too pale nor too high-coloured, Apelles shall copy his own *Campaspe*. And lastly, Aetion shall give her *Roxana's* lips. Nay, we can do better:

have we not Homer, best of painters, though a Euphranor and an Apelles be present? Let him colour all like the limbs of Menelaus, which he says were 'ivory tinged with red.' He too shall paint her calm 'ox- eyes,' and the Theban poet shall help him to give them their 'violet' hue. Homer shall add her smile, her white arms, her rosy finger-tips, and so complete the resemblance to golden Aphrodite, to whom he has compared Brises' daughter with far less reason. So far we may trust our sculptors and painters and poets:

but for her crowning glory, for the grace—nay, the choir of Graces and Loves that encircle her—who shall portray them?

Poly. This was no earthly vision, Lycinus; surely she must have dropped from the clouds.—And what was she doing?

Ly. In her hands was an open scroll; half read (so I surmised) and half to be read. As she passed, she was making some remark to one of her company; what it was I did not catch. But when she smiled, ah! then, Polystratus, I beheld teeth whose whiteness, whose unbroken regularity, who shall describe? Imagine a lovely necklace of gleaming pearls, all of a size; and imagine those dazzling rows set off by ruby lips. In that glimpse, I realized what Homer meant by his 'carven ivory.' Other women's teeth differ in size; or they project; or there are gaps:

here, all was equality and evenness; pearl joined to pearl in unbroken line. Oh, 'twas a wondrous sight, of beauty more than human.

Poly. Stay. I know now whom you mean, as well from your description as from her nationality. You said that there were eunuchs in her train?

Ly. Yes; and soldiers too.

Poly. My simple friend, the lady you have been describing is a celebrity, and possesses the affections of an Emperor.

Ly. And her name?

Poly. Adds one more to the list of her charms; for it is the same as that of Abradatas's wife.[52] You know Xenophon's enthusiastic account of that beautiful and virtuous woman?—you have read it a dozen times.

Ly. Yes; and every time I read it, it is as if she stood before me. I almost hear her uttering the words the historian has put into her mouth, and see her arming her husband and sending him forth to battle.

Poly. Ah, my dear Lycinus, *this* lady has passed you but once, like a lightning flash; and your praises, I perceive, are all for those external charms that strike the eye. You are yet a stranger to her nobility of soul; you know not that higher, more god-like beauty. *I* am her fellow-countryman, I know her, and have conversed with her many times. You are aware that gentleness, humanity, magnanimity, modesty, culture, are things that I prize more than beauty-and rightly; to do otherwise would be as absurd as to value raiment above the body. Where physical perfection goes hand-in-hand with spiritual excellence, there alone (as I maintain) is true beauty. I could show you many a woman whose outward loveliness is marred by what is within; who has but to open her lips, and beauty stands confessed a faded, withered thing, the mean, unlovely handmaid of that odious mistress, her soul. Such women are like Egyptian temples:

the shrine is fair and stately, wrought of costly marble, decked out with gilding and painting:

but seek the God within, and you find an ape—an ibis—a goat—a cat. Of how many women is the same thing true! Beauty unadorned is not enough:

and her true adornments are not purple and jewels, but those others that I have mentioned, modesty, courtesy, humanity, virtue and all that waits on virtue.

Ly. Why then, Polystratus, you shall give me story for story, good measure, shaken together, out of your abundance:

paint me the portrait of her soul, that I may be no more her half-admirer.

[52] See *Panthea* in Notes.

Poly. This will be no light task, my friend. It is one thing to commend what all the world can see, and quite another to reveal what is hidden. I too shall want help with my portrait. Nor will sculptors and painters suffice me:

I must have philosophers; it is by their canons that I must adjust the proportions of the figure, if I am to attain to the perfection of ancient models.

To begin then. Of her clear, liquid voice Homer might have said, with far more truth than of aged Nestor's, that

honey from those lips distilled.

The pitch, exquisitely soft, as far removed from masculine bass as from ultra-feminine treble, is that of a boy before his voice breaks; sweet, seductive, suavely penetrating; it ceases, and still vibrating murmurs play, echo-like, about the listener's ears, and Persuasion leaves her honeyed track upon his mind. But oh! the joy, to hear her sing, and sing to the lyre's accompaniment. Let swans and halcyons and cicalas then be mute. There is no music like hers; Philomela's self, 'full-throated songstress' though she be, is all unskilled beside her. Methinks Orpheus and Amphion, whose spell drew even lifeless things to hear them, would have dropped their lyres and stood listening in silence to that voice. What should Thracian Orpheus, what should Amphion, whose days upon Cithaeron were divided betwixt his lyre and his herd,—what should they know of true concord, of accurate rhythm, of accentuation and time, of the harmonious adaptation of lyre and voice, of easy and graceful execution? Yes; once hear her sing, Lycinus, and you will know something of Sirens as well as of Gorgons:

you have experienced petrifaction; you will next learn what it is to stand entranced, forgetting country and kindred. Wax will not avail you:

her song will penetrate through all; for therein is every grace that Terpsichore, Melpomene, Calliope herself, could inspire. In a word, imagine that you hear such notes as should issue from those lips, those teeth that you have seen. Her perfect intonation, her pure Ionic accent, her ready Attic eloquence, need not surprise you; these are her birthright; for is not Smyrna Athens' daughter? And what more natural than that she should love poetry, and make it her chief study? Homer is her fellow citizen.—There you have my first portrait; the portrait of a sweet-voiced songstress, though it fall far short of its original. And now for others. For I do not propose to make one of many, as you did. I aim higher:

the complex picture of so many beauties wrought into one, however artful be the composition, cannot escape inconsistency:

with me, each separate virtue of her soul shall sit for its own portrait.

Ly. What a banquet awaits me! Here, assuredly, is good measure. Mete it out; I ask for nothing better.

Poly. I proceed then to the delineation of Culture, the confessed mistress of all mental excellences, particularly of all acquired ones:

I must render her features in all their manifold variety; not even here shall my portraiture be inferior to your own. I paint her, then, with every grace that Helicon can give. Each of the Muses has but her single accomplishment, be it tragedy or history or hymn:

all these Culture shall have, and with them the gifts of Hermes and of Apollo. The poet's graceful numbers, the orator's persuasive power, the historian's learning, the sage's counsel, all these shall be her adornments; the colours shall be imperishable, and laid on with no niggardly brush. It is not my fault, if I am unable to point to any classical model for the portrait:

the records of antiquity afford no precedent for a culture so highly developed.—May I hang this beside the other? I think it is a passable likeness.

Ly. Passable! My dear Polystratus, it is sublime; exquisitely finished in every line.

Poly. Next I have to depict Wisdom; and here I shall have occasion for many models, most of them ancient; one comes, like the lady herself, from Ionia. The artists shall be Aeschines and Socrates his master, most realistic of painters, for their heart was in their work. We could choose no better model of wisdom than Milesian Aspasia, the admired of the admirable 'Olympian'[53]; her political knowledge and insight, her shrewdness and penetration, shall all be transferred to our canvas in their perfect measure. Aspasia, however, is only preserved to us in miniature:

our proportions must be those of a colossus.

Ly. Explain.

Poly. The portraits will be alike, but not on the same scale. There is a difference between the little republic of ancient Athens, and the Roman Empire of to-day; and there will be the same difference in *scale* (however close the resemblance in other respects) between our huge canvas and that miniature. A second and a third model may be found in Theano, and in the poetess of Lesbos; nay, we may add Diotima too. Theano shall give grandeur to the picture, Sappho elegance; and Diotima shall be represented as well by her wisdom and sagacity, as by the qualities for which Socrates commended her. The portrait is complete. Let it be hung.

Ly. 'Tis a fine piece of work. Proceed.

Poly. Courtesy, benevolence:

that is now my subject. I have to show forth her gentle disposition, her graciousness to suppliants. She shall appear in the likeness of Theano— Antenor's Theano this time—, of Arete and her daughter Nausicaa, and of every other who in her high station has borne herself with constancy. Next comes constancy of another kind,—constancy in love; its original, the daughter of Icarius, 'constant' and 'wise,' as Homer draws her; am I doing more than justice to his Penelope? And there is another:

our lady's namesake, Abradatas's wife; of her we have already spoken.

Ly. Once more, noble work, Polystratus. And now your task must be drawing to a close:

---

[53] See *Pericles* in Notes.

here is a whole soul depicted; its every virtue praised.

Poly. Not yet:

the highest praise remains. Born to magnificence, she clothes not herself in the pride of wealth; listens not to Fortune's flattering tale, who tells her she is more than human; but walks upon the common ground, far removed from all thought of arrogance and ostentation. Every man is her equal; her greeting, her smile are for all who approach her; and how acceptable is the kindness of a superior, when it is free from every touch of condescension! When the power of the great turns not to insolence but to beneficence, we feel that Fortune has bestowed her gifts aright. Here alone Envy has no place. For how should one man grudge another his prosperity when he sees him using it with moderation, not, like the Homeric Ate, an oppressor of the weak, trampling on men's necks? It is otherwise with those meaner souls—victims of their own ignoble vanity—, who, when Fortune has raised them suddenly beyond their hopes into her winged aerial car, know no rest, can never look behind them, but must ever press upwards. To such the end soon comes:

Icarus-like, with melted wax and moulting feathers, they fall headlong into the billows, a derision to mankind. The Daedaluses use their waxen wings with moderation:

they are but men; they husband their strength accordingly, and are content to fly a little higher than the waves,—so little that the sun never finds them dry; and that prudence is their salvation.

Therein lies this lady's highest praise. She has her reward:

all men pray that her wings may never droop, and that blessings may increase upon her.

Ly. And may the prayer be granted! She deserves every blessing:

she is not outwardly fair alone, like Helen, but has a soul within more fair, more lovely than her body. It is a fitting crown to the happiness of our benevolent and gracious Emperor, that in his day such a woman should be born; should be his, and her affections his. It is blessedness indeed, to possess one of whom we may say with Homer that she contends with golden Aphrodite in beauty, and in works is the equal of Athene. Who of womankind shall be compared to her

In comeliness, in wit, in goodly works?

Poly. Who indeed?—Lycinus, I have a proposal to make. Let us combine our portraits, yours of the body and mine of the soul, and throw them into a literary form, for the enjoyment of our generation and of all posterity. Such a work will be more enduring than those of Apelles and Parrhasius and Polygnotus; it will be far removed from creations of wood and wax and colour, being inspired by the Muses, in whom alone is that true portraiture that shows forth in one likeness a lovely body and a virtuous soul.

DEFENCE OF THE 'PORTRAIT-STUDY'

Polystratus. Lycinus

Poly. Well, here is the lady's comment. _Your pages are most kind and complimentary, I am sure, Lycinus. No one would have so over-praised me who had not felt kindly towards me. But if you would know my real feeling, here it is. I never do much like the complaisant; they always strike me as insincere and wanting in frankness. But when it comes to a set panegyric, in which my much magnified virtues are painted in glaring colours, I blush and would fain stop my ears, and feel that I am rather being made fun of than commended.

Praise is tolerable up to the point at which the object of it can still believe in the existence of the qualities attributed to him; pass that point, and he is revolted and finds the flatterer out. Of course I know there are plenty of people who are glad enough to have non-existent qualities added to their praises; who do not mind being called young and lusty in their decline, or Nireuses and Phaons though they are hideous; who, Pelias-like, expect praise to metamorphose or rejuvenate them.

But they are mistaken. Praise would indeed be a most precious commodity if there were any way of converting its extravagances into solid fact. But there being none, they can only be compared to an ugly man on whom one should clap a beautiful mask, and who should then be proud of those looks that any one could take from him and break to pieces; revealed in his true likeness, he would be only the more ridiculous for the contrast between casket and treasure. Or, if you will, imagine a little man on stilts measuring heights with people who have eighteen inches the better of him in stocking feet_.

And then she told this story. There was a noble lady, fair and comely in all respects except that she was short and ill-proportioned. A poet wrote an ode in her honour, and included among her beauties that of tallness; her slender height was illustrated from the poplar. She was in ecstasies, as though the verses were making her grow, and kept waving her hand. Which the poet seeing, and realizing her appetite for praise, recited the lines again and again, till at last one of the company whispered in his ear, 'Stop, my good man; you will be making her get up.'

She added a similar but still more absurd anecdote of Stratonice the wife of Seleucus, who offered a talent to the poet who should best celebrate her hair. As a matter of fact she was bald, with not a hair to call her own. But what matter what her head was like, or that every one knew how a long illness had treated her? she listened to these abandoned poets telling of hyacinthine locks, plaiting thick tresses, and making imaginary curls as crisp as parsley.

All such surrenders to flattery were laughed to scorn, with the addition that many people were just as fond of being flattered and fooled by portrait-painters as these by verbal artists. *What these people look for in a painter* (she said) *is readiness to improve nature:*

389

Some of them insist upon the artist's taking a little off their noses, deepening the shade of their eyes, or otherwise idealizing them to order; it quite escapes them that the garlands they afterwards put on the picture are offered to another person who bears no relation to themselves.

And so she went on, finding much in your composition to approve, but displeased in particular with your likening her to Hera and Aphrodite. *Such comparisons are far too high for me,* she said, *or indeed for any of womankind. Why, I would not have had you put me on a level with women of the Heroic Age, with a Penelope, an Arete, a Theano; how much less with the chief of the Goddesses. Where the Gods are concerned* (she continued; and mark her here), *I am very apprehensive and timid. I fear that to accept a panegyric like this would be to make a Cassiopeia of myself; though indeed* she *only challenged the Nereids, and stopped short of Hera and Aphrodite.*

So, Lycinus, she insisted that you must recast all this; otherwise she must call the Goddesses to witness that you had written against her wishes, and leave you to the knowledge that the piece would be an annoyance to her, if it circulated in its present shape, so lacking in reverence and piety. The outrage on reverence would be put down to her, if she allowed herself to be likened to her of Cnidus and her of the Garden. She would have you bear in mind the close of your discourse, where you spoke of the unassuming modesty that attempted no superhuman flights, but kept near the earth. It was inconsistent with that to take the same woman up to heaven and compare her with Goddesses.

She would like to be allowed as much sense as Alexander; he, when his architect proposed to transform Mount Athos into a vast image of the King with a pair of cities in his hands, shrank from the grandiose proposal; such presumption was beyond him; such patent megalomania must be suppressed; leave Athos alone, he said, and do not degrade a mighty mountain to the similitude of a poor human body. This only showed the greatness of Alexander, and itself constituted in the eyes of all future generations a monument higher than any Athos; to be able to scorn so extraordinary an honour was itself magnanimity.

So she commends your work of art, and your selective method, but cannot recognize the likeness. She does not come up to the description, nor near it, for indeed no woman could. Accordingly she sends you back your laudation, and pays homage to the originals from which you drew it. Confine your praises within the limits of humanity; if the shoe is too big, it may chance to trip her up. Then there was another point which I was to impress upon you.

I often hear, she said,—*but whether it is true, you men know better than I—that at Olympia the victors are not allowed to have their statues set up larger than life; the Stewards see to it that no one transgresses this rule, examining the statues even more scrupulously than they did the competitor's qualification. Take care that we do not get convicted of false proportions, and find our statue thrown down by the Stewards.*

390

And now I have given you her message. It is for you, Lycinus, to overhaul your work, and by removing these blemishes avoid the offence. They shocked and made her nervous as I read; she kept on addressing the Goddesses in propitiatory words; and such feelings may surely be permitted to her sex. For that matter, to be quite frank, I shared them to some extent. At the first hearing I found no offence; but as soon as she put her finger on the fault, I began to agree. You know what happens with visible objects; if we look at them at close quarters, just under our eyes, I mean, we distinguish nothing clearly; but stepping back to the right distance, we get a clear conception of what is right and what is wrong about them. That was my experience here.

After all, to compare a mortal to Hera and Aphrodite is cheapening the Goddesses, and nothing else. In such comparisons the small is not so much magnified as the great is diminished and reduced. If a giant and a dwarf were walking together, and their heights had to be equalized, no efforts of the dwarf could effect it, however much he stood on tiptoe; the giant must stoop and make himself out shorter than he is. So in this sort of portraiture:

the human is not so much exalted by the similitude as the divine is belittled and pulled down. If indeed a lack of earthly beauties forced the artist upon scaling Heaven, he might perhaps be acquitted of blasphemy; but your enterprise was so needless; why Aphrodite and Hera, when you have all mortal beauty to choose from?

Prune and chasten, then, Lycinus. All this is not quite like you, who never used to be over-ready with your commendation; you seem to have gone now to the opposite extreme of prodigality, and developed from a niggard into a spendthrift of praise. Do not be ashamed to make alterations in what you have already published, either. They say Phidias did as much after finishing his Olympian Zeus. He stood behind the doors when he had opened them for the first time to let the work be seen, and listened to the comments favourable or the reverse. One found the nose too broad, another the face too long, and so on. When the company was gone, he shut himself up again to correct and adapt his statue to the prevailing taste. Advice so many-headed was not to be despised; the many must after all see further than the one, though that one be Phidias. There is the counsel of a friend and well-wisher to back up the lady's message.

Ly. Why, Polystratus, I never knew what an orator you were. After that eloquent close-packed indictment of my booklet, I almost despair of the defence. You and she were not quite judicial, though; you less than she, in condemning the accused when its counsel was not in court. It is always easy to win a walk-over, you know; so no wonder we were convicted, not being allowed to speak or given the ear of the court. But, still more monstrous, you were accusers and jury at once. Well, what am I to do? accept the verdict and hold my tongue? pen a palinode like Stesichorus? or will you grant an appeal?

Poly. Surely, if you have anything to say for yourself. For you will be heard not by opponents, as you say, but by friends. Indeed, my place is with you in the dock.

Ly. How I wish I could, have spoken in her own presence! that would have been far better; but I must do it by proxy. However, if you will report me to her as well as you did her to me, I will adventure.

Poly. Trust me to do justice to the defence; but put it shortly, in mercy to my memory.

Ly. So severe an indictment should by rights be met at length; but for your sake I will cut it short. Put these considerations before her from me, then.

Poly. No, not that way, please. Make your speech, just as though she were listening, and I will reproduce you to her.

Ly. Very well, then. She is here; she has just delivered the oration which you have described to me; it is now counsel's turn. And yet—I must confide my feelings to you—you have made my undertaking somehow more formidable; you see the beads gather on my brow; my courage goes; I seem to see her there; my situation bewilders me. Yet begin I will; how can I draw back when she is there?

Poly. Ah, but her face promises a kindly hearing; see how bright and gracious. Pluck up heart, man, and begin.

Ly. Most noble lady, in what you term the great and excessive praise that I bestowed upon you, I find no such high testimony to your merits as that which you have borne yourself by your surprise at the attribution of divinity. That one thing surpasses all that I have said of you, and my only excuse for not having added this trait to my portrait is that I was not aware of it; if I had been, no other should have had precedence of it. In this light I find myself, far from exaggerating, to have fallen much short of the truth. Consider the magnitude of this omission, the convincing demonstration of a sterling character and a right disposition which I lost; for those will be the best in human relations who are most earnest in their dealings with the divine. Why, were it decided that I must correct my words and retouch my statue, I should do it not by presuming to take away from it, but by adding this as its crowning grace. But from another point of view I have a great debt of gratitude to acknowledge. I commend your natural modesty, and your freedom from that vanity and pride which so exalted a position as yours might excuse. The best witness to my correctness is just the exception that you have taken to my words. That instead of receiving the praise I offered as your right you should be disturbed at it and call it excessive, is the proof of your unassuming modesty. Nevertheless, the more you reveal that this is your view of praise, the stronger proof you give of your own worthiness to be praised. You are an exact illustration of what Diogenes said when some one asked him how he might become famous:

— 'by despising fame.' So if I were asked who most deserve praise, I should answer, Those who refuse it.

But I am perhaps straying from the point. What I have to defend is the having likened you, in giving your outward form, to the Cnidian and the Garden *Aphrodite*, to *Hera* and *Athene*; such comparisons you find out of all proportion. I will deal directly with them, then. It has indeed been said long ago that poets and painters are irresponsible; that is still more true, I conceive, of panegyrists, even humble prose ones like myself who are not run away with by their metre. Panegyric is a chartered thing, with no standard quantitative measure to which it must conform; its one and only aim is to express deep admiration and set its object in the most enviable light. However, I do not intend to take that line of defence; you might think I did so because I had no other open.

But I have. I refer you to the proper formula of panegyric, which requires the author to introduce illustrations, and depends mainly on their goodness for success. Now this goodness is shown not when the illustration is just like the thing illustrated, nor yet when it is inferior, but when it is as high above it as may be. If in praising a dog one should remark that it was bigger than a fox or a cat, would you regard him as a skilful panegyrist? certainly not. Or if he calls it the equal of a wolf, he has not made very much of it so either. Where is the right thing to be found? why, in likening the dog's size and spirit to the lion's. So the poet who would praise Orion's dog called it the lion-queller. There you have the perfect panegyric of the dog. Or take Milo of Croton, Glaucus of Carystus, or Polydamas; to say of them by way of panegyric that each of them was stronger than a woman would be to make oneself a laughing-stock; one man instead of the woman would not much mend matters. But what, pray, does a famous poet make of Glaucus?—

> To match those hands not e'en the might
> Of Pollux' self had dared;
> Alcmena's son, that iron wight,
> Had shrunk—

See what Gods he equals him to, or rather what Gods he puts him above. And Glaucus took no exception to being praised at the expense of his art's patron deities; nor yet did they send any judgement on athlete or poet for irreverence; both continued to be honoured in Greece, one for his might, and the other for this even more than for his other odes. Do not be surprised, then, that when I wished to conform to the canons of my art and find an illustration, I took an exalted one, as reason was that I should.

You used the word flattery. To dislike those who practise it is only what you should do, and I honour you for it. But I would have you distinguish between panegyric proper and the flatterer's exaggeration of it. The flatterer praises for selfish ends, cares little for truth, and makes it his business to magnify indiscriminately; most of his effects consist in lying additions of his own; he thinks nothing of making Thersites handsomer than Achilles, or telling Nestor he is younger than any of the host; he will swear Croesus's son hears better than Melampus, and give Phineus better sight than Lynceus, if he sees his way to a profit on the lie. But the panegyrist pure and simple, instead of lying outright, or inventing a quality that does not exist, takes the virtues his subject really does possess, though possibly not in large measure, and makes the most of them. The horse is really distinguished among the animals we know for light-footed speed; well, in praising a horse, he will hazard:

The corn-stalks brake not 'neath his airy tread.

He will not be frightened of 'whirlwind-footed steeds.' If his theme is a noble house, with everything handsome about it,

Zeus on Olympus dwells in such a home,

we shall be told. But your flatterer would use that line about the swineherd's hovel, if he saw a chance of getting anything out of the swineherd. Demetrius Poliorcetes had a flatterer called Cynaethus who, when he was gravelled for lack of matter, found some in a cough that troubled his patron—he cleared his throat so musically!

There you have one criterion:

flatterers do not draw the line at a lie if it will please their patrons; panegyrists aim merely at bringing into relief what really exists. But there is another great difference:

the flatterers exaggerate as much as ever they can; the panegyrists in the midst of exaggeration observe the limitations of decency. And now that you have one or two of the many tests for flattery and panegyric proper, I hope you will not treat all praise as suspect, but make distinctions and assign each specimen to its true class.

By your leave I will proceed to apply the two definitions to what I wrote; which of them fits it? If it had been an ugly woman that I likened to the Cnidian statue, I should deserve to be thought a toady, further gone in flattery than Cynaethus. But as it was one for whose charms I can call all men to witness, my shot was not so far out.

Now you will perhaps say—nay, you have said already—Praise my beauty, if you will; but the praise should not have been of that invidious kind which compares a woman to Goddesses. Well, I will keep truth at arm's length no longer; I did *not*, dear lady, compare you to Goddesses, but to the handiwork in marble and bronze and ivory of certain good artists. There is no impiety, surely, in illustrating mortal beauty by the work of mortal hands—unless you take the thing that Phidias fashioned to be indeed Athene, or Praxiteles's not much later work at Cnidus to be the heavenly Aphrodite. But would that be quite a worthy conception of divine beings? I take the real presentment of them to be beyond the reach of human imitation.

But granting even that it had been the actual Goddesses to whom I likened you, it would be no new track, of which I had been the pioneer; it had been trodden before by many a great poet, most of all by your fellow citizen Homer, who will kindly now come and share my defence, on pain of sharing my sentence. I will ask him, then—or rather you for him; for it is one of your merits to have all his finest passages by heart—what think you, then, of his saying about the captive Briseis that in her mourning for Patroclus she was 'Golden Aphrodite's peer'? A little further on, Aphrodite alone not meeting the case, it is:

So spake that weeping dame, a match for Goddesses.

When he talks like that, do you take offence and fling the book away, or has *he* your licence to expatiate in panegyric? Whether he has yours or not, he has that of all these centuries, wherein not a critic has found fault with him for it, not he that dared to scourge his statue[54], not he whose marginal pen [55] bastarded so many of his verses. Now, shall he have leave to match with Golden Aphrodite a barbarian woman, and her in tears, while I, lest I should describe the beauty that you like not to hear of, am forbidden to compare certain images to a lady who is ever bright and smiling—that beauty which mortals share with Gods?

When he had Agamemnon in hand, he was most chary of divine similitudes, to be sure! what economy and moderation in his use of them! Let us see—eyes and head from Zeus, belt from Ares, chest from Posidon; why, he deals the man out piecemeal among the host of Heaven. Elsewhere, Agamemnon is 'like baleful Ares'; others have their heavenly models; Priam's son (a Phrygian, mark) is 'of form divine,' the son of Peleus is again and again 'a match for Gods.' But let us come back to the feminine instances You remember, of course,

—a match For Artemis or golden Aphrodite;

and

Like Artemis adown the mountain slope.

But he does not even limit himself to comparing the whole man to a God; Euphorbus's mere hair is called like the Graces—when it is dabbled with blood, too. In fact the practice is so universal that no branch of poetry can do without its ornaments from Heaven. Either let all these be blotted, or let me have the same licence. Moreover, illustration is so irresponsible that Homer allows himself to convey his compliments to Goddesses by using creatures inferior to them. Hera is ox-eyed. Another poet colours Aphrodite's eyes from the violet. As for fingers like the rose, it takes but little of Homer's society to bring us acquainted with them.

Still, so far we do not get beyond mere looks; a man is only called *like* a God. But think of the wholesale adaptation of their names, by Dionysiuses, Hephaestions, Zenos, Posidoniuses, Hermaeuses. Leto, wife of Evagoras, King of Cyprus, even dispensed with adaptation; but her divine namesake, who could have turned her into stone like Niobe, took no offence. What need to

---

[54] Zoilus, called Homeromastix.
[55] Aristarclius.

mention that the most religious race on earth, the Egyptian, never tires of divine names? most of those it uses hail from Heaven.

Consequently, there is not the smallest occasion for you to be nervous about the panegyric. If what I wrote contains anything offensive to the deity, you are not responsible, unless you consider we are responsible for all that goes in at our ears; no, I shall pay the penalty—as soon as the Gods have settled with Homer and the other poets. Ah, and they have not done so yet with the best of all philosophers[56], for saying that man is a likeness of God. But now, though I could say much more, madam, I must have compassion upon Polystratus's memory, and cease.

Poly. I am not so sure I am equal to it, Lycinus, as it is. You have made it long, and exceeded your time limit. However, I will do my best. See, I scurry off with my fingers in my ears, that no alien sound may find its way in to disturb the arrangement; I do not want to be hissed by my audience.

Ly. Well, the responsibility for a correct report lies with you alone. And having now duly instructed you, I will retire for the present. But when the verdict is brought into court, I will be there to learn the result.

---

[56] Lucian's 'best of all philosophers' might be Plato, who is their spokesman in 'The Fisher' (see Sections 14, 22), or Epicurus, in the light of two passages in the 'Alexander' (Sections 47, 61) in which he almost declares himself an Epicurean. The exact words are not found in Plato, though several similar expressions are quoted; words of Epicurus appear to be translated in Cicero, *De nat. Deorum*, Book I, xviii s. f., hominis esse specie deos confitendum est:

we must admit that the Gods are in the image of man.

TOXARIS:
A DIALOGUE OF FRIENDSHIP

Mnesippus. Toxaris

Mne. Now, Toxaris:

do you mean to tell me that you people actually *sacrifice* to Orestes and Pylades? do you take them for Gods?

Tox. Sacrifice to them? of course we do. It does not follow that we think they are Gods:

they were good men.

Mne. And in Scythia 'good men' receive sacrifice just the same as Gods?

Tox. Not only that, but we honour them with feasts and public gatherings.

Mne. But what do you expect from them? They are shades now, so their goodwill can be no object.

Tox. Why, as to that, I think it may be just as well to have a good understanding even with shades. But that is not all:

in honouring the dead we consider that we are also doing the best we can for the living. Our idea is that by preserving the memory of the noblest of mankind, we induce many people to follow their example.

Mne. Ah, there you are right. But what could you find to admire in Orestes and Pylades, that you should exalt them to godhead? They were strangers to you:

strangers, did I say? they were enemies! Why, when they were shipwrecked on your coast, and your ancestors laid hands on them, and took them off to be sacrificed to Artemis, they assaulted the gaolers, overpowered the garrison, slew the king, carried off the priestess, laid impious hands on the Goddess herself, and so took ship, snapping their fingers at Scythia and her laws. If you honour men for this kind of thing, there will be plenty of people to follow their example, and you will have your hands full. You may judge for yourselves, from ancient precedent, whether it will suit you to have so many Oresteses and Pyladeses putting into your ports. It seems to me that it will soon end in your having no religion left at all:

God after God will be expatriated in the same manner, and then I suppose you will supply their place by deifying their kidnappers, thus rewarding sacrilege with sacrifice. If this is not your motive in honouring Orestes and Pylades, I shall be glad to know what other service they have rendered you, that you should change your minds about them, and admit them to divine honours. Your ancestors did their best to offer them up to Artemis:

you offer up victims to them. It seems an absurd inconsistency.

Tox. Now, in the first place, the incident you refer to is very much to their credit. Think of those two entering on that vast undertaking by themselves:

sailing away from their country to the distant Euxine[57]—that sea unknown in those days to the Greeks, or known only to the Argonauts— unmoved by the stories they heard of it, undeterred by the inhospitable name it then bore, which I suppose referred to the savage nations that dwelt upon its shores; think of their courageous bearing after they were captured; how escape alone would not serve them, but they must avenge their wrong upon the king, and carry Artemis away over the seas. Are not these admirable deeds, and shall not the doers be counted as Gods by all who esteem prowess? However, this is not our motive in giving them divine honours.

Mne. Proceed. What else of godlike and sublime was in their conduct? Because from the seafaring point of view, there are any number of merchants whose divinity I will maintain against theirs:

the Phoenicians, in particular, have sailed to every port in Greek and foreign waters, let alone the Euxine, the Maeotian Lake and the Bosphorus; year after year they explore every coast, only returning home at the approach of winter. Hucksters though they be for the most part, and fishmongers, you must deify them all, to be consistent.

Tox. Now, now, Mnesippus, listen to me, and you shall see how much more candid we barbarians are in our valuation of good men than you Greeks. In Argos and Mycenae there is not so much as a respectable tomb raised to Orestes and Pylades:

in Scythia, they have their temple, which is very appropriately dedicated to the two friends in common, their sacrifices, and every honour. The fact of their being foreigners does not prevent us from recognizing their virtues. We do not inquire into the nationality of noble souls:

we can hear without envy of the illustrious deeds of our enemies; we do justice to their merits, and count them Scythians in deed if not in name. What particularly excites our reverent admiration in the present case is the unparalleled loyalty of the two friends; in them we have a model from which every man may learn how he must share good and evil fortune with his friends, if he would enjoy the esteem of all good Scythians. The sufferings they endured with and for one another our ancestors recorded on a brazen pillar in the Oresteum; and they made it law, that the education of their children should begin with committing to memory all that is inscribed thereon. More easily shall a child forget his own father's name than be at fault in the achievements of Orestes and Pylades. Again, in the temple corridor are pictures by the artists of old, illustrating the story set forth on the pillar. Orestes is first shown on shipboard, with his friend at his side. Next, the ship has gone to pieces on the rocks; Orestes is captured and bound; already Iphigenia prepares the two victims for sacrifice. But on the opposite wall we see that Orestes has broken free; he slays Thoas and many a Scythian; and the last scene shows them sailing away, with Iphigenia and the Goddess; the Scythians clutch vainly at the

---

[57] See *Euxine* in Notes.

receding vessel; they cling to the rudder, they strive to clamber on board; at last, utterly baffled, they swim back to the shore, wounded or terrified. It is at this point in their conflict with the Scythians that the devotion of the friends is best illustrated:

the painter makes each of them disregard his own enemies, and ward off his friend's assailants, seeking to intercept the arrows before they can reach him, and counting lightly of death, if he can save his friend, and receive in his own person the wounds that are meant for the other. Such devotion, such loyal and loving partnership in danger, such true and steadfast affection, we held to be more than human; it indicated a spirit not to be found in common men. While the gale is prosperous, we all take it very much amiss if our friends will not share equally with us:

but let the wind shift ever so little, and we leave them to weather the storm by themselves. I must tell you that in Scythia no quality is more highly esteemed than this of friendship; there is nothing on which a Scythian prides himself so much as on sharing the toils and dangers of his friend; just as nothing is a greater reproach among us than treachery to a friend. We honour Orestes and Pylades, then, because they excelled in the Scythian virtue of loyalty, which we place above all others; and it is for this that we have bestowed on them the name of Coraci, which in our language means spirits of friendship.

Mne. Ah, Toxaris, so archery is not the only accomplishment of the Scythians, I find; they excel in rhetorical as well as in military skill. You have persuaded me already that you were right in deifying Orestes and Pylades, though I thought differently just now. I had no conception, either, what a painter you were. Your description of the pictures in the Oresteum was most vivid;—that battle-scene, and the way in which the two intercepted one another's wounds. Only I should never have thought that the Scythians would set such a high value on friendship:

they are such a wild, inhospitable race; I should have said they had more to do with anger and hatred and enmity than with friendship, even for their nearest relations, judging by what one is told; it is said, for instance, that they devour their fathers' corpses.

Tox. Well, which of the two is the more dutiful and pious in general, Greek or Scythian, we will not discuss just now:

but that we are more loyal friends than you, and that we treat friendship more seriously, is easily shown. Now please do not be angry with me, in the name of all your Gods:

but I am going to mention a few points I have observed during my stay in this country. I can see that you are all admirably well qualified to talk about friendship:

but when it comes to putting your words into practice, there is a considerable falling off; it is enough for you to have demonstrated what an excellent thing friendship is, and somehow or other, at the critical moment, you make off, and leave your fine words to look after themselves. Similarly, when your tragedians represent this subject on the stage, you are loud in your applause; the spectacle of one friend risking his life for another generally brings tears to your eyes:

but you are quite incapable of rendering any such signal services yourselves; once let your friends get into difficulties, and all those tragic reminiscences take wing like so many dreams; you are then the very image of the silent mask which the actor has thrown aside:

its mouth is open to its fullest extent, but not a syllable does it utter. It is the other way with us:

we are as much superior to you in the practice of friendship, as we are inferior in expounding the theory of it.

Now, what do you say to this proposal? let us leave out of the question all the cases of ancient friendship that either of us might enumerate (there you would have the advantage of me:

you could produce all the poets on your side, most credible of witnesses, with their Achilles and Patroclus, their Theseus and Pirithous, and others, all celebrated in the most charming verses); and instead let each of us advance a few instances of devotion that have occurred within his own experience, among our respective countrymen; these we will relate in detail, and whoever can show the best friendships is the winner, and announces his country as victorious. Mighty issues are at stake:

I for my part would rather be worsted in single combat, and lose my right hand, as the Scythian custom is, than yield to any man on the question of friendship, above all to a Greek; for am I not a Scythian?

Mne. I have got my work cut out for me, if I am to engage an old soldier like Toxaris, with a whole arsenal of keen words at his command. Well, I am not such a craven as to decline the challenge, when my country's honour is at stake. Could those two overcome the host of Scythians represented in the legend, and in the ancient pictures you have just described so impressively,— and shall Greece, her peoples and her cities, be condemned for want of one to plead her cause? Strange indeed, if that were so; I should deserve to lose not my hand like you, but my tongue. Well now, is the number of friendships to be limited, or does wealth of instances itself constitute one claim to superiority?

Tox. Oh no; number counts for nothing, that must be understood. We have the same number, and it is simply a question whether yours are better and more pointed than mine; if they are, of course, the wounds you inflict will be the more deadly, and I shall be the first to succumb.

Mne. Very well. Let us fix the number:

I say five each.

Tox. Five be it, and you begin. But you must be sworn first:

because the subject naturally lends itself to fictitious treatment; there is no checking anything. When you have sworn, it would be impious to doubt your word.

Mne. Very well, if you think it necessary. Have you any preference among our Gods? How would the God of Friendship meet the case?

Tox. Excellently; and when my turn comes, I will employ the national oath of the Scythians.

Mne. Zeus the God of Friendship be my witness, that all I shall now relate is derived either from my own experience, or from such careful inquiry as I was able to make of others; and is free from all imaginative additions of my own. I will begin with, the friendship of Agathocles and Dinias. The story is well known in Ionia. This Agathocles was a native of Samos, and lived not many years ago. Though his conduct showed him to be the best of friends, he was of no better family and in no better circumstances than the generality of the Samians. From boyhood he had been the friend of Dinias, the son of Lyson, an Ephesian. Dinias, it seems, was enormously wealthy, and as his wealth was newly acquired, it is not to be wondered at that he had plenty of acquaintances besides Agathocles; persons who were quite qualified to share his pleasures, and to be his boon-companions, but who were very far indeed from being friends. For some time Agathocles—little as he cared for such a life— played his convivial part with the rest, Dinias making no distinction between him and the parasites. Finally, however, he took to finding fault with his friend's conduct, and gave great offence:

his continual allusions to Dinias's ancestry, and his exhortations to him to husband the fortune which had cost his father such labour to acquire, seemed to his friend to be in indifferent taste. He gave up asking Agathocles to join in his revels, contented himself with the company of his parasites, and sought to elude his friend's observation. Well, the misguided youth was presently persuaded by his flatterers that he had made a conquest of Chariclea, the wife of Demonax, an eminent Ephesian, holding the highest office in that city. He was kept well supplied with billets-doux, half-faded flowers, bitten apples, and all the stock-in-trade of those intriguing dames whose business it is to fan an artificial passion that vanity has inspired. There is no more seductive bait to young men who value themselves on their personal attractions, than the belief that they have made an impression; they are sure to fall into the trap. Chariclea was a charming little woman, but sadly wanting in reserve:

any one might enjoy her favours, and on the easiest of terms; the most casual glance was sure to meet with encouragement; there was never any fear of a repulse from Chariclea. With more than professional skill, she could draw on a hesitating lover till his subjugation was complete:

then, when she was sure of him, she had a variety of devices for inflaming his passion:

she could storm, and she could flatter; and flattery would be succeeded by contempt, or by a feigned preference for his rival;—in short, her resources were infinite; she was armed against her lovers at every point. This was the lady whom Dinias's parasites now associated with them; they played their subordinate part well, and between them fairly hustled the boy into a passion for Chariclea. Such a finished mistress of the art of perdition, who had ruined plenty of victims before, and acted love-scenes and swallowed fine fortunes without number, was not likely to let this simple inexperienced youth out of her clutches:

she struck her talons into him on every side, and secured her quarry so effectually, that she was involved in his destruction,—to say nothing of the miseries of the hapless victim. She got to work at once with the billets-doux. Her maid was for ever coming with news of tears and sleepless nights:

'her poor mistress was ready to hang herself for love.' The ingenuous youth was at length driven to conclude that his attractions were too much for the ladies of Ephesus; he yielded to the girl's entreaties, and waited upon her mistress. The rest, of course, was easy. How was he to resist this pretty woman, with her captivating manners, her well-timed tears, her parenthetic sighs? Lingering farewells, joyful welcomes, judicious airs and graces, song and lyre,— all were brought to bear upon him. Dinias was soon a lost man, over head and ears in love; and Chariclea prepared to give the finishing stroke. She informed him that he was about to become a father, which was enough in itself to inflame the amorous simpleton; and she discontinued her visits to him; her husband, she said, had discovered her passion, and was watching her. This was altogether too much for Dinias:

he was inconsolable; wept, sent messages by his parasites, flung his arms about her statue—a marble one which he had had made—, shrieked forth her name in loud lamentation, and finally threw himself down upon the ground and rolled about in a positive frenzy. Her apples and her flowers drew forth presents which were on quite another scale of munificence:

houses and farms, servants, exquisite fabrics, and gold to any extent. To make a long story short, the house of Lyson, which had the reputation of being the wealthiest in Ionia, was quite cleared out. No sooner was this the case, than Chariclea abandoned Dinias, and went off in pursuit of a certain golden youth of Crete, irresistible as he, and not less gullible. Deserted alike by her and by his parasites (who followed the chase of the fortunate Cretan), Dinias presented himself before Agathocles, who had long been aware of his friend's situation. He swallowed his first feelings of embarrassment, and made a clean breast of it all:

his love, his ruin, his mistress's disdain, his Cretan rival; and ended by protesting that without Chariclea he could not live. Agathocles did not think it necessary to remind Dinias just then how he alone had been excluded from his friendship, and how parasites had been preferred to him:

instead, he went off and sold his family residence in Samos—the only property he possessed—and brought him the proceeds, 750 pounds. Dinias had no sooner received the money, than it became evident that he had somehow recovered his good looks, in the opinion of Chariclea:

once more the maid-servant and the notes, with reproaches for his long neglect; once more, too, the throng of parasites; they saw that there were still pickings to be had. Dinias arrived at her house, by agreement, at about bedtime, and was already inside, when Demonax—whether he had an understanding with his wife in the matter, as some say, or had got his information independently—sprang out from concealment, gave orders to his servants to make the door fast and to secure Dinias, and then drew his sword, breathing fire and flagellation against the paramour. Dinias, realizing his danger, caught up a heavy bar that lay near, and dispatched Demonax with a blow on the temple; then, turning to Chariclea, he dealt blow after blow with the same weapon, and finally plunged her husband's sword into her body. The domestics stood by, dumb with amazement and terror; and when at length they attempted to seize him, he rushed at them with the sword, put them to flight, and slipped away from the fatal scene. The rest of that night he and Agathocles spent at the latter's house, pondering on the deed and its probable consequences. The news soon spread, and in the morning officers came to arrest Dinias. He made no attempt to deny the murder, and was conducted into the presence of the then Prefect of Asia, who sent him up to the Emperor. He presently returned, under sentence of perpetual banishment to Gyarus, one of the Cyclades. All this time, Agathocles had never left his side:

with unfaltering devotion, he accompanied him to Italy, and was the only friend who stood by him in his trial. And now even in his banishment he would not desert him, but condemned himself to share the sentence; and when the necessaries of life failed them, he hired himself out as a diver in the purple-fishery, and with the proceeds of his industry supported Dinias and tended him in his sickness till the end. Even when all was over, he would not return to his own home, but remained on the island, thinking it shame even in death to desert his friend. There you have the history of a Greek friendship, and one of recent date; I think it can scarcely be as much as five years ago that Agathocles died on Gyarus.

Tox. I wish I were at liberty to doubt the truth of your story:

but alas! you speak under oath. Your Agathocles is a truly Scythian friend; I only hope there are no more of the same kind to come.

Mne. See what you think of the next—Euthydicus of Chalcidice. I heard his story from Simylus, a shipmaster of Megara, who vowed that he had been an eyewitness of what he related. He set sail from Italy about the setting of the Pleiads, bound for Athens, with a miscellaneous shipload of passengers, among whom were Euthydicus and his comrade Damon, also of Chalcidice. They were of about the same age. Euthydicus was a powerful man, in robust health; Damon was pale and weakly, and looked as if he were just recovering from a long illness. They had a good voyage as far as Sicily:

but they had no sooner passed through the Straits into the Ionian Sea, than a tremendous storm overtook them. I need not detain you with descriptions of mountainous billows and whirlwinds and hail and the other adjuncts of a storm:

suffice it to say, that they were compelled to take in all sail, and trail cables after them to break the force of the waves, and in this way made Zacynthus by about midnight. At this point Damon, being seasick, as was natural in such a heavy sea, was leaning over the side, when (as I suppose) an unusually violent lurch of the vessel in his direction, combining with the rush of water across the deck, hurled him headlong into the sea. The poor wretch was not even naked, or he might have had a chance of swimming:

it was all he could do to keep himself above water, and get out a cry for help. Euthydicus was lying in his berth undressed. He heard the cry, flung himself into the sea, and succeeded in overtaking the exhausted Damon; and a powerful moonlight enabled those on deck to see him swimming at his side for a considerable distance, and supporting him. 'We all felt for them,' said Simylus, 'and longed to give them some assistance, but the gale was too much for us:

we did, however, throw out a number of corks and spars on the chance of their getting hold of some of them, and being carried to shore; and finally we threw over the gangway, which was of some size.'—Now only think:

could any man give a surer proof of affection, than by throwing himself into a furious sea like that to share the death of his friend? Picture to yourself the surging billows, the roar of crashing waters, the hissing foam, the darkness, the hopeless prospect:

look at Damon,—he is at his last gasp, he barely keeps himself up, he holds out his hands imploringly to his friend:

and lastly look at Euthydicus, as he leaps into the water, and swims by his side, with only one thought in his mind,—Damon must not be the first to perish;—and you will see that Euthydicus too was no bad friend.

Tox. I tremble for their fate:

were they drowned, or did some miraculous providence deliver them?

Mne. Oh, they were saved all right; and they are in Athens at this day, both of them, studying philosophy. Simylus's story closes with the events of the night:

Damon has fallen overboard, Euthydicus has jumped in to his rescue, and the pair are left swimming about till they are lost in the darkness. Euthydicus himself tells the rest. It seems that first they came across some pieces of cork, which helped to support them; and they managed with much ado to keep afloat, till about dawn they saw the gangway, swam up to it, clambered on, and were carried to Zacynthus without further trouble. These, I think, are passable instances of friendship; and my third is no way inferior to them, as you shall hear.

Eudamidas of Corinth, though he was himself in very narrow circumstances, had two friends who were well-to-do, Aretaeus his fellow townsman, and Charixenus of Sicyon. When Eudamidas died, he left a will behind him which I dare say would excite most people's ridicule:

404

but what the generous Toxaris, with his respect for friendship and his ambition to secure its highest honours for his country, may think of the matter, is another question. The terms of the will—but first I should explain that Eudamidas left behind him an aged mother and a daughter of marriageable years;—the will, then, was as follows:

To Aretaeus I bequeath my mother, to tend and to cherish in her old age:

and to Charixenus my daughter, to give in marriage with such dowry as his circumstances will admit of:

and should anything befall either of the legatees, then let his portion pass to the survivor. The reading of this will caused some merriment among the hearers, who knew of Eudamidas's poverty, but did not know anything of the friendship existing between him and his heirs. They went off much tickled at the handsome legacy that Aretaeus and Charixenus (lucky dogs!) had come in for:

'Eudamidas,' as they expressed it, 'was apparently to have a death-interest in the property of the legatees.' However, the latter had no sooner heard the will read, than they proceeded to execute the testator's intentions. Charixenus only survived Eudamidas by five days:

but Aretaeus, most generous of heirs, accepted the double bequest, is supporting the aged mother at this day, and has only lately given the daughter in marriage, allowing to her and to his own daughter portions of 500 pounds each, out of his whole property of 1,250 pounds; the two marriages were arranged to take place on the same day. What do you think of him, Toxaris? This is something like friendship, is it not,—to accept such a bequest as this, and to show such respect for a friend's last wishes? May we pass this as one of my five?

Tox. Excellent as was the behaviour of Aretaeus, I admire still more Eudamidas's confidence in his friends. It shows that he would have done as much for them; even if nothing had been said about it in their wills, he would have been the first to come forward and claim the inheritance as natural heir.

Mne. Very true. And now I come to Number Four—Zenothemis of Massilia, son of Charmoleos. He was pointed out to me when I was in Italy on public business:

a fine, handsome man, and to all appearance well off. But by his side (he was just driving away on a journey) sat his wife, a woman of most repulsive appearance; all her right side was withered; she had lost one eye; in short, she was a positive fright. I expressed my surprise that a man in the prime of manly beauty should endure to have such a woman seated by him. My informant, who was a Massiliot himself, and knew how the marriage had come about, gave me all the particulars. 'The father of this unsightly woman,' he said, 'was Menecrates; and he and Zenothemis were friends in days when both were men of wealth and rank. The property of Menecrates, however, was afterwards confiscated by the Six Hundred, and he himself disfranchised, on the ground

405

that he had proposed an unconstitutional measure; this being the regular penalty in Massilia for such offences. The sentence was in itself a heavy blow to Menecrates, and it was aggravated by the sudden change from wealth to poverty and from honour to dishonour. But most of all he was troubled about this daughter:

she was now eighteen years old, and it was time that he found her a husband; yet with her unfortunate appearance it was not probable that any one, however poor or obscure, would have taken her, even with all the wealth her father had possessed previous to his sentence; it was said, too, that she was subject to fits at every increase of the moon. He was bewailing his hard lot to Zenothemis, when the latter interrupted him:

"Menecrates," he said, "be sure that you shall want for nothing, and that your daughter shall find a match suitable to her rank." So saying, he took his friend by the hand, brought him into his house, assigned him a share of his great wealth, and ordered a banquet to be prepared, at which he entertained Menecrates and his friends, giving the former to understand that he had prevailed upon one of his acquaintance to marry the girl. When dinner was over, and libations had been poured to the Gods, Zenothemis filled a goblet and passed it to Menecrates:

"Accept," he cried, "from your son-in-law the cup of friendship. This day I wed your daughter Cydimache. The dowry I have had long since; 60,000 pounds was the sum." *"You?"* exclaimed Menecrates; "Heaven forbid that I should be so mad as to suffer you, in the pride of your youth, to be yoked to this unfortunate girl!" But even while he spoke, Zenothemis was conducting his bride to the marriage-chamber, and presently returned to announce that she was his wedded wife. Since that day, he has lived with her on the most affectionate terms; and you see for yourself that he takes her about with him wherever he goes. As to his being ashamed of his wife, one would rather suppose that he was proud of her; and his conduct in this respect shows how lightly he esteems beauty and wealth and reputation, in comparison with friendship and his friend; for Menecrates is not less his friend because the Six Hundred have condemned him. To be sure, Fortune has already given him one compensation:

his ugly wife has borne him a most beautiful child. Only a few days ago, he carried his child into the Senate-house, crowned with an olive-wreath, and dressed in black, to excite the pity of the senators on his grandfather's behalf:

the babe smiled upon them, and clapped his little hands together, which so moved the senators that they repealed the sentence against Menecrates, who is now reinstated in his rights, thanks to the pleadings of his tiny advocate.'

Such was the Massiliot's story. As you see, it was no slight service that Zenothemis rendered to his friend; I fancy there are not many Scythians who would do the same; they are said to be very nice even in their selection of concubines.

I have still one friend to produce, and I think none is more worthy of remembrance than Demetrius of Sunium. He and Antiphilus of the deme of Alopece had been playmates in their childhood, and grown up side by side. They subsequently took ship for Egypt, and carried on their studies there together, Demetrius practising the Cynic philosophy under the famous sophist of Rhodes, while Antiphilus, it seems, was to be a doctor. Well, on one occasion Demetrius had gone up country to see the Pyramids, and the statue of Memnon. He had heard it said that the Pyramids in spite of their great height cast no shadow, and that a sound proceeded from the statue at sunrise:

all this he wished to see and hear for himself, and he had now been away up the Nile six months. During his absence, Antiphilus, who had remained behind (not liking the idea of the heat and the long journey), became involved in troubles which required all the assistance that faithful friendship could have rendered. He had a Syrian slave, whose name was also Syrus. This man had made common cause with a number of temple-robbers, had forced his way with them into the temple of Anubis, and robbed the God of a pair of golden cups, a caduceus, also of gold, some silver images of Cynocephali and other treasures; all of which the rest entrusted to Syrus's charge. Later on they were caught trying to dispose of some of their booty, and were taken up; and being put on the rack, immediately confessed the whole truth. They were accordingly conducted to Antiphilus's house, where they produced the stolen treasure from a dark corner under a bed. Syrus was immediately arrested, and his master Antiphilus with him:

the latter being dragged away from the very presence of his teacher during lecture- time. There was none to help him:

his former acquaintances turned their backs on the desecrator of Anubis's temple, and made it a matter of conscience that they had ever sat at the same table with him. As to his other two servants, they got together all his belongings, and ran off.

Antiphilus had now lain long in captivity. He was looked upon as the vilest criminal of all in the prison; and the native gaoler, a superstitious man, considered that he was avenging the God's wrongs and securing his favour by harsh treatment of Antiphilus. His attempts to clear himself of the charge of sacrilege only served to set him in the light of a hardened offender, and materially to increase the detestation in which he was held. His health was beginning to give way under the strain, and no wonder:

his bed was the bare ground, and all night he was unable so much as to stretch his legs, which were then secured in the stocks; in the daytime, the collar and one manacle sufficed, but at night he had to submit to being bound hand and foot. The stench, too, and the closeness of the dungeon, in which so many prisoners were huddled together gasping for breath, and the difficulty of getting any sleep, owing to the clanking of chains,—all combined to make the situation intolerable to one who was quite unaccustomed to endure such hardships. At last, when Antiphilus had given up all hope, and refused to take any nourishment, Demetrius arrived, ignorant of all that had passed in his absence. He no sooner learnt the truth, than he flew to the prison. It was now evening, and he was refused admittance, the gaoler having long since bolted the door and retired to rest, leaving his slaves to keep guard. Morning came, and after many entreaties he was allowed to enter. Suffering had altered Antiphilus beyond recognition, and for long Demetrius sought him in vain:

like men who seek their slain relatives on the day after a battle, when death has already changed them, he went from prisoner to prisoner, examining each in turn; and had he not called on Antiphilus by name, it would have been long before he could have recognized him, so great was the change that misery had wrought. Antiphilus heard the voice, and uttered a cry; then, as his friend approached, he brushed the dry matted hair from his face, and revealed his identity. At the unexpected sight of one another, the two friends instantly fell down in a swoon. But presently Demetrius recovered, and raised Antiphilus from the ground:

he obtained from him an exact account of all that had happened, and bade him be of good cheer; then, tearing his cloak in two, he threw one half over himself, and gave the other to his friend, first ripping off the squalid, threadbare rags in which he was clothed. From that hour, Demetrius was unfailing in his attendance. From early morning till noon, he hired himself out as a porter to the merchants in the harbour, and thus made a considerable wage. Returning to the prison when his work was over, he would give a part of his earnings to the gaoler, thus securing his obsequious goodwill, and the rest sufficed him amply for supplying his friend's needs. For the remainder of the day, he would stay by Antiphilus, administering consolation to him; and at nightfall made himself a litter of leaves near the prison door, and there took his rest. So things went on for some time, Demetrius having free entrance to the prison, and Antiphilus's misery being much alleviated thereby. But presently a certain robber died in the gaol, apparently from the effects of poison; a strict watch was kept, and admittance was refused to all applicants alike, to the great distress of Demetrius, who could think of no other means of obtaining access to his friend than by going to the Prefect and professing complicity in the temple robbery. As the result of this declaration, he was immediately led off to prison, and with great difficulty prevailed upon the gaoler after many entreaties to place him next to Antiphilus, and under the same collar. It was now that his devotion to his friend appeared in the strongest light. Ill though he was himself, he thought nothing of his own sufferings:

his only care was to lighten the affliction of his friend, and to procure him as much rest as possible; and the companionship in misery certainly lightened their load. Finally an event happened which brought their misfortunes to an end. One of the prisoners had somehow got hold of a file. He took a number of the others into his confidence, filed through the chain which held them together by means of their collars, and set all at liberty. The guards being few were easily slain; and the prisoners burst out of the gaol *en masse*. They then scattered, and each took refuge for the moment where he could, most of them being subsequently recaptured. Demetrius and Antiphilus, however, remained in the prison, and even secured Syrus when he was about to escape. The next morning the Prefect, hearing what had happened, sent men in pursuit of the other prisoners, and Demetrius and Antiphilus, being summoned to his presence, were released from their fetters, and commended for not having run away like the rest. The friends, however, declined to accept their dismissal on such terms:

Demetrius protested loudly against the injustice which would be done to them if they were to pass for criminals, who owed their discharge to mercy, or to their discretion in not having run away. They insisted that the judge should examine carefully into the facts of their case. He at length did so; and was convinced of their innocence, did justice to their characters, and, with a warm commendation of Demetrius's conduct, dismissed them; but not before he had expressed his regret at the unjust sentence under which they had suffered, and made each of them a present from his own purse,—400 pounds to Antiphilus, and twice that sum to Demetrius. Antiphilus is still in Egypt at the present time, but Demetrius went off to India to visit the Brahmins, leaving his 800 pounds with Antiphilus. He could now, he said, leave his friend with a clear conscience. His own wants were simple, and as long as they continued so, he had no need of money:

on the other hand, Antiphilus, in his present easy circumstances, had as little need of a friend.

See, Toxaris, what a Greek friend can do! You were so hard just now upon our rhetorical vanity, that I forbear to give you the admirable pleadings of Demetrius in court:

not one word did he say in his own behalf; all was for Antiphilus; he wept and implored, and sought to take all the guilt upon himself; till at last the confession of Syrus under torture cleared them both. These loyal friends whose stories I have related were the first that occurred to my memory; where I have given five instances, I might have given fifty. And now I am silent:

it is your turn to speak. I need not tell you to make the most of your Scythians, and bring them out triumphant if you can:

you will do that for your own sake, if you set any value on that right hand of yours. Quit you, then, like a man. You would look foolish if, after your truly professional panegyric of Orestes and Pylades, your art were to fail you in your country's need.

Tox. I honour you for your disinterested encouragement:

apparently you are under no uneasiness as to the loss of your tongue, in the event of my winning. Well, I will begin:

and you will get no flowery language from me; it is not our Scythian way, especially when the deeds we handle dwarf description. Be prepared for something very different from the subjects of your own eulogy:

here will be no marryings of ugly and dowerless women, no five-hundred-pound-portionings of friends' daughters, nor even surrenderings of one's person to gaolers, with the certain prospect of a speedy release. These are very cheap manifestations; the lofty, the heroic, is altogether wanting. I have to speak of blood and war and death for friendship's sake; you will learn that all you have related is child's-play, when compared with the deeds of the Scythians. After all, it is natural enough:

what should you do but admire these trifles? Living in the midst of peace, you have no scope for the exhibition of an exalted friendship, just as in a calm we cannot tell a good pilot from a bad; we must wait till a storm comes; then we know. We, on the contrary, live in a state of perpetual warfare, now invading, now receding, now contending for pasturage or booty. There is the true sphere of friendship; and there is the reason that its ties among us are drawn so close; friendship we hold to be the one invincible, irresistible weapon.

But before I begin, I should like to describe to you our manner of making friends. Friendships are not formed with us, as with you, over the wine-cups, nor are they determined by considerations of age or neighbourhood. We wait till we see a brave man, capable of valiant deeds, and to him we all turn our attention. Friendship with us is like courtship with you:

rather than fail of our object, and undergo the disgrace of a rejection, we are content to urge our suit patiently, and to give our constant attendance. At length a friend is accepted, and the engagement is concluded with our most solemn oath:

'to live together and if need be to die for one another.' That vow is faithfully kept:

once let the friends draw blood from their fingers into a cup, dip the points of their swords therein, and drink of that draught together, and from that moment nothing can part them. Such a treaty of friendship may include three persons, but no more:

a man of many friends we consider to be no better than a woman who is at the service of every lover; we feel no further security in a friendship that is divided between so many objects.

I will commence with the recent story of Dandamis. In our conflict with the Sauromatae, Dandamis's friend Amizoces had been taken captive,—oh, but first I must take the Scythian oath, as we agreed at the start. I swear by Wind and Scimetar that I will speak nothing but truth of the Scythian friendships.

Mne. You need not have troubled to swear, as far as I am concerned. However, you showed judgement in not swearing by a God.

Tox. What can you mean? Wind and Scimetar not Gods? Are you now to learn that life and death are the highest considerations among mankind? When we swear by Wind and Scimetar, we do so because Wind is the cause of life and Scimetar of death.

Mne. On that principle, you get a good many other Gods besides Scimetar, and as good as he:

there is Arrow, and Spear, and Hemlock, and Halter, and so on. Death is a God who assumes many shapes; numberless are the roads that lead into his presence.

Tox. Now you are just trying to spoil my story with these quibbling objections. I gave *you* a fair hearing.

Mne. You are quite right, Toxaris; it shall not occur again, be easy on that score. I'll be so quiet, you would never know I was here at all.

Tox. Four days after Dandamis and Amizoces had shared the cup of blood, the Sauromatae invaded our territory with 10,000 horse, their infantry being estimated at three times that number. The invasion was unexpected, and we were completely routed; many of our warriors were slain, and the rest taken captive, with the exception of a few who managed to swim across to the opposite bank of the river, on which half our host was encamped, with a part of the waggons. The reason of this arrangement I do not know; but our leaders had seen good to divide our camp between the two banks of the Tanais. The enemy at once set to work to secure their booty and collect the captives; they plundered the camp, and took possession of the waggons, most of them with their occupants; and we had the mortification of seeing our wives and concubines mishandled before our very eyes. Amizoces was among the prisoners, and while he was being dragged along he called upon his friend by name, to witness his captivity and to remember the cup of blood. Dandamis heard him, and without a moment's delay plunged into the river in the sight of all, and swam across to the enemy. The Sauromatae rushed upon him, and were about to transfix him with their raised javelins, when he raised the cry of Zirin. The man who pronounces that word is safe from their weapons:

it indicates that he is the bearer of ransom, and he is received accordingly. Being conducted into the presence of their chief, he demanded the liberation of Amizoces, and was told in reply, that his friend would only be released upon payment of a high ransom. 'All that was once mine,' said Dandamis, 'has become your booty:

but if one who is stripped of all can have anything yet left to give, it is at your disposal. Name your terms:

take me, if you will, in his place, and use me as seems best to you.' 'To detain the person of one who comes with the Zirin on his lips is out of the question:

but you may take back your friend on paying me a part of your possessions.' 'What will you have?' asked Dandamis. 'Your eyes,' was the reply. Dandamis submitted:

his eyes were plucked out, and the Sauromatae had their ransom. He returned leaning on his friend, and they swam across together, and reached us in safety.

There was comfort for all of us in this act of Dandamis. Our defeat, it seemed, was no defeat, after all:

our most precious possessions had escaped the hands of our enemies; loyal friendship, noble resolution, these were still our own. On the Sauromatae it had the contrary effect:

they did not at all like the idea of engaging with such determined adversaries on equal terms; gaining an advantage of them by means of a surprise was quite another matter. The end of it was, that when night came on they left behind the greater part of the herds, burnt the waggons, and beat a hasty retreat. As for Amizoces, he could not endure to see, when Dandamis was blind:

he blinded himself, and the two now sit at home, supported in all honour at the public expense.

Can you match that, friend? I think not, though I should give you ten new chances on the top of your five; ay, and release you from your oath, too, for that matter, leaving you free to exaggerate as much as you choose. Besides, I have given you just the bare facts. Now, if *you* had been telling Dandamis's story, what embroidery we should have had! The supplications of Dandamis, the blinding process, his remarks on the occasion, the circumstances of his return, the effusive greetings of the Scythians, and all the *ad captandum* artifices that you Greeks understand so well.

• And now let me introduce you to another friend, not inferior to Dandamis,—a cousin of Amizoces, Belitta by name. Belitta was once hunting with his friend Basthes, when the latter was torn from his horse by a lion. Already the brute had fallen upon him, and was clutching him by the throat and beginning to tear him to pieces, when Belitta, leaping to earth, rushed upon him from behind, and attempted to drag him off, and to turn his rage upon himself, thrusting his hands into the brute's mouth, and doing his best to extricate Basthes from those teeth. He succeeded at last:

the lion, abandoning his half dead prey, turned upon Belitta, grappled with him, and slew him; but not before Belitta had plunged a scimetar into his breast. Thus all three died together; and we buried them, the two friends in one grave, the lion in another close by.

For my third instance, I shall give you the friendship of Macentes, Lonchates, and Arsacomas. This Arsacomas had been on a visit to Leucanor, king of Bosphorus, in connexion with the tribute annually paid to us by that country, which tribute was then three months overdue; and while there he had fallen in love with Mazaea, the king's daughter. Mazaea was an extremely fine woman, and Arsacomas, seeing her at the king's table, had been much smitten with her charms. The question of the tribute was at length settled, Arsacomas had his answer, and the king was now entertaining him prior to his departure. It is the custom for suitors in that country to make their proposals at table, stating at the same time their qualifications. Now in the present case there were a number of suitors—kings and sons of kings, among whom were Tigrapates the prince of the Lazi and Adyrmachus the chief of the Machlyans. What each suitor has to do is, first to declare his intentions, and quietly take his seat at table with the rest; then, when dinner is over, he calls for a goblet, pours libation upon the table, and makes his proposal for the lady's hand, saying whatever he can for himself in the way of birth, wealth, and dominion. Many suitors, then, had already preferred their request in due form, enumerating their realms and possessions, when at last Arsacomas called for a cup. He did not make a libation, because it is not the Scythian custom to do so; we should consider it an insult to Heaven to pour away good wine:

instead, he drank it all off at one draught, and then addressed the king. 'Sire,' he said, 'give *me* your daughter Mazaea to wife:

if wealth and possessions count for anything, I am a fitter husband for her than these.' Leucanor was surprised:

he knew that Arsacomas was but a poor commoner among the Scythians. 'What herds, what waggons have you, Arsacomas?' he asked; 'these are the wealth of your people.' 'Waggons and herds I have none,' was Arsacomas's reply:

'but I have two excellent friends, whose like you will not find in all Scythia.' His answer only excited ridicule; it was attributed to drunkenness, and no further notice was taken of him. Adyrmachus was preferred to the other suitors, and was to take his bride away the next morning to his Maeotian home. Arsacomas on his return informed his friends of the slight that had been put upon him by the king, and of the ridicule to which he had been subjected on account of his supposed poverty. 'And yet,' he added, 'I told him of my wealth:

told him that I had the friendship of Lonchates and Macentes, a more precious and more lasting possession than his kingdom of Bosphorus. But he made light of it; he jeered at us; and gave his daughter to Adyrmachus the Machlyan, because he had ten golden cups, and eighty waggons of four seats, and a number of sheep and oxen. It seems that herds and lumbering waggons and superfluous beakers are to count for more than brave men. My friends, I am doubly wounded:

I love Mazaea, and I cannot forget the humiliation which I have suffered before so many witnesses, and in which you are both equally involved. Ever since we were united in friendship, are we not one flesh? are not our joys and our sorrows the same? If this be so, each of us has his share in this disgrace.' 'Not only so,' rejoined Lonchates; 'each of us labours under the whole ignominy of the affront.' 'And what is to be our course?' asked Macentes. 'We will divide the work,' replied the other. 'I for my part undertake to present Arsacomas with the head of Leucanor:

you must bring him his bride.' 'I agree. And you, Arsacomas, can stay at home; and as we are likely to want an army before we have done, you must be getting together horses and arms, and raise what men you can, A man like you will have no difficulty in getting plenty of people to join him, and there are all our relations; besides, you can sit on the ox-hide.' This being settled, Lonchates set off just as he was for the Bosphorus, and Macentes for Machlyene, each on horseback; while Arsacomas remained behind, consulting with his acquaintance, raising forces from among the relations of the three, and, finally, taking his seat on the ox-hide.

Our custom of the hide is as follows. When a man has been injured by another, and desires vengeance, but feels that he is no match for his opponent, he sacrifices an ox, cuts up the flesh and cooks it, and spreads out the hide upon the ground. On this hide he takes his seat, holding his hands behind him, so as to suggest that his arms are tied in that position, this being the natural attitude of a suppliant among us. Meanwhile, the flesh of the ox has been laid out; and the man's relations and any others who feel so disposed come up and take a portion thereof, and, setting their right foot on the hide, promise whatever assistance is in their power:

one will engage to furnish and maintain five horsemen, another ten, a third some larger number; while others, according to their ability, promise heavy or light-armed infantry, and the poorest, who have nothing else to give, offer their own personal services. The number of persons assembled on the hide is sometimes very considerable; nor could any troops be more reliable or more invincible than those which are collected in this manner, being as they are under a vow; for the act of stepping on to the hide constitutes an oath. By this means, then, Arsacomas raised something like 5,000 cavalry and 20,000 heavy and light armed.

Meanwhile, Lonchates arrived unknown in Bosphorus, and presented himself co the king, who was occupied at the moment in affairs of state. 'I come,' he said, 'on public business from Scythia:

but I have also a private communication of high import to make to your Majesty.' The king bade him proceed. 'As to my public errand, it is the old story:

we protest against your herdsmen's crossing the Rocks and encroaching on the plains. And with reference to the robbers of whom you complain, I am instructed to say that our government is not responsible for their incursions, which are the work of private individuals, actuated merely by the love of booty; accordingly, you are at liberty to punish as many of them as you can secure, And now for my own news. You will shortly be invaded by a large host under Arsacomas the son of Mariantas, who was lately at your court as an ambassador. I suppose the cause of his resentment is your refusing him your daughter's hand. He has now been on the ox-hide for seven days, and has got together a considerable force.' 'I had heard,' exclaimed Leucanor, 'that an army was being raised on the hide:

but who was raising it, and what was its destination, I had no idea.' 'You know now,' said Lonchates. 'Arsacomas is a personal enemy of mine:

the superior esteem in which I am held, and the preference shown for me by our elders, are things which he cannot forgive. Now promise me your other daughter Barcetis:

apart from my present services, I shall be no discreditable son-in-law:

promise me this, and in no long time I will return bringing you the head of Arsacomas.' 'I promise,' cried the king, in great perturbation; for he realized the provocation he had given to Arsacomas, and had a wholesome respect for the Scythians at all times. 'Swear,' insisted Lonchates, 'that you will not go back from your promise.' The king was already raising up his hand to Heaven, when the other interrupted him. 'Wait!' he exclaimed; 'not here! these people must not know what is the subject of our oath. Let us go into the temple of Ares yonder, and swear with closed doors, where none may hear. If Arsacomas should get wind of this, I am likely to be offered up as a preliminary sacrifice; he has a good number of men already.' 'To the temple, then, let us go,' said the king; and he ordered the guards to remain aloof, and forbade any one to approach the temple unless summoned by him. As soon as they were inside, and the guards had withdrawn, Lonchates drew his sword, and putting his left hand on the king's mouth to prevent his crying out, plunged it into his breast; then, cutting off his head, he went out from the temple carrying it under his cloak; affecting all the time to be speaking to the king, and promising that he would not be long, as if the king had sent him on some errand. He thus succeeded in reaching the place where he had left his horse tethered, leapt on to his back, and rode off into Scythia. There was no pursuit:

the people of Bosphorus took some time to discover what had happened; and then they were occupied with disputes as to the succession. Thus Lonchates fulfilled his promise, and handed the head of Leucanor to Arsacomas.

The news of this reached Macentes while he was on his way to Machlyene, and on his arrival there he was the first to announce the king's death. 'You, Adyrmachus,' he added, 'are his son-in-law, and are now summoned to the throne. Ride on in advance, and establish your claim while all is still unsettled. Your bride can follow with the waggons; the presence of Leucanor's daughter will be of assistance to you in securing the support of the Bosphorans. I myself am an Alanian, and am related to this lady by the mother's side:

Leucanor's wife, Mastira, was of my family. I now come to you from Mastira's brothers in Alania:

they would have you make the best of your way to Bosphorus at once, or you will find your crown on the head of Eubiotus, Leucanor's bastard brother, who is a friend to Scythia, and detested by the Alanians.' In language and dress, Macentes resembled an Alanian; for in these respects there is no difference between Scythians and Alanians, except that the Alanians do not wear such long hair as we do. Macentes had completed the resemblance by cropping his hair to the right shortness, and was thus enabled to pass for a kinsman of Mastira and Mazaea. 'And now, Adyrmachus,' he concluded, 'I am ready to go with you to Bosphorus; or, if you prefer it, I will escort your bride.' 'If you will do the latter,' replied Adyrmachus, 'I shall be particularly obliged, since you are

Mazaea's kinsman. If you go with us, it is but one horseman more; whereas no one could be such a suitable escort for my wife.' And so it was settled:

Adyrmachus rode off, and left Mazaea, who was still a maid, in the care of Macentes. During the day, Macentes accompanied Mazaea in the waggon:

but at nightfall he placed her on horseback (he had taken care that there should be a horseman in attendance), and, mounting behind her, abandoned his former course along the Maeotian Lake, and struck off into the interior, keeping the Mitraean Mountains on his right. He allowed Mazaea some time for rest, and completed the whole journey from Machlyene to Scythia on the third day; his horse stood still for a few moments after arrival, and then dropped down dead. 'Behold,' said Macentes, presenting Mazaea to Arsacomas, 'behold your promised bride.' Arsacomas, amazed at so unexpected a sight, was beginning to express his gratitude:

but Macentes bade him hold his peace. 'You speak,' he exclaimed, 'as if you and I were different persons, when you thank me for what I have done. It is as if my left hand should say to my right:

Thank you for tending my wound; thank you for your generous sympathy with my pain. That would be no more absurd than for us—who have long been united, and have become (so far as such a thing may be) one flesh—to make such ado because one part of us has done its duty by the whole; the limb is but serving its own interest in promoting the welfare of the body.' And that was how Macentes received his friend's thanks.

Adyrmachus, on hearing of the trick that had been played upon him, did not pursue his journey to Bosphorus; indeed, Eubiotus was already on the throne, having been summoned thither from his home in Sarmatia. He therefore returned to his own country, collected a large army, and marched across the mountains into Scythia. He was presently followed by Eubiotus himself, at the head of a miscellaneous army of Greeks, together with 20,000 each of his Alanian and Sarmatian allies. The two joined forces, and the result was an army of 90,000 men, one third of whom were mounted bowmen. We Scythians (I say *we*, because I myself took part in this enterprise, and was maintaining a hundred horse on the hide)—we Scythians then, numbering in all not much less than 30,000 men, including cavalry, awaited their onset, under the command of Arsacomas. As soon as we saw them approaching, we too advanced, sending on our cavalry ahead. After a long and obstinate engagement, our lines were broken, and we began to give ground; and finally our whole army was cut clean in two. One half had not suffered a decisive defeat; with these it was rather a retreat than a flight, nor did the Alanians venture to follow up their advantage for any distance. But the other and smaller division was completely surrounded by the Alanians and Machlyans, and was being shot down on every side by the copious discharge of arrows and javelins; the position became intolerable, and most of our men were beginning to throw down their arms. In this latter division were Lonchates and Macentes. They had borne the brunt of the attack, and both were wounded:

416

Lonchates had a spear-thrust in his thigh, and Macentes, besides a cut on the head from an axe, had had his shoulder damaged by a pike. Arsacomas, seeing their condition (he was with us in the other division), could not endure the thought of turning his back on his friends:

plunging the spurs into his horse, and raising a shout, he rode through the midst of the enemy, with his scimetar raised on high. The Machlyans were unable to withstand the fury of his onset; their ranks divided, and made way for him to pass. Having rescued his friends from their danger, he rallied the rest of the troops; and charging upon Adyrmachus brought down the scimetar on his neck, and cleft him in two as far as the waist. Adyrmachus once slain, the whole of the Machlyans and Alanians soon scattered, and the Greeks followed their example. Thus did we turn defeat into victory; and had not night come to interrupt us, we should have pursued the fugitives for a considerable distance, slaying as we went. The next day came messengers from the enemy suing for reconciliation, the Bosphorans undertaking to double their tribute, and the Machlyans to leave hostages; whilst the Alanians promised to expiate their guilt by reducing the Sindians to submission, that tribe having been for some time in revolt against us. These terms we accepted, at the instance of Arsacomas and Lonchates, who conducted the negotiations and concluded the peace.

Such, Mnesippus, are the deeds that Scythians will do for friendship's sake.

Mne. Truly deeds of high emprise; quite a legendary look about them. With Wind's and Scimetar's good leave, I think a man might be excused for doubting their truth.

Tox. Now, honestly, Mnesippus, does not that doubt look a little like envy? However, doubt if you will:

that shall not deter me from relating other Scythian exploits of the same kind which have happened within my experience.

Mne. Brevity, friend, is all I ask. Your story is apt to run away with you. Up hill and down dale you go, through Scythia and Machlyene, off again to Bosphorus, then back to Scythia, till my taciturnity is exhausted.

Tox. I am schooled. Brevity you shall have; I will not run you off your ears this time. My next story shall be of a service rendered to myself, by my friend Sisinnes. Induced by the desire for Greek culture, I had left my home and was on my way to Athens. The ship put in at Amastris, which comes in the natural route from Scythia, being on the shore of the Euxine, not far from Carambis. Sisinnes, who had been my friend from childhood, bore me company on this voyage. We had transferred all our belongings from the ship to an inn near the harbour; and whilst we were busy in the market, suspecting nothing wrong, some thieves had forced the door of our room and carried off everything, not leaving us even enough to go on with for that day. Well, when we got back and found what had happened, we thought it was no use trying to get legal redress from our landlord, or from the neighbours; there were too many of them; and if we *had* told our story,—how we had been robbed of four hundred darics and our clothes and rugs and everything, most people would only have thought we were making a fuss about a trifle. So we had to think what was to be done:

here we were, absolutely destitute, in a foreign country. For my part, I thought I might as well put a sword through my ribs there and then, and have done with it, rather than endure the humiliation that might be forced upon us by hunger and thirst. Sisinnes took a more cheerful view, and implored me to do nothing of the kind:

'I shall think of something,' he said, 'and we may do well yet.' For the moment, he made enough to get us some food by carrying up timber from the harbour. The next morning, he took a walk in the market, where it seems he saw a company of fine likely young fellows, who as it turned out were hired as gladiators, and were to perform two days after. He found out all about them, and then came back to me. 'Toxaris,' he exclaimed, 'consider your poverty at an end! In two days' time, I will make a rich man of you.' We got through those two days somehow, and then came the show, in which we took our places as spectators, Sisinnes bidding me prepare myself for all the novel delights of a Greek amphitheatre. The first thing we saw on sitting down was a number of wild beasts:

some of them were being assailed by javelins, others hunted by dogs, and others again were let loose upon certain men who were tied hand and foot, and whom we supposed to be criminals. The gladiators next made their appearance. The herald led forward a strapping young fellow, and announced that any one who was prepared to stand up against him might step into the arena and take his reward, which would be 400 pounds. Sisinnes rose from his seat, jumped down into the ring, expressed his willingness to fight, and demanded arms. He received the money, and brought it to me. 'If I win,' he said, 'we will go off together, and are amply provided for:

if I fall, you will bury me and return to Scythia.' I was much moved.

He now received his arms, and put them on; with the exception, however, of the helmet, for he fought bareheaded. He was the first to be wounded, his adversary's curved sword drawing a stream of blood from his groin. I was half dead with fear. However, Sisinnes was biding his time:

the other now assailed him with more confidence, and Sisinnes made a lunge at his breast, and drove the sword clean through, so that his adversary fell lifeless at his feet. He himself, exhausted by the loss of blood, sank down upon the corpse, and life almost deserted him; but I ran to his assistance, raised him up, and spoke words of comfort. The victory was won, and he was free to depart; I therefore picked him up and carried him home. My efforts were at last successful:

he rallied, and is living in Scythia to this day, having married my sister. He is still lame, however, from his wound. Observe:

this did not take place in Machlyene, nor yet in Alania; there is no lack of witnesses to the truth of the story this time; many an Amastrian here in Athens would remember the fight of Sisinnes.

One more story, that of Abauchas, and I have done. Abauchas once arrived in the capital of the Borysthenians, with his wife, of whom he was extremely fond, and two children; one, a boy, was still at the breast, the other was a girl of seven. With him also was his friend Gyndanes, who was still suffering from the effects of a wound he had received on the journey:

they had been attacked by some robbers, and Gyndanes in resisting them had been stabbed in the thigh, and was still unable to stand on account of the pain. One night they were all asleep in the upper story, when a tremendous fire broke out; the whole building was wrapped in flames, and every means of exit blocked. Abauchas started up, and leaving his sobbing children, and shaking off his wife, who clung to him and implored him to save her, he caught up his friend in his arms, and just managed to force his way down without being utterly consumed by the flames. His wife followed, carrying the boy, and bade the girl come after her; but, scorched almost to a cinder, she was compelled to drop the child from her arms, and barely succeeded in leaping through the flames; the little girl too only just escaped with her life. Abauchas was afterwards reproached with having abandoned his own wife and children to rescue Gyndanes. 'I can beget other children easily enough,' said he:

'nor was it certain how these would turn out:

but it would be long before I got such another friend as Gyndanes; of his affection I have been abundantly satisfied by experience.'

There, Mnesippus, you have *my* little selection. The next thing is to settle whether my hand or your tongue is to be amputated. Who is umpire?

Mne. Umpire we have none; we forgot that. I tell you what:

we have wasted our arrows this time, but some other day we will appoint an arbitrator, and submit other friendships to his judgement; and then off shall come your hand, or out shall come my tongue, as the case may be. Perhaps, though, this is rather a primitive way of doing things. As you seem to think a great deal of friendship, and as I consider it to be the highest blessing of humanity, what is there to prevent our vowing eternal friendship on the spot? We shall both have the satisfaction of winning then, and shall get a substantial prize into the bargain:

two right hands each instead of one, two tongues, four eyes, four feet;—everything in duplicate. The union of two friends—or three, let us say—is like Geryon in the pictures:

a six-handed, three-headed individual; my private opinion is, that there was not one Geryon, but three Geryons, all acting in concert, as friends should.

Tox. Done with you, then.

Mne. And, Toxaris,—we will dispense with the blood-and- scimetar ceremony. Our present conversation, and the similarity of our aims, are a much better security than that sanguinary cup of yours. Friendship, as I take it, should be voluntary, not compulsory.

Tox. Well said. From this day, I am your friend, you mine; I your guest here in Greece, you mine if ever you come to Scythia.

Mne. Scythia! I would go further than Scythia, to meet with such friends as Toxaris's narratives have shown him to be.

ZEUS CROSS-EXAMINED

Cyniscus. Zeus

Cyn. Zeus:

I am not going to trouble you with requests for a fortune or a throne; you get prayers enough of that sort from other people, and from your habit of convenient deafness I gather that you experience a difficulty in answering them. But there is one thing I should like, which would cost you no trouble to grant.

Zeus. Well, Cyniscus? You shall not be disappointed, if your expectations are as reasonable as you say.

Cyn. I want to ask you a plain question.

Zeus. Such a modest petition is soon granted; ask what you will.

Cyn. Well then:

you know your Homer and Hesiod, of course? Is it all true that they sing of Destiny and the Fates—that whatever they spin for a man at his birth must inevitably come about?

Zeus. Unquestionably. Nothing is independent of their control. From their spindle hangs the life of all created things; whose end is predetermined even from the moment of their birth; and that law knows no change.

Cyn. Then when Homer says, for instance, in another place,

Lest unto Hell thou go, *outstripping Fate,*

he is talking nonsense, of course?

Zeus. Absolute nonsense. Such a thing is impossible:

the law of the Fates, the thread of Destiny, is over all. No; so long as the poets are under the inspiration of the Muses, they speak truth:

but once let those Goddesses leave them to their own devices, and they make blunders and contradict themselves. Nor can we blame them:

they are but men; how should they know truth, when the divinity whose mouthpieces they were is departed from them?

Cyn. That point is settled, then. But there is another thing I want to know. There are three Fates, are there not,—Clotho, Lachesis, and Atropus?

Zeus. Quite so.

Cyn. But one also hears a great deal about Destiny and Fortune. Who are they, and what is the extent of their power? Is it equal to that of the Fates? or greater perhaps? People are always talking about the insuperable might of Fortune and Destiny.

Zeus. It is not proper, Cyniscus, that you should know all. But what made you ask me about the Fates?

Cyn. Ah, you must tell me one thing more first. Do the Fates also control you Gods? Do *you* depend from their thread?

Zeus. We do. Why do you smile?

Cyn. I was thinking of that bit in Homer, where he makes you address the Gods in council, and threaten to suspend all the world from a golden cord. You said, you know, that you would let the cord down from Heaven, and all the Gods together, if they liked, might take hold of it and try to pull you down, and they would never do it:

whereas you, if you had a mind to it, could easily pull them up,
And Earth and Sea withal.

I listened to that passage with shuddering reverence; I was much impressed with the idea of your strength. Yet now I understand that you and your cord and your threats all depend from a mere cobweb. It seems to me Clotho should be the one to boast:

she has you dangling from her distaff, like a sprat at the end of a fishing-line.

Zeus. I do not catch the drift of your questions.

Cyn. Come, I will speak my mind; and in the name of Destiny and the Fates take not my candour amiss. If the case stands thus, if the Fates are mistresses of all, and their decisions unalterable, then why do men sacrifice to *you*, and bring hecatombs, and pray for good at *your* hands? If our prayers can neither save us from evil nor procure us any boon from Heaven, I fail to see what we get for our trouble.

Zeus. These are nice questions! I see how it is,—you have been with the sophists; accursed race! who would deny us all concern in human affairs. Yes, these are just the points they raise, impiously seeking to pervert mankind from the way of sacrifice and prayer:

it is all thrown away, forsooth! the Gods take no thought for mankind; they have no power on the earth.—Ah well; they will be sorry for it some day.

Cyn. Now, by Clotho's own spindle, my questions are free from all sophistic taint. How it has come about, I know not; but one word has brought up another, and the end of it is—there is no use in sacrifice. Let us begin again. I will put you a few more questions; answer me frankly, but think before you speak, this time.

Zeus. Well; if you have the time to waste on such tomfoolery.

Cyn. Everything proceeds from the Fates, you say?

Zeus. Yes.

Cyn. And is it in your power to unspin what they have spun?

Zeus. It is not.

Cyn. Shall I proceed, or is the inference clear?

Zeus. Oh, clear enough. But you seem to think that people sacrifice to us from ulterior motives; that they are driving a bargain with us, *buying* blessings, as it were:

not at all; it is a disinterested testimony to our superior merit.

Cyn. There you are, then. As you say, sacrifice answers no useful purpose; it is just our good-natured way of acknowledging your superiority. And mind you, if we had a sophist here, he would want to know all about that superiority. You are our fellow slaves, he would say; if the Fates are our mistresses, they are also yours. Your immortality will not serve you; that only makes things worse. We mortals, after all, are liberated by death:

422

but for you there is no end to the evil; that long thread of yours means eternal servitude.

Zeus. But this eternity is an eternity of happiness; the life of Gods is one round of blessings.

Cyn. Not all Gods' lives. Even in Heaven there are distinctions, not to say mismanagement. *You* are happy, of course:

you are king, and you can haul up earth and sea as it were a bucket from the well. But look at Hephaestus:

a cripple; a common blacksmith. Look at Prometheus:

he gets nailed up on Caucasus. And I need not remind you that your own father lies fettered in Tartarus at this hour. It seems, too, that Gods are liable to fall in love; and to receive wounds; nay, they may even have to take service with mortal men; witness your brother Posidon, and Apollo, servants to Laomedon and to Admetus. I see no great happiness in all this; some of you I dare say have a very pleasant time of it, but not so others. I might have added, that you are subject to robbery like the rest of us; your temples get plundered, and the richest of you becomes a pauper in the twinkling of an eye. To more than one of you it has even happened to be melted down, if he was a gold or a silver God. All destiny, of course.

Zeus. Take care, Cyniscus:

you are going too far. You will repent of this one day.

Cyn. Spare your threats:

you know that nothing can happen to me, except what Fate has settled first. I notice, for instance, that even temple-robbers do not always get punished; most of them, indeed, slip through your hands. Not destined to be caught, I suppose.

Zeus. I knew it! you are one of those who would abolish Providence.

Cyn. You seem to be very much afraid of these gentlemen, for some reason. Not one word can I say, but you must think I picked it up from them. Oblige me by answering another question; I could desire no better authority than yours. What is this Providence? Is she a Fate too? or some greater, a mistress of the Fates?

Zeus. I have already told you that there are things which it is not proper for you to know. You said you were only going to ask me one question, instead of which you go on quibbling without end. I see what it is you are at:

you want to make out that we Gods take no thought for human affairs.

Cyn. It is nothing to do with me:

it was you who said just now that the Fates ordained everything. Have you thought better of it? Are you going to retract what you said? Are the Gods going to push Destiny aside and make a bid for government?

Zeus. Not at all; but the Fates work *through us.*

Cyn. I see:

you are their servants, their underlings. But that comes to the same thing: it is still they who design; you are only their tools, their instruments.

Zeus. How do you make that out?

Cyn. I suppose it is pretty much the same as with a carpenter's adze and drill:

they do assist him in his work, but no one would describe them as the workmen; we do not say that a ship has been turned out by such and such an adze, or by such and such a drill; we name the shipwright. In the same way, Destiny and the Fates are the universal shipwrights, and you are their drills and adzes; and it seems to me that instead of paying their respects and their sacrifices to you, men ought to sacrifice to Destiny, and implore *her* favours; though even that would not meet the case, because I take it that things are settled once and for all, and that the Fates themselves are not at liberty to chop and change. If some one gave the spindle a turn in the wrong direction, and undid all Clotho's work, Atropus would have something to say on the subject.

Zeus. So! You would deprive even the Fates of honour? You seem determined to reduce all to one level. Well, we Gods have at least one claim on you:

we do prophesy and foretell what the Fates have disposed.

Cyn. Now even granting that you do, what is the use of knowing what one has to expect, when one can by no possibility take any precautions? Are you going to tell me that a man who finds out that he is to die by a steel point can escape the doom by shutting himself up? Not he. Fate will take him out hunting, and there will be his steel:

Adrastus will hurl his spear at the boar, miss the brute, and get Croesus's son; Fate's inflexible law directs his aim. The full absurdity of the thing is seen in the case of Laius:

Seek not for offspring in the Gods' despite;
Beget a child, and thou begett'st thy slayer.

Was not this advice superfluous, seeing that the end must come? Accordingly we find that the oracle does not deter Laius from begetting a son, nor that son from being his slayer. On the whole, I cannot see that your prophecies entitle you to reward, even setting aside the obscurity of the oracles, which are generally contrived to cut both ways. You omitted to mention, for instance, whether Croesus—'the Halys crossed'—should destroy his own or Cyrus's mighty realm.' It might be either, so far as the oracle goes.

Zeus. Apollo was angry with Croesus. When Croesus boiled that lamb and tortoise together in the cauldron, he was making trial of Apollo.

Cyn. Gods ought not to be angry. After all, I suppose it was fated that the Lydian should misinterpret that oracle; his case only serves to illustrate that general ignorance of the future, which Destiny has appointed for mankind. At that rate, your prophetic power too seems to be in her hands.

Zeus. You leave us nothing, then? We exercise no control, we are not entitled to sacrifice, we are very drills and adzes. But you may well despise me:

why do I sit here listening to all this, with my thunder-bolt beneath my arm?

Cyn. Nay, smite, if the thunder-bolt is my destiny. I shall think none the worse of you; I shall know it is all Clotho's doing; I will not even blame the bolt that wounds me. And by the way— talking of thunder-bolts—there is one thing I will ask you and Destiny to explain; you can answer for her. Why is it that you leave all the pirates and temple-robbers and ruffians and perjurers to themselves, and direct your shafts (as you are always doing) against an oak-tree or a stone or a harmless mast, or even an honest, God-fearing traveller? ... No answer? Is this one of the things it is not proper for me to know?

Zeus. It is, Cyniscus. You are a meddlesome fellow; I don't know where you picked up all these ideas.

Cyn. Well, I suppose I must not ask you all (Providence and Destiny and you) why honest Phocion died in utter poverty and destitution, like Aristides before him, while those two unwhipped puppies, Callias and Alcibiades, and the ruffian Midias, and that Aeginetan libertine Charops, who starved his own mother to death, were all rolling in money? nor again why Socrates was handed over to the Eleven instead of Meletus? nor yet why the effeminate Sardanapalus was a king, and one high-minded Persian after another went to the cross for refusing to countenance his doings? I say nothing of our own days, in which villains and money-grubbers prosper, and honest men are oppressed with want and sickness and a thousand distresses, and can hardly call their souls their own.

Zeus. Surely you know, Cyniscus, what punishments await the evil-doers after death, and how happy will be the lot of the righteous?

Cyn. Ah, to be sure:

Hades—Tityus—Tantalus. Whether there is such a place as Hades, I shall be able to satisfy myself when I die. In the meantime, I had rather live a pleasant life here, and have a score or so of vultures at my liver when I am dead, than thirst like Tantalus in this world, on the chance of drinking with the heroes in the Isles of the Blest, and reclining in the fields of Elysium.

Zeus. What! you doubt that there are punishments and rewards to come? You doubt of that judgement-seat before which every soul is arraigned?

Cyn. I *have* heard mention of a judge in that connexion; one Minos, a Cretan. Ah, yes, tell me about him:

they say he is your son?

Zeus. And what of him?

Cyn. Whom does he punish in particular?

Zeus. Whom but the wicked? Murderers, for instance, and temple-robbers.

Cyn. And whom does he send to dwell with the heroes?

Zeus. Good men and God-fearing, who have led virtuous lives.

Cyn. Why?

Zeus. Because they deserve punishment and reward respectively.

Cyn. Suppose a man commits a crime accidentally:
does he punish him just the same?

Zeus. Certainly not.

Cyn. Similarly, if a man involuntarily performed a good action, he would not reward him?

Zeus. No.

Cyn. Then there is no one for him to reward or punish.

Zeus. How so?

Cyn. Why, we men do nothing of our own free will:

we are obeying an irresistible impulse,—that is, if there is any truth in what we settled just now, about Fate's being the cause of everything. Does a man commit a murder? Fate is the murderess. Does he rob a temple? He has her instructions for it. So if there is going to be any justice in Minos's sentences, he will punish Destiny, not Sisyphus; Fate, not Tantalus. What harm did these men do? They only obeyed orders.

Zeus. I am not going to speak to you any more. You are an unscrupulous man; a sophist. I shall go away and leave you to yourself.

Cyn. I wanted to ask you where the Fates lived; and how they managed to attend to all the details of such a vast mass of business, just those three. I do not envy them their lot; they must have a busy time of it, with so much on their hands. Their destiny, apparently, is no better than other people's. I would not exchange with them, if I had the choice; I had rather be poorer than I am, than sit before such a spindleful, watching every thread.—But never mind, if you would rather not answer. Your previous replies have quite cleared up my doubts about Destiny and Providence; and for the rest, I expect I was not destined to hear it.

ZEUS TRAGOEDUS

Hermes. Hera. Colossus. Heracles. Athene. Posidon. Momus.
Hermagoras. Zeus. Aphrodite. Apollo, Timocles. Damis

    Herm. Wherefore thus brooding, Zeus? wherefore apart,
And palely pacing, as Earth's sages use?
Let me thy counsel know, thy cares partake;
And find thy comfort in a faithful fool.

    Ath. Cronides, lord of lords, and all our sire,
I clasp thy knees; grant thou what I require;
A boon the lightning-eyed Tritonia asks:

Speak, rend the veil thy secret thought that masks;
Reveal what care thy mind within thee gnaws,
Blanches thy cheek, and this deep moaning draws.

    Zeus. Speech hath no utterance of surpassing fear,
Tragedy holds no misery or woe,
But our divinest essence soon shall taste.

    Ath. Alas, how dire a prelude to thy tale!

    Zeus. O brood maleficent, teemed from Earth's dark womb! And
thou, Prometheus, how hast thou wrought me woe!

    Ath. Possess us; are not we thine own familiars?

    Zeus. With a whirr and a crash
Let the levin-bolt dash—
Ah, whither?

    Hera. A truce to your passion, Zeus. *We* have not these good people's
gift for farce or recitation; *we* have not swallowed Euripides whole, and cannot
play up to you. Do you suppose we do not know how to account for your
annoyance?

    Zeus. Thou knowst not; else thy waitings had been loud.

    Hera. Don't tell me; it's a love affair; that's what's the matter with you.
However, you won't have any 'wailings' from me; I am too much hardened to
neglect. I suppose you have discovered some new Danae or Semele or Europa
whose charms are troubling you; and so you are meditating a transformation
into a bull or satyr, or a descent through the roof into your beloved's bosom as
a shower of gold; all the symptoms—your groans and your tears and your
white face—point to love and nothing else.

    Zeus. Happy ignorance, that sees not what perils now forbid love and
such toys!

    Hera. Is your name Zeus, or not? and, if so, what else can possibly annoy
you but love?

    Zeus. Hera, our condition is most precarious; it is touch- and-go, as they
call it, whether we are still to enjoy reverence and honour from the earth, or be
utterly neglected and become of no account.

Hera. Has Earth produced a new brood of giants? Have the Titans broken their chains, overpowered their guards, and taken up arms against us once more?

Zeus. Nay, fear not that; Hell threatens not the Gods.

Hera. What can the matter be, then? To hear you, one might think it was Polus or Aristodemus, not Zeus; and why, pray, if something of that sort is not bothering you?

Zeus. My dear, a discussion somehow arose yesterday between Timocles the Stoic and Damis the Epicurean; there was a numerous and respectable audience (which particularly annoyed me), and they had an argument on the subject of Providence. Damis questioned the existence of the Gods, and utterly denied their interest in or government of events, while Timocles, good man, did his best to champion our cause. A great crowd gathered round; but no conclusion was reached. They broke up with an understanding that the inquiry should be completed another day; and now they are all agog to see which will win and prove his case. You all see how parlous and precarious is our position, depending on a single mortal. These are the alternatives for us:

to be dismissed as mere empty names, or (if Timocles prevails) to enjoy our customary honours.

Hera. This is really a serious matter; your ranting was not so uncalled-for, Zeus.

Zeus. You fancied me thinking of some Danae or Antiope; and this was the dread reality. Now, Hermes, Hera, Athene, what is our course? We await your contribution to our plans.

Herm. My opinion is that an assembly be summoned and the community taken into counsel.

Hera. And I concur.

Ath. Sire, I dissent entirely; you should not fill Heaven with apprehensions, nor let your own uneasiness be visible, but take private measures to assure Timocles's victory and Damis's being laughed out of court.

Herm. It cannot be kept quiet, Zeus; the philosophers' debate is public, and you will be accused of despotic methods, if you maintain reserve on a matter of so great and general interest.

Zeus. Make proclamation and summon all, then. I approve your judgement.

Herm. Here, assemble, all ye Gods; don't waste time, come along, here you are; we are going to have an important meeting.

Zeus. What, Hermes? so bald, so plain, so prosy an announcement—on this momentous occasion?

Herm. Why, how would you like it done?

Zeus. Some metre, a little poetic sonority, would make the style impressive, and they would be more likely to come.

Herm. Ah, Zeus, that is work for epic poets or reciters, and I am no good at poetry. I should be sure to put in too many feet, or leave out some, and spoil the thing; they would only laugh at my rude verses. Why, I've known Apollo himself laughed at for some of his oracles; and prophecy has the advantage of obscurity, which gives the hearers something better to do than scanning verses.

Zeus. Well, well, Hermes, you can make lines from Homer the chief ingredient of your composition; summon us in his words; you remember them, of course.

Herm. I cannot say they are exactly on the tip of my tongue; however, I'll do my best:

> Let ne'er a God (tum, tum), nor eke a Goddess,
> Nor yet of Ocean's rivers one be wanting,
> Nor nymphs; but gather to great Zeus's council;
> And all that feast on glorious hecatombs,
> Yea, middle and lower classes of Divinity,
> Or nameless ones that snuff fat altar-fumes

Zeus. Good, Hermes; that is an excellent proclamation:

see, here they come pell-mell; now receive and place them in correct precedence, according to their material or workmanship; gold in the front row, silver next, then the ivory ones, then those of stone or bronze. A cross-division will give precedence to the creations of Phidias, Alcamenes, Myron, Euphranor, and artists of that calibre, while the common inartistic jobs can be huddled together in the far corner, hold their tongues, and just make up the rank and file of our assembly.

Herm. All right; they shall have their proper places. But here is a point:

suppose one of them is gold, and heavy at that, but not finely finished, quite amateurish and ill proportioned, in fact—is he to take precedence of Myron's and Polyclitus's bronze, or Phidias's and Alcamenes's marble? or is workmanship to count most?

Zeus. It should by rights. Never mind, put the gold first.

Herm. I see; property qualification, comparative wealth, is the test, not merit.—Gold to the front row, please.—Zeus, the front row will be exclusively barbarian, I observe. You see the peculiarity of the Greek contingent:

they have grace and beauty and artistic workmanship, but they are all marble or bronze—the most costly of them only ivory with just an occasional gleam of gold, the merest surface-plating; and even those are wood inside, harbouring whole colonies of mice. Whereas Bendis here, Anubis there, Attis next door, and Mithras and Men, are all of solid gold, heavy and intrinsically precious.

Pos. Hermes, is it in order that this dog-faced Egyptian person should sit in front of me, Posidon?

Herm. Certainly. You see, Earth-shaker, the Corinthians had no gold at the time, so Lysippus made you of paltry bronze; Dog- face is a whole gold-mine richer than you. You must put up with being moved back, and not object to the owner of such a golden snout being preferred.

Aph. Then, Hermes, find me a place in the front row; I am golden.

Herm. Not so, Aphrodite, if I can trust my eyes; I am purblind, or you are white marble; you were quarried, I take it, from Pentelicus, turned by Praxiteles's fancy into Aphrodite, and handed over to the Cnidians.

Aph. Wait; my witness is unexceptionable—Homer. 'The Golden Aphrodite' he calls me, up and down his poems.

Herm. Oh, yes, no doubt; *he* called Apollo rich, 'rolling in gold'; but now where will you find Apollo? Somewhere in the third-class seats; his crown has been taken off and his harp pegs stolen by the pirates, you see. So *you* may think yourself lucky with a place above the fourth.

Col. Well, who will dare dispute *my* claim? Am I not the Sun? and look at my height. If the Rhodians had not decided on such grandiose dimensions for me, the same outlay would have furnished forth a round dozen of your golden Gods; I ought to be valued proportionally. And then, besides the size, there is the workmanship and careful finish.

Herm. What shall I do, Zeus? Here is a difficulty again—too much for me. Going by material, he is bronze; but, reckoning the talents his bronze cost, he would be above the first class.

Zeus. What business has he here dwarfing the rest and blocking up all the bench?—Why, my excellent Rhodian, you may be as superior to the golden ones as you will; but how can you possibly go in the front row? Every one would have to get up, to let you sit; half that broad beam of yours would fill the whole House. I must ask you to assist our deliberations standing; you can bend down your head to the meeting.

Herm. Now here is another problem. Both bronze, equal aesthetically, being both from Lysippus's studio, and, to crown all, nothing to choose between them for birth—two sons of yours, Zeus—Dionysus and Heracles. Which is to be first? You can see for yourself, they mean to stand upon their order.

Zeus. We are wasting time, Hermes; the debate should have been in full swing by now. Tell them to sit anyhow, according to taste; we will have an *ad hoc* meeting another day, and then I shall know how to settle the question of precedence.

Herm. My goodness, what a noise! what low vulgar bawling! listen— 'Hurry up with that carving!' 'Do pass the nectar!' 'Why no more ambrosia?' 'When are those hecatombs coming?' 'Here, shares in that victim!'

Zeus. Call them to order, Hermes; this nonsense must cease, before I can give them the order of the day.

Herm. They do not all know Greek; and I haven't the gift of tongues, to make myself understood by Scythians and Persians and Thracians and Celts. Perhaps I had better hold up my hand and signal for silence.

Zeus. Do.

430

Herm. Good; they are as quiet as if they were so many teachers of elocution. Now is the time for your speech; see, they are all hanging on your lips.

Zeus. Why—there is something wrong with me—Hermes, my boy —I will be frank with you. You know how confident and impressive I always was as a public speaker?

Herm. I know; I used to be in such a fright; you threatened sometimes to let down your golden cord and heave up earth and sea from their foundations, Gods included.

Zeus. But to-day, my child—it may be this terrible crisis— it may be the size of the audience—there is a vast number of Gods here, isn't there—anyhow, my thoughts are all mixed, I shiver, my tongue seems tied. What is most absurd of all, my exordium is gone clean out of my head; and I had prepared it on purpose to produce a good impression at the start.

Herm. You have spoiled everything, Zeus. They cannot make out your silence; they are expecting to hear of some terrible disaster, to account for your delay.

Zeus. What do you think? Reel off the exordium in Homer?

Herm. Which one?

Zeus. Lend me your ears, Gods all and Goddesses.

Herm. Rubbish! you made quite exhibition enough of yourself in that vein in our cabinet council. However, you might, if you like, drop your metrical fustian, and adapt any one of Demosthenes's Philippics with a few alterations. That is the fashionable method with speakers nowadays.

Zeus. Ah, that is a royal road to eloquence—simplifies matters very much for a man in difficulties.

Herm. Go ahead, then.

Zeus. Men of—Heaven, I presume that you would be willing to pay a great price, if you could know what in the world has occasioned the present summons. Which being so, it is fitting that you should give a ready hearing to my words. Now, whereas the present crisis, Heavenians, may almost be said to lift up a voice and bid us take vigorous hold on opportunity, it seems to me that we are letting it slip from our nerveless grasp. And I wish now (I can't remember any more) to exhibit clearly to you the apprehensions which have led to my summoning you.

As you are all aware, Mnesitheus the ship's-captain yesterday made his votive offering for the narrow escape of his vessel off Caphereus, and those of us whom he had invited attended the banquet in Piraeus. After the libations you went your several ways. I myself, as it was not very late, walked up to town for an afternoon stroll in Ceramicus, reflecting as I went on the parsimony of Mnesitheus. When the ship was driving against the cliff, and already inside the circle of reef, he had vowed whole hecatombs:

what he offered in fact, with sixteen Gods to entertain, was a single cock—an old bird afflicted with catarrh—and half a dozen grains of frankincense; these were all mildewed, so that they at once fizzled out on the embers, hardly giving enough smoke to tickle the olfactories. Engaged in these thoughts I reached the Poecile, and there found a great crowd gathered; there were some inside the Portico, a large number outside, and a few seated on the benches vociferating as loud as they could. Guessing correctly that these were philosophers of the militant variety, I had a mind to stop and hear what they were saying. I was enveloped in a good thick cloud, under cover of which I assumed their habit, lengthened my beard, and so made a passable philosopher; then I elbowed my way through the crowd and got in undetected. I found an accomplished scoundrel and a pattern of human virtue at daggers drawn; they were Damis the Epicurean and Timocles the Stoic. The latter was bathed in perspiration, and his voice showed signs of wear, while Damis goaded him on to further exertions with mocking laughter.

The bone of contention was ourselves. Damis—the reptile!—maintained that we did not concern ourselves in thought or act with human affairs, and practically denied our existence; that was what it came to. And he found some support. Timocles was on our side, and loyally, passionately, unshrinkingly did he champion the cause; he extolled our Providence, and illustrated the orderly discerning character of our influence and government. He too had his party; but he was exhausted and quite husky; and the majority were inclining to Damis. I saw how much was at stake, and ordered Night to come on and break up the meeting. They accordingly dispersed, agreeing to conclude the inquiry next day. I kept among the crowd on its way home, heard its commendations of Damis, and found that his views were far the more popular, though some still protested against condemning Timocles out of hand, and preferred to see what he would say for himself to-morrow.

You now know the occasion of this meeting—no light one, ye Gods, if you reflect how entirely our dignity, our revenue, our honour, depend on mankind. If they should accept as true either our absolute non-existence or, short of that, our indifference to them, farewell to our earthly sacrifices, attributes, honours; we shall sit starving and ineffectual in Heaven; our beloved feasts and assemblies, games and sacrifices, vigils and processions—all will be no more. So mighty is the issue; believe me, it behoves us all to search out salvation; and where lies salvation? In the victory and acceptance of Timocles, in laughter that shall drown the voice of Damis. For I doubt the unaided powers of Timocles, if our help be not accorded him.

Hermes, make formal proclamation, and let the debate commence.

Herm. Hear, keep silence, clamour not. Of full and qualified Gods, speak who will. Why, what means this? Doth none rise? Cower ye confounded at these momentous tidings?

Mo.

Away, ye dull as earth, as water weak!

But *I* could find plenty to say, Zeus, if free speech were granted me.

Zeus. Speak, Momus, and fear not. You will use your freedom, surely, for the common good.

Mo. Hear, then, ye Gods; for out of the abundance of the heart the mouth speaketh. You must know, I foresaw all this clearly—our difficulty— the growth of these agitators; it is ourselves who are responsible for their impudence; I swear to you, we need not blame Epicurus nor his friends and successors, for the prevalence of these ideas. Why, what can one expect men to think, when they see all life topsy-turvy—the good neglected, pining in poverty, disease, and slavery, detestable scoundrels honoured, rolling in wealth, and ordering their betters about, temple-robbers undetected and unpunished, the innocent constantly crucified and bastinadoed? With this evidence before them, it is only natural they should conclude against our existence. All the more when they hear the oracles saying that some one

      The Halys crossed, o'erthrows a mighty realm, but not specifying
  whether that realm is his own or his enemy's;

    or again

   O sacred Salamis, thou shalt slay
Full many a mother's son.

The Greeks were mothers' sons as well as the Persians, I suppose. Or again, when they hear the ballads about our loves, our wounds, captivities, thraldoms, quarrels, and endless vicissitudes (mark you, we claim all the while to be blissful and serene), are they not justified in ridiculing and belittling us? And then we say it is outrageous if a few people who are not quite fools expose the absurdity and reject Providence; why, we ought to be glad enough that a few still go on sacrificing to blunderers like us.

And at this point, Zeus—this meeting is private; the human element is not represented among us (except by Heracles, Dionysus, Ganymede, and Asclepius, and they are naturalized)—at this point, answer me a question frankly:

    did your interest in mankind ever carry you so far as to sift the good from the bad? The answer is in the negative, I know. Very well, then; had not a Theseus, on his way from Troezen to Athens, exterminated the malefactors as an incidental amusement, Sciron and Pityocamptes and Cercyon and the rest of them might have gone on battening on the slaughter of travellers, for all you and your Providence would have done. Had not an old-fashioned thoughtful Eurystheus, benevolently collecting information of local troubles, sent this energetic enterprising servant of his about, the mighty Zeus would never have given a thought to the Hydra or the Stymphalian birds, the Thracian horses and the drunken insolence of Centaurs.

If the truth must out, we sit here with a single eye to one thing— does a man sacrifice and feed the altars fat? Everything else drifts as it may. We get our deserts, and shall continue to get them, when men open their eyes by degrees and find that sacrifices and processions bring them no profit. Before long you will find we are the laughing-stock of people like Epicurus,

Metrodorus, Damis, who will have mastered and muzzled our advocates. With whom does it lie to check and remedy this state of things? Why, with you, who have brought it on. As for Momus, what is dishonour to him? He was never among the recipients of honour, while you were still prosperous; your banquetings were too exclusive.

Zeus. He was ever a cross-grained censor; we need not mind his maundering, Gods. We have it from the admirable Demosthenes:

imputations, blame, criticism, these are easy things; they tax no one's capacity:

what calls for a statesman is the suggesting of a better course; and that is what I rely upon the rest of you for; let us do our best without his help.

Pos. As for me, I live ordinarily under water, as you know, and follow an independent policy in the depths; that policy is to save sailors, set ships on their way, and keep the winds quiet, as best I may. However, I do take an interest in your politics too, and my opinion is that this Damis should be got rid of before the debate; the thunderbolt would do it, or some means could be found; else he might win—you say he is a plausible fellow, Zeus. It would teach them that there is a reckoning for telling such tales about us, too.

Zeus. You must be jesting, Posidon; you cannot have forgotten that we have no say in the matter? It is the Fates that spin a man's thread, whether he be destined to the thunderbolt or the sword, to fever or consumption. If it had depended on me, do you suppose I should have let those temple-robbers get off unblasted from Pisa the other day?—two of my curls shorn off, weighing half a dozen pounds apiece. Would *you* have stood it, when that fisherman from Oreus stole your trident at Geraestus? Moreover, they will think we are sensitive and angry; they will suspect that the reason why we get the man out of the way without waiting to see him matched with Timocles is that we are afraid of his arguments; they will say we are just securing judgement by default.

Pos. Dear, dear! I thought I had hit upon a good short cut to our object.

Zeus. Nonsense, there is something fishy about it, Posidon; and it is a dull notion too, to destroy your adversary beforehand; he dies unvanquished, and leaves his argument behind him still debatable and undecided.

Pos. Then the rest of you must think of something better, if 'fishy' is the best word you have for me.

Apol. If we beardless juniors were competent to address the meeting, *I* might perhaps have contributed usefully to the discussion.

Mo. Oh, Apollo, the inquiry is so important that seniority may be waived, and any one allowed his say; a pretty thing to split hairs about legal competence at a supreme crisis! But *you* are surely qualified by this time; your minority is prehistoric, your name is on the Privy-Council roll, your senatorial rank dates back almost to Cronus. Pray spare us these juvenile airs, and give us your views freely; you need not be bashful about your smooth chin; you have a father's rights in Asclepius's great bush of a beard. Moreover, you never had a better opportunity of showing your wisdom, if your philosophic *seances* with the Muses on Helicon have not been thrown away.

Apol. Why, it does not lie with you to give me leave, Momus; Zeus must do that; and if he bids, I may find words that shall be not all uncultured, but worthy of my Heliconian studies.

Zeus. Speak, son; thou hast my leave.

Apol. This Timocles is a good pious man, and an excellent Stoic scholar; his learning has gained him a wide and paying connexion among young men; in private lessons his manner is indeed very convincing. But in public speaking he is timid, cannot produce his voice, and has a provincial accent; the consequence is, he gets laughed at in company, lacks fluency, stammers and loses his thread—especially when he emphasizes these defects by an attempt at flowers of speech. As far as intelligence goes, he is extremely acute and subtle, so the Stoic experts say; but he spoils it all by the feebleness of his oral explanations; he is confused and unintelligible, deals in paradoxes, and when he is interrogated, explains *ignotum per ignotius*; his audience does not grasp his meaning, and therefore laughs at him. I think lucidity a most important point; there is nothing one should be so careful about as to be comprehensible.

Mo. You praise lucidity, Apollo; your theory is excellent, though your practice does not quite conform; your oracles are crooked and enigmatic, and generally rely upon a safe ambiguity; a second prophet is required to say what they mean. But what is your solution of the problem? How are we to cure Timocles of the impediment in his speech?

Apol. If possible, we should provide him with an able counsel (there are plenty such) to be inspired by him and give adequate expression to his ideas.

Mo. Your sapience is beardless indeed—*in statu pupillari*, one may say. A learned gathering:

Timocles with counsel by his side to interpret his ideas. Damis speaking *in propria persona* with his own tongue, his opponent employing a go-between into whose ears he privately pours inspiration, and the go-between producing ornate periods, without, I dare say, understanding what he is told—most entertaining for the listeners! We shall get nothing out of that device.

But, reverend sir, you claim the gift of prophecy, and it has brought you in good pay—golden ingots on one occasion?—why not seize this opportunity of exhibiting your art? You might tell us which of the disputants will win; a prophet knows the future, of course.

Apol. I have no tripod or incense here; no substitute for the divining-well of Castaly.

Mo. Aha! you are caught! you will not come to the scratch.

Zeus. Speak, my son, in spite of all; give not this enemy occasion to blaspheme; let him not flout thy powers with tripod and water and frankincense, as though thine art were lost without them.

Apol. Father, it were better done at Delphi or at Colophon, with all the customary instruments to hand. Yet, bare and unprovided as I am, I will essay to tell whether of them twain shall prevail.—If the metre is a little rough, you must make allowances.

Mo. Go on, then; but remember, Apollo:

lucidity; no 'able counsel,' no solutions that want solving themselves. It is not a question of lamb and tortoise boiling[58] in Lydia now; you know what we want to get at.

Zeus. What will thine utterance be? How dread, even now, is the making ready! The altered hue, the rolling eyes, the floating locks, the frenzied gesture—all is possession, horror, mystery.

Apol.

Who lists may hear Apollo's soothfast rede
Of stiff debate, heroic challenge ringing
Shrill, and each headpiece lined with fence of proof.
Alternate clack the strokes in whirling strife;
Sore buffeted, quakes and shivers heart of oak.
But when grasshopper feels the vulture's talons,
Then the storm-boding ravens croak their last,
Prevail the mules, butts his swift foals the ass.

Zeus. Why that ribald laughter, Momus? It is no laughing matter. Stop, stop, fool; you'll choke yourself.

Mo. Well, such a clear simple oracle puts one in spirits.

Zeus. Indeed? Then perhaps you will kindly expound it.

Mo. No need of a Themistocles this time; it is absolutely plain. The oracle just says in so many words that he is a quack, and we pack-asses (quite true) and mules to believe in him; we have not as much sense, it adds, as a grasshopper.

Herac. Father, I am only an alien, but I am not afraid to give my opinion. Let them begin their debate. Then, if Timocles gets the best of it, we can let the meeting go on, in our own interest; on the other hand, if things look bad, I will give the Portico a shake, if you like, and bring it down on Damis; a confounded fellow like that is not to insult us.

Zeus. Now by Heracles—I can swear by you, I certainly cannot swear by your plan—what a crude—what a shockingly philistine suggestion! What! destroy all those people for one man's wickedness? and the Portico thrown in, with the Miltiades and Cynaegirus on the field of Marathon? Why, if these were ruined, how could the orators ever make another speech, with the best of their stock-in-trade taken from them? Besides, while you were alive, you might possibly have done a thing like that; but now that you are a God, you surely understand that only the Fates are competent, and we cannot interfere?

Herac. Then when I slew the lion or the Hydra, was I only the Fates' instrument?

Zeus. Of course you were.

---

[58] See *Croesus* in Notes.

Herac. And now, suppose any one insults me, or robs my temple, or upsets an image of me, am I not to pulverize him, just because the Fates have not decreed it long ago?

Zeus. Certainly not.

Herac. Then allow me to speak my mind;
I'm a blunt man; I call a spade a spade.

If this is the state of things with you, good-bye for me to your honours and altar-steam and fat of victims; I shall be off to Hades. There, if I show my bow ready for action, the ghosts of the monsters I have slain will be frightened, at least.

Zeus. Oh, splendid! 'Thine own lips testify against thee,' says the book; you would have saved Damis some trouble by putting this in his mouth.

But who is this breathless messenger? Bronze—a nice clean figure and outline—*chevelure* rather out of date. Ah, he must be your brother, Hermes, who stands in the Market by the Poecile; I see he is all over pitch; that is what comes of having casts taken of you every day. My son, why this haste? Have you important news from Earth?

Hermag. Momentous news, calling for infinite energy.

Zeus. Speak, tarry not, if any peril else hath escaped our vigilance.

Hermag.
   It chanced of late that by the statuaries
My breast and back were plastered o'er with pitch;
A mock cuirass tight-clinging hung, to ape
My bronze, and take the seal of its impression.
When lo, a crowd! therein a pallid pair
Sparring amain, vociferating logic;
'Twas Damis and—

Zeus. Truce to your iambics, my excellent Hermagoras; I know the pair. But tell me whether the fight has been going on long.

Hermag. Not yet; they were still skirmishing—slinging invective at long range.

Zeus. Then we have only, Gods, to look over and listen. Let the Hours unbar, draw back the clouds, and open the doors of Heaven.

Upon my word, what a vast gathering! And I do not quite like the looks of Timocles; he is trembling; he has lost his head; he will spoil everything; it is perfectly plain, he will not be able to stand up to Damis. Well, there is one thing left us:
   we can pray for him
Inwardly, silently, lest Damis hear.

_Ti. What, you miscreant, no Gods? no Providence?

Da. No, no; you answer my question first; what makes you believe in them?

Ti. None of that, now; the_ onus probandi _is with you, scoundrel.

Da. None of that, now; it is with you.

Zeus_. At this game ours is much the better man—louder-voiced, rougher-tempered. Good, Timocles; stick to invective; that is your strong point; once you get off that, he will hook and hold you up like a fish.

_Ti. I solemnly swear I will not answer first.

Da. Well, put your questions, then; so much you score by your oath. But no abuse, please.

Ti. Done. Tell me, then, and be damned to you, do you deny that the Gods exercise providence?

Da. I do.

Ti. What, are all the events we see uncontrolled, then?

Da. Yes.

Ti. And the regulation of the universe is not under any God's care?

Da. No.

Ti. And everything moves casually, by blind tendency?

Da. Yes.

Ti. Gentlemen, can you tolerate such sentiments? Stone the blasphemer.

Da. What do you mean by hounding them against me? Who are you, that you should protest in the Gods' name? They do not even protest in their own; they have sent no judgement on me, and they have had time enough to hear me, if they have ears.

Ti. They do hear you; they do; and some day their vengeance will find you out.

Da. Pray when are they likely to have time to spare for me? They are far too busy, according to you, with all the infinite concerns of the universe on their hands. That is why they have never punished you for your perjuries and—well, for the rest of your performances, let me say, not to break our compact about abuse. And yet I am at a loss to conceive any more convincing proof they could have given of their Providence, than if they had trounced you as you deserve. But no doubt they are from home—t'other side of Oceanus, possibly, on a visit to 'the blameless Ethiopians.' We know they have a way of going there to dinner, self-invited sometimes.

Ti. What answer is possible to such ribaldry?

Da. The answer I have been waiting for all this time; you can tell me what made you believe in divine Providence.

Ti. Firstly, the order of nature—the sun running his regular course, the moon the same, the circling seasons, the growth of plants, the generation of living things, the ingenious adaptations in these latter for nutrition, thought, movement, locomotion; look at a carpenter or a shoemaker, for instance; and the thing is infinite. All these effects, and no effecting Providence?

Da. You beg the question; whether the effects are produced by Providence is just what is not yet proved. Your description of nature I accept; it does not follow that there is definite design in it; it is not impossible that things now similar and homogeneous have developed from widely different origins. But you give the name 'order' to mere blind tendency. And you will be

438

very angry if one follows your appreciative catalogue of nature in all its variety, but stops short of accepting it as a proof of detailed Providence. So, as the play says,

Here lurks a fallacy; bring me sounder proof.

Ti. I cannot admit that further proof is required; nevertheless, I will give you one. Will you allow Homer to have been an admirable poet?

Da. Surely.

Ti. Well,_ he _maintains Providence, and warrants my belief.

Da. Magnificent! why, every one will grant you Homer's poetic excellence; but not that he, or any other poet for that matter, is good authority on questions of this sort._ Their _object, of course, is not truth, but fascination; they call in the charms of metre, they take tales for the vehicle of what instruction they give, and in short all their efforts are directed to pleasure.

But I should be glad to hear which parts of Homer you pin your faith to. Where he tells how the daughter, the brother, and the wife of Zeus conspired to imprison him? If Thetis had not been moved to compassion and called Briareus, you remember, our excellent Zeus would have been seized and manacled; and his gratitude to her induced him to delude Agamemnon with a lying dream, and bring about the deaths of a number of Greeks. Do you see? The reason was that, if he had struck and blasted Agamemnon's self with a thunderbolt, his double dealing would have come to light. Or perhaps you found the Diomede story most convincing?— Diomede wounded Aphrodite, and afterwards Ares himself, at Athene's instigation; and then the Gods actually fell to blows and went a-tilting—without distinction of sex; Athene overthrew Ares, exhausted no doubt with his previous wound from Diomede; and

Hermes the stark and stanch 'gainst Leto stood.

Or did you put your trust in Artemis? She was a sensitive lady, who resented not being invited to Oeneus's banquet, and by way of vengeance sent a monstrous irresistible boar to ravage his country. Is it with tales like these that Homer has prevailed on you?

Zeus_. Goodness me, what a shout, Gods! they are all cheering Damis. And our man seems posed; he is frightened and trembles; he is going to throw up the sponge, I am certain of it; he looks round for a gap to get away through.

_Ti. And will you scout Euripides too, then? Again and again he brings Gods on the stage, and shows them upholding virtue in the Heroes, but chastising wickedness and impiety (like yours).

Da. My noble philosopher, if that is how the tragedians have convinced you, you have only two alternatives:

you must suppose that divinity is temporarily lodged either in the actor—a Polus, an Aristodemus, a Satyrus—, or else in the actual masks, buskins, long tunics, cloaks, gloves, stomachers, padding, and ornamental paraphernalia in general of tragedy—a manifest absurdity; for when Euripides can speak his own sentiments unfettered by dramatic necessity, observe the freedom of his remarks:

Dost see this aether stretching infinite,
And girdling earth with close yet soft embrace?
That reckon thou thy Zeus, that name thy God.

And again,

Zeus, whatever Zeus may be (for, save by hearsay,
I know not)—;

and there is more of the same sort.

Ti. Well, but all men—ay, all nations—have acknowledged and, feted Gods; was it all delusion?

Da. Thank you; a timely reminder; national observances show better than anything else how vague religious theory is. Confusion is endless, and beliefs as many as believers. Scythia makes offerings to a scimetar, Thrace to the Samian runaway Zamolxis, Phrygia to a Month-God, Ethiopia to a Day-Goddess, Cyllene to Phales, Assyria to a dove, Persia to fire, Egypt to water. In Egypt, though, besides the universal worship of water, Memphis has a private cult of the ox, Pelusium of the onion, other cities of the ibis or the crocodile, others again of baboon, cat, or monkey. Nay, the very villages have their specialities: one deifies the right shoulder, and another across the river the left; one a half skull, another an earthenware bowl or platter. Come, my fine fellow, is it not all ridiculous?

Mo_. What did I tell you, Gods? All this was sure to come out and be carefully overhauled.

Zeus. You did, Momus, and your strictures were justified; if once we come safe out of this present peril, I will try to introduce reforms.

_Ti. Infidel! where do you find the source of oracles and prophecies, if not in the Gods and their Providence?

Da. About oracles, friend, the less said the better; I shall ask you to choose your instances, you see. Will Apollo's answer to the Lydian suit you? That was as symmetrical as a double-edged knife; or say, it faced both ways, like those Hermae which are made double, alike whether you look at front or back. Consider; will Croesus's passage of the Halys destroy his own realm, or Cyrus's? Tet the wretched Sardian paid a long price for his ambidextrous hexameter.

Mo_. The man is realizing just my worst apprehensions. Where is our handsome musician now? Ah, there you are; go down and plead your own cause against him.

Zeus. Hush, Momus; you are murdering our feelings; it is no time for recrimination.

_Ti. Have a care, Damis; this is sacrilege, no less; what you say amounts to razing the temples and upsetting the altars.

Da. Oh, not_ all _the altars; what harm do they do, so long as incense and perfume is the worst of it? As for Artemis's altar at Tauri, though, and her hideous feasts, I should like it overturned from base to cornice.

440

*Zeus_*. Whence comes this resistless plague among us? There is none of us he spares; he is as free with his tongue as a tub orator,

And grips by turns the innocent and guilty.

Mo. The innocent? You will not find many of those among us, Zeus. He will soon come to laying hands upon some of the great and eminent, I dare say.

_*Ti*. Do you close your ears even to Zeus's thunder, atheist?

Da. I clearly cannot shut out the thunder; whether it is Zeus's thunder, you know better than I perhaps; you may have interviewed the Gods. Travellers from Crete tell another story:

there is a tomb there with an inscribed pillar, stating that Zeus is long dead, and not going to thunder any more.

*Mo_*. I could have told you that was coming long ago. What, Zeus? pale? and your teeth chattering? What is the matter? You should cheer up, and treat such manikins with lofty contempt.

Zeus. Contempt? See what a number of them there is—how set against us they are already—and he has them fast by the ears.

Mo. Well, but you have only to choose, and you can let down your golden cord, and then every man of them

With earth and sky and all thou canst draw up.

_*Ti*. Blasphemer, have you ever been a voyage?

Da. Many.

Ti. Well, then, the wind struck the canvas and filled the sails, and it or the oars gave you way, but there was a person responsible for steering and for the safety of the ship?

Da. Certainly.

Ti. Now that ship would not have sailed, without a steersman; and do you suppose that this great universe drifts unsteered and uncontrolled?

*Zeus_*. Good, this time, Timocles; a cogent illustration, that.

_*Da*. But, you pattern of piety, the earthly navigator makes his plans, takes his measures, gives his orders, with a single eye to efficiency; there is nothing useless or purposeless on board; everything is to make navigation easy or possible; but as for the navigator for whom you claim the management of this vast ship, he and his crew show no reason or appropriateness in any of their arrangements; the forestays, as likely as not, are made fast to the stern, and both sheets to the bows; the anchor will be gold, the beak lead, decoration below the water-line, and unsightliness above.

As for the men, you will find some lazy awkward coward in second or third command, or a fine swimmer, active as a cat aloft, and a handy man generally, chosen out of all the rest to—pump. It is just the same with the passengers:

here is a gaolbird accommodated with a seat next the captain and treated with reverence, there a debauchee or parricide or temple-robber in honourable possession of the best place, while crowds of respectable people are packed together in a corner and hustled by their real inferiors. Consider what sort of a

441

voyage Socrates and Aristides and Phocion had of it, on short rations, not venturing, for the filth, to stretch out their legs on the bare deck; and on the other hand what a comfortable, luxurious, contemptuous life it was for Callias or Midias or Sardanapalus.

That is how things go on board your ship, sir wiseacre; and who shall count the wrecks? If there had been a captain supervising and directing, in the first place he would have known the difference between good and bad passengers, and in the second he would have given them their deserts; the better would have had the better accommodation above by his side, and the worse gone below; with some of the better he would have shared his meals and his counsels. So too for the crew:

the keen sailor would have been made look-out man or captain of the watch, or given some sort of precedence, and the lazy shirker have tasted the rope's end half a dozen times a day. The metaphorical ship, your worship, is likely to be capsized by its captain's incompetence.

Mo_. He is sweeping on to victory, with wind and tide.

Zeus. Too probable, Momus. And Timocles never gets hold of an effective idea; he can only ladle out trite commonplaces higgledy-piggledy—no sooner heard than refuted.

_Ti. Well, well; my ship leaves you unconvinced; I must drop my sheet-anchor, then; that at least is unbreakable.

Zeus_. I wonder what it is.

Ti. See whether this is a sound syllogism; can you upset it?—If there are altars, there are Gods:

there are _altars; therefore, there are Gods. Now then.

Da. Ha, ha, ha! I will answer as soon as I can get done with laughing.

Ti. Will you never stop? At least tell me what the joke is.

Da. Why, you don't see that your anchor (sheet-anchor, too) hangs by a mere thread. You defend on connexion between the existence of Gods and the existence of altars, and fancy yourself safe at anchor! As you admit that this was your sheet-anchor, there is nothing further to detain us.

Ti. You retire; you confess yourself beaten, then?

Da. Yes; we have seen you take sanctuary at the altars under persecution. At those altars I am ready (the sheet-anchor be my witness) to swear peace and cease from strife.

Ti. Tou are playing with me, are you, you vile body-snatcher, you loathsome well-whipped scum! As if we didn't know who your father was, how your mother was a harlot! You strangled your own brother, you live in fornication, you debauch the young, you unabashed lecher! Don't be in such a hurry; here is something for you to take with you; this broken pot will serve me to cut your foul throat.

Zeus_. Damis makes off with a laugh, and the other after him, calling him names, mad at his insolence. He will get him on the head with that pottery, I know. And now, what are we to do?

442

Herm. Why, the man in the comedy was not far out:

Put a good face on 't, and thou hast no harm.

It is no such terrible disaster, if a few people go away infected. There are plenty who take the other view—a majority of Greeks, the body and dregs of the people, and the barbarians to a man.

Zeus. Ah, Hermes, but there is a great deal in Darius's remark about Zopyrus—I would rather have had one ally like Damis than be the lord of a thousand Babylons.

THE COCK

Micyllus. A Cock

Mi. Detested bird! May Zeus crunch your every bone! Shrill, envious brute:

to wake me from delightful dreams of wealth and magic blessedness with those piercing, deafening notes! Am I not even in sleep to find a refuge from Poverty, Poverty more vile than your vile self? Why, it cannot be midnight yet:

all is hushed; numbness—sure messenger of approaching dawn—has not yet performed its morning office upon my limbs:

and this wakeful brute (one would think he was guarding the golden fleece) starts crowing before night has fairly begun. But he shall pay for it.— Yes; only wait till daylight comes, and my stick shall avenge me; I am not going to flounder about after you in the dark.

Cock. Why, master, I meant to give you a pleasant surprise:

I borrowed what I could from the night, that you might be up early and break the back of your work; think, if you get a shoe done before sunrise, you are so much the nearer to earning your day's bread. However, if you prefer to sleep, I have done; I will be mute as any fish. Only you may find your rich dreams followed by a hungry awakening.

Mi. God of portents! Heracles preserve us from the evil to come! My cock has spoken with a human voice.

Cock. And what if he has? Is that so very portentous?

Mi. I should think it was. All Gods avert the omen!

Cock. Micyllus, I am afraid your education has been sadly neglected. If you had read your Homer, you would know that Achilles's horse Xanthus declined to have anything more to do with neighing, and stood on the field of battle spouting whole hexameters; *he* was not content with plain prose like me; he even took to prophecy, and foretold to Achilles what should befall him. Nor was this considered anything out of the way; Achilles saw nothing portentous about it, nor did he invoke Heracles on the occasion. What a fuss you would have made, if the keel of the Argo had addressed a remark to you, or the leaves of the Dodonaean oak had opened their mouths and prophesied; or if you had seen ox- hides crawling about, and heard the half-cooked flesh of the beasts bellowing on the spit! As for me, considering my connexion with Hermes—most loquacious, most argumentative of Gods—and my familiar intercourse with mankind, it was only to be expected that I should pick up your language pretty quickly. Nay, there is a still better reason for my conversational powers, which I don't mind telling you, if you will promise to keep quiet about it.

Mi. Am I dreaming still, or is this bird really talking to me?—In Hermes' name then, good creature, out with your better reason; I will be mum, never fear; it shall go no further. Why, who would believe the story, when I told him that I had it from a cock?

Cock. Listen. You will doubtless be surprised to learn that not so long ago the cock who stands before you was a man.

Mi. Why, to be sure, I have heard something like this before about a cock. It was the story of a young man called Alectryon[59]; he was a friend of Ares,—used to join in his revels and junketings, and give him a hand in his love affairs. Whenever Ares went to pay a sly visit to Aphrodite, he used to take Alectryon with him, and as he was particularly afraid that the Sun would see him, and tell Hephaestus, he would always leave Alectryon at the door, so that he might give him warning when the Sun was up. But one day Alectryon fell asleep, and unwittingly betrayed his trust; the consequence was that the Sun got a peep at the lovers, while Ares was having a comfortable nap, relying on Alectryon to tell him if any one came. Hephaestus heard of it, and caught them in that cage of his, which he had long had waiting for them. When Ares was released, he was so angry with Alectryon that he turned him into a cock, armour and all, as is shown by his crest; and that is what makes you cocks in such a hurry to crow at dawn, to let us know that the Sun is coming up presently; it is your way of apologizing to Ares, though crowing will not mend matters now.

Cock. Yes, there is that story too:
but that is nothing to do with mine; I only became a cock quite lately.

Mi. But what I want to know is, how did it happen?

Cock. Did you ever hear of Pythagoras of Samos, son of Mnesarchus?

Mi. What, that sophist quack, who forbade the eating of meat, and would have banished beans from our tables (no beans, indeed! my favourite food!), and who wanted people to go for five years without speaking?

Cock. And who, I may add, was Euphorbus before he was Pythagoras.

Mi. He was a knave and a humbug, that Pythagoras, by all accounts.

Cock. That Pythagoras, my worthy friend, is now before you in person:
spare his feelings, especially as you know nothing about his real character.

Mi. Portent upon portent! a cock philosopher! But proceed, son of Mnesarchus:
how came you to change from man to bird, from Samos to Tanagra? 'Tis an unconvincing story; I find a difficulty in swallowing it. I have noticed two things about you already, which do not look much like Pythagoras.

Cock. Yes?

Mi. For one thing, you are garrulous; I might say noisy. Now, if I am not mistaken, Pythagoras advocated a course of five years' silence at a stretch. As for the other, it is rank heresy. You will remember that yesterday, not having anything else to give you, I brought you some beans:

---

[59] Alectryon is the Greek word for a cock.

and you,—you gobbled them up without thinking twice about it! Either you lied when you told me you were Pythagoras, or else you have sinned against your own laws:

in eating those beans, you have as good as bolted your own father's head.

Cock. Ah, you don't understand, Micyllus. There is a reason for these things:

different diets suit different creatures. I was a philosopher in those days:

accordingly I abstained from beans. Now, on the contrary, I propose to eat beans; they are an unexceptionable diet for birds. And now if you like I will tell you how from being Pythagoras I have come to be—what you see me; and all about the other lives I have lived, and what were the good points of each.

Mi. Tell on; there is nothing I should like better. Indeed, if I were given my choice between hearing your story, and having my late dream of riches over again, I don't know which I should decide on. 'Twas a sweet vision, of joys above all price:

yet not above the tale of my cock's adventures.

Cock. What, still puzzling over the import of a dream? Still busy with vain phantoms, chasing a visionary happiness through your head, that 'fleeting' joy, as the poet calls it?

Mi. Ah, cock, cock, I shall never forget it. That dream has left its honeyed spell on my eyelids; 'tis all I can do to open them; they would fain close once more in sleep. As a feather tickles the ear, so did that vision tickle my imagination.

Cock. Bless me, you seem to be very hard hit. Dreams are winged, so they say, and their flight circumscribed by sleep:

this one seems to have broken bounds, and taken up its abode in wakeful eyes, transferring thither its honeyed spell, its lifelike presence. Tell me this dream of your desire.

Mi. With all my heart; it is a joy to remember it, and to speak of it. But what about your transformations?

Cock. They must wait till you have done dreaming, and wiped the honey from your eyelids. So you begin:

I want to see which gates the dream came through, the ivory or the horn.

Mi. Through neither.

Cock. Well, but these are the only two that Homer mentions.

Mi. Homer may go hang:

what does a babbling poet know about dreams? Pauper dreams may come through those gates, for all I know; that was the kind that Homer saw, and not over clearly at that, as he was blind. But *my* beauty came through golden gates, golden himself and clothed in gold and bringing gold.

Cock. Enough of gold, most gentle Midas; for to a Midas- prayer it is that I trace your vision; you must have dreamt whole minefuls.

Mi. Gold upon gold was there; picture if you can that glorious lightning-flash! What is it that Pindar says about gold? Can you help me to it? He says water is best, and then very properly proceeds to sing the praises of gold; it comes at the beginning of the book, and a beautiful ode it is.

Cock. What about this?

Chiefest of all good we hold

Water:

even so doth gold,

Like a fire that flameth through the night,

Shine mid lordly wealth most lordly bright.

Mi. The very words; I could fancy that Pindar had seen my vision. And now, my philosophic cock, I will proceed to details. That I did not dine at home last night, you are already aware; the wealthy Eucrates had met me in the morning, and told me to come to dinner after my bath at his usual hour.

Cock. Too well do I know it, after starving all day long. It was quite late before you came home—half-seas over—and gave me those five beans; rather short commons for a cock who has been an athlete in his day, and contended at Olympia, not without distinction.

Mi. Well, so when I got back, and had given you the beans, I went to sleep, and

Through the ambrosial night a dream divine—

ah, divine indeed!—

Cock. Wait:

let us have Eucrates first. What sort of a dinner was it? Tell me all about it. Seize the opportunity:

dine once more in waking dream; chew the cud of prandial reminiscence.

Mi. I thought all that would bore you; however, if you are curious, all right. I had never dined at a great house in my life before, when yesterday, in a lucky hour for me, I fell in with Eucrates. After saluting him respectfully as usual, I was making off—not to bring discredit on him by walking at his side in my shabby clothes—when he spoke to me:

'Micyllus,' he said, 'it is my daughter's birthday to-day, and I have invited a number of friends to celebrate it. One of them, I hear, is indisposed, and will not be able to come; you can take his place, always provided that I do not hear from him, for at present I do not know whether to expect him or not.' I made my bow, and departed, praying that ague, pleurisy, and gout might light upon the invalid whose appetite I had the honour to represent. I thought bath-time would never come; I could not keep my eyes off the dial:

where was the shadow now? could I go yet? At last it really was time:

I scraped the dirt off, and made myself smart, turning my cloak inside out, so that the clean side might be uppermost. Among the numerous guests assembled at the door, whom should I see but the very man whose understudy I was to be, the invalid, in a litter! He was evidently in a sad way; groaning and coughing and spitting in the most alarmingly emphatic manner; ghostly pale, puffy, and not much less, I reckoned, than sixty years old. He was a philosopher, so they said,—one of those who fill boys' heads with nonsensical

447

ideas. Certainly his beard was well adapted to the part he played; it cried aloud
for the barber. Archibius the doctor asked him what induced him to venture
out in that state of health. 'Oh,' says he, 'a man must not shirk his duties, least
of all a philosopher; no matter if a thousand ailments stand in his way.
Eucrates would have taken it as a slight.' 'You're out there,' I cried; 'Eucrates
would be only too glad if you would cough out your soul at home instead of
doing it at his table.' He made as if he had not heard my jest; he was above
such things. Presently in came Eucrates from his bath, and seeing Thesmopolis
(the philosopher), 'Ah, Professor,' says he, 'I am glad to see you here; not that
it would have made any difference, even if you had stayed at home; I should
have had everything sent over to you.' And with that he took the philosopher's
hand, and with the help of the slaves, conducted him in. I thought it was time
for me to be going about my business:

however, Eucrates turned round to me, and seeing how glum I looked,
'Micyllus,' says he, after a good deal of humming and ha'ing, 'you must join us;
we shall find room for you; I can send my boy to dine with his mother and the
women.' It had very nearly turned out a wild-goose chase, but not quite:

I walked in, feeling rather ashamed of myself for having done the boy
out of his dinner. We were now to take our places. Thesmopolis was first
hoisted into his, with some difficulty, by five stalwart youths, who propped
him up on every side with cushions to keep him in his place and enable him to
hold out to the end. As no one else was disposed to have him for a neighbour,
that privilege was assigned to me without ceremony. And then dinner was
brought in:

such dainties, Pythagoras, such variety! and everything served on gold or
silver. Golden cups, smart servants, musicians, jesters,— altogether, it was
delightful. Thesmopolis, though, annoyed me a good deal:

he kept on worrying about virtue, and explaining how two negatives
make one positive, and how when it is day it is not night; among other things,
he would have it that I had horns. I wanted none of his philosophy, but on he
went, quite spoiling my pleasure; it was impossible to listen to the music and
singing. So that is what the dinner was like.

Cock. Not much of a one, especially with that old fool for your
neighbour.

Mi. And now for the dream, which was about no other than Eucrates.
How it came about I don't know, but Eucrates was childless, and was on his
death-bed; he sent for me and made his will, leaving everything to me, and
soon after died. I now came into the property, and ladled out gold and silver
by the bucketful from springs that never dried; furniture and plate, clothes and
servants, all were mine. I drove abroad, the admiration of all eyes and the envy
of all hearts, lolling in my carriage behind a pair of creams, with a crowd of
attendants on horseback and on foot in front of me, and a larger crowd behind.
Dressed in Eucrates's splendid clothes, my fingers loaded with a score or so of
rings, I ordered a magnificent feast to be prepared for the entertainment of my

friends. The next moment they were there,—it happens so in dreams; dinner was brought in, the wine splashed in the cups. I was pledging each of my friends in turn in beakers of gold, and the biscuits were just being brought in, when that unlucky crow of yours spoilt all:

over went the tables, and away flew my visionary wealth to all the quarters of Heaven. Had I not some reason to be annoyed with you? I could have gone on with that dream for three nights on end.

Cock. Is the love of gold so absorbing a passion? Gold the only thing you can find to admire? The possession of gold the sole happiness?

Mi. I am not the only one, Pythagoras. Why, you yourself (when you were Euphorbus) used to go to battle with your hair adorned with gold and silver, though iron would have been more to the point than gold under the circumstances; however, you thought differently, and fought with a golden circlet about your brow; which I suppose is why Homer compares your hair to that of the Graces in gold and silver clasped.

No doubt its charm would be greatly enhanced by the glitter of the interwoven gold. After all, though, you, my golden-haired friend, were but the son of Panthus; one can understand your respect for gold. But the father of Gods and men, the son of Cronus and Rhea himself, could find no surer way to the heart of his Argive enchantress[60]—or to those of her gaolers—than this same metal; you know the story, how he turned himself into gold, and came showering down through the roof into the presence of his beloved? Need I say more? Need I point out the useful purposes that gold serves? the beauty and wisdom and strength, the honour and glory it confers on its possessors, at a moment's notice turning obscurity and infamy into world-wide fame? You know my neighbour and fellow craftsman, Simon, who supped with me not long since? 'Twas at the Saturnalia, the day I made that pease-pudding, with the two slices of sausage in it?

Cock. I know:

the little snub-nosed fellow, who went off with our pudding-basin under his arm,—the only one we had; I saw him with these eyes.

Mi. So it was he who stole that basin! and he swore by all his Gods that he knew nothing of it! But you should have called out, and told me how we were being plundered.

Cock. I did crow; it was all I could do just then. But what were you going to say about Simon?

Mi. He had a cousin, Drimylus, who was tremendously rich. During his lifetime, Drimylus never gave him a penny; and no wonder, for he never laid a finger on his money himself. But the other day he died, and Simon has come in for everything. No more dirty rags for him now, no more trencher-licking:

---

[60] Danae.

he drives abroad clothed in purple and scarlet; slaves and horses are his, golden cups and ivory-footed tables, and men prostrate themselves before him. As for me, he will not so much as look at me:

it was only the other day that I met him, and said, 'Good day, Simon':

he flew into a rage:

'Tell that beggar,' he said, 'not to cut down my name; it is Simonides, not Simon.' And that is not all,—the women are in love with him too, and Simon is coy and cold:

some he receives graciously, but the neglected ones declare they will hang themselves. See what gold can do! It is like Aphrodite's girdle, transforming the unsightly and making them lovely to behold. What say the poets?

Happy the hand that grasps thee, Gold!

and again,

Gold hath dominion over mortal men.

But what are you laughing at?

Cock. Ah, Micyllus, I see that you are no wiser than your neighbours; you have the usual mistaken notions about the rich, whose life, I assure you, is far more miserable than your own. I ought to know:

I have tried everything, and been poor man and rich man times out of number. You will find out all about it before long.

Mi. Ah, to be sure, it is your turn now. Tell me how you came to be changed into a cock, and what each of your lives was like.

Cock. Very well; and I may remark, by way of preface, that of all the lives I have ever known none was happier than yours.

Mi. Than mine? Exasperating fowl! All I say is, may you have one like it! Now then:

begin from Euphorbus, and tell me how you came to be Pythagoras, and so on, down to the cock. I'll warrant you have not been through all those different lives without seeing some strange sights, and having your adventures.

Cock. How my spirit first proceeded from Apollo, and took flight to earth, and entered into a human form, and what was the nature of the crime thus expiated,—all this would take too long to tell; nor is it fitting either for me to speak of such matters or for you to hear of them. I pass to the time when I became Euphorbus,—

Mi. Wait a minute:

have I ever been changed in this way?

Cock. You have.

Mi. Then who was I, do you know? I am curious about that.

Cock. Why, you were an Indian ant, of the gold-digging species.

Mi. What could induce me, misguided insect that I was, to leave that life without so much as a grain of gold-dust to supply my needs in this one? And what am I going to be next? I suppose you can tell me. If it is anything good, I'll hang myself this moment from the very perch on which you stand.

Cock. That I can on no account divulge. To resume. When I was Euphorbus, I fought at Troy, and was slain by Menelaus. Some time then elapsed before I entered into the body of Pythagoras. During this interval, I remained without a habitation, waiting till Mnesarchus had prepared one for me.

Mi. What, without meat or drink?

Cock. Oh yes; these are mere bodily requirements.

Mi. Well, first I will have about the Trojan war. Did it all happen as Homer describes?

Cock. Homer! What should he know of the matter? He was a camel in Bactria all the time. I may tell you that things were not on such a tremendous scale in those days as is commonly supposed:

Ajax was not so very tall, nor Helen so very beautiful. I saw her:

she had a fair complexion, to be sure, and her neck was long enough to suggest her swan parentage[61]:

but then she was such an age—as old as Hecuba, almost. You see, Theseus had carried her off first, and she had lived with him at Aphidnae:

now Theseus was a contemporary of Heracles, and the former capture of Troy, by Heracles, had taken place in the generation before mine; my father, who told me all this, remembered seeing Heracles when he was himself a boy.

Mi. Well, and Achilles:

was he so much better than other people, or is that all stuff and nonsense?

Cock. Ah, I never came across Achilles; I am not very strong on the Greeks; I was on the other side, of course. There is one thing, though:

I made pretty short work of his friend Patroclus— ran him clean through with my spear.

Mi. After which Menelaus settled you with still greater facility. Well, that will do for Troy. And when you were Pythagoras?

Cock. When I was Pythagoras, I was—not to deceive you—a sophist; that is the long and short of it. At the same time, I was not uncultured, not unversed in polite learning. I travelled in Egypt, cultivated the acquaintance of the priests, and learnt wisdom from their mouths; I penetrated into their temples and mastered the sacred books of Orus and Isis; finally, I took ship to Italy, where I made such an impression on the Greeks that they reckoned me among the Gods.

Mi. I have heard all about that; and also how you were supposed to have risen from the dead, and how you had a golden thigh, and favoured the public with a sight of it on occasion. But what put it into your head to make that law about meat and beans?

Cock. Ah, don't ask me that, Micyllus.

Mi. But why not?

---

[61] See *Helen* in Notes.

Cock. I am ashamed to answer you.

Mi. Come, out with it! I am your friend and fellow lodger; we will drop the 'master' now.

Cock. There was neither common sense nor philosophy in that law. The fact is, I saw that if I did just the same as other people, I should draw very few admirers; my prestige, I considered, would be in proportion to my originality. Hence these innovations, the motive of which I wrapped up in mystery; each man was left to make his own conjecture, that all might be equally impressed by my oracular obscurity. There now! you are laughing at me; it is your turn this time.

Mi. I am laughing much more at the folk of Cortona and Metapontum and Tarentum, and the rest of those mute disciples who worshipped the ground you trod on. And in what form was your spirit next clothed, after it had put off Pythagoras?

Cock. In that of Aspasia, the Milesian courtesan.

Mi. Dear, dear! And your versatility has even changed sexes? My gallant cock has positively laid eggs in his time? Pythagoras has carded and spun? Pythagoras the mistress—and the mother—of a Pericles? My Pythagoras no better than he should be?

Cock. I do not stand alone. I had the example of Tiresias and of Caeneus; your gibes touch them as well as me.

Mi. And did you like being a man best, or receiving the addresses of Pericles?

Cock. Ha! the question that Tiresias paid so dearly for answering!

Mi. Never mind, then,—Euripides has settled the point; he says he would

    rather bear the shock of battle thrice
Than once the pangs of labour.

Cock. Ah, just a word in your ear:

    those pangs will shortly be your own; more than once, in the course of a lengthy career, you will be a woman.

Mi. Strangulation on the bird! Does he think we all hail from Miletus or Samos? Yes, I said Samos; Pythagoras has had his admirers, by all accounts, as well as Aspasia. However;—what was your sex next time?

Cock. I was the Cynic Crates.

Mi. Castor and Pollux! What a change was there!

Cock. Then it was a king; then a pauper, and presently a satrap, and after that came horse, jackdaw, frog, and I know not how many more; there is no reckoning them up in detail. Latterly, I have been a cock several times. I liked the life; many is the king, many the pauper and millionaire, with whom I took service in that capacity before I came to you. In your lamentations about poverty, and your admiration of the rich, I find an unfailing source of entertainment; little do you know what those rich have to put up with! If you had any idea of their anxieties, you would laugh to think how you had been deceived as to the blessedness of wealth.

Mi. Well, Pythagoras,—or is there any other name you prefer? I shall throw you out, perhaps, if I keep on calling you different things?

Cock. Euphorbus or Pythagoras, Aspasia or Crates, it is all the same to me; one is as much my name as another. Or stay:

not to be wanting in respect to a bird whose humble exterior contains so many souls, you had better use the evidence of your own eyes and call me Cock.

Mi. Then, cock, as you have tried wellnigh every kind of life, you can next give me a clear description of the lives of rich and poor respectively; we will see if there was any truth in your assertion, that I was better off than the rich.

Cock. Well now, look at it this way. To begin with, you are very little troubled with military matters. Suppose there is talk of an invasion:

you are under no uneasiness about the destruction of your crops, or the cutting-up of your gardens, or the ruin of your vines; at the first sound of the trumpet (if you even hear it), all you have to think of is, how to convey your own person out of harm's way. Well, the rich have got to provide for that too, and they have the mortification into the bargain of looking on while their lands are being ravaged. Is a war-tax to be levied? It all falls on them. When you take the field, theirs are the posts of honour—and danger:

whereas you, with no worse encumbrance than your wicker shield, are in the best of trim for taking care of yourself; and when the time comes for the general to offer up a sacrifice of thanksgiving for his victory, your presence may be relied on at the festive scene.

Then again, in time of peace, you, as one of the commons, march up to the Assembly to lord it over the rich, who tremble and crouch before you, and seek to propitiate you with grants. They must labour, that you may be supplied with baths and games and spectacles and the like to your satisfaction; you are their censor and critic, their stern taskmaster, who will not always hear before condemning; nay, you may give them a smart shower of stones, if the fancy takes you, or confiscate their property. The informer's tongue has no terrors for you; no burglar will scale or undermine *your* walls in search of gold; you are not troubled with book-keeping or debt-collecting; you have no rascally steward to wrangle with; none of the thousand worries of the rich distract you. No, you patch your shoe, and you take your tenpence; and at dusk up you jump from your bench, get a bath if you are in the humour for it, buy yourself a haddock or some sprats or a few heads of garlic, and make merry therewith; Poverty, best of philosophers, is your companion, and you are seldom at a loss for a song. And what is the result? Health and strength, and a hardiness that sets cold at defiance. Your work keeps you keen-set; the ills that seem insuperable to other men find a tough customer in you. Why, no serious sickness ever comes near you:

fever, perhaps, lays a light hand on you now and again; you let him have his way for a day or two, and then you are up again, and shake the pest off; he beats a hasty retreat, not liking the look of a man who drinks cold water at that rate, and has such a short way with the doctors. But look at the rich:

name the disease to which these creatures are not subjected by their intemperance; gout, consumption, pneumonia, dropsy,—they all come of high feeding. Some of these men are like Icarus:

they fly too high, they get near the sun, not realizing that their wings are fastened with wax; and then some day there is a great splash, and they have disappeared headlong into the deep. Others there are who follow Daedalus's example; such minds eschew the upper air, and keep their wax within splashing distance of the sea; these generally get safely to their journey's end.

Mi. Shrewd, sensible fellows.

Cock. Yes, but among the others you may see some ugly shipwrecks. Croesus is plucked of his feathers, and mounts a pyre for the amusement of the Persians. A tyranny capsizes, and the lordly Dionysius is discovered teaching Corinthian children their alphabet.

Mi. You tell me, cock, that you have been a king yourself:

now how did *you* find the life? I expect you had a pleasant time of it, living on the very fat of the land?

Cock. Do not remind me of that miserable existence. A pleasant time! So people thought, no doubt:

I knew better; it was vexation upon vexation.

Mi. You surprise me. How should that be? It sounds unlikely.

Cock. The country over which I ruled was both extensive and fertile. Its population and the beauty of its cities alike entitled it to the highest consideration. It possessed navigable rivers and excellent harbours. My army was large, my pike-men numerous, my cavalry in a high state of efficiency; it was the same with my fleet; and my wealth was beyond calculation. No circumstance of kingly pomp was wanting; gold plate in abundance, everything on the most magnificent scale. I could not leave my palace without receiving the reverential greetings of the public, who looked on me as a God, and crowded together to see me pass; some enthusiasts would even betake themselves to the roofs of the houses, lest any detail of my equipage, clothes, crown or attendants should escape them. I could make allowance for the ignorance of my subjects, but this did not prevent me from pitying myself, when I reflected on the vexations and worries of my position. I was like those colossal statues, the work of Phidias, Myron or Praxiteles:

they too look extremely well from outside:

'tis Posidon with his trident, Zeus with his thunderbolt, all ivory and gold:

but take a peep inside, and what have we? One tangle of bars, bolts, nails, planks, wedges, with pitch and mortar and everything that is unsightly; not to mention a possible colony of rats or mice. There you have royalty.

Mi. But you have not told me what is the mortar, what the bolts and bars and other unsightlinesses that lurk behind a throne. Admiration, dominion, divine honours,—these no doubt fit your simile; there is a touch of the godlike about them. But now let me have the inside of your colossus.

Cock. And where shall I begin? With fear and suspicion? The resentments of courtiers and the machinations of conspirators? Scant and broken sleep, troubled dreams, perplexities, forebodings? Or again with the hurry of business—fiscal—legal—military? Orders to be issued, treaties to be drawn up, estimates to be formed? As for pleasure, such a thing is not to be dreamt of; no, one man must think for all, toil incessantly for all. The Achaean host is snoring to a man:

But   sweet   sleep   came   not   nigh   to   Atreus'   son,
Who pondered many things within his heart.

Lydian Croesus is troubled because his son is dumb; Persian Artaxerxes, because Clearchus is raising a host for Cyrus; Dionysius, because Dion whispers in Syracusan ears; Alexander, because Parmenio is praised. Perdiccas has no peace for Ptolemy, Ptolemy none for Seleucus. And there are other griefs than these:

his favourite is cold; his concubine loves another; there is talk of a rebellion; there has been muttering among a half-dozen of his guards. And the bitterness of it is, that his nearest and dearest are those whom he is most called on to distrust; from them he must ever look for harm. One we see poisoned by his son, another by his own favourite; and a third will probably fare no better.

Mi. Whew! I like not this, my cock. Methinks there is safety in bent backs and leather-cutting, and none in golden loving-cups; I will pledge no man in hemlock or in aconite. All *I* have to fear is that my knife may slip out of the line, and draw a drop or two from my fingers:

but your kings would seem to sit down to dinner with Death, and to lead dogs' lives into the bargain. They go at last; and then they are more like play-actors than anything else—like such a one as you may see taking the part of Cecrops or Sisyphus or Telephus. He has his diadem and his ivory-hilted sword, his waving hair and spangled cloak:

but accidents will happen,— suppose he makes a false step:

down he comes on the middle of the stage, and the audience roars with laughter. For there is his mask, crumpled up, diadem and all, and his own bloody coxcomb showing underneath it; his legs are laid bare to the knees, and you see the dirty rags inside his fine robe, and the great lumbering buskins. Ha, ha, friend cock, have I learnt to turn a simile already? Well, there are my views on tyranny. Now for the horses and dogs and frogs and fishes:

how did you like that kind of thing?

Cock. Your question would take a long time to answer; more time than we can spare. But—to sum up my experience in two words— every one of

455

these creatures has an easier life of it than man. Their aims, their wants, are all confined to the body:

such a thing as a tax-farming horse or a litigant frog, a jackdaw sophist, a gnat confectioner, or a cock pander, is unknown; they leave such things to humanity.

Mi. It may be as you say. But, cock (I don't mind making a clean breast of it to you), I have had a fancy all my life for being rich, and I am as bad as ever; nay, worse, for there is the dream, still flaunting its gold before my eyes; and that confounded Simon, too,—it chokes me to think of him rolling in luxury.

Cock. I'll put that right. It is still dark, get up and come with me. You shall pay a visit to Simon and other rich men, and see how things stand with them.

Mi. But the doors are locked. Would you have me break in?

Cock. Oh no; but I have a certain privilege from Hermes, my patron: you see my longest tail-feather, the curling one that hangs down,—

Mi. There are two curling ones that hang down.

Cock. The one on the right. By allowing any one to pluck out that feather and carry it, I give him the power, for as long as I like, of opening all doors and seeing everything, himself unseen.

Mi. Cock, you are a positive conjurer. Only give me the feather, and it shall not be long before Simon's wealth shifts its quarters; I'll slip in and make a clean sweep. His teeth shall tug leather again.

Cock. That must not be. I have my instructions from Hermes, and if my feather is put to any such purpose, I am to call out and expose the offender.

Mi. Hermes, of all people, grudge a man a little thievery? I'll not believe it of him. However, let us start; I promise not to touch the gold ... if I can help it.

Cock. You must pluck out the feather first.... What's this? You have taken both!

Mi. Better to be on the safe side. And it would look so bad to have one half of your tail gone and not the other.

Cock. Well. Where shall we go first? To Simon's?

Mi. Yes, yes, Simon first. Simonides it is, nowadays; two syllables is not enough for him since he has come into money.... Here we are; what do I do next?

Cock. Apply the feather to the bolt.

Mi. So. Heracles! it might be a key; the door flies open.

Cock. Walk in; you go first. Do you see him? He is sitting up over his accounts.

Mi. See him! I should think I did. What a light! That lamp wants a drink. And what makes Simon so pale? He is shrivelled up to nothing. That comes of his worries; there is nothing else the matter with him, that I have heard of.

456

Cock. Listen, and you will understand.

Si. That seventeen thousand in the hole under my bed is safe enough; not a soul saw me that time. But I believe Sosylus caught me hiding the four thousand under the manger:

he is not the most industrious of grooms, he was never too fond of work; but he *lives* in that stable now. And I expect that is not all that has gone, by a long way. What was Tibius doing with those fine great kippers yesterday? And they tell me he paid no less a sum than four shillings for a pair of earrings for his wife. God help me, it's *my* money they're flinging about. I'm not easy about all that plate either:

what if some one should knock a hole in the wall, and make off with it? Many is the one that envies me, and has an eye on my gold; my neighbour Micyllus is as bad as any of them.

Mi. Hear, hear! He is as bad as Simon; he walks off with other people's pudding-basins under his arm.

Cock. Hush! we shall be caught.

Si. There's nothing like sitting up, and having everything under one's own eye. I'll jump up and go my rounds…. You there! you burglar! I see you…. Ah, it is but a post; all is well. I'll pull up the gold and count it again; I may have missed something just now…. Hark! a step! I knew it; he is upon me! I am beset with enemies. The world conspires against me. Where is my dagger? Only let me catch …—I'll put the gold back.

Cock. There:

now you have seen Simon at home. Let us go on to another house, while there is still some of the night left.

Mi. The worm! what a life! I wish all my enemies such wealth as his. I'll just lend him a box on the ear, and then I am ready.

Si. Who was that? Some one struck me! Ah! I am robbed!

Mi. Whine away, Simon, and sit up of nights till you are as yellow as the gold you clutch.—I should like to go to Gniphon the usurer's next; it is quite close…. Again the door opens to us.

Cock. He is sitting up too, look. It is an anxious time with him; he is reckoning his interest. His fingers are worn to the bone. Presently he will have to leave all this, and become a cockroach, or a gnat, or a bluebottle.

Mi. Senseless brute! it will hardly be a change for the worse. He, like Simon, is pretty well thinned down by his calculations. Let us try some one else.

Cock. What about your friend Eucrates? See, the door stands open; let us go in.

Mi. An hour ago, all this was mine!

Cock. Still the golden dream!—Look at the hoary old reprobate:

with one of his own slaves!

Mi. Monstrous! And his wife is not much better; she takes her paramour from the kitchen.

457

Cock. Well? Is the inheritance to your liking? Will you have it all?

Mi. I will starve first. Good-bye to gold and high living. Preserve me from my own servants, and I will call myself rich on twopence-halfpenny.

Cock. Well, well, we must be getting home; see, it is just dawn. The rest must wait for another day.

ICAROMENIPPUS, AN AERIAL EXPEDITION

Menippus and a Friend

Me. Let me see, now. First stage, Earth to Moon, 350 miles. Second stage, up to the Sun, 500 leagues. Then the third, to the actual Heaven and Zeus's citadel, might be put at a day's journey for an eagle in light marching order.

Fr. In the name of goodness, Menippus, what are these astronomical sums you are doing under your breath? I have been dogging yon for some time, listening to your suns and moons, queerly mixed up with common earthly stages and leagues.

Me. Ah, you must not be surprised if my talk is rather exalted and ethereal; I was making out the mileage of my journey.

Fr. Oh, I see; using stars to steer by, like the Phoenicians?

Me. Oh no, travelling among them.

Fr. Well, to be sure, it must have been a longish dream, if you lost yourself in it for whole leagues.

Me. Dream, my good man? I am just come straight from Zeus. Dream, indeed!

Fr. How? What? Our Menippus a literal godsend from Heaven?

Me. 'Tis even so; from very Zeus I come this day, eyes and ears yet full of wonders. Oh, doubt, if you will. That my fortune should pass belief makes it only the more gratifying.

Fr. Nay, my worshipful Olympian, how should I, 'a man begotten, treading this poor earth,' doubt him who transcends the clouds, a 'denizen of Heaven,' as Homer says? But vouchsafe to tell me how you were uplifted, and where you got your mighty tall ladder. There is hardly enough of Ganymede in your looks to suggest that you were carried off by the eagle for a cupbearer.

Me. I see you are bent on making a jest of it. Well, it *is* extraordinary; you could not be expected to see that it is not a romance. The fact is, I needed neither ladder nor amorous eagle; I had wings of my own.

Fr. Stranger and stranger! this beats Daedalus. What, you turned into a hawk or a crow on the sly?

Me. Now that is not a bad shot; it was Daedalus's wing trick that I tried.

Fr. Well, talk of foolhardiness! did you like the idea of falling into the sea, and giving us a *Mare Menippeum* after the precedent of the *Icarium*?

Me. No fear. Icarus's feathers were fastened with wax, and of course, directly the sun warmed this, he moulted and fell. No wax for me, thank you.

Fr. How did you manage, then? I declare I shall be believing you soon, if you go on like this.

Me. Well, I caught a fine eagle, and also a particularly powerful vulture, and cut off their wings above the shoulder- joint.... But no; if you are not in a hurry, I may as well give you the enterprise from the beginning.

Fr. Do, do; I am rapt aloft by your words already, my mouth open for your *bonne bouche*; as you love me, leave me not in those upper regions hung up by the ears!

Me. Listen, then; it would be a sorry sight, a friend deserted, with his mouth open, and *sus. per aures.*—Well, a very short survey of life had convinced me of the absurdity and meanness and insecurity that pervade all human objects, such as wealth, office, power. I was filled with contempt for them, realized that to care for them was to lose all chance of what deserved care, and determined to grovel no more, but fix my gaze upon the great All. Here I found my first problem in what wise men call the universal order; I could not tell how it came into being, who made it, what was its beginning, or what its end. But my next step, which was the examination of details, landed me in yet worse perplexity. I found the stars dotted quite casually about the sky, and I wanted to know what the sun was. Especially the phenomena of the moon struck me as extraordinary, and quite passed my comprehension; there must be some mystery to account for those many phases, I conjectured. Nor could I feel any greater certainty about such things as the passage of lightning, the roll of thunder, the descent of rain and snow and hail.

In this state of mind, the best I could think of was to get at the truth of it all from the people called philosophers; they of course would be able to give it me. So I selected the best of them, if solemnity of visage, pallor of complexion and length of beard are any criterion—for there could not be a moment's doubt of their soaring words and heaven-high thoughts—and in their hands I placed myself. For a considerable sum down, and more to be paid when they should have perfected me in wisdom, I was to be made an airy metaphysician and instructed in the order of the universe. Unfortunately, so far from dispelling my previous ignorance, they perplexed me more and more, with their daily drenches of beginnings and ends, atoms and voids, matters and forms. My greatest difficulty was that, though they differed among themselves, and all they said was full of inconsistency and contradiction, they expected me to believe them, each pulling me in his own direction.

Fr. How absurd that wise men should quarrel about facts, and hold different opinions on the same things!

Me. Ah, but keep your laughter till you have heard something of their pretentious mystifications. To begin with, their feet are on the ground; they are no taller than the rest of us 'men that walk the earth'; they are no sharper-sighted than their neighbours, some of them purblind, indeed, with age or indolence; and yet they say they can distinguish the limits of the sky, they measure the sun's circumference, take their walks in the supra-lunar regions, and specify the sizes and shapes of the stars as though they had fallen from them; often one of them could not tell you correctly the number of miles from Megara to Athens, but has no hesitation about the distance in feet from the sun to the moon. How high the atmosphere is, how deep the sea, how far it is round the earth— they have the figures for all that; and moreover, they have

460

only to draw some circles, arrange a few triangles and squares, add certain complicated spheres, and lo, they have the cubic contents of Heaven.

Then, how reasonable and modest of them, dealing with subjects so debatable, to issue their views without a hint of uncertainty; thus it must be and it shall be; *contra gentes* they will have it so; they will tell you on oath the sun is a molten mass, the moon inhabited, and the stars water-drinkers, moisture being drawn up by the sun's rope and bucket and equitably distributed among them.

How their theories conflict is soon apparent; next-door neighbours? no, they are miles apart. In the first place, their views of the world differ. Some say it had no beginning, and cannot end; others boldly talk of its creator and his procedure; what particularly entertained me was that these latter set up a contriver of the universe, but fail to mention where he came from, or what he stood on while about his elaborate task, though it is by no means obvious how there could be place or time before the universe came into being.

Fr. You really do make them out very audacious conjurers.

Me. My dear fellow, I wish I could give you their lucubrations on ideas and incorporeals, on finite and infinite. Over that point, now, there is fierce battle; some circumscribe the All, others will have it unlimited. At the same time they declare for a plurality of worlds, and speak scornfully of others who make only one. And there is a bellicose person who maintains that war is the father of the universe. [62]

As to Gods, I need hardly deal with that question. For some of them God is a number; some swear by dogs and geese and plane-trees. [63] Some again banish all other Gods, and attribute the control of the universe to a single one; I got rather depressed on learning how small the supply of divinity was. But I was comforted by the lavish souls who not only make many, but classify; there was a First God, and second and third classes of divinity. Yet again, some regard the divine nature as unsubstantial and without form, while others conceive it as a substance. Then they were not all disposed to recognize a Providence; some relieve the Gods of all care, as we relieve the superannuated of their civic duties; in fact, they treat them exactly like supernumeraries on the stage. The last step is also taken, of saying that Gods do not exist at all, and leaving the world to drift along without a master or a guiding hand.

Well, when I heard all this, I dared not disbelieve people whose voices and beards were equally suggestive of Zeus. But I knew not where to turn for a theory that was not open to exception, nor combated by one as soon as propounded by another. I found myself in the state Homer has described; many a time I would vigorously start believing one of these gentlemen;

---

[62] Variously attributed to Heraclitus, who denies the possibility of repose, and insists that all things are in a state of flux; and to Empedocles, who makes all change and becoming depend on the interaction of the two principles, attraction and repulsion.

[63] Socrates made a practice of substituting these for the names of Gods in his oaths.

But then came second thoughts.

So in my distress I began to despair of ever getting any knowledge about these things on earth; the only possible escape from perplexity would be to take to myself wings and go up to Heaven. Partly the wish was father to the thought; but it was confirmed by Aesop's Fables, from which it appears that Heaven is accessible to eagles, beetles, and sometimes camels. It was pretty clear that I could not possibly develop feathers of my own. But if I were to wear vulture's or eagle's wings—the only kinds equal to a man's weight—I might perhaps succeed. I caught the birds, and effectually amputated the eagle's right, and the vulture's left wing. These I fastened together, attached them to my shoulders with broad thick straps, and provided grips for my hands near the end of the quill-feathers. Then I made experiments, first jumping up and helping the jump by flapping my hands, or imitating the way a goose raises itself without leaving the ground and combines running with flight. Finding the machine obedient, I next made a bolder venture, went up the Acropolis, and launched myself from the cliff right over the theatre.

Getting safely to the bottom that time, my aspirations shot up aloft. I took to starting from Parnes or Hymettus, flying to Geranea, thence to the top of the Acrocorinthus, and over Pholoe and Erymanthus to Taygetus. The training for my venture was now complete; my powers were developed, and equal to a lofty flight; no more fledgeling essays for me. I went up Olympus, provisioning myself as lightly as possible. The moment was come; I soared skywards, giddy at first with that great void below, but soon conquering this difficulty. When I approached the Moon, long after parting from the clouds, I was conscious of fatigue, especially in the left or vulture's wing. So I alighted and sat down to rest, having a bird's-eye view of the Earth, like the Homeric Zeus,   Surveying now the Thracian horsemen's land,   Now Mysia, and again, as the fancy took me, Greece or Persia or India. From all which I drew a manifold delight.

Fr. Oh well, Menippus, tell me all about it. I do not want to miss a single one of your travel experiences; if you picked up any stray information, let me have that too. I promise myself a great many facts about the shape of the Earth, and how everything on it looked to you from your point of vantage.

Me. And you will not be disappointed there, friend. So do your best to get up to the Moon, with my story for travelling companion and showman of the terrestrial scene.

Imagine yourself first descrying a tiny Earth, far smaller than the Moon looks; on turning my eyes down, I could not think for some time what had become of our mighty mountains and vast sea. If I had not caught sight of the Colossus of Rhodes and the Pharus tower, I assure you I should never have made out the Earth at all. But their height and projection, with the faint shimmer of Ocean in the sun, showed me it must be the Earth I was looking at. Then, when once I had got my sight properly focused, the whole human race was clear to me, not merely in the shape of nations and cities, but the individuals, sailing, fighting, ploughing, going to law; the women, the beasts, and in short every breed 'that feedeth on earth's foison.'

Fr. Most unconvincing and contradictory. Just now you were searching for the Earth, it was so diminished by distance, and if the Colossus had not betrayed it, you would have taken it for something else; and now you develop suddenly into a Lynceus, and distinguish everything upon it, the men, the beasts, one might almost say the gnat-swarms. Explain, please.

Me. Why, to be sure! how did I come to leave out so essential a particular? I had made out the Earth, you see, but could not distinguish any details; the distance was so great, quite beyond the scope of my vision; so I was much chagrined and baffled. At this moment of depression—I was very near tears—who should come up behind me but Empedocles the physicist? His complexion was like charcoal variegated with ashes, as if he had been baked. I will not deny that I felt some tremors at the sight of him, taking him for some lunar spirit. But he said:

'Do not be afraid, Menippus;

A mortal I, no God; how vain thy dreams.

I am Empedocles the physicist. When I threw myself into the crater in such a hurry, the smoke of Etna whirled me off up here; and now I live in the Moon, doing a good deal of high thinking on a diet of dew. So I have come to help you out of your difficulty; you are distressed, I take it, at not being able to see everything on the Earth.' 'Thank you so much, you good Empedocles,' I said; 'as soon as my wings have brought me back to Greece, I will remember to pour libations to you up the chimney, and salute you on the first of every month with three moonward yawns.' 'Endymion be my witness,' he replied, 'I had no thought of such a bargain; I was touched by the sight of your distress. Now, what do you think is the way to sharpen your sight?'

'I have no idea, unless you were to remove the mist from my eyes for me; the sight seems quite bleared.' 'Oh, you can do without me; the thing that gives sharp sight you have brought with you from Earth.' 'Unconsciously, then; what is it?' 'Why, you know that you have on an eagle's right wing?' 'Of course I do; but what have wings and eyes to do with one another?' 'Only this,' he said; 'the eagle is far the strongest-eyed of all living things, the only one that can look straight at the sun; the test of the true royal eagle is, his meeting its rays without blinking.' 'So I have heard; I wish I had taken out my own eyes when I was starting, and substituted the eagle's. I am an imperfect specimen now I am here, not up to the royal standard at all, but like the rejected bastards.' 'Well, you can very soon acquire one royal eye. If you will stand up for a minute, keep the vulture wing still, and work the other, your right eye, corresponding to that wing, will gain strength. As for the other, its dimness cannot possibly be obviated, as it belongs to the inferior member.' 'Oh, I shall be quite content with aquiline vision for the right eye only,' I said; 'I have often observed that carpenters in ruling their wood find one better than two.' So saying, I proceeded to carry out my instructions at once. Empedocles began gradually to disappear, and at last vanished in smoke.

I had no sooner flapped the wing than a flood of light enveloped me, and things that before I had not even been aware of became perfectly clear. I turned my eyes down earthwards, and with ease discerned cities, men, and all that was going on, not merely in the open, but in the fancied security of houses. There was Ptolemy in his sister's arms, the son of Lysimachus plotting against his father, Seleucus's son Antiochus making signs to his step-mother Stratonice, Alexander of Pherae being murdered by his wife, Antigonus corrupting his daughter-in-law, the son of Attalus putting the poison in his cup; Arsaces was in the act of slaying his mistress, while the eunuch Arbaces drew his sword upon him; the guards were dragging Spatinus the Mede out from the banquet by the foot, with the lump on his brow from the golden cup. Similar sights were to be seen in the palaces of Libya and Scythia and Thrace— adulteries, murders, treasons, robberies, perjuries, suspicions, and monstrous betrayals.

Such was the entertainment afforded me by royalty; private life was much more amusing; for I could make that out too. I saw Hermodorus the Epicurean perjuring himself for 40 pounds, Agathocles the Stoic suing a pupil for his fees, lawyer Clinias stealing a bowl from the temple of Asclepius, and Herophilus the cynic sleeping in a brothel. Not to mention the multitude of burglars, litigants, usurers, duns; oh, it was a fine representative show!

Fr. I must say, Menippus, I should have liked the details here too; it all seems to have been very much to your taste.

Me. I could not go through the whole of it, even to please you; to take it in with the eyes kept one busy. But the main divisions were very much what Homer gives from the shield of Achilles:

here junketings and marriages, there courts and councils, in another compartment a sacrifice, and hard by a mourning. If I glanced at Getica, I would see the Getae at war; at Scythia, there were the Scythians wandering about on their waggons; half a turn in another direction gave me Egyptians at the plough, or Phoenicians chaffering, Cilician pirates, Spartan flagellants, Athenians at law.

All this was simultaneous, you understand; and you must try to conceive what a queer jumble it all made. It was as if a man were to collect a number of choristers, or rather of choruses,[64] and then tell each individual to disregard the others and start a strain of his own; if each did his best, went his own way, and tried to drown his neighbour, can you imagine what the musical effect would be?

Fr. A very ridiculous confusion.

Me. Well, friend, such are the earthly dancers; the life of man is just such a discordant performance; not only are the voices jangled, but the steps are not uniform, the motions not concerted, the objects not agreed upon—until the

---

[64] The Greek chorus combined singing with dancing.

impresario dismisses them one by one from the stage, with a 'not wanted.' Then they are all alike, and quiet enough, confounding no longer their undisciplined rival strains. But as long as the show lasts in its marvellous diversity, there is plenty of food for laughter in its vagaries.

The people who most amused me, however, were those who dispute about boundaries, or pride themselves on cultivating the plain of Sicyon, or holding the Oenoe side of Marathon, or a thousand acres at Acharnae. The whole of Greece, as I then saw it, might measure some four inches; how much smaller Athens on the same scale. So I realized what sort of sized basis for their pride remains to our rich men. The widest-acred of them all, methought, was the proud cultivator of an Epicurean atom. Then I looked at the Peloponnese, my eyes fell on the Cynurian district, and the thought occurred that it was for this little plot, no broader than an Egyptian lentil, that all those Argives and Spartans fell in a single day. Or if I saw a man puffed up by the possession of seven or eight gold rings and half as many gold cups, again my lungs would begin to crow; why, Pangaeus with all its mines was about the size of a grain of millet.

Fr. You lucky man! what a rare sight you had! And how big, now, did the towns and the people look from there?

Me. You must often have seen a community of ants, some of them a seething mass, some going abroad, others coming back to town. One is a scavenger, another a bustling porter loaded with a bit of bean-pod or half a wheat grain. They no doubt have, on their modest myrmecic scale, their architects and politicians, their magistrates and composers and philosophers. At any rate, what men and cities suggested to me was just so many ant-hills. If you think the similitude too disparaging, look into the Thessalian legends, and you will find that the most warlike tribe there was the Myrmidons, or ants turned men. Well, when I had had enough of contemplation and laughter, I roused myself and soared

To join the Gods, where dwells the Lord of storms.

I had only flown a couple of hundred yards, when Selene's feminine voice reached me:

'Menippus, do me an errand to Zeus, and I will wish you a pleasant journey.' 'You have only to name it,' I said, 'provided it is not something to carry.' 'It is a simple message of entreaty to Zeus. I am tired to death, you must know, of being slandered by these philosophers; they have no better occupation than impertinent curiosity about me—What am I? how big am I? why am I halved? why am I gibbous? I am inhabited; I am just a mirror hung over the sea; I am—whatever their latest fancy suggests. It is the last straw when they say my light is stolen, sham, imported from the sun, and keep on doing their best to get up jealousy and ill feeling between brother and sister. They might have been contented with making *him* out a stone or a red-hot lump.

'These gentry who in the day look so stern and manly, dress so gravely, and are so revered by common men, would be surprised to learn how much I

465

know of their vile nightly abominations. I see them all, though I never tell; it would be too indecent to make revelations, and show up the contrast between their nightly doings and their public performances; so, if I catch one of them in adultery or theft or other nocturnal adventure, I pull my cloud veil over me; I do not want the vulgar to see old men disgracing their long beards and their virtuous calling. But they go on giving tongue and worrying me all the same, and, so help me Night, I have thought many a time of going a long, long way off, out of reach of their impertinent tongues. Will you remember to tell Zeus all this? and you may add that I cannot remain at my post unless he will pulverize the physicists, muzzle the logicians, raze the Porch, burn the Academy, and put an end to strolling in the Lyceum. That might secure me a little peace from these daily mensurations.'

'I will remember,' said I, and resumed my upward flight to Heaven, through

A region where nor ox nor man had wrought.

For the Moon was soon but a small object, with the Earth entirely hidden behind it. Three days' flight through the stars, with the Sun on my right hand, brought me close to Heaven; and my first idea was to go straight in as I was; I should easily pass unobserved in virtue of my half-eagleship; for of course the eagle was Zeus's familiar; on second thoughts, though, my vulture wing would very soon betray me. So, thinking it better not to run any risks, I went up to the door and knocked. Hermes opened, took my name, and hurried off to inform Zeus. After a brief wait I was asked to step in; I was now trembling with apprehension, and I found that the Gods, who were all seated together, were not quite easy themselves. The unexpected nature of the visit was slightly disturbing to them, and they had visions of all mankind arriving at my heels by the same conveyance.

But Zeus bent upon me a Titanic glance, awful, penetrating, and spoke:

Who art thou? where thy city? who thy kin?

At the sound, I nearly died of fear, but remained upright, though mute and paralysed by that thunderous voice. I gradually recovered, began at the beginning, and gave a clear account of myself—how I had been possessed with curiosity about the heavens, had gone to the philosophers, found their accounts conflicting, and grown tired of being logically rent in twain; so I came to my great idea, my wings, and ultimately to Heaven; I added Selene's message. Zeus smiled and slightly unbent his brow. 'What of Otus and Ephialtes now?' he said; 'here is Menippus scaling Heaven! Well, well, for to-day consider yourself our guest. To-morrow we will treat with you of your business, and send you on your way.' And therewith he rose and walked to the acoustic centre of Heaven, it being prayer time.

As he went, he put questions to me about earthly affairs, beginning with, What was wheat a quarter in Greece? had we suffered much from cold last winter? and did the vegetables want more rain? Then he wished to know whether any of Phidias's kin were alive, why there had been no Diasia at Athens all these years, whether his Olympieum was ever going to be completed, and had the robbers of his temple at Dodona been caught? I answered all these questions, and he proceeded:

—'Tell me, Menippus, what are men's feelings towards me?' 'What should they be, Lord, but those of absolute reverence, as to the King of all Gods?' 'Now, now, chaffing as usual,' he said; 'I know their fickleness very well, for all your dissimulation. There was a time when I was their prophet, their healer, and their all,

And Zeus filled every street and gathering-place.

In those days Dodona and Pisa were glorious and far-famed, and I could not get a view for the clouds of sacrificial steam. But now Apollo has set up his oracle at Delphi, Asclepius his temple of health at Pergamum, Bendis and Anubis and Artemis their shrines in Thrace, Egypt, Ephesus; and to these all run; theirs the festal gatherings and the hecatombs. As for me, I am superannuated; they think themselves very generous if they offer me a victim at Olympia at four-year intervals. My altars are cold as Plato's *Laws* or Chrysippus's *Syllogisms*.'

So talking, we reached the spot where he was to sit and listen to the prayers. There was a row of openings with lids like well-covers, and a chair of gold by each. Zeus took his seat at the first, lifted off the lid and inclined his ear. From every quarter of Earth were coming the most various and contradictory petitions; for I too bent down my head and listened. Here are specimens. 'O Zeus, that I might be king!' 'O Zeus, that my onions and garlic might thrive!' 'Ye Gods, a speedy death for my father!' Or again, 'Would that I might succeed to my wife's property!' 'Grant that my plot against my brother be not detected.' 'Let me win my suit.' 'Give me an Olympic garland.' Of those at sea, one prayed for a north, another for a south wind; the farmer asked for rain, the fuller for sun. Zeus listened, and gave each prayer careful consideration, but without promising to grant them all;

Our Father this bestowed, and that withheld.

Righteous prayers he allowed to come up through the hole, received and laid them down at his right, while he sent the unholy ones packing with a downward puff of breath, that Heaven might not be defiled by their entrance. In one case I saw him puzzled; two men praying for opposite things and promising the same sacrifices, he could not tell which of them to favour, and experienced a truly Academic suspense of judgement, showing a reserve and equilibrium worthy of Pyrrho himself.

The prayers disposed of, he went on to the next chair and opening, and attended to oaths and their takers. These done with, and Hermodorus the Epicurean annihilated, he proceeded to the next chair to deal with omens, prophetic voices, and auguries. Then came the turn of the sacrifice aperture, through which the smoke came up and communicated to Zeus the name of the devotee it represented. After that, he was free to give his wind and weather orders:

—Rain for Scythia to-day, a thunderstorm for Libya, snow for Greece. The north wind he instructed to blow in Lydia, the west to raise a storm in the Adriatic, the south to take a rest; a thousand bushels of hail to be distributed over Cappadocia.

His work was now pretty well completed, and as it was just dinner time, we went to the banquet hall. Hermes received me, and gave me my place next to a group of Gods whose alien origin left them in a rather doubtful position—Pan, the Corybants, Attis, and Sabazius. I was supplied with bread by Demeter, wine by Dionysus, meat by Heracles, myrtle-blossoms by Aphrodite, and sprats by Posidon. But I also got a sly taste of ambrosia and nectar; good-natured Ganymede, as often as he saw that Zeus's attention was engaged elsewhere, brought round the nectar and indulged me with a half- pint or so. The Gods, as Homer (who I think must have had the same opportunities of observation as myself) somewhere says, neither eat bread nor drink the ruddy wine; they heap their plates with ambrosia, and are nectar-bibbers; but their choicest dainties are the smoke of sacrifice ascending with rich fumes, and the blood of victims poured by their worshippers round the altars. During dinner, Apollo harped, Silenus danced his wild measures, the Muses uprose and sang to us from Hesiod's *Birth of Gods*, and the first of Pindar's odes. When we had our fill and had well drunken, we slumbered, each where he was.

Slept all the Gods, and men with plumed helms,
That livelong night; but me kind sleep forsook;

for I had much upon my mind; most of all, how came it that Apollo, in all that time, had never grown a beard? and how was night possible in Heaven, with the sun always there taking his share of the good cheer? So I had but a short nap of it. And in the morning Zeus arose, and bade summon an assembly.

When all were gathered, he thus commenced:

—'The immediate occasion of my summoning you is the arrival of this stranger yesterday. But I have long intended to take counsel with you regarding the philosophers, and now, urged by Selene and her complaints, I have determined to defer the consideration of the question no longer. There is a class which has recently become conspicuous among men; they are idle, quarrelsome, vain, irritable, lickerish, silly, puffed up, arrogant, and, in Homeric phrase, vain cumberers of the earth. These men have divided themselves into bands, each dwelling in a separate word-maze of its own construction, and call themselves Stoics, Epicureans, Peripatetics, and more farcical names yet. Then they take to themselves the holy name of Virtue, and with uplifted brows and flowing beards exhibit the deceitful semblance that hides immoral lives; their model is the tragic actor, from whom if you strip off the mask and the gold-spangled robe, there is nothing left but a paltry fellow hired for a few shillings to play a part.

'Nevertheless, quite undeterred by their own characters, they scorn the human and travesty the divine; they gather a company of guileless youths, and feed them with solemn chatter upon Virtue and quibbling verbal puzzles; in their pupils' presence they are all for fortitude and temperance, and have no words bad enough for wealth and pleasure:

when they are by themselves, there is no limit to their gluttony, their lechery, their licking of dirty pence. But the head and front of their offending is this:

they neither work themselves nor help others' work; they are useless drones,

Of no avail in council nor in war;

which notwithstanding, they censure others; they store up poisoned words, they con invectives, they heap their neighbours with reproaches; their highest honours are for him who shall be loudest and most overbearing and boldest in abuse.

'Ask one of these brawling bawling censors, And what do *you* do? in God's name, what shall we call *your* contribution to progress? and he would reply, if conscience and truth were anything to him:

I consider it superfluous to sail the sea or till the earth or fight for my country or follow a trade; but I have a loud voice and a dirty body; I eschew warm water and go barefoot through the winter; I am a Momus who can always pick holes in other people's coats; if a rich man keeps a costly table or a mistress, I make it my business to be properly horrified; but if my familiar friend is lying sick, in need of help and care, I am not aware of it. Such, your Godheads, is the nature of this vermin.

'There is a special insolence in those who call themselves Epicureans; these go so far as to lay their hands on our character; we take no interest in human affairs, they say, and in fact have nothing to do with the course of events. And this is a serious question for you; if once they infect their generation with this view, you will learn what hunger means. Who will sacrifice to you, if he does not expect to profit by it? As to Selene's complaints, you all heard them yesterday from this stranger's lips. And now decide upon such measures as shall advantage mankind and secure your own safety.'

Zeus had no sooner closed his speech than clamour prevailed, all crying at once:

Blast! burn! annihilate! to the pit with them! to Tartarus! to the Giants! Zeus ordered silence again, and then, 'Your wishes,' he said, 'shall be executed; they shall all be annihilated, and their logic with them. But just at present chastisement is not lawful; you are aware that we are now in the four months of the long vacation; the formal notice has lately been issued. In the spring of next year, the baleful levin-bolt shall give them the fate they deserve.'

He spake, and sealed his word with lowering brows.

'As to Menippus,' he added, 'my pleasure is this. He shall be deprived of his wings, and so incapacitated for repeating his visit, but shall to-day be conveyed back to Earth by Hermes.' So saying, he dismissed the assembly. The Cyllenian accordingly lifted me up by the right ear, and yesterday evening deposited me in the Ceramicus. And now, friend, you have all the latest from Heaven. I must be off to the Poecile, to let the philosophers loitering there know the luck they are in.

THE DOUBLE INDICTMENT

Zeus. Hermes. Justice. Pan. Several Athenians. The Academy. The Porch. Epicurus. Virtue. Luxury. Diogenes. Rhetoric. A Syrian. Dialogue

Zeus. A curse on all those philosophers who will have it that none but the Gods are happy! If they could but know what we have to put up with on men's account, they would not envy us our nectar and our ambrosia. They take Homer's word for it all,—the word of a blind quack; 'tis he who pronounces us blessed, and expatiates on heavenly glories, he who could not see in front of his own nose. Look at the Sun, now. He yokes that chariot, and is riding through the heavens from morn till night, clothed in his garment of fire, and dispensing his rays abroad; not so much breathing-space as goes to the scratching of an ear; once let his horses catch him napping, and they have the bit between their teeth and are off 'cross country, with the result that the Earth is scorched to a cinder. The Moon is no better off:

she is kept up into the small hours to light the reveller and the diner-out upon their homeward path. And then Apollo,—*he* has his work cut out for him:

with such a press of oracular business, it is much if he has any ears left to hear with:

he is wanted at Delphi; the next minute, he must be off to Colophon; then away to Xanthus; then back at a trot to Clarus; then it is Delos, then Branchidae;—in short, he is at the beck of every priestess who has taken her draught of holy water, munched her laurel-leaf, and made the tripod rock; it is now or never; if he is not there that minute to reel off the required oracle, his credit is gone. The traps they set for him too! He must have a dog's nose for lamb and tortoise in the pot, or his Lydian customer[65] departs, laughing him to scorn. As for Asclepius, he has no peace for his patients:

his eyes are acquainted with horror, and his hands with loathsomeness; another's sickness is his pain. To say nothing of the work that the Winds have to get through, what with sowing and winnowing and getting the ships along; or of Sleep, always on the wing, with Dream at his side all night giving a helping hand. Men have to thank us for all this:

every one of us contributes his share to their well-being. And the others have an easy time of it, compared to me, to me the King and Father of all. The annoyances I have to put up with! the worry of thinking of all these things at once! I must keep an eye on all the rest, to begin with, or they would be making some silly mistake; and as for the work I have to do with my own hands, there is no end to it; such complications! it is all I can do to get through with it. It is not as if I had only the main issues to attend to, the rain and hail and wind and lightning, and as soon as I had arranged them could sit down, feeling that my own particular work was over:

---

[65] See *Croesus* in Notes.

no, besides all that, I must be looking every way at once, Argus-eyed for theft and perjury, as for sacrifice; the moment a libation has been poured, it is for me to locate the savoury smoke that rises; for me it is to hear the cry of the sick man and of the sailor; at one and the same moment, a hecatomb demands my presence at Olympia, a battle in the plain of Babylon; hail is due in Thrace, dinner in Ethiopia; 'tis too much! And do what I may, it is hard to give satisfaction. Many is the time that all besides, both Gods and men of plumed helm, have slept the long night through, while unto Zeus sweet slumber has not come nigh. If I nod for a moment, behold, Epicurus is justified, and our indifference to the affairs of Earth made manifest; and if once men lend an ear to that doctrine, the consequences will be serious:

our temples will go ungarlanded; the streets will be redolent no longer of roast meat, the bowl no longer yield us libation; our altars will be cold, sacrifice and oblation will be at an end, and utter starvation must ensue. Hence like a pilot I stand up at the helm all alone, tiller in hand, while every soul on board is asleep, and probably drunk; no rest, no food for me, while I ponder in my mind and breast on the common safety; and my reward? to be called the Lord of all! I should like to ask those philosophers who assign us the monopoly of blessedness, when they suppose we find time for nectar and ambrosia among our ceaseless occupations. Look at the mildewed, cob-webbed stack of petitions mouldering on their files in our chancery, for want of time to attend to them:

look only at the cases pending between men and the various Arts and Sciences; venerable relics, some of them! Angry protests against the delays of the law reach me from all quarters; men cannot understand that it is from no neglect of ours that these judgements have been postponed; it is simply pressure of business—pressure of blessedness, if they will have it so.

Her. I myself, father, have heard a great deal of dissatisfaction expressed on Earth, only I did not like to mention it to you. However, as you have introduced the subject yourself, I may say that the discontent is general:

men do not venture to express their resentment openly, but there are mutterings in corners about the delay. It is high time they were all put out of their suspense, for better or for worse.

Zeus. And what would you have me do, my boy? hold a session at once? or shall we say next year?

Her. Oh, at once, by all means.

Zeus. To work, then:

fly down, and make proclamation in the following terms:

All litigant parties to assemble this day on Areopagus:

Justice to assign them their juries from the whole body of the Athenians, the number of the jury to be in proportion to the amount of damages claimed; any party doubting the justice of his sentence to have the right of appeal to me.

And you, my daughter, take your seat by the side of the Dread Goddesses[66], cast lots for the order of the trials, and superintend the formation of juries.

Just. You would have me return to Earth, once more to be driven thence in ignominious flight by the intolerable taunts of Injustice?

Zeus. Hope for better things. The philosophers have quite convinced every one by this time of your superiority. The son of Sophroniscus was particularly strong on your merits:

he laid it down that Justice was the highest Good.

Just. Yes; and very serviceable his dissertations on Justice were to him, were they not, when he was handed over to the Eleven, and thrown into prison, and drank the hemlock? Poor man, he had not even time to sacrifice the cock he owed to Asclepius. His accusers were too much for him altogether, and *their* philosophy had Injustice for its object.

Zeus. But in those days philosophy was not generally known, and had but few exponents; it is not surprising that the scale turned in favour of Anytus and Meletus. But now it is different:

look at the number of cloaks and sticks and wallets that are about; everywhere philosophers, long-bearded, book in hand, maintain your cause; the public walks are filled with their contending hosts, and every man of them calls Virtue his nurse. Numbers have abandoned their former professions to pounce upon wallet and cloak; these ready-made philosophers, carpenters once or cobblers, now duly tanned to the true Ethiopian hue, are singing your praises high and low. 'He that falls on shipboard strikes wood,' says the proverb; and the eye, wheresoever it fall, will light on philosophers.

Just. Yes, father, but they frighten me:

they quarrel so among themselves; and when they talk about me, they only expose their own little minds. And, from what I hear, most of those who make so free with my name show no inclination at all to put my principles into practice. I may count upon finding their doors closed to *me*.

Injustice has been beforehand with me.

Zeus. Come, child, they are not all so bad, and if you can find a few honest men it will be something. Now, off with you both, and see if you can't get a few cases settled up to-day.

Her. Well, Justice:

yonder is our road:

straight in the line for Sunium, to the foot of Hymettus, taking Parnes on our right; you see those two hills? You have quite forgotten the way, I suppose, in all this time? Now, now:

weeping? why so vexed? There is nothing to fear. Things are quite different in these days:

the Scirons and Pityocampteses and Busirises and Phalarises who used to frighten you so are all dead:

---

[66] See *Erinnyes* in Notes.

Wisdom, the Academy, the Porch, now hold sway everywhere. They are all your admirers; their talk is all of you; they yearn to see you descend to them once more.

Just. Tell me, Hermes,—you if any one must know the truth; you are generally busy either in the Gymnasium or else in the Market, making proclamation to the Assembly,—what are the Athenians like now? shall I be able to live with them?

Her. We are brother and sister, it is only right that I should tell you the truth. Well then, Philosophy has made a considerable change for the better in most of them; at the worst, their respect for the cloth is some check on their misdeeds. At the same time—not to conceal anything—you will find villains amongst them; and you will find some who are neither quite philosophers nor quite knaves. The fact is, Philosophy's dyeing process is still going on. Some have absorbed the full quantity of dye; these are perfect specimens of her art, and show no admixture of other colours; with them you will find a ready reception. But others, owing to their original impurities, are not yet completely saturated; they are better than the generality of mankind, but they are not all they should be; they are piebald or spotted or dappled. Others again there are who have contented themselves with merely rubbing a fingertip in the soot on the outside of the cauldron, and smearing themselves with that; after which they consider the dyeing process complete. But you, of course, will only live with the best. Meanwhile, here we are, close to Attica; we must now leave Sunium on our right, and diverge towards the Acropolis. Good:

terra firma. You had better sit down somewhere here on the Areopagus, in the direction of the Pnyx, and wait whilst I make Zeus's proclamation. I shall go up into the Acropolis; that will be the easiest way of making every one hear the summons.

Just. Before you go, Hermes, tell me who this is coming along; a man with horns and a pipe and shaggy legs.

Her. Why, you must know Pan, most festive of all Dionysus's followers? He used to live on Mount Parthenius:

but at the time of the Persian expedition under Datis, when the barbarians landed at Marathon, he volunteered in the Athenian service; and ever since then he has had the cave yonder at the foot of the Acropolis, a little past the Pelasgicum, and pays his taxes like any other naturalized foreigner. Seeing us so near at hand, I suppose he is coming up to make his compliments.

Pan. Hail, Justice and Hermes!

Just. Hail, Pan; chief of Satyrs in dance and song, and most gallant of Athens' soldiers!

Pan. But what brings you here, Hermes?

Her. Justice will explain; I must be off to the Acropolis on my errand.

Just. Zeus has sent me down, Pan, to preside in the law- court.—And how do you like Athens?

Pan. Well, the fact is, I am a good deal disappointed:

they do not treat me with the consideration to which I am entitled, after repelling that tremendous barbarian invasion. All they do is to come up to my cave two or three times a year with a particularly high-scented goat, and sacrifice him:

I am permitted to look on whilst they enjoy the feast, and am complimented with a perfunctory dance. However, there is some joking and merrymaking on the occasion, and that I find rather fun.

Just. And, Pan,—have they become more virtuous under the hands of the philosophers?

Pan. Philosophers? Oh! people with beards just like mine; sepulchral beings, who are always getting together and jabbering?

Just. Those are they.

Pan. I can't understand a word they say; their philosophy is too much for me. I am mountain-bred; smart city-language is not in my line; sophists and philosophers are not known in Arcadia. I am a good hand at flute or pipe; I can mind goats, I can dance, I can fight at a pinch, and that is all. But I hear them all day long, bawling out a string of hard words about virtue, and nature, and ideas, and things incorporeal. They are good enough friends when the argument begins, but their voices mount higher and higher as they go on, and end in a scream; they get more and more excited, and all try to speak at once; they grow red in the face, their necks swell, and their veins stand out, for all the world like a flute-player on a high note. The argument is turned upside down, they forget what they are trying to prove, and finally go off abusing one another and brushing the sweat from their brows; victory rests with him who can show the boldest front and the loudest voice, and hold his ground the longest. The people, especially those who have nothing better to do, adore them, and stand spellbound under their confident bawlings. For all that I could see, they were no better than humbugs, and I was none too pleased at their copying my beard. If there were any use in their noise, if the talking did any good to the public, I should not have a word to say against them:

but, to tell you the plain unvarnished truth, I have more than once looked out from my peep-hole yonder and seen them—

Just. Hush, Pan:

was not that Hermes making the proclamation?

Pan. I thought so.

Her. Be it known to all men that we purpose on this seventh day of March to hold a court of justice, and Fortune defend the right! All litigant parties to assemble on Areopagus, where Justice will assign the juries and preside over the trials in person. The juries to be taken from the whole Athenian people; the pay to be sixpence for each case; the number of jurors to vary with the nature of the accusation. Any parties who had commenced legal proceedings and have died in the interim to be sent up by Aeacus. Any party doubting the justice of his sentence may appeal; the appeal to he heard by Zeus.

Pan. Talk about noise! how they shout! And what a hurry they are in to get here! See how one hales another up the hill! Here comes Hermes himself. Well, I leave you to your juries and your evidence; you are accustomed to it. I will return to my cave, and there play over one of those amorous ditties with which I love to upbraid Echo. As to rhetoric and law-pleadings, I hear enough of those every day in this very court of Areopagus.

Her. We had better summon the parties, Justice.

Just. True. Only look at the crowd, bustling and buzzing about the hilltop like a swarm of wasps!

First Ath. I've got you, curse you.

Second Ath. Pooh! a trumped-up charge.

Third Ath. At last! you shall get your deserts this time.

Fourth Ath. Your villany shall be unmasked.

Fifth Ath. My jury first, Hermes.

Sixth Ath. Come along:
 into court with you, rascal.

Seventh Ath. You needn't throttle me.

Just. Do you know what I think we had better do, Hermes? Put off all the other cases for to-morrow, and only take to-day the charges brought by Arts, Professions, and Philosophies. Pick me out all of that kind.

Her. Drink *v.* the Academy, *re* Polemon, kidnapped.

Just. Seven jurors.

Her. Porch *v.* Pleasure. Defendant is charged with seducing Dionysius, plaintiff's admirer.

Just. Five will do for that.

Her. Luxury *v.* Virtue, *re* Aristippus.

Just. Five again.

Her. Bank *v.* Diogenes, alleged to have run away from plaintiff's service.

Just. Three only.

Her. Painting *v.* Pyrrho. Desertion from the ranks.

Just. That will want nine.

Her. What about these two charges just brought against a rhetorician?

Just. No, those can stand over; we must work off the arrears first.

Her. Well, these cases are of just the same kind. They are not old ones, it is true, but they are very like those you have taken, and might fairly be heard with them.

Just. That looks rather like favouritism, Hermes. However, as you like; only these must be the last; we have got quite enough. What are they?

Her. Rhetoric *v.* a Syrian[67], for neglect; Dialogue *v.* the same, for assault.

Just. And who is this Syrian? There is no name given.

Her. That is all:
 the Syrian rhetorician; he can have a jury without having a name.

---

[67] i.e. Lucian. See Volume I, Introduction, Section I, Life.

Just. So! here on Areopagus I am to give juries to outsiders, who ought to be tried on the other side of the Euphrates? Well, give him eleven, and they can hear both cases.

Her. That's right; it will save a lot of expense.

Just. First case:

the Academy *versus* Drink. Let the jury take their seats. Mark the time,' Hermes. Drink, open the case.... Not a word? can you do nothing but nod?— Hermes, go and see what is the matter with her.

Her. She says she cannot plead, she would only be laughed at; wine has tied her tongue. As you see, she can hardly stand.

Just. Well, there are plenty of able counsel present, ready to shout themselves hoarse for sixpence; let her employ one of them.

Her. No one will have anything to do with such a client in open court. But she makes a very reasonable proposal.

Just. Yes?

Her. The Academy is always ready to take both sides; she makes a point of contradicting herself plausibly. 'Let her speak first on my behalf,' says Drink, 'and then on her own.'

Just. A novel form of procedure. However, go on, Academy; speak on both sides, if you find it so easy.

Acad. First, gentlemen of the jury, let me state the case for 16 Drink, as her time is now being taken.

My unfortunate client, gentlemen, has been cruelly wronged:

I have torn from her the one slave on whose loyalty and affection she could rely, the only one who saw nothing censurable in her conduct. I allude to Polemon, whose days, from morning to night, were spent in revel; who in broad daylight sought the publicity of the Market in the company of music— girls and singers; ever drunk, ever headachy, ever garlanded. In support of my statements, I appeal to every man in Athens to say whether he had ever seen Polemon sober. But in an evil hour for him, his revels, which had brought him to so many other doors, brought him at length to my own. I laid hands on him, tore him away by brute force from the plaintiff, and made him my own; giving him water to drink, teaching him sobriety, and stripping him of his garlands. He, who should have been sitting over his wine, now became acquainted with the perverse, the harassing, the pernicious quibbles of philosophy. Alas! the ruddy glow has departed from his cheek; he is pale and wasted; his songs are all forgotten; there are times when he will sit far on into the night, tasting neither meat nor drink, while he reels out the meaningless platitudes with which I have so abundantly supplied him. I have even incited him to attack the character of my client, and to utter a thousand base insinuations against her good fame.

The case of Drink is now complete. I proceed to state my own. Let my time be taken.

Just. What will the defendant have to say to that, I wonder? Give her the same time allowance.

Acad. Nothing, gentlemen of the jury, could sound more plausible than the arguments advanced by my learned friend on her client's behalf. And yet, if you will give me your favourable attention, I shall convince you that the plaintiff has suffered no wrong at my hands. This Polemon, whom plaintiff claims as her servant, so far from having any natural connexion with her, is one whose excellent parts entitle him to claim kinship and affinity with myself. He was still a boy, his powers were yet unformed, when plaintiff, aided and abetted by Pleasure—ever her partner in crime—seized upon him, and delivered him over into the clutches of debauchery and dissipation, under whose corrupt influence the unfortunate young man utterly lost all sense of shame. Those very facts that plaintiff supposed to be so many arguments in her favour will be found, on the contrary, to make for my own case. From early morning (as my learned friend has just observed) did the misguided Polemon, with aching head and garlanded, stagger through the open market to the noise of flutes, never sober, brawling with all he met; a reproach to his ancestors and his city, a laughing-stock to foreigners. One day he reached my door. He found it open:

I was discoursing to a company of my disciples, as is my wont, upon virtue and temperance. He stood there, with the flute-girl at his side and the garlands on his head, and sought at first to drown our conversation with his noisy outcry. But we paid no heed to him, and little by little our words produced a sobering effect, for Drink had not entire possession of him:

he bade the flute-girl cease, tore off his garlands, and looked with shame at his luxurious dress. Like one waking from deep sleep, he saw himself as he was, and repented of his past life; the flush of drunkenness faded and vanished from his cheek, and was succeeded by a blush of shame; at last, not (as plaintiff would have you believe) in response to any invitation of mine, nor under any compulsion, but of his own free will, and in the conviction of my superiority, he renounced his former mistress there and then, and entered my service. Bring him into court. You shall see for yourselves, gentlemen, what he has become under my treatment. Behold that Polemon whom I found drunk, unable to speak or stand upright, an object of ridicule:

I turned him from his evil ways; I taught him sobriety; and I present him to you, no longer a slave, but a decent and orderly citizen, a credit to his nation. In conclusion let me say that the change I have wrought in him has won me the gratitude not only of Polemon himself but of all his friends. Which of us has been the more profitable companion for him, it is now for the jury to decide.

Her. Come, gentlemen, get up and give your votes. There is no time to be lost; we have other cases coming on.

Just. Academy wins, by six votes to one.

Her. I am not surprised to find that Drink has one adherent. Jurors in the case of Porch *v.* Pleasure *re* Dionysius take their seats! The lady of the frescoes[68] may begin; her time is noted.

Porch. I am not ignorant, gentlemen, of the attractions of my adversary. I see how your eyes turn in her direction; she has your smiles, I your contempt, because my hair is close-cropped, and my expression stern and masculine. Yet if you will give me a fair hearing, I fear her not; for justice is on my side. Nay, it is with these same meretricious attractions of hers that my accusation is concerned:

it was by her specious appearance that she beguiled the virtuous Dionysius, my lover, and drew him to herself. The present case is in fact closely allied with that of Drink and the Academy, with which your colleagues have just dealt. The question now before you is this:

are men to live the lives of swine, wallowing in voluptuousness, with never a high or noble thought:

or are they to set virtue above enjoyment, and follow the dictates of freedom and philosophy, fearing not to grapple with pain, nor seeking the degrading service of pleasure, as though happiness were to be found in a pot of honey or a cake of figs? These are the baits my adversary throws out for fools, and toil the bugbear with which she frightens them:

her artifices seldom fail; and among her victims is this unfortunate whom she has constrained to rebel against my authority. She had to wait till she found him on a sick-bed; never while he was himself would he have listened to her proposals. Yet what right have *I* to complain? She spares not even the Gods; she impugns the wisdom of Providence; she is guilty of blasphemy; you have a double penalty to impose, if you would be wise. I hear that she has not even been at the pains of preparing a defence:

Epicurus is to speak for her! She does not stand upon ceremony with you, gentlemen.—Ask her what Heracles would have been, what your own Theseus would have been, if they had listened to the voice of pleasure, and shrunk back from toil:

their toils were the only check upon wickedness, which else must have overrun the whole Earth. And now I have done; I am no lover of long speeches. Yet if my adversary would consent to answer a few questions, her worthlessness would soon appear. Let me remind you, gentlemen, of your oath:

give your votes in accordance with that oath, and believe not Epicurus, when he tells you that the Gods take no thought for the things of Earth.

Her. Stand down, madam. Epicurus will now speak on behalf of pleasure.

Epi. I shall not detain you long, gentlemen of the jury; there is no occasion for me to do so. If it were true, as the plaintiff asserts, that Dionysius was her lover, and that my client by means of drugs or incantations had

---

[68] See *Poecile* in Notes.

constrained him to withdraw his affections from the plaintiff and transfer them to herself,—if this were true, then my client might fairly be accused of witchcraft, nor could her wicked practices upon her rival's admirers escape condemnation. On the other hand, if a free citizen of a free state, deciding for himself in a matter where the law is silent, takes a violent aversion to this lady's person, concludes that the blessedness with which she promises to crown his labours is neither more nor less than moonshine, and accordingly makes the best of his way out of her labyrinthine maze of argument into the attractive arms of Pleasure, bursts the bonds of verbal subtlety, exchanges credulity for common sense, and pronounces, with great justice, that toil is toilsome, and that pleasure is pleasant,—I ask, is this shipwrecked mariner to be excluded from the calm haven of his desire, and hurled back headlong into a sea of toil? is this poor suppliant at the altar of Mercy—in other words of Pleasure— is he to be delivered over into the power of perplexity,—and all on the chance that his hot climb up the steep hill of Virtue may be rewarded with a glimpse of that celebrated lady on the top, and his life of toil followed by a hereafter of happiness? We could scarcely ask for a better judge of the matter than Dionysius himself. He was as familiar with the Stoic doctrines as any man, and held at one time that virtue was the only Good:

but he presently discovered that toil was an evil:

he then chose what seemed to him the better course. He would no doubt observe that those philosophers who had so much to say on the subject of patience and endurance under toil were secretly the servants of Pleasure, carefully abiding by her laws in their own homes, though they made so free with her name in their discourses. They cannot bear to be detected in any relaxation, or any departure from their principles:

but, poor men, they lead a Tantalus life of it in consequence, and when they *do* get a chance of sinning without being found out, they drink down pleasure by the bucketful. Depend on it, if some one would make them a present of Gyges's ring of invisibility, or Hades's cap, they would cut the acquaintance of toil without further ceremony, and elbow their way into the presence of Pleasure; they would all be Dionysiuses then. As long as Dionysius was well, he thought that there was some good in all this talk about endurance; but when he fell ill, and found out what pain really was, he perceived that his body was of another school than the Porch, and held quite other tenets:

he was converted, realized that he was flesh and blood, and from that day ceased to behave as if he were made of marble; he knew now that the man who talks nonsense about the iniquity of pleasure

But toys with words:

his thoughts are bent elsewhither.

And now, gentlemen, I leave you to your vote.

Porch. Not yet! Let me ask him a few questions.

Epi. Yes? I am ready.

Porch. You hold toil to be an evil?

480

Epi. I do.

Porch. And pleasure a good?

Epi. Unquestionably.

Porch. Do you recognize the distinction between *differentia* and *indifferentia*? between *praeposita* and *rejecta*?

Epi. Why, certainly.

Her. Madam, this discussion must cease; the jury say they do not understand word-chopping. They will now give their votes.

Porch. Ah; I should have won, if I could have tried him with my third figure of *self-evidents*.

Just. Who wins?

Her. Unanimous verdict for Pleasure.

Porch. I appeal to Zeus.

Just. By all means. Next case, Hermes.

Her. Luxury *v.* Virtue, *re* Aristippus; Aristippus must appear in person.

Vir. I ought to speak first. Aristippus is mine; his words and his deeds alike proclaim him mine.

Lux. On the contrary, any one who will observe his garlands and his purple robes and his perfumes will agree that he is mine.

Just. Peace! This suit must stand over, until Zeus has decided the appeal *re* Dionysius. The cases are similar. If Porch wins her appeal, Aristippus shall be adjudged to Virtue:

if not, Luxury must have him. Bring the next case. By the way, those jurors must not have their fee; they have not earned it.

Her. So the poor old gentlemen have climbed up all this way for nothing!

Just. Well, they must be content with a third. Now go away, all of you, and don't be cross; you shall have another chance.

Her. Diogenes of Sinope wanted! Bank, it is for you to speak.

Diog. Look here, Madam Justice, if she doesn't stop bothering, I shall have assault and battery to answer for before long, instead of desertion; my stick is ready.

Just. What is the meaning of this? Bank has run away, and Diogenes after her, with his stick raised. Poor Bank! I am afraid she will be roughly handled. Call Pyrrho.

Her. Here is Painting, but Pyrrho has never come up. I knew how it would be.

Just. And what was his reason?

Her. He holds that there is no such thing as a true decision.

Just. Then judgement goes against him by default. Now for the Syrian advocate. The indictments were only filed a day or two ago; there was no such hurry. However——. We will first take the case in which Rhetoric is plaintiff. How people crowd in to hear it!

Her. Just so:

481

the case has not had time to get stale, you see; it has the charm of novelty, the indictment, as you say, having only been filed yesterday. The prospect, too, of hearing the Syrian defend himself against two such plaintiffs as Rhetoric and Dialogue, one after the other, is a great attraction. Well, Rhetoric, when are you going to begin?

Rhet. Before all things, men of Athens, I pray the Gods that you may listen to me throughout this trial with feelings not less warm than those that I have ever entertained towards my country and towards each one of you, my countrymen. And if, further, I pray them so to dispose your hearts that you will suffer me to conduct my case in accordance with my original intention and design, without interruption from my adversary, I shall be asking no more than justice. When I listen to the defendant's words, and then reflect upon the treatment I have received from him, I know not how I am to reconcile the two. You will presently find him holding a language scarcely distinguishable from my own:

yet examine into his conduct, and you will see, from the lengths to which he has already gone, that I am justified in taking steps to prevent his going yet further. But enough of preamble:

I am wasting time that might be better employed in accusing my adversary.

Gentlemen, the defendant was no more than a boy—he still spoke with his native accent, and might at any moment have exhibited himself in the garb of an Assyrian—when I found him wandering up and down Ionia, at a loss for employment. I took him in hand; I gave him an education; and, convinced of his capabilities and of his devotion to me (for he was my very humble servant in those days, and had no admiration to spare for any one else), I turned my back upon the many suitors who sought my hand, upon the wealthy, the brilliant and the high-born, and betrothed myself to this monster of ingratitude; upon this obscure pauper boy I bestowed the rich dowry of my surpassing eloquence, brought him to be enrolled among my own people, and made him my fellow citizen, to the bitter mortification of his unsuccessful rivals. When he formed the resolution of travelling, in order to make his good fortune known to the world, I did not remain behind:

I accompanied him everywhere, from city to city, shedding my lustre upon him, and clothing him in honour and renown. Of our travels in Greece and Ionia, I say nothing:

he expressed a wish to visit Italy:

I sailed the Ionian Sea with him, and attended him even as far as Gaul, scattering plenty in his path.

For a long time he consulted my wishes in everything, was unfailing in his attendance upon me, and never passed a night away from my side. But no sooner had he secured an adequate provision, no sooner did he consider his reputation established, than his countenance changed towards me:

he assumed a haughty air, and neglected, nay, utterly abandoned me; having conceived a violent affection for the bearded old person yonder, whom you may know from his dress to be Dialogue, and who passes for a son of Philosophy. With this Dialogue, in spite of the disparity of age, he is now living; and is not ashamed to clip the wings of free, high-soaring eloquence, and submit himself to the comedian's fetters of bald question and answer. He, whose thoughts should have found utterance in thundering oratory, is content to weave a puny network of conversation. Such things may draw a smile from his audience, a nod, an unimpassioned wave of the hand, a murmur of approbation:

they can never hope to evoke the deafening uproar of universal applause. And this, gentlemen, is the fascination under which he looks coldly upon me; I commend his taste! They say, indeed, that he is not on the best of terms even with his beloved Dialogue; apparently I am not the only victim of his overweening pride. Does not such ingratitude as this render him liable to the penalties imposed by the marriage-laws? He leaves me, his lawful wife, to whom he is indebted alike for wealth and reputation, leaves me to neglect, and goes off in pursuit of novelty; and that, at a time when all eyes are turned upon me, when all men write me their protectress. I hold out against the entreaties of countless suitors:

they knock, and my doors remain closed to them; they call loudly upon my name, but I scorn their empty clamours, and answer them not. All is in vain:

he will not return to me, nor withdraw his eyes from this new love. In Heaven's name, what does he expect to get from him? what has Dialogue but his cloak?

In conclusion, gentlemen:

should he attempt to employ my art in his defence, suffer him not thus unscrupulously to sharpen my own sword against me; bid him defend himself, if he can, with the weapons of his adored Dialogue.

Her. Now there, madam, you are unreasonable:

how can he possibly make a dialogue of it all by himself? No, no; let him deliver a regular speech, just the same as other people.

Syrian. In view, gentlemen, of the indignation that plaintiff has expressed at the idea of my employing her gift of eloquence in order to maintain my cause at large, I shall confine myself to a brief and summary refutation of her charges, and shall then leave the whole matter to your discernment.

Gentlemen, all that the plaintiff has said is true. She educated me; she bore me company in my travels; she made a Greek of me. She has each of these claims to a husband's gratitude. I have now to give my reasons for abandoning her, and cultivating the acquaintance of Dialogue:

and, believe me, no motive of self- interest shall induce me to misrepresent the facts. I found, then, that the discreet bearing, the seemly dress, which had distinguished her in the days of her union with the illustrious demesman of Paeania[69], were now thrown aside:

I saw her tricked out and bedizened, rouged and painted like a courtesan. My suspicions were aroused, and I began to watch the direction of her eyes. To make a long story short, our street was nightly infested with the serenades of her tipsy gallants, some of whom, not content with knocking at our doors, threw aside all restraint, and forced their way into the house. These attentions amused and delighted my wife:

she was commonly to be seen leaning over the parapet and listening to the loose ditties that were bawled up from below; and when she thought she was unobserved, she would even open the door, and admit the gallant to her shameless embraces. Such things were not to be endured:

I was loth to bring her into the divorce-court, and accordingly sought the hospitality of Dialogue, who was my near neighbour.

Such, gentlemen, are the grievous wrongs that plaintiff has suffered at my hands. Even had the provocation I have described been wanting, my age (I was then nearly forty years old) called upon me to withdraw from the turmoil of the law-courts, and suffer the 'gentlemen of the jury' to rest in peace. Tyrants enough had been arraigned, princes enough been eulogized:

it was time to retreat to the walks of Academy or the Lyceum, there to enjoy, in the delightful society of Dialogue, that tranquil discourse which aims not at noisy acclamations. I might say much more, but I forbear:

you, gentlemen, will give your votes in accordance with the dictates of conscience. *Just.* Who wins?

Her. The Syrian has all votes but one.

Just. And that one a rhetorician's, I suppose. Dialogue will now address the same jury. Gentlemen, you will remain and hear this second case, and will receive a double fee.

Dia. If I had had my choice, gentlemen, I should have addressed you in the conversational style to which I am accustomed, instead of delivering a long harangue. However, I must conform to the custom of the law-courts, though I have neither skill nor experience in such matters. So much by way of exordium:

and now for the outrage committed on me by the defendant. In former days, gentlemen, I was a person of exalted character:

my speculations turned upon the Gods, and Nature, and the *Annus Magnus*; I trod those aerial plains wherein Zeus on winged car is borne along through the heights. My flight had actually brought me to the heavenly vault; I was just setting foot upon the upper surface of that dome, when this Syrian took it upon himself to drag me down, break my wings, and reduce me to the common level of humanity. Whisking off the seemly tragic mask I then wore, he clapped on in its place a comic one that was little short of ludicrous:

---

[69] Demosthenes.

his next step was to huddle me into a corner with Jest, Lampoon, Cynicism, and the comedians Eupolis and Aristophanes, persons with a horrible knack of making light of sacred things, and girding at all that is as it should be. But the climax was reached when he unearthed a barking, snarling old Cynic, Menippus by name, and thrust *his* company upon me; a grim bulldog, if ever there was one; a treacherous brute that will snap at you while his tail is yet wagging. Could any man be more abominably misused? Stripped of my proper attire, I am made to play the buffoon, and to give expression to every whimsical absurdity that his caprice dictates. And, as if that were not preposterous enough, he has forbidden me either to walk on my feet or to rise on the wings of poesy:

I am a ridiculous cross between prose and verse; a monster of incongruity; a literary Centaur.

Her. Now, Syrian:

what do you say to that?

Syrian. Gentlemen of the jury, I am surprised. Nothing could be more unexpected than the charge Dialogue has brought against me. When I first took him in hand, he was regarded by the world at large as one whose interminable discussions had soured his temper and exhausted his vitality. His labours entitled him to respect, but he had none of the attractive qualities that could secure him popularity. My first step was to accustom him to walk upon the common ground like the rest of mankind; my next, to make him presentable, by giving him a good bath and teaching him to smile. Finally, I assigned him Comedy as his yokefellow, thus gaining him the confidence of his hearers, who until then would as soon have thought of picking up a hedgehog as of venturing into the thorny presence of Dialogue.

But I know what the grievance is:

he wants me to sit and discourse subtle nothings with him about the immortality of the soul, and the exact number of pints of pure homogeneous essence that went to the making of the universe, and the claims of rhetoric to be called a shadow of a fraction of statecraft, or a fourth part of flattery. He takes a curious pleasure in refinements of this kind; it tickles his vanity most deliciously to be told that not every man can see so far into the ideal as he. Evidently he expects *me* to conform to his taste in this respect; he is still hankering after those lost wings; his eyes are turned upwards; he cannot see the things that lie before his feet. I think there is nothing else he can complain of. He cannot say that I, who pass for a barbarian, have torn off his Greek dress, and replaced it with one like my own:

that would have been another matter; to deprive him of his native garb were indeed a crime.

Gentlemen, I have made my defence, as far as in me lies:

I trust that your present verdict will confirm the former one.

Her. Well I never! All ten are for you again. Only one dissentient, and he the same one as before. True to his envious principles, he must ever give his

485

vote against his betters. The jurors may now leave the court. The remaining cases will come on to-morrow.

THE PARASITE, A DEMONSTRATION
THAT SPONGING IS A PROFESSION

Tychiades. Simon

Tyc. I am curious about you, Simon. Ordinary people, free and slaves alike, have some trade or profession that enables them to benefit themselves and others; you seem to be an exception.

Si. I do not quite see what you mean, Tychiades; put it a little clearer.

Tyc. I want to know whether you have a profession of any sort; for instance, are you a musician?

Si. Certainly not.

Tyc. A doctor?

Si. No.

Tyc. A mathematician?

Si. No.

Tyc. Do you teach rhetoric, then? I need not ask about philosophy; you have about as much to do with that as sin has.

Si. Less, if possible. Do not imagine that you are enlightening me upon my failings. I acknowledge myself a sinner—worse than you take me for.

Tyc. Very well. But possibly you have abstained from these professions because nothing great is easy. Perhaps a trade is more in your way; are you a carpenter or cobbler? Your circumstances are hardly such as to make a trade superfluous.

Si. Quite true. Well, I have no skill in any of these.

Tye. But in——?

Si. An excellent one, in my opinion; if you were acquainted with it you would agree, I am sure. I can claim to be a practical master in the art by this time; whether I can give an account of my faith is another question.

Tyc. What is it?

Si. No, I do not think I have got up the theory of it sufficiently. For the present, rest assured that I have a profession, and cease your strictures on that head. Its nature you shall know another time.

Tyc. No, no; I will not be put off like that.

Si. Well, I am afraid my profession would be rather a shock to you.

Tyc. I like shocks.

Si. Well, I will tell you some day.

Tyc. Now, I say; or else I shall know you are ashamed of it.

Si. Well, then, I sponge.

Tyc. Why, what sane man would call sponging a profession?

Si. I, for one. And if you think I am not sane, put down my innocence of other professions to insanity, and let that be my sufficient excuse. My lady Insanity, they say, is unkind to her votaries in most respects; but at least she excuses their offences, which she makes herself responsible for, like a schoolmaster or tutor.

Tyc. So sponging is an art, eh?

Si. It is; and I profess it.

Tyc. So you are a sponger?

Si. What an awful reproach!

Tyc. What! you do not blush to call yourself a sponger?

Si. On the contrary, I should be ashamed of not calling myself so.

Tyc. And when we want to distinguish you for the benefit of any one who does not know you, but has occasion to find you out, we must say 'the sponger,' naturally?

Si. The name will be more welcome to me than 'statuary' to Phidias; I am as proud of my profession as Phidias of his Zeus.

Tyc. Ha, ha, ha! Excuse me—just a particular that occurred to me.

Si. Namely——?

Tyc. Think of the address of your letters—Simon the Sponger!

Si. Simon the Sponger, Dion the Philosopher. I shall like mine as well as he his.

Tyc. Well, well, your taste in titles concerns me very little. Come now to the next absurdity.

Si. Which is——?

Tyc. The getting it entered on the list of arts. When any one asks what the art is, how do we describe it? Letters we know, Medicine we know; Sponging?

Si. My own opinion is, that it has an exceptionally good right to the name of art. If you care to listen, I will explain, though I have not got this properly into shape, as I remarked before.

Tyc. Oh, a brief exposition will do, provided it is true.

Si. I think, if you agree, we had better examine Art generically first; that will enable us to go into the question whether the specific arts really belong under it.

Tyc. Well, what is Art? Of course you know that?

Si. Quite well.

Tyc. Out with it, then, as you know.

Si. An art, as I once heard a wise man say, is a body of perceptions regularly employed for some useful purpose in human life.

Tyc. And he was quite right.

Si. So, if sponging has all these marks, it must be an art?

Tyc. If, yes.

Si. Well, now we will bring to bear on sponging each of these essential elements of Art, and see whether its character rings true, or returns a cracked note like bad pottery when it is tapped. It has got to be, like all art, a body of perceptions. Well, we find at once that our artist has to distinguish critically the man who will entertain him satisfactorily and not give him reason to wish that he had sponged elsewhere. Now, in as much as assaying—which is no more than the power of distinguishing between false and true coin—is a recognized profession, you will hardly refuse the same status to that which distinguishes between false and true *men*; the genuineness of men is more obscure than that of coins; this indeed is the gist of the wise Euripides's complaint:

But among men how tell the base apart?
Virtue and vice stamp not the outward flesh.

So much the greater the sponger's art, which beats prophecy in the certainty of its conclusions upon problems so difficult.

Next, there is the faculty of so directing your words and actions as to effect intimacy and convince your patron of your devotion:

is that consistent with weak understanding or perception?

Tyc. Certainly not.

Si. Then at table one has to outshine other people, and show the difference between amateur and professional:

is that to be done without thought and ingenuity?

Tyc. No, indeed.

Si. Or perhaps you fancy that any outsider who will take the trouble can tell a good dinner from a bad one. Well, the mighty Plato says, if the guest is not versed in cookery, the dressing of the banquet will be but unworthily judged.

The next point to be established is, that sponging depends not merely on perceptions, but on perceptions regularly employed. Nothing simpler. The perceptions on which other arts are based frequently remain unemployed by their owner for days, nights, months, or years, without his art's perishing; whereas, if those of the sponger were to miss their daily exercise, not merely his art would perish, but he with it.

There remains the 'useful purpose in human life'; it would take a madman to question that here. I find nothing that serves a more useful purpose in human life than eating and drinking; without them you cannot live.

Tyc. That is true.

Si. Moreover, sponging is not to be classed with beauty and strength, and so called a quality instead of an art?

Tyc. No.

Si. And, in the sphere of art, it does not denote the negative condition, of unskilfulness. That never brings its owner prosperity. Take an instance:

if a man who did not understand navigation took charge of a ship in a stormy sea, would he be safe?

Tyc. Not he.

Si. Why, now? Because he wants the art which would enable him to save his life?

Tyc. Exactly.

Si. It follows that, if sponging was the negative of art, the sponger would not save his life by its means?

Tyc. Yes.

Si. A man is saved by art, not by the absence of it?

Tyc. Quite so.

Si. So sponging is an art?

Tyc. Apparently.

Si. Let me add that I have often known even good navigators and skilful drivers come to grief, resulting with the latter in bruises and with the former in death but no one will tell you of a sponger who ever made shipwreck. Very well, then, sponging is neither the negative of art, nor is it a quality; but it is a body of perceptions regularly employed. So it emerges from the present discussion an art.

Tyc. That seems to be the upshot. But now proceed to give us a good definition of your art.

Si. Well thought of. And I fancy this will about do:

Sponging is the art of eating and drinking, and of the talk by which these may be secured; its end is Pleasure.

Tyc. A very good definition, I think. But I warn you that your end will bring you into conflict with some of the philosophers.

St. Ah well, if sponging agrees with Happiness about the end, we may be content.

And that it does I will soon show you. The wise Homer, admiring the sponger's life as the only blissful enviable one, has this:

I say no fairer end may be attained
Than when the people is attuned to mirth,
. . . . . and groans the festal board
With meat and bread, and the cup-bearer's ladle
From flowing bowl to cup the sweet wine dips.

As if this had not made his admiration quite clear enough, he lays a little more emphasis, good man, on his personal opinion:

This in my heart I count the highest bliss.

Moreover, the character to whom he entrusts these words is not just any one; it is the wisest of the Greeks. Well now, if Odysseus had cared to say a word for the end approved by the Stoics, he had plenty of chances—when he brought back Philoctetes from Lemnos, when he sacked Troy, when he stopped the Greeks from giving up, or when he made his way into Troy by scourging himself and putting on rags bad enough for any Stoic. But no; he never said theirs was a fairer end. And again, when he was living an Epicurean life with Calypso, when he could spend idle luxurious days, enjoying the daughter of Atlas and giving the rein to every soft emotion, even then he had not his fairer end; that was still the life of the sponger. Banqueter was the word used for sponger in his day; what does he say? I must quote the lines again; nothing like repetition:

490

'The banqueters in order set'; and 'groans the festal board With meat and bread.'

It was a remarkable piece of impudence on Epicurus's part to appropriate the end that belongs to sponging for his system of Happiness. That it *was* a bit of larceny—Epicurus having nothing, and the sponger much, to do with Pleasure—I will soon show you. I take it that Pleasure means, first, bodily tranquillity, and secondly, an untroubled soul. Well, the sponger attains both, Epicurus neither. A man who is busy inquiring into the earth's shape, the infinity of worlds, the sun's size, astronomic distances, the elements, the existence or non-existence of Gods, and who is engaged in incessant controversies about the end—he is a prey not merely to human, but to cosmic perturbations. Whereas the sponger, convinced that all is for the best in the best of all possible worlds, living secure and calm with no such perplexities to trouble him, eats and sleeps and lies on his back, letting his hands and feet look after themselves, like Odysseus on his passage home from Scheria.

But here is an independent refutation of Epicurus's pretensions to Pleasure. Our Epicurus, whoever his Wisdom may be, either is, or is not, supplied with victuals. If he is not, so far from having a pleasurable life, he will have no life at all. If he is, does he get them out of his own means, or from some one else? If the latter, he is a sponger, and not what he says he is; if the former, he will not have a pleasurable life.

Tyc. How so?

Si. Why, if his food is provided out of his own means, that way of life has many consequences; reckon them up. You will admit that, if the principle of your life is to be pleasure, all your appetites have to be satisfied?

Tyc. I agree.

Si. Well, a large income may possibly meet that requirement, a scanty one certainly not; consequently, a poor man cannot be a philosopher, or in other words attain the end, which is Pleasure. But neither will the rich, who lavishes his substance on his desires, attain it. And why? Because spending has many worries inseparably attached to it; your cook disappoints you, and you must either have strained relations with him, or else purchase peace and quiet by feeding badly and missing your pleasure. Then similar difficulties attend your steward's management of the house. You must admit all this.

Tyc. Oh, certainly, I agree.

Si. In fact, something or other is sure to happen and cut off Epicurus from his end. Now the sponger has no cook to be angry with, no farm, steward or money to be annoyed at the loss of; at the same time he lives on the fat of the land, and is the one person who can eat and drink without the worries from which others cannot escape.

That sponging is an art, has now been abundantly proved; it remains to show its superiority; and this I shall take in two divisions:

first, it has a general superiority to all the arts; and, secondly, it is superior to each of them separately. The general superiority is this:

491

the arts have to be instilled by dint of toil, threats and blows—regrettable necessities, all of them; my own art, of which the acquisition costs no toil, is perhaps the only exception. Who ever came away from dinner in tears? with the schoolroom it is different; or who ever went out to dinner with the dismal expression characteristic of going to school? No, the sponger needs no pressing to get him to table; he is devoted to his profession; it is the other apprentices who hate theirs, to the point of running away, sometimes. And it is worth your notice that a parent's usual reward for a child who makes progress in the ordinary arts is just the thing that the sponger gets regularly. The lad has done his writing well, they say; let him have something nice:

what vile writing! let him go without. Oh, the mouth is very useful for reward and punishment.

Again, with the other arts the result comes only after the learning is done; their fruits alone are agreeable; 'long and steep the road thereto.' Sponging is once more an exception, in that profit and learning here go hand in hand; you grasp your end as soon as you begin. And whereas all other arts are practised solely for the sustenance they will ultimately bring, the sponger has his sustenance from the day he starts. You realize, of course, that the farmer's object in farming is something else than farming, the carpenter's something different from abstract carpentering; but the sponger has no ulterior object; occupation and pre-occupation are for him one and the same.

Then it is no news to any one that other professions slave habitually, and get just one or two holidays a month; States keep some monthly and some yearly festivals; these are their times of enjoyment. But the sponger has thirty festivals a month; every day is a red-letter day with him.

Once more, success in the other arts presupposes a diet as abstemious as any invalid's; eat and drink to your heart's content, and you make no progress in your studies.

Other arts, again, are useless to their professor unless he has his plant; you cannot play the flute if you have not one to play; lyrical music requires a lyre, horsemanship a horse. But of ours one of the excellences and conveniences is that no instrument is required for its exercise.

Other arts we pay, this we are paid, to learn.

Further, while the rest have their teachers, no one teaches sponging; it is a gift from Heaven, as Socrates said of poetry.

Then do not forget that, while the others have to be suspended during a journey or a voyage, this may be in full swing under those circumstances too.

Tyc. No doubt about that.

Si. Another point that strikes me is that other arts feel the need of this one, but not vice versa.

Tyc. Well, but is the appropriation of what belongs to others no offence?

Si. Of course it is.

Tyc. Well, the sponger does that; why is he privileged to offend?

Si. Ah, I know nothing about that. But now look here:

you know how common and mean are the beginnings of the other arts; that of sponging, on the contrary, is noble. Friendship, that theme of the encomiast, is neither more nor less, you will find, than the beginning of sponging.

Tyc. How do you make that out?

Si. Well, no one asks an enemy, a stranger, or even a mere acquaintance, to dinner; the man must be his friend before he will share bit and sup with him, and admit him to initiation in these sacred mysteries. I know I have often heard people say, Friend, indeed! by what right? he has never eaten or drunk with us. You see; only the man who has done that is a friend to be trusted.

Next take a sound proof, though not the only one, that it is the most royal of the arts:

at the rest of them men have to work (not to mention toil and sweat) in the sitting or standing posture, which marks them for the absolute slaves of their art, whereas the sponger is free to recline like a king.

As to his happy condition, I need no more than allude to the wise Homer's words; he it is, and he alone, that 'planteth not, nor ploughs'; he 'reapeth where he hath not ploughed nor sown.'

Again, while knavery and folly are no bar to rhetoric, mathematics, or copper-working, no knave or fool can get on as a sponger.

Tyc. Dear, dear, what an amazing profession! I am almost tempted to exchange my own for it.

Si. I consider I have now established its superiority to art in general; let us next show how it excels individual arts. And it would be silly to compare it with the trades; I leave that to its detractors, and undertake to prove it superior to the greatest and most honourable professions. Such by universal acknowledgement are Rhetoric and Philosophy; indeed, some people insist that no name but science is grand enough for them; so if I prove sponging to be far above even these, *a fortiori* it will excel the others as Nausicaa her maids.

Now, its first superiority it enjoys over Philosophy and Rhetoric alike, and this is in the matter of real existence; it can claim that, they cannot. Instead of our having a single consistent notion of Rhetoric, some of us consider it an art, some the negation of art, some a mere artfulness, and so on. Similarly there is no unity in Philosophy's subject, or in its relation to it; Epicurus takes one view, the Stoics another, the Academy, the Peripatetics, others; in fact Philosophy has as many definitions as definers. So far at least victory wavers between them, and their profession cannot be called *one*. The conclusion is obvious; I utterly deny that what has no real existence can be an art. To illustrate:

there is one and only one Arithmetic; twice two is four whether here or in Persia; Greeks and barbarians have no quarrel over that; but philosophies are many and various, agreed neither upon their beginnings nor their ends.

Tyc. Perfectly true; they call Philosophy one, but they make it many.

Si. Well, such a want of harmony might be excused in other arts, they being of a contingent nature, and the perceptions on which they are based not being immutable. But that *Philosophy* should lack unity, and even conflict with itself like instruments out of tune—how can that be tolerated? Philosophy, then, is not one, for I find its diversity infinite. And it cannot be many, because it is Philosophy, not philosophies.

The real existence of Rhetoric must incur the same criticism. That with the same subject-matter all professors should not agree, but maintain conflicting opinions, amounts to a demonstration:

that which is differently apprehended cannot exist. The inquiry whether a thing is this or that, in place of agreement that it is one, is tantamount to a negation of its existence.

How different is the case of Sponging! for Greeks or barbarians, *one* in nature and subject and method. No one will tell you that these sponge this way, and those that; there are no spongers with peculiar principles, to match those of Stoics and Epicureans, that I know of; they are all agreed; their conduct and their end alike harmonious. Sponging, I take it on this showing, is just Wisdom itself.

Tyc. Yes, I think you have dealt with that point sufficiently; apart from that, how do you show the inferiority of Philosophy to your art?

Si. I must first mention that no sponger was ever in love with Philosophy; but many philosophers are recorded to have set their hearts on Sponging, to which they still remain constant.

Tyc. Philosophers caring to sponge? Names, please.

Si. Names? You know them well enough; you only play at not knowing because you regard it as a slur on their characters, instead of as the credit it is.

Tyc. Simon, I solemnly assure you I cannot think where you will find your instances.

Si. Honour bright? Then I conclude you never patronize their biographers, or you could not hesitate about my reference.

Tyc. Seriously, I long to hear their names.

Si. Oh, I will give you a list; not bad names either; the *elite*, if I am correctly informed; they will rather surprise you. Aeschines the Socratic, now, author of dialogues as witty as they are long, brought them with him to Sicily in the hope that they would gain him the royal notice of Dionysius; having given a reading of the *Miltiades*, and found himself famous, he settled down in Sicily to sponge on Dionysius and forget Socratic composition.

Again, I suppose you will pass Aristippus of Cyrene as a distinguished philosopher?

Tyc. Assuredly.

Si. Well, he was living there too at the same time and on the same terms. Dionysius reckoned him the best of all spongers; he had indeed a special gift that way; the prince used to send his cooks to him daily for instruction. He, I think, was really an ornament to the profession.

Well then, Plato, the noblest of you all, came to Sicily with the same view; he did a few days' sponging, but found himself incompetent and had to leave. He went back to Athens, took considerable pains with himself, and then had another try, with exactly the same result, however. Plato's Sicilian disaster seems to me to bear comparison with that of Nicias.

Tyc. Your authority for all this, pray?

Si. Oh, there are plenty of authorities; but I will specify Aristoxenus the musician, a weighty one enough, and himself attached as a sponger to Neleus. Then you of course know that Euripides held this relation to Archelaus till the day of his death, and Anaxarchus to Alexander.

As for Aristotle, that tiro in all arts was a tiro here too.

I have shown you, then, and without exaggeration, the philosophic passion for sponging. On the other hand, no one can point to a sponger who ever cared to philosophize.

But of course, if never to be hungry, thirsty, or cold, is to be happy, the sponger is the man who is in that position. Cold hungry philosophers you may see any day, but never a cold hungry sponger; the man would not be a sponger, that is all, but a wretched pauper, no better than a philosopher.

Tyc. Well, let that pass. And now what about those many points in which your art is superior to Rhetoric and Philosophy?

Si. Human life, my dear sir, has its times and seasons; there is peace time and there is war time. These provide unfailing tests for the character of arts and their professors. Shall we take war time first, and see who will do best for himself and for his city under those conditions?

Tyc. Ah, now comes the tug of war. It tickles me, this queer match between sponger and philosopher.

Si. Well, to make the thing more natural, and enable you to take it seriously, let us picture the circumstances. Sudden news has come of a hostile invasion; it has to be met; we are not going to sit still while our outlying territory is laid waste; the commander-in-chief issues orders for a general muster of all liable to serve; the troops gather, including philosophers, rhetoricians, and spongers. We had better strip them first, as the proper preliminary to arming. Now, my dear sir, have a look at them individually and see how they shape. Some of them you will find thin and white with underfeeding—all goose-flesh, as if they were lying wounded already. Now, when you think of a hard day, a stand-up fight with press and dust and wounds, what is it but a sorry jest to talk of such starvelings' being able to stand it?

Now go and inspect the sponger. Full-bodied, flesh a nice colour, neither white like a woman's nor tanned like a slave's; you can see his spirit; he has a keen look, as a gentleman should, and a high, full-blooded one to boot; none of your shrinking feminine glances when you are going to war! A noble pike-man that, and a noble corpse, for that matter, if a noble death is his fate.

495

But why deal in conjecture when there are facts to hand? I make the simple statement that in war, of all the rhetoricians and philosophers who ever lived, most never ventured outside the city walls, and the few who did, under compulsion, take their places in the ranks left their posts and went home.

Tyc. A bold extravagant assertion. Well, prove it.

Si. Rhetoricians, then. Of these, Isocrates, so far from serving in war, never even ventured into a law-court; he was afraid, because his voice was weak, I understand. Well, then Demades, Aeschines, and Philocrates, directly the Macedonian war broke out, were frightened into betraying their country and themselves to Philip. They simply espoused his interests in Athenian politics; and any other Athenian who took the same side was their friend. As for Hyperides, Demosthenes, and Lycurgus, supposed to be bolder spirits, and always raising scenes in the assembly with their abuse of Philip, how did they ever show their prowess in the war? Hyperides and Lycurgus never went out, did not so much as dare show their noses beyond the gates; they sat snug inside in a domestic state of siege, composing poor little decrees and resolutions. And their great chieftain, who had no gentler words for Philip in the assembly than 'the brute from Macedon, which cannot produce even a slave worth buying'— well, he did take heart of grace and go to Boeotia the day before; but battle had not been joined when he threw away his shield and made off. You must have heard this before; it was common talk not only at Athens, but in Thrace and Scythia, whence the creature was derived.

Tyc. Yes, I know all that. But then these are orators, trained to speak, not to fight. But the philosophers; you cannot say the same of them.

Si. Oh, yes; they discuss manliness every day, and do a great deal more towards wearing out the word Virtue than the orators; but you will find them still greater cowards and shirkers.—How do I know?—In the first place, can any one name a philosopher killed in battle? No, they either do not serve, or else run away. Antisthenes, Diogenes, Crates, Zeno, Plato, Aeschines, Aristotle, and all their company, never set eyes on a battle array. Their wise Socrates was the solitary one who dared to go out; and in the battle of Delium he ran away from Mount Parnes and got safe to the gymnasium of Taureas. It was a far more civilized proceeding, according to his ideas, to sit there talking soft nonsense to handsome striplings and posing the company with quibbles, than to cross spears with a grown Spartan.

Tyc. Well, I have heard these stories before, and from people who had no satirical intent. So I acquit you of slandering them by way of magnifying your own profession.

But come now, if you don't mind, to the sponger's military behaviour; and also tell me whether there is any sponging recorded of the ancients.

Si. My dear fellow, the most uneducated of us has surely heard enough of Homer to know that he makes the best of his heroes spongers. The great Nestor, whose tongue distilled honeyed speech, sponged on the King; Achilles was, and was known for, the most upright of the Greeks in form and in mind;

but neither for him, for Ajax, nor for Diomede, has Agamemnon such admiring praise as for Nestor. It is not for ten Ajaxes or Achilleses that he prays; no, Troy would have been taken long ago, if he had had in his host ten men like—that old sponger. Idomeneus, of Zeus's own kindred, is also represented in the same relation to Agamemnon.

Tyc. I know the passages; but I do not feel sure of the sense in which they were spongers.

Si. Well, recall the lines in which Agamemnon addresses Idomeneus.

Tyc. How do they go?

Si.

For thee the cup stands ever full,
Even as for me, whene'er it lists thee drink.

When he speaks of the cup ever full, he means not that it is perpetually ready (when Idomeneus is fighting or sleeping, for instance), but that he has had the peculiar privilege all through his life of sharing the King's table without that special invitation which is necessary for his other followers. Ajax, after a glorious single combat with Hector, 'they brought to lordly Agamemnon,' we are told; he, you see, is admitted to the royal table (and high time too) as an honour; whereas Idomeneus and Nestor were the King's regular table companions; at least that is my idea. Nestor I take to have been an exceedingly good and skilful sponger on royalty; Agamemnon was not his first patron; he had served his apprenticeship under Caeneus and Exadius. And but for Agamemnon's death I imagine he would never have relinquished the profession.

Tyc. Yes, that was a first-class sponger. Can you give me any more?

Si. Why, Tychiades, what else was Patroclus's relation to Achilles? and he was as fine a fellow, all round, as any Greek of them all. Judging by his actions, I cannot make out that he was inferior to Achilles himself. When Hector had forced the gates and was fighting inside by the ships, it was Patroclus who repelled him and extinguished the flames which had got a hold on Protesilaus's ship; yet one would not have said the people aboard her were inefficient—Ajax and Teucer they were, one as good in the *melee* as the other with his bow. A great number of the barbarians, including Sarpedon the son of Zeus, fell to this sponger. His own death was no common one. It took only one man, Achilles, to slay Hector; Paris was enough for Achilles himself; but two men and a God went to the killing of the sponger. And his last words bore no resemblance to those of the mighty Hector, who prostrated himself before Achilles and besought him to let his relations have his body; no, they were such as might be expected from one of his profession. Here they are:

———

But of thy like I would have faced a score,
And all the score my spear had given to death.

Tyc. Yes, you have proved him a good man; but can you show him to have been not Achilles's friend, but a sponger?

497

Si. I will produce you his own statement to that effect.

Tyc. What a miracle-worker you are!

Si. Listen to the lines, then:

Achilles, lay my bones not far from thine;
Thou and thine fed me; let me lie by thee.

    And a little further on he says:

    Peleus me received,
And nurtured gently, and thy henchman named,

that is, gave him the right of sponging; if he had meant to allude to Patroclus
as his son's friend, he would not have used the word henchman; for he was a
free man. What is a henchman, slaves and friends being excluded? Why,
obviously a sponger. Accordingly Homer uses the same word of Meriones's
relation to Idomeneus. And by the way it is not Idomeneus, though he was son
of Zeus, that he describes as 'peer of Ares'; it is the sponger Meriones.

Again, did not Aristogiton, poor and of mean extraction, as Thucydides
describes him, sponge on Harmodius? He was also, of course, in love with
him—a quite natural relation between the two classes. This sponger it was,
then, who delivered Athens from tyranny, and now adorns the marketplace in
bronze, side by side with the object of his passion. And now I have given you
an example or two of the profession.

But what sort of a guess do you make at the sponger's behaviour in war?
In the first place, he will fight on a full belly, as Odysseus advises. You must
feed the man who is to fight, he says, however early in the morning it may
happen to be. The time that others spend in fitting on helmet or breastplate
with nervous care, or in anticipating the horrors of battle, he will devote to
putting away his food with a cheerful countenance, and as soon as business
begins you will find him in front. His patron will take his place behind him,
sheltering under his shield as Teucer under Ajax's; when missiles begin to fly
the sponger will expose himself for his patron, whose safety he values more
than his own.

Should he fall in battle, neither officer nor comrade need feel ashamed of
that great body, which now reclines as appropriate an ornament of the battlefield as it once was of the dining-room. A pretty sight is a philosopher's body
by its side, withered, squalid, and bearded; he was dead before the fight began,
poor weakling. Who would not despise the city whose guards are such
miserable creatures? Who would not suppose, seeing these pallid, hairy
manikins scattered on the ground, that it had none to fight for it, and so had
turned out its gaol-birds to fill the ranks? That is how the spongers differ from
the rhetoricians and philosophers in war.

Then in peace time, sponging seems to me as much better than philosophy as peace itself than war. Be kind enough to glance first at the scenes of peace.

Tyc. I do not quite know what they are; but let us glance at them, by all means.

Si. Well, you will let me describe as civil scenes the market, the courts, the wrestling-schools and gymnasia, the hunting field and the dining-room?

Tyc. Certainly.

Si. To market and courts the sponger gives a wide berth they are the haunts of chicanery; there is no satisfaction to be got out of them. But at wrestling-school and gymnasium he is in his element; he is their chief glory. Show me a philosopher or orator who is in the same class with him when he strips in the wrestling- school; look at them in the gymnasium; they shame instead of adorning it. And in a lonely place none of them would face the onset of a wild beast; the sponger will, though, and find no difficulty in disposing of it; his table familiarity with it has bred contempt. A stag or a wild boar may put up its bristles; he will not mind; the boar may whet its tusks against him; he only returns the compliment. As for hares, he is more deadly to them than a greyhound. And then in the dining-room, where is his match, to jest or to eat? Who will contribute most to entertainment, he with his song and his joke, or a person who has not a laugh in him, sits in a threadbare cloak, and keeps his eyes on the ground as if he was at a funeral and not a dinner? If you ask me, I think a philosopher has about as much business in a dining-room as a bull in a china-shop.

But enough of this. What impression does one get of the sponger's actual life, when one compares it with the other? First it will be found that he is indifferent to reputation, and does not care a jot what people think about him, whereas all rhetoricians and philosophers without exception are the slaves of vanity, reputation, and what is worse, of money. No one could be more careless of the pebbles on the shore than the sponger is of money; he would as soon touch fire as gold. But the rhetoricians and, as if that were not bad enough, the professed philosophers, are beneath contempt in this respect. No need to illustrate in the case of the rhetoricians; but of the philosophers whose repute stands highest at present, one was lately convicted of taking a bribe for his verdict in a law-suit, and another expects a salary for giving a prince his company, and counts it no shame to go into exile in his old age, and hire himself out for pay like some Indian or Scythian captive. The very name his conduct has earned him calls no blush to his cheek.

But their susceptibilities are by no means limited to these; pain, temper, jealousy, and all sorts of desires, must be added; all of which the sponger is beyond the reach of; he does not yield to temper because on the one hand he has fortitude, and on the other hand he has no one to irritate him. Or if he is by any chance moved to wrath, there is nothing disagreeable or sullen about it; it entertains and amuses merely. As to pain, he has less of that to endure than anybody, one of his profession's recommendations and privileges being just that immunity. He has neither money, house, slave, wife, nor children—those hostages to Fortune. He desires neither fame, wealth, nor beauty.

Tyc. He will feel pain if the supplies run short, I presume.

Si. Ah, but you see, he is not a sponger if that happens. A courageous man is not courageous if he has no courage, a sensible one not sensible if he has no sense. He could not be a sponger under those conditions. We are discussing the sponger, not the non- sponger. If the courageous is so in virtue of his courage, the sensible sensible in virtue of his sense, then the sponger is a sponger in virtue of sponging. Take that away, and we shall be dealing with something else, and not with a sponger at all.

Tyc. So his supplies will never run short?

Si. Manifestly. So he is as free from that sort of pain as from others.

Then all philosophers and rhetoricians are timorous creatures together. You may generally see them carrying sticks on their walks; well, of course they would not go armed if they were not afraid. And they bar their doors elaborately, for fear of night attacks. Now our man just latches his room door, so that the wind may not blow it open; if there is a noise in the night, it is all the same to him as if there were none; he will travel a lonely road and wear no sword; he does not know what fear is. But I am always seeing philosophers, though there is nothing to be afraid of, carrying bows and arrows; as for their sticks, they take them to bath or breakfast with them.

Again, no one can accuse a sponger of adultery, violence, rape, or in fact of any crime whatsoever. One guilty of such offences will not be sponging, but ruining himself. If he is caught in adultery, his style thenceforth is taken from his offence. Just as a piece of cowardice brings a man not repute, but disrepute, so, I take it, the sponger who commits an offence loses his previous title and gets in exchange that proper to the offence. Of such offences on the part of rhetoricians and philosophers, on the other hand, we have not only abundant examples in our own time, but records against the ancients in their own writings. There is an Apology of Socrates, of Aeschines, of Hyperides, of Demosthenes, and indeed of most of their kind. There is no sponger's apology extant, and you will never hear of anybody's bringing a suit against one.

Now I suppose you will tell me that the sponger's life may be better than theirs, but his death is worse. Not a bit of it; it is a far happier one. We know very well that all or most philosophers have had the wretched fate they deserved, some by poison after condemnation for heinous crimes, some by burning alive, some by strangury, some in exile. No one can adduce a sponger's death to match these; he eats and drinks, and dies a blissful death. If you are told that any died a violent one, be sure it was nothing worse than indigestion.

Tyc. I must say, you have done well for your kind against the philosophers. And now look at it from the patron's point of view; does he get his money's worth? It strikes me the rich man does the kindness, confers the favour, finds the food, and it is all a little discreditable to the man who takes them.

Si. Now, really, Tychiades, that is rather silly of you. Can you not see that a rich man, if he had the gold of Gyges, is yet poor as long as he dines alone, and no better than a tramp if he goes abroad unattended? A soldier without his arms, a dress without its purple, a horse without its trappings, are poor things; and a rich man without his sponger is a mean, cheap spectacle. The sponger gives lustre to the patron, never the patron to the other.

Moreover, none of the reproach that you imagine attaches to sponging; you refer, of course, to the difference in their degrees; but then it is an advantage to the rich man to keep the other; apart from his ornamental use, he is a most valuable bodyguard. In battle no one will be over ready to undertake the rich man with such a comrade at his side; and you can hardly, having him, die by poison. Who would dare attempt such a thing, with him tasting your food and drink? So he brings you not only credit, but insurance. His affection is such that he will run all risks; he would never leave his patron to face the dangers of the table alone; no, he would rather eat and die with him.

Tyc. You have stated your case without missing a point, Simon. Do not tell me you were unprepared again; you have been trained in a good school, man. But one thing more I should like to know. There is a nasty sound about the word sponger, don't you think?

Si. See whether I have a satisfactory answer to that. Oblige me by giving what you consider the right answers to my questions. Sponging is an old word; what does it really mean?

Tyc. Getting your dinner at some one else's expense.

Si. Dining out, in fact?

Tyc. Yes.

Si. And we may call a sponger an out-diner?

Tyc. The gravamen's in that; he should dine at home.

Si. A few more answers, please. Of these pairs, which do you consider the best? Which would you take, if you had the choice?—To sail, or to out-sail?

Tyc. The latter.

Si. To run or out-run?

Tyc. The latter.

Si. Ride or out-ride, shoot or out-shoot?

Tyc. Still the same.

Si. So I presume an out-diner is better than a diner?

Tyc. Indisputable. Henceforward I shall come to you morning and afternoon like a schoolboy for lessons. And I am sure you ought to do your very best for me, as your first pupil. The first child is always the mother's joy, you know.[70]

---

[70] It has been necessary, in Section 60, to tamper a little with the Greek in order to get the point, such as it is; but it has not been seriously misrepresented.

ANACHARSIS, A DISCUSSION OF PHYSICAL TRAINING

Anacharsis. Solon

An. Why do your young men behave like this, Solon? Some of them grappling and tripping each other, some throttling, struggling, intertwining in the clay like so many pigs wallowing. And yet their first proceeding after they have stripped-I noticed that-is to oil and scrape each other quite amicably; but then I do not know what comes over them—they put down their heads and begin to push, and crash their foreheads together like a pair of rival rams. There, look! that one has lifted the other right off his legs, and dropped him on the ground; now he has fallen on top, and will not let him get his head up, but presses it down into the clay; and to finish him off he twines his legs tight round his belly, thrusts his elbow hard against his throat, and throttles the wretched victim, who meanwhile is patting his shoulder; that will be a form of supplication; he is asking not to be quite choked to death. Regardless of their fresh oil, they get all filthy, smother themselves in mud and sweat till they might as well not have been anointed, and present, to me at least, the most ludicrous resemblance to eels slipping through a man's hands.

Then here in the open court are others doing just the same, except that, instead of the clay, they have for floor a depression filled with deep sand, with which they sprinkle one another, scraping up the dust on purpose, like fowls; I suppose they want their interfacings to be tighter; the sand is to neutralize the slipperiness of the oil, and by drying it up to give a firmer grip.

And here are others, sanded too, but on their legs, going at each other with blows and kicks. We shall surely see this poor fellow spit out his teeth in a minute; his mouth is all full of blood and sand; he has had a blow on the jaw from the other's fist, you see. Why does not the official there separate them and put an end to it? I guess that he is an official from his purple; but no, he encourages them, and commends the one who gave that blow.

Wherever you look, every one busy-rising on his toes, jumping up and kicking the air, or something.

Now I want to know what is the good of it all. To me it looks more like madness than anything else. It will not be very easy to convince me that people who behave like this are not wrong in their heads.

So. It is quite natural it should strike you that way, being so novel, and so utterly contrary to Scythian customs. Similarly you have no doubt many methods and habits that would seem extraordinary enough to us Greeks, v if we were spectators of them as you now are of ours. But be reassured, my dear sir; these proceedings are not madness; it is no spirit of violence that sets them hitting each other, wallowing in clay, and sprinkling dust. The thing has its use, and its delight too, resulting in admirable physical condition. If you make some stay, as I imagine you will, in Greece, you are bound to be either a clay-bob or a dust-bob before long; you will be so taken with the pleasure and profit of the pursuit.

503

An. Hands off, please. No, I wish you all joy of your pleasures and your profits; but if any of you treats me like that, he will find out that we do not wear scimetars for ornament.

But would you mind giving a name to all this? What are we to say they are doing?

So. The place is called a gymnasium, and is dedicated to the Lycean Apollo. You see his statue there; the one leaning on the pillar, with a bow in the left hand. The right arm bent over the head indicates that the God is resting after some great exertion.

Of the exercises here, that in the clay is called wrestling; the youths in the dust are also called wrestlers, and those who strike each other standing are engaged in what we call the pancratium. But we have other gymnasiums for boxing, quoit-throwing, and high- jumping; and in all these we hold contests, the winner in which is honoured above all his contemporaries, and receives prizes.

An. Ah, and what are the prizes, now?

So. At Olympia a wreath of wild olive, at the Isthmus one of pine, at Nemea of parsley, at Pytho some of the God's sacred apples, and at our Panathenaea oil pressed from the temple olives. What are you laughing at, Anacharsis? Are the prizes too small?

An. Oh dear no; your prize-list is most imposing; the givers may well plume themselves on their munificence, and the competitors be monstrous keen on winning. Who would not go through this amount of preparatory toil, and take his chance of a choking or a dislocation, for apples or parsley? It is obviously impossible for any one who has a fancy to a supply of apples, or a wreath of parsley or pine, to get them without a mud plaster on his face, or a kick in the stomach from his competitor. O *So.* My dear sir, it is not the things' intrinsic value that we look at. They are the symbols of victory, labels of the winners; it is the fame attaching to them that is worth any price to their holders; that is why the man whose quest of honour leads through toil is content to take his kicks. No toil, no honour; he who covets that must start with enduring hardship; when he has done that, he may begin to look for the pleasure and profit his labours are to bring.

An. Which pleasure and profit consists in their being seen in their wreaths by every one, and congratulated on their victory by those who before commiserated their pain; their happiness lies in their exchange of apples and parsley for toil.

So. Ah, you certainly do not understand our ways yet. You will revise your opinions before long, when you go to the great festivals and see the crowds gathering to look on, the stands filling up, the competitors receiving their ovations, and the victor being idolized.

An. Why, Solon, that is just where the humiliation comes in; they are treated like this not in something like privacy, but with all these spectators to watch the affronts they endure—who, I am to believe, count them happy when they see them dripping with blood or being throttled; for such are the happy concomitants of victory. In my country, if a man strikes a citizen, knocks him down, or tears his clothes, our elders punish him severely, even though there were only one or two witnesses, not like your vast Olympic or Isthmian gatherings. However, though I cannot help pitying the competitors, I am still more astonished at the spectators; you tell me the chief people from all over Greece attend; how can they leave their serious concerns and waste time on such things? How they can like it passes my comprehension—to look on at people being struck and knocked about, dashed to the ground and pounded by one another.

So. If the Olympia, Isthmia, or Panathenaea were only on now, those object-lessons might have been enough to convince you that our keenness is not thrown away. I cannot make you apprehend the delights of them by description; you should be there sitting in the middle of the spectators, looking at the men's courage and physical beauty, their marvellous condition, effective skill and invincible strength, their enterprise, their emulation, their unconquerable spirit, and their unwearied pursuit of victory. Oh, I know very well, you would never have been tired of talking about your favourites, backing them with voice and hand.

An. I dare say, and with laugh and flout too. All the fine things in your list, your courages and conditions, your beauties and enterprises, I see you wasting in no high cause; your country is not in danger, your land not being ravaged, your friends or relations not being haled away. The more ridiculous that such patterns of perfection as you make them out should endure the misery all for nothing, and spoil their beauty and their fine figures with sand and black eyes, just for the triumphant possession of an apple or a sprig of wild olive. Oh, how I love to think of those prizes! By the way, do all who enter get them?

So. No, indeed. There is only one winner.

An. And do you mean to say such a number can be found to toil for a remote uncertainty of success, knowing that the winner cannot be more than one, and the failures must be many, with their bruises, or their wounds very likely, for sole reward?

So. Dear me; you have no idea yet of what is a good political constitution, or you would never depreciate the best of our customs. If you ever take the trouble to inquire how a State may best be organized, and its citizens best developed, you will find yourself commending these practices and the earnestness with which we cultivate them; then you will realize what good effects are inseparable from those toils which seem for the moment to tax our energies to no purpose.

An. Well, Solon, why did I come all the way from Scythia, why did I make the long stormy passage of the Euxine, but to learn the laws of Greece, observe your customs, and work out the best constitution? That was why I chose you of all Athenians for my friend and host; I had heard of you; I had

505

been told you were a legislator, you had devised the most admirable customs, introduced institutions of great excellence, and in fact built up what you call a constitution. Before all things, then, teach me; make me your pupil. Nothing would please me more than to sit by your side without bit or sup for as long as you could hold out, and listen open-mouthed to what you have to say of constitution and laws.

So. The whole thing can hardly be so shortly disposed of, friend. You must take the different departments, one by one, and find out our views upon the Gods, then upon parents, upon marriage, and so for the rest. But I will let you know at once what we think about the young, and how we treat them when higher things begin to dawn upon their intelligence, when their frames begin to set and to be capable of endurance. Then you will grasp our purpose in imposing these exercises upon them and insisting on physical effort; our view is not bounded by the contests, and directed to their carrying off prizes there—of course only a small proportion of them ever reach that point; no; the indirect benefit that we secure for their city and themselves is of more importance. There is another contest in which all good citizens get prizes, and its wreaths are not of pine or wild olive or parsley, but of complete human happiness, including individual freedom and political independence, wealth and repute, enjoyment of our ancient ritual, security of our dear ones, and all the choicest boons a man might ask of Heaven. It is of these materials that the wreath I tell you of is woven; and they are provided by that contest for which this training and these toils are the preparation.

An. You strange man! you had all these grand prizes up your sleeve, and you told me a tale of apples and parsley and tufts of wild olive and pine.

So. Ah, you will not think those such trifles either, when you take my meaning. They are manifestations of the same spirit, all small parts of that greater contest, and of the wreath of happiness I told you of. But it is true that instead of beginning at the beginning I was carried away to the meetings at the Isthmus and Olympia and Nemea. However, we have plenty of time, and you profess curiosity; it is a simple matter to go back to the beginning, to that many-prized contest which I tell you is the real end of all.

An. That will be better; we are more likely to prosper on the high road; perhaps I shall even be cured of my inclination to laugh at any one I see priding himself on his olive or parsley wreath. But I propose that we go into the shade over there and sit down on the benches, not to be interrupted by these rounds of cheering. And indeed I must confess I have had enough of this sun; how it scorches one's bare head! I did not want to look like a foreigner, so I left my hat at home. But the year is at its hottest; the dog-star, as you call it, is burning everything up, and not leaving a drop of moisture in the air; and the noonday sun right overhead gives an absolutely intolerable heat. I cannot make out how you at your age, so far from dripping like me, never turn a hair; instead of looking about for some hospitable shade, you take your sunning quite kindly.

So. Ah, Anacharsis, these useless toils, these perpetual clay-baths, these miseries in the sand and the open air, are prophylactics against the sun's rays; *we* need no hats to ward off his shafts. But come along.

And you are not to regard me as an authority whose statements are to be accepted as matter of faith; wherever you think I have not made out my case, you are to contradict me at once and get the thing straight. So we shall stand to win; either you, after relieving your mind of all objections that strike you, will reach a firm conviction, or, failing that, I shall have found out my mistake. And in the latter case, Athens will owe you a debt that she cannot be too quick to acknowledge; for your instructions and corrections of my ideas will redound to her advantage. I shall keep nothing back; I shall produce it all in public, stand up in the assembly and say:

Men of Athens, I drew up for you such laws as I thought would most advantage you; but this stranger—and at that word I point to you, Anacharsis—*this stranger from Scythia has been wise enough to show me my mistake and teach me better ways. Let his name be inscribed as your benefactor's; set him up in bronze beside your name-Gods, or by Athene on the citadel.* And be assured that Athens will not be ashamed to learn what is for her good from a barbarian and an alien.

An. Ah, now I have a specimen of that Attic irony which I have so often heard of. I am an unsettled wanderer who lives on his cart and goes from land to land, who has never dwelt in a city, nor even seen one till now; how should I lay down a constitution, or give lessons to a people that is one with the soil it lives on[71], and for all these ages has enjoyed the blessings of perfect order in this ancient city? How, above all, instruct that Solon whose native gift all men say it is to know how a state may best be governed, and what laws will bring it happiness? Nevertheless, you shall be my legislator too; I will contradict you, where I think you wrong, for my own better instruction. And here we are, safely covered from the sun's pursuit, and this cool stone invites us to take our ease. Start now and give me your reasons. Why seize upon the rising generation so young, and subject them to such toils? How do you develop perfect virtue out of clay and training? What is the exact contribution to it of dust and summersaults? That and that only is my first curiosity. All the rest you shall give me by degrees as occasion rises later. But, Solon, one thing you must bear in mind:

you are talking to a barbarian. What I mean is, you must be simple, and brief; I am afraid I shall forget the beginning, if a very abundant flow follows.

So. Why, you had better work the sluice yourself, whenever the word-stream is either turbid or diverging into a wrong channel. As for mere continuance, you can cut that up by questions. However, so long as what I have to say is not irrelevant, I do not know that length matters. There is an ancient procedure in the Areopagus, our murder court. When the members have

---

[71] See *Athenians* in Notes.

ascended the hill, and taken their seats to decide a case of murder or deliberate maiming or arson, each side is allowed to address the court in turn, prosecution and defence being conducted either by the principals or by counsel. As long as they speak to the matter in hand, the court listens silently and patiently. But if either prefaces his speech with an appeal to its benevolence, or attempts to stir its compassion or indignation by irrelevant considerations —and the legal profession have numberless ways of playing upon juries—, the usher at once comes up and silences him. The court is not to be trifled with or have its food disguised with condiments, but to be shown the bare facts. Now, Anacharsis, I hereby create you a temporary Areopagite; you shall hear me according to that court's practice, and silence me if you find me cajoling you; but as long as I keep to the point, I may speak at large. For there is no sun here to make length a burden to you; we have plenty of shade and plenty of time.

An. That sounds reasonable. And I take it very kindly that you should have given me this incidental view of the proceedings on the Areopagus; they are very remarkable, quite a pattern of the way a judicial decision should be arrived at. Let your speech be regulated accordingly, and the Areopagite of your appointment shall listen as his office requires.

So. Well, I must start with a brief preliminary statement of our views upon city and citizens. A city in our conception is not the buildings—walls, temples, docks, and so forth; these are no more than the local habitation that provides the members of the community with shelter and safety; it is in the citizens that we find the root of the matter; they it is that replenish and organize and achieve and guard, corresponding in the city to the soul in man. Holding this view, we are not indifferent, as you see, to our city's body; that we adorn with all the beauty we can impart to it; it is provided with internal buildings, and fenced as securely as may be with external walls. But our first, our engrossing preoccupation is to make our citizens noble of spirit and strong of body. So they will in peace time make the most of themselves and their political unity, while in war they will bring their city through safe with its freedom and well-being unimpaired. Their early breeding we leave to their mothers, nurses, and tutors, who are to rear them in the elements of a liberal education. But as soon as they attain to a knowledge of good and evil, when reverence and shame and fear and ambition spring up in them, when their bodies begin to set and strengthen and be equal to toil, then we take them over, and appoint them both a course of mental instruction and discipline, and one of bodily endurance. We are not satisfied with mere spontaneous development either for body or soul; we think that the addition of systematic teaching will improve the gifted and reform the inferior. We conform our practice to that of the farmer, who shelters and fences his plants while they are yet small and tender, to protect them from the winds, but, as soon as the shoot has gathered substance, prunes it and lets the winds beat upon it and knock it about, and makes it thereby the more fruitful.

We first kindle their minds with music and arithmetic, teach them to write and to read with expression. Then, as they get on, we versify, for the better impressing their memories, the sayings of wise men, the deeds of old time, or moral tales. And as they hear of worship won and works that live in song, they yearn ever more, and are fired to emulation, that they too may be sung and marvelled at by them that come after, and have their Hesiod and their Homer. And when they attain their civil rights, and it is time for them to take their share in governing—but all this, it may be, is irrelevant. My subject was not how we train their souls, but why we think fit to subject them to the toils we do. I will silence myself without waiting for the usher, or for you, my Areopagite, who have been too considerate, methinks, in letting me maunder on out of bounds all this way.

An. Another point of Areopagite procedure, please, Solon. When a speaker passes over essential matters in silence, has the court no penalty for him?

So. Why? I do not take you.

An. Why, you propose to pass by the question of the soul, which is the noblest and the most attractive to me, and discuss the less essential matters of gymnasiums and physical exercise.

So. You see, my dear sir, I have my eye on our original conditions; I do not want to divert the word-stream; it might confuse your memory with its irregular flow. However, I will do what I can in the way of a mere summary for this branch of the subject; as for a detailed examination of it, that must be deferred.

Well, we regulate their sentiments partly by teaching them the laws of the land, which are inscribed in large letters and exposed at the public expense for all to read, enjoining certain acts and forbidding others, and partly by making them attend good men, who teach them to speak with propriety, act with justice, content themselves with political equality, eschew evil, ensue good, and abstain from violence; sophist and philosopher are the names by which these teachers are known. Moreover, we pay for their admission to the theatre, where the contemplation of ancient heroes and villains in tragedy or comedy has its educational effect of warning or encouragement. To the comic writers we further give the licence of mockery and invective against any of their fellow citizens whose conduct they find discreditable; such exposure may act both directly upon the culprits, and upon others by way of example.

An. Ah, I have seen the tragedians and comedians you speak of, at least if the former are men in heavy stilted shoes, and clothes all picked out with gold bands; they have absurd head- pieces with vast open mouths, from inside which comes an enormous voice, while they take great strides which it seems to me must be dangerous in those shoes. I think there was a festival to Dionysus going on at the time. Then the comedians are shorter, go on their own feet, are more human, and smaller-voiced; but their head-pieces are still more ridiculous, so much so that the audience was laughing at them like one man.

509

But to the others, the tall ones, every one listened with a dismal face; I suppose they were sorry for them, having to drag about those great clogs.

So. Oh no, it was not for the actors that they were sorry. The poet was probably setting forth some sad tale of long ago, with fine speeches that appealed to the audience's feelings and drew tears from them. I dare say you observed also some flute-players, with other persons who stood in a circle and sang in chorus. These too are things that have their uses. Well, our youths' souls are made susceptible and developed by these and similar influences.

Then their bodily training, to which your curiosity was especially directed, is as follows. When their first pithless tenderness is past, we strip them and aim at hardening them to the temperature of the various seasons, till heat does not incommode nor frost paralyse them. Then we anoint them with oil by way of softening them into suppleness. It would be absurd that leather, dead stuff as it is, should be made tougher and more lasting by being softened with oil, and the living body get no advantage from the same process. Accordingly we devise elaborate gymnastic exercises, appoint instructors of each variety, and teach one boxing, another the pancratium. They are to be habituated to endurance, to meet blows half way, and never shrink from a wound. This method works two admirable effects in them:

makes them spirited and heedless of bodily danger, and at the same time strong and enduring. Those whom you saw lowering their heads and wrestling learn to fall safely and pick themselves up lightly, to shove and grapple and twist, to endure throttling, and to heave an adversary off his legs. *Their* acquirements are not unserviceable either; the one great thing they gain is beyond dispute; their bodies are hardened and strengthened by this rough treatment. Add another advantage of some importance:

it is all so much practice against the day of battle. Obviously a man thus trained, when he meets a real enemy, will grapple and throw him the quicker, or if he falls will know better how to get up again. All through we are reckoning with that real test in arms; we expect much better results from our material if we supple and exercise their bodies before the armour goes on, so increasing their strength and efficiency, making them light and wiry in themselves (though the enemy will rather be impressed with their weight).

You see how it will act. Something may surely be expected from those in arms who even without them would be considered awkward customers; they show no inert pasty masses of flesh, no cadaverous skinniness, they are not shade-blighted women; they do not quiver and run with sweat at the least exertion, and pant under their helmets as soon as a midday sun like this adds to the burden. What would be the use of creatures who should be overpowered by thirst and dust, unnerved at sight of blood, and as good as dead before they came within bow-shot or spear-thrust of the enemy? But our fellows are ruddy and sunburnt and steady-eyed, there is spirit and fire and virility in their looks, they are in prime condition, neither shrunken and withered nor running to corpulence, but well and truly proportioned; the waste superfluity of their tissues they have sweated out; the stuff that gives strength and activity, purged from all inferior admixture, remains part of their substance. The winnowing fan has its counterpart in our gymnastics, which blow away chaff and husks, and sift and collect the clean grain.

The inevitable result is sound health and great capacity of enduring fatigue. A man like this does not sweat for a trifle, and seldom shows signs of distress. Returning to my winnowing simile— if you were to set fire on the one hand to pure wheat grain, and on the other to its chaff and straw, the latter would surely blaze up much the quicker; the grain would burn only gradually, without a blaze and not all at once; it would smoulder slowly and take much longer to consume. Well, disease or fatigue being similarly applied to this sort of body will not easily find weak spots, nor get the mastery of it lightly. Its interior is in good order, its exterior strongly fortified against such assaults, so that it gives neither admission nor entertainment to the destroying agencies of sun or frost. To any place that begins to weaken under toil comes an accession from the abundant internal heat collected and stored up against the day of need; it fills the vacancy, restores the vital force, and lengthens endurance to the utmost. Past exertion means not dissipation but increase of force, which can be fanned into fresh life.

Further, we accustom them to running, both of the long distance and of the sprinting kind. And they have to run not on hard ground with a good footing, but in deep sand on which you can neither tread firmly nor get a good push off, the foot sinking in. Then, to fit them to leap a trench or other obstacle, we make them practise with leaden dumb-bells in their hands. And again there are distance matches with the javelin. Yes, and you saw in the gymnasium a bronze disk like a small buckler, but without handle or straps; you tried it as it lay there, and found it heavy and, owing to its smooth surface, hard to handle. Well, that they hurl upwards and forwards, trying who can get furthest and outdo his competitors—an exercise that strengthens the shoulders and braces the fingers and toes.

As to the clay and dust that first moved your laughter, I will tell you now why they are provided. In the first place, that a fall may be not on a hard surface, but soft and safe. Secondly, greater slipperiness is secured by sweat and clay combined (you compared them to eels, you remember); now this is neither useless nor absurd, but contributes appreciably to strength and activity. An adversary in that condition must be gripped tightly enough to baffle his attempts at escape. To lift up a man who is all over clay, sweat, and oil, and who is doing his very best to get away and slip through your fingers, is no light task, I assure you. And I repeat that all these things have their military uses too: you may want to take up a wounded friend and convey him out of danger; you may want to heave an enemy over your head and make off with him. So we give them still harder tasks in training, that they may be abundantly equal to the less.

The function we assign to dust is just the reverse, to prevent one who is gripped from getting loose. After learning in the clay to retain their hold on the elusive, they are accustomed in turn to escape themselves even from a firm grasp. Also, we believe the dust forms a plaster that keeps in excessive sweat, prevents waste of power, and obviates the ill effects of the wind playing upon a body when its pores are all relaxed and open. Besides which, it cleanses the skin and makes it glossy. I should like to put side by side one of the white creatures who live sheltered lives and, after washing off his dust and clay, any of the Lyceum frequenters you should select, and then ask you which you would rather resemble. I know you would make your choice at the first glance, without waiting to see what they could do; you would rather be solid and well-knit than delicate and soft and white for want of the blood that had hidden itself away out of sight.

Such are the exercises we prescribe to our young men, Anacharsis; we look to find them good guardians of their country and bulwarks of our freedom; thus we defeat our enemies if they invade us, and so far overawe our immediate neighbours that they mostly acknowledge our supremacy and pay us tribute. During peace also we find our account in their being free from vulgar ambitions and from the insolence generated by idleness; they have these things to fill their lives and occupy their leisure. I told you of a prize that all may win and of a supreme political happiness; these are attained when we find our youth in the highest condition alike for peace and war, intent upon all that is noblest.

An. I see, Solon; when an enemy invades, you anoint yourselves with oil, dust yourselves over, and go forth sparring at them; then they of course cower before you and run away, afraid of getting a handful of your sand in their open mouths, or of your dancing round to get behind them, twining your legs tight round their bellies, and throttling them with your elbows rammed well in under their chin-pieces. It is true they will try the effect of arrows and javelins; but you are so sunburnt and full-blooded, the missiles will hurt you no more than if you were statues; you are not chaff and husks; you will not be readily disposed of by the blows you get; much time and attention will be required before you at last, cut to pieces with deep wounds, have a few drops of blood extracted from you. Have I misunderstood your figure, or is this a fair deduction from it?

But perhaps you will take the equipment of your tragedians and comedians, and when you get your marching orders put on those wide-mouthed headpieces, to scare the foe with their appalling terrors; of course, and you can put the stilted things on your feet; they will be light for running away (if that should be advisable), or, if you are in pursuit, the strides they lend themselves to will make your enemy's escape impossible. Seriously now, are not these refinements of yours all child's play—something for your idle, slack youngsters to do? If you really want to be free and happy, you must have other exercises than these; your training must be a genuine martial one; no toy

512

contests with friends, but real ones with enemies; danger must be an element in your character- development. Never mind dust and oil; teach them to use bow and javelin; and none of your light darts diverted by a puff of wind; let it be a ponderous spear that whistles as it flies; to which add stones, a handful each, the axe, the shield, the breastplate, and the helmet.

On your present system, I cannot help thinking you should be very grateful to some God for not having allowed you to perish under the attack of any half-armed band. Why, if I were to draw this little dagger at my girdle and run amuck at your collective youth, I could take the gymnasium without more ado; they would all run away and not dare face the cold steel; they would skip round the statues, hide behind pillars, and whimper and quake till I laughed again. We should have no more of the ruddy frames they now display; they would be another colour then, all white with terror. That is the temper that deep peace has infused into you; you could not endure the sight of a single plume on an enemy's crest.

So. Ah, Anacharsis, the Thracians who invaded us with Eumolpus told another tale; so did your women who assailed Athens with Hippolyta; so every one who has met us in the field. My dear sir, it does not follow from our exercising our youths without arms that we expose them in the same condition to the real thing; the independent bodily development once complete, training in arms follows; and to this they come much the fitter for their previous work.

An. Where is your military gymnasium, then? I have been all over Athens, and seen no sign of it.

So. But if you stay longer you will find that every man has arms enough, for use at the proper time; you will see our plumes and horse-trappings, our horses and horsemen; these last amounting to a quarter of our citizens. But to carry arms and be girded with scimetars we consider unnecessary in peace time; indeed there is a fine for going armed in town without due cause, or producing weapons in public. *You* of course may be pardoned for living in arms. The want of walls gives conspiracy its chance; you have many enemies; you never know when somebody may come upon you in your sleep, pull you out of your cart, and dispatch you. And then, in the mutual distrust inseparable from an independence that recognizes no law or constitution, the sword must be always at hand to repel violence.

An. Oho, you think the wearing of arms, except on occasion, unnecessary; you are careful of your weapons, avoid wear and tear for them, and put them away for use when the time comes; but the bodies of your youth you keep at work even when no danger presses; you knock them about and dissolve them in sweat; instead of husbanding their strength for the day of need, you expend it idly on clay and dust. How is that?

So. I fancy you conceive of force as something similar to wine or water or liquid of some sort. You are afraid of its dribbling away in exercise as those might from an earthenware jar, and by its disappearance leaving the body, which is supposed to have no internal reserves, empty and dry. That is not the case; the greater the drain upon it in the course of exercise, the greater the supply; did you ever hear a story about the Hydra? cut off one of its heads, and two immediately sprang up in its place. No, it is the unexercised and fibreless, in whom no adequate store of material has ever been laid up, that will peak and pine under toil. There is a similar difference between a fire and a lamp; the same breath that kindles the former and soon excites it to greater heat will put out the latter, which is but ill provided to resist the blast; it has a precarious tenure, you see.

An. Ah, I cannot get hold of all that, Solon; it is too subtle for me—wants exact thought and keen intelligence. But I wish you would tell me—at the Olympic, Isthmian, Pythian, and other Games, attended, you tell me, by crowds to see your youth contend, why do you have no martial events? Instead, you put them in a conspicuous place and exhibit them kicking and cuffing one another, and when they win give them apples or wild olive. Now your reason for that would be worth hearing.

So. Well, we think it will increase their keenness for exercise to see the champions at it honoured and proclaimed by name among the assembled Greeks. It is the thought of having to strip before such a crowd that makes them take pains with their condition; they do not want to be a shameful spectacle, so each does his best to deserve success. And the prizes, as I said before, are not small things—to be applauded by the spectators, to be the mark of all eyes and fingers as the best of one's contemporaries. Accordingly, numbers of spectators, not too old for training, depart with a passion thus engendered for toilsome excellence. Ah, Anacharsis, if the love of fair fame were to be wiped out of our lives, what good would remain? Who would care to do a glorious deed? But as things are you may form your conclusions from what you see. These who are so keen for victory when they have no weapons and only a sprig of wild olive or an apple to contend for, how would they behave in martial array, with country and wives and children and altars at stake?

I wonder what your feelings would be if you saw our quail and cock fights, and the excitement they raise. You would laugh, no doubt, especially when you were told that they are enjoined by law, and that all of military age must attend and watch how the birds spar till they are utterly exhausted. And yet it is not a thing to laugh at either; a spirit of contempt for danger is thus instilled into men's souls; shall they yield to cocks in nobility and courage? shall they let wounds or weariness or discomfort incapacitate them before there is need? But as for testing our men in arms and looking on while they gash one another, no, thank you! that would be brutality and savagery, besides the bad policy of butchering our bravest, who would serve us best against our enemies.

You say you are going to visit the rest of Greece also. Well, if you go to Sparta, remember not to laugh at them either, nor think their labour is all in vain, when they charge and strike one another over a ball in the theatre; or perhaps they will go into a place enclosed by water, divide into two troops, and handle one another as severely as enemies (except that they too have no arms), until the Lycurgites drive the Heraclids, or vice versa, out of the enclosure and into the water; it is all over then; not another blow breaks the peace. Still worse, you may see them being scourged at the altar, streaming with blood, while their parents look on—the mothers, far from being distressed by the sight, actually making them hold out with threats, imploring them to endure pain to the last extremity and not be unmanned by suffering. There are many instances of their dying under the trial; while they had life and their people's eyes were on them, they would not give up, nor concede anything to bodily pain; and you will find their statues there, set up *honoris causa* by the Spartan state. Seeing these things, never take them for madmen, nor say that, since it is neither a tyrant's bidding nor a conqueror's ordinance, they victimize themselves for no good reason. Lycurgus their lawgiver would have many reasonable remarks to make to you on the subject, and give you his grounds for thus afflicting them; he was not moved by enmity or hatred; he was not wasting the state's young blood for nothing; he only thought it proper that defenders of their country should have endurance in the highest degree and be entirely superior to fear. However, you need no Lycurgus to tell you; you can surely see for yourself that, if one of these men were captured in war, no tortures would wring a Spartan secret out of him; he would take his scourging with a smile, and try whether the scourger would not be tired sooner than the scourged.

An. Solon, did Lycurgus take his whippings at the fighting age, or did he make these spirited regulations on the safe basis of superannuation?

So. It was in his old age, after returning from Crete, that he legislated. He had been attracted to Crete by hearing that their laws were the best possible, devised by Minos, son of Zeus.

An. Well, and why did you not copy Lycurgus and whip your young men? It is a fine institution quite worthy of yourselves.

So. Oh, we were content with our native exercises; we are not much given to imitating other nations.

An. No, no; you realize what a thing it is to be stripped and scourged with one's hands up, without benefit to oneself or one's country. If I do happen to be at Sparta when this performance is on, I shall expect a public stoning at their hands for laughing at it all, when I see them being whipped like robbers or thieves or such malefactors. Really, I think a state that submits to such ridiculous treatment at its own hands wants a dose of hellebore.

So. Friend, do not plume yourself on winning an undefended case where you have it all your own way in the absence of your opponents. In Sparta you will find some one to plead properly for their customs. But now, as I have described ours to you, not apparently to your satisfaction, I may fairly ask you to take your turn and tell me how you train your youth in Scythia; what exercises do you bring them up in? how do you make good men of them?

An. Quite a fair demand, Solon; I will give you the Scythian customs; there is no grandeur about them; they are not much like yours; for we would

515

never take a single box on the ears, we are such cowards; but such as they are, you shall have them. We must put off our talk till to-morrow, though, if you do not mind; I want to think quietly over what you have said, and collect materials for what I am to say myself. On that understanding let us go home; for it is getting late.

OF MOURNING

The behaviour of the average man in a time of bereavement, his own language and the remarks offered him by way of consolation, are things that will reward the attention of a curious observer. The mourner takes it for granted that a terrible blow has fallen both upon himself and upon the object of his lamentations:

yet for all he knows to the contrary (and here I appeal to Pluto and Persephone) the departed one, so far from being entitled to commiseration, may find himself in improved circumstances. The feelings of the bereaved party are in fact guided solely by custom and convention. The procedure in such cases—but no:

let me first state the popular beliefs on the subject of death itself; we shall then understand the motives for the elaborate ceremonial with which it is attended.

The vulgar (as philosophers call the generality of mankind), implicitly taking as their text-book the fictions of Homer and Hesiod and other poets, assume the existence of a deep subterranean hole called Hades; spacious, murky, and sunless, but by some mysterious means sufficiently lighted to render all its details visible. Its king is a brother of Zeus, one Pluto; whose name—so an able philologer assures me—contains a complimentary allusion to his ghostly wealth. As to the nature of his government, and the condition of his subjects, the authority allotted to him extends over all the dead, who, from the moment that they come under his control, are kept in unbreakable fetters; Shades are on no account permitted to return to Earth; to this rule there have been only two or three exceptions since the beginning of the world, and these were made for very urgent reasons. His realm is encompassed by vast rivers, whose very names inspire awe:

Cocytus, Pyriphlegethon, and the like. Most formidable of all, and first to arrest the progress of the new-comer, is Acheron, that lake which none may pass save by the ferryman's boat; it is too deep to be waded, too broad for the swimmer, and even defies the flight of birds deceased. At the very beginning of the descent is a gate of adamant:

here Aeacus, a nephew of the king, stands on guard. By his side is a three-headed dog, a grim brute; to new arrivals, however, he is friendly enough, reserving his bark, and the yawning horror of his jaws, for the would-be runaway. On the inner shore of the lake is a meadow, wherein grows asphodel; here, too, is the fountain that makes war on memory, and is hence called Lethe. All these particulars the ancients would doubtless obtain from the Thessalian queen Alcestis and her fellow-countryman Protesilaus, from Theseus the son of Aegeus, and from the hero of the Odyssey. These witnesses (whose evidence is entitled to our most respectful acceptance) did not, as I gather, drink of the waters of Lethe; because then they would not have remembered. According to them, the supreme power is entirely in the hands of Pluto and Persephone,

517

who, however, are assisted in the labours of government by a host of underlings:

such are the Furies, the Pains, the Fears; such too is Hermes, though he is not always in attendance. Judicial powers are vested in two satraps or viceroys, Minos and Rhadamanthus, both Cretans, and both sons of Zeus. By them all good and just men who have followed the precepts of virtue are sent off in large detachments to form colonies, as it were, in the Elysian Plain, and there to lead the perfect life. Evil-doers, on the contrary, are handed over to the Furies, who conduct them to the place of the wicked, where they are punished in due proportion to their iniquities. What a variety of torments is there presented! The rack, the fire, the gnawing vulture; here Ixion spins upon his wheel, there Sisyphus rolls his stone. I have not forgotten Tantalus; but he stands elsewhere, stands parched on the Lake's very brink, like to die of thirst, poor wretch! Then there is the numerous class of neutral characters; these wander about the meadow; formless phantoms, that evade the touch like smoke. It seems that they depend for their nourishment upon the libations and victims offered by us upon their tombs; accordingly, a Shade who has no surviving friends or relations passes a hungry time of it in the lower world.

So profoundly have the common people been impressed with these doctrines that, when a man dies, the first act of his relations is to put a penny into his mouth, that he may have wherewithal to pay the ferryman:

they do not stop to inquire what is the local currency, whether Attic or Macedonian or Aeginetan; nor does it occur to them how much better it would be for the departed one if the fare were not forthcoming,—because then the ferryman would decline to take him, and he would be sent back into the living world. Lest the Stygian Lake should prove inadequate to the requirements of ghostly toilets, the corpse is next washed, anointed with the choicest unguents to arrest the progress of decay, crowned with fresh flowers, and laid out in sumptuous raiment; an obvious precaution, this last; it would not do for the deceased to take a chill on the journey, nor to exhibit himself to Cerberus with nothing on. Lamentation follows. The women wail; men and women alike weep and beat their breasts and rend their hair and lacerate their cheeks; clothes are also torn on the occasion, and dust sprinkled on the head. The survivors are thus reduced to a more pitiable condition than the deceased:

while they in all probability are rolling about and dashing their heads on the ground, he, bravely attired and gloriously garlanded, reposes gracefully upon his lofty bier, adorned as it were for some pageant. The mother—nay, it is the father, as likely as not,—now advances from among the relatives, falls upon the bier (to heighten the dramatic effect, we will suppose its occupant to be young and handsome), and utters wild and meaningless ejaculations; the corpse cannot speak, otherwise it might have something to say in reply. His son—the father exclaims, with a mournful emphasis on every word,—his beloved son is no more; he is gone; torn away before his hour was come, leaving him alone to mourn; he has never married, never begotten children, never been on the field of battle, never laid hand to the plough, never reached old age; never again will he make merry, never again know the joys of love, never, alas! tipple at the convivial board among his comrades. And so on, and so on. He imagines his son to be still coveting these things, and coveting them in vain. But this is nothing:

time after time men have been known to slaughter horses upon the tomb, and concubines and pages; to burn clothes and other finery, or bury it, in the idea that the deceased will find a profitable use for such things in the lower world. Now the afflicted senior, in delivering the tragic utterances I have suggested above, and others of the same kind, is not, as I understand it, consulting the interests of his son (who he knows will not hear him, though he shout louder than Stentor), nor yet his own; he is perfectly aware of his sentiments, and has no occasion to bellow them into his own ear. The natural conclusion is, that this tomfoolery is for the benefit of the spectators; and all the time he has not an idea where his son is, or what may be his condition; he cannot even have reflected upon human life generally, or he would know that the loss of it is no such great matter. Let us imagine that the son has obtained leave from Aeacus and Pluto to take a peep into the daylight, and put a stop to these parental maunderings. 'Confound it, sir,' he might exclaim, 'what is the noise about? You bore me. Enough of hair-plucking and face- scratching. When you call me an ill-fated wretch, you abuse a better man than yourself, and a more fortunate. Why are you so sorry for me? Is it because I am not a bald, bent, wrinkled old cripple like yourself? Is it because I have not lived to be a battered wreck, nor seen a thousand moons wax and wane, only to make a fool of myself at the last before a crowd? Can your sapience point to any single convenience of life, of which we are deprived in the lower world? I know what you will say:

clothes and good dinners, wine and women, without which you think I shall be inconsolable. Are you now to learn that freedom from hunger and thirst is better than meat and drink, and insensibility to cold better than plenty of clothes? Come, I see you need enlightenment; I will show you how lamentation ought to be done. Make a fresh start, thus:

Alas, my son! Hunger and thirst and cold are his no longer! He is gone, gone beyond the reach of sickness; he fears not fever any more, nor enemies nor tyrants. Never again, my son, shall love disturb your peace, impair your health, make hourly inroads on your purse; oh, heavy change! Never can you reach contemptible old age, never be an eyesore to your juniors!—Confess, now, that my lamentation has the advantage of yours, in veracity, as in absurdity.

'Perhaps it is the pitchy darkness of the infernal regions that runs in your head? is that the trouble? Are you afraid I shall be suffocated in the confinement of the tomb? You should reflect that my eyes will presently decay, or (if such is your good pleasure) be consumed with fire; after which I shall have no occasion to notice either light or darkness. However, let that pass. But

519

all this lamentation, now; this fluting and beating of breasts; these wholly disproportionate wailings:

how am I the better for it all? And what do I want with a garlanded column over my grave? And what good do you suppose you are going to do by pouring wine on it? do you expect it to filter through all the way to Hades? As to the victims, you must surely see for yourselves that all the solid nutriment is whisked away heavenwards in the form of smoke, leaving us Shades precisely as we were; the residue, being dust, is useless; or is it your theory that Shades batten on ashes? Pluto's realm is not so barren, nor asphodel so scarce with us, that we must apply to you for provisions.—What with this winding-sheet and these woollen bandages, my jaws have been effectually sealed up, or, by Tisiphone, I should have burst out laughing long before this at the stuff you talk and the things you do.'

And at the word Death sealed his lips for ever.

Thus far our corpse, leaning on one side, supported on an elbow. Can we doubt that he is in the right of it? And yet these simpletons, not content with their own noise, must call in professional assistance:

an artist in grief, with a fine repertoire of cut-and-dried sorrows at his command, assumes the direction of this inane choir, and supplies a theme for their woful acclamations. So far, all men are fools alike:

but at this point national peculiarities make their appearance. The Greeks burn their dead, the Persians bury them; the Indian glazes the body, the Scythian eats it, the Egyptian embalms it. In Egypt, indeed, the corpse, duly dried, is actually placed at table,—I have seen it done; and it is quite a common thing for an Egyptian to relieve himself from pecuniary embarrassment by a timely visit to the pawnbroker, with his brother or father deceased. The childish futility of pyramids and mounds and columns, with their short-lived inscriptions, is obvious. But some people go further, and attempt to plead the cause of the deceased with his infernal judges, or testify to his merits, by means of funeral games and laudatory epitaphs. The final absurdity is the funeral feast, at which the assembled relatives strive to console the parents, and to prevail upon them to take food; and, Heaven knows, they are willing enough to be persuaded, being almost prostrated by a three days' fast. 'How long is this to go on?' some one expostulates. 'Suffer the spirit of your departed saint to rest in peace. Or if mourn you will, then for that very reason you must eat, that your strength may be proportioned to your grief.' At this point, a couple of lines of Homer go the round of the company:

Ev'n fair-haired Niobe forgat not food,
and
Not fasting mourn th' Achaeans for their dead.

The parents are persuaded, though they go to work at first in a somewhat shamefaced manner; they do not want it to be thought that after their bereavement they are still subject to the infirmities of the flesh.

Such are some of the absurdities that may be observed in mourners; for I have by no means exhausted the list. And all springs from the vulgar error, that Death is the worst thing that can befall a man.

THE RHETORICIAN'S VADE MECUM

You ask, young man, how you may become a rhetorician, and win yourself the imposing and reverend style of Professor. You tell me life is for you not worth living, if you cannot clothe yourself in that power of the word which shall make you invincible and irresistible, the cynosure of all men's admiration, the desired of all Grecian ears. Your one wish is to be shown the way to that goal. And small blame, youngster, to one who in the days of his youth sets his gaze upon the things that are highest, and knowing not how he shall attain, comes as you now come to me with the privileged demand for counsel. Take then the best of it that I can give, doubting nothing but you shall speedily be a man accomplished to see the right and to give it expression, if you will henceforth abide by what you now hear from me, practise it with assiduity, and go confidently on your way till it brings you to the desired end.

The object of your pursuit is no poor one, worth but a moderate endeavour; to grasp it you might be content to toil and watch and endure to the utmost; mark how many they are who once were but cyphers, but whom words have raised to fame and opulence, ay, and to noble lineage.

Yet fear not, nor be appalled, when you contemplate the greatness of your aim, by thought of the thousand toils first to be accomplished. It is by no rough mountainous perspiring track that I shall lead you; else were I no better than those other guides who point you to the common way, long, steep, toilsome, nay, for the most part desperate. What should commend my counsel to you is even this:

a road most pleasant and most brief, a carriage road of downward slope, shall bring you in all delight and ease, at what leisurely effortless pace you will, through flowery meadows and plenteous shade, to that summit which you shall mount and hold untired and there lie feasting, the while you survey from your height those panting ones who took the other track; they are yet in the first stage of their climb, forcing their slow way amid rough or slippery crags, with many a headlong fall and many a wound from those sharp rocks. But you will long have been up, and garlanded and blest; you have slept, and waked to find that Rhetoric has lavished upon you all her gifts at once.

Fine promises, these, are they not? But pray let it not stir your doubts, that I offer to make most easy that which is most sweet. It was but plucking a few leaves from Helicon, and the shepherd Hesiod was a poet, possessed of the Muses and singing the birth of Gods and Heroes; and may not a rhetorician ('tis no such proud title as that of poet) be quickly made, if one but knows the speediest way?

Let me tell you of an idea that came to nothing for want of faith, and brought no profit to the man it was offered to. Alexander had fought Arbela, deposed Darius, and was lord of Persia; his orders had to be conveyed to every part of his empire by dispatch-runners. Now from Persia to Egypt was a long journey; to make the necessary circuit round the mountains, cross Babylonia into Arabia, traverse a great desert, and so finally reach Egypt, took at the best full twenty days. And as Alexander had intelligence of disturbances in Egypt, it was an inconvenience not to be able to send instructions rapidly to his lieutenants there. A Sidonian trader came to him and offered to shorten the distance:

if a man cut straight across the mountains, which could be done in three days, he would be in Egypt without more ado. This was a fact; but Alexander took the man for an impostor, and would have nothing to say to him. That is the reception any surprisingly good offer may expect from most men.

Be not like them. A trial will soon show you that you may fly over the mountains from Persia to Egypt, and in a day, in part of a day, take rank as rhetorician. But first I will be your Cebes and give you word-pictures of the two different ways leading to that Rhetoric, with which I see you so in love. Imagine her seated on a height, fair and comely; her right hand holds an Amalthea's horn heaped high with all fruits, and at her other side you are to see Wealth standing in all his golden glamour. In attendance too are Repute and Might; and all about your lady's person flutter and cling embodied Praises like tiny Loves. Or you may have seen a painted Nilus; he reclines himself upon a crocodile or hippopotamus, with which his stream abounds, and round him play the tiny children they call in Egypt his *Cubits*; so play the Praises about Rhetoric. Add yourself, the lover, who long to be straightway at the top, that you may wed her, and all that is hers be yours; for him that weds her she must endow with her worldly goods.

When you have reached the mountain, you at first despair of scaling it; you seem to have set yourself the task that Aornus[72] presented to the Macedonians; how sheer it was on every side! it was true, they thought, even a bird could hardly soar that height; to take it would be work for a Dionysus or Heracles. Then in a little while you discern two roads; or no, one is no more than a track, narrow, thorny, rough, promising thirst and sweat. But I need say no more of it; Hesiod has described it long ago The other is broad, and fringed with flowers and well watered and—not to keep you back with vain repetitions from the prize even now within your grasp—such a road as I told you of but now.

This much, however, I must add:

that rough steep way shows not many steps of travellers; a few there are, but of ancient date. It was my own ill fortune to go up by it, expending needless toil; but I could see from far off how level and direct was that other, though I did not use it; in my young days I was perverse, and put trust in the poet who told me that the Good is won by toil. He was in error; I see that the many who toil not are more richly rewarded for their fortunate choice of route and method. But the question is now of you; I know that when you come to the parting of the ways you will doubt—you doubt even now—which turn to

<hr />

[72] i.e., birdless.

take. What you must do, then, to find the easiest ascent, and blessedness, and your bride, and universal fame, I will tell you. Enough that *I* have been cheated into toil; for you let all grow unsown and unploughed as in the age of gold.

A strong severe-looking man will at once come up to you; he has a firm step, a deeply sunburnt body, a decided eye and wide-awake air; it is the guide of the rough track. This absurd person makes foolish suggestions that you should employ him, and points you out the footmarks of Demosthenes, Plato, and others; they are larger than what we make, but mostly half obliterated by time; he tells you you will attain bliss and have Rhetoric to your lawful wife, if you stick as closely to these as a rope-walker to his rope; but diverge for a moment, make a false step, or incline your weight too much either way, and farewell to your path and your bride. He will exhort you to imitate these ancients, and offer you antiquated models that lend themselves as little to imitation as old sculpture, say the clean-cut, sinewy, hard, firmly outlined productions of Hegesias, or the school of Critius and Nesiotes; and he will tell you that toil and vigilance, abstinence and perseverance, are indispensable, if you would accomplish your journey. Most mortifying of all, the time he will stipulate for is immense, years upon years; he does not so much as mention days or months; whole Olympiads are his units; you feel tired at the mere sound of them, and ready to relinquish the happiness you had set your heart upon. And as if this was not enough, he wishes to be paid handsomely for your trouble, and must have a good sum down before he will even put you in the way.

So he will talk—a conceited primitive old-world personage; for models he offers you old masters long dead and done with, and expects you to exhume rusty speeches as if they were buried treasures; you are to copy a certain cutler's son[73] or one who called the clerk Atrometus father[74]; he forgets that we are at peace now, with no invading Philip or hectoring Alexander to give a temporary value to that sort of eloquence; and he has never heard of our new road to Rhetoric, short, easy, and direct. Let him not prevail with you; heed not him at all; in his charge, if you do not first break your neck, you will wear yourself into a premature old age. If you are really in love, and would enjoy Rhetoric before your prime is past, and be made much of by her, dismiss this hairy specimen of ultra- virility, and leave him to climb by himself or with what dupes he can make, panting and perspiring to his heart's content.

Go you to the other road, where you will find much good company, but in especial one man. Is he clever? is he engaging? Mark the negligent ease of his gait, his neck's willowy curve, his languishing glance; these words are honey, that breath perfume; was ever head scratched with so graceful a forefinger? and those locks —were there but more of them left—how hyacinthine their wavy order! he is tender as Sardanapalus or Cinyras; 'tis Agathon's self, loveliest of

---

[73] Demosthenes.
[74] Aeschines.

tragedy-makers. Take these traits, that seeing you may know him; I would not have you miss so divine an apparition, the darling of Aphrodite and the Graces. Yet how needless! were he to come near while your eyes were closed, and unbar those Hymettian lips to the voice that dwells within, you could not want the thought that this was none of us who munch the fruits of earth, but some spirit from afar that on honeydew hath fed, and drunk the milk of Paradise. Him seek; trust yourself to him, and you shall be in a trice rhetorician and man of note, and in his own great phrase, King of Words, mounted without an effort of your own upon the chariot of discourse. For here is the lore he shall impart to his disciple.

But let him describe it himself. For one so eloquent it is absurd that I should speak; my histrionic talent is not equal to so mighty a task; I might trip, and break the heroic mask in my fall. He thus addresses you, then, with a touch of the hand to those scanty curls, and the usual charming delicate smile; you might take him— so engaging is his utterance—for a Glycera, a Malthace, or her comic and meretricious majesty, Thais herself. What has a refined bewitching orator to do with the vulgar masculine?

Listen now to his modest remarks. _Dear sir, was it Apollo sent you here? did he call me best of rhetoricians, as when Chaerephon asked and was told who was wisest of his generation? If it has not been so, if you have come directed only by the amazement and applause, the wonder and despair, that attend my achievements, then shall you soon learn whether there is divinity or no in him whom you have sought. Look not for a greatness that may find its parallel in this man or that; a Tityus, an Otus, an Ephialtes there may have been; but here is a portent and a marvel greater far than they. You are to hear a voice that puts to silence all others, as the trumpet the flute, as the cicala the bee, as the choir the tuning-fork.

But you wish to be a rhetorician yourself; well, you could have applied in no better quarter; my dear young friend, you have only to follow my instructions and example, and keep carefully in mind the rules I lay down for your guidance. Indeed you may start this moment without a tremor; never let it disturb you that you have not been through the laborious preliminaries with which the ordinary system besets the path of fools; they are quite unnecessary. Stay not to find your slippers, as the song has it; your naked feet will do as well; writing is a not uncommon accomplishment, but I do not insist upon it; it is one thing, and rhetoric is another.

I will first give you a list of the equipment and supplies for your journey that you must bring with you from home, with a view to making your way rapidly. After that, I will show you as we go along some practical illustrations, add a few verbal precepts, and before set of sun you shall be as superior a rhetorician as myself, the absolute microcosm of your profession. Bring then above all ignorance, to which add confidence, audacity, and effrontery; as for diffidence, equity, moderation, and shame, you will please leave them at home; they are not merely needless, they are encumbrances. The loudest voice you can come by, please, a ready falsetto, and a gait modelled on my own. That exhausts the real necessaries; very often there would be no occasion for anything further. But I recommend bright colours or white for your clothes; the Tarentine stuff that lets the body show through is best; for shoes, wear either the Attic woman's shape with the open network, or else the Sicyonians that show white lining. Always have a train of attendants, and a book in your hand.

The rest you will take in with your eyes and ears as we go. I will tell you the rules you must observe, if Rhetoric is to recognize and admit you; otherwise she will turn from you and drive you away as an uninitiated intruder upon her mysteries. You must first be exceedingly careful about your appearance; your clothes must be quite the thing. Next, you must scrape up some fifteen old Attic words—say twenty for an outside estimate; and these you must rehearse diligently till you have them at the tip of your tongue; let us say *sundry, whereupon, say you so, in some wise, my masters;* that is the sort of thing; these are for general garnish, you understand; and you need not concern yourself about any little dissimilarity, repulsion, discord, between them and the rest; so long as your upper garment is fair and bright, what matter if there is coarse serge beneath it?

Next, fill your quiver with queer mysterious words used once or twice by the ancients, ready to be discharged at a moment's notice in conversation. This will attract the attention of the common herd, who will take you for a wonder, so much better educated than themselves. Put on your clothes? of course not;_ invest yourself. *Will you sit in the porch, when there is a* parvys *to hand? No earnest-money for us; let it be an* arles-penny. *And no breakfast-time, pray, but* undern. *You may also do a little word-formation of your own on occasion, and enact that a person good, at exposition shall be known as a* clarifier, *a sensible one as a* cogitant, *or a pantomime as a* manuactor. _If you commit a blunder or provincialism, you have only to carry it off boldly with an instant reference to the authority of some poet or historian, who need not exist or ever have existed; your phrase has his approval, and he was a wise man and a past master in language. As for your reading, leave the ancients alone; never mind a foolish Isocrates, a tasteless Demosthenes, a frigid Plato; study the works of the last generation; you will find the declamations, as they call them, a plenteous store on which to draw at need.

When the time comes for you to perform, and the audience have proposed subjects and invented cases for discussion, you should get rid of the difficult ones by calling them trivial, and complain that there is nothing in this selection that can really test a man's powers. When they have chosen, do not hesitate a moment, but start; the tongue is an unruly member; do not attempt to rule it; never care whether your firstly is logics firstly, or your secondly and thirdly in the right order; just say what comes; you may greave your head and helmet your legs, but whatever you do, move, keep going, never pause. If your subject is assault or adultery in Athens, cite the Indians and Medes. Always have your Marathon and your Cynaegirus handy; they are indispensable. Hardly less so are a fleet crossing Mount Athos, an army treading the Hellespont, a sun eclipsed by Persian arrows, a flying Xerxes, an admired Leonidas, an inscriptive Othryades. Salamis, Artemisium, and Plataea, should also be in constant use. All this dressed as usual with our seasoning-garnish aforesaid—that persuasive flavour of *sundry* and *methinks*; do not wait till these seem to be called for; they are pretty words, quite apart from their relevancy.

If a fancy for impassioned_ recitative _comes over you, indulge it as long as you will, and air your falsetto. If your matter is not of the right poetic sort, you may consider yourself to have met the requirements if you run over the names of the jury in a rhythmic manner. Appeal constantly to the pathetic instinct, smite your thigh, mouth your words well, punctuate with loud sighs, and let your very back be eloquent as you pace to and fro. If the audience fails to applaud, take offence, and give your offence words; if they get up and prepare to go out in disgust, tell them to sit down again; discipline must be maintained.

It will win you credit for copiousness, if you start with the Trojan War—you may if you like go right back to the nuptials of Deucalion and Pyrrha—and thence trace your subject down to to-day. People of sense, remember, are rare, and they will probably hold their tongues out of charity; or if they do comment, it will be put down to jealousy. The rest are awed by your costume, your voice, gait, motions, falsetto, shoes, and_ sundry_; when they see how you perspire and pant, they cannot admit a moment's doubt of your being a very fine rhetorical performer. With them, your mere rapidity is a miracle quite sufficient to establish your character. Never prepare notes, then, nor think out a subject beforehand; that shows one up at once.

Your friends' feet will be loud on the floor, in payment for the dinners you give them; if they observe you in difficulties, they will come to the rescue, and give you a chance, in the relief afforded by rounds of applause, of thinking how to go on. A devoted *claque* of your own, by the way, is among your requirements. Its use while you are performing I have given; and as you walk home afterwards, discussing the points you made, you should be absolutely surrounded by them as a bodyguard. If you meet acquaintances on the way, talk very big about yourself, put a good value on your merits, and never mind about their feelings. Ask them, Where is Demosthenes now? Or wonder *which* of the ancients comes nearest you.

But dear me, I had very nearly passed over the most important and effectual of all aids to reputation:

the pouring of ridicule upon your rivals. If a man has a fine style, its beauties are borrowed; if a sober one, it is bad altogether. When you go to a recitation, arrive late, which makes you conspicuous; and when all are listening intently, interject some inappropriate commendation that will distract and annoy the audience; they will be so sickened with your offensive words that they cannot listen. And then do not wave your hand too much—warm approval is rather low; and as to jumping up, never do it more than once or twice. A slight smile is your best expression; make it clear that you do not think much of the thing. Only let your ears be critical, and you are sure of finding plenty to condemn. In fact, all the qualities needed are easily come by—audacity, effrontery, ready lying, indifference to perjury, impartial jealousy, hatred, abuse, and skilful slander— that is all you want to win you speedy credit and renown. So much for your visible public life.

And in private you need draw the line at nothing, gambling, drink, fornication, nor adultery; the last you should boast of, whether truly or not; make no secret of it, but exhibit your notes from real or imaginary frail ones. One of your aims should be to pass for a pretty fellow, in much favour with the ladies; the report will be professionally useful to you, your influence with the sex being accounted for by your rhetorical eminence.

Master these instructions, young man—they are surely simple enough not to overtax your powers—, and I confidently promise that you shall soon be a first-class rhetorician like myself; after which I need not tell you what great and what rapid advancement Rhetoric will put in your way. You have but to look at me. My father was an obscure person barely above a slave; he had in fact been one south of Xois and Thmuis; my mother a common sempstress. I was myself not without pretensions to beauty in my youth, which earned me a bare living from a miserly ill-conditioned admirer; but I discovered this easy short-cut, made my way to the top—for I had, if I may be bold to say it, all the qualifications I told you of, confidence, ignorance, and effrontery—, and at once found myself in a position to change my name of Pothinus to one that levels me with the children of Zeus and Leda. I then established myself in an old dame's house, where I earned my keep by professing a passion for her seventy years and her half-dozen remaining teeth, dentist's gold and all. However, poverty reconciled me to my task; even for those cold coffin kisses,_ fames *was* condimentum optimum. _And it was by the merest ill luck that I missed inheriting her wealth—that damned slave who peached about the poison I had bought!

I was turned out neck and crop, but even so I did not starve. I have my professional position and am well known in the courts— especially for collusion and the corruption-agency which I keep for credulous litigants. My cases generally go against me; but the palms at my door[75] are fresh and flower-crowned—springes to catch woodcocks, you know. Then, to be the object of universal detestation, to be distinguished only less for the badness of one's

---

[75] Now stretch your throat, unhappy man! now raise
　Your clamours, that, when hoarse, a bunch of bays,
　Stuck in your garret window, may declare,
　That some victorious pleader nestles there.
Juvenal, vii. 118 (Gifford).

character than for that of one's speeches, to be pointed at by every finger as the famous champion of all-round villany—this seems to me no inconsiderable attainment. And now you have my advice; take it with the blessing of the great Goddess Lubricity. It is the same that I gave myself long ago; and very thankful I have been to myself for it._

Ah! our admirable friend seems to have done. If you decide to take his advice, you may regard yourself as practically arrived at your goal. Keep his rules, and your path is clear; you may dominate the courts, triumph in the lecture-room, be smiled on by the fair; your bride shall be not, like your lawgiver and teacher's, an old woman off the comic stage, but lovely dame Rhetoric. Plato told of Zeus sweeping on in his winged car; you shall use the figure as fitly of yourself. And I? why, I lack spirit and courage; I will stand out of your way. I will resign—nay, I have resigned—my high place about our lady's person to you; for I cannot pay my court to her like the new school. Do your walk over, then, hear your name announced, take your plaudits; I ask you only to remember that you owe the victory not to your speed, but to your discovery of the easy down-hill route.[76]

---

[76] It is apparent from the later half of this piece that the satire is aimed at an individual. He is generally identified with Julius Pollux. This Pollux (1) was contemporary (floruit A.D. 183) with Lucian. (2) Explains by his name the reference to Leda's children (Castor and Pollux) in Section 24. (3) Published an Onomasticon, or classified vocabulary; cf. Sections 16, 17. (4) Published a collection of declamations, or school rhetorical exercises on set themes; cf. Section 17. (5) Came from Egypt; cf. Section 24; Xois and Thmuis were in that country. (6) Is said to have been appointed professor of rhetoric at Athens by Commodus purely on account of his mellifluous voice; cf. Section 19.

It is supposed that *Lexiphanes* (in the dialogue of that name, which has much in common with the present satire) is also Julius Pollux.

THE LIAR

Tychiades. Philocles

Tyc. Philocles, what *is* it that makes most men so fond of a lie? Can you explain it? Their delight in romancing themselves is only equalled by the earnest attention with which they receive other people's efforts in the same direction.

Phi. Why, in some cases there is no lack of motives for lying,—motives of self-interest.

Tyc. Ah, but that is neither here nor there. I am not speaking of men who lie with an object. There is some excuse for that:

indeed, it is sometimes to their credit, when they deceive their country's enemies, for instance, or when mendacity is but the medicine to heal their sickness. Odysseus, seeking to preserve his life and bring his companions safe home, was a liar of that kind. The men I mean are innocent of any ulterior motive:

they prefer a lie to truth, simply on its own merits; they like lying, it is their favourite occupation; there is no necessity in the case. Now what good can they get out of it?

Phi. Why, have you ever known any one with such a strong natural turn for lying?

Tyc. Any number of them.

Phi. Then I can only say they must be fools, if they really prefer evil to good.

Tyc. Oh, that is not it. I could point you out plenty of men of first-rate ability, sensible enough in all other respects, who have somehow picked up this vice of romancing. It makes me quite angry:

what satisfaction can there be to men of their good qualities in deceiving themselves and their neighbours? There are instances among the ancients with which you must be more familiar than I. Look at Herodotus, or Ctesias of Cnidus; or, to go further back, take the poets—Homer himself:

here are men of world-wide celebrity, perpetuating their mendacity in black and white; not content with deceiving their hearers, they must send their lies down to posterity, under the protection of the most admirable verse. Many a time I have blushed for them, as I read of the mutilation of Uranus, the fetters of Prometheus, the revolt of the Giants, the torments of Hell; enamoured Zeus taking the shape of bull or swan; women turning into birds and bears; Pegasuses, Chimaeras, Gorgons, Cyclopes, and the rest of it; monstrous medley! fit only to charm the imaginations of children for whom Mormo and Lamia have still their terrors. However, poets, I suppose, will be poets. But when it comes to national lies, when one finds whole cities bouncing collectively like one man, how is one to keep one's countenance? A Cretan will look you in the face, and tell you that yonder is Zeus's tomb. In Athens, you are informed that Erichthonius sprang out of the Earth, and that the first

530

Athenians grew up from the soil like so many cabbages; and this story assumes quite a sober aspect when compared with that of the Sparti, for whom the Thebans claim descent from a dragon's teeth. If you presume to doubt these stories, if you choose to exert your common sense, and leave Triptolemus's winged aerial car, and Pan's Marathonian exploits, and Orithyia's mishap, to the stronger digestions of a Coroebus and a Margites, you are a fool and a blasphemer, for questioning such palpable truths. Such is the power of lies!

Phi. I must say I think there is some excuse, Tychiades, both for your national liars and for the poets. The latter are quite right in throwing in a little mythology:

it has a very pleasing effect, and is just the thing to secure the attention of their hearers. On the other hand, the Athenians and the Thebans and the rest are only trying to add to the lustre of their respective cities. Take away the legendary treasures of Greece, and you condemn the whole race of ciceroni to starvation:

sightseers do not want the truth; they would not take it at a gift. However, I surrender to your ridicule any one who has no such motive, and yet rejoices in lies.

Tyc. Very well:

now I have just been with the great Eucrates, who treated me to a whole string of old wives' tales. I came away in the middle of it; he was too much for me altogether; Furies could not have driven me out more effectually than his marvel-working tongue.

Phi. What, Eucrates, of all credible witnesses? That venerably bearded sexagenarian, with his philosophic leanings? I could never have believed that he would lend his countenance to other people's lies, much less that *he* was capable of such things himself

Tyc. My dear sir, you should have heard the stuff he told me; the way in which he vouched for the truth of it all too, solemnly staking the lives of his children on his veracity! I stared at him in amazement, not knowing what to make of it:

one moment I thought he must be out of his mind; the next I concluded he had been a humbug all along, an ape in a lion's skin. Oh, it was monstrous.

Phi. Do tell me all about it; I am curious to see the quackery that shelters beneath so long a beard.

Tyc. I often look in on Eucrates when I have time on my hands, but to-day I had gone there to see Leontichus; he is a friend of mine, you know, and I understood from his boy that he had gone off early to inquire after Eucrates's health, I had not heard that there was anything the matter with him, but this was an additional reason for paying him a visit. When I got there, Leontichus had just gone away, so Eucrates said; but he had a number of other visitors. There was Cleodemus the Peripatetic and Dinomachus the Stoic, and Ion. You know Ion? he is the man who fancies himself so much on his knowledge of Plato; if you take his word for it, he is the only man who has ever really got to the bottom of that philosopher's meaning, or is qualified to act as his interpreter. There is a company for you; Wisdom and Virtue personified, the *elite* of every school, most reverend gentlemen all of them; it almost frightened one. Then there was Antigonus the doctor, who I suppose attended in his professional capacity. Eucrates seemed to be better already:

he had come to an understanding with the gout, which had now settled down in his feet again. He motioned me to a seat on the couch beside him. His voice sank to the proper invalid level when he saw me coming, but on my way in I had overheard him bellowing away most lustily. I made him the usual compliments—explained that this was the first I had heard of his illness, and that I had come to him post-haste—and sat down at his side, in very gingerly fashion, lest I should touch his feet. There had been a good deal of talk already about gout, and this was still going on; each man had his pet prescription to offer. Cleodemus was giving his. 'In the left hand take up the tooth of a field-mouse, which has been killed in the manner described, and attach it to the skin of a freshly flayed lion; then bind the skin about your legs, and the pain will instantly cease.' 'A lion's skin?' says Dinomachus; 'I understood it was an uncovered hind's. That sounds more likely:

a hind has more pace, you see, and is particularly strong in the feet. A lion is a brave beast, I grant you; his fat, his right fore-paw, and his beard-bristles, are all very efficacious, if you know the proper incantation to use with each; but they would hardly be much use for gout.' 'Ah, yes; that is what I used to think for a long time:

a hind was fast, so her skin must be the one for the purpose. But I know better now:

a Libyan, who understands these things, tells me that lions are faster than stags; they must be, he says, because how else could they catch them? 'All agreed that the Libyan's argument was convincing. When I asked what good incantations could do, and how an internal complaint could be cured by external attachments, I only got laughed at for my pains; evidently they set me down as a simpleton, ignorant of the merest truisms, that no one in his senses would think of disputing. However, I thought doctor Antigonus seemed rather pleased at my question. I expect his professional advice had been slighted:

he wanted to lower Eucrates's tone,—cut down his wine, and put him on a vegetable diet. 'What, Tychiades,' says Cleodemus, with a faint grin,' you don't believe these remedies are good for anything?' 'I should have to be pretty far gone,' I replied, 'before I could admit that external things, which have no communication with the internal causes of disease, are going to work by means of incantations and stuff, and effect a cure merely by being hung on. You might take the skin of the Nemean lion himself, with a dozen of field-mice tacked on, and you would do no good. Why, I have seen a live lion limping before now, hide and all complete.' 'Ah, you have a great deal to learn,' cried Dinomachus; 'you have never taken the trouble to inquire into the operation of these valuable remedies. It would not surprise me to hear you disputing the most palpable facts, such as the curing of tumours and intermittent fevers, the charming of reptiles, and so on; things that every old woman can effect in these days. And this being so, why should not the same principles be extended further?' 'Nail drives out nail,' I replied; 'you argue in a circle. How do I know that these cures are brought about by the means to which you attribute them? You have first to show inductively that it is in the course of nature for a fever or a tumour to take fright and bolt at the sound of holy names and foreign incantations; till then, your instances are no better than old wives' tales.' 'In other words, you do not believe in the existence of the Gods, since you maintain that cures cannot be wrought by the use of holy names?' 'Nay, say not so, my dear Dinomachus,' I answered; 'the Gods may exist, and these things may yet be lies. I respect the Gods:

I see the cures performed by them, I see their beneficence at work in restoring the sick through the medium of the medical faculty and their drugs. Asclepius, and his sons after him, compounded soothing medicines and healed the sick, —without the lion's-skin-and-field-mouse process.'

'Never mind Asclepius,' cried Ion. 'I will tell you of a strange thing that happened when I was a boy of fourteen or so. Some one came and told my father that Midas, his gardener, a sturdy fellow and a good workman, had been bitten that morning by an adder, and was now lying prostrate, mortification having set in the leg. He had been tying the vine-branches to the trellis-work, when the reptile crept up and bit him on the great toe, getting off to its hole before he could catch it; and he was now in a terrible way. Before our informant had finished speaking, we saw Midas being carried up by his fellow servants on a stretcher:

his whole body was swollen, livid and mortifying, and life appeared to be almost extinct. My father was very much troubled about it; but a friend of his who was there assured him there was no cause for uneasiness. 'I know of a Babylonian,' he said, 'what they call a Chaldaean; I will go and fetch him at once, and he will put the man right.' To make a long story short, the Babylonian came, and by means of an incantation expelled the venom from the body, and restored Midas to health; besides the incantation, however, he used a splinter of stone chipped from the monument of a virgin; this he applied to Midas's foot. And as if that were not enough (Midas, I may mention, actually picked up the stretcher on which he had been brought, and took it off with him into the vineyard! and it was all done by an incantation and a bit of stone), the Chaldaean followed it up with an exhibition nothing short of miraculous. Early in the morning he went into the field, pronounced seven names of sacred import, taken from an old book, purified the ground by going thrice round it with sulphur and burning torches, and thereby drove every single reptile off the estate! They came as if drawn by a spell:

venomous toads and snakes of every description, asp and adder, cerastes and acontias; only one old serpent, disabled apparently by age, ignored the summons. The Chaldaean declared that the number was not complete, appointed the youngest of the snakes as his ambassador, and sent him to fetch the old serpent who presently arrived. Having got them all together, he blew upon them; and imagine our astonishment when every one of them was immediately consumed!'

'Ion,' said I, 'about that one who was so old:

did the ambassador snake give him an arm, or had he a stick to lean on?' 'Ah, you will have your joke,' Cleodemus put in; 'I was an unbeliever myself once—worse than you; in fact I considered it absolutely impossible to give credit to such things. I held out for a long time, but all my scruples were overcome the first time I saw the Flying Stranger; a Hyperborean, he was; I have his own word for it. There was no more to be said after that:

there was he travelling through the air in broad daylight, walking on the water, or strolling through fire, perfectly at his ease!' 'What,' I exclaimed,' you saw this Hyperborean actually flying and walking on water?' 'I did; he wore brogues, as the Hyperboreans usually do. I need not detain you with the everyday manifestations of his power:

how he would make people fall in love, call up spirits, resuscitate corpses, bring down the Moon, and show you Hecate herself, as large as life. But I will just tell you of a thing I saw him do at Glaucias's. It was not long after Glaucias's father, Alexicles, had died. Glaucias, on coming into the property, had fallen in love with Chrysis, Demaenetus's daughter. I was teaching him philosophy at the time, and if it had not been for this love-affair he would have thoroughly mastered the Peripatetic doctrines:

at eighteen years old that boy had been through his physics, and begun analysis. Well, he was in a dreadful way, and told me all about his love troubles. It was clearly my duty to introduce him to this Hyperborean wizard, which I accordingly did; his preliminary fee, to cover the expenses of sacrifice, was to be 15 pounds, and he was to have another 60 pounds if Glaucias succeeded with Chrysis. Well, as soon as the moon was full, that being the time usually chosen for these enchantments, he dug a trench in the courtyard of the house, and commenced operations, at about midnight, by summoning Glaucias's father, who had now been dead for seven months. The old man did not approve of his son's passion, and was very angry at first; however, he was prevailed on to give his consent. Hecate was next ordered to appear, with Cerberus in her train, and the Moon was brought down, and went through a variety of transformations; she appeared first in the form of a woman, but presently she turned into a most magnificent ox, and after that into a puppy. At length the Hyperborean moulded a clay Eros, and ordered it to *go and fetch Chrysis*. Off went the image, and before long there was a knock at the door, and there stood Chrysis. She came in and threw her arms about Glaucias's neck; you would have said she was dying for love of him; and she stayed on till at last we heard cocks crowing. Away flew the Moon into Heaven, Hecate disappeared under ground, all the apparitions vanished, and we saw Chrysis out of the house just about dawn.—Now, Tychiades, if you had seen that, it would have been enough to convince you that there was something in incantations.'

'Exactly,' I replied. 'If I had seen it, I should have been convinced:

as it is, you must bear with me if I have not your eyes for the miraculous. But as to Chrysis, I know her for a most inflammable lady. I do not see what occasion there was for the clay ambassador and the Moon, or for a wizard all the way from the land of the Hyperboreans; why, Chrysis would go that distance herself for the sum of twenty shillings; 'tis a form of incantation she cannot resist. She is the exact opposite of an apparition:

apparitions, you tell me, take flight at the clash of brass or iron, whereas if Chrysis hears the chink of silver, she flies to the spot. By the way, I like your wizard:

instead of making all the wealthiest women in love with himself, and getting thousands out of them, he condescends to pick up 15 pounds by rendering Glaucias irresistible.'

'This is sheer folly,' said Ion; 'you are determined not to believe any one. I shall be glad, now, to hear your views on the subject of those who cure demoniacal possession; the effect of *their* exorcisms is clear enough, and they have spirits to deal with. I need not enlarge on the subject:

look at that Syrian adept from Palestine:

every one knows how time after time he has found a man thrown down on the ground in a lunatic fit, foaming at the mouth and rolling his eyes; and how he has got him on to his feet again and sent him away in his right mind; and a handsome fee he takes for freeing men from such horrors. He stands over them as they lie, and asks the spirit whence it is. The patient says not a word, but the spirit in him makes answer, in Greek or in some foreign tongue as the case may be, stating where it comes from, and how it entered into him. Then with adjurations, and if need be with threats, the Syrian constrains it to come out of the man. I myself once saw one coming out:

it was of a dark, smoky complexion.' 'Ah, that is nothing for you,' I replied; 'your eyes can discern those *ideas* which are set forth in the works of Plato, the founder of your school:

now they make a very faint impression on the dull optics of us ordinary men.'

'Do you suppose,' asked Eucrates, 'that he is the only man who has seen such things? Plenty of people besides Ion have met with spirits, by night and by day. As for me, if I have seen one apparition, I have seen a thousand. I used not to like them at first, but I am accustomed to them now, and think nothing of it; especially since the Arab gave me my ring of gallows-iron, and taught me the incantation with all those names in it. But perhaps you will doubt my word too?' 'Doubt the word of Eucrates, the learned son of Dino? Never! least of all when he unbosoms himself in the liberty of his own house.' 'Well, what I am going to tell you about the statue was witnessed night after night by all my household, from the eldest to the youngest, and any one of them could tell you

535

the story as well as myself.' 'What statue is this?' 'Have you never noticed as you came in that beautiful one in the court, by Demetrius the portrait-sculptor?' 'Is that the one with the quoit,—leaning forward for the throw, with his face turned back towards the hand that holds the quoit, and one knee bent, ready to rise as he lets it go?' 'Ah, that is a fine piece of work, too,—a Myron; but I don't mean that, nor the beautiful Polyclitus next it, the Youth tying on the Fillet. No, forget all you pass on your right as you come in; the Tyrannicides[77] of Critius and Nesiotes are on that side too:

— but did you never notice one just by the fountain?—bald, pot-bellied, half-naked; beard partly caught by the wind; protruding veins? that is the one I mean; it looks as if it must be a portrait, and is thought to be Pelichus, the Corinthian general.' 'Ah, to be sure, I have seen it,' I replied; 'it is to the right of the Cronus; the head is crowned with fillets and withered garlands, and the breast gilded.' 'Yes, I had that done, when he cured me of the tertian ague; I had been at Death's door with it.' 'Bravo, Pelichus!' I exclaimed; 'so he was a doctor too?' 'Not was, but is. Beware of trifling with him, or he may pay you a visit before long. Well do I know what virtue is in that statue with which you make so merry. Can you doubt that he who cures the ague may also inflict it at will?' 'I implore his favour,' I cried; 'may he be as merciful as he is mighty! And what are his other doings, to which all your household are witnesses?' 'At nightfall,' said Eucrates, 'he descends from his pedestal, and walks all round the house; one or other of us is continually meeting with him; sometimes he is singing. He has never done any harm to any one:

all we have to do when we see him is to step aside, and he passes on his way without molesting us. He is fond of taking a bath; you may hear him splashing about in the water all night long.' 'Perhaps,' I suggested, 'it is not Pelichus at all, but Talos the Cretan, the son of Minos? He was of bronze, and used to walk all round the island. Or if only he were made of wood instead of bronze, he might quite well be one of Daedalus's ingenious mechanisms—you say he plays truant from his pedestal just like them—and not the work of Demetrius at all.' 'Take care, Tychiades; you will be sorry for this some day. I have not forgotten what happened to the thief who stole his monthly pennies.' 'The sacrilegious villain!' cried Ion; 'I hope he got a lesson. How was he punished? Do tell me:

never mind Tychiades; he can be as incredulous as he likes.' 'At the feet of the statue a number of pence were laid, and other coins were attached to his thigh by means of wax; some of these were silver, and there were also silver plates, all being the thank-offerings of those whom he had cured of fever. Now we had a scamp of a Libyan groom, who took it into his head to filch all this coin under cover of night. He waited till the statue had descended from his pedestal, and then put his plan into effect. Pelichus detected the robbery as soon as he got back; and this is how he found the offender out and punished

---

[77] Harmodius and Aristogiton.

him. He caused the wretch to wander about in the court all night long, unable to find his way out, just as if he had been in a maze; till at daybreak he was caught with the stolen property in his possession. His guilt was clear, and he received a sound flogging there and then; and before long he died a villain's death. It seems from his own confession that he was scourged every night; and each succeeding morning the weals were to be seen on his body.—*Now*, Tychiades, let me hear you laugh at Pelichus:

I am a dotard, am I not? a relic from the time of Minos?'

'My dear Eucrates,' said I, 'if bronze is bronze, and if that statue was cast by Demetrius of Alopece, who dealt not in Gods but in men, then I cannot anticipate any danger from a statue of Pelichus; even the menaces of the original would not have alarmed me particularly.'

Here Antigonus, the doctor, put in a word. 'I myself,' he informed his host, 'have a Hippocrates in bronze, some eighteen inches high. Now the moment my candle is out, he goes clattering about all over the house, slamming the door, turning all my boxes upside down, and mixing up all my drugs; especially when his annual sacrifice is overdue.' 'What are we coming to?' I cried; 'Hippocrates must have sacrifices, must he? he must be feasted with all pomp and circumstance, and punctually to the day, or his leechship is angry? Why, he ought to be only too pleased to be complimented with a cup of mead or a garland, like other dead men.'

'Now here,' Eucrates went on, 'is a thing that I saw happen five years ago, in the presence of witnesses. It was during the vintage. I had left the labourers busy in the vineyard at midday, and was walking off into the wood, occupied with my own thoughts. I had already got under the shade of the trees, when I heard dogs barking, and supposed that my boy Mnason was amusing himself in the chase as usual, and had penetrated into the copse with his friends. However, that was not it:

presently there was an earthquake; I heard a voice like a thunderclap, and saw a terrible woman approaching, not much less than three hundred feet high. She carried a torch in her left hand, and a sword in her right; the sword might be thirty feet long. Her lower extremities were those of a dragon; but the upper half was like Medusa—as to the eyes, I mean; they were quite awful in their expression. Instead of hair, she had clusters of snakes writhing about her neck, and curling over her shoulders. See here:

it makes my flesh creep, only to speak of it!' And he showed us all his arm, with the hair standing on end.

Ion and Dinomachus and Cleodemus and the rest of them drank down every word. The narrator led them by their venerable noses, and this least convincing of colossal bogies, this hundred-yarder, was the object of their mute adorations. And these (I was reflecting all the time)—these are the admired teachers from whom our youth are to learn wisdom! Two circumstances distinguish them from babies:

they have white hair, and they have beards:

but when it comes to swallowing a lie, they are babes and more than babes.

Dinomachus, for instance, wanted to know 'how big were the Goddess's dogs?' 'They were taller than Indian elephants,' he was assured, 'and as black, with coarse, matted coats. At the sight of her, I stood stock still, and turned the seal of my Arab's ring inwards; whereupon Hecate smote upon the ground with her dragon's foot, and caused a vast chasm to open, wide as the mouth of Hell. Into this she presently leaped, and was lost to sight. I began to pluck up courage, and looked over the edge; but first I took hold of a tree that grew near, for fear I should be giddy, and fall in. And then I saw the whole of Hades:

there was Pyriphlegethon, the Lake of Acheron, Cerberus, the Shades. I even recognized some of them:

I made out my father quite distinctly; he was still wearing the same clothes in which we buried him.' 'And what were the spirits doing?' asked Ion. 'Doing? Oh, they were just lying about on the asphodel, among their friends and kinsmen, all arranged according to their clans and tribes.' 'There now!' exclaimed Ion; 'after that I should like to hear the Epicureans say another word against the divine Plato and his account of the spiritual world. I suppose you did not happen to see Socrates or Plato among the Shades?' 'Yes, I did; I saw Socrates; not very plainly, though; I only went by the bald head and corpulent figure. Plato I did *not* make out; I will speak the plain truth; we are all friends here. I had just had a good look at everything, when the chasm began to close up; some of the servants who came to look for me (Pyrrhias here was among them) arrived while the gap was still visible.—Pyrrhias, is that the fact?' 'Indeed it is,' says Pyrrhias; 'what is more, I heard a dog barking in the hole, and if I am not mistaken I caught a glimmer of torchlight.' I could not help a smile; it was handsome in Pyrrhias, this of the bark and the torchlight.

'Your experience,' observed Cleodemus, 'is by no means without precedent. In fact I saw something of the same kind myself, not long ago. I had been ill, and Antigonus here was attending me. The fever had been on me for seven days, and was now aggravated by the excessive heat. All my attendants were outside, having closed the door and left me to myself; those were your orders, you know, Antigonus; I was to get some sleep if I could. Well, I woke up to find a handsome young man standing at my side, in a white cloak. He raised me up from the bed, and conducted me through a sort of chasm into Hades; I knew where I was at once, because I saw Tantalus and Tityus and Sisyphus. Not to go into details, I came to the Judgement-hall, and there were Aeacus and Charon and the Fates and the Furies. One person of a majestic appearance—Pluto, I suppose it was—sat reading out the names of those who were due to die, their term of life having lapsed. The young man took me and set me before him, but Pluto flew into a rage:

"Away with him," he said to my conductor; "his thread is not yet out; go and fetch Demylus the smith; *he* has had his spindleful and more." I ran off home, nothing loath. My fever had now disappeared, and I told everybody that Demylus was as good as dead. He lived close by, and was said to have some illness, and it was not long before we heard the voices of mourners in his house.'

'This need not surprise us,' remarked Antigonus; 'I know of a man who rose from the dead twenty days after he had been buried; I attended him both before his death and after his resurrection.' 'I should have thought,' said I, 'that the body must have putrefied in all that time, or if not that, that he must have collapsed for want of nourishment. Was your patient a second Epimenides?'

At this point in the conversation, Eucrates's sons came in from the gymnasium, one of them quite a young man, the other a boy of fifteen or so. After saluting the company, they took their seats on the couch at their father's side, and a chair was brought for me. The appearance of the boys seemed to remind Eucrates of something:

laying a hand upon each of them, he addressed me as follows. 'Tychiades, if what I am now about to tell you is anything but the truth, then may I never have joy of these lads. It is well known to every one how fond I was of my sainted wife, their mother; and I showed it in my treatment of her, not only in her lifetime, but even after her death; for I ordered all the jewels and clothes that she had valued to be burnt upon her pyre. Now on the seventh day after her death, I was sitting here on this very couch, as it might be now, trying to find comfort for my affliction in Plato's book about the soul. I was quietly reading this, when Demaenete herself appeared, and sat down at my side exactly as Eucratides is doing now.' Here he pointed to the younger boy, who had turned quite pale during this narrative, and now shuddered in childish terror. 'The moment I saw her,' he continued, 'I threw my arms about her neck and wept aloud. She bade me cease; and complained that though I had consulted her wishes in everything else, I had neglected to burn one of her golden sandals, which she said had fallen under a chest. We had been unable to find this sandal, and had only burnt the fellow to it. While we were still conversing, a hateful little Maltese terrier that lay under the couch started barking, and my wife immediately vanished. The sandal, however, was found beneath the chest, and was eventually burnt.—Do you still doubt, Tychiades, in the face of one convincing piece of evidence after another?' 'God forbid!' I cried; 'the doubter who should presume, thus to brazen it out in the face of Truth would deserve to have a golden sandal applied to him after the nursery fashion.'

Arignotus the Pythagorean now came in—the 'divine' Arignotus, as he is called; the philosopher of the long hair and the solemn countenance, you know, of whose wisdom we hear so much. I breathed again when I saw him. 'Ah!' thought I, 'the very man we want! here is the axe to hew their lies asunder. The sage will soon pull them up when he hears their cock-and-bull stories. Fortune has brought a *deus ex machina* upon the scene.' He sat down (Cleodemus rising to make room for him) and inquired after Eucrates's health.

539

Eucrates replied that he was better. 'And what,' Arignotus next asked, 'is the subject of your learned conversation? I overheard your voices as I came in, and doubt not that your time will prove to have been profitably employed.' Eucrates pointed to me. 'We were only trying,' he said, 'to convince this man of adamant that there are such things as supernatural beings and ghosts, and that the spirits of the dead walk the earth and manifest themselves to whomsoever they will.' Moved by the august presence of Arignotus, I blushed, and hung my head. 'Ah, but, Eucrates,' said he, 'perhaps all that Tychiades means is, that a spirit only walks if its owner met with a violent end, if he was strangled, for instance, or beheaded or crucified, and not if he died a natural death. If that is what he means, there is great justice in his contention.' 'No, no,' says Dinomachus, 'he maintains that there is absolutely no such thing as an apparition.' 'What is this I hear?' asked Arignotus, scowling upon me; 'you deny the existence of the supernatural, when there is scarcely a man who has not seen some evidence of it?' 'Therein lies my exculpation,' I replied:

'I do not believe in the supernatural, because, unlike the rest of mankind, I do not see it:

if I saw, I should doubtless believe, just as you all do.' 'Well,' said he, 'next time you are in Corinth, ask for the house of Eubatides, near the Craneum; and when you have found it, go up to Tibius the door-keeper, and tell him you would like to see the spot on which Arignotus the Pythagorean unearthed the demon, whose expulsion rendered the house habitable again.' 'What was that about, Arignotus?' asked Eucrates.

'The house,' replied the other, 'was haunted, and had been uninhabited for years:

each intending occupant had been at once driven out of it in abject terror by a most grim and formidable apparition. Finally it had fallen into a ruinous state, the roof was giving way, and in short no one would have thought of entering it. Well, when I heard about this, I got my books together (I have a considerable number of Egyptian works on these subjects) and went off to the house about bed-time, undeterred by the remonstrances of my host, who considered that I was walking into the jaws of Death, and would almost have detained me by force when he learnt my destination. I took a lamp and entered alone, and putting down my light in the principal room, I sat on the floor quietly reading. The spirit now made his appearance, thinking that he had to do with an ordinary person, and that he would frighten me as he had frightened so many others. He was pitch-black, with a tangled mass of hair. He drew near, and assailed me from all quarters, trying every means to get the better of me, and changing in a moment from dog to bull, from bull to lion. Armed with my most appalling adjuration, uttered in the Egyptian tongue, I drove him spell-bound into the corner of a dark room, marked the spot at which he disappeared, and passed the rest of the night in peace. In the morning, to the amazement of all beholders (for every one had given me up for lost, and expected to find me lying dead like former occupants), I issued from

540

the house, and carried to Eubatides the welcome news that it was now cleared of its grim visitant, and fit to serve as a human habitation. He and a number of others, whom curiosity had prompted to join us, followed me to the spot at which I had seen the demon vanish. I instructed them to take spades and pick-axes and dig:

they did so; and at about a fathom's depth we discovered a mouldering corpse, of which nothing but the bones remained entire. We took the skeleton up, and placed it in a grave; and from that day to this the house has never been troubled with apparitions.'

After such a story as this-coming as it did from Arignotus, who was generally looked up to as a man of inspired wisdom—my incredulous attitude towards the supernatural was loudly condemned on all hands. However, I was not frightened by his long hair, nor by his reputation. 'Dear, dear!' I exclaimed, 'so Arignotus, the sole mainstay of Truth, is as bad as the rest of them, as full of windy imaginings! Our treasure proves to be but ashes.' 'Now look here, Tychiades,' said Arignotus, 'you will not believe me, nor Dinomachus, nor Cleodemus here, nor yet Eucrates:

we shall be glad to know who is your great authority on the other side, who is to outweigh us all?' 'No less a person,' I replied, 'than the sage of Abdera, the wondrous Democritus himself. *His* disbelief in apparitions is sufficiently clear. When he had shut himself up in that tomb outside the city gates, there to spend his days and nights in literary labours, certain young fellows, who had a mind to play their pranks on the philosopher and give him a fright, got themselves up in black palls and skull-masks, formed a ring round him, and treated him to a brisk dance. Was Democritus alarmed at the ghosts? Not he:

"Come, enough of that nonsense," was all he had to say to them; and that without so much as looking up, or taking pen from paper. Evidently *he* had quite made up his mind about disembodied spirits.' 'Which simply proves,' retorted Eucrates, 'that Democritus was no wiser than yourself. Now I am going to tell you of another thing that happened to me personally; I did not get the story second-hand. Even you, Tychiades, will scarcely hold out against so convincing a narrative.

'When I was a young man, I passed some time in Egypt, my father having sent me to that country for my education. I took it into my head to sail up the Nile to Coptus, and thence pay a visit to the statue of Memnon, and hear the curious sound that proceeds from it at sunrise. In this respect, I was more fortunate than most people, who hear nothing but an indistinct voice:

Memnon actually opened his lips, and delivered me an oracle in seven hexameters; it is foreign to my present purpose, or I would quote you the very lines. Well now, one of my fellow passengers on the way up was a scribe of Memphis, an extraordinarily able man, versed in all the lore of the Egyptians. He was said to have passed twenty-three years of his life underground in the tombs, studying occult sciences under the instruction of Isis herself.' 'You must

541

mean the divine Pancrates, my teacher,' exclaimed Arignotus; 'tall, clean-shaven, snub-nosed, protruding lips, rather thin in the legs; dresses entirely in linen, has a thoughtful expression, and speaks Greek with a slight accent?' 'Yes, it was Pancrates himself. I knew nothing about him at first, but whenever we anchored I used to see him doing the most marvellous things,—for instance, he would actually ride on the crocodiles' backs, and swim about among the brutes, and they would fawn upon him and wag their tails; and then I realized that he was no common man. I made some advances, and by imperceptible degrees came to be on quite a friendly footing with him, and was admitted to a share in his mysterious arts. The end of it was, that he prevailed on me to leave all my servants behind at Memphis, and accompany him alone; assuring me that we should not want for attendance. This plan we accordingly followed from that time onwards. Whenever we came to an inn, he used to take up the bar of the door, or a broom, or perhaps a pestle, dress it up in clothes, and utter a certain incantation; whereupon the thing would begin to walk about, so that every one took it for a man. It would go off and draw water, buy and cook provisions, and make itself generally useful. When we had no further occasion for its services, there was another incantation, after which the broom was a broom once more, or the pestle a pestle. I could never get him to teach me this incantation, though it was not for want of trying; open as he was about everything else, he guarded this one secret jealously. At last one day I hid in a dark corner, and overheard the magic syllables; they were three in number. The Egyptian gave the pestle its instructions, and then went off to the market. Well, next day he was again busy in the market:

so I took the pestle, dressed it, pronounced the three syllables exactly as he had done, and ordered it to become a water-carrier. It brought me the pitcher full; and then I said:

Stop:

be water-carrier no longer, but pestle as heretofore. But the thing would take no notice of me:

it went on drawing water the whole time, until at last the house was full of it. This was awkward:

if Pancrates came back, he would be angry, I thought (and so indeed it turned out). I took an axe, and cut the pestle in two. The result was that both halves took pitchers and fetched water; I had two water-carriers instead of one. This was still going on, when Pancrates appeared. He saw how things stood, and turned the water-carriers back into wood; and then he withdrew himself from me, and went away, whither I knew not.'

'And you can actually make a man out of a pestle to this day?' asked Dinomachus. 'Yes, I can do *that,* but that is only half the process:

I cannot turn it back again into its original form; if once it became a water-carrier, its activity would swamp the house.'

'Oh, stop!' I cried:

'if the thought that you are old men is not enough to deter you from talking this trash, at least remember who is present:

if you do not want to fill these boys' heads with ghosts and hobgoblins, postpone your grotesque horrors for a more suitable occasion. Have some mercy on the lads:

do not accustom them to listen to a tangle of superstitious stuff that will cling to them for the rest of their lives, and make them start at their own shadows.'

'Ah, talking of superstition, now,' says Eucrates, 'that reminds me:

what do you make of oracles, for instance, and omens? of inspired utterances, of voices from the shrine, of the priestess's prophetic lines? You will deny all that too, of course? If I were to tell you of a certain magic ring in my possession, the seal of which is a portrait of the Pythian Apollo, and actually *speaks* to me, I suppose you would decline to believe it, you would think I was bragging? But I must tell you all of what I heard in the temple of Amphilochus at Mallus, when that hero appeared to me in person and gave me counsel, and of what I saw with my own eyes on that occasion; and again of all I saw at Pergamum and heard at Patara. It was on my way home from Egypt that the oracle of Mallus was mentioned to me as a particularly intelligible and veracious one:

I was told that any question, duly written down on a tablet and handed to the priest, would receive a plain, definite answer. I thought it would be a good thing to take the oracle on my way home, and consult the God as to my future.'

I saw what was coming:

this was but the prologue to a whole tragedy of the oracular. It was clear enough that I was not wanted, and as I did not feel called upon to pose as the sole champion of the cause of Truth among so many, I took my leave there and then, while Eucrates was still upon the high seas between Egypt and Mallus. 'I must go and find Leontichus,' I explained; 'I have to see him about something. Meanwhile, you gentlemen, to whom human affairs are not sufficient occupation, may solicit the insertion of divine fingers into your mythologic pie.' And with that I went out. Relieved of my presence, I doubt not that they fell to with a will on their banquet of mendacity.

That is what I got by going to Eucrates's; and, upon my word, Philocles, my overloaded stomach needs an emetic as much as if I had been drinking new wine. I would pay something for the drug that should work oblivion in me:

I fear the effects of haunting reminiscence; monsters, demons, Hecates, seem to pass before my eyes.

Phi. I am not much better off. They tell us it is not only the mad dog that inflicts hydrophobia:

his human victim's bite is as deadly as his own, and communicates the evil as surely. You, it seems, have been bitten with many bites by the liar

543

Eucrates, and have passed it on to me; no otherwise can I explain the demoniacal poison that runs in my veins.

Tyc. What matter, friend? Truth and good sense:

these are the drugs for our ailment; let us employ them, and that empty thing, a lie, need have no terrors for us. F.

DIONYSUS, AN INTRODUCTORY LECTURE

When Dionysus invaded India—for I may tell you a Bacchic legend, may I not?—it is recorded that the natives so underrated him that his approach only amused them at first; or rather, his rashness filled them with compassion; he would so soon be trampled to death by their elephants, if he took the field against them. Their scouts had doubtless given them amazing details about his army:

the rank and file were frantic mad women crowned with ivy, clad in fawn- skins, with little pikes that had no steel about them, but were ivy-wreathed like themselves, and toy bucklers that tinkled at a touch; they took the tambourines for shields, you see; and then there were a few bumpkins among them, stark naked, who danced wildly, and had tails, and horns like a new-born kid's.

Their general, who rode on a car drawn by panthers, was quite beardless, with not even a vestige of fluff on his face, had horns, was crowned with grape-clusters, his hair tied with a fillet, his cloak purple, and his shoes of gold. Of his lieutenants, one was short, thick-set, paunchy, and flat-nosed, with great upright ears; he trembled perpetually, leant upon a narthex-wand, rode mostly upon an ass, wore saffron to his superior's purple, and was a very suitable general of division for him. The other was a half-human hybrid, with hairy legs, horns, and flowing beard, passionate and quick-tempered; with a reed-pipe in his left hand, and waving a crooked staff in his right, he skipped round and round the host, a terror to the women, who let their dishevelled tresses fly abroad as he came, with cries of Evoe—the name of their lord, guessed the scouts. Their flocks had suffered, they added, the young had been seized alive and torn piecemeal by the women; they ate raw flesh, it seemed.

All this was food for laughter, as well it might be, to the Indians and their king:

Take the field? array their hosts against him? no, indeed; at worst they might match their women with his, if he still came on; for themselves such a victory would be a disgrace; a set of mad women, a general in a snood, a little old drunkard, a half- soldier, and a few naked dancers; why should they murder such a droll crew? However, when they heard how the God was wasting their land with fire, giving cities and citizens to the flames, burning their forests, and making one great conflagration of all India—for fire is the Bacchic instrument, Dionysus's very birthright—, then they lost no more time, but armed; they girthed, bitted, and castled their elephants, and out they marched; not that they had ceased to scorn; but now they were angry too, and in a hurry to crush this beardless warrior with all his host.

When the two armies came to sight of one another, the Indians drew up their elephants in front and advanced their phalanx; on the other side, Dionysus held the centre, Silenus led his right, and Pan his left wing; his colonels and captains were the satyrs, and the word for the day *evoe.*

Straightway tambourines clattered, cymbals sounded to battle, a satyr blew the war-note on his horn, Silenus's ass sent forth a martial bray, and the maenads leapt shrill-voiced on the foe, girt with serpents and baring now the steel of their thyrsus-heads. In a moment Indians and elephants turned and fled disordered, before even a missile could carry across; and the end was that they were smitten and led captive by the objects of their laughter; they had learnt the lesson that it is not safe to take the first report, and scorn an enemy of whom nothing is known.

But you wonder what all this is about—suspect me, possibly, of being only too fresh from the company of Bacchus. Perhaps the explanation, involving a comparison of myself with Gods, will only more convince you of my exalted or my drunken mood; it is, that ordinary people are affected by literary novelties (my own productions, for instance) much as the Indians were by that experience. They have an idea that literary satyr-dances, absurdities, pure farce, are to be expected from me, and, however they reach their conception of me, they incline to one of two attitudes. Some of them avoid my readings altogether, seeing no reason for climbing down from their elephants and paying attention to revelling women and skipping satyrs; others come with their preconceived idea, and when they find that the thyrsus-head has a steel point under it, they are too much startled by the surprise to venture approval. I confidently promise them, however, that if they will attend the rite repeatedly now as in days of yore, if my old boon-companions will call to mind the revels that once we shared, not be too shy of satyrs and Silenuses, and drink deep of the bowl I bring, the frenzy shall take hold upon them too, till their *evoes* vie with mine.

Well, they are free to listen or not; let them take their choice. Meanwhile, we are still in India, and I should like to give you another fact from that country, again a link between Dionysus and our business. In the territory of the Machlaeans, who occupy the left bank of the Indus right down to the sea, there is a grove, of no great size, but enclosed both round about and overhead, light being almost excluded by the profusion of ivy and vine. In it are three springs of fair pellucid water, called, one of them the satyrs' well, the second Pan's, and the other that of Silenus. The Indians enter this grove once a year at the festival of Dionysus, and taste the wells, not promiscuously, however, but according to age; the satyrs' well is for the young, Pan's for the middle-aged, and Silenus's for those at my time of life.

What effect their draught produces on the children, what doings the men are spurred to, Pan-ridden, must not detain us; but the behaviour of the old under their water intoxication has its interest. As soon as one of them has drunk, and Silenus has possessed him, he falls dumb for a space like one in vinous lethargy; then on a sudden his voice is strong, his articulation clear, his intonation musical; from dead silence issues a stream of talk; the gag would scarce restrain him from incessant chatter; tale upon tale he reels you off. Yet all is sense and order withal; his words are as many, and find their place as well, as those 'winter snowflakes' of Homer's orator. You may talk of his swan- song if you will, mindful of his years; but you must add that his chirping is quick and lively as the grasshopper's, till evening comes; then the fit is past; he falls silent, and is his common self again. But the greatest wonder I have yet to tell:

if he leave unfinished the tale he was upon, and the setting sun cut him short, then at his next year's draught he will resume it where the inspiration of this year deserted him.

Gentlemen, I have been pointing Momus-like at my own foibles; I need not trouble you with the application; you can make out the resemblance for yourselves. But if you find me babbling, you know now what has loosed my tongue; and if there is shrewdness in any of my words, then to Silenus be the thanks.

HERACLES, AN INTRODUCTORY LECTURE

Our Heracles is known among the Gauls under the local name of Ogmius; and the appearance he presents in their pictures is truly grotesque. They make him out as old as old can be:

the few hairs he has left (he is quite bald in front) are dead white, and his skin is wrinkled and tanned as black as any old salt's. You would take him for some infernal deity, for Charon or Iapetus,—any one rather than Heracles. Such as he is, however, he has all the proper attributes of that God:

the lion's-skin hangs over his shoulders, his right hand grasps the club, his left the strung bow, and a quiver is slung at his side; nothing is wanting to the Heraclean equipment.

Now I thought at first that this was just a cut at the Greek Gods; that in taking these liberties with the personal appearance of Heracles, the Gauls were merely exacting pictorial vengeance for his invasion of their territory; for in his search after the herds of Geryon he had overrun and plundered most of the peoples of the West. However, I have yet to mention the most remarkable feature in the portrait. This ancient Heracles drags after him a vast crowd of men, all of whom are fastened by the ears with thin chains composed of gold and amber, and looking more like beautiful necklaces than anything else. From this flimsy bondage they make no attempt to escape, though escape must be easy. There is not the slightest show of resistance:

instead of planting their heels in the ground and dragging back, they follow with joyful alacrity, singing their captor's praises the while; and from the eagerness with which they hurry after him to prevent the chains from tightening, one would say that release is the last thing they desire. Nor will I conceal from you what struck me as the most curious circumstance of all. Heracles's right hand is occupied with the club, and his left with the bow:

how is he to hold the ends of the chains? The painter solves the difficulty by boring a hole in the tip of the God's tongue, and making that the means of attachment; his head is turned round, and he regards his followers with a smiling countenance.

For a long time I stood staring at this in amazement:

I knew not what to make of it, and was beginning to feel somewhat nettled, when I was addressed in admirable Greek by a Gaul who stood at my side, and who besides possessing a scholarly acquaintance with the Gallic mythology, proved to be not unfamiliar with our own. 'Sir,' he said, 'I see this picture puzzles you:

let me solve the riddle. We Gauls connect eloquence not with Hermes, as you do, but with the mightier Heracles. Nor need it surprise you to see him represented as an old man. It is the prerogative of eloquence, that it reaches perfection in old age; at least if we may believe your poets, who tell us that

Youth is the sport of every random gust,

whereas old age

Hath that to say that passes youthful wit.

Thus we find that from Nestor's lips honey is distilled; and that the words of the Trojan counsellors are compared to the lily, which, if I have not forgotten my Greek, is the name of a flower. Hence, if you will consider the relation that exists between tongue and ear, you will find nothing more natural than the way in which our Heracles, who is Eloquence personified, draws men along with their ears tied to his tongue. Nor is any slight intended by the hole bored through that member:

I recollect a passage in one of your comic poets in which we are told that

There is a hole in every glib tongue's tip.

Indeed, we refer the achievements of the original Heracles, from first to last, to his wisdom and persuasive eloquence. His shafts, as I take it, are no other than his words; swift, keen-pointed, true-aimed to do deadly execution on the soul.' And in conclusion he reminded me of our own phrase, 'winged words.'

Now while I was debating within myself the advisability of appearing before you, and of submitting myself for a second time to the verdict of this enormous jury, old as I am, and long unused to lecturing, the thought of this Heracles portrait came to my relief. I had been afraid that some of you would consider it a piece of youthful audacity inexcusable in one of my years. 'Thy force,' some Homeric youth might remark with crushing effect, 'is spent; dull age hath borne thee down'; and he might add, in playful allusion to my gouty toes,

Slow are thy steeds, and weakness waits upon thee.

But the thought of having that venerable hero to keep me in countenance emboldens me to risk everything:

I am no older than he. Good-bye, then, to bodily perfections, to strength and speed and beauty; Love, when he sees my grey beard, is welcome to fly past, as the poet of Teos[78] has it, with rush of gilded wings; 'tis all one to Hippoclides. Old age is Wisdom's youth, the day of her glorious flower:

let her draw whom she can by the ears; let her shoot her bolts freely; no fear now lest the supply run short. There is the old man's comfort, on the strength of which he ventures to drag down his boat, which has long lain high and dry, provision her as best he may, and once more put out to sea.

Never did I stand in more need of a generous breeze, to fill my sails and speed me on my way:

may the Gods dispose you to contribute thereto; so shall I not be found wanting, and of me, as of Odysseus, it shall be said

How stout a thigh lurked 'neath the old man's rags!

---

[78] Anacreon.

SWANS AND AMBER

You have no doubt a proper faith in the amber legend—how it is the tears shed by poplars on the Eridanus for Phaethon, the said poplars being his sisters, who were changed to trees in the course of their mourning, and continue to distil their lacrimal amber. That was what the poets taught me, and I looked forward, if ever fortune should bring me to the Eridanus, to standing under a poplar, catching a few tears in a fold of my dress, and having a supply of the commodity.

Sure enough, I found myself there not long ago upon another errand, and had occasion to go up the Eridanus; but, though I was all eyes, I saw neither poplars nor amber, and the natives had not so much as heard of Phaethon. I started my inquiries by asking when we should come to the amber poplars; the boatmen only laughed, and requested explanations. I told them the story:

Phaethon was a son of Helius, and when he grew up came to his father and asked if he might drive his car, and be the day-maker just that once. His father consented, but he was thrown out and killed, and his mourning sisters 'in this land of yours,' I said, 'where he fell on the Eridanus, turned into poplars, and still weep amber for him.'

'What liar took you in like that, sir?' they said; 'we never saw a coachman spilt; and where are the poplars? why, do you suppose, if it was true, we would row or tow up stream for sixpences? we should only have to collect poplar-tears to be rich men.' This truth impressed me a good deal; I said no more, and was painfully conscious of my childishness in trusting the poets; they deal in such extravagant fictions, they come to scorn sober fact. Here was one hope gone; I had set my heart upon it, and was as much chagrined as if I had dropped the amber out of my hands; I had had all my plans ready for the various uses to which it was to be put.

However, there was one thing I still thought I really should find there, and that was flocks of swans singing on the banks. We were still on the way up, and I applied to the boatmen again:

'About what time do the swans take post for their famous musical entertainment?—Apollo's fellow craftsmen, you know, who were changed here from men to birds, and still sing in memory of their ancient art.'

But they only jeered at me:

'Are you going to lie all day about our country and our river, pray? We are always on the water; we have worked all our lives on the Eridanus; well, we do see a swan now and again in the marshes; and a harsh feeble croak their note is; crows or jackdaws are sirens to them; as for sweet singing such as you tell of, not a ghost of it. We cannot make out where you folk get all these tales about us.'

Such disappointments are the natural consequence of trusting picturesque reporters. Well now, I am afraid the newcomers among you, who hear me for the first time, may have been expecting swans and amber from me, and may presently depart laughing at the people who encouraged them to look for such literary treasures. But I solemnly aver that no one has ever heard or ever shall hear me making any such claims. Other persons in plenty you may find who are Eridanuses, rich not in amber, but in very gold, and more melodious far than the poets' swans. But you see how plain and unromantic is my material; song is not in me. Any one who expects great things from me will be like a man looking at an object in water. Its image is magnified by an optical effect; he takes the reality to correspond to the appearance, and when he fishes it up is disgusted to find it so small. So I pour out the water, exhibit my wares, and warn you not to hope for a large haul; if you do, you have only yourselves to blame.

THE FLY, AN APPRECIATION

The fly is not the smallest of winged things, on a level with gnats, midges, and still tinier creatures; it is as much larger than they as smaller than the bee. It has not feathers of the usual sort, is not fledged all over like some, nor provided with quill- feathers like other birds, but resembles locusts, grasshoppers, and bees in being gauze-winged, this sort of wing being as much more delicate than the ordinary as Indian fabrics are lighter and softer than Greek. Moreover, close inspection of them when spread out and moving in the sun will show them to be peacock-hued.

Its flight is accompanied neither by the incessant wing-beat of the bat, the jump of the locust, nor the buzz of the wasp, but carries it easily in any direction. It has the further merit of a music neither sullen as with the gnat kind, deep as with the bee, nor grim and threatening as with the wasp; it is as much more tuneful than they as the flute is sweeter than trumpet or cymbals.

As for the rest of its person, the head is very slenderly attached by the neck, easily turned, and not all of one piece with the body as in the locust; the eyes are projecting and horny; the chest strong, with the legs springing freely from it instead of lying close like a wasp's. The belly also is well fortified, and looks like a breastplate, with its broad bands and scales. Its weapons are not in the tail as with wasp and bee, but in its mouth and proboscis; with the latter, in which it is like the elephant, it forages, takes hold of things, and by means of a sucker at its tip attaches itself firmly to them. This proboscis is also supplied with a projecting tooth, with which the fly makes a puncture, and so drinks blood. It does drink milk, but also likes blood, which it gets without hurting its prey much. Of its six legs, four only are for walking, and the front pair serves for hands; you may see it standing on four legs and holding up a morsel in these hands, which it consumes in very human fashion.

It does not come into being in its ultimate shape, but starts as a worm in the dead body of man or animal; then it gradually develops legs, puts forth wings and becomes a flying instead of a creeping thing, which generates in turn and produces a little worm, one day to be a fly. Living with man, sharing his food and his table, it tastes everything except his oil, to drink which is death to it. In any case it soon perishes, having but a short span of life allotted to it, but while it lives it loves the light, and is active only under its influence; at night it rests, neither flying nor buzzing, but retiring and keeping quiet.

I am able to record its considerable wisdom, shown in evading the plots of its enemy the spider. It is always on the look-out for his ambushes, and in the most circumspect way dodges about, that it may not be caught, netted, and entangled in his meshes. Its valour and spirit require no mention of mine; Homer, mightiest-voiced of poets, seeking a compliment for the greatest of heroes, likens his spirit not to a lion's, a panther's, a boar's, but to the courage of the fly, to its unshrinking and persistent assault; mark, it is not mere audacity, but courage, that he attributes to it. Though you drive it off, he says, it will not leave you; it will have its bite. He is so earnest an admirer of the fly that he alludes to it not once nor twice, but constantly; a mention of it is felt to be a poetic ornament. Now it is its multitudinous descent upon the milk that he celebrates; now he is in want of an illustration for Athene as she wards off a spear from the vitals of Menelaus; so he makes her a mother caring for her sleeping child, and in comes the fly again. Moreover he gives them that pretty epithet, 'thick- clust'ring'; and 'nations' is his dignified word for a swarm of them.

The fly's force is shown by the fact that its bite pierces not merely the human skin, but that of cattle and horses; it annoys the elephant by getting into the folds of its hide, and letting it know the efficiency of even a tiny trunk. There is much ease and freedom about their love affairs, which are not disposed of so expeditiously as by the domestic fowl; the act of union is prolonged, and is found quite compatible with flight. A fly will live and breathe for some time after its head is cut off.

The most remarkable point about its natural history is that which I am now to mention. It is the one fact that Plato seems to me to have overlooked in his discourse of the soul and its immortality. If a little ashes be sprinkled on a dead fly, it gets up, experiences a second birth, and starts life afresh, which is recognized as a convincing proof that its soul is immortal, inasmuch as after it has departed it returns, recognizes and reanimates the body, and enables it to fly; so is confirmed the tale about Hermotimus of Clazomenae—how his soul frequently left him and went off on its own account, and afterwards returning occupied the body again and restored the man to life.

It toils not, but lives at its ease, profiting by the labours of others, and finding everywhere a table spread for it. For it the goats are milked, for its behoof and man's the honey is stored, to its palate the *chef* adapts his sauces; it tastes before the king himself, walks upon his table, shares his meal, and has the use of all that is his.

Nest, home, local habitation, it has none; like the Scythians, it elects to lead a wandering life, and where night finds it, there is its hearth and its chamber. But as I said, it works no deeds of darkness; 'live openly' is its motto; its principle is to do no villany that, done in the face of day, would dishonour it.

Legend tells how Myia (the fly's ancient name) was once a maiden, exceeding fair, but over-given to talk and chatter and song, Selene's rival for the love of Endymion. When the young man slept, she was for ever waking him with her gossip and tunes and merriment, till he lost patience, and Selene in wrath turned her to what she now is. And therefore it is that she still, in memory of Endymion, grudges all sleepers their rest, and most of all the young and tender. Her very bite and blood-thirst tell not of savagery, but of love and human kindness; she is but enjoying mankind as she may, and sipping beauty.

In ancient times there was a woman of her name, a poetess wise and beautiful, and another a famous Attic courtesan, of whom the comic poet wrote:

As deep as to his heart fair Myia bit him.

The comic Muse, we see, disdained not the name, nor refused it the hospitality of the boards; and parents took no shame to give it to their daughters. Tragedy goes further and speaks of the fly in high terms of praise, as witness the following:

Foul shame the little fly, with might courageous,
Should leap upon men's limbs, athirst for blood,
But men-at-arms shrink from the foeman's steel!

I might add many details about Pythagoras's daughter Myia, were not her story too well known.

There are also flies of very large size, called generally soldier- flies, or dog-flies; these have a hoarse buzz, a very rapid flight, and quite long lives; they last the winter through without food, mostly in sheltered nooks below the roof; the most remarkable fact about these is that they are hermaphrodites.

But I must break off; not that my subject is exhausted; only that to exhaust such a subject is too like breaking a butterfly on the wheel.

REMARKS ADDRESSED TO AN ILLITERATE BOOK-FANCIER

Let me tell you, that you are choosing the worst way to attain your object. You think that by buying up all the best books you can lay your hands on, you will pass for a man of literary tastes:

not a bit of it; you are merely exposing thereby your own ignorance of literature. Why, you cannot even buy the right things:

any casual recommendation is enough to guide your choice; you are as clay in the hands of the unscrupulous amateur, and as good as cash down to any dealer. How are you to know the difference between genuine old books that are worth money, and trash whose only merit is that it is falling to pieces? You are reduced to taking the worms and moths into your confidence; their activity is your sole clue to the value of a book; as to the accuracy and fidelity of the copyist, that is quite beyond you.

And supposing even that you had managed to pick out such veritable treasures as the exquisite editions of Callinus, or those of the far-famed Atticus, most conscientious of publishers,—what does it profit you? Their beauty means nothing to you, my poor friend; you will get precisely as much enjoyment out of them as a blind lover would derive from the possession of a handsome mistress. Your eyes, to be sure, are open; you do see your books, goodness knows, see them till you must be sick of the sight; you even read a bit here and there, in a scrambling fashion, your lips still busy with one sentence while your eyes are on the next. But what is the use of that? You cannot tell good from bad:

you miss the writer's general drift, you miss his subtle arrangements of words:

the chaste elegance of a pure style, the false ring of the counterfeit,—'tis all one to you.

Are we to understand that you possess literary discernment without the assistance of any study? And how should that be? perhaps, like Hesiod, you received a laurel-branch from the Muses? As to that, I doubt whether you have so much as heard of Helicon, the reputed haunt of those Goddesses; your youthful pursuits were not those of a Hesiod; take not the Muses' names in vain. They might not have any scruples about appearing to a hardy, hairy, sunburnt shepherd:

but as for coming near such a one as you (you will excuse my particularizing further just now, when I appeal to you in the name of the Goddess of Lebanon?) they would scorn the thought; instead of laurel, you would have tamarisk and mallow-leaves about your back; the waters of Olmeum and Hippocrene are for thirsty sheep and stainless shepherds, they must not be polluted by unclean lips. I grant you a very creditable stock of effrontery:

but you will scarcely have the assurance to call yourself an educated man; you will scarcely pretend that your acquaintance with literature is more than skin-deep, or give us the names of your teacher and your fellow students?

No; you think you are going to work off all arrears by the simple expedient of buying a number of books. But there again:

you may get together the works of Demosthenes, and his eight beautiful copies of Thucydides, all in the orator's own handwriting, and all the manuscripts that Sulla sent away from Athens to Italy,—and you will be no nearer to culture at the end of it, though you should sleep with them under your pillow, or paste them together and wear them as a garment; an ape is still an ape, says the proverb, though his trappings be of gold. So it is with you:

you have always a book in your hand, you are always reading; but what it is all about, you have not an idea; you do but prick up asinine ears at the lyre's sound. Books would be precious things indeed, if the mere possession of them guaranteed culture to their owner. You rich men would have it all your own way then; we paupers could not stand against you, if learning were a marketable commodity; and as for the dealers, no one would presume to contest the point of culture with men who have whole shopfuls of books at their disposal. However, you will find on examination that these privileged persons are scarcely less ignorant than yourself. They have just your vile accent, and are as deficient in intelligence as one would expect men to be who have never learnt to distinguish good from bad. Now you see, *you* have merely bought a few odd volumes from them:

they are at the fountain-head, and are handling books day and night. Judge from this how much good your purchases are likely to do you; unless you think that your very book-cases acquire a tincture of learning, from the bare fact of their housing so many ancient manuscripts.

Oblige me by answering some questions; or rather, as circumstances will not admit of your answering, just nod or shake your head. If the flute of Timotheus, or that of Ismenias, which its owner sold in Corinth for a couple of thousand pounds, were to fall into the hands of a person who did not know how to play the instrument, would that make him a flute-player? would his acquisition leave him any wiser than it found him? You very properly shake your head. A man might possess the instrument of a Marsyas or an Olympus, and still he would not be able to play it if he had never learnt. Take another case:

a man gets hold of Heracles's bow and arrows:

but he is no Philoctetes; he has neither that marksman's strength nor his eye. What do you say? will he acquit himself creditably? Again you shake your head. The same will be the case with the ignorant pilot who is entrusted with a ship, or with the unpractised rider on horseback. Nothing is wanting to the beauty and efficiency of the vessel, and the horse may be a Median or a Thessalian or a Koppa[79]:

yet I take it that the incompetence of their respective owners will be made clear; am I right? And now let me ask your assent to one more proposition:

if an illiterate person like yourself goes in for buying books, he is thereby laying himself open to ridicule. You hesitate? Yet surely nothing could be clearer:

who could observe such a man at work, and abstain from the inevitable allusion to pearls and swine?

There was a wealthy man in Asia, not many years ago, who was so unfortunate as to lose both his feet; I think he had been travelling through snow-drifts, and had got them frost-bitten. Well, of course, it was a very hard case; and in ordering a pair of wooden feet, by means of which he contrived to get along with the assistance of servants, he was no doubt only making the best of a bad job. But the absurd thing was, that he would always make a point of having the smartest and newest of shoes to set off his stumps—feet, I mean. Now are you any wiser than he, when for the adornment of that hobbling, wooden understanding of yours you go to the expense of such golden shoes as would tax the agility of a sound-limbed intellect?

Among your other purchases are several copies of Homer. Get some one to turn up the second book of the Iliad, and read to you. There is only one part you need trouble about; the rest does not apply to your case. I refer to the harangue of a certain ludicrous, maimed, distorted creature called Thersites. Now imagine this Thersites, such as he is there depicted, to have clothed himself in the armour of Achilles. What will be the result? Will he be converted there and then into a stalwart, comely warrior, clearing the river at a bound, and staining its waters with Phrygian blood? Will he prove a slayer of Asteropaeuses and Lycaons, and finally of Hectors, he who cannot so much as bear Achilles's spear upon his shoulders? Of course not. He will simply be ridiculous:

the weight of the shield will cause him to stagger, and will presently bring him on to his nose; beneath the helmet, as often as he looks up, will be seen that squint; the Achillean greaves will be a sad drag to his progress, and the rise and fall of the breast-plate will tell a tale of a humped-back; in short, neither the armourer nor the owner of the arms will have much to boast of. You are just like Thersites, if only you could see it. When you take in hand your fine volume, purple-cased, gilt-bossed, and begin reading with that accent of yours, maiming and murdering its contents, you make yourself ridiculous to all educated men:

---

[79] The brand of the obsolete letter Koppa is supposed to have denoted the Corinthian breed.

your own toadies commend you, but they generally get in a chuckle too, as they catch one another's eye.

Let me tell you a story of what happened once at Delphi. A native of Tarentum, Evangelus by name, a person of some note in his own city, conceived the ambition of winning a prize in the Pythian Games. Well, he saw at once that the athletic contests were quite out of the question; he had neither the strength nor the agility required. A musical victory, on the other hand, would be an easy matter; so at least he was persuaded by his vile parasites, who used to burst into a roar of applause the moment he touched the strings of his lyre. He arrived at Delphi in great style:

among other things, he had provided himself with gold-bespangled garments, and a beautiful golden laurel-wreath, with full-size emerald berries. As for his lyre, that was a most gorgeous and costly affair—solid gold throughout, and ornamented with all kinds of gems, and with figures of Apollo and Orpheus and the Muses, a wonder to all beholders. The eventful day at length arrived. There were three competitors, of whom Evangelus was to come second. Thespis the Theban performed first, and acquitted himself creditably; and then Evangelus appeared, resplendent in gold and emeralds, beryls and jacinths, the effect being heightened by his purple robe, which made a background to the gold; the house was all excitement and wondering anticipation. As singing and playing were an essential part of the competition, Evangelus now struck up with a few meaningless, disconnected notes, assaulting his lyre with such needless violence that he broke three strings at the start; and when he began to sing with his discordant pipe of a voice the whole audience was convulsed with laughter, and the stewards, enraged at his presumption, scourged him out of the theatre. Our golden Evangelus now presented a very queer spectacle, as the floggers drove him across the stage, weeping and bloody- limbed, and stooping to pick up the gems that had fallen from the lyre; for that instrument had come in for its share of the castigation. His place was presently taken by one Eumelus of Elis:

his lyre was an old one, with wooden pegs, and his clothes and crown would scarcely have fetched ten shillings between them. But for all that his well-managed voice and admirable execution caused him to be proclaimed the victor; and he was very merry over the unavailing splendours of his rival's gem-studded instrument. 'Evangelus,' he is reported to have said to him, 'yours is the golden laurel—you can afford it:

I am a pauper, and must put up with the Delphian wreath. No one will be sorry for your defeat; your arrogance and incompetence have made you an object of detestation; that is all your equipment has done for you.' Here again the application is obvious; Evangelus differing from you only in his sensibility to public ridicule.

I have also an old Lesbian story which is very much to the point. It is said that after Orpheus had been torn to pieces by the Thracian women, his head and his lyre were carried down the Hebrus into the sea; the head, it seems, floated down upon the lyre, singing Orpheus's dirge as it went, while the winds blew an accompaniment upon the strings. In this manner they reached the coast of Lesbos; the head was then taken up and buried on the site of the present temple of Bacchus, and the lyre was long preserved as a relic in the temple of Apollo. Later on, however, Neanthus, son of the tyrant Pittacus, hearing how the lyre had charmed beasts and trees and stones, and how after Orpheus's destruction it had played of its own accord, conceived a violent fancy for the instrument, and by means of a considerable bribe prevailed upon the priest to give him the genuine lyre, and replace it with one of similar appearance. Not thinking it advisable to display his acquisition in the city in broad daylight, he waited till night, and then, putting it under his cloak, walked off into the outskirts; and there this youth, who had not a note of music in him, produced his instrument and began jangling on the strings, expecting such divine strains to issue therefrom as would subdue all souls, and prove him the fortunate heir to Orpheus's power. He went on till a number of dogs collected at the sound and tore him limb from limb; thus far, at least, his fate resembled that of Orpheus, though his power of attraction extended only to hostile dogs. It was abundantly proved that the charm lay not in the lyre, but solely in those peculiar gifts of song and music that had been bestowed upon Orpheus by his mother; as to the lyre, it was just like other lyres.

But there:

what need to go back to Orpheus and Neanthus? We have instances in our own days:

I believe the man is still alive who paid 120 pounds for the earthenware lamp of Epictetus the Stoic. I suppose he thought he had only to read by the light of that lamp, and the wisdom of Epictetus would be communicated to him in his dreams, and he himself assume the likeness of that venerable sage. And it was only a day or two ago that another enthusiast paid down 250 pounds for the staff dropped by the Cynic Proteus[80] when he leaped upon the pyre. He treasures this relic, and shows it off just as the people of Tegea do the hide of the Calydonian boar[81], or the Thebans the bones of Geryon, or the Memphians Isis' hair. Now the original owner of this precious staff was one who for ignorance and vulgarity would have borne away the palm from yourself.—My friend, you are in a bad way:

a stick across the head is what you want.

They say that when Dionysius took to tragedy-writing he made such sad stuff of it that Philoxenus was more than once thrown into the quarries because he could not control his laughter. Finding that his efforts only made him ridiculous, Dionysius was at some pains to procure the tablets on which Aeschylus had been wont to write. He looked to draw divine inspiration from them:

---

[80] See *Peregrine* in Notes.
[81] See *Oenevs* in Notes.

as it turned out, however, he now wrote considerably worse rubbish than before. Among the contents of the tablets I may quote:

'Twas Dionysius' wife, Doridion.
Here is another:

Most serviceable woman! thou art gone!
Genuine tablet that, and the next:

Men that are fools are their own folly's butt.

Taken with reference to yourself, by the way, nothing could be more to the point than this last line; Dionysius's tablets deserved gilding, if only for that.

What is your idea, now, in all this rolling and unrolling of scrolls? To what end the gluing and the trimming, the cedar-oil and saffron, the leather cases and the bosses? Much good your purchases have been to you; one sees that already:

why, your language—no, I am wrong there, you are as dumb as a fish—but your life, your unmentionable vices, make every one hate the sight of you; if that is what books do, one cannot keep too clear of them. There are two ways in which a man may derive benefit from the study of the ancients:

he may learn to express himself, or he may improve his morals by their example and warning; when it is clear that he has not profited in either of these respects, what are his books but a habitation for mice and vermin, and a source of castigation to negligent servants?

And how very foolish you must look when any one finds you with a book in your hand (and you are never to be seen without) and asks you who is your orator, your poet, or your historian:

you have seen the title, of course, and can answer that question pat:

but then one word brings up another, and some criticism, favourable or the reverse, is passed upon the contents of your volume:

you are dumb and helpless; you pray for the earth to open and swallow you; you stand like Bellerophon with the warrant for your own execution in your hand.

Once in Corinth Demetrius the Cynic found some illiterate person reading aloud from a very handsome volume, the Bacchae of Euripides, I think it was. He had got to the place where the messenger is relating the destruction of Pentheus by Agave, when Demetrius snatched the book from him and tore it in two:

'Better,' he exclaimed, 'that Pentheus should suffer one rending at my hands than many at yours.'

I have often wondered, though I have never been able to satisfy myself, what it is that makes you such an ardent buyer of books. The idea of your making any profitable use of them is one that nobody who has the slightest acquaintance with you would entertain for a moment:

does the bald man buy a comb, the blind a mirror, the deaf a flute-player? the eunuch a concubine, the landsman an oar, the pilot a plough? Are you merely seizing an opportunity of displaying your wealth? Is it just your way of showing the public that you can afford to spend money even on things that are of no use to you? Why, even a Syrian like myself knows that if you had not got your name foisted into that old man's will, you would have been starving by this time, and all your books must have been put up to sale.

Only one possible explanation remains:

your toadies have made you believe that in addition to your charms of person you have an extraordinary gift for rhetoric, history, and philosophy; and you buy books merely to countenance their flatteries. It seems that you actually hold forth to them at table; and they, poor thirsty frogs, must croak dry-throated applause till they burst, or there is no drink for them. You are a most curiously gullible person:

you take in every word they say to you. You were made to believe at one time that your features resembled those of a certain Emperor. We had had a pseudo-Alexander, and a pseudo-Philip, the fuller, and there was a pseudo-Nero as recently as our own grandfathers' times:

you were for adding one more to the noble army of pseudos. After all, it was nothing for an illiterate fool like you to take such a fancy into his head, and walk about with his chin in the air, aping the gait and dress and expression of his supposed model:

even the Epirot king Pyrrhus, remarkable man that he was in other respects, had the same foible, and was persuaded by his flatterers that he was like Alexander, Alexander the Great, that is. In point of fact, I have seen Pyrrhus's portrait, and the two—to borrow a musical phrase— are about as much like one another as bass and treble; and yet he was convinced he was the image of Alexander. However, if that were all, it would be rather too bad of me to insult Pyrrhus by the comparison:

but I am justified by the sequel; it suits your case so exactly. When once Pyrrhus had got this fancy into his head, every one else ran mad for company, till at last an old woman of Larissa, who did not know Pyrrhus, told him the plain truth, and cured his delusion. After showing her portraits of Philip, Perdiccas, Alexander, Casander, and other kings, Pyrrhus finally asked her which of these he resembled, taking it as a matter of course that she would fix upon Alexander:

however, she considered for some time, and at length informed him that he was most like Batrachion the cook, there being a cook of that name in Larissa who *was* very like Pyrrhus. What particular theatrical pander *you* most resemble I will not pretend to decide:

all I can state with certainty is that to this day you pass for a raving madman on the strength of this fancy.. After such an instance of your critical discernment, we need not be surprised to find that your flatterers have inspired you with the further ambition of being taken for a scholar.

But I am talking nonsense. The cause of your bibliomania is clear enough; I must have been dozing, or I should have seen it long ago. This is your idea of strategy:

you know the Emperor's scholarly tastes, and his respect for culture, and you think it will be worth something to you if he hears of your literary pursuits. Once let your name be mentioned to him as a great buyer and collector of books, and you reckon that your fortune is made. Vile creature! and is the Emperor drugged with mandragora that he should hear of this and never know the rest, your daylight iniquities, your tipplings, your monstrous nightly debauches? Know you not that an Emperor has many eyes and many ears? Yet *your* deeds are such as cannot be concealed from the blind or the deaf. I may tell you at once, as you seem not to know it, that a man's hopes of the Imperial favour depend not on his book-bills, but on his character and daily life. Are you counting upon Atticus and Callinus, the copyists, to put in a good word for you? Then you are deceived:

those relentless gentlemen propose, with the Gods' good leave, to grind you down and reduce you to utter destitution. Come to your senses while there is yet time:

sell your library to some scholar, and whilst you are about it sell your new house too, and wipe off part of your debt to the slave-dealers.

You see, you will ride both these hobbies at once; there is the trouble:

besides your expensive books you must have your superannuated minions; you are insatiable in these pursuits, and you cannot follow both without money. Now observe how precious a thing is counsel. I recommend you to dispense with the superfluous, and confine your attention to your other foible; in other words, keep your money for the slave-dealers, or your private supplies will run short, and you will be reduced to calling in the services of freemen, who will want every penny you possess; otherwise there is nothing to prevent them from telling how your time is spent when you are in liquor. Only the other day I heard some very ugly stories about you—backed, too, by ocular evidence:

the bystanders on that occasion are my witnesses how angry I was on your account; I was in two minds about giving the fellow a thrashing; and the annoying part of it was that he appealed to more than one witness who had had the same experience and told just the same tale. Let this be a warning to you to economize, so that you may be able to have your enjoyments at home in all security. I do not suggest that you should give up these practices:

that is quite hopeless; the dog that has gnawed leather once will gnaw leather always.

On the other hand, you can easily do without books. Your education is complete; you have nothing more to learn; you have the ancients as it were on the tip of your tongue; all history is known to you; you are a master of the choice and management of words, you have got the true Attic vocabulary; the multitude of your books has made a ripe scholar of you. (You love flattery, and there is no reason why I should not indulge you as well as another.)

But I am rather curious on one point:

what are your favourite books among so many? Plato? Antisthenes? Archilochus? Hipponax? Or are they passed over in favour of the orators? Do you ever read the speech of Aeschines against Timarchus? All that sort of thing I suppose you have by heart. And have you grappled with Aristophanes and Eupolis? Did you ever go through the *Baptae*[82]? Well then, you must surely have come on some embarrassing home-truths in that play? It is difficult to imagine that mind of yours bent upon literary studies, and those hands turning over the pages. When do you do your reading? In the daytime, or at night? If the former, you must do it when no one is looking:

and if the latter, is it done in the midst of more engrossing pursuits, or do you work it in before your rhetorical outpourings? As you reverence Cotytto, venture not again into the paths of literature; have done with books, and keep to your own peculiar business. If you had any sense of shame, to be sure, you would abandon that too:

think of Phaedra's indignant protest against her sex:

Darkness is their accomplice, yet they fear not,
Fear not the chamber-walls, their confidants.

But no:

you are determined not to be cured. Very well:

buy book upon book, shut them safely up, and reap the glory that comes of possession:

only, let that be enough; presume not to touch nor read; pollute not with that tongue the poetry and eloquence of the ancients; what harm have they ever done to you?

All this advice is thrown away, I know that. Shall an Ethiopian change his skin? You will go on buying books that you cannot use— to the amusement of educated men, who derive profit not from the price of a book, nor from its handsome appearance, but from the sense and sound of its contents. You think by the multitude of books to supply the deficiencies of your education, and to throw dust in our eyes. Did you but know it, you are exactly like the quack doctors, who provide themselves with silver cupping-glasses, gold-handled lancets, and ivory cases for their instruments; they are quite incapable of using them when the time comes, and have to give place to some properly qualified surgeon, who produces a lancet with a keen edge and a rusty handle, and affords immediate relief to the sufferer. Or here is a better parallel:

take the case of the barbers:

---

[82] See Cotytto in Notes.

you will find that the skilled practitioners have just the razor, scissors, and mirror that their work requires:

the impostors' razors are numerous, and their mirrors magnificent. However, that does not serve to conceal their incompetence, and the result is most amusing:

the average man gets his hair cut by one of their more capable neighbours, and then goes and arranges it before *their* glasses. That is just what your books are good for—to lend to other people; you are quite incapable of using them yourself. Not that you ever have lent any one a single volume; true to your dog-in-the-manger principles, you neither eat the corn yourself, nor give the horse a chance.

There you have my candid opinion about your books:

I shall find other opportunities of dealing with your disreputable conduct in general.

SLANDER, A WARNING

A TERRIBLE thing is ignorance, the source of endless human woes, spreading a mist over facts, obscuring truth, and casting a gloom upon the individual life. We are all walkers in darkness--or say, our experience is that of blind men, knocking helplessly against the real, and stepping high to clear the imaginary, failing to see what is close at their feet, and in terror of being hurt by something that is leagues away. Whatever we do, we are perpetually slipping. about. This it is that has found the tragic poets a thousand themes, Labdacids, Pelopids, and all their kind. Inquiry would show that most of the calamities put upon the boards are arranged by ignorance as by some supernatural stage-manager. This is true enough as a generality; but I refer more particularly to the false reports about intimates and friends that have ruined families, razed cities, driven fathers into frenzy against their offspring, embroiled brother with brother, children with parents, and lover with beloved. Many are the friendships that have been cut short, many the households set by the ears, because slander has found ready credence.

By way of precaution against it, then, it is my design to sketch the nature, the origin, and effects of slander, though indeed the picture is already in existence, by the hand of Apelles. He had been traduced in the ears of Ptolemy as an accomplice of Theodotas in the Tyrian conspiracy. As a matter of fact he had never seen Tyre, and knew nothing of Theodotas beyond the information that he was an officer of Ptolemy's in charge of Phoenicia. However, that did not prevent another painter called Antiphilus, who was jealous of his court influence and professional skill, from reporting his supposed complicity to Ptolemy:

he had seen him at Theodotas's table in Phoenicia, whispering in his ear all through dinner; he finally got as far as making Apelles out prime instigator of the Tyrian revolt and the capture of Pelusium.

Ptolemy was not distinguished for sagacity; he had been brought up on the royal diet of adulation; and the incredible tale so inflamed and carried him away that the probabilities of the case never struck him:

the traducer was a professional rival; a painter's insignificance was hardly equal to the part; and this particular painter had had nothing but good at his hands, having been exalted by him above his fellows. But no, he did not even find out whether Apelles had ever made a voyage to Tyre; it pleased him to fall into a passion and make the palace ring with denunciations of the ingrate, the plotter, the conspirator. Luckily one of the prisoners, between disgust at Antiphilus's effrontery and compassion for Apelles, stated that the poor man had never been told a word of their designs; but for this, he would have paid with his head for his non-complicity in the Tyrian troubles.

Ptolemy was sufficiently ashamed of himself, we learn, to make Apelles a present of £25,000, besides handing Antiphilus over to him as a slave. The painter was impressed by his experience, and took his revenge upon Slander in a picture.

On the right sits a man with long ears almost of the Midas pattern, stretching out a hand to Slander, who is still some way off, but coming. About him are two females whom I take for Ignorance and Assumption. Slander, approaching from the left, is an extraordinarily beautiful woman, but with a heated, excitable air that suggests delusion and impulsiveness; in her left hand is a lighted torch, and with her right she is haling a youth by the hair; he holds up hands to heaven and calls the

Gods to witness his innocence. Showing Slander the way is a man with piercing eyes, but pale, deformed, and shrunken as from long illness; one may easily guess him to be Envy. Two female attendants encourage Slander, acting as tire-women, and adding touches to her beauty; according to the *cicerone*, one of these is Malice, and the other Deceit. Following behind in mourning guise, black-robed and with torn hair, comes (I think he named her) Repentance. She looks tearfully behind her, awaiting shame-faced the approach of Truth. That was how Apelles translated his peril into paint.

I propose that we too execute in his spirit a portrait of Slander and her surroundings; and to avoid vagueness let us start with a definition or outline. Slander, we will say, is an undefended indictment, concealed from its object, and owing its success to one-sided half-informed procedure. Now we have something to go upon. Further, our actors, as in comedy[83], are three--the slanderer, the slandered, and the recipient of the slander; let us take each in turn and see how his case works out.

And first for our chief character, the manufacturer of the slander. That he is not a good man needs no proof; no good man will injure his neighbour; good men's reputation, and their credit for kindness, is based on the benefits they confer upon their friends, not on unfounded disparagement of others and the ousting of them from their friends' affections.

Secondly, it is easy to realize that such a person offends against justice, law, and piety, and is a pest to all who associate with him. Equality in everything, and contentment with your proper share, are the essentials of justice; inequality and overreaching, of injustice; that every one will admit. It is not less clear that the man who secretly slanders the absent is guilty of over-reaching; he is insisting on entire possession of his hearer, appropriating and enclosing his ears, guarding them against impartiality by blocking them with prejudice. Such procedure is unjust to the last degree; we have the testimony of the best law-givers for that; Solon and Draco made every juror swear that he would hear indifferently, and view both parties with equal benevolence, till the defence should have been compared with the prosecution and proved better or

---

[83] Cratinus was the first to limit the number of actors to three. . . There were no further innovations, and the number of the actors in comedy was permanently fixed at three.' Haigh's *Attic Theatre*.

worse than it. Before such balancing of the speeches, they considered that the forming of a conclusion must be impious and unholy. We may indeed literally suppose Heaven to be offended, if we license the accuser to say what he will, and then, closing our own ears or the defendant's mouth, allow our judgement to be dictated by the first speech. No one can say, then, that the uttering of slander is reconcilable with the requirements of justice, of law, or of the juror's oath. If it is objected that the lawgivers are no sufficient authority for such extreme justice and impartiality, I fall back on the prince of poets, who has expressed a sound opinion, or let me say, laid down a sound law on the subject:

> or give thy judgement,
> till both sides are heard.

He too was doubtless very well aware that, of all the ills that flesh is heir to, none is more grievous or more iniquitous than that a man should be condemned unjudged and unheard. That is precisely what the slanderer tries to effect by exposing the slandered without trial to his hearer's wrath, and precluding defence by the secrecy of his denunciation.

Every such person is a skulker and a coward; he will not come into the open; he is an ambuscader shooting from a lurking-place, whose opponent cannot meet him nor have it out with him, but must be shot down helplessly before he knows that war is afoot; there could be no clearer proof that his allegations are baseless. Of course a man who knows he is bringing true charges does the exposure in public, challengers inquiry, and faces examination; just so no one who can win a pitched battle will resort to ambush and deceit.

It is in kings' courts that these creatures are mostly found; they thrive in the atmosphere of dominion and power, where envy is rife, suspicions innumerable, and the opportunities for flattery and back-biting endless. Where hopes are higher, there envy is more intense, hatred more reckless, and jealousy more unscrupulous. They all keep close watch upon one another, spying like duellists for a weak spot. Every one would be first, and to that end shoves and elbows his neighbour aside, and does his best to pull back or trip the man in front of him. One whose equipment is limited to goodness is very soon thrown down, dragged about, and finally thrust forth with ignominy; while he who is prepared to flatter, and can make servility plausible, is high in credit, gets first to his end, and triumphs. These people bear out the words of Homer:

> Th' impartial War-God slayeth him that slew.

Convinced that the prize is great, they elaborate their mutual stratagems, among which slander is at once the speediest and the most uncertain; high are the hopes with which this child of envy or hatred is born; pitiful, gloomy and disastrous the end to which it comes.

Success is by no means the easy simple matter it may be supposed; it demands much skill and tact, with the most concentrated attention. Slander would never do the harm it does, if it were not made plausible; it would never prevail against truth, that strongest of all things, if it were not dressed up into really attractive bait.

The chief mark for it is the man who is in favour, and therefore enviable in the eyes of his distanced competitors; they all regard him as standing in their light, and let fly at him; every one thinks he will be first if he can only dispose of this conspicuous person and spoil him of his favour. You, may see the same thing among runners at the games. The good runner, from the moment the barrier falls, simply makes the best of his way; his thoughts are on the winning-post, his hopes of victory in his feet; he leaves his neighbour alone and does not concern himself at all with his competitors. It is the ill qualified, with no prospect of winning by his speed, who resorts to foul play; his one pre-occupation is how he may stop, impede, curb the real runner, because failing that his own victory is out of the question. The persons we are concerned with race in like manner for the favour of the great. The one who forges ahead is at once the object of plots, is taken at a disadvantage by his enemies when his thoughts are elsewhere, and got rid of, while they get credit for devotion by the harm they do to others.

The credibility of the slander is by no means left to take care of itself; it is the chief object of their solicitude; they are extremely cautious against inconsistencies or contradictions. The usual method is to seize upon real characteristics of a victim, and only paint these in darker colours, which allows verisimilitude. A man is a doctor; they make him out a poisoner; wealth figures as tyranny; the tyrant's ready tool is a ready traitor too.

Sometimes, however, the hint is taken from the hearer's own nature; the villains succeed by using a bait that will tempt *him*. They know he is jealous, and they tell him:

'He beckoned to your wife at dinner, and sighed as he gazed at her; and Stratonice--well, did not seem offended.' Or he writes poetry, and piques himself upon it; then, 'Philoxenus had great sport pulling your poem to pieces--said the metre was faulty and the composition vile.' A devout religious person is told that his friend is an atheist and a blasphemer, rejects belief and denies Providence. That is quite enough; the venom has entered at the ear and inflamed the brain; the man does not wait for confirmation, but abandons his friend.

In a word, they invent and say the kind of thing that they know will be most irritating to their hearer, and having a full knowledge of his vulnerable point, concentrate their fire upon it; he is to be too much flustered by rage to have time for investigation; the very surprise of what he is told is to be so convincing to him that he will not hear, even if his friend is willing to plead.

That slander, indeed, is especially effective which is unwelcome; Demetrius the Platonic was reported to Ptolemy Dionysus for a water drinker, and for the only man who had declined to put on female attire at the Dionysia. He was summoned next morning, and had to drink in public, dress up in gauze, clash and dance to the cymbals, or he would have been put to death for disapproving the King's life, and setting up for a critic of his luxurious ways.

At Alexander's court there was no more fatal imputation than that of refusing worship and adoration to Hephaestion. Alexander had been so fond of him that to appoint him a God after his death was, for such a worker of marvels, nothing out of the way. The various cities at once built temples to him, holy ground was consecrated, altars, offerings and festivals instituted to this new divinity; if a man would be believed, he must swear by Hephaestion. For smiling at these proceedings, or showing the slightest lack of reverence, the penalty was death. The flatterers cherished, fanned, and put the bellows to this childish fancy of Alexander's; they had visions and manifestations of Hephaestion to relate; they invented cures and attributed oracles to him; they did not stop short of doing sacrifice to this God of Help and Protection. Alexander was delighted, and ended by believing in it all; it gratified his vanity to think that he was now not only a God's son, but a God-maker. It would be interesting to know how many of his friends in those days found that what the new divinity did for them was to supply a charge of irreverence on which they might be dismissed and deprived of the King's favour.

Agathocles of Samos was a valued officer of his, who very narrowly escaped being thrown into a lion's cage; the offence reported against him was shedding tears as he passed Hephaestion's tomb. The tale goes that he was saved by Perdiccas, who swore, by all the Gods and Hephaestion, that the God had appeared plainly to him as he was hunting, and charged him to bid Alexander spare Agathocles:

his tears had meant neither scepticism nor mourning, but been merely a tribute to the friendship that was gone.

Flattery and slander had just then their opportunity in Alexander's emotional condition. In a siege, the assailants do not attempt a part of the defences that is high, precipitous, or solid; they direct all their force at some rotten, low, or neglected point, expecting to get in and effect the capture most easily so. Similarly the slanderer finds out where the soul is weak or corrupt or accessible, there makes his assault, there applies his engines, or effects an entry at a point where there are no defenders to mark his approach. Once in, he soon has all in flames; fire and sword and devastation clear out the previous occupants; how else should it be when a soul is captured and enslaved?

His siege-train includes deceit, falsehood, perjury, insinuation, effrontery, and a thousand other moral laxities. But the chief of them all is Flattery, the blood relation, the sister indeed, of Slander. No heart so high, so fenced with adamant, but Flattery will master it, with the aid of Slander undermining and sapping its foundations.

That is what goes on outside. But within there are traitorous parties working to the same end, stretching hands of help to the attack, opening the gates, and doing their utmost to bring the capture about. There are those ever-present human frailties, fickleness and satiety; there is the appetite for the surprising. We all delight, I cannot tell why, in whisperings and insinuations. I know people whose ears are as agreeably titillated with slander as their skin with a feather.

Supported by all these allies, the attack prevails; victory is hardly in doubt for a moment; there is no defence or resistance to the assault; the hearer surrenders without reluctance, and the slandered knows nothing of what is going on; as when a town is stormed by night, he has his throat cut in his sleep.

The most pitiful thing is when, all unconscious of how matters stand, he comes to his friend with a cheerful countenance, having nothing to be ashamed of, and talks and behaves as usual, just as if the toils were not all round him. Then if the other has any nobility or generous spirit of fair play in him, he gives vent to his anger and pours out his soul; after which he allows him to answer, and so finds out how he has been abused.

But if he is mean and ignoble, he receives him with a lip smile, while he is gnashing his teeth in covert rage, wrathfully brooding in the soul's dark depth, as the poet describes it. I know nothing so characteristic of a warped slavish nature as to bite the lip while you nurse your spite and cultivate your secret hatred, one thing in your heart and another on your tongue, playing with the gay looks of comedy a lamentable sinister tragedy. This is especially apt to occur, when the slander conies from one who is known for an old friend of the slandered. When that is the case, a man pays no attention to anything the victim or his apologists may say; that old friendship affords a sufficient presumption of truth; he forgets that estrangements, unknown to outsiders, constantly part the greatest friends; and sometimes a man will try to escape the consequences of his own faults by attributing similar ones to his neighbour and getting his denunciation in first. It may be taken, indeed, that no one will venture to slander an enemy; that is too unconvincing; the motive is so obvious. It is the supposed friend that is the most promising object, the idea being to give your hearer absolute proof of your devotion to him by sacrificing your dearest to his interests.

It must be added that there are persons who, if they subsequently learn that they have condemned a friend in error, are too much ashamed of that error to receive or look him in the face again; you might suppose the discovery of his innocence was a personal injury to them.

It is not, then, too much to say that life is made miserable by these lightly and incuriously credited slanders. Antea said to Proetus, after she had solicited and been scorned by Bellerophon;

Die thou the death, if thou slay not the man

That so would have enforc'd my chastity!

By the machinations of this lascivious woman, the young man came near perishing in his combat with the Chimera, as the penalty for continence and loyalty to his host. And Phaedra, who made a similar charge against her stepson, succeeded in bringing down upon Hippolytus a father's curse, though God knows how innocent he was.

'Ah, yes,' I fancy some one objecting; 'but the traducer sometimes deserves credit, being known for a just and a wise man; then he ought to be listened to, as one incapable of villany.' What? was there ever a juster man than Aristides? yet he led the opposition to Themistocles and incited the people against him, pricked by the same political ambition as he. Aristides was a just man in all other relations; but he was human, he had a gall, he was open to likes and dislikes.

And if the story of Palamedes is true, the wisest of the Greeks, a great man in other respects too, stands convicted of hatching that insidious plot[84]; the ties that bind kinsmen, friends, and comrades in danger, had to yield to jealousy. To be a man is to be subject to this temptation.

It is superfluous to refer to Socrates, misrepresented to the Athenians as an impious plotter, to Themistocles or Miltiades, suspected after all their victories of betraying Greece; such examples are innumerable, and most of them familiar.

What, then, should a man of sense do, when he finds one friend's virtue pitted against another's truth? Why, surely, learn from Homer's parable of the Sirens; he advises sailing past these ear-charmers; we should stuff up our ears; we should not open them freely to the prejudiced, but station there a competent hall-porter in the shape of Judgement, who shall inspect every vocal visitor, and take it on himself to admit the worthy, but shut the door in the face of others. How absurd to have such an official at our house door, and leave our ears and understandings open to intrusion!

So, when any one comes to you with a tale, examine it on its merits, regardless of the informant's age, general conduct, or skill in speech. The more plausible he is, the greater need of care. Never trust another's judgement--it may be in reality only his dislike--but reserve the inquiry to yourself; let envy, if such it was, recoil upon the backbiter, your trial of the two men's characters be an open one, and your award of contempt and approval deliberate. To award them earlier, carried away by the first word of slander--why, God bless me, how puerile and mean and iniquitous it all is!

And the cause of it, as we started with saying, is ignorance, and the mystery that conceals men's characters. Would some God unveil all lives to us, Slander would retire discomfited to the bottomless pit; for the illumination of truth would be over all.

---

[84] Odysseus.

THE HALL

As Alexander stood gazing at the transparent loveliness of the Cydnus, the thought of a plunge into those generous depths, of the delicious shock of ice-cold waters amid summer heat, was too much for him; and could he have foreseen the illness that was to result from it, I believe he would have had his bath just the same. With such an example before him, can any one whose pursuits are literary miss a chance of airing his eloquence amid the glories of this spacious hall, wherein gold sheds all its lustre, whose walls are decked with the flowers of art, whose light is as the light of the sun? Shall he who might cause this roof to ring with applause, and contribute his humble share to the splendours of the place,--shall such a one content himself with examining and admiring its beauties without a word, and so depart, like one that is dumb, or silent from envy? No man of taste or artistic sensibility, none but a dull ignorant boor, would consent thus to cut himself off from the highest of enjoyments, or could need to be reminded of the difference between the ordinary spectator and the educated man. The former, when he has carried his eyes around and upwards in silent admiration, and clasped ecstatic hands, has done all that can be expected of him; he ventures not on words, lest they should prove inadequate to his subject. With the cultured observer, it is otherwise:

he, surely, will not rest content with feasting his eyes on beauty; he will not stand speechless amid his splendid surroundings, but will set his mind to work, and as far as in him lies pay verbal tribute. Nor will his tribute consist in mere praise of the building. It was well enough, no doubt, for the islander Telemachus to express his boyish amazement in the palace of Menelaus, and to liken that prince's gold and ivory to the glories of Heaven;--his limited experience afforded him no earthly parallel:

but here, the very use to which the hall is put, and the distinguished quality of the audience, are an essential part of the praise bestowed upon it.

Nothing, surely, could be more delightful than to find this noble building thrown open for the reception of eloquent praise, its atmosphere laden with panegyric, its very walls reechoing, cavern-like, to every syllable, prolonging each cadence, dwelling on each period;--nay, they are themselves an audience, most appreciative of audiences, that stores up the speaker's words in memory, and recompenses his efforts with a meed of most harmonious flattery. Even so do the rocks resound to the shepherd's flute; the notes come ringing back again, and simple rustics think it is the voice of some maid, who dwells among the crags, and from the depths of her rocky haunt makes answer to their songs and their cries.

I feel as if a certain mental exaltation resulted from this magnificence:

it is suggestive; the imagination is stimulated. It would scarcely be too much to say that through the medium of the eyes Beauty is borne in upon the mind, and suffers no thought to find utterance before it has received her impress. We hold it for true that Achilles' wrath was whetted against the Phrygians by the sight of his new armour, and that as he donned it for the first time his lust of battle was uplifted on wings:

and why should not a beautiful building similarly be a whet to the zeal of the orator? Luxuriant grass, a fine plane-tree and a clear spring, hard by Ilissus, were inspiration enough for Socrates:

in such a spot he could sit bantering Phaedrus, refuting Lysias, and invoking the Muses; never doubting--indelicate old person--but that those virgin Goddesses would grace his retirement with their presence, and take part in his amorous discourse. But to such a place as this we may surely

hope that they will come uninvited, We can offer them something better than the shade of a plane-tree, though for that upon Ilissus' bank we should substitute the golden one of the Persian King. His tree had one claim to admiration--it was expensive:

but for symmetry and proportion and beautiful workmanship, nothing of that kind was thrown in; the gold was gold, an uncouth manifestation of solid wealth, calculated to excite envy in the beholder, and to procure congratulations for the possessor, but far from creditable to the artist. The line of the Arsacidae cared nothing for beauty; they did not appeal to men's taste; not *How may I win approval?* but *How may I dazzle?* was the question they asked themselves. The barbarian has a keen appreciation of gold:

to the treasures of art he is blind.

But I see about me in this Hall beauties that were never designed to please barbarians, nor to gratify the vulgar ostentation of Persian monarchs. Poverty is not here the sole requirement of the critic:

taste is also necessary; nor will the eyes deliver judgement without the assistance of Reason. The eastern aspect, procuring us, as in the temples of old, that first welcome peep of the sun in his new-born glory, and suffering his rays to pour in without stint through the open doors, the adaptation of length to breadth and breadth to height, the free admission of light at every stage of the Sun's course,--all is charmingly contrived, and redounds to the credit of the architect. What admirable judgement has been shown, too, in the structure and decoration of the roof! nothing wanting, yet nothing superfluous; the gilding is exactly what was required to achieve elegance without empty display; it is precisely that little touch of adornment with which a beautiful and modest woman sets off her loveliness; it is the slender necklace about her neck, the light ring upon her finger, the earrings, the brooch, the fillet that imprisons her luxuriant hair, and, like the purple stripe upon a robe, enhances its beauty. Contrast with this the artifices of courtesans, and particularly of the most unlovely among them, whose robes are *all* of purple, and their necks loaded with golden chains, who hope to render themselves attractive by their extravagance, and by external adornments to supply the deficiencies of Nature; their arms, they think, will look more dazzlingly white if gold glitters upon them, a clumsy foot pass unobserved if hidden in a golden sandal, and the face be irresistible that appears beneath a halo of gold. The modest house, far from resorting to such meretricious charms, uses as little gold as may be; I think she knows that she would have no cause to blush, though she should display her beauty stripped of all adornment.

And so it is with this Hall. The roof--the head, as I may say,--comely in itself, is not without its golden embellishments:

yet they are but as the stars, whose fires gleam here and there, pranked in the darkness of the sky. Were that sky all fire, it would be beautiful to us no longer, only terrible. Observe, too, that the gold is not otiose, not merely an ornament among ornaments, put there to flatter the eye:

it diffuses soft radiance from end to end of the building, and the walls are tinged with its warm glow. Striking upon the gilded beams, and mingling its brightness with theirs, the daylight glances down upon us

with a clearness and a richness not all its own. Such are the glories overhead, whose praises might best be sung by him who told of Helen's high-vaulted chamber, and Olympus' dazzling peak.

And for the rest, the frescoed walls, with their exquisite colouring, so clear, so highly finished, so true to nature, to what can I compare them but to a flowery meadow in spring? Even so the comparison halts. Those flowers wither and decay and shed their beauty:

but here is one eternal spring; this meadow fades not, its flowers are everlasting; for no hand is put forth to pluck away their sweetness, only the eye feeds thereon. And what eye would not delight to feed on joys so varied? What orator would not feel that his credit was at stake, and so be fired with ambition to surpass himself, rather than be found wanting to his theme?

The contemplation of beautiful objects is of all things the most inspiring, and not to men only. I think even a horse must feel some increase of pleasure in galloping over smooth, soft fields, that give an easy footing, and ring back no defiance to his hoofs:

it is then that he goes his best; the beauty of his surroundings puts him on his mettle; he will not be beaten,

if pace counts for anything. And look at the peacock. Spring has just begun; never are flowers a gladder sight than now; it is as if they were really brighter, their hues more fresh, than at other times. Watch the bird, as he struts forth into some meadow:

he spreads his feathers, and displays them to the Sun; up goes his tail, a towered circle of flowery plumage; for with him too it is spring, and the meadow challenges him to do his utmost. See how he turns about, and shows forth his gorgeous beauty. As the sun's rays strike upon him, the wonder grows:

there is a subtle transmutation of colours, one glory vanishing and giving place to another. The change is nowhere more apparent than in those rainbow rings at the ends of his feathers:

here a slight movement turns bronze to gold, and (such is the potency of light) purple becomes green, because sun is exchanged for shadow. As for the sea, I need not remind you how inviting, how attractive, is its appearance on a calm day:

the veriest landlubber must long to be upon it, and sail far away from the shore, as he marks how the light breeze fills the sails and speeds the vessel on its gentle gliding course over the crests of the waves.

The beauty of this Hall has a similar power over the orator, encouraging him, stimulating him to fresh effort, enlarging his ambition. The spell was irresistible:

I have yielded to it, and come hither to address you, as though drawn by wryneck's or by Siren's charm; nor am I without hope that my words, bald though they be in themselves, may yet borrow something from that atmosphere of beauty in which they are here clothed as in a garment.

Scarcely have I pronounced these last words, when a certain Theory (and a very sound one, too, if we can take its own word for it), which has been interrupting me all along, and doing its best to break my speech off, informs me that there is no truth in my statements, and expresses its surprise at my assertion that gilding and mural decoration are favourable to the display of rhetorical skill. The very contrary, it maintains, is the case. On second thoughts, it may as well come forward and plead its own cause; you, gentlemen, will kindly serve as jury, and hear what it has to say in favour of the cheap and nasty in architecture, considered as rhetorical conditions. My own sentiments on this subject you have already heard, nor is there any occasion for me to repeat them. The Theory is therefore at liberty to speak; I will withdraw for a while, and hold my tongue.

'Gentlemen of the jury,' it begins, 'a splendid tribute has been paid to this Hall by the last speaker; and I for my part am so far from having any fault to find with the building, that I propose to supply the deficiencies of his encomium; for by magnifying its glories, I am so much the nearer to proving my point, which is, its unsuitableness to the purposes of the orator. And first I shall ask your permission to avail myself of his simile of feminine adornments. In my opinion, it is not enough to say that lavish ornament adds nothing to feminine beauty:

it actually takes away from it. Dazzled by gold and costly gems, how should the beholder do justice to the charms of a clear complexion, to neck, and eye, and arm, and finger? Sards and emeralds, bracelets and necklaces, claim all his attention, and the lady has the mortification of finding herself eclipsed by her own jewels, whose engrossed admirers can spare no words, and barely a casual glance for herself. The same fate, it seems to me, awaits the orator who exhibits his skill amid these wondrous works of art:

his praises are obscured, quite swallowed up, in the splendour of the things he praises. It is as if a man should bring a wax light to feed a mighty conflagration, or set up an ant for exhibition on a camel's or an elephant's back. That is one pitfall for the orator. And there is another:

the distracting influence of that resonant music that echoes through the Hall, making voluminous answer to his words, nay, drowning them in the utterance; surely as trumpet quells flute, or the sea-roar the boatswain's pipe, if he presume to contend with the crash of waves, so surely shall the orator's puny voice be overmastered by this mighty music, and seem like silence.

'Then again, my opponent spoke of the stimulating, the encouraging effect produced on the speaker by architectural beauty. I should have said that the effect was rather dispiriting than otherwise:

the speaker's thoughts are scattered, and his confidence shaken, as he reflects on the disgrace that must attach to mean words uttered beneath a noble roof. There could be no more crushing ignominy; he is precisely in the position of a warrior in brilliant armour who sets the example of flight, and whose cowardice is only emphasized by his splendid equipment. To this principle I should refer the conduct of Homer's model orator, who, so far from attaching any importance to externals, affected the bearing of a man that was altogether witless; his design was to bring his eloquence into stronger relief by the studied ungracefulness of his attitude.

'The orator's mind, too, is so engrossed with what he sees, that it is absolutely impossible for him to preserve the thread of his discourse; he cannot think of what he is saying, so imperatively do the sights around him claim his attention. It is not to be expected that he will do himself justice:

he is too full of his subject. And I might add that his supposed hearers, when they come into such a building as this, are no longer hearers of *his* eloquence, but spectators of *its* beauties; he must be a Thamyris, an Amphion, an Orpheus among orators who could gain their attention in such circumstances. Once let a man cross this threshold, and a blaze of beauty envelops his senses; he is all eyes, and to the orator is "as one that marketh not";--unless, indeed, he be altogether blind, or take a hint from the court of Areopagus, and give audience in the dark. Compare the story of the Sirens with that of the Gorgons, if you would know how insignificant is the power of words in comparison with that of visible objects. The enchantments of the former were at the best a matter of time; they did but flatter the ear with pleasing songs; if the mariner landed, he remained long on their hands, and it has even happened to them to be disregarded altogether. But the beauty of the Gorgons, irresistible in might, won its way to the inmost soul, and wrought amazement and dumbness in the beholder; admiration (so the legend goes) turned him to stone. All that my opponent has just said about the peacock illustrates my point:

that bird charms not the ear, but the eye. Take a swan, take a nightingale, and set her singing:

now put a silent peacock at her side, and I will tell you which bird has the attention of the company. The songstress may go hang now; so invincible a thing is the pleasure of the eyes. Shall I call evidence? A sage, then, shall be my witness, how far mightier are the things of the eye than those of the ear. Usher, call me Herodotus, son of Lyxes, of Halicarnassus.--Ah, since he has been so obliging as to hear the summons, let him step into the box. You will excuse the Ionic dialect; it is his way.'

Gentlemen of the jury, the Theory hath spoken sooth. Give good heed to that he saith, how sight is a better thing than hearing; for a man shall sooner trust his eyes than his ears.

'You hear him, gentlemen? He gives the preference to sight, and rightly. For words have wings; they are no sooner out of the mouth than they take flight and are lost:

but the delight of the eyes is ever present, ever draws the beholder to itself. Judge, then, the difficulty the orator must experience in contending with such a rival as this Hall, whose beauty attracts every eye.

'But my weightiest argument I have kept till now:

you, gentlemen, throughout the hearing of this case, have been gazing with admiration on roof and wall, scanning each picture in its turn. I do not reproach you:

you have done what every man must do, when he beholds workmanship so exquisite, subjects so varied. Here are works whose perfect technique, applied as it is to the illustration of all that is useful in history and mythology, holds out an irresistible challenge to the judgement of the connoisseur. Now I would not have your eyes altogether glued to those walls; I would fain have some share of your attention:

let me try, therefore, to give you word-pictures of these originals; I think it may not be uninteresting to you to hear a description of those very objects which your eyes view with such admiration. And you will perhaps count it a point in my favour, that I, and not my antagonist, have hit upon this means of doubling your pleasure. It is a hazardous enterprise, I need not say,--without materials or models to put together picture upon picture; this word-painting is but sketchy work.

'On our right as we enter, we have a story half Argive, half Ethiopian. Perseus slays the sea-monster, and sets Andromeda free; it will not be long ere he leads her away as his bride; an episode, this, in his Gorgon expedition. The artist has given us much in a small space:

maiden modesty, girlish terror, are here portrayed in the countenance of Andromeda, who from her high rock gazes down upon the strife, and marks the devoted courage of her lover, the grim aspect of his bestial antagonist. As that bristling horror approaches, with awful gaping jaws, Perseus in his left hand displays the Gorgon's head, while his right grasps the drawn sword. All of the monster that falls beneath Medusa's eyes is stone already; and all of him that yet lives the scimetar hews to pieces.

577

'In the next picture, a tale of retributive justice is dramatically set forth. The painter seems to have taken his hint from Euripides or Sophocles; each of them has portrayed this incident. The two young men are friends:

Pylades of Phocis, and Orestes, who is thought to be dead. They have stolen into the palace unobserved, and together they slay Aegisthus Clytemnestra has already been dispatched:

her body lies, half-naked, upon a bed; all the household stand aghast at the deed; some cry out, others look about for means of escape. A fine thought of the painter's:

the matricide is but slightly indicated, as a thing achieved:

with the slaying of the paramour, it is otherwise; there is something deliberate in the manner in which the lads go about their work.

'Next comes a more tender scene. We behold a comely God, and a beautiful boy. The boy is Branchus:

sitting on a rock, he holds out a hare to tease his dog, who is shown in the act of jumping for it. Apollo looks on, well pleased:

half of his smile is for the dog's eagerness, and half for the mischievous boy.

'Once more Perseus; an earlier adventure, this time. He is cutting off Medusa's head, while Athene screens him from her sight. Although the blow is struck, he has never seen his handiwork, only the reflection of the head upon the shield; he knows the price of a single glance at the reality.

'High upon the middle wall, facing the door, a shrine of Athene is modelled. The statue of the Goddess is in white marble. She is not shown in martial guise; it is the Goddess of War in time of peace.

'We have seen Athene in marble:

next we see her in painting. She flies from the pursuit of amorous Hephaestus; it was to this moment that Erichthonius owed his origin.

'The next picture deals with the ancient story of Orion. He   is blind, and on his shoulder carries Cedalion, who directs the sightless eyes towards the East. The rising Sun heals his infirmity; and there stands Hephaestus on Lemnos, watching the cure.

'Then we have Odysseus, seeking by feigned madness to avoid joining the expedition of the Atridae, whose messengers have already appeared to summon him. Nothing could be more convincing than his plough-chariot, his ill-assorted team, and his apparent unconsciousness of all that is going forward. But his paternal feeling betrays him. Palamedes, penetrating his secret, seizes upon Telemachus, and threatens him with drawn sword. If the other can act madness, *he* can act anger. The father in Odysseus is revealed:

he is frightened into sanity, and throws aside the mask.

'Last of all is Medea, burning with jealousy, glaring askance , upon her children, and thinking dreadful thoughts. See, the sword even now is in her hand:

and there sit the victims, smiling; they see the sword, yet have no thought of what is to come.

'Need I say, gentlemen, how the sight of all these pictures draws away the attention of the audience upon them, and leaves the orator without a single hearer? If I have described them at length, it was not in order to impress you with the headstrong audacity of my opponent, in voluntarily thrusting himself upon an audience so ill-disposed. I seek not to call down your condemnation nor your resentment upon him, nor do I ask you to refuse him a hearing:

rather I would have you assist his endeavours, listen to him, if you can, with closed eyes, and remember the difficulty of his undertaking; when you, his judges, have become his fellow workers, he will still have much ado to escape the imputation of bringing discredit upon this magnificent Hall. And if it seem strange to you that I should plead thus on my antagonist's behalf, you must attribute it to my fondness for this same Hall, which makes me anxious that every man who speaks in it should come off creditably, be he who he may.'

PATRIOTISM

IT is a truism with no pretensions to novelty that there is nothing sweeter than one's country. Does that imply that, though there is nothing pleasanter, there may be something grander or more divine? Why, of all that men reckon grand and divine their country is the source and teacher, originating, developing, inculcating. For great and brilliant and splendidly equipped cities many men have admiration, but for their own all men have love. No man--not the most enthusiastic sightseer that ever was--is so dazzled by foreign wonders as to forget his own land.

He who boasts that he is a citizen of no mean city misses, it seems to me, the true patriotism; he suggests that it would be a mortification to him to belong to a State less distinguished. It is country in the abstract that I delight rather to honour. It is well enough when you are comparing States to investigate the questions of size or beauty or markets; but when it is a matter of choosing a country, no one would exchange his own for one more glorious; he may wish that his own resembled those more highly blest, but he will choose it, defects and all.

It is the same with loyal sons, or good fathers. A young man who has the right stuff in him will honour no man above his father; nor will a father set his affections on some other young man to the neglect of his son. On the contrary, fathers are so convinced of their children's being better than they really are, that they reckon them the handsomest, the tallest, the most accomplished of their generation. Any one who does not judge his offspring thus I cannot allow to have the father's eye.

The fatherland! it is the first and the nearest of all names. It is true there is nothing nearer than a father; but a man who duly honours his father, according to the dictates of law and nature, will yet be right to honour his fatherland in still higher degree; for that father himself belongs to the fatherland; so does his father's father, and all his house back and back, till the line ends with the Gods our fathers.

The Gods too love the lands of their nativity; though they may be supposed to concern themselves with human affairs in general, claiming the whole of earth and sea as theirs, yet each of them honours above all other lands the one that gave him birth. That State is more majestic which a God calls his country, that isle has an added sanctity in which poesy affirms that one was born. Those are acceptable offerings, which a man has come to their respective homes to make. And if Gods are patriotic, shall not men be more so?

For it was from his own country that every man looked his first upon the Sun; that God, though he be common to all men, yet each reckons among his country Gods, because in that country he was revealed to him. There speech came to him, the speech that belonged to that soil, and there he got knowledge of the Gods. If his country be such that to attain true culture he must seek another, yet even for that culture let him thank his country; the word State he could never have known, had not his country shown him that States existed.

And surely men gather culture and learning, that they may thereby render themselves more serviceable to their country; they amass wealth that they may outdo their neighbours in devoting it to their country's good. And 'tis no more than reason; it is not for those who have received the greatest of all benefits to prove thankless; if we are grateful, as we doubtless should be, to the individual benefactor, much more ought we to give our country her due; against neglect of parents the various States have laws; we should account our country the common mother of us all, and recompense her who bred us, and taught us that there were laws.

The man was never known who so forgot his country as to be indifferent to it when established in another State. All who fare ill abroad are perpetually thinking how country is the best of all good things; and those who fare well, whatever their general prosperity, are ever conscious of the one thing lacking:

they do not live at home, but are exiles; and exile is a reproach. Those again whose sojourn has brought them distinction by way of garnered wealth or honourable fame, acknowledged culture or approved courage, all of them, you will find, yearn for their native land, where are the spectators of their triumphs that they would most desire. A man's longing for home is indeed in direct proportion to his credit abroad.

Even the young have the patriotic sentiment; but in the old it is as much more keen as their sense is greater. Every old man directs his efforts and his prayers to ending his life in his own land; where he began to live, there would he lay his bones, in the soil that formed him, and join his fathers in the grave. It is a dread fate to be condemned to exile even in death, and lie in alien earth.

But if you would know the true man's feeling for his country, it is in the born citizen that you must study it. The merely naturalized are a sort of bastards ever ready for another change; they know not nor love the name of country, but think they may find what they need in one place as well as another; their standard of happiness is the pleasures of the belly. Those whose country is their true mother love the land whereon they were born and bred, though it be narrow and rough and poor of soil. If they cannot vaunt the goodness of the land, they are still at no loss for praises of their country; if they see others making much of bounteous plains and meadows variegated with all plants that grow, they too can call up their country's praise; another may breed good horses; what matter? theirs breeds good men.

A man is fain to be at home, though the home be but anislet; though he might have fortune among strangers, he will not take immortality there; to be buried in his own land is better. Brighter to him the smoke of home than the fire of other lands.

In such honour everywhere is the name of country that you will find legislators all the world over punishing the worst offences with exile, as the heaviest penalty at their command. And it is just the same with generals on service. When the men are taking their places for battle, no such encouragement as to tell them they are fighting for their country. No one will disgrace himself after that if he can help it; the name of country turns even a coward into a brave man.

DIPSAS, THE THIRST-SNAKE

THE southern parts of Libya are all deep sand and parched soil, a desert of wide extent that produces nothing, one vast plain destitute of grass, herb, vegetation, and water; or if a remnant of the scanty rain stands here and there in a hollow place, it is turbid and evil-smelling, undrinkable even in the extremity of thirst. The land is consequently uninhabited; savage, dried up, barren, droughty, how should it support life? The mere temperature, an atmosphere that is rather fire than air, and a haze of burning sand, make the district quite inaccessible.

On its borders dwell the Garamantians, a lightly clad, agile tribe of tent-dwellers subsisting mainly by the chase. These are the only people who occasionally penetrate the desert, in pursuit of game. They wait till rain falls, about the winter solstice, mitigating the excessive heat, moistening the sand, and making it just passable. Their quarry consists chiefly of wild asses, the giant ostrich that runs instead of flying, and monkeys, to which the elephant is sometimes added; these are the only creatures sufficiently proof against thirst and capable of bearing that incessant fiery sunshine. But the Garamantians, as soon as they have consumed the provisions they brought with them, instantly hurry back, in fear of the sand's recovering its heat and becoming difficult or impassable, in which case they would be trapped, and lose their lives as well as their game. For if the sun draws up the vapour, dries the ground rapidly, and has an access of heat, throwing into its rays the fresh vigour derived from that moisture which is its aliment, there is then no escape.

But all that I have yet mentioned, heat, thirst, desolation, barrenness, you will count less formidable than what I now come to, a sufficient reason in itself for avoiding that land. It is beset by all sorts of reptiles, of huge size, in enormous numbers, hideous and venomous beyond belief or cure. Some of them have burrows in the sand, others live on the surface--toads, asps, vipers, horned snakes and stinging beetles, lance-snakes, reversible snakes[85], dragons, and two kinds of scorpion, one of great size and many joints that runs on the ground, the other aerial, with gauzy wings like those of the locust, grasshopper, or bat. With the multitude of flying things like these, that part of Libya has no attraction for the traveller.

But the direst of all the reptiles bred in the sand is the dipsas or thirst-snake; it is of no great size, and resembles the viper; its bite is sharp, and the venom acts at once, inducing agonies to which there is no relief. The flesh is burnt up and mortified, the victims feel as if on fire, and yell like men at the stake. But the most overpowering of their torments is that indicated by the creature's name. They have an intolerable thirst; and the remarkable thing is, the more they drink, the more they want to drink, the appetite growing with

---

[85] The amphisbaena, supposed to have a head at each end and move either way.

what it feeds on. You will never quench their thirst, though you give them all the water in Nile or Danube; water will be fuel, as much as if you tried to put out a fire with oil.

Doctors explain this by saying that .the venom is originally thick, and gains in activity when diluted with the drink, becoming naturally more fluid and circulating more widely.

I have not seen a man in this condition, and I pray Heaven I never may behold such human sufferings; I am happy to say I have not set foot upon Libyan soil. But I have had an epitaph repeated to me, which a friend assured me he had read on the grave of a victim. My friend, going from Libya to Egypt, had taken the only practicable land route by the Great Syrtis. He there found a tomb on the beach at the sea's very edge, with a pillar setting forth the manner of death. On it a man was carved in the attitude familiar in pictures of Tantalus, standing by a lake's side scooping up water to drink; the dipsas was wound about his foot, in which its fangs were fastened, while a number of women with jars were pouring water over him. Hard by were lying eggs like those of the ostrich hunted, as I mentioned, by the Gararnantians. And then there was the epitaph, which it may be worth while to give you:

> See the envenom'd cravings Tantalus
>   Could find no thirst-assuaging charm to still,
> The cask that daughter-brood of Danaus,
>   For ever filling, might not ever fill.

There are four more lines about the eggs, and how he was bitten while taking them; but I forget how they go.

The neighbouring tribes, however, do collect and value these eggs, and not only for food; they use the empty shells for vessels and make cups of them; for, as there is nothing but sand for material, they have no pottery. A particularly large egg is a find; bisected, it furnishes two hats big enough for the human head.

Accordingly the dipsas conceals himself near the eggs, and when a man comes, crawls out and bites the unfortunate, who then goes through the experiences just described, drinking and increasing his thirst and getting no relief.

Now, gentlemen, I have not told you all this to show you I could do as well as the poet Nicander, nor yet by way of proof that I have taken some trouble with the natural history of Libyan reptiles; that would be more in the doctor's line, who must know about such things with a view to treatment. No, it is only that I am conscious (and now pray do not be offended by my going to the reptiles for my illustration)--I am conscious of the same feelings towards you as a dipsas victim has towards drink; the more I have of your company, the more of it I want; my thirst for it rages uncontrollably; I shall never have enough of this drink. And no wonder; where else could one find such clear sparkling water? You must pardon me, then, if, bitten to the soul (most agreeably and wholesomely bitten), I put my head under the fountain and gulp the liquor down. My only prayer is that the stream that flows from you may never fail; never may your willingness to listen run dry and leave me thirstily gaping! On my side there is no reason why drinking should not go on for ever; the wise Plato says that you cannot have too much of a good thing.

A WORD WITH HESIOD

Lycinus. Hesiod

Ly. As to your being a first-rate poet, Hesiod, we do not doubt that, any more than we doubt your having received the gift from the Muses, together with that laurel-branch; it is sufficiently proved by the noble inspiration that breathes in every line of your works. But there is one point on which we may be excused for feeling some perplexity. You begin by telling us that your divine gifts were bestowed upon you by Heaven in order that you might sing of the glories that have been, and tell of that which is to come. Well, now, one half of your duties you have admirably performed. You have traced back the genealogy of the Gods to Chaos and Ge and Uranus and Eros; you have specified the feminine virtues; and you have given advice to the farmer, adding complete information with reference to the Pleiads, the seasons suitable for ploughing, reaping, and sailing,--and I know not what besides. But that far diviner gift, which would have been of so much more practical utility to your readers, you do not exercise at all:

the soothsaying department is entirely overlooked. We find no parallel in your poems to those prophetic utterances which Calchas, and Telemus, and Polyidus, and Phineus--persons less favoured by the Muses than yourself--were wont to dispense freely to all applicants. Now in these circumstances, you must plead guilty to one of three charges. Either the alleged promise of the Muses to disclose the future to you was never given, and you are--excuse the expression-- a liar:

or it was given, and fulfilled, but you, niggard, have quietly pocketed the information, and refuse to impart it to them that have need:

or, thirdly, you *have* composed a number of prophetic works, but have not yet given them to the world; they are reserved for some more suitable occasion. I do not presume to suggest, as a fourth possibility, that the Muses have only fulfilled half of their promise, and revoked the other,-- which, observe, is recorded first in your poem. Now, if *you* will not enlighten me on this subject, who can? As the Gods are 'givers of good,' so you, their friends and pupils, should impart your knowledge frankly, and set our doubts at rest.

Hes. My poor friend, there is one very simple answer to all your questions:

I might tell you that not one of my poems is my own work; all is the Muses', and to them I might refer you for all that has been said and left unsaid. For what came of my own knowledge, of pasturage, of milking, of driving afield, and all that belongs to the herdsman's art, I may fairly be held responsible:

but for the Goddesses,--they give whatso they will to whom they will.-- Apart from this, however, I have the usual poet's apology. The poet, I conceive, is not to be called to account in this minute fashion, syllable by syllable. If in the fervour of composition a word slip in unawares, search not too narrowly; remember that with us metre and euphony have much to answer for; and then there are certain amplifications--certain elegances--that insinuate themselves into a verse, one scarce knows how. Sir, you would rob us of our highest prerogative, our freedom, our unfettered movement. Blind to the flowers of poetry, you are intent upon its thorns, upon those little flaws that give a handle to malicious criticism. But there! you are not the only offender, nor I the only victim:

in the trivial defects of Homer, my fellow craftsman, many a carping spirit has found material for similar hair-splitting disquisitions.--Come, now, I will meet my accuser on fair ground, face to   face. Read, fellow, in my *Works and Days*:

mark the inspired prophecies there set forth:

the doom foretold to the negligent, the success promised to him that labours aright and in due season.

> One basket shall suffice to store thy grain,

> And men shall not regard thee.

Could there be a more timely warning, balanced as it is by the prospect of abundance held out to him that follows the true method of agriculture?

Ly. Admirable; and spoken like a true herdsman. There is no doubting the divine afflatus after that:

left to yourself, you cannot so much as defend your own poems. At the same time, this is not quite the sort of thing we expect of Hesiod and the Muses combined. You see, in this particular branch of prophecy, you are quite outclassed by the farmers:

they are perfectly qualified to inform us that if the rain comes there will be a heavy crop, and that a drought, on the other hand, will inevitably be followed by scarcity; that midsummer is not a good time to begin ploughing if you wish your seed to do anything, and that you will find no grain in the ear if you reap it when it is green. Nor do we want a prophet to tell us that the sower must be followed by a labourer armed with a spade, to cover up the seed; otherwise, the birds will come and consume his prospective harvest. Call these useful suggestions, if you like:

but they are very far from my idea of prophecy. I expect a prophet to penetrate into secrets wholly hidden from our eyes:

the prophet informs Minos that he will find his son drowned in a jar of honey; he explains to the Achaeans the cause of Apollo's resentment; he specifies the precise year in which Troy will be captured. That *is* prophecy. But if the term is to be so extended, then I shall be glad to have my own claims recognized without loss of time. I undertake, without the assistance of Castalian waters, laurel-branches, or Delphian tripods, to foretell and prognosticate:

That if a man walk out on a cold morning with nothing on, he will take a severe chill; and particularly if it happens to be raining or hailing at the time. And I further prophesy:

That his chill will be accompanied by the usual fever, together with other circumstances which it would be superfluous to mention.

No, Hesiod:

your defence will not do; nor will your prophecies. But I dare say there is something in what you said at first--that you knew not what you wrote, by reason of the divine afflatus versifying within you. And that afflatus was no such great matter, either:

afflatuses should not promise more than they mean to perform.

THE SHIP:
OR, THE WISHES

Lycinus. Timolaus. Samippus. Adimantus

Ly. Said I not well? More easily shall a corpse lie mouldering in the sun, and the vulture mark it not, than any strange sight escape Timolaus, no matter though he must run all the way to Corinth at a stretch for it.--Indefatigable sightseer!

Ti. Well, Lycinus, what do you expect? One has nothing to do, and just then one hears that a great monster of an Egyptian corn-ship has put in to Piraeus. What is more, I believe you and Samippus came down on precisely the same errand.

Ly. So we did, so we did, and Adimantus with us; only he has got lost somewhere in the crowd of spectators. We came all together to the ship; and going on board you were in front, Samippus, if I remember, and Adimantus next, and I was behind, hanging on to him for dear life; he gave me a hand all up the gangway, because I had never taken my shoes off, and he had; but I saw no more of him after that, either on board or when we came ashore.

Sa. You see when it was we lost him, Lycinus? It must have been when that nice-looking boy came up from the hold, you know, with the beautiful clean linen, and his hair parted in the middle and done up in a knot behind. If I know anything of Adimantus, he no sooner saw that charming sight, than he said good-bye to the Egyptian ship-wright who was showing us round; and now stands urging his tearful suit. You know; his way; tears come natural to him in these affairs of the heart.

Ly. Well, but, Samippus, this boy was nothing great, that he should make such a conquest; Adimantus has the beauties of Athens at his beck; nice gentlemanly boys, with good Greek, on their tongues, and the mark of the gymnasium on every muscle; a man may languish under *their* rigours with some credit. As for this fellow, to say nothing of his dark skin, and protruding lips, and spindle shanks, his words came tumbling out in a heap, one on the top of another; it was Greek, of course, but the voice, the accent were Egyptian born. And then his hair:

no freeman ever had his hair tied up in a knot behind like that.

Ti. Oh, but that is a sign of noble birth in Egypt, Lycinus. All gentlemen's sons wear their hair done up till they reach manhood. It was the other way with our ancestors:

the topknot, and the golden grasshopper to keep it together, were the proper thing for old men in their time.

Sa. Very much to the point, Timolaus; you allude to the remarks in Thucydides's preface, about our old luxurious habits, as preserved in the Asiatic colonies

589

Ly. Of course! I remember now where it was we lost Adimantus. It was when we were standing all that time looking up at the mast, counting the layers of hides, and watching that marvellous fellow going up the shrouds, and running along the yards, perfectly comfortable, with just a hand on the yard-tackling.

Sa. So it was. Well, now what are we to do? Shall we wait for him here, or do you think I had better go back on board?

Ti. No, no, let us walk on; he has probably gone tearing off home, not being able to find us. Anyhow, he knows the way; he will never get lost for want of us to take care of him.

Ly. It is rather a shame, perhaps, to go off and leave one's friend to shift for himself. However, I agree, if Samippus does.

Sa. Certainly I do. We may find the gymnasium open still. --I say, though, what a size that ship was! 180 feet long, the man said, and something over a quarter of that in width; and from deck to keel, the maximum depth, through the hold, 44 feet. And then the height of the mast, with its huge yard; and what a forestay it takes to hold it! And the lofty stern with its gradual curve, and its gilded beak, balanced at the other end by the long rising sweep of the prow, and the figures of her name-goddess, Isis, on either side. As to the other ornamental details, the paintings and the scarlet topsail, I was more struck by the anchors, and the capstans and windlasses, and the stern cabins. The crew was like a small army. And they were saying she carried as much corn as would feed every soul in Attica for a year. And all depends for its safety on one little old atomy of a man, who controls that great rudder with a mere broomstick of a tiller! He was pointed out to me; Heron was his name, I think; a woolly-pated fellow, half-bald.

Ti. He is a wonderful hand at it, so the crew say; a very Proteus in sea-cunning. Did they tell you how he brought them here, and all their adventures? how they were saved by a star?

Ly. No; you can tell us about that now.

Ti. I had it from the master, a nice intelligent fellow to talk to. They set sail with a moderate wind from Pharus, and sighted Acamas on the seventh day. Then a west wind got up, and they were carried as far east as Sidon. On their way thence they came in for a heavy gale, and the tenth day brought them through the Straits to the Chelidon Isles; and there they very nearly went to the bottom. I have sailed past the Chelidons myself, and I know the sort of seas you get there, especially if the wind is SW. by S.; it is just there, of course, that the division takes place between the Lycian and Pamphylian waters; and the surge caused by the numerous currents gets broken at the headland, whose rocks have been sharpened by the action of the water till they are like razors; the result is a stupendous crash of waters, the waves often rising to the very top of the crags. This was the kind of thing they found themselves in for, according to the master,--and on a pitch dark night! However, the Gods were moved by their distress, and showed them a fire that enabled them to identify the Lycian coast; and a bright star--either Castor or Pollux--appeared at the masthead, and guided the ship into the open sea on their left; just in time, for she was making straight for the cliff. Having once lost their proper course, they sailed on through the Aegean, bearing up against the Etesian winds, until they came to anchor in Piraeus yesterday, being the seventieth day of the voyage; you see how far they had been carried out of their way; whereas if they had taken Crete on their right, they would have doubled Malea, and been at Rome by this time.

Ly. A pretty pilot this Heron, and no mistake, to get so far out in his reckoning; a man after Nereus's heart!--But look! that is surely Adimantus?

Ti. Adimantus it is. Let us hail him. Adimantus! . . . Son of Strombichus! . . . of the deme of Myrrhinus! He must be offended with us, or else he is deaf; it is certainly he.

Ly. I can make him out quite clearly now; his cloak, his walk, his cropped head. Let us mend our pace, and catch him up.--We shall have to pull you by the cloak, and compel you to turn round, Adimantus; you will take no notice of our shouts. You seem like one rapt in contemplation; you are pondering on matters of no light import?

Ad. Oh, it is nothing serious. An idle fancy, that came to me as I walked, and engrossed my attention, so that I never heard you.

Ly. And the fancy? Tell us without reserve, unless it is a very delicate matter. And even if it is, you know, we have all been through the Mysteries; we can keep a secret.

Ad. No, I had rather not tell you; you would think it so childish.

Ly. Can it be a love affair? Speak on; *those* mysteries too are not unknown to us; we have been initiated in full torchlight.

Ad. Oh dear, no; nothing of that kind.--No; I was making myself an imaginary present of a fortune--that 'vain, deluding joy,' as it has been called; I had just reached the pinnacle of luxury and affluence when you arrived.

Ly. Then all I have to say is, 'Halves!' Come, out with your wealth! We are Adimantus's friends:

let us share his superfluities.

Ad. Well, I lost sight of you at once on the ship--the moment I had got you safely up, Lycinus. I was measuring the thickness of the anchor, and you disappeared somewhere. However, I went on and saw everything, and then I asked one of the sailors how much the vessel brought in to her owner in an average year. Three thousand pounds, he said, was the lowest reckoning. So afterwards, on the way back, I was thinking:

Suppose some God took it into his head to make *me* a present of that ship; what a glorious life I should have of it, and my friends too! Sometimes I could make the trip myself, at other times I could send my men. On the strength of that three thousand, I had already built myself a house, nicely situated just above the Poecile--I would have nothing more to say to my ancestral abode on the banks of the Ilissus,--and was in treaty for my wardrobe and slaves and chariots and stable. And now behold me on board, the envy of every passenger, and the terror of my I crew, who regarded me as next thing to a king; I was getting matters shipshape, and taking a last look at the port in the distance, when up comes Lycinus, capsizes the vessel, just as she is scudding before a wishing wind, and sends all my wealth to the bottom.

Ly. Well, you are a man of spirit:

lay hands on me, and away with me to the governor, for the buccaneer that I am. A flagrant case of piracy; on the high roads, too, between Athens and Piraeus. Stay, though; perhaps we can compound the matter. What do you say to *five* ships, larger and finer ones than your Egyptian; above all, warranted not to sink?--each to bring you, shall we say, five cargoes of corn per annum? Though I foresee that you will be the most unbearable of shipowners when you have got them. The possession of this one made you deaf to our salutations; give you five more--three-masters all of them, and imperishable--and the result is obvious:

you will not know your friends when you see them. And so, good voyage to your worship; we will establish ourselves at Piraeus, and question all who land from Egypt or Italy, as to whether they came across Adimantus's great ship, the Isis, anywhere.

Ad. There now; that was why I refused to tell you about it at first; I knew you would make a jest and a laughing-stock of my Wish. So now I shall stop here till you have got on ahead, and then I shall go another voyage on my ship. I like talking to my sailors much better than being jeered at by you.

Ly. That will never do. We shall hang about, and go on board too.

Ad. I shall go on first, and haul up the gangway.

Ly. Then we shall swim across and board you. You seem to think there will be no difficulty about your acquiring these great ships without building them or paying for them; why should not *we* obtain from the Gods the privilege of swimming for an indefinite distance without getting tired? You made no objection to our company the other day, you know, when we all went across together to Aegina, to see the rites of Hecate, in that tiny little boat, at sixpence a head; and now you are furious at the idea of our going on board with you; you go on ahead, and haul up the gangway. You forget yourself, my Shipowner; you wax fat and kick; you withhold from Nemesis her due. See what comes of houses in fashionable quarters, and great retinues. Well, please remember to bring us back some of those exquisite smoked fish from the Nile, or some myrrh from Canopus, or an ibis from Memphis;--I suppose you would scarcely have room for a pyramid?

Ti. That is enough, Lycinus. Spare his blushes. You have quite swamped his ship; she is laughter-logged, and can weather it no longer. Now, we have still some distance before us; let us break it up into four parts, and each have so many furlongs, in which he may demand of the Gods what he will. This will lighten our journey, and amuse us into the bargain; we shall revel in a delightful waking dream of unlimited prosperity; for each of us will have full control of his own Wish, and it will be understood that the Gods must grant everything, however impracticable. Above all, it will give us an idea who would make the best use of the supposed wealth; we shall see what kind of a man it would have made of him.

Sa. A good idea. I am your man; I undertake to wish when my turn comes. We need not ask Adimantus whether

he agrees; he has one foot on board already. We must have Lycinus's sanction, however.

Ly. Why, let us to our wealth, if so it must be. Where all is prosperity, I would not be thought to cast an evil eye.

Ad. Who begins?

Ly. You; and then Samippus, and then Timolaus. I shall only want the last hundred yards or so before the Gate for mine, and a quick hundred, too.

Ad. Well, I stick to my ship still; only I shall wish some more things, as it is allowed. May the God of Luck say Yes to all! I will have the ship, and everything in her; the cargo, the merchants, the women, the sailors, and anything else that is particularly nice to have.

Sa. You forget one thing you have on board--

Ad. Oh, the boy with the hair; yes, him too. And instead of the present cargo of wheat, I will have the same bulk of coined gold, all sovereigns.

Ly. Hullo! The ship will sink. Wheat and gold to the same bulk are not of the same weight.

Ad. Now, don't make envious remarks. When your turn comes, you can have the whole of Fames turned into a mass of gold if you like, and I shall say nothing.

Ly. Oh, I was only thinking of your safety. I don't want all hands to go down with the golden cargo. It would not matter so much about us, but the poor boy would be drowned; he can't swim.

Ti. Oh, that will be all right. The dolphins will pick him up and get him to shore. Shall a paltry musician be rescued by them for a song's sake, a lifeless Melicertes be carried on their backs to the Isthmus, and Adimantus's latest purchase find never an amorous dolphin at his need?

Ad. Timolaus, you are just as bad as Lycinus, with your superfluous sneers. You ought to know better; it was all your idea.

Ti. You should make it more plausible. Find a treasure under your bed; that would save unloading the gold, and getting it up to town.

Ad. Oh yes! It shall be dug up from under the Hermes in our court; a thousand bushels of coined gold. Well; my first thought has been for a handsome house,--'the homestead first and chiefest,' says Hesiod; and my purchases in the neighbourhood are now complete; there remains my property at Delphi, and the sea-front at Eleusis; and a little something at the Isthmus (I might want to stop there for the games); and the plain of Sicyon; and in short every scrap of land in the country where there is nice shade, or a good stream, or fine fruit; I reserve them all. We will eat off gold plate; and our cups shall weigh 100 lb. apiece; I will have none of the flimsy ware that appears on Echecrates's table.

Ly. I dare say! And how is your cupbearer going to hand you a thing of that weight, when he has filled it? And how will you like taking it from him? It would tax the muscles of a Sisyphus, let alone a cupbearer's.

Ad. Oh, don't keep on picking holes in my Wish. I shall have tables and couches of solid gold, if I like; and servants too, if you say another word.

Ly. Well, take care, or you will be like Midas, with nothing but gold to eat and drink; and die of a right royal hunger, a martyr to superabundance.

Ad. Your turn will come presently, Lycinus, and then you can be as realistic as you like. To proceed:

I must have purple raiment, and every luxury, and sleep as late as I like; with friends to come and pay court to me, and every one bowing down to the ground; and they will all have to wait about at my doors from early morning-- the great Cleaenetus and Democritus among them; oh yes, and when they come and try to get in before every one else, seven great foreign giants of porters shall slam the door in their faces, just as theirs do now. And as soon as I feel inclined, I shall peep out like the rising sun, and some of that set I shall simply ignore; but if there is some poor man there, like me before I got the treasure, I shall have a kind word for him:

'You must come and have dinner with me, after your bath; you know my hour.' The great men will all choke with envy when they see my chariots and horses, and my handsome slaves--two thousand choice ones, of all ages. Well, so the dinner service is to be of gold,--no silver for me, it is much too cheap-- and I shall have smoked fish from Spain; wine from Italy; oil from Spain again; our own honey, but it must be clarified without heat; delicacies from all quarters; wild boars; hares; all sorts of birds, pheasants, Indian peacocks, Numidian capons; and special cooks for everything, artists in sauce and seasoning. And when I call for a beaker or goblet to pledge any one, he shall take it home with him. As to the people who now pass for rich, they, I need not say, will be paupers to me. Dionicus will give up displaying his silver plate and cup in processions, when he sees that my slaves eat off nothing but silver. I should set apart something for the public service, too; a monthly distribution of £4 a head to citizens, and half that to foreigners; and the most beautiful theatres and baths you can imagine; and the sea should be brought along a great canal up to the Double Gates, and there would be a harbour close by, so that my ship could be seen lying at anchor from the Ceramicus. And of you who are my friends, Samippus should have twenty bushels of coined gold paid out to him by my steward; Timolaus, five quarts; and Lycinus one quart, strict measure, because he talks too much, and sneers at my Wish. That is how I would live; revelling in every luxury without stint, superlatively rich. I have done. Hermes bring it all to pass!

Ly. Have you realized on what a slender thread all this wealth depends? Once let that break, and all is gone; your treasure is but dust and ashes.

594

Ad. How so?

Ly. Why, it is not clear how long this life of affluence is to last. Who knows? You may be sitting one day at your solid gold table, just putting out your hand for a slice of that peacock or capon, when, at that very moment, off flies *animula vagula*, and Adimantus after her, leaving his all a prey to crows and vultures. Need I enumerate instances? There have been rich men who have died before they knew what it was to be rich; others have lived to be robbed of their possessions by some malign spirit who waits upon wealth. The cases of Croesus and Polycrates are familiar to you. Their riches were greater far than yours; yet at one stroke they lost all. But leaving them out of the case, do you consider that you have good security for the continuance of your health? Look at the number of rich men whose lives are made miserable by their infirmities:

some are crippled, others are blind, others have internal diseases. Say what you will, I am sure that for double your wealth you would not consent to be a weakling like rich Phanomachus; not to mention the artful designs, the robberies, the envy, and the unpopularity that are inseparable from wealth. See what troubles your treasure will land you in!

Ad. You are always against me, Lycinus. I shall cancel your quart now, for this last piece of spite.

Ly. That is so like a rich man, to draw back and break his promise; a good beginning! Now, Samippus, it is your turn to wish.

Sa. Well, I am a landsman; I come from Mantinea, you know, in Arcadia; so I shall not ask for a ship; I could make no show with that in my country. Nor will I insult the generosity of the Gods by asking for so much gold down. I understand there is no boon so great, but their power and Timolaus's law can compass it; we are to wish away without ceremony, he says,--they will refuse us nothing. Well then, I wish to be a king. But I will not succeed to a hereditary throne, like Alexander of Macedon, Ptolemy, Mithridates and the rest of them. No, I will begin as a brigand, in a troop of thirty or so, brisk companions ready at need. Then little by little we shall grow to be 300; then 1,000, and presently 10,000; and at last we shall total 50,000 heavy-armed, and 5,000 horse. I shall be elected their chieftain by general consent, having shown myself to be the best qualified for the command and conduct of their affairs. Already, you see, I have the advantage of ordinary kings:

I am elected to the command on my own merits; I am no hereditary monarch, reaping the fruits of my predecessor's labours. That would be like Adimantus, with his treasure; but there is much more satisfaction in knowing that your power is the work of your own hands.

Ly. Now really, this *is* a Wish, and no mistake; the very acme of blessedness; to be commander of that vast company, chosen on your own merits by 50,000 men! A genius, a master! of strategy and king-craft has been quietly growing up in Mantinea, and we not a whit the wiser! But I interrupt. Proceed, O King, at the head of your troops; dispose your forces, infantry and cavalry. Whither, I wonder, goes this mighty host, issuing from Arcadia? Who are to be the first victims?

Sa. I'll tell you; or you can come with us, if you like. I will put you in command of the cavalry.

Ly. Why, as to that, your Majesty, I am much beholden to you for the honour; accept my most oriental prostrations; and manuflexions. But, with all respect to your diadem, and the perpendicularity of your tiara, you would do well to take one of these stout fellows instead. I am sadly deficient in horsemanship; indeed, I was never on a horse in my life. I am afraid that when the trumpet sounded to advance, I might fall off, and be trampled, in the general confusion, under some of those numerous hoofs. Or again, my spirited charger might get the bit between his teeth, and carry me right into the midst of the enemy. If I am to remain in possession of saddle and bridle, I shall have to be tied on.

Ad. All right, Samippus, I will command the cavalry; Lycinus can have the right wing. I have the first claim on you, after all those bushels of sovereigns.

Sa. Let us see what my troopers think of you for a leader. All in favour of Adimantus, hold up their hands.

Ad. All hands go up, look.

Sa. You command the cavalry, then, and Lycinus the right wing. Timolaus will have the left wing. I am in the centre, like the Persian monarchs when they take the field in person. Well; after due observance paid to Zeus, king of kings, we advance along the hill-road to Corinth. Greece being now subjugated (for no resistance will be offered to our enormous host, we shall merely walk over), we get our troops on to the galleys, and the horses on to the transports (arrangements having been made at Cenchreae for the requisite number of vessels, with adequate provision and so on), cross the Aegean, and land in Ionia. Here we sacrifice to Artemis, and finding the various cities unfortified, take easy possession of them, put in governors, and march on in the direction of Syria. On the way we pass through Caria, Lycia, Pamphylia, Pisidia, the mountains and sea-board of Cilicia, and so at last reach the Euphrates.

Ly. If your Majesty has no objection, I will stay behind and be Pacha of Greece. I am a poor-spirited fellow; to go all that way from home is not to my liking at all. You evidently meditate an attack upon the Parthians and Armenians, warlike folk, and unerring shots. Let some one else have the right wing, and let me play Antipater here at home. Some arrow, from the walls of Susa or Bactra, might find a chink in my armour, and let daylight through me; and there would be a melancholy end of my strategic career.

Sa. Oh coward, to desert your post! The penalty for that is decapitation.--We are now at the Euphrates, and have thrown our bridge across. All is secured in our rear by the subordinates whom I have placed in charge of the various districts; officers have also been dispatched for the reduction of

Phoenicia and Palestine, and, subsequently, of Egypt. Now, Lycinus, you cross first, with the right wing; I next, and Timolaus after me. Last comes Adimantus with the cavalry. We have now crossed Mesopotamia, and no enemy has yet shown himself; town after town has voluntarily given itself up; we reach Babylon; we enter its gates without warning, and the city is ours. The Persian king meanwhile is at Ctesiphon. He hears of our approach and withdraws to Seleucia, where he proceeds to muster his full strength of cavalry, bowmen, and slingers. Our scouts report that the force already collected numbers something like a million, including two hundred thousand mounted bowmen; and the Armenian, Caspian, and Bactrian contingents are still to come; only the neighbouring districts, the suburbs, as it were, of the empire, have contributed as yet. With such ease does the Persian monarch raise a million of men! It is now time for us to think what we are to do next.

Ad. Well, I say that you should all march for Ctesiphon, leaving me to secure Babylon with the cavalry.

Sa. Are you going to show the white feather too, Adimantus, now that the danger is near?--Timolaus, what is your advice?

Ti. We must march upon the enemy in full force, before they have had time to strengthen their hands with the reinforcements that are pouring in from all quarters; let us engage them whilst they are still making their several ways to Seleucia.

Sa. There is something in that. What do you recommend, Lycinus?

Ly Well, we have all been on our legs till we are tired out; there was the early walk down, and we must be a good three miles now on the way home; and the sun is extremely powerful--it is just about noon:

how would it be to sit down for a bit on that ruined column under the olive trees, till we are sufficiently restored to complete the journey?

Sa. O *sancta simplicitas!* Did you think that you were at Athens all this time? You are in the plain before Babylon, in a great camp,--engaged in a council of war.

Ly. Why, so I am. I forgot; we are drunk, of course; it is against rules to talk sense.

Sa. Well, now, please, to the attack. Bear yourselves gallantly in this hour of danger:

be not less than Greeks. See, the enemy are upon us. Our watchword is 'Lord of Battles.' The moment the trumpet sounds, raise the war-cry, clash spear upon shield, and lose no time in coming to close quarters, out of danger of their arrows; otherwise the bowmen will give us a warm reception. No sooner do we get to work than Timolaus with his left wing routs their right; in the centre the conflict is even; for I have the native Persian troops against me, and the king is in their midst. The whole strength of their cavalry bears down upon our right wing; play the man, therefore, Lycinus; and encourage your troops to receive the charge.

Ly. Just my luck! Every single trooper of them is making straight for me, as if I were the only foeman worthy of their steel. If they go on like this, I think I shall have to turn tail and make for the gymnasium, and leave you to fight it out.

Sa. Nonsense; you have almost beaten them already. Now, observe, the king challenges me to single combat; honour forbids that I should draw back; I accordingly engage him.

Ly. To be sure; and are promptly wounded. No king should omit to receive a wound, when empire is at stake.

Sa. Well, yes; I do get just a scratch; it is well out of sight, however, so the scar will be no disfigurement. On the other hand, observe the fury of my charge:

I send my spear through horse and rider at one stroke; cut off the royal head; remove the diadem therefrom, and am saluted as king with universal prostrations. That applies only to the barbarians; from you who are Greeks I shall have merely the usual title of commander-in-chief. You may imagine the rest:

the Samippopolises I shall found, the cities I shall storm and destroy for slighting my supremacy. The wealthy Cydias will come in for the largest share of my attention; I have not forgotten his gradual encroachments on my property, in the days when we were neighbours.

Ly. Stop there, Samippus; after such a victory, it is high time you retired to Babylon, to keep festival. Three-quarters of a mile is your allowance of dominion, as I reckon it. Timolaus now selects his wish.

Sa. Well, tell me what you think of mine?

Ly. It seems to me, most sapient monarch, to involve considerably more trouble and annoyance than that of Adimantus. While he lives luxuriously, and hands about gold cups--hundred-pounders--to his guests, you are sustaining wounds in single combat. From morning till night, all is worry and anxiety with you. You have not only the public enemies to fear:

there are the numberless conspiracies, the envy and hatred of your courtiers; you have flatterers enough, but not one friend; their seeming goodwill is the work of fear or ambition. As to enjoyment, you can never dream of such a thing. You have to content yourself with glory and gold embroidery and purple; with the victor's garland, and the king's bodyguard; beyond these there is nothing but intolerable toil and continual discomfort. You are either negotiating with ambassadors, or judging cases, or issuing mandates to your subjects. Here a tribe revolts:

there an enemy invades. All is fear and suspicion. The world may think you happy; but you know better. And surely it is a very humiliating circumstance that you should be apt to fall ill, just like ordinary people? Fevers seem not to understand that you are a king; nor does Death stand in any awe of your bodyguard; when the fancy takes him, he comes, and carries you off lamenting; what cares he for the diadem? Fallen from your high estate, dragged from your kingly throne, you go the same road as the rest of us; there is no 'benefit of royalty' among the timid flock of shades. You leave behind you upon earth some massive tomb, some stately column, some pyramid of noble outline; but it will be too late then for vanity to enjoy these things; and the statues and temples, the offerings of obsequious cities, nay, your great name itself, all will presently decay, and vanish, and be of no further account. Take it at the best; let all endure for ages:

what will it profit your senseless clay? And it is for this that you are to live uneasy days, ever scheming, fearing, toiling!--Timolaus, the wish is with you. We shall expect better things from your judgement and experience.

Ti. See if you can find anything questionable or reprehensible in what I propose. As to treasure-heaps and bushels of coin, I will have none of them; nor monarchy, with the wars and terrors it involves. You rightly censured such things, precarious as they are, exposed to endless machinations, and bringing with them more vexation than pleasure. No; my wish is that Hermes should appear and present me with certain rings. possessed of certain powers. One should ensure its wearer continual health and strength, invulnerability, insensibility to pain. Another, like that of Gyges, should make me invisible. A third should give me the strength to pick up with ease a weight that ten thousand men could barely move. Then I must be able to fly to any height above the earth; a ring for that, Again, I shall want to be able to put people to sleep upon occasion and at my approach all doors must immediately fly open; all bolts yield, all bars withdraw. One ring may secure these points. There remains yet one, the most precious of them all; for with it on my finger I am the desire of every woman and boy, ay, of whole nations; not one escapes me; I am in all hearts, on all tongues. Women will hang themselves for the vehemence of their passion, boys will go mad. Happy will those few be reckoned on whom I cast a glance; and those whom I scorn will pine away for grief. Hyacinth, Hylas, Phaon, will sink into insignificance beside me. And all this I hold on no brief tenure; the limitations of human life are not for me. I shall live a thousand years, ever renewing my youth, and casting off the slough of old age every time I get to seventeen.--With these rings I shall lack nothing. All that is another's is mine:

for can I not open his doors, put his guards to sleep, and walk in unperceived? Instead of sending to India or to the Hyperboreans for their curiosities, their treasures, their wines or their delicacies, I can fly thither myself, and take my fill of all. The phoenix of India, the griffin, that winged monster, are sights unknown to others:

I shall see them. I alone shall know the sources of the Nile, the lands that are uninhabited, the Antipodes, if such there be, dwelling on the other side of the earth. Nay, I may learn the nature of the stars, the moon, the sun itself; for fire cannot harm me. And think of the joy of announcing the Olympian victor's name in Babylon, on the day of the contest! or of having one's breakfast in Syria, and one's dinner in Italy! Had I an enemy, I could be even with him, thanks to my invisibility, by cracking his skull with a rock; my friends, on the other hand, I might subsidize with showers of gold as they lay asleep. Have we some overweening tyrant, who insults us with his wealth? I carry him off a couple of miles or so, and drop him over the nearest precipice. I could enjoy the company of my beloved without let or hindrance, going secretly in after I had put every one else in the house to sleep. What a thing it would be to hover overhead, out of range, and watch contending armies! If I liked, I could take the part of the vanquished, send their conquerors to sleep, rally the fugitives and give them the victory. In short, the affairs of humanity would be my diversion; all things would be in my power; mankind would account me a God. Here is the perfection of happiness, secure and indestructible, backed as it is by health and longevity. What faults have you to find, Lycinus?

Ly. None; it is not safe to thwart a man who has wings, and the strength of ten thousand. I have only one question to ask. Did you ever, among all the nations you passed in your flight, meet with a similar case of mental aberration? a man of mature years riding about on a finger-ring, moving whole mountains with a touch; bald and snub-nosed, yet the desire of all eyes? Ah, there was another point. What is to prevent one single ring from doing all the work? Why go about with your left hand loaded,--a ring to every finger? nay, they overflow; the right hand must be forced into the service. And you have left out the most important ring of all, the one to stop your drivelling at this absurd rate. Perhaps you consider that a stiffish dose of hellebore would serve the turn?

Ti. Now, positively, Lycinus, you must have a try yourself. You find fault with everybody else; this time we should like to hear your version of a really unexceptionable wish.

Ly. What do I want with a wish? Here we are at the gates. What with the valiant Samippus's single combat at Babylon, and your breakfasts in Syria and dinners in Italy, you have used up my ground between you; and you are heartily welcome. I have no fancy for a short-lived visionary wealth, with the humiliating sequel of barley-bread and no butter. That will be your fate presently. Your bliss and your wealth will take wings; you will wake from your charming dreams of treasure and diadems, to find that your domestic arrangements are of quite another kind, like the actors who take the king's part in tragedies;--their late majesties King Agamemnon and King Creon usually return to very short commons on leaving the theatre. Some depression, some discontent at your existing arrangements, is to be expected on the occasion. You will be the worst off, Timolaus. Your flying-machine will come to grief, like that of Icarus; you will descend from the skies, and foot it on the ground; and all those rings will slip off and be lost. As for me, I am content with the exquisite amusement afforded me by your various wishes; I would not exchange it for all the treasure in the world, Babylon included. And you call yourselves philosophers!

DIALOGUES OF THE HETAERAE

I

Glycera. Thais

Gly. Thais, that Acarnanian soldier, who used to be so fond of Abrotonum, and then fell in love with me--he was decorated, and wore a military cloak--do you know the man I mean? I suppose you have forgotten him?

Th. Oh no, dear, I know; why, he shared our table last harvest festival. Well? you look as if you had something to tell me about him.

Gly. That wicked Gorgona (such a *friend* of mine, to be sure!)--she has stolen him away from me.

Th. What! he has given you up, and taken her in your place?

Gly. Yes, dear; isn't it *horrid* of her?

Th. Well, Glycera darling, it is wicked, of course; but it is not very surprising; it is what all we poor girls do. You mustn't be too much vexed; I shouldn't blame her, if I were you; Abrotonum never blamed you about him, you know; and you were friends, too. But *I* cannot think what he *finds* in her; where are his eyes? has he never found out how thin her hair is? what a lot of forehead she shows! and her lips! all livid; they might be a dead woman's; and that scraggy neck, veined all over; and what an amount of nose! I grant you she is tall and straight; and she has quite a nice smile.

Gly. Oh, Thais, you don't think it was her *looks* caught him. Don't you know? her mother Chrysarium is a witch; she knows Thessalian charms, and can draw down the moon; they do say she flies o' nights. It was she bewitched him with drugs in his drink, and now they are making their harvest out of him.

Th. Ah well, dear, you will get a harvest out of some one else; never mind him.

II

Myrtium. Pamphilus. Doris

Myr. Well, Pamphilus? So I hear you are to marry Phido the shipmaster's daughter,--if you have not done so already! And this is the end of your vows and tears! All is over and forgotten! And I so near my time! Yes, that is all I have to thank my lover for; that, and the prospect of having a child to bring up; and you know what that means to us poor girls. I mean to keep the child, especially if it is a boy:

it will be some comfort to me to call him after you; and perhaps some day you will be sorry, when he comes to reproach you for betraying his poor mother. I can't say much for the lady's looks. I saw her only the other day, with her mother, at the Thesmophoria; little did I know then that she was to rob me of my Pamphilus! Hadn't you better see what she is like first? Take a good look at her eyes; and try not to mind the colour, and the cast (she has such a squint!). Or no:

there is no need for you to see her:

you have seen Phido; you know what a face *he* has.

Pa. How much more nonsense are you going to talk about shipowners and marriages? What do I know about brides, ugly or pretty? If you mean Phido of Alopece, I never knew he had a grown-up daughter at all. Why, now I think of it, he is not even on speaking terms with my father. They were at law not long ago--something about a shipping contract. He owed my father a talent, I think it was, and refused to pay; so he was had up before the Admiralty Court, and my father never got paid in full, after all, so he said. Do you suppose if I wanted to marry I should pass over Demeas's daughter in favour of Phido's? Demeas was general last year, and she is my cousin on the mother's side. Who has been telling you all this? Is it just a cobweb spun in that jealous little brain of yours?

Myr. Pamphilus! You mean to say you are not going to be married?

Pa. Are you mad, or what is the matter with you? We did not have much to drink yesterday.

Myr. Ask Doris; it is all her fault. I sent her out to buy some wool, and to offer up prayer to Artemis for me. And she said that she met Lesbia, and Lesbia------Doris, tell him what Lesbia said, unless you invented it all yourself.

Dor. May I die, miss, if I said a word more than the truth! Just by the town-hall Lesbia met me, and 'Doris,' says she, smiling, 'your young gentleman is to marry Phido's daughter. And if you don't believe me,' says she, 'look up their street, and you will see everything crowned with garlands, and a fine bustle going on; flutes playing, and people singing the wedding-song'

Pa. Well; and you did?

Dor. That I did, sir; and it was all as Lesbia had said.

Pa. Ah, now I see! You have told your mistress nothing but the truth; and there was some ground for what Lesbia told you. However, it is a false alarm. The wedding is not at our house. I remember now. When I went back home yesterday, after leaving you, 'Pamphilus,' said my mother, here is neighbour Aristaenetus's son, Charmides, who is no older than you, just going to marry and settle down:

when are *you* going to turn over a new leaf? ' And then I dropped off to sleep. I went out early this morning, so that I saw nothing of all that Doris has seen. If you doubt my word, Doris can go again; and look more carefully this time, Doris; mark the house, not the street only, and you will find that the garlands are next door.

Myr. I breathe again! Pamphilus, if it had been true, I should have killed myself!

Pa. True, indeed! Am I mad, that I should forget Myrtium, so soon to become the mother of my child?

III

Philinna. Her Mother

Mother. You must be mad, Philinna; what *was* the matter with you at the dinner last night? Diphilus was in tears this morning when he came and told me how he had been treated. You were tipsy, he said, and made an exhibition of yourself, dancing when he asked you not to; then you kissed his friend Lamprias, and when Diphilus did not like that, you left him and went and put your arms round Lamprias; and he choking with rage all the time. And afterwards you would not go near him, but let him cry by himself, and kept singing and teasing him.

Phi. Ah, mother, he never told you how *he* behaved; if you knew how rude he was, you would not take his part. He neglected me and made up to Thais, Lamprias's girl, before Lamprias came. I was angry, and let him see what I thought of him, and then he took hold of Thais's ear, bent her neck back and gave her--oh, such a kiss! I thought it would never end. So I began to cry; but he only laughed, and kept whispering to her--about me, of course; Thais was looking at me and smiling. However, when they heard Lamprias coming, and had had enough of each other at last, I did take my place by him all the same, not to give him an excuse for a fuss afterwards. It was Thais got up and danced first, showing her ankles ever so much, as if no one else had pretty ones. And when she stopped, Lamprias never said a word, but Diphilus praised her to the skies--such perfect time! such varied steps! foot and music always right; and what a lovely ankle! and so on, and so on; it might have been the *Sosandra* of Calamis he was complimenting, and not Thais; what she is really like, *you* know well enough. And how she insulted me, too! 'If some one is not ashamed of her spindle-shanks,' she said, 'she will get up and dance now.' Well, that is all, mammy; of course I did get up and dance. What was I to do? take it quietly and make her words seem true and let her be queen?

Mother. You are too touchy, my lass; you should have taken no notice. But go on.

Phi. Well, the others applauded, but Diphilus lay on his back and looked up at the ceiling, till I was tired and gave up. Mother. But what about kissing Lamprias? is that true? and going across and embracing him? Well, why don't you speak? Those are things I cannot forgive.

Phi. I wanted to pay him out.

Mother. And then not sitting near him! singing while he was in tears! Think how poor we are, girl; you forget how much we have had from him, and what last winter would have been if Aphrodite had not sent him to us.

Phi. I dare say! and I am to let him outrage my feelings just for that?

Mother. Oh, be as angry as you like, but no tit for tat. You ought to know that if a lover's feelings are outraged his love ends, and he finds out his folly. You have always been too hard on the lad; pull too tight, and the rope breaks, you know.

IV

Melitta. Bacchis

Me. Bacchis, don't you know any of those old women--there are any number of them about, 'Thessalians,' they call them--they have incantations, you know, and they can make a man in love with you, no matter how much he

603

hated you before? Do go and bring me one, there's a dear! I'd give the clothes off my back, jewellery and all, to see Charinus here again, and to have him hate Simiche as he hates me at this moment.

Ba. Melitta! You mean to tell me that Charinus has gone off after Simiche, and that after making his people so angry because he wouldn't marry the heiress, all for your sake? She was to have brought him five talents, so they said. I have not forgotten what you told me about that.

Me. Oh, that is all over now; I have not had a glimpse of him for the last five days. No; he and Simiche are with his friend Pammenes enjoying themselves.

Ba. Poor darling! But it can't have been a trifle that drove him away: what was it all about?

Me. I don't know exactly. All I can say is, that he came back the other day from Piraeus (his father had sent him there to collect some money), and wouldn't even look at me! I ran to meet him, expecting him to take me in his arms, instead of which he pushed me away! 'Go to Hermotimus the shipowner,' he said; 'go and read what is written on the column in the Ceramicus; you will find your name there, and his.' Hermotimus? column? what do you mean?' said I. But he would tell me nothing more; he went to bed without any dinner, and never gave me so much as a look. I tried everything:

I lavished all my endearments on him, and did all I could to make him look at me. Nothing would soften him:

all he said was, 'If you keep on bothering, I shall go away this minute, I don't care what time it is.'

Ba. But you *did* know Hermotimus, I suppose?

Me. My dear, if I ever so much as heard of a Hermotimus who was a ship-owner, may I be more wretched than I am now!--Next morning, at cock-crow, Charinus got up, and went off. I remembered his saying something about my name being written up in the Ceramicus, so I sent Acis to have a look; and all she found was just this, chalked up close by the Dipylus, on the right as you come in:

Melitta loves Hermotimus; and again a little lower down:

Hermotimus the ship-owner loves Melitta.

Ba. Ah, mischievous boys! I see what it is! Some one must have written it up to tease Charinus, knowing how jealous he is. And he took it all in at once! I must speak to him if I see him anywhere. He is a mere child, quite unsophisticated.

Me. If you see him, yes:

but you are not likely to. He has shut himself up with Simiche; his people have been asking for him, they think he is here still. No, Bacchis, I want one of those old women; she would put all to rights.

Ba. Well, love, I know a capital witch; she comes from Syria, such a brisk, vigorous old thing! Once when Phanias had quarrelled with me in the

604

same way, all about nothing, she brought us together again, after four whole months; I had quite given hire up, but her spells drew him back.

Me. What was her fee? do you remember

Ba. Oh, she was most reasonable:

one drachma, and a loaf of bread. Then you have to provide salt, of course, and sulphur, and a torch, and seven pennies. And besides this, you must mix her a bowl of wine, which she has to drink all by herself; and then there must be something belonging to the man, his coat, or his shoes, or a lock of hair, or something.

Me. I have got his shoes.

Ba. She hangs them up on a peg, and fumigates them with the sulphur, throwing a little salt into the fire, and muttering both your names. Then she brings out her magic wheel, and spins it, and rattles off an incantation, such horrid, outlandish words! Well, she had scarcely finished, when; sure enough, in came Phanias; Phoebis (that was the girl he was with) had begged and implored him not to go, and his friends declared it was a shame; but the spell was too strong for them. Oh yes, and she taught me a splendid charm against Phoebis. I was to mark her footsteps, and rub out the last of them, putting my right foot into her left footprint, and my left into her right; and then I was to say:

My foot on thy foot; I trample thee down! I did it exactly as she told me.

Me. Oh, Bacchis, dear, do be quick and fetch the witch. Acis, you see to the bread and sulphur and things.

VII

Musarium. Her Mother

Mother. Well, child, if we get another gallant like Chaereas, we must make some offerings; the earthly Aphrodite shall have a white kid, the heavenly one in the Gardens a heifer, and our lady of windfalls a garland. How well off we shall be, positively rolling in wealth! You see how much this boy brings in; not an obol, not a dress, not a pair of shoes, not a box of ointment, has he ever given you; it is all professions and promises and distant prospects; always, *if* my father *should------*, and I *should* inherit, everything *would* be yours. And according to you, he swears you shall be his wife.

Mu. Oh yes, mother, he swore it, by the two Goddesses[86] and Polias.

Mother. And you believe it, no doubt. So much so that the other day, when he had a subscription to pay and nothing to pay with, you gave him your ring without asking me, and the price of it went in drink. Another time it was the pair of Ionian necklaces that Praxias the Chian captain got made in Ephesus and brought you; two darics apiece they weighed; a club-dinner with

---

[86] Demeter and Persephone.

the men of his year it was that time. As for shirts and linen, those are trifles not worth mention. A mighty catch he has been, to be sure!

Mu. He is so handsome with his smooth chin; and he loves me, and cries as he tells me so; and he is the son of Laches the Areopagite and Dinomache; and we shall be his *real* wife and mother-in-law, you know; we have great expectations, if only the old man would go to bye-bye.

Mother. So when we want shoes, and the shoemaker expects to be paid, we are to tell him we have no money, 'but take a few expectations.' And the baker the same. And on rent-day we shall ask the man to wait till Laches of Collytus is dead; he shall have it after the wedding. Well, I should be ashamed to be the only pretty girl that could not show an earring or a chain or a bit of lace.

Mu. Oh well, mother, are the rest of them happier or better-looking than I am?

Mother. No; but they have more sense; they know their business better than to pin their faith to the idle words of a boy with a mouthful of lover's oaths. But you go in for constancy and true love, and will have nothing to say to anybody but your Chaereas. There was that farmer from Acharnae the other day; his chin was smooth too; and he brought the two minae he had just got for his father's wine; but oh dear me no! you send him away with a sneer; none but your Adonis for you.

Mu. Mother, you could not expect me to desert Chaereas and let that nasty working-man (faugh!) come near me. Poor Chaereas! he is a pet and a duck.

Mother. Well, the Acharnian did smell rather of the farm. But there was Antiphon--son to Menecrates--and a whole mina; why not him? he is handsome, and a gentleman, and no older than Chaereas.

Mu. Ah, but Chaereas vowed he would cut both our throats if he caught me with him.

Mother. The first time such a thing was ever threatened, I suppose. So you will go without your lovers for this, and be as good a girl as if you were a priestess of Demeter instead of what you are. And if that were all!--but to-day is harvest festival; and where is his present?

Mu. Mammy dear, he has none to give.

Mother. They don't all find it so hard to get round their fathers; why can't he get a slave to wheedle him? why not tell his mother he will go off for a soldier if she doesn't let him have some money? instead of which he haunts and tyrannizes over us, neither giving himself nor letting us take from those who would. Do you expect to be eighteen all your life, Musarium? or that Chaereas will be of the same mind when he has his fortune, and his mother finds a marriage that will bring ' him another? You don't suppose he will remember tears and kisses and vows, with five talents of dowry to distract him

Mu. Oh yes, he will. They have done everything to make him marry now; and he wouldn't! that shows.

Mother. I only hope it shows true. I shall remind you of all this when the time comes.

VIII

Ampelis. Chrysis

Am. Well, but, Chrysis, I don't call a man in love at all, if he doesn't get jealous, and storm, and slap one, and clip one's hair, and tear one's clothes to pieces.

Ch. Is that the only way to tell?

Am. To tell a serious passion, yes. The kisses and tears and vows, the constant attendance,--all that only shows that he's beginning to be in love; it's still coming on. But the real flame is jealousy, pure and simple. So if Gorgias is jealous, and slaps you, as you say, you may hope for the best; pray that he may always go on as he has begun!

Ch. Go on slapping me?

Am. No, no; but getting angry if you ever look at any one else. If he were not in love with you, why should he mind your having another lover?

Ch. Oh, but I *haven't!* It's all a mistake! He took it into his head that old Moneybags had been paying me attentions, because I just happened to mention his name once.

Am. Well, that's very nice, too. You want him to think that there are rich men after you. It will make him all the more angry, and all the more liberal; he'll be afraid of being cut out by his rivals.

Ch. But Gorgias never gives me anything. He only storms and slaps.

Am. Oh, you wait. Nothing tames them like jealousy.

Ch. Ampelis, I believe you *want* me to be slapped!

Am. Nonsense! All I mean is this:

if you want to make a man wildly in love with you, let him see that you can do without him. When he thinks that he has you all to himself, he is apt to cool down. You see I've had twenty years' experience:

whereas you, I suppose, are about eighteen, perhaps not that. Come now; I'll tell you what happened to me, not so many years ago. Demophantus was my admirer in those days; the usurer, you know, at the back of the Poecile. He had never given me more than five drachmae at a time, and he wanted to have everything his own way. The fact was, my dear, his love was only skin-deep. There were no sighs or tears with him; no knocking me up at unearthly hours; he would spend an evening with me now and then--very occasionally--and that was all. But one day when he called, I was 'not at home'; I had Callides the painter with me (he had given me ten drachmae). Well, at the time Demophantus said some very rude things, and walked off. However, the days went by, and I never sent to him; and at last (finding that Callides had been with me again) even Demophantus began to catch fire, and to get into a passion about it; so one day he stood outside, and waited till he found the door open:

607

my dear, I don't know what he didn't do! cried, beat me, vowed he would murder me, tore my clothes dreadfully! And it all ended with his giving me a talent; after which I saw no one else for eight months on end. His wife told everybody that I had bewitched him with some drug. 'Twas easy to see what the drug had been:

jealousy. Now you should try the same drug upon Gorgias. The boy will have money, if anything happens to his father.

IX

Dorcas. Pannychis. Philostratus. Polemon

Dor. Oh, miss, we are lost, lost! Here is Polemon back from the wars a rich man, they say. I saw him myself in a mantle with a purple border and a clasp, and a whole train of men at his back. His friends when they caught sight of him crowded round to get their greetings in. I made out in the train his man who went abroad with him. So I said How d'ye do, and then asked, 'Do tell me, Parmenon, how you got on; have you made anything to repay you for all your fighting?'

Pa. Ah, you should not have begun with that. Thanks to all the Gods you were not killed (you ought to have said), and most of all to Zeus who guards the stranger and Athene who rules the battle! My mistress was always trying to find out how you were doing and where you were. And if you had added that she was always weeping and talking of Polemon, that would have been still better.

Dor. Oh, I said all that right at the beginning; but I never thought of telling you that; I wanted to get on to the news. This was how I began to Parmenon:

'Did you and your master's ears burn, Parmenon?' I said; 'mistress was always talking of him and crying; and when any one came back from the last battle and reported that many had been killed, she would tear her hair and beat her breast, and grieve so every time!'

Pa. Ah, that was right, Dorcas.

Dor. And then after a little while I went on to the other questions. And he said, 'Oh, yes, we have come back great men.'

Pa. What, straight off like that? never a word of how Polemon had talked or thought of me, or prayed he might find me alive?

Dor. Yes, he said a good deal of that. But his real news was enormous riches--gold, raiment, slaves, ivory. As for the money, they didn't count it, but measured it by the bushel, and it took some time that way. On Parmenon's own finger was a huge queer-shaped ring with one of those three-coloured stones, the outer part red. I left him when he wanted to give me the history of how they crossed the Halys and killed somebody called Tiridates, and how Polemon distinguished himself in the battle with the Pisidians. I ran off to tell you, and give you time to think. Suppose Polemon were to come--and you may be sure he will, as soon as he has got rid of his company--and find when he asked after you that Philostratus was here; what *would* he do?

Pa. Oh, Dorcas, we *must* find some way out of it. It would be shabby to send Philostratus about his business so soon after having that talent from him; and he is a merchant, and if he keeps all his promises-------. And on the other hand, it is a pity not to be at home to Polemon now he is come back such a great man; besides, he is so jealous; when he was poor, there was no getting on with him for it; and what will he be like now?

Dor. Here he comes.

Pa. Oh, Dorcas, what *am* I to do? I shall faint; how I tremble!

Dor. Why, here is Philostratus too.

Pa. Oh, what will become of me? oh that the earth would swallow me up!

Phi. Well, my dear, where is that wine?

Pa. (Now he has gone and done it!) Ah, Polemon, so you are back at last; are you well?

Po. Who is this person coming to you? What, no answer? Oh, mighty fine, Pannychis! Here have I come on the wings of love--the whole way from Thermopylae in five days; and all for a woman like this! But I deserve it; I ought to be grateful; I shall not be plundered any more, that is something.

Phi. And who may you be, good sir?

Po. Polemon, deme Stiria, tribe Pandionis; will that do for you? late colonel, now general of division, and Pannychis's lover, so long as he supposed a mere man was good enough for her.

Phi. At present, however, sir free-lance, Pannychis is mine. She has had one talent, and will have another as soon as my cargoes are disposed of. Come along, Pannychis; the colonel can keep his colonelling for the Odrysians.

Dor. She is a free woman; it is for her to say whether she will come along or not.

Pa. What shall I do, Dorcas?

Dor. Better go in; Polemon is too angry to talk to now, and a little jealousy will only whet his appetite.

Pa. Well, if you think so, let us go in.

Po. I give you both fair warning that you drink your last drink to-day; I ought to know by this time how to part soul from body. Parmenon, the Thracians. Full armour, battle array, this alley blocked. Pikemen in the centre, slingers and archers on the flanks, and the remainder in the rear.

Phi. You take us for babies, Mr. Mercenary, to judge from your appeal to our imaginations. Now I wonder whether you ever shed as much blood as runs in a cock's veins, or ever looked on war; to stretch a point in your favour, I dare say you may have been corporal in charge of a bit of wall somewhere.

Po. You will know ere long, when you look upon our serried ranks of glittering steel.

Phi. Oh, pack up your traps and come, by all means. I and my Tibius--I have only one man, you see--will scatter you so wide with a few stones and bricks that you shall never find one another again.

XI

Tryphaena. Charmides

Try. Well, to be sure! Get a girl to keep company with you, and then turn your back on her! Nothing but tears and groans! The wine was not good enough, I suppose, and you didn't want a *tête-à-tête* dinner. Oh yes, I saw you were crying at dinner too. And now it is one continued wail like a baby's. What is it all about, Charmides? *do* tell me; let me get that much out of my evening with you.

Ch. Love is killing me, Tryphaena; I can stand it no longer.

Try. It is not love for me, that is clear. You would not be so cold to me, and push me away when I want to put my arms round you. It really is not fair to keep me off like this! Never mind, tell me who it is; perhaps I may help you to her; I know one ought to make oneself useful.

Ch. Oh, you two know each other quite well; she is quite a celebrity.

Try. Name, name, Charmides!

Ch. Well then--Philematium.

Try. Which? there are two of them; one in Piraeus, who has only just come there; Damyllus the governor's son is in love with her; is it that one? or the other, the one they call The Trap?

Ch. Yes, that is she; she has caught me and got me tight, poor mouse.

Try. And the tears were all for her?

Ch. Even so.

Try. Is this recent? or how long has it been going on?

Ch. Oh, it is nothing new. I saw her first at the Dionysia; that makes seven months.

Try. Had you a full view of her, or did you just see her face and as much as a woman of forty-five likes to show?

Ch. Oh, come! I have her word for it she will be two-and-twenty next birthday.

Try. Well, which are you going to trust--her word, or your own eyes? Just take a careful look at her temples some day; that is the only place where her own hair shows; all the rest is a thick wig; but at the temples, when the dye fades a little, you can easily detect the grey. But that is nothing; insist on seeing more than her face.

Ch. Oh, but I am not favoured so far as that.

Try. No, I should think not. She knows what the effect would be; why, she is all over--oh, talk of leopard-skins! And it was she made you cry like that, was it? I dare say, now, she was very cruel and scornful?

Ch. Yes, she was, dear; and such a lot of money as she has from me! Just now she wants a thousand drachmas; well, I am dependent on my father, and he is very close, and I could not very well get it; so she is at home to Moschion, and will not see me. That is why you are here; I thought it might vex her.

Try. Well, I'm sure I never never would have come if I had been told what it was for--just to vex somebody else, and that somebody old coffin-ripe Philematium! I shall go away; for that matter the third cock-crow is past.

Ch. No, no, not so fast, Tryphaena. If it is all true—the wig, the dye, and the leopard-skin--I shall hate the sight of her.

Try. If your mother has ever seen her at the bath, ask her. As to the age, you had better ask your grandfather about that, if he is alive.

Ch. Well, as that is what she is like, come up close to me. Give me your arms--and your lips--and let us be friends. Philematium be hanged!

XII

Joessa. Pythias. Lysias

Jo. Cross boy! But I deserve it all! I ought to have treated you as any other girl would do,--bothered you for money, and been engaged when you called, and made you cheat your father or rob your mother to get presents for me; instead of which, I have always let you in from the very first time, and it has never cost you a penny, Lysias. Think of all the lovers I have sent away:

Ethocles, now a Chairman of Committees, and Pasion the shipowner, and young Melissus, who had just come into all his father's money. I would not have a word to say to one of them; I kept myself for you, hard-hearted Phaon that you are! I was fool enough to believe all your vows, and have been living like a Penelope for your sake; mother is furious about it, and is always talking at me to her friends. And now that you feel sure of me, and know how I dote on you, what is the consequence? You flirt with Lycaena under my very eyes, just to vex me; you sit next to *me* at dinner, and pay compliments to Magidium, a mere music-girl, and hurt my feelings, and make me cry. And that wine-party the other day, with Thraso and Diphilus, when Cymbalium the flute-girl was there, and Pyrallis:

you know how I hate that girl:

as for Cymbalium, whom you kissed no less than five times, I didn't mind so much about that,--it must have been sufficient punishment in itself:

--but the way in which you were always making signs to Pyrallis to notice your cup, and whispering to the boy, when you gave it back to him, that he was not to fill it for any one but Pyrallis! and that piece of apple that you bit off and shot across right into her lap, when you saw that Diphilus was occupied with Thraso,--you never even tried to conceal it from me! and she kissed it, and hid it away beneath her girdle. What is the meaning of it all? What have I ever done to you? Did I ever displease you? ever look at any other man? Do I not live for you alone? A brave thing, is it not, Lysias, to vex a poor weak woman who loves you to distraction! There is a Nemesis who watches such deeds. You will be sorry some day, perhaps, when you hear of my hanging myself, or jumping head first into a well; for die I will, one way or another, rather than live to be an eyesore to you. There will be an achievement for you to boast of! You need not look at me like that, nor gnash your teeth:

if you have anything to say against me, here is Pythias; let her judge between us. Oh, you are going away without a word?--You see what I have to put up with, Pythias!

Py. Monster! He cares nothing for her tears. He must be made of stone instead of flesh and blood. But the truth is, my dear, you have spoilt him, by letting him see how fond you are of him. It is a great mistake to make so much of them; they get uppish. Don't cry, dear:

take my advice, and shut him out once or twice; it will be his turn to dote on you then.

Jo. Shut him out? Don't breathe a word of such a thing! I only wish he would wait till I turned him out!

Py. Why, here he is back again.

Jo. Pythias! What *have* you done? If he should have overheard that about shutting him out!

Ly. I am coming back on your account, Pythias, not on hers; I will never look at her again, after what she has done:

but I don't want *you* to think badly of me; it shall not be said that Lysias was hard-hearted.

Py. Exactly what I *was* saying.

Ly. But what would you have me do? This girl, who is so tearful now, has been disloyal to me, and received another lover; I actually found them together!

Py. Well, after all------. But when did you make this discovery?

Ly. It must have been something like five days ago; yes, it was, because it was on the second, and to-day is the seventh. My father had found out about this precious Joessa, and how long it had been going on, and he locked me in, and gave the porter orders not to open to me. Well, I wasn't going to be kept away from her, so I told Dromo to slip along the courtyard to the lowest part of the wall, and then let me mount on his back; I knew I could easily get over that way. To make a long story short, I got out, and came here. It was midnight, and I found the door carefully barred. Instead of knocking, I quietly lifted the door off its hinges (it was not the first time I had done so) and passed noiselessly in. Every one was asleep. I groped my way along the wall, and stopped at the bedside.

Jo. Good Heavens! What is coming? I am in torment!

Ly. I perceived from the breathing that there was more than one person there, and thought at first that Lyde must be sleeping with her. Pythias, I was mistaken! My hands passed over a smooth, beardless *man's* face; the fellow was close-cropped, and reeked of scent like any woman. I had not brought my sword with me, or you may be sure I should have known what to do with it-- What are you both laughing at? Is it so amusing, Pythias?

Jo. Oh, Lysias! is that all? Why, it was Pythias who was sleeping with me!

Py. Joessa, don't tell him!

Jo. Why not? Lysias, dear, it was Pythias; I had asked her to come and sleep with me; I was so lonely without you.

Ly. Pythias? Then her hair has grown pretty fast in five days.

Jo. She has been ill, and her hair was falling off, and she had to have it cropped. And now she has got false hair. Pythias, show him that it is so. Behold your rival, Lysias! this is the young gentleman of whom you were jealous.

Ly. And what lover would not have been jealous? I had the evidence of my hands, remember.

Jo. Well, you know better now. Suppose I were to return you evil for evil? What should you say to that? It is my turn to be angry with you now.

Ly. No, you mustn't be angry. We will have some wine, and Pythias must join us; the truce cannot be ratified without her.

Jo. Of course not. A pretty scrape you have led me into, Pythias, you nice young man!

Py. The nice young man has led you out of it again too, so you must forgive him. I say, Lysias, you need not tell any one--about my hair, you know.

XIII

Leontichus. Chenidas. Hymnis

Le. And then that battle with the Galatians; tell her about that, Chenidas--how I rode out in front on the grey, and the Galatians (brave fellows, those Galatians, too)--but they ran away directly they saw me; not a man stood his ground. That time, you know, I used my lance for a javelin, and sent it through their captain and his horse as well; and then, as some of them were left--the phalanx was broken up, you see, but a certain number had rallied--well, I pulled out my trusty blade, rode at them as hard as I could go, knocked over half a dozen of the front rank with the mere rush of my horse, brought down my sword on one of the officers, and clove his head in two halves, helmet and all. The rest of you came up shortly, you remember, when they were already running.

Che. Oh, but that duel of yours with the satrap in Paphlagonia! that was a fine display, too.

Le. Well remembered; yes, that was not so bad, either. A great big fellow that satrap was, supposed to be a champion fighter too--thought nothing of Greek science. Out he came, and challenged all comers to single combat. There was consternation among our officers, from the lowest to the general himself-- though he was a pretty good man. Aristaechmus the Aetolian he was--very strong on the javelin; I was only a colonel then. However, I was not afraid. I shook off the friends who clung to me--they were anxious about me when they saw the barbarian resplendent in his gilded armour, towering high with his terrible plume and brandishing his lance--

Che. Yes, *I* was afraid that time; you remember how I clung to you and besought you not to sacrifice yourself; life would not have been worth living, if you had fallen.

Le. I ventured it, though. Out I went, as well armed as the Paphlagonian, all gold like him. What a shout there was on both sides! the barbarians recognized me too; they knew my buckler and medals and plume. Who was it they all compared me to, Chenidas?

Che. Why, who should it be? Achilles, of course; the son of Peleus and Thetis, of course. Your helmet was so magnificent, your purple so rich, your buckler so dazzling.

Le. We met. The barbarian drew first blood--just a scratch with his lance a little above the knee; but my great spear drove through his shield and right into the breast-bone. Then I ran up, just sliced his head off with my sword, and came back carrying his arms, the head spiked on my spear dripping gore upon me.

Hym. How horrid, Leontichus! what disgusting frightful tales you tell about yourself! What girl would look at a man who likes such nastiness--let alone drink or sleep with him? I am going away.

Le. Pooh! I double your pay.

Hym. No, nothing shall induce me to sleep with a murderer.

Le. Don't be afraid, my dear. All that was in Paphlagonia. I am a man of peace now.

Hym. No, you are unclean; the blood of the barbarian's head on the spear has dripped over you! I embrace and kiss a man like that? the Graces forbid! he is no better than the executioner.

Le. I am certain you would be in love with me if you had seen me in my armour.

Hym. I tell you it makes me sick and frightened even to hear of such things; I see the shades and ghosts of the slain; that poor officer with his head cloven! what would it be if I saw the thing done, and the blood, and the bodies lying there? I am sure I should die; I never saw a chicken killed, even.

Le. Such a coward, girl? so poor of heart? I thought you would like to hear it.

Hym. Well, try the Lemnian women, or the daughters of Danaus, if you want to please with that sort of tale. I shall run home to my mother, while there is some daylight left. Come along, Grammis. Good-bye, mightiest of colonels, and murderer of however many it is!

Le. Stay, girl, stay.--Why, she is gone!

Che. Well, Leontichus, you frightened the simple little thing with your nodding plumes and your incredible exploits. I saw her getting pale as far back as the officer story; her face was all puckered up and quivering when you split his head.

Le. I thought it would make me more attractive. Well, but it was your fault too; you started the duel.

Che. Well, I had to chime in when I saw what you were bragging for. But you laid it on so thick. Pass the cutting off the wretched Paphlagonian's head,

614

what did you want to spike it on a spear for, and let the blood run down on you?

Le. That was a bit too strong, I admit; the rest was rather well put together. Well, go and persuade her to come back.

Che. Shall I tell her you lied to make her think you a fine fellow?

Le. Oh, plague upon it!

Che. It 's the only way. Choose--a mighty champion, and loathed, or a confessed liar, and--Hymnis?

Le. Bad is the best; but I say Hymnis. Go to her, then, Chenidas, and say I lied--in parts.

XIV

Dorion. Myrtale

Do. So, Myrtale! You ruin me first, and then close your doors on me! It was another tale when I brought you all those presents:

I was your love, then; your lord, your life. But you have squeezed me dry now, and have got hold of that Bithynian merchant; so I am left to whimper on the wrong side of the door, while he, the favoured lover, enjoys your embraces, and is to become a father soon, so you tell him.

Myr. Come, Dorion, that is too much! Ruined you, indeed! A lot you ever gave me! Let us go through the list of your presents, from the very beginning.

Do. Very well; let us. First, a pair of shoes from Sicyon, two drachmae. Remember two drachmae.

Myr. Ah, but you were here for two nights.

Do. A box of Phoenician ointment, when I came back from Syria; the box of alabaster. The same price, as I'm a seaman!

Myr. Well, and when you sailed again, didn't I give you that waistcoat, that you might have something to wear when you were rowing? It was Epiurus the boatswain's, that waistcoat; he left it here one night by mistake.

Do. Epiurus recognized it, and took it away from me in Samos, only the other day; and a rare tussle we had before he got it. Then there were those onions I brought you from Cyprus, and five haddocks and four perch, the time we came back from the Bosphorus. Oh, and a whole basket of ship's bread-- eight loaves of it; and a jar of figs from Caria. Another time it was a pair of slippers from Patara, gilded ones, you ungrateful girl! Ah, and I was forgetting that great cheese from Gythium.

Myr. Say five drachmae the lot.

Do. It was all that my pay would run to, Myrtale; I was but a common seaman in those days. I have risen to be mate now, my haughty miss. And didn't I put down a solid drachma for you at the feet of Aphrodite's statue, when it was her feast the other day? Then I gave your mother two drachmae to buy shoes with; and Lyde there,--many is the copper I have slipped into her hand, by twos and threes. Put all that together, and it makes a seaman's fortune.

Myr. Onions and haddocks.

Do. Yes; 'twas all I had; if I were rich, I should not be a sailor. I have never brought my own mother so much as a head of garlic. I should like to know what sort of presents the Bithynian makes you?

Myr. Look at this dress:
he bought it me; and this necklace, the thick one.

Do. Pooh, you have had that for years.

Myr. No, the one you knew was much lighter, and it had no emeralds. My earrings were a present of his too, and so was that rug; and he gave me two minae the other day, besides paying our rent. Rather different from Patara slippers, and Gythium cheeses and stuff!

Do. And how do you like him for a lover? you say nothing about that. He is fifty years old if he is a day; his hair is all gone in front, and he has the complexion of a lobster. Did you ever notice his teeth? And so accomplished too! it is a treat to hear him when he sings and tries to make himself agreeable; what is it they tell me about an ass that would learn the lyre? Well, I wish you joy of him; you deserve no better luck; and may the child be like his father! As for me, I'll find some Delphis or Cymbalium that's more in my line; your neighbour, perhaps, the flute-girl; anyhow, I shall get some one. We can't all afford necklaces and rugs and two minae presents.

Myr. How I envy the lucky girl who gets you, Dorion! What onions she will have from Cyprus! what cheeses next time you come from Gythium!

XV

Cochlis. Parthenis

Co. Crying, Parthenis! what is it? how do your pipes come to be broken?

Par. Oh! oh! I have been beaten by Crocale's lover--that tall Aetolian soldier; he found me playing at Crocale's, hired by his rival Gorgus. He broke in while they were at dinner, smashed my pipes, upset the table, and emptied out the wine-bowl. Gorgus (the country fellow, you know) he pulled out of the dining-room by the hair of his head, and the two of them, Dinomachus (I think they call him) and a fellow soldier, stood over thumping him. Oh, Cochlis, I doubt whether he will live; there was a great rush of blood from his nostrils, and his face is all swollen and livid.

Co. Is the man mad? or was it just a drunken freak?

Par. All jealousy, my dear--love run wild. Crocale had asked two talents, I believe, if Dinomachus wanted her all to himself. He refused; so she shut the door in his face, I was told, and would not let him in at all. Instead of him she took Gorgus of Oenoë, a well-to-do farmer and a nice man; they were drinking together, and she had got me in to play the pipes. Well, the wine was going, I was striking up one of those Lydian tunes, the farmer standing up to dance, Crocale clapping, and all as merry as could be. Suddenly there was a noise and a shout, crash went the front door, and a moment after in burst eight great strong men, that brute among them. Everything was upside down directly, Gorgus on the ground, as I told you, being thumped and kicked. Crocale got away somehow and took refuge with Thespias next door. Dinomachus boxed my ears, and 'Go to blazes!' he said, throwing me the broken pipes. I am running to tell master about it now. And the farmer is going to find some of his friends in town and get the brute summonsed in the police-court.

Co. Yes, bruises and the courts--that is all we get out of the military. They tell you they are generals and colonels, and then when it comes to paying, 'Oh, wait for settling day,' they say; 'then I shall get my pay, and put everything right.' I wish they were all dead, they and their bragging. But I never have anything to do with them; it is the best way. Give me a fisherman or a sailor or farmer no better than myself, with few compliments and plenty of money. These plume-tossing word-warriors! they are nothing but noise, Parthenis.

THE DEATH OF PEREGRINE

LUCIAN to CRONIUS. Greeting.

Poor dear Peregrine--or Proteus, as he loved to call himself,--has quite come up to his namesake in Homer. We have seen him under many shapes:

countless have been his transformations for glory's sake; and now--'tis his last appearance--we see him in the shape of fire. So vast was his ambition. Yes, Cronius; all that is left of the best of men is a handful of ashes. It's just like Empedocles; only with a difference. That philosopher would fain have sneaked into his crater unobserved:

not so our high-souled friend. He bides his time till all Greece is mustered in full force--constructs a pyre of the largest dimensions--and jumps on top in the eyes of all the world, having briefly addressed the nation a few days before on the subject of his daring enterprise! I fancy I see you chuckling away at the old dotard; or rather I hear you blurting out the inevitable comments--' Mere imbecility Mere clap-trap'--Mere . . .' everything else that we are accustomed to attribute to these gentry. But then you are far enough off to be comparatively safe:

now *I* made my remarks before a vast audience, in the very moment of cremation (and before it for that matter), exciting thereby the indignation of all the old fool's admirers, though there were a few who joined in the laugh against him. I can tell you, I was within an ace of being torn limb from limb by the Cynics, like Actaeon among the dogs, or his cousin Pentheus among the Maenads.--But I must sketch you the whole drama in detail. As to our author, I say nothing:

you know the man, you know the sublime utterances that marked his earthly course, outvoicing Sophocles and Aeschylus.

Well, the first thing I did when I got to Elis was to take a turn in the gymnasium, listening the while to the discordant yells of some Cynic or other;--the usual platitudes, you know;--ringing commendations of Virtue--indiscriminate slaughter of characters--finally, a peroration on the subject of Proteus. I must try and give you the exact words, as far as I can remember them; you will recognize the true Cynic yell, I'll be bound; you have heard it before.

'Proteus,' he cried, 'Proteus vain-glorious? Who dares name the word? Earth! Sun! Seas! Rivers! God of our fathers, Heracles! Was it for this that he suffered bondage in Syria? that he forgave his country a debt of a million odd? that he was cast out of Rome,--he whose brilliance exceeds the Sun, fit rival of the Lord of Olympus? 'Tis his good will to depart from life by fire, and they call it vain-glory! What other end had Heracles? 'Twas the thunderbolt, methinks, that slew Asclepius, Dionysus[87]? 'Twas in the crater that Empedocles sought death?'

Theagenes (our friend with the lungs) had got thus far, when I asked one of the bystanders what all this meant about 'fire,' and what Heracles and Empedocles had got to do with Proteus?--'Proteus,' he replied, 'will shortly cremate himself, at the Olympic games.'--'But how,' I asked, 'and why?' He did his best to explain, but the Cynic went on bawling, and it was quite out of the question to attend to anything else. I waited on to the end. It was one torrent of wild panegyric on Proteus. The sage of Sinope, Antisthenes his master,--nay, Socrates himself--none of them were so much as to be compared with him. Zeus was invited to contend for the preeminence. Subsequently however it seemed advisable to leave the two on some sort of equality. 'The world,' he cried in conclusion, 'has seen but two works of surpassing excellence, the Olympian Zeus, and--Proteus. The one we owe to the creative genius of Phidias; the other is Nature's handiwork. And now, this godlike statue departs from among mankind; borne upon wings of fire, he seeks the heavens, and leaves us desolate.' He had worked himself up into a state of perspiration over all this; and when it was over he was very absurd, and cried, and tore his hair,--taking care not to pull too hard; and was finally taken away by some compassionate Cynics, sobbing violently all the time.

Well, after him, up jumped somebody else, before the crowd had time to disperse; pouring his libation upon the glowing embers of the previous sacrifice. He commenced operations with a loud guffaw--there was no doubting its sincerity--after which he addressed us as follows. 'Theagenes (Heaven forgive him!) concluded his vile rant with the tears of Heraclitus:

I, on the other hand, propose to begin with the laughs of Democritus.' Another hearty guffaw, in which most of us were fain to join. 'One simply can't help it,' he remarked, pulling himself together, 'when one hears such sad stuff talked, and sees old men practically standing on their heads for the public amusement,--and all to keep their grubby little reputations alive! Now, if you want to know all about this " statue " which proposes to cremate itself, I'm your man. I have marked his career from the first, and followed his intellectual development; and I learnt a good deal from his fellow citizens, and others whose authority was unquestionable.

'To begin then, this piece of perfect workmanship, straight from Nature's mould, this type of true proportion, had barely come of age, when he was caught in adultery; in Armenia this was; he received a brisk drubbing for his pains, and finally made a jump of it from the roof, and so got off. His next exploit was the corruption of a handsome boy. This would have brought him before the Governor, by rights; but the parents were poor, and he bought them

---

[87] The allusion to Dionysus is unexplained. The Greek requires a fiery death, not the fiery birth, for which see *Dionysus* and *Semele* in Notes.

off to the tune of a hundred and twenty pounds. But perhaps it is hardly worth while mentioning trifles of this kind. Our clay, you see, is yet unwrought :

the "perfect workmanship" is still to come. That business about his father makes rather good hearing:

only you know all about that;--how the old fellow would hang on, though he was past sixty already, till Proteus could stand it no longer, and put a noose about his neck. Well, this began to be talked about; so he passed sentence of banishment on himself, and wandered about from place to place.

It was now that he came across the priests and scribes of the Christians, in Palestine, and picked up their queer creed. I can tell you, he pretty soon convinced them of his superiority; prophet, elder, ruler of the Synagogue--he was everything at once; expounded their books, commented on them, wrote books himself. They took him for a God, accepted his laws, and declared him their president. The Christians, you know, worship a *man* to this day,--the distinguished personage who introduced their novel rites, and was crucified on that account. Well, the end of it was that Proteus was arrested and thrown into prison. This was the very thing to lend an air to his favourite arts of clap-trap and wonder-working; he was now a made man. The Christians took it all very seriously:

he was no sooner in prison, than they began trying every means to get him out again,--but without success. Everything else that could be done for him they most devoutly did. They thought of nothing else. Orphans and ancient widows might be seen hanging about the prison from break of day. Their officials bribed the gaolers to let them sleep inside with him. Elegant dinners were conveyed in; their sacred writings were read; and our old friend Peregrine (as he was still called in those days) became for them "the modern Socrates." In some of the Asiatic cities, too, the Christian communities put themselves to the expense of sending deputations, with offers of sympathy, assistance, and legal advice. The activity of these people, in dealing with any matter that affects their community, is something extraordinary; they spare no trouble, no expense. Peregrine, all this time, was making quite an income on the strength of his bondage; money came pouring in. You see, these misguided creatures start with the general conviction that they are immortal for all time, which explains the contempt of death and voluntary self-devotion which are so common among them; and then it was impressed on them by their original lawgiver that they are all brothers, from the moment that they are converted, and deny the gods of Greece, and worship the crucified sage, and live after his laws. All this they take quite on trust, with the result that they despise all worldly goods alike, regarding them merely as common property. Now an adroit, unscrupulous fellow, who has seen the world, has only to get among these simple souls, and his fortune is pretty soon made; he plays with them.

'To return, however, to Peregrine. The governor of Syria perceived his mental warp:

"he must make a name, though he die for it:

" now philosophy was the governor's hobby; he discharged him--wouldn't hear of his being punished--and Peregrine returned to Armenia. He found it too hot to hold him. He was threatened from all quarters with prosecutions for parricide. Then again, the greater part of his property had disappeared in his absence:

nothing was left but the land, which might be worth a matter of four thousand pounds. The whole estate, as the old man left it, would come perhaps to eight thousand. Theagenes was talking nonsense when he said a million odd. Why, the whole city, with its five nearest neighbours thrown in, men, cattle, and goods of every description , would never fetch that sum.--Meanwhile, indictments and accusations were brewing:

an attack might be looked for at any moment:

as for the common people, they were in a state of furious indignation and grief at the foul butchery of a harmless old man; for so he was described. In these trying circumstances, observe the ingenuity and resource of the sagacious Proteus. He makes his appearance in the assembly:

his hair (even in these early days) is long, his cloak is shabby; at his side is slung the philosopher's wallet, his hand grasps the philosopher's staff; truly a tragic figure, every inch of him. Thus equipped, he presents himself before the public, with the announcement that the property left him by his father of blessed memory is entirely at their disposal! Being a needy folk, with a keen eye to charity, they received the information with ready applause:

"Here is true philosophy; true patriotism; the spirit of Diogenes and Crates is here!" As for his enemies, they were dumb; and if any one did venture an allusion to parricide, he was promptly stoned.

'Proteus now set out again on his wanderings. The Christians were meat and drink to him; under their protection he lacked nothing, and this luxurious state of things went on for some time. At last he got into trouble even with them; I suppose they caught him partaking of some of their forbidden meats. They would have nothing more to do with him, and he thought the best way out of his difficulties would be, to change his mind about that property, and try and get it back. He accordingly sent in a petition to the emperor, suing for its restitution. But as the people of Parium sent up a deputation to remonstrate, nothing came of it all; he was told that as he had been under no compulsion in making his dispositions, he must abide by them.

'Pilgrimage number three, to Egypt, to see Agathobulus. Here he went through a most interesting course of discipline:

shaved half his head bare; anointed his face with mud; grossly exposed himself before a large concourse of spectators, as a practical illustration of "Stoic indifference"; received castigation with a birch rod; administered the same; and mystified the public with a number of still more extravagant follies. Thus prepared, he took ship to Italy, and was scarcely on dry land again when he began abusing everybody, especially the Emperor, on whose indulgence and good nature he knew that he could safely rely. The Emperor, as you may

621

suppose, was not greatly concerned at his invectives; and it was his theory that no one in the garb of philosophy should be called to account for his words, least of all a specialist in scandal. Proteus's reputation throve upon neglect. The crack-brained philosopher became the cynosure of unsophisticated eyes; and he grew at last to be so unbearable that the city prefect judiciously expelled him:

"we do not require philosophers of your school," he explained. Even this made for his notoriety:

he was in every one's mouth as the philosopher who was banished for being too outspoken, and saying what he thought. He took rank with Musonius, Dion, Epictetus, and others who have been in the same predicament.

'Finally, Proteus arrives in Greece; and what does he do there? He makes himself offensive in Elis; he instigates Greece to revolt against Rome; he finds a man of enlarged views and established character[88], a public benefactor in general, and in particular the originator of the water-supply to Olympia, which saved that great assembly from perishing of thirst--and he has nothing but hard words for him; "Greece is demoralized," he cries; "the spectators of the games should have done without water, ay, and died if need be,"--and so many of them would have done, from the violence of the epidemics then raging in consequence of the drought. And all the time Proteus was drinking of that very water! At this there was a general rush to stone him, which pretty nearly succeeded; it was all our magnanimous friend could do, for the time being, to find salvation at the altar of Zeus. He spent the four following years in composing a speech, which he delivered in public at the next Olympic games; it consisted of encomiums on the donor of the water-supply and explanations of his flight on the former occasion. But by this time people had lost all curiosity about him; his prestige was quite gone; everything fell flat, and he could devise no more novelties for the amazement of chance-comers, nor elicit the admiration and applause for which he had always so passionately longed. Hence this last bold venture of the funeral-pyre. So long ago as the last Olympic Games he published his intention of cremating himself at the next. That is what all this mystification is about, this digging of pits we hear of, and collecting of firewood; these glowing accounts of fortitude hereafter to be shown. Now, in the first place, it seems to me that a man has no business to run away from life:

he ought to wait till his time comes. But if nothing else will serve, if positively he must away still there is no need of pyres and such-like solemn paraphernalia:

there are plenty of ways of dying without this; let him choose one of them, and have done with it. Or if a fiery end is so attractively Heraclean, what was to prevent his quietly selecting some well-wooded mountain top, and doing his cremation all by himself, with Theagenes or somebody to play

---

[88] See *Herodes Atticus* in Notes.

Philoctetes to his Heracles? But no; he must roast in full concourse, at Olympia, as it might be on a stage; and, so help me Heracles, he is not far out, if justice is to be done on all parricides and unbelievers. Nay, if we look at it that way, this is but dilatory work:

he might have been packed into Phalaris's bull years ago, and he would have had no more than his deserts,--a mouthful of flame and sudden death is too good for him. For by all I can learn burning is the quickest of deaths; a man has but to open his mouth, and all is over.

But I suppose what runs in his mind is the imposing spectacle of a man being burnt alive in the holy place, in which ordinary mortality may not so much as be buried. There was another man, once on a time, who wanted to be famous. I dare say you have heard of him. When he found there was no other way, he set fire to the temple of Artemis at Ephesus. Proteus's design reminds me of that. The passion for fame must wholly possess him, body and soul. He says, of course, that it is all for the benefit of the human race,--to teach them to scorn death, and to show fortitude in trying circumstances. Now I should just like to ask you a question; it is no use asking him. How would you like it, if the criminal classes were to profit by his lesson in fortitude, and learn to scorn death, and burning, and so on? You would not like it at all. Then how is Proteus going to draw the line? How is he going to improve the honest men, without hardening and encouraging the rogues? Suppose it even to be practicable that none should be present at the spectacle but such as will make a good use of it. Again I ask:

do you want your sons to conceive an ambition of this sort? Of course not. However, I need not have raised that point:

not a soul, even among his own disciples, will be caught by his enthusiasm. That is where I think Theagenes is so much to blame:

in all else he is a zealous adherent:

yet when his master sets out "to be with Heracles,"--he stops behind, he won't go! though it is but a single header into the flames, and in a moment endless felicity is his. It is not zeal, to have the same kind of stick and coat and scrip as another man; any one can do that; it is both safe and easy. Zeal must appear in the end, in the consummation:

let him get together his pyre of fig-tree faggots, as green as may be, and gasp out his last amid the smoke! For as to merely being burnt, Heracles and Asclepius have no monopoly there:

temple-robbers and murderers may be seen experiencing the same fate in the ordinary course of law. Smoke is the only death, if you want to have it all to yourselves.

'Besides, if Heracles really ever did anything so stupendous at all, he was driven to it by frenzy; he was being consumed alive by the Centaur's blood,--so the play tells us. But what point is there in Proteus's throwing himself into the fire? Ah, of course:

he wants to set an example of fortitude, like the Brahmins, to whom Theagenes thought it necessary to corn-pare him. Well, I suppose there may be fools and empty-headed enthusiasts in India as elsewhere? Anyhow, he might stick to his models. The Brahmins never jump straight into the fire:

Onesicritus, Alexander's pilot, saw Calanus burn himself, and according to him, when the pyre has been got ready, they stand quietly roasting in front of it, and when they do get on top, there they sit, smouldering away in a dignified manner, never budging an inch. I see nothing so great in Proteus's just jumping in and being swallowed by the flames. As likely as not he would jump out when he was half done; only, as I understand, he is taking care to have the pyre in a good deep hole.

'Some say that he is beginning to think better of it; that   he reports certain dreams, to the effect that Zeus will not suffer the holy place to be profaned. Let him be easy on that score. I dare swear that not a God of them will have any objection to a rogue's dying a rogue's death. To be sure, he won't easily get out of it now. His Cynic friends egg him on and thrust him pyre-wards; they keep his ambition aglow; there shall be no flinching, if *they* can help it! If Proteus would take a couple of them with him in the fatal leap, it would be the first good action he has ever performed.

'Not even "Proteus" will serve now, they were saying:

he has changed his name to Phoenix; that Indian bird being credited with bringing a prolonged existence to an end upon a pyre. He tells strange tales too, and quotes oracles—guaranteed old--to the effect that he is to be a guardian spirit of the night. Evidently he has conceived a fancy for an altar, andlooks to have his statue set up, all of gold. And upon my word it is as likely as not that among the simple vulgar will be found some to declare that Proteus has cured them of the ague, and that in the darkness they have met with the "guardian spirit of the night." And as the ancient Proteus, the son of Zeus, the great original, had the gift of prophecy, I suppose these precious disciples of the modern one will be for getting up an oracle and a shrine upon the scene of cremation. Mark my words:

we shall find we have got Protean priests of the scourge; priests of the branding-iron; priests of some strange thing or other; or--who knows?--nocturnal rites in his honour, with a torchlightprocession about the pyre. I heard but now, from a friend, of Theagenes's producing a prophecy of the Sibyl on this subject:

he quoted the very words:

> What time the noblest of the Cynic host
> Within the Thunderer's court shall light a fire,
> And leap into its midst, and thence ascend
> To great Olympus--then shall all mankind,
> Who eat the furrow's fruit, give honour due

To the Night-wanderer. His seat shall be

Hard by Hephaestus and lord Heracles.

That's the oracle that Theagenes says he heard from the Sibyl. Now I'll give him one of Bacis's on the same subject. Bacis speaks very much to the point as follows:

What time the Cynic many-named shall leap,

Stirred in his heart with mad desire for fame,

Into hot fire--then shall the Fox-dogs all,

His followers, go hence as went the Wolf.

And him that shuns Hephaestus' fiery might

Th' Achaeans all shall straightway slay with stones;

Lest, cool in courage, he essay warm words,

Stuffing with gold of usury his scrip;

For in fair Patrae he hath thrice five talents.

What say you, friends? Can Bacis turn an oracle too, as well as the Sibyl? Apparently it is time for the esteemed followers of Proteus to select their spots for "evaporation," as they call burning.'

A universal shout from the audience greeted this conclusion:

'Away with them to the fire! 'tis all they are good for.' The orator descended, beaming.

But Nestor marked the uproar--

The shouts no sooner reached Theagenes's ears, than he was back on the platform, bawling out all manner of scandal against the last speaker (I don't know what this capital fellow was called). However, I left Theagenes there, bursting with indignation, and went off to see the games, as I heard the stewards were already on the course. So much for Elis.

On our arrival at Olympia, we found the vestibule full of people, all talking about Proteus. Some were inveighing against him, others commended his purpose; and most of them had come to blows about it when, just after the Heralds' contest, in came Proteus himself, with a multitudinous escort, and gave us a speech, all about himself;--the life he had lived, the risks he had run, the trials he had undergone in the cause of philosophy. He had a great deal to say, but I heard very little of it; there was such a crowd. Presently I began to think I should be squeezed to death in the crush (I saw this actually happen to several people), so off I went, having had enough of this sophist in love with death, and his anticipatory epitaph. Thus much I heard, however. Upon a golden life he desired to set a golden crown. He had lived like Heracles:

like Heracles he must die, and mingle with the upper air. 'Tis my aim,' he continued, 'to benefit mankind; to teach them how contemptible a thing is death. To this end, the world shall be my Philoctetes.' The simpler souls among his audience wept, crying 'Live, Proteus; live for Greece!' Others were of sterner stuff, and expressed hearty approval of his determination. This discomposed the old man considerably. His idea had been that they would never let him go near the pyre; that they would all cling about him and insist on his continuing a compulsory existence. He had the complexion of a corpse before:

but this wholly unexpected blow of approbation made him turn several degrees paler:

he trembled--and broke off.

Conceive my amusement! Pity it was impossible to feel for such morbid vanity:

among all who have ever been afflicted with this scourge, Proteus stands pre-eminent. However, he had a fine following, and drank his fill of notoriety, as he gazed on the host of his admirers; poor man! he forgot that criminals on the way to the cross, or in the executioner's hands, have a greater escort by far.

And now the games were over. They were the best I had ever; seen, though this makes my fourth visit to Olympia. In the general rush of departure, I got left behind, finding it impossible to procure a conveyance.

After repeated postponements, Proteus had finally announced a late hour of the night for his exhibition. Accordingly, at about midnight I got up (I had found lodgings with a friend), and set out for Harpine; for here was the pyre, just two miles and a half from Olympia, going East along the racecourse. We found on arrival that the pyre had been placed in a hole, about six feet deep. To ensure speedy ignition, it had been composed chiefly of pine-torches, with brushwood stuffed in between.

As soon as the moon had risen--for her presence too was required at the glorious spectacle--Proteus advanced, in his usual costume, accompanied by the chiefs of the Cynics; conspicuous among them came the pride of Patrae, torch in hand; nobly qualified for the part he was to play. Proteus too had his torch. They drew near to the pyre, and kindled it at several points; as it contained nothing but torches and brushwood, a fine blaze was the result. Then Proteus-- are you attending, Cronius?--Proteus threw aside his scrip, and cloak, and club- -' his club of Heracles--and stood before us in scrupulously unclean linen. He demanded frankincense, to throw upon the fire; being supplied he first threw it on, then, turning to the South (another tragic touch, this of the South), he exclaimed:

'Gods of my mother, Gods of my father, receive me with favour.' And with these words he leapt into the pyre. There was nothing more to be seen, however; the towering mass of flames enveloped him completely.

Again, sweet sir, you smile over the conclusion of my tragedy. As for me, I saw nothing much in his appealing to his mother's Gods, but when he included his *father's* in the invocation, I laughed outright; it reminded me of the parricide story. The Cynics stood dry-eyed about the pyre, gazing upon the flames in silent manifestation of their grief. At last, when I was half dead with suppressed laughter, I addressed them. 'Intelligent sirs,' I said, 'let us go away.

No pleasure is to be derived from seeing an old man roasted, and there is a horrible smell of burning. Are you waiting for some painter to come along and take a sketch of you, to match the pictures of Socrates in prison, with his companions at his side?' They were very angry and abusive at first, and some took to their sticks:

but when I threatened to pick a few of them up and throw them on to the fire to keep their master company, they quieted down and peace was restored.

Curious reflections were running in my mind, Cronius, as I made my way back. 'How strange a thing is this same ambition!' I said to myself; ''tis the one irresistible passion; irresistible to the noblest of mankind, as we account them,--how much more to such as Proteus, whose wild, foolish life may well end upon the pyre!' At this point I met a number of people coming out to assist at the spectacle, thinking to find Proteus still alive; for among the various rumours of the preceding day, one had been, that before entering the fire he was to greet the rising sun, which to be sure is said to be the Brahmin practice. Most of them turned back when I told them that all was over; all but those enthusiasts who could not rest without seeing the identical spot, and snatching some relic from the flames. After this, you may be sure, my work was cut out for me:

I had to tell them all about it, and to undergo a minute cross-examination from everybody. If it was some one I liked the look of, I confined myself to plain prose, as in the present narrative:

but for the benefit of the curious simple, I put in a few dramatic touches on my own account. No sooner had Proteus thrown himself upon the kindled pyre, than there was a tremendous earthquake, I informed them; the ground rumbled beneath us; and a vulture flew out from the midst of the flames, and away into the sky, exclaiming in human accents

'I rise from Earth, I seek Olympus.'

They listened with amazement and shuddering reverence. 'Did the vulture fly East or West?' they wanted to know. I answered whichever came uppermost.

On getting back to Olympia, I stopped to listen to an old man who was giving an account of these proceedings; a credible witness, if ever there was one, to judge by his long beard and dignified appearance in general. He told us, among other things, that only a short time before, just after the cremation, Proteus had appeared to him in white raiment; and that he had now left him walking with serene countenance in the Colonnade of Echoes, crowned with olive; and on the top of all this he brought in the vulture, solemnly swore that he had seen it himself flying away from the pyre,--my own vulture, which I had but just let fly, as a satire on crass stupidity!

Only think what work we shall have with him hereafter! Significant bees will settle on the spot; grasshoppers beyond calculation will chirrup; crows will perch there, as over Hesiod's grave,--and all the rest of it. As for statues, several, I know, are to be put up at once, by Elis and other places, to which, I understand, he had sent letters. These letters, they say, were dispatched to almost all cities of any importance:

they contain certain exhortations and schemes of reform, as it were a legacy. Certain of his followers were specially appointed by him for this service: *Couriers to the Grave* and *Grand Deputies of the Shades* were to be their titles.

Such was the end of this misguided man; one who, to give his character in a word, never to his last day suffered his gaze to rest on Truth; whose words, whose actions had but one aim,--notoriety and vulgar applause. 'Twas the love of applause that drove him to the pyre, where applause could no longer reach his ears, nor gratify his vanity.

One anecdote, and I have done; it will keep you in amusement for some time to come. I told you long ago, on my return from Syria, how I had come on the same ship with him from Troas, and what airs he put on during the voyage, and about the handsome youth whom he converted to Cynicism, by way of having an Alcibiades all of his own, and how he woke up one night in mid-ocean to find a storm breaking on us, and a heavy sea rolling, and how the superb philosopher, for whom Death had no terrors, was found wailing among the women. All that you know. But a short time before his death, about a week or so, he had a little too much for dinner, I suppose, and was taken ill in the night, and had a sharp attack of fever. Alexander was the physician called in to attend him, and it was from him I got the story. He said he found Proteus rolling on the ground, unable to endure the fever, and making passionate demands for water. Alexander said no to this:

and he told him that if he really wanted to die, here was death, unbidden, at his very door; he had only to attend the summons; there was no need of a pyre. 'No, no,' says Proteus; 'any one may die that way; there's no distinction in it.'

So much for Alexander. I myself, not so long ago, saw Proteus with some irritant rubbed on his eyes to purge them of rheum. Evidently we are to infer that there is no admission for blear eyes in the kingdom of Aeacus. 'Twas as if a man on the way to be crucified were to concern himself about a sprained finger. Think if Democritus had seen all this! How would he have taken it? The laughing philosopher might have done justice to Proteus. I doubt, indeed, whether he ever had such a good excuse for his mirth.

Be that as it may, you, my friend, shall have your laugh; especially when you hear Proteus's name mentioned with admiration.

THE RUNAWAYS

Apollo. Zeus. Philosophy. Heracles. Hermes. Three Masters. An Innkeeper. Orpheus. Innkeeper's Wife. Three Runaway Slaves

Apol. Father, is this true, about a man's publicly throwing himself upon a pyre, at the Olympian Games? He was quite an old man, it seems, and rather a good hand at anything in the sensational line. Selene told us about it:

she says she actually saw him burning.

Zeus. Quite true, my boy; only too true!

Apol. Oh? the old gentleman deserved a better fate?

Zeus. Why, as to that, I dare say he did. But I was alluding to the smell, which incommoded me extremely; the odour of roast man, I need hardly tell you, is far from pleasant. I made the best of my way to Arabia at once, or, upon my word, those awful fumes would have been the death of me. Even in that fragrant land of frankincense and spices I could scarcely get the villanous stench out of my nostrils; the mere recollection of it makes me feel queer.

Apol. But what was his object, father? Was there anything to be got by jumping on to a pyre, and being converted to cinders?

Zeus. Ah, if you come to that, you must call Empedocles to account first: *he* jumped into a crater, in Sicily.

Apol. Poor fellow! he must have been in a sad way. But what was the inducement in the present case?

Zeus. I'll quote you his own words. He made a speech, explaining his motives to the public. As far as I remember, he said--but who comes here in such haste? There must be something wrong:

she is crying; some one has been ill-treating her. Why, it is Philosophy, in a sad way, calling out to me. Why are you crying, child? and what brings you here, away from the world? More misdeeds of the ignorant herd? a repetition of the Socrates and Anytus affair? is that it?

Phi. No, father, nothing of that kind. The common people have been most polite and respectful; they are my most devout admirers,--worshippers, I might almost say; not that they understand much of what I tell them. No; it was those--I don't know what to call them--but the people who pretend to be on such friendly terms with me, and are always using my name;--the wretches!

Zeus. Oh, it's the philosophers who have been misbehaving themselves?

Phi. No, no, father; they have been just as badly treated as I have.

Zeus. Then if it is neither the philosophers nor the common people, who is it that you complain of?

Phi. There are some people who are between the two:

they are not philosophers, and yet they are not like the rest of mankind. They are got up to look like philosophers; they have the dress, the walk, the expression; they call me mistress, write philosopher after their names, and declare themselves my disciples and followers:

but they are evil men, made up of folly and impudence and wickedness; a disgrace to my name. It was their misconduct that drove me away.

Zeus. Poor child! it is too bad of them. And what have they been doing to you exactly?

Phi. Judge for yourself whether the provocation was a slight one. When formerly you looked down upon the world, and saw that it was filled with iniquity and transgression, and was become the troubled abode of sin and folly, you had compassion on the frailty of ignorant mankind, and sent me down to them:

you bade me see to it, that wickedness and violence and brutality should cease from among them; I was to lift their eyes upwards to the truth, and cause them to live together in unity. Remember your words on that occasion:

'Behold, my daughter, the misdeeds of mankind; behold how ignorance has wrought upon them. I feel compassion for them, and have chosen you from among all the Gods to heal their ills; for who else should heal them? '

Zeus. I said that, and more. Yes? and how did they receive you at your first descent? and what is the trouble now?

Phi. My first flight was not directed towards Greece. I thought it best to begin with the hardest part of my task, which I took to be the instruction of the barbarians. With the Greeks I anticipated no difficulty; I had supposed that they would accept my yoke without hesitation. First, then, I went to the Indians, the mightiest nation upon earth. I had little trouble in persuading them to descend from their elephants and follow me. The Brahmins, who dwell between Oxydracae and the country of the Nechrei, are mine to a man:

they live according to my laws, and are respected by all their neighbours; and the manner of their death is truly wonderful.

Zeus. Ah, to be sure:

the Gymnosophists. I have heard a great deal of them. Among other things, they ascend gigantic pyres, and sit quietly burning to death without moving a muscle. However, that is no such great matter:

I saw it done at Olympia only the other day. You would be there, no doubt,--when that old man burnt himself?

Phi. No, father:

I was afraid to go near Olympia, on account of those hateful men I was telling you of; I saw that numbers of them were going there, to make their barking clamour heard in the temple, and to abuse all comers. Accordingly I know nothing of this cremation. But to continue:

after I had left the Brahmins, I went straight to Ethiopia, and thence to Egypt, where I associated with the priests and prophets, and taught them of the Gods. Then to Babylon, to instruct the Chaldaeans and Mages. Next came Scythia, and after Scythia, Thrace; here Eumolpus and Orpheus were my companions. I sent them on into Greece before me; Eumolpus, whom I had thoroughly instructed in theology, was to institute the sacred mysteries,

Orpheus to win men by the power of music. I followed close behind them. On my first arrival, the Greeks received me without enthusiasm:

they did not, however, wholly reject my advances; by slow degrees I gained over seven men to be my companions and disciples, and Samos, Ephesus, and Abdera,[89] each added one to the little company. And then there sprang up--I scarce know how--the tribe of sophists:

men who had but little of my spirit, yet were not wholly alien to me; a motley Centaur breed, in whom vanity and wisdom meeting were moulded into one incongruous whole. They clung not entirely to ignorance, but theirs was not the steady eye that could meet the gaze of Philosophy; and if at moments my semblance flashed phantom-like across their dulled vision, they held that in that dim shadow they had seen all that was to be seen. It was this pride that nourished the vain, unprofitable science that they mistook for invincible wisdom; the science of quaint conceits, ingenious paradoxes, and labyrinthine dilemmas. My followers would have restrained them, and exposed their errors:

but they grew angry, and conspired against them, and in the end brought them under the power of the law, which condemned them to drink of hemlock. Doubtless I should have done well to renounce humanity there and then, and take my flight:

but Antisthenes and Diogenes, and after them Crates, and our friend Menippus, prevailed upon me to tarry yet a little longer. Would that I had never yielded! I should have been spared much pain in the sequel.

Zeus. But, my dear, you are merely giving way to your feelings, instead of telling me what your wrongs were.

Phi. Then hear them, father. There is a vile race upon the earth, composed for the most part of serfs and menials, creatures whose occupations have never suffered them to become acquainted with philosophy; whose earliest years have been spent in the drudgery of the fields, in learning those base arts for which they are most fitted--the fuller's trade, the joiner's, the cobbler's--or in carding wool, that housewives may have ease in their spinning, and the thread be fit for warp and woof. Thus employed, they knew not in their youth so much as the name of Philosophy. But they had no sooner reached manhood, than they perceived the respect paid to my followers; how men submitted to their blunt speech, valued their advice, deferred to their judgement, and cowered beneath their censure; all this they saw, and held that here was a life for a king. The learning, indeed, that befits a philosopher would have taken them long to acquire, if it was not utterly out of their reach. On the other hand, their own miserly handicrafts barely rewarded their toil with a sufficiency. To some, too, servitude was in itself an oppression:

they knew it, in fact, for the intolerable thing it is. But they bethought them that there was still one chance left; their sheet-anchor, as sailors say. They took refuge with my lady Folly, called in the assistance of Boldness, Ignorance,

---

[89] Pythagoras, Heraclitus, Democritus.

and Impudence, ever their untiring coadjutors, and provided themselves with a stock of bran-new invectives; these they have ever ready on their tongues; 'tis their sole equipment; noble provision, is it not, for a philosopher? Nothing could be more plausible than the philosophic disguise they now assume, reminding one of the fabled ass of Cyme, in Aesop, who clothed himself in a lion's skin, and, stoutly braying, sought to play the lion's part; the beast, I doubt not, had his adherents. The externals of philosophy, as you know, are easily aped:

it is a simple matter to assume the cloak and wallet, walk with a stick, and bawl, and bark, and bray, against all corners. They know that they are safe; their cloth protects them. Liberty is thus within their grasp:

no need to ask their master's leave; should he attempt to reclaim them, their sticks are at his service. No more short commons for them now, no more of crusts whose dryness is mitigated only by herbs or salt fish:

they have choice of meats, drink the best of wines, and take money where they will, *shearing the sheep*, as they call it when they levy contributions, in the certainty that many will give, from respect to their garb or fear of their tongues. They foresee, of course, that they will be on the same footing as genuine philosophers; so long as their exterior is conformable, no one is likely to make critical distinctions. They take care not to risk exposure:

at the first hint of a rational argument, they shout their opponent down, withdraw into the stronghold of personal abuse, and flourish their ever-ready cudgels. Question their practice, and you will hear much of their principles:

offer to examine those principles, and you are referred to their conduct. The city swarms with these vermin, particularly with those who profess the tenets of Diogenes, Antisthenes, and Crates. Followers of the Dog, they care little to excel in the canine virtues; they are neither trusty guardians nor affectionate, faithful servants:

but for noise and greed and thievery and wantonness, for cringing, fawning cupboard-love,--there, indeed, they are perfect. Before long you will see every trade at a standstill, the workmen all at large:

for every man of them knows that, whilst he is bent over his work from morning to night, toiling and drudging for a starvation wage, idle impostors are living in the midst of plenty, commanding charity where they will, with no word of thanks to the giver, and a curse on him that withholds the gift. Surely (he will say to himself) the golden age is returned, and the heavens shall rain honey into my mouth.

And would that that were all! But they have other ways of bringing discredit upon us, besides the baseness of their origin. When beauty comes within the reach of these grave and reverend gentlemen, they are guilty of excesses that I will not pollute my lips with mentioning. They have been known, like Trojan Paris, to seduce the wives of their own hosts, and to quote the authority of Plato for leaving these fair converts at the disposal of all their acquaintance; they little knew the true meaning of that inspired philosopher's community of women. I will not tire you with a description of their drunken orgies; observe, however, that these are the men who preach against drunkenness and adultery and avarice and lewdness. Could any contrast be greater than that presented by their words and their deeds? They speak their detestation of flattery:

a Gnathonides and a Struthias are less fulsome than they. They bid men tell the truth:

yet their own tongues cannot move but to utter lies. To hear them, you would say they were at war with pleasure, and Epicurus their bitterest foe:

yet nothing do they do but for pleasure's sake. Querulous, irritable, passionate as cradled babes, they are a derision to the beholder; the veriest trifle serves to move their ire, to bring the purple to their cheeks, ungoverned fury to their eyes, foam--call it rather venom--to their lips. Preserve me from their turbid rantings! *Gold I ask not, nor silver; be one penny all my wealth, to purchase beans withal. And for my drink, a river, a spring, shall furnish me.* But presently it turns out that what they want is not pence, nor shillings, but whole fortunes. He must be a thriving merchant, whose cargoes will bring him in such profits as these men suck out of philosophy. They are sufficiently provided at last, and then off goes the hated uniform:

lands and houses are bought, and soft raiment, and comely pages. Inquire of them now for Crates's wallet, Antisthenes's cloak, Diogenes's tub:

they know nothing of the matter. When men see these things, they spit in the face of philosophy; they think that all philosophers are the same, and blame me their teacher. It is long since I have won over any to my side. I toil like Penelope at the loom, and one moment undoes all that I have done. Ignorance and Wickedness watch my unavailing labours, and smile.

Zeus. Really, Philosophy has been shamefully treated. We must take some measures with these rascals. Let us think what is to be done. The single stroke of the thunderbolt is too quick a death.

Apol. Father, I have a suggestion to make. By their neglect of the Muses, these vile quacks have incurred my own resentment as well as Philosophy's. They are not worthy to die by your hand. Instead, I would advise your sending Hermes to them, with full authority to punish them at his discretion.

With his forensic experience, he will be at no loss to distinguish between the true philosopher and the false. The former will receive merited praise:

on the latter he will inflict such chastisement as the circumstances demand.

Zeus. A sensible proposal. Heracles, you can go too; take Philosophy with you, and lose no time. Think:

this will make your thirteenth Labour, and a creditable one too, the extermination of these reptiles.

Hera. Rather than meddle with them, I would give the Augean stables a second clean-out. However, let us be starting, Philosophy.

Phi. If I must, I must.

Her. Yes, come along, and we will polish off a few to-day.--Which way, Philosophy? You know where they are to be found. Somewhere in Greece, of course?

Phi. Oh no; the few that there are in Greece are genuine philosophers. Attic poverty is not at all to the liking of the impostors; we must look for them in places where gold and silver mines abound.

Her. Straight to Thrace, then?

Hera. Yes, Thrace, and I will show you the way. I know every inch of Thrace; I have been there so often. Look here, this is our route.

Her. Yes?

Hera. You see those two magnificent mountains (the big one is Haemus, and the other Rhodope), and the fertile plain that spreads between them, running to the very foot of either? These three grand, rugged crests that stand out so proudly yonder form as it were a triple citadel to the city that lies beneath; you can see it now, look.

Her. Superb! A queen among cities; her splendours reach us even here. And what is the great river that flows so close beneath the walls?

Hera. The Hebrus, and the city was built by Philip. Well, we have left the clouds behind us now; let us try our fortune on terra firma.

Her. Very good; and what comes next? How do we hunt our vermin down?

Hera. Ah, that is where you come in, Mr. Crier:
oblige us by crying them without loss of time.

Her. There is only one objection to that:
I do not know what they are called. What names am I to say, Philosophy? and how shall I describe them?

Phi. I am not sure of their names, as I have never come into contact with them. To judge from their grasping propensities, however, you can hardly go wrong with Cteso, Ctesippus, Ctesicles, Euctemon, Polyctetus[90].

Her. To be sure. But who are these men? They seem to be looking for something too. Why, they are coming up to speak to us.

Innkeeper and Masters. Excuse us, madam, and gentlemen, but have you come across a company of three rascals conducting a woman--a very masculine-looking female, with hair cut short in the Spartan fashion?

Phi. Ha! the very people we are looking for!

Masters. Indeed, madam? But these are three runaway slaves. The woman was kidnapped by them, and we want to get her back.

Her. *Our* business with them I will tell you afterwards. For the present, let us make a joint proclamation.

Disappeared. A Paphlagonian slave, formerly of Sinope. Any person giving information as to his whereabouts will be rewarded; the amount of the reward to be fixed by the informant. Description. Name:

---

[90] *Ctesis* is Greek for 'gain'.

634

begins with CTE. Complexion:
sallow. Hair:
close-cropped, with long beard.
Dress:
a coarse cloak with wallet. Temper:
bad. Education:
none. Voice:
harsh. Manner:
offensive.

First Master. Why, what is all this about? His name used to be Cantharus when he was with. me. He had long hair, and no beard, and was apprenticed to my trade; I am a fuller, and he was in my shop, dressing cloth.

Phi. Yes, it is the same; but he has dressed to some purpose this time, and has become a philosopher.

First Master. Cantharus a philosopher! I like that. And where do I come in?

Second and Third Masters. Oh well, we shall get them all now. This lady knows all about them, it seems.

Phi. Heracles, who is this comely person with a lyre?

Hera. It is Orpheus. I was on the Argo with him. He was the best of boatswains; it was quite a pleasure to row to his singing. Welcome, my musical friend:

you have not forgotten Heracles, I hope?

Or. And welcome to all of you, Philosophy, Heracles, Hermes. I should like my reward, please:

I can lay my finger on your man.

Her. Then show us the way. It is useless, of course, to offer gold to the gifted son of Calliope?

Or. Oh, quite.--I will show you the house, but not the man. His tongue might avenge him; scurrility is his strong point.

Her. Lead on.

Or. It is this house close by. And now I shall leave you; l have no wish to set eyes on him.

Her. Hush! Was that a woman's voice, reciting Homer?

Phi. It was. Let us listen.

Innkeeper's Wife.

More   than   the   gates   of   Hell   I   hate   that   man
Who, loving gold, cloaketh his love with lies.

Her. At that rate, madam, you will have to quarrel with Cantharus:

He with his kindly host hath dealt amiss.

Innkeeper. That 's me. I took him in, and he ran away with my wife.

Innk. Wife.

Wine-witted knave, deer-hearted and dog-eyed,

Thersites, babbler loose, that nought availest

In council, nought in arms; most valiant daw,

That with thine aimless chatter chidest kings,--

First Master. My rascal to a T.

Innk. Wife.

The dog in thee--for thou art dog and goat

And lion--doth a blasting fury breathe.

Innkeeper. Wife, wife! the dogs have been too many for you; ay, and for your virtue, so men say.

Her. Hope for the best; some little Cerberus or Geryon shall call you father, and Heracles have employment again.--Ah, no need to knock:

here they come.

First Master. Ha, Cantharus, have I got you? What, nothing to say for yourself? Let us see what you have in that wallet; beans, no doubt, or a crust of bread.

Her. Bread, indeed! Gold, a purseful of it!

Hera. That need not surprise you. In Greece, you see, he was a Cynic, but here he is all for golden Chrysippus. Next you will see him dangling, Cleanthes-like[91], by his beard, and serve the dirty fellow right.

Second Master. Ha, you rascal there, am I mistaken, or are you my lost Lecythio? Lecythio it is. What a figure! Lecythio a philosopher! I'll believe anything after this.

Her. Does none of you know anything about this other? Third Master. Oh yes, he is mine; but he may go hang for me.

Her. And why is that?

Third Master. Ah, he 's a sadly leaky vessel, is Rosolio, as we used to call him.

Her. Gracious Heracles! did you hear that? Rosolio with wallet and stick!--Friend, here is your wife again.

Innkeeper. Thank you for nothing. I'll have no woman brought to bed of an old book in my house.

Her. How am I to understand that?

Innkeeper. Why, the Three-headed Dog is a book, master? Her. Ay, and so was the Man with the Three Hats, for that matter.

Masters. We leave the rest to you, sir.

Her. This is my judgement. Let the woman return beneath her husband's roof, or many-headed monsters will come of it. These two truant sparks I hand over to their owners:

let them follow their trades as heretofore; Lecythio wash clothes, and Rosolio patch them;--not, however, before his back has felt the mallow-stalk.

---

[91] See *Cleanthes* in Notes.

And for Cantharus, first let the men of pitch take him, and plaster him without mercy; and be their pitch the vilest procurable. Then let him be led forth to stand upon the snowy slopes of Haemus, naked and fettered.

Can. Mercy! have mercy on me! Ah me! I am undone!

First Master. So tragic? Come, follow me to the plasterers; and off with that lion's-skin, lest you be taken for other than an ass.

SATURNALIA

Cronus. His Priest

Pr. Cronus, you are in authority just now, I understand; to you our sacrifices and ceremonies are directed; now, what can I make surest of getting if I ask it of you at this holy season?

Cro. You had better make up your own mind what to pray for, unless you expect your ruler to be a *clairvoyant* and know what you would like to ask. Then, I will do my best not to disappoint you.

Pr. Oh, I have done that long ago. No originality about it; the usual thing, please,---wealth, plenty of gold, landed proprietorship, a train of slaves, gay soft raiment, silver, ivory, in fact everything that is worth anything. Best of Cronuses, give me some of these; your priest should profit by your rule, and not be the one man who has to go without all his life.

Cro. Of course! *ultra vires*; these are not mine to give. So do not sulk at being refused; ask Zeus for them; he will be in authority again soon enough. Mine is a limited monarchy, you see. To begin with, it only lasts a week; that over, I am a private person, just a man in the street. Secondly, during my week the serious is barred; no business allowed. Drinking and being drunk, noise and games and dice, appointing of kings and feasting of slaves, singing naked, clapping of tremulous hands, an occasional ducking of corked faces in icy water,--such are the functions over which I preside. But the great things, wealth and gold and such, Zeus distributes as he will.

Pr. He is not very free with them, though, Cronus. I am tired of asking for them, as I do at the top of my voice. He never listens; he shakes his aegis, gets the thunderbolt ready for action, puts on a stern look and scares you out of worrying him. He does consent now and then, and make a man rich; but his selection is most casual; he will pass over the good and sensible, and set fools and knaves up to the lips in wealth, gaolbirds or debauchees most of them. But I want to know what are the things *you* can do.

Cro. Oh, they are not to be sneezed at; it does not come to so very little, if you make allowance for my general limitations. Perhaps you think it a trifle always to win at dice, and be able to count on the sice when the ace is the best the others can throw? Anyhow, there are plenty who get as much as they can eat just because the die likes them and does what it can for them. Others you may see naked, swimming for their lives; and what was the reef that wrecked them, pray? that little die. Or again, to enjoy your wine, to sing the best song at table, at the slaves' feast to see the other waiters[92] ducked for incompetence, while you are acclaimed victor and carry off the sausage prize is all that nothing? Or you find yourself absolute monarch by favour of the knucklebone, can have no ridiculous commands laid on you, and can lay them on the rest:

---

[92] See *Saturnalia* in Notes.

one must shout out a libel on himself, another dance naked, or pick up the flute-girl and carry her thrice round the house; how is that for a sample of my open-handedness? If you complain that the sovereignty is not real nor lasting, that is unreasonable of you; you see that I, the giver of it, have a short-lived tenure myself. Well, anything that is in my power--draughts, monarchy, song, and the rest I have mentioned--you can ask, and welcome; *I* will not scare you with aegis and thunderbolt.

Pr. Most kind Titan, such gifts I require not of you. Give me the answer that was my first desire, and then count yourself to have repaid my sacrifice sufficiently; you shall have my receipt in full.

Cro. Put your question. An answer you shall have, if my knowledge is equal to it.

Pr. First, then, is the common story true? used you to eat the children Rhea bore you? and did she steal away Zeus, and give you a stone to swallow for a baby? did he when he grew to manhood make victorious war upon you and drive you from your kingdom, bind and cast you into Tartarus, you and all the powers that ranged themselves with you?

Cro. Fellow, were it any but this festive season, when 'tis lawful to be drunken, and slaves have licence to revile their lords, the reward for thy question, for this thy rudeness to a grey-haired aged God, had been the knowledge that wrath is yet permitted me.

Pr. It is not *my* story, you know, Cronus; it is Homer's and Hesiod's; I might say, only I don't quite like to, that it is the belief of the generality.

Cro. That conceited shepherd[93]? you do not suppose he knew anything worth knowing about me? Why, think. Is a man conceivable--let alone a God--who would devour his own children?--wittingly, I mean; of course he might be a Thyestes and have a wicked brother; that is different. However, even granting that, I ask you whether he could help knowing he had a stone in his mouth instead of a baby; I envy him his teeth, that is all. The fact is, there was no war, and Zeus did not depose me; I voluntarily abdicated and retired from the cares of office. That I am not in fetters or in Tartarus you can see for yourself, or you must be as blind as Homer.

Pr. But what possessed you to abdicate?

Cro. Well, the long and short of it is, as I grew old and gouty --that last, by the way, accounts for the fetters of the story--I found the men of these latter days getting out of hand; I had to be for ever running up and down swinging the thunderbolt and blasting perjurers, temple-robbers, oppressors; I could get no peace; younger blood was wanted. So I had the happy thought of abdicating in Zeus's favour. Independently of that, I thought it a good thing to divide up my authority--I had sons to take it on--and to have a pleasant easy time, free of all the petition business and the embarrassment of contradictory prayers, no thundering or lightening to do, no lamentable necessity for sending

---

[93] Hesiod.

discharges of hail. None of that now; I am on the shelf, and I like it, sipping neat nectar and talking over old times with Iapetus and the others that were boys with me. And He is king, and has troubles by the thousand. But it occurred to me to reserve these few days for the employments I have mentioned; during them I resume my authority, that men may remember what life was like in my days, when all things grew without sowing or ploughing of theirs--no ears of corn, but loaves complete and meat ready cooked--, when wine flowed in rivers, and there were fountains of milk and honey; all men were good and all men were gold. Such is the purpose of this my brief reign; therefore the merry noise on every side, the song and the games; therefore the slave and the free as one. When I was king, slavery was not.

 Pr. Dear me, now! and I accounted for your kindness to slaves and prisoners from the story again; I thought that, as you were a slave yourself, you were paying slaves a compliment in memory of your own fetters.

 Cro. Cease your ribald jests.

 Pr. Quite so; I will. But here is another question, please. Used mortals to play draughts in your time?

 Cro. Surely; but not for hundreds or thousands of pounds like you; nuts were their highest stake; a man might lose without a sigh or a tear, when losing could not mean starvation.

 Pr. Wise men! though, as they were solid gold themselves, they were out of temptation. It occurred to me when you mentioned that--suppose any one were to import one of your solid gold men into our age and exhibit him, what sort of a reception would the poor thing get? They would tear him to pieces, not a doubt of it. I see them rushing at him like the Maenads at Pentheus, the Thracian women at Orpheus, or his hounds at Actaeon, trying which could get the biggest bit of him; even in the holidays they do not forget their avarice; most of them regard the holy season as a sort of harvest. In which persuasion some of them loot their friends' tables, others complain, quite unreasonably, of you, or smash their innocent dice in revenge for losses due to their own folly.

 But tell me this, now:

 as you are such a delicate old deity, why pick out the most disagreeable time, when all is wrapt in snow, and the north wind blows, everything is hard frozen, trees dry and bare and leafless, meadows have lost their flowery beauty, and men are hunched up cowering over the fire like so many octogenarians,-- why this season of all others for your festival? It is no time for the old or the luxurious.

 Cro. Fellow, your questions are many, and no good substitute for the flowing bowl. You have filched a good portion of my carnival with your impertinent philosophizings. Let them go, and we will make merry and clap our hands and take our holiday licence, play draughts for nuts in the good old way, elect our kings and do them fealty. I am minded to verify the saw, that old age is second childhood.

Pr. Now dry be his cup when he thirsts, to whom such words come amiss! Cronus, a bowl with you! 'tis enough that you have made answer to my former questions. By the way, I think of reducing our little interview to writing, my questions and your so affable answers, for submission to those friends whose discretion may be trusted.

CRONOSOLON

The words of Cronosolon, priest and prophet of Cronus, and holiday lawgiver.

The regulations to be observed by the poor I have sent expressly to them in another scroll, and am well assured that they will abide by the same, failing which, they will be obnoxious to the heavy penalties enacted against the disobedient. And you, ye rich, see to it that ye transgress not nor disregard the instructions following. Be it known to him that shall so do, that he scorneth not me the lawgiver, but Cronus' self, who hath appeared, in no dream, but these two days gone to my waking senses, and appointed me to give holiday laws. No bondsman was he, nor foul to look upon, as painters have limned him after poets' foolish tales. His sickle was indeed full sharp; but he was cheerful of countenance, strong of limb, and royally arrayed. Such was his semblance; and his words, wherein too was divinity, it is fitting you hear.

He beheld me pacing downcast, meditative, and straightway knew--as how should a God not know?--the cause of my sorrow, and how I was ill content with poverty and with the unseasonable thinness of my raiment. For there was frost and north wind and ice and snow, and I but ill fenced against them. The feast was moreover at hand, and I might see others making ready for sacrifice and good cheer, but for me things looked not that way. He came upon me from behind and touched and thrilled my ear, as is the manner of his approach, and spake:

'O Cronosolon, wherefore this troubled mien?' 'Is there not a cause, lord,' I said, 'when I look on pestilent loathly fellows passing rich, engrossing all luxury, but I and many another skilled in liberal arts have want and trouble to our bed-fellows? And thou, even thou, lord, wilt not say it shall not he, nor order things anew and make us equal.' 'In common life,' then said he, ''tis no light matter to change the lots that Clotho and her sister Fates have laid upon you; but as touching the feast, I will set right your poverty; and let the settling be after this manner. Go, O Cronosolon, indite me certain laws for observance in the feast days, that the rich feast not by themselves, but impart of their good things to you.' Then said I, 'I know not how.'

'But I,' quoth he, 'will teach you.' And therewith he began and taught me. And when I was perfect, 'And certify them,' he said, 'that if they do not hereafter, this sharp sickle that I bear is no toy; 'twere odd if I could maim therewith Uranus my father, but not do as much for the rich that transgress my laws; they shall be fitted to serve the Mother of the Gods with alms-box and pipe and timbrel.' Thus he threatened; wherefore ye will do well to observe his decrees.

FIRST TABLE OF THE LAWS

All business, be it public or private, is forbidden during the feast days, save such as tends to sport and solace and delight. Let none follow their avocations saving cooks and bakers.

All men shall be equal, slave and free, rich and poor, one with another.

Anger, resentment, threats, are contrary to law.

During the feast days, no man shall be called to account of his stewardship.

No man shall in these days count his money nor inspect his wardrobe, nor make an inventory.

Athletic training shall cease.

No discourse shall be either composed or delivered, except it be witty and lusty, conducing to mirth and jollity.

SECOND TABLE OF THE LAWS

In good time against the feast every rich man shall inscribe in a table-book the names of his several friends, and shall provide money to a tithe of his yearly incomings, together with the superfluity of his raiment, and such ware as is too coarse for his own service, and a goodly quantity of silver vessels. These shall be all in readiness.

On the eve of the feast the rich shall hold a purification, and drive forth from their houses parsimony and avarice and covetousness and all other such leanings that dwell with the most of them. And their houses being purged they shall make offering to Zeus the Enricher, and to Hermes the Giver, and to Apollo the Generous. And at afternoon the table-book of their friends shall be read to them.

Then shall they with their own hands allot to each friend his fitting share, and send it before set of sun.

And the carriers shall be not more than three or four, the trustiest of a man's servants, and well on in years. And let him write in a letter what is the gift, and its amount, that the carriers be not suspect to giver or receiver. And the said servants shall drink one cup each man, and depart, and ask no more.

To such as have culture let all be sent in double measure; it is fitting that they have two portions.

The message that goeth with a gift shall be modest and brief; let no man humble his friend, nor commend his own gift.

Rich shall not send gifts to rich, nor entertain his peer at the feast.

Of the things made ready for sending, none shall be reserved; let no man give and un-give.

He that by absence missed his share of yester-year shall now receive that too.

Let the rich discharge debts for their friends that are poor, and their rent if they owe and cannot pay it.

Let it be their care above all to know in time the needs of every man.

The receiver for his part should be not over-curious, but account great whatsoever is sent him. Yet are a flask of wine, a hare, or a fat fowl, not to be held sufficient gifts; rather they bring the feast into mockery. For the poor man's return gift, if he have learning, let it be an ancient book, but of good omen and festive humour, or a writing of his own after his ability; and the rich man shall receive the same with a glad countenance, and take and read it forthwith; if he reject or fling it aside, be it known to him that he hath incurred that penalty of the sickle, though he himself hath sent all he should. For the unlearned, let him send a garland or grains of frankincense.

If a poor man send, to one that is rich, raiment or silver or gold beyond his means, the gift shall be impounded and sold, and the price thereof cast into the treasury of Cronus; and on the morrow the poor man shall receive from the rich stripes upon his hands with a rod not less than twelve score and ten.

LAWS OF THE BOARD

The bath hour shall be noon, and before it nuts and draughts.

Every man shall take place as chance may direct; dignities and birth and wealth shall give no precedence.

All shall he served with the same wine; the rich host shall not say, For my colic, or for my megrims, I must drink the better.

Every man's portion of meat shall be alike. The attendants shall favour none, nor yet in their serving shall they be deaf to any, nor pass any by before his pleasure be known. They shall not set great portions before him, and small before him, nor give this one a dainty and that one refuse, but all shall be equal. Let the butler have a quick eye and ear for all from his point of vantage, and heed his master least. And be the cups large or small at choice.

It shall be any man's right to call a health; and let all drink to all if they will, when the host has set the wine a-going. But no man shall be bound to drink, if he be no strong toper.

It shall not be free to any who will to bring an unpractised dancer or musician to the dinner.

Let the limit to jesting be, that the feelings of none be wounded.

The stake at draughts shall be nuts alone; if any play for money, he shall fast on the morrow.

When the rich man shall feast his slaves, let his friends serve with him.

These laws every rich man shall engrave on a brazen pillar and set them in the centre of his hall and there read them. And be it known that, so long as that pillar stands, neither famine nor sickness nor fire nor any mischance shall come upon the house. But if it be removed--which God avert!--then evil shall be that house's doom.

SATURNALIAN LETTERS

I

I to Cronus, Greeting.

I have written to you before telling you of my condition, how poverty was likely to exclude me from the festival you have proclaimed. I remember observing how unreasonable it was that some of us should be in the lap of wealth and luxury, and never give a share of their good things to the poor, while others are dying of hunger with your holy season just upon them. But as you did not answer, I thought I might as well refresh your memory. Dear good Cronus, you ought really to remove this inequality and pool all the good things before telling us to make merry. The world is peopled with camels and ants now, nothing between the two. Or, to put it another way, kindly imagine an actor, with one foot mounted on the tragic stilt and the other bare; if he walks like that, he must be a giant or a dwarf according to the leg he stands on; our lives are about as equal as his heights. Those who are taken on by manager Fortune and supplied with stilts come the hero over us, while the rest pad it on the ground, though you may take my word for it we could rant and stalk with the best of them if we were given the same chance.

Now the poets inform me that in the old days when you were king it was otherwise with men; earth bestowed her gifts upon them unsown and unploughed, every man's table was spread automatically, rivers ran wine and milk and honey. Most wonderful of all, the men themselves were gold, and poverty never came near them. As for us, we can hardly pass for lead; some yet meaner material must be found. In the sweat of our face the most of us eat bread. Poverty, distress, and helplessness, sighs and lamentations and pinings for what is not, such is the staple of man's life, the poor man's at least. All which, believe me, would be much less painful to us, if there were not the felicity of the rich to emphasize it. They have their chests of gold and silver, their stored wardrobes, their slaves and carriages and house property and farms, and, not content with keeping to themselves their superfluity in all these, they will scarce fling a glance to the generality of us.

Ah, Cronus, there is the sting that rankles beyond endurance --that one should loll on cloth of finest purple, overload his stomach with all delicacies, and keep perpetual feast with guests to wish him joy, while I and my like dream over the problematic acquisition of a sixpence to provide us a loaf white or brown, and send us to bed with a smack of cress or thyme or onion in our mouths. Now, good Cronus, either reform this altogether and feed us alike, or at the least induce the rich not to enjoy their good things alone; from their bushels of gold let them scatter a poor pint among us; the raiment that they would never feel the loss of though the moth were to consume it utterly, seeing that in any case it must perish by mere lapse of time, let them devote to covering our nakedness rather than to propagating mildew in their chests and drawers.

Further let them entertain us by fours and fives, and not as they now do, but more on principles of equality; let us all share alike. The way now is for one to gorge himself on some dainty, keeping the servant waiting about him till he is pleased to have done; but when it reaches us, as we are in the act of helping ourselves it is whisked off, and we have but that fleeting glimpse of the entrée or fag-end of a sweet. Or in comes a sucking-pig; half of it, including the head, falls to the host; the rest of us share the bones, slightly disguised. And pray charge the butlers not to make us call unto seven times, but bring us our wine when we ask for it first; and let it be a full-sized cup and a bumper, as it is for their masters. And the same wine, please, for every one at table; where is the legal authority for my host's growing mellow on the choicest bouquet while my stomach is turned with mere must?

These things if you correct and reform, you will have made life life, and your feast a feast. If not we will leave the feasting to them, and just kneel down and pray that as they come from the bath the slave may knock down and spill their wine, the cook smoke their sauce and absent-mindedly pour the pea-soup over the caviare, the dog steal in while the scullions are busy and make away with the whole of the sausage and most of the pastry. Boar and buck and sucking-pigs, may they rival in their roasting Homer's oxen of the Sun! only let them not confine themselves to crawling[94], but jump up and make off to the mountains with their spits sticking in them! and may the fat fowls, all plucked and trussed, fly far away and rob them of their unsociable delights!

But we can touch them more closely than that. May Indian gold-ants[95] come by night, unearth their hoards and convey them to their own state treasury! May their wardrobe-keepers be negligent, and our good friends the mice make sieve-work of their raiment, fit for nothing but tunny-nets! May every pretty curled minion, every Hyacinth and Achilles and Narcissus they keep, turn bald as he hands the cup! let his hair fall off and his chin grow bristly, till he is like the peak-bearded fellows on the comic stage, hairy and prickly on cheek and temple, and on the top smooth and bare! These are specimens of the petitions we will send up, if they will not moderate their selfishness, acknowledge themselves trustees for the public, and let us have our fair share.

---

[94] Homer, *Od.* xii. 395. Odysseus's crew had killed and begun to cook the oxen of the Sun. 'And soon thereafter the Gods chewed forth signs and wonders to my company. The skins were creeping, and the flesh bellowing upon the spits, both the roast and raw, and there was a sound as of the voice of kine.'--*Butcher and Lang.*

[95] Herodotus, iii. 102. 'And in this desert and sandy tract' (in North India) 'are produced ants, which are in size smaller than dogs but larger than foxes. . . These ants there make their dwelling under ground and carry up the sand just in the same manner as the ants found in the land of the Hellenes . . . and the sand which is brought up contains gold.'--*Macaulay's translation.*

II

Cronus to his well-beloved me, Greeting.

My good man, why this absurdity of writing to me about the state of the world, and advising redistribution of property? It is none of my business; the present ruler must see to that. It is an odd thing you should be the only person unaware that I have long abdicated; my sons now administer various departments, of which the one that concerns you is mainly in the hands of Zeus; my own charge is confined to draughts and merry-making, song and good cheer, and that for one week only. As for the weightier matters you speak of, removal of inequalities and reducing of all men to one level of poverty or riches, Zeus must do your business for you. On the other hand, if any man is wronged or defrauded of his holiday privileges, that is a matter within my competence; and I am writing to the rich on the subject of dinners, and that pint of gold, and the raiment, directing them to send you what the season requires. The poor are reasonable there; it is right and proper for the rich to do these things, unless it turns out that they have good reasons to the contrary.

Speaking generally, however, I must tell you that you are all in error; it is quite a misconception to imagine the rich in perfect bliss; they have no monopoly of life's pleasures because they can eat expensive food, drink too much good wine, revel in beauty, and go in soft raiment. You have no idea of how it works out. The resulting anxieties are very considerable. A ceaseless watch must be kept, or stewards will be lazy and dishonest, wine go sour, and grain be weeviled; the burglar will be off with the rich man's plate; agitators will persuade the people that he is meditating a *coup d'état*. And these are but a minute fraction of their troubles; if you could know their apprehensions and cares, you would think riches a thing to be avoided at all costs.

Why, look at me; if wealth and dominion were good things, do you suppose I should have been fool enough to relinquish them, make room for others, and sit down like a common man content with a subordinate position? No, it was because I knew all the conditions the rich and powerful cannot escape that I had the sense to abdicate.

You made a great fuss in your letter about *their* gorging on boar's head and pastry while *your* festival consists of a mouthful of cress or thyme or onion. Now, what are the facts? As to the immediate sensation, on the palate, there is little to choose between the two diets--not much to complain of in either; but with the after effects it is quite otherwise. *You* get up next morning without either the headache the rich man's wine leaves behind, or the disgusting queasiness that results from his surfeit of food. To these effects he adds those of nights given to lust and debauchery, and as likely as not reaps the fruit of his luxury in consumption, pneumonia, or dropsy. It is quite a difficult matter to find a rich man who is not deathly pale; most of them by the time they are old men use eight legs belonging to other people instead of their own two; they are gold without and rags within, like the stage hero's robes. No fish dinners for you, I admit; you hardly know what fish tastes like; but then observe, no gout or pneumonia either, nor other ailments due to other excesses. Apart from that. though, the rich themselves do not enjoy their daily over-indulgence in these things; you may see them as eager, and more, for a dinner of herbs as ever you are for game.

I say nothing of their other vexations--one has a disreputable son, another a wife who prefers his slave to himself, another realizes that his minion yields to necessity what he would not to affection; there are numberless things, in fact, that you know nothing about; you only see their gold and purple, or catch sight of them behind their high-steppers, and open your mouths and abase yourselves before them. If you left them severely alone, if you did not turn to stare at their silver-plated carriages, if you did not while they were talking eye their emerald rings, or finger their clothes and admire the fineness of the texture, if you let them keep their riches to themselves, in short, I can assure you they would seek you out and implore the favour of your company; you see, they must show you their couches and tables and goblets, the sole good of which is in the being known to possess them.

You will find that most of their acquisitions are made for you; they are not for their own use, but for your astonishment. I am one that knows both lives, and I write this for your consolation. You should keep the feast with the thought in your minds that both parties will soon leave this earthly scene, they resigning their wealth, and you your poverty. However, I will write to them as I promised, and am confident that they will not disregard what I say.

III

Cronus to the Rich, Greeting.

I lately received a letter from the poor, complaining that you give them no share of your prosperity. They petitioned me in general terms to institute community of goods and let each have his part:

it was only right that equality should be established, instead of one's having a superfluity while another was cut off from pleasure altogether. I told them that had better be left to Zeus; but their particular festival grievances I considered to belong to my own jurisdiction, and so I undertook to write to you. These demands of theirs are moderate enough, it seems to me. How can we possibly keep the feast (they ask), when we are numb with frost and pinched with hunger? if I meant them to participate, I must compel you to bestow on them any clothes that you do not require, or find too heavy for your own use, and also to vouchsafe them just a slight sprinkling of gold. If you do this, they engage not to dispute your right to your property any further in the court of Zeus. Otherwise they will demand redistribution the next time he takes his seat upon the bench. Well, this is no heavy call, considering the vast property on the possession of which I congratulate you.

They also requested me to mention the subject of dinners; you were to ask them to dinner, instead of closing your doors and living daintily by yourselves. When you do entertain a few of them at long intervals, they say you make it rather a humiliation than an enjoyment; everything is done to degrade them--that monstrous piece of snobbishness, for instance, the giving different people different wines. It is really a little discreditable to them that they do not get up and walk out in such a case, leaving you in sole possession. But that is not all; they tell me there is not *enough* to drink either; your butlers' ears are as impervious as those of Odysseus's crew. Other vulgarities I can hardly bring myself to name. The helpings and the waiters are complained of; the latter linger about you till you are full to repletion, but post by your poor guests at a run--with other meannesses hardly conceivable in the house of a gentleman. For mirth and good-fellowship it is essential that all the company be on the same footing; if your carver does not secure equality, better not have one, but a general scramble.

It rests with you to obviate these complaints and secure honour and affection; a liberality that costs you nothing appreciable will impress itself permanently by its timeliness on the memory of recipients. Why, your cities would not be habitable, if you had not poor fellow citizens to make their numberless contributions to your well-being; you would have no admirers of your wealth if you lived alone with it in the obscurity of isolation. Let there be plenty to see it and to marvel at your silver and your exquisite tables; let them drink to your health, and as they drink examine the goblet, feel and guess at its weight, enjoy its storied workmanship enhanced by and enhancing the preciousness of the material. So you may not only gain a reputation for goodness and geniality, but also escape envy; that is a feeling not directed against people who let others participate in their prosperity to a reasonable extent; every one prays that they may live long to enjoy it. Your present practice results in an unsatisfying life, with none to see your happiness, but plenty to grudge you your wealth.

It is surely not so agreeable to gorge yourself alone, like a lion or an old wolf that has deserted the pack, as to have the company of well-bred people who do their best to make things pleasant. In the first place they banish dull silence from your table, and are ready with a good story, a harmless jest, or some other contribution to entertainment; that is the way to please the Gods of wine and love and beauty. And secondly they win you love by spreading abroad next morning your hospitable fame. These are things that would be cheap at a considerable price.

For I put it to you whether, if blindness were a regular concomitant of poverty (fancy is free), you would be indifferent to the want of any one to impress with your purple clothes and attendant crowds and massive rings. I will not dwell on the certainty that plots and ill-feeling will be excited against you by your exclusiveness; suffice it to say that the curses they threaten to imprecate upon you are positively horrible; God forbid they should really be driven to it! You would never taste sausage or pastry more; if the dog's depredations stopped short of completeness, you would still find a fishy flavour in your soup, the boar and the buck would effect an escape to the mountains from off the very roasting-jack, and your birds (no matter for their being plucked) would be off with a whiz and a whirr to the poor men's tables. Worst of all, your pretty cup-bearers would turn bald in a twinkling--the wine, by the way, having previously all been spilt. I now leave you to make up your minds on the course that the festival proprieties and your own safety recommend; these people are extremely poor; a little relief will gain you friends worth having at a trifling cost.

IV

The Rich to Cronus, Greeting.

Do you really suppose, Sire, that these letters of the poor have gone exclusively to *your* address? Zeus is quite deaf with their clamour, their appeals for redistribution, their complaints of Destiny for her unfairness and of us for refusing them relief. But Zeus is Zeus; *he* knows where the fault lies, and consequently pays them very little attention. However, as the authority is at present with you, to you we will address our defence. Having before our eyes all that you have laid down on the beauty of assisting out of our abundance those who are in want, and the delight of associating and making merry with the poor, we adopted the principle of treating them on such equal terms that a guest could not possibly have anything to complain of.

On their side, they started with professions of wanting very little indeed; but that was only the thin edge of the wedge. Now, if their demands are not instantly and literally satisfied, there is bad temper and offence and talk; their tales may be as false as they will, every one believes them: they have been there; they must know! Our only choice was between a refusal that meant detestation, and a total surrender that meant speedy ruin and transfer to the begging class for ourselves.

But the worst is to come. At table that filling of the stomach (of which we have by no means the monopoly) does not so completely occupy them but that, when they have drunk a drop too much, they find time for familiarities with the attendants or saucy compliments to the ladies. Then, after being ill at our tables, they go home, and next day reproach us with the hunger and thirst they feelingly describe. If you doubt the accuracy of this account, we refer you to your own quondam guest Ixion, who being hospitably received by you and treated as one of yourselves distinguished himself by his drunken addresses to Hera.

For these among other reasons we determined to protect ourselves by giving them the entrée no longer. But if they engage under your guarantee to make only the moderate demands they now profess, and to abstain from outraging their hosts' feelings, what is ours shall be theirs; we shall be only too glad of their company. We will comply with your suggestions about the clothes and, as far as may be, about the gold, and in fact will do our duty. We ask them on their side to give up trading on our hospitality, and to be our friends instead of our toadies and parasites. If only the' will behave themselves, you shall have no reason to complain of us.

A FEAST OF LAPITHAE

Philo. Lycinus

Phi. Ah, Lycinus, I hear you had a very varied entertainment dining with Aristaenetus last night; a philosophic debate followed by a sharp difference of opinion, I understand; if Charinus's information was correct, it went as far as blows, and the conference had a bloody end.

Ly. Charinus? he was not there; what can he know about it? *Phi.* Dionicus the doctor had told him, he said; he was one of you, was he not?

Ly. Yes, but only later on; he came when the fray was already a promising one, though no blows had yet been struck. I doubt whether he could have any intelligible account to give, as he had not followed the beginning of the rivalry that was to end in bloodshed.

Phi. Just so; Charinus told me to apply to you, if I wanted a true description of all the details. Dionicus had mentioned that he had not been there all through, but said you knew the whole of the facts, and would remember the arguments too, as you are a real student and take more than an outside interest in that sort of thing. So no more ceremony, please, but spread me this most tempting of banquets; its attractions are enhanced by the fact that we shall enjoy it soberly, quietly, without bloodshed or danger, whatever regrettable words or deeds the old men's weak heads or the young men's vinous exaltation may have led them into.

Ly. What an indiscreet demand, Philo! What, make the story public? give a full description of what men do in their cups? A veil should be drawn over such things; they should be ascribed to Dionysus; I am not at all sure that he will pardon the man who holds aloof from his mystic influence. I should like to be sure that it does not betray an evil nature if you dwell too curiously on what you should forget as you leave the dining-room. 'Babble wet, But dry forget,' goes the rhyme. It was not right of Dionicus to blab to Charinus, bespattering great philosophers with stale wine-rinsings. No, get thee behind me; my lips are sealed.

Phi. Coquette! and you have mistaken your man too; I am quite aware that you are more eager to tell than I to hear:

I believe, if you had no one to listen, you would find a pillar or statue and out with the whole tale to it in one torrent. If I try to make off now, you will never let me go till I have done my listening; you will hold on to me and pursue me and solicit me. Then it will be my turn to coquet. Oh, very well; do not trouble to tell me; good-bye; I will get it out of some one else.

Ly. Oh, you needn't be so hasty. I will tell you, if you are so set upon it; only don't repeat it to everybody.

Phi. If I know anything whatever of you, you will take good care of that; you will not leave me many to repeat it to.

Now begin with telling me what Aristaenetus was giving the banquet for; was it his boy Zeno's wedding?

Ly. No, his girl Cleanthis's--to the son of Eucritus the banker, a student of philosophy.

Phi. I know; a fine lad; only a lad, though; old enough to marry?

Ly. Well, he was the most *suitable* to be had, I suppose. He is a well-behaved youngster, has taken up philosophy, and is sole heir to a rich father; so he was the selected bridegroom.

Phi. Ah, no doubt Eucritus's money is a consideration. Well, and who were the guests?

Ly. Why, I need not give you the whole list; what you want is the philosophers and men of letters. There was the old Stoic Zenothemis, and with him 'Labyrinth' Diphilus; Aristaenetus's son Zeno is his pupil. The Peripatetics were represented by Cleodemus--the ready, argumentative person--you know him; 'Sword,' and 'Cleaver,' his disciples call him. And then there was Hermon the Epicurean; directly he came in, there were queer looks and edgings away in the Stoic contingent; he might have been a parricide or an outlaw, by the way they treated him. These had been asked as Aristaenetus's personal friends and intimates, under which head come also Histiaeus the literary man and Dionysodorus the rhetorician.

Then Chaereas (that is the bridegroom's name) was responsible for his tutor Ion the Platonic--a grave reverend man remarkable for the composure of his expression. He is generally spoken of as 'The Standard,' so infallible is his judgement. As he walked up the room, everybody got out of his way and saluted him like some higher being; the great Ion's presence is like an angel's visit.

When nearly all the guests had arrived, and we were to take our places, the ladies occupied the whole of the table to the right of the entrance; there were a good many of them, surrounding the closely veiled bride. The table at the far end accommodated the general company, in due precedence.

At the one opposite the ladies, Eucritus had the first place, with Aristaenetus next him. Then a doubt arose whether the next was Zenothemis the Stoic's, in virtue of his years, or Hermon the Epicurean's, who is priest of the Twin Gods [96], and also of the noblest blood in the land. Zenothemis found the solution. 'Aristaenetus,' he said, 'if you place me below this Epicurean (I need not use worse language than *that*), I at once leave the room'; and calling his servant he made as if to depart. 'Have your way, Zenothemis,' said Hermon, 'though, whatever your contempt for Epicurus, etiquette would have suggested your giving way to my priesthood, if I had no other claims.' 'Priest and Epicurean! that is a good joke,' retorted Zenothemis, and took the place, with Hermon next him, however. Then came Cleodemus the Peripatetic, Ion with

---

[96] Castor and Pollux.

the bridegroom, myself, Diphilus and his pupil Zeno, then Dionysodorus the rhetorician and Histiaeus the literary man.

Phi. Upon my word, a very temple of the Muses, peopled mainly with the learned! I congratulate Aristaenetus on choosing for his guests on so auspicious an occasion these patterns of wisdom; he skimmed the cream off every sect in a most catholic spirit.

Ly. Oh, yes, he is not one's idea of the rich man at all; he cares for culture, and gives most of his time to those who have it.

Well, we fell to, quietly at first, on the ample and varied fare. But you do not want a catalogue of soups and pastry and sauces; there was plenty of everything. At this stage Cleodemus bent down to Ion, and said:

'Do you see how the old man' (this was Zenothemis; I could overhear their talk) 'is stuffing down the good things--his dress gets a good deal of the gravy--and what a lot he hands back to his servant? he thinks we cannot see him, and does not care whether there will be enough to go round. Just call Lycinus's attention to him.' This was quite unnecessary, as I had had an excellent view of it for some time.

Just after Cleodemus had said this, in burst Alcidamas the cynic. He had not been asked, but put a good face upon it with the usual 'No summons Menelaus waits.' The general opinion clearly was that he was an impudent rogue, and various people struck in with what came to hand:

'What, Menelaus, art distraught?' or, 'It liked not Agamemnon, Atreus' son,' and other neat tags suited to the occasion; but these were all asides; no one ventured to make them audible to him. Alcidamas is a man uncommonly 'good at the war-cry'; he will bark you louder than any dog of them all, literal or metaphorical; my gentlemen all knew he was their better, and lay low.

Aristaenetus told him he was quite right to come; would he take a chair and sit behind Histiaeus and Dionysodorus? 'Stuff!' he said; 'a soft womanish trick, to sit on a chair or a stool! one might as well loll at one's food half on one's back, like all of you on this soft couch with purple cushions under you. As for me, I will take my dinner standing and walking about the room. If I get tired, I will lay my old cloak on the ground and prop myself on my elbow like Heracles in the pictures.' 'Just as you please,' said Aristaenetus; and after that Alcidamas fed walking round, shifting his quarters like the Scythians according to where pasturage was richest, and following the servants up as they carried the dishes.

However, he did not let feeding interrupt his energetic expositions of virtue and vice, and his scoffs at gold and silver. What was the good of this multitude of wonderful cups, he wanted to know, when earthenware would serve the purpose? Aristaenetus got rid of his obtrusiveness for the moment by signing to his servant to hand the cynic a huge goblet of potent liquor. It seemed a happy thought; but he little knew the woes that were to flow from that goblet. When Alcidamas got it, he was quiet for a while, throwing himself on the ground in dishabille as he had threatened, with his elbow planted vertically, just in the attitude of the painters' *Heracles with Pholus*.

By this time the wine was flowing pretty freely everywhere; healths were drunk, conversation was general, and the lights had come in. I now noticed the boy standing near Cleodemus--a good-looking cup-bearer--to have an odd smile on. I suppose I am to give you all the by-play of the dinner, especially any tender incidents. Well, so I was trying to get at the reason for the smile. In a little while he came to take Cleodemus's cup from him; he gave the boy's fingers a pinch, and handed him up a couple of shillings, I think it was, with the cup. The smile appeared again in response to the pinch, but I imagine he failed to notice the coins; he did not get hold of them; they went ringing on the floor, and there were two blushing faces to be seen. Those round, however, could not tell whose the money was, the boy saying he had not dropped it, and Cleodemus, at whose place it had been heard to fall, not confessing to the loss. So the matter was soon done with; hardly any one had grasped the situation-- only Aristaenetus, as far as I could gather. He shifted the boy soon after, effecting the transfer without any fuss, and assigned Cleodemus a strong grown-up fellow who might be a mule or horse groom. So much for that business; it would have seriously compromised Cleodemus if it had attracted general attention; but it was smothered forthwith by Aristaenetus's tactful handling of the offence.

Alcidamas the cynic, who had now emptied his goblet, after finding out the bride's name, called for silence; he then faced the ladies, and cried out in a loud voice:

'Cleanthis, I drink to you in the name of my patron Heracles.' There was a general laugh; upon which, 'You vile scum,' says he, 'you laugh, do you, because I invoke our God Heracles as I toast the bride? Let me tell you that, if she will not pledge me, she shall never bear a son as brave of spirit, as free of judgement, as strong of body, as myself.' And he proceeded to show us more of the said body, till it was scarcely decent. The company irritated him by laughing again; he stood there with a wandering wrathful eye, and looked as if he were going to make trouble. He would probably have brought down his stick on somebody's head, but for the timely arrival of an enormous cake, the sight of which mollified him; he quieted down, and accompanied its progress, eating hard.

The rest were mostly flushed with wine by this time, and the room was full of clamour. Dionysodorus the rhetorician was alternately delivering speeches of his own composition and receiving the plaudits of the servants behind. Histiaeus, the literary man below him, was making an eclectic mixture of Pindar, Hesiod, and Anacreon, whose collaboration produced a most remarkable ode, some of it really prophetic of what was soon to come--'Then hide met stubborn hide,' for instance, and 'Uprose the wailings and the prayers of men.' Zenothemis too had taken a scroll in small writing from his servant, which he was reading aloud.

Now came one of the usual slight breaks in the procession of dishes; and Aristaenetus, to avoid the embarrassment of a blank, told his jester to come in and talk or perform, by way of putting the company still more at their ease. So in came an ugly fellow with a shaven head--just a few hairs standing upright on the crown. He danced with dislocations and contortions, which made him still more absurd, then improvised and delivered some anapaests in an Egyptian accent, and wound up with witticisms on the guests.

Most of them took these in good part; but when it came to Alcidamas's turn, and he called him a Maltese poodle[97], Alcidamas, who had shown signs of jealousy for some time and did not at all like the way he was holding every one's attention, lost his temper. He threw off his cloak and challenged the fellow to a bout of pancratium; otherwise he would let him feel his stick. So poor Satyrion, as the jester was called, had to accept the challenge and stand up. A charming spectacle--the philosopher sparring and exchanging blows with a buffoon! Some of us were scandalized and some amused, till Alcidamas found he had his bellyful, being no match for the tough little fellow. They gave us a good laugh.

It was now, not long after this match, that Dionicus the doctor came in. He had been detained, he said, by a brain-fever case; the patient was Polyprepon the piper, and thereby hung a tale. He had no sooner entered the room, not knowing how far gone the man was, when he jumped up, secured the door, drew a dagger, and handed him the pipes, with an order to play them; and when Dionicus could not, he took a strap and inflicted chastisement on the palms of his hands. To escape from this perilous position, Dionicus proposed a match, with a scale of forfeits to be exacted with the strap. He played first himself, and then handed over the pipes, receiving in exchange the strap and dagger. These he lost no time in sending out of window into the open court, after which it was safe to grapple with him and shout for help; the neighbours broke open the door and rescued him. He showed us his wealed hands and some scratches on his face. His story had as distinguished a success as the jester before; he then squeezed himself in by Histiaeus and dined on what was left. His coming was providential, and he most useful in the sequel.

There now appeared a messenger who said he brought a communication from Hetoemocles the Stoic, which his master had directed him to read publicly, and then return. With Aristaenetus's permission he took it to the lamp, and began reading.

Phi. The usual thing, I suppose--a panegyric on the bride, or an epithalamium?

Ly. Just what we took it for; however, it was quite another story. Here are the contents:

-----

[97] Alcidamas being a cynic, or 'dog.'

HETOEMOCLES THE PHILOSOPHER TO ARISTAENETUS, GREETING.

My views on dining are easily deducible from my whole past life; though daily importuned by far richer men than you to join them, I invariably refuse; I know too well the tumults and follies that attend the wine-cup. But if there is one whose neglect I may fairly resent, it is yourself; the fruit of my long and unremitting attentions to you is to find myself not on the roll of your friends; I, your next-door neighbour, am singled out for exclusion. The sting of it is in the personal ingratitude; happiness for me is not found in a plate of wild boar or hare or pastry; these I get in abundance at the houses of people who understand the proprieties; this very day I might have dined (and well, by all accounts) with my pupil Pammenes; but he pressed me to no purpose; I was reserving myself, poor fool, for you. But you pass me by, and feast others. I ought not to be surprised; you have not acquired the power of distinguishing merit; you have no apprehensive imagination. I know whence the blow comes; it is from your precious philosophers, Zenothemis and The Labyrinth, whose mouths (though I would not boast) I could stop with a single syllogism. Let either of them tell me, What is Philosophy? or, not to go beyond the merest elements, how does condition differ from constitution? for I will not resort to real puzzles, as the Horns *the* Sorites *, or the* Reaper[98]. *Well, I wish you joy of their company. As for me, holding as I do that nothing is good but what is right, I shall get over a slight like this.*

You will be kind enough not to resort later to the well-worn excuse of having forgotten in the bustle of your engagements; I have spoken to you twice to-day, in the morning at your house, and later when you were sacrificing at the Anaceum. This is to let your guests know the rights of the case.

If you think it is the dinner I care about, reflect upon the story of Oeneus; you will observe that, when he omitted Artemis alone from the Gods to whom he offered sacrifice, she resented it. Homer's account of it states that he

> *Forgot or ne'er bethought him--woeful blindness!*
> *Euripides's begins,*
> *This land of Calydon, across the gulf*
> *From Pelops' land, with all its fertile plains--;*
> *and Sophocles's,*
> *Upon the tilth of Oeneus Leto's child,*
> *Far-darting Goddess, loosed a monstrous boar.*

I quote you but these few of the many passages upon the incident, just to suggest the qualities of him whom you have passed over, to entertain, and to have your son taught by, Diphilus! natural enough; of course, the lad fancies him, and finds him an agreeable master! If tale-telling were not beneath me, I

---

[98] See *Puzzles* in Notes.

would add a piece of information that, if you choose, you can get confirmed by the boy's attendant Zopyrus. But a wedding is not a time for unpleasantness or denunciations, especially of offences so vile. Diphilus deserves it richly at my hands, indeed--two pupils he has stolen from me--; but for the good name of Philosophy I will hold my hand.

My man has instructions, if you should offer him a portion of wild boar or venison or sesame cake to bring me in lieu of my dinner, to refuse it. I would not have you find the motive of my letter in such desires.

My dear fellow, I went all hot and cold as this was read; I was praying that the earth might swallow me up when I saw everybody laughing at the different points; the most amused were those who knew Hetoemocles and his white hair and reverend looks; it was such a surprise to find the reality behind that imposing beard and serious countenance. I felt sure Aristaenetus had passed him over not in neglect, but because he supposed he would never accept an invitation or have anything to do with festivities; he had thought it out of the question, and not worth trying.

As soon as the man stopped reading, all eyes were turned on Zeno and Diphilus, who were pale with apprehension, and confirmed by their embarrassment the insinuations of Hetoemocles. Aristaenetus was uneasy and disturbed, but urged us to drink, and tried to smooth the matter over with an attempt at a smile; he told the man he would see to it, and dismissed him. Zeno disappeared shortly after; his attendant had signed to him, as from his father, to retire.

Cleodemus had been on the look-out for an opportunity; he was spoiling for a fight with the Stoics, and chafing over the difficulty of starting the subject:

but the letter had struck the right key, and off he went. 'Now we see the productions of your fine Chrysippus, your glorious Zeno, your Cleanthes--a few poor catch-words, some fruitless posers, a philosophic exterior, and a large supply of--Hetoemocleses. What ripe wisdom does this letter reveal, with its conclusion that Aristaenetus is an Oeneus, and Hetoemocles an Artemis! How auspicious, how suitable to the occasion, its tone '

To be sure,' chimed in Hermon, his left-hand neighbour; he had no doubt heard that Aristaenetus had bespoken a wild boar, and thought the introduction of the one at Calydon appropriate. Aristaenetus, I adjure you by the domestic altar, let hint taste the victim, or we shall have the old man starving, and withering away like his Meleager. Though indeed it would not be so very hard on him; such a fate is one of Chrysippus's *things indifferent.*'

Here Zenothemis woke up and thundered out:

'Chrysippus? you name that name? because a pretender like Hetoemocles comes short of his profession, you argue from him to the real sages, to Cleanthes and Zeno? And who are the men, pray, who hold such language? Why, Hermon, who shore the curls, the solid golden curls, of the Dioscuri, and who will yet receive his barber's fee from the executioner. And

Cleodemus, who was caught in adultery with his pupil Sostratus's wife, and paid the shameful penalty. Silence would better become the owners of such consciences.' 'Who trades in his own wife's favours? ' retorted Cleodemus; 'I do not do that, and I do not undertake to keep my foreign pupil's purse and then swear by Polias the deposit was never made; I do not lend money at fifty per cent, and I do not hale my pupils into court if fees are not paid to the day.' 'You will hardly deny, though,' said Zenothemis, 'that you supplied Crito with the poison for his father.'

And therewith, his cup being in his hand, about half full of wine, he emptied it over the pair; and Ion, whose worst guilt was being their neighbour, came in for a good deal of it. Hermon bent forward, dried his head, and entered a protest. Cleodemus, having no wine to reply with, leant over and spat at Zenothemis; at the same time he clutched the old man's beard with his left hand, and was aiming a blow which would have killed him, when Aristaenetus arrested it, stepped over Zenothemis, and lay down between the two, making himself a buffer in the interests of peace.

All this time, Philo, my thoughts were busy enough with the old commonplace, that after all it is no use having all theory at your finger's ends, if you do not conform your conduct to the right. Here were these masters of precept making themselves perfectly ridiculous in practice. Then it was borne in upon me that possibly the vulgar notion is right, and culture only misleads the people who are too much wrapt up in books and bookish ideas. Of all that philosophic company there was not a man--not so much as an accidental exception--who could pass muster; if his conduct did not condemn him, his words did yet more fatally. I could not make the wine responsible, either; the author of that letter was fasting and sober.

Things seemed to go by contraries; you might see the ordinary people behaving quite properly at table; no rioting and disorder there; the most they did was to laugh at and, no doubt, censure the others, whom they had been accustomed to respect and to credit with the qualities their appearance suggested. It was the wise men who made beasts of themselves, abused each other, over-fed, shouted and came to blows. I thought one could find no better illustration for our dinner than the poets' story of Eris. When she was not invited to Peleus's nuptials, she threw that apple on the table which brought about the great Trojan war. Hetoemocles's letter was just such an apple, woeful Iliad and all. For buffer-Aristaenetus had proved ineffectual, and the quarrel between Zenothemis and Cleodemus was proceeding.

For the present,' said the latter, 'I am satisfied with exposing your ignorance; to-morrow I will give you your deserts more adequately. Pray explain, Zenothemis, or the reputable Diphilus

for you, how it is that you Stoics class the acquisition of wealth 1 among the things indifferent, and then concentrate your whole efforts upon it, hang perpetually about the rich to that end, lend money, screw out your usury, and take pay for your teaching. Or again, if you hate pleasure and condemn the

Epicureans, how comes it that you will do and endure the meanest things for it? you resent it if you are not asked out; and when you are, you eat so much, and convey so much more to your servant's keeping'--and he interrupted himself to make a grab at the napkin that Zenothemis's boy was holding, full of all sorts of provender; he meant to get it away and empty the contents on the floor; but the boy held on too tight.

'Quite right, Cleodemus,' said Hermon; 'let them tell us   why they condemn pleasure, and yet expect more of it than any one else.' 'No, no,' says Zenothemis; 'you give us *your* grounds, Cleodemus, for saying wealth is *not* a thing indifferent.' 'No, I tell you; let us have *your* case.' So the see-saw went on, till Ion came out of his retirement and called a truce:

'I will give you,' he said, 'a theme worthy of the occasion; and you shall speak and listen without trying for personal triumphs; take a leaf from our Plato this time.' 'Hear, hear,' from the company, especially from Aristaenetus and Eucritus, who hailed this escape from unpleasantness. The former now went back to his own place, confident of peace.

The 'repast,' as they call it, had just made its appearance; each guest was served with a bird, a slice of wild boar, a portion of hare, a fried fish, some sesame cakes and sweet-meats--all these to be taken home if the guest chose. Every man had not a separate dish, however; Aristaenetus and Eucritus shared one little table, from which each was to take what belonged to him; so Zenothemis the Stoic and Hermon the Epicurean; Cleodemus and Ion had the third table, the bridegroom and I the next; Diphilus had a double portion, by the absence of Zeno. Remember these details, Philo; you will find they bear on the story.

Phi. Trust me.

Ly. Ion proceeded:

'I will start, then, if you wish it.' He reflected a moment, and then:

'With so much talent in the room, no less a subject might seem indicated than Ideas [99], Incorporeals, and the Immortality of the Soul. On the other hand our divergent views might make that too controversial; so I will take the question of marriage, and say what seems appropriate. The counsel of perfection here would be to dispense with it, and be satisfied, according to the prescription of Plato and Socrates, with contemplating male beauty. So, and only so, is absolute virtue to be attained. But if marriage is admitted as a practical necessity, then we should adopt the Platonic system of holding our wives in common, thus obviating rivalry.'

The unseasonableness of these remarks raised a laugh. And Dionysodorus had another criticism:

'Spare us these provincialisms,' he said; 'or give us your authority for "rivality."' 'Such carpings are beneath contempt,' was the polite reply.

---

[99] See *Plato* in Notes.

Dionysodorus was about to return the compliment with interest, when our good man of letters intervened:

'Stop,' said Histiaeus, 'and let me read you an epithalamium.'

He at once went off at score; and I think I can reproduce the effusion:

> Or like, in Aristaenetus's hall,
>   Cleanthis, softly nurtured bright princess,
> Surpassing other beauties virginal,
>   Cythera's Queen, or Helen's loveliness.
> Bridegroom, the best of your contemporaries,
>   Nireus's and Achilles' peer, rejoice!
> While we in hymeneal voluntaries
>   Over the pair keep lifting up our voice.

By the time the laughter that not unnaturally followed had subsided, it was time to pack up our 'repasts'; Aristaenetus and Eucritus took each his intended portion; Chaereas and I, Ion and Cleodemus, did likewise. But as Zeno was not there, Diphilus expected to come in for his share too. He said everything on that table was his, and disputed possession with the servants. There was a tug of war between them just like that over the body of Patroclus; at last he was worsted and had to let go, to the huge amusement of all, which he heightened by taking the thing as a most serious wrong.

As I told you, Hermon and Zenothemis were neighbours, the latter having the upper place. Their portions were equal enough except in one respect, and the division was peaceful until that was reached. But the bird on Hermon's side was--by chance, no doubt--the fatter. The moment came for them to take their respective birds. At this point--now attend carefully, please, Philo; here is the kernel of the whole affair--at this point Zenothemis let his own bird lie, and took the fatter one before Hermon. But Hermon was not going to be put upon; he laid hold of it too. Then their voices were lifted up, they closed, belaboured each other's faces with the birds, clutched each other's beards, and called for assistance, Hermon appealing to Cleodemus, Zenothemis to Alcidamas and Diphilus. The allies took their sides, Ion alone preserving neutrality.

The hosts engaged. Zenothemis lifted a goblet from the table where it stood before Aristaenetus, and hurled it at Hermon;

> And him it missed, but found another mark,

laying open the bridegroom's skull with a sound deep gash.

This opened the lips of the ladies; most of them indeed jumped down into the battle's interspace, led by the young man's mother, as soon as she saw his blood flowing; the bride too was startled from her place by terror for him. Meanwhile Alcidamas was in his glory maintaining the cause of Zenothemis; down came his stick on Cleodemus's skull, he injured Hermon's jaw, and severely wounded several of the servants who tried to protect them. The other side were not beaten, however; Cleodemus with levelled finger was gouging out Zenothemis's eye, not to mention fastening on his nose and biting a piece off it; and when Diphilus came to Zenothemis's rescue, Hermon pitched him head first from the couch.

Histiaeus too was wounded in trying to part the pair; it was a kick in the teeth, I think, from Cleodemus, who took him for Diphilus. So the poor man of letters lay 'disgorging blood,' as his own Homer describes it. It was a scene of tumult and tears. The women were hanging over Chaereas and wailing, the other men trying to restore peace. The great centre of destruction was Alcidamas, who after routing the forces immediately opposed to him was striking at whatever presented itself. Many a man had fallen there, be sure, had he not broken his stick. I was standing close up to the wall watching the proceedings in which I took no part; Histiaeus's fate had taught me the dangers of intervention. It was a sight to recall the Lapithae and Centaurs--tables upside down, blood in streams, bowls hurtling in the air.

At last Alcidamas upset the lamp, there was a great darkness, and confusion was worse confounded. It was not so easy to procure another light, and many a horrid deed was done in the dark. When some one came at last with a lamp, Alcidamas was discovered stripping and applying compulsion to the flute-girl, and Dionysodorus proved to have been as incongruously engaged; as he stood up, a goblet rolled out of his bosom. His account of the matter was that Ion had picked it up in the confusion, and given it him to save it from damage! for which piece of carefulness Ion was willing to receive credit.

So the party came to an end, tears being resold in the laughter at Alcidamas, Dionysodorus and Ion. The wounded were borne off in sad case, especially old Zenothemis, holding one hand on his nose and the other on his eye, and bellowing out that the agony was more than he could bear. Hermon was in poor condition himself, having lost a couple of teeth; but he could not let this piece of evidence go; 'Bear in mind, Zenothemis,' he called out, 'that you do *not* consider pain a thing indifferent.' The bridegroom, who had been seen to by Dionicus, was also taken off with his head in bandages--in the carriage in which he was to have taken his bride home. It had been a sorry wedding-feast for him, poor fellow. Dionicus had done what he could for the rest, they were taken home to bed, and very ill most of them were on the way. Alcidamas stayed where he was; it was impossible to get rid of him, as he had thrown himself down anyhow across a couch and fallen asleep.

And now you know all about the banquet, my dear Philo; a tragedy epilogue seems called for:

Hidden power sways each hour:

Men propose, the Gods dispose:

661

Fail surmises, come surprises.

It was the unexpected that came to pass here, at any rate. Well, live and learn; I know now that a quiet man had better keep clear of these feasts of reason.

DEMOSTHENES
AN ENCOMIUM

A LITTLE before noon on the sixteenth, I was walking in the Porch--it was on the left-hand side as you go out--, when Thersagoras appeared; I dare say he is known to some of you--short, hook-nosed, fair-complexioned, and virile. He drew nearer, and I spoke:

'Thersagoras the poet. Whence, and whither?' 'From home, hither,' he replied. 'Just a stroll?' I asked. 'Why, I do need a stroll too,' he said. 'I got up in the small hours, impressed with the duty of making a poetic offering on Homer's birthday.' 'Very proper,' said I; 'a good way of paying for the education he has given you.' 'That was how I began,' he continued, 'and time has glided by till now it is just upon noon; that was what I meant by saying I wanted a stroll.

'However, I wanted something else much more--an inter view with this gentleman' (and he pointed to the Homer; you know the one on the right of the Ptolemies' shrine, with the hair hanging loose); 'I came to greet him, and to pray for a good flow of verse.' 'Ah,' I sighed, 'if prayers would do it! in that case *I* should have given Demosthenes a worrying for assistance against *his* birthday. If prayers availed, I would join my wishes to yours; for the boons we desire are the same.' 'Well, I put down to Homer,' he replied, 'my facility of this night and morning; ardours divine and mystic have possessed me. But you shall judge. Here are my tablets, which I have brought with designs upon any idle friend I might light upon; and you, I rejoice to see, are idle.'

'Ah, you lucky man!' I exclaimed; 'you are like the winner of the three miles, who had washed off the dust, and could amuse himself for the rest of the day. He was minded to crack a story with the wrestler, when the wrestling was next on the programme; but the wrestler asked him whether he had felt like cracking stories when he toed the line just now. You have won your poetic three miles, and want me to minister to your amusement just as I am shivering at the thought of my hundred yards.' He laughed:

'Why, how will it make things worse for you? '

'Ah, you probably consider Demosthenes of much less account than Homer. *You* are very proud of your eulogy on Homer; and is Demosthenes a light matter to *me*?' 'A trumped up charge,' he exclaimed; 'I am not going to sow dissension between these two mighty ones, though it is true my own allegiance is rather to Homer.'

'Good,' I said, 'and you must allow me to give mine to Demosthenes. But, though you do not disqualify my subject, I am sure you think poetry the only real treatment; you feel about mere rhetoric what the cavalryman feels as he gallops past the infantry.' 'I hope I am not so mad as that,' he said, 'though a considerable touch of madness is required of him who would pass the gates of poetry.' 'If you come to that, prose cannot do without some divine inspiration either, if it is not to be flat and common.' He admitted that at once:

'I often delight myself with comparing passages from Demosthenes and other prose writers with Homer in point of vehemence, pungency, fire. "Flown with wine" I pair off against the revellings and dancings and debauchery of Philip; "One presage that ne'er fails[100]" finds its counterpart in "It is for brave men, founding themselves upon brave hopes--"; "How would old Peleus, lord of steeds, repine--" is matched by "What a cry of lamentation would go up from the men of those days who laid down their lives for glory and freedom--"; "fluent Python" reminds me of Odysseus's "snow-flake speech"; "If 'twere our lot neither to age nor die," I illustrate by "For every man's life must end in death, though he shut himself up in a narrow chamber for safer keeping." In fact the instances are numberless in which they attack their meaning by the same road.

'I love too to study his feelings and moods and transitions, the variety with which he combats weariness, his resumptions after digression, the charm of his opportune illustrations, and the never-failing native purity of his style.

'It has often struck me about Demosthenes--for I will tell the whole truth out--that that looser of the bonds of speech rebukes Athenian slackness with a dignity that is lacking in the "Greekesses" used by Homer of the Greeks; and again he maintains the tragic intensity proper to the great Hellenic drama more consistently than the poet who inserts speeches at the very crisis of battle and allows energy to evaporate in words.

'As often as I read Demosthenes, the balanced clauses, the rhythmic movement and cadence, make me forget that this is not my beloved poetry; for Homer too abounds in contrast and parallel, in figures startling or simple. It is a provision of nature, I suppose, that each faculty should have its proper equipment attached to it. How should I scorn your Muse? I know her powers too well.

'None the less, I consider my task of a Homeric encomium twice as difficult as your praise of Demosthenes; not because it must be in verse, but from the nature of the material; *I* cannot lay down a foundation of fact to build the edifice of praise upon; there is nothing but the poems themselves. Everything else is uncertain--his country, his family, his time. If there had been any uncertainty about them,

> Debate and strife had not divided men;

but as it is, they give him for a country Ios or Colophon or Cumae, Chios, Smyrna, or Egyptian Thebes, or half a hundred other places; his father may be Macon the Lydian, or he may be a river; his mother is now Melanope, and now in default of satisfactory human descent a dryad; his time is the Heroic Age, or else perhaps it is the Ionic. There is no knowing for certain whether he was

---

[100] Homer, *Il.* xii. 243. 'One omen is best--to fight for our own country.'

before or after Hesiod, even; and no wonder, considering that some object to his very name, and will have him Melesigenes instead. So too with his poverty, and his blindness. However, all these questions are best left alone. So you see the arena open to my panegyric is extremely limited; my theme is a poet and not a man of action; I can infer and collect his wisdom only from his verses.

'Your work, now, can be reeled smoothly off out of hand; you have your definite known facts; the butcher's meat is there, only needing to be garnished with the sauce of your words. History supplies you with the greatness and distinction of Demosthenes; it is all known; his country was Athens, the splendid, the famous, the bulwark of Hellas. Now if *I* could have laid hands on Athens, I might have used the poet's right to introduce the loves and judgements and sojourns there of the Gods, the gifts they lavished on it, the tale of Eleusis. As for its laws and courts and festivals, its Piraeus and its colonies, the memorials set up in it of victory by land and sea, Demosthenes himself is the authority for saying that no words could do justice to them. My material would have been inexhaustible; and I could not have been accused of hanging up my true theme; the formula of panegyric includes the arraying of the man in the splendours of his country. So too Isocrates ekes out his *Helen* by introducing Theseus. It is true that poets have their privileges; and perhaps *you* have to be more careful about your proportions; there must not be *too* much sack to the proverbial halfpennyworth of bread.

'Well then, let Athens go; but your discourse at once finds another support in his father's wealth--that "golden base" which Pindar likes--; for to be responsible for providing a warship was to be among the richest Athenians in those days. And though he died while Demosthenes was quite a child, we are not to count his orphan state a disaster; it led to the distinction that brought his splendid gifts into notice.

'Tradition gives us no hint of how Homer was educated or developed his powers; the panegyrist must plunge straight into his works, and can find nothing to talk about in his breeding and training and pupilage; he has not even the resource of that Hesiodic sprig of bay which could make a facile poet out of a shepherd. But think of *your* abundance in this branch of the subject. There is Callistratus and all the mighty roll of orators, Alcidamas, Isocrates, Isaeus, Eubulides. Then again, at Athens even those who were subject to paternal control had countless temptations to indulgence, youth is the susceptible time, a neglected ward could have lived as irregular a life as he chose, and yet the objects that Demosthenes set up for himself were philosophy and patriotism, and the doors they took him to not Phryne's, but those of Aristotle and Theophrastus, Xenocrates and Plato.

'And so, my dear sir, your way is open to a disquisition upon the two kinds of human love, the one sprung of a desire that is like the sea, outrageous, fierce, stormily rocking the soul; it is a true sea wave, which the earthly Aphrodite sets rolling with the tempestuous passions of youth; but the other is the steady drawing of a golden cord from heaven; it does not scorch and pierce and leave festering wounds; it impels towards the pure and unsullied ideal of absolute beauty, and is a sane madness in those souls which "yet hold of Zeus and nurse the spark divine."

'Love will find out the way, though that way involve a shaven head, a cavern dwelling, a discouraging mirror and punitive sword, a disciplining of the tongue, a belated apprenticeship to the actor's art, a straining of the memory, a conquest over clamour, and a borrowing of night hours to lengthen toilsome days[101]. All this your Demosthenes endured, and who knows not what an orator it made of him? his speech packed with thought and terse of language, himself convincing in his knowledge of human nature, as splendid in the elevation as mighty in the force of his sentiments, the master and not the slave of his words and his ideas, ever fresh with the graces of his art. He is the one orator whose speech has, in the bold phrase of Leosthenes, at once the breath of life and the strength of wrought iron.

Callisthenes remarked of Aeschylus that he wrote his tragedies in wine, which lent vigour and warmth to his work. With Demosthenes it was otherwise; he composed not on wine but on water; whence the witticism of Demades, that most men's tongues are regulated by water[102], but Demosthenes's pen was subject to the same influence. And Pytheas detected the smell of the midnight oil in the very perfection of the speeches. Well, there is much in common between your subject and mine, so far as this branch of them is concerned; on Homer's *poems* I was no worse off than you are.

'But when you come to your hero's acts of humanity, his pecuniary sacrifices, his grand political achievements ' (and he was going on in full swing to the rest of the catalogue, when I interrupted, with a laugh:

'Must I be dowsed with the remainder of your canful, good bath-man?' 'Most certainly,' he retorted, and went straight on), 'the public entertainments he gave, the public burdens he assumed, the ships, the wall, the trench he contributed to, the prisoners he ransomed, the girls he portioned, his admirable policy, the embassies he served on, the laws he got passed, the mighty issues he was concerned in--why, then I cannot but laugh to see your contracted brows; as if a recital of the exploits of Demosthenes *could* lack matter!'

'I believe you think, my good man,' I protested, 'that I have never had the deeds of Demosthenes drummed into me; I should be singular among rhetoricians, then.' 'It was on the assumption,' he said, 'implied by you, that we want assistance. But perhaps your case is a very different one; is the light so bright that you cannot manage to fix your eyes on the dazzling glory of Demosthenes? Well, I was rather like that about Homer at first. Indeed, I came very near turning mine away, thinking I could not possibly face my subject. However, I got over it somehow or other; became gradually inured, as it were,

---

[101] See *Demosthenes* in Notes.
[102] Speeches in the law courts had a time limit appointed, which was measured by the water-clock or clepsydra, generally called simply 'the water,' 'my water,' 'his water,' &c.

superior to the weakness of vision that would have condemned me for a bastard eagle and no true son of Homer.

'But now here is another great advantage that I consider you have over me. The poetic faculty has a single aim; from which it follows that Homer's glory must be laid hold of at once and as a whole. You on the other hand, if you were to attempt dealing with the whole Demosthenes all at once, would never know what to say; you would waver and not be able to set your thoughts to work. You would be like the *gourmand* at a Sicilian banquet, or the aesthete who has a thousand delightful sights and sounds presented to him at once; they do not know which way to turn for their conflicting desires. I suspect that you too are distracted and find concentration impossible; all round you are the varied attractions--his magnanimity, his fire, his orderly life, his oratorical force and practical courage, the endless opportunities of gain that he scorned, his justice, humanity, honour, spirit, sagacity, and each of all his great services to his country. It may well be that, when you behold on this side decrees, ambassadors, speeches, laws, on the other, fleets, Euboea, Boeotia, Chios, Rhodes, the Hellespont, Byzantium, you are pulled to and fro among these too numerous invitations, and cannot tell which to accept.

'Pindar once found himself in a similar difficulty with an overabundant theme:

> Ismenus? Melia's distaff golden-bright?
> Cadmus? the race from dragon's teeth that came?
> Thebe's dark circlet? the all-daring might
> Of Heracles? great Bacchus' merry fame?
> White-armed Harmonia's bridal?--Ay, but which?
> My Muse, we 're poor in that we are too rich.

You, I dare say, are in the same quandary. Logic and life, rhetoric and philosophy, popularity and death--ay, but which?

The maze is quite easy to escape from, though; you have only to take hold of one single clue, no matter which--his oratory, if you will, so that it is taken by itself--, and stick to that one throughout your present discourse. You will have ample material; his oratory is not of the Periclean type. Pericles could lighten and thunder, and he could hit the right nail on the head; so much tradition tells us; but we have nothing to judge for ourselves by, no doubt because, beyond the momentary impression produced, there was in his performances no element of permanence, nothing that could stand the searching test of time. But with Demosthenes's work--well, that it will be your province to deal with, if your choice goes that way.

Or if you prefer his character, or his policy, it will be well to isolate some particular detail--if you are greedy you may pick out two or three--which will give you quite enough to go upon; so great was he at every point. And for such specializing we have Homer's example; the compliments he pays his heroes are attached to parts of them, their feet, their heads, their hair, even their shields or something they have on; and the Gods seem to have had no objection to poets' basing their praises merely on a distaff, a bow, or the aegis; a limb or a quality must pass still more easily; and as for good actions, it is impossible to give an exhaustive list of them. Demosthenes accordingly will not blame you for confining your eulogy to *one* of his merits, especially as to celebrate the whole of them worthily would be beyond even *his* powers.'

When Thersagoras had finished this harangue, I remarked:

'Your intention is plain; I am to be convinced that you are more than a good poet; so you have constructed your prose Demosthenes as a pendant to your verse Homer.' 'No, no,' he said; 'what made me run on so long was the idea that, if I could ease your mind by showing how light your task was, I should have secured my listener.' 'Then let me tell you that *your* object has not been furthered, and my case has only been aggravated.' 'A fine doctor I seem to be!' he said. 'Not knowing where the difficulty lies,' I continued, 'you are a doctor who mistakes his patient's ailment and treats him for another.' 'How so?'

'You have been prescribing for the troubles that would attend a first attempt; unfortunately it is years and years since I got through that stage, and your remedies are quite out of date.' 'Why, then,' he exclaimed, 'the cure is complete; nobody is nervous about a road of which he knows every inch.'

'Ah, but then I have set my heart upon reversing the feat that Anniceris of Cyrene exhibited to Plato and his friends. To show what a fine driver he was, he drove round the Academy time after time exactly in his own track, which looked after it as if it had only been traversed once. Now my endeavour is just the opposite, to *avoid* my old tracks; and it is by no means so easy to keep out of the ruts.' 'Pauson's is the trick for you,' he said. 'What is that? I never heard of it.'

'Pauson the painter was commissioned to do a horse rolling. He painted one galloping in a cloud of dust. As he was at work upon it, his patron came in, and complained that this was not what he had ordered. Pauson just turned the picture upside down and told his man to hold it so for inspection; there was the horse rolling on its back.' 'You dear innocent!' I said; 'do you suppose I have kept my picture turned the same way all these years? It has been shifted and tilted at every conceivable angle, till I begin to have apprehensions of ending like Proteus.' 'And how was that?' 'Oh, I mean the issue of his attempts to evade human observation; when he had exhausted all shapes of animals and plants and elements, finding no metamorphosis left him, he had to be Proteus again.'

'You have more shifts than ever Proteus had,' he said, 'to get off hearing my poem.'

'Oh, do not say that,' said I; 'off goes my burden of care, and I am at your service. Perhaps when you have got over your own pains of child-birth you will show more feeling for my delicate state.'

He liked the offer, we settled down on a convenient stone step, and I listened to some excellent poetry. In the middle of reading he was seized with an idea, did up his tablets, and said:

'You shall have your hearer's fee, as well deserved as an Athenian's after a day in court or assembly. Thank me, please.' 'I do, before I know what for. But what may it be?' 'It was in the Macedonian royal archives that I came across the book;

I was delighted with it at the time, and took considerable trouble to secure it; it has just come into my head that I have it at home. It contains, among details of Antipater's management of the household, facts about Demosthenes that I think you will find worth your best attention.' 'You shall have payment on the spot,' I said, 'in the shape of an audience for the rest of your verses; and moreover I shall not part with you till your promise is fulfilled. You have given me a luscious Homer birthday dinner; and it seems you are to be at the charges of the Demosthenes one too.'

He read to the end, we stayed long enough for me to give the poem its meed of praise, and then adjourned to his house, where after some search the book was found. I took it away with me, and on further acquaintance was so much impressed by it that I shall do no editing, but read it you *totidem verbis*. Asclepius is not less honoured if his worshippers, in default of original compositions, have the hymns of Isodemus or Sophocles performed before him; there is a failure nowadays in the supply of new plays for Dionysus; but those who produce the works of old masters at the proper season have the credit all the same of honouring the God.

This book, then (the part of the state records that concerns us is the conversation I shall give you)--the book informs us that Archias's name was announced to Antipater. In case any of my younger hearers should not know the fact already, this Archias had been charged with the arrest of all exiles. In particular, he was to get Demosthenes from Calauria into Antipater's presence, but rather by persuasion than by force. Antipater was excited about it, hoping that Demosthenes might arrive any day. So, hearing that Archias was come from Calauria, he gave orders for his instant admittance.

When he entered--but you shall have the conversation as it stands.

Archias. Antipater

Ar. Is it well with you, Antipater?

Ant. It is well, if you have brought Demosthenes.

Ar. I have brought him as I might. I have the urn that holds his remains

Ant. Ha? my hopes are dashed. What avail ashes and urns, if I have not Demosthenes?

Ar. The soul, O King, may not be prisoned in a man's own despite.

Ant. Why took you him not alive?

Ar. We took him.

Ant. And he has died on the way?

Ar. He died where he was, in Calauria.

Ant. Your neglect is to blame; you took not due care of him.

Ar. Nay, it lies not at our door.

Ant. What mean you? These are riddles, Archias; you took him alive, and you have him not?

Ar. Was it not your charge that we should use no force at first? Yet indeed we should have fared no better if we had; we did intend it.

Ant. You did not well, even in the intention; it may be your violence killed him.

Ar. No, we killed him not; but if we could not persuade him, there was nothing for it but force. But, O King, how had you been the better off, if he had come alive? you could have done no more than kill him.

Ant. Peace, Archias! methinks you comprehend neither the nature of Demosthenes, nor my mind. You think there is no more in the finding of Demosthenes than in the hunting down such scoundrels as Himeraeus or Aristonicus or Eucrates; these are like swollen torrents--mean fellows in themselves, to whom a passing storm gives brief importance; they make a brave show while the disturbance lasts; but they are as sure to vanish soon as the wind to fall at evening. The recreant Hyperides is another--a selfish demagogue, who took no shame to curry favour with the mob by libelling Demosthenes, and make himself its instrument for ends that his dupes soon wished they had never attained; for the libels had not long borne their fruit before the libelled was reinstated with more honour than Alcibiades himself. But what reeked Hyperides? he scrupled not to use against what had once been dearest to him the tongue that he deserved, even by that iniquity, to lose.

Ar. How.? was Demosthenes not our enemy of enemies?

Ant. Not in the eyes of one who cares for an honourable nature, and loves a sincere consistent character. The noble is noble, though it be in an enemy; and virtue has no country. Am I meaner than Xerxes? he could admire Bulis and Sperchis the Spartans, and release them when they were in his power. No man that ever lived do I admire more than Demosthenes; twice I was in his company at Athens (in hurried times, it is true), and I have heard much from others, and there is his work to judge by. And what moves me is not his skill in speech. You might well suppose so; Python was nothing, matched with him, and the Attic orators but babes in comparison with his finish and intensity, the music of his words, the clearness of his thoughts, his chains of proof, his cumulative blows. We found our mistake when we listened to Python and his promises; we had gathered the Greeks to Athens to see the Athenians confuted; it was Demosthenes who confuted us. But no words of mine can describe the power of his eloquence.

Yet to that I give but a secondary place, as a tool the man used. It was the man himself I marvelled at, his spirit and his wisdom, and the steadiness of soul that steered a straight course through all the tempests of fortune with never a craven impulse. And Philip was of my mind about him; when a speech of his before the Athenian assembly against Philip was reported, Parmenio was angry, and made some bitter jest upon him. But Philip said:

Ah, Parmenio, he has a right to say what he pleases; he is the only popular orator in all Greece whose name is missing in my secret service accounts, though I would far rather have put myself in his hands than in those of clerks and third-rate actors. All the tribe of them are down for gold, timber, rents, cattle, land, in Boeotia if not in Macedonia[103]; but the walls of Byzantium are not more proof against the battering-ram than Demosthenes against gold.

This is the way I look at it, Parmenio. An Athenian who speaking in Athens prefers me to his country shall have of my money, but not of my friendship; as for one who hates me for his country's sake, I will assault him as I would a citadel, a wall, a dock, a trench, but I have only admiration for his virtue, and congratulations for the State that possesses him. The other kind I should like to crush as soon as they have served my purpose; but him I would sooner have here with us than the Illyrian and Triballian horse and all my mercenaries; arguments that carry conviction, weight of intellect, I do not put below force of arms.

That was to Parmenio; and he said much the same to me. At the time of the Athenian expedition under Diopithes, I was very anxious, but Philip laughed at me heartily, and said:

Are you afraid of these town-bred generals and their men? Their fleet, their Piraeus, their docks, I snap my fingers at them. What is to be looked for from people whose worship is of Dionysus, whose life is in feasting and dancing? If Demosthenes, and not a man besides, had been subtracted from Athens, we should have had it with less trouble than Thebes or Thessaly; deceit and force, energy and corruption, would soon have done the thing. But he is ever awake; he misses no occasion; he makes move for move and counters every stroke. Not a trick of ours, not an attempt begun or only thought of, but he has intelligence of it; in a word he is the obstacle that stands between us and the swift attainment of our ends. It was little fault of his that we took Amphipolis, that we won Olynthus, Phocis, Thermopylae, that we are masters of the Hellespont.

He rouses his reluctant countrymen out of their opiate sleep, applies to their indolence the knife and cautery of frank statement, and little he cares whether they like it or not. He transfers the revenues from state theatre to state armament, re-creates with his navy bill a fleet disorganized to the verge of extinction, restores patriotism to the place from which it had long been ousted by the passion for legal fees, uplifts the eyes of a degenerate race to the deeds of their fathers and emulation of Marathon and Salamis, and fits them for Hellenic leagues and combinations. You cannot escape his vigilance, he is not

---

[103] To get a meaning, I translate as though the Greek, instead of οὐ Βοιωτίας οὐδ' ἔνθα τι μή, were ὁ μὲν Βοιωτίας, ὁ δ' ἔνθα.

to be wheedled, you can no more buy him than the Persian King could buy the great Aristides.

This is the direction your fears should take, Antipater; never mind all the war-ships and all the fleets. What Themistocles and Pericles were to the Athens of old, that is Demosthenes to Athens to-day, as shrewd as Themistocles, as high of soul as Pericles. He it was that gained them the control of Euboea and Megara, the Hellespont and Boeotia. It is well indeed that they give the command to such as Chores or Diopithes or Proxenus, and keep Demosthenes to the platform at home. If they had given into his hands their arms and ships and troops, their strategy and their money, I doubt he would have put me on my mettle to keep Macedonia; even now that he has no weapon but his decrees, he is with us at every turn, his hand is upon us; the ways and means are of his finding, the force of his gathering; it is he that sends armadas afar, he that joins power to power, he that meets our every change of plan.

This was his tone about Demosthenes on many other occasions too; he put it down as one of his debts to fortune that armies were never led by the man whose mere words were so many battering-rams and catapults worked from Athens to the shattering and confounding of his plans. As to Chaeronea, even the victory made no difference; he continued to impress upon us how precarious a position this one man had contrived for us.

Things went unexpectedly well; their generals were cowards and their troops undisciplined, and the caprice of fortune, which has so often served us well, brought us out victorious; but he had reduced me to hazarding my kingdom and my life on that single throw; he had brought the most powerful cities into line, he had united Greece, he had forced Athens and Thebes and all Boeotia, Corinth, Euboea, Megara--the might of Greece, in short--to play the game out to its end, and had arrested me before I reached Attic soil.

He never ceased to speak thus about Demosthenes. If any one told him the Athenian democracy was a formidable rival, 'Demosthenes,' he would say, 'is my only rival; Athens without him is no better than Aenianes or Thessalians.' Whenever Philip sent embassies to the various states, if Athens had sent any one else to argue against his men, he always gained his point with ease; but when it was Demosthenes, he would tell us the embassy had come to naught:

there was not much setting up of trophies over speeches of Demosthenes.

Such was Philip's opinion. Now I am no Philip at the best, and do you suppose, Archias, that if I could have got a man like Demosthenes, I should have found nothing better to do with him than sending him like an ox to the slaughter? or should I have made him my right-hand man in the management of Greece and of the empire? I was instinctively attracted long ago by his public record--an attraction heightened by the witness of Aristotle. He constantly assured both Alexander and myself that among all the vast number of his pupils he had found none comparable to Demosthenes in natural genius and persevering self-development, none whose intellect was at once so weighty and so agile, none who spoke his opinions so freely or maintained them so courageously.

But you (said Aristotle) *confuse him with an Eubulus, a Phrynon, a Philocrates, and think to convert with gifts a man who has actually lavished his inheritance half on needy Athenians and half on Athens; you vainly imagine that you can intimidate one who has long ago resolved to set his life upon his country's doubtful fortunes; if he arraigns your proceedings, you try denunciation; why, the nearer terrors of the Assembly find him unmoved. You do not realize that the mainspring of his policy is patriotism, and that the only personal advantage he expects from it is the improvement of his own nature.*

All this it was, Archias, that made me long to have him with me, to hear from his own lips what he thought about the state of things, and be able at any time of need, abandoning the flatterers who infest us, to hear the plain words of an independent mind and profit by sincere advice. And I might fairly have drawn his attention to the ungrateful nature of those Athenians for whom he had risked all when he might have had firmer and less unconscionable friends.

Ar. O King, your other ends you might have gained, but that you would have told him to no purpose; his love of Athens was a madness beyond cure.

Ant. It was so indeed; 'twere vain to deny it. But how died he?

Ar. O King, there is further wonder in store for you. We who have had the scene before our eyes are as startled and as unbelieving yet as when we saw it. He must long ago have determined how to die; his preparation shows it. He was seated within the temple, and our arguments of the days before had been spent on him in vain.

Ant. Ay? and what were they?

Ar. Long and kindly I urged him, with promises on your part, not that I looked to see them kept (for I knew not then, and took you to be wroth with him), but in hopes they might prevail.

Ant. And what hearing did he give them? Keep nothing back; I would I were there now, hearing him with my own ears; failing which, do you hide nothing from me. 'Tis worth much to learn the bearing of a true man in the last moments of his life, whether he gave way and played the coward, or kept his course unfaltering even to the end.

Ar. Ah, in him was no bending to the storm; how far from it! With a smiling allusion to my former life, he told me I was not actor enough to make your lies convincing.

Ant. Ha? he left life for want of belief in my promises?

Ar. Not so; hear to the end, and you will see his distrust was not all for you. Since you bid me speak, O King, he told me there was no oath that could bind a Macedonian; it was nothing strange that they should use against Demosthenes the weapon that had won them Amphipolis, and Olynthus, and Oropus. And much more of the like; I had writers there, that his words might be preserved for you. *Archias* (he said), *the prospect of death or torture would be enough to keep me out of Antipater's presence. And if you tell me true, I must be on my guard against the worse danger of receiving life itself as a present at his hands, and deserting, to serve Macedonia, that post which I have sworn to hold for Greece.*

Life were a thing to be desired, Archias, were it purchased for me by the power of Piraeus (a war-ship, my gift, has floated there), by the wall and trench of which I bore the cost, by the tribe Pandionis whose festival charges I took upon me, by the spirit of Solon and Draco, by unmuzzled statesmen and a free people, by martial levies and naval organization, by the virtues and the victories of our fathers, by the affection of fellow citizens who have crowned me many a time, and by the might of a Greece whose guardian I have never ceased to be. Or again, if life is to be owed to compassion, though it be mean enough, yet compassion I might endure among the kindred of the captives I have ransomed, the fathers whose daughters I have helped to portion, and the men whose debts I have joined in paying.

But if the island empire and the sea may not save me, I ask my safety from the Posidon at whose altar and under whose sanctuary I stand. And if Posidon's power avails not to keep his temple inviolate, if he scorns not to surrender Demosthenes to Archias, then welcome death; I will not transfer my worship to Antipater. I might have had Macedonia more at my devotion than Athens, might be now a partaker in your fortunes, if I would have ranged myself with Callimedon, and Pytheas, and Demades. When things were far gone, I might yet have made a shift, if I had not had respect to the daughters of Erechtheus and to Codrus. Fortune might desert, I would not follow her; for death is a haven of safety, which he who reaches will do no baseness more. Archias, I will not be at this late day a stain upon the name of Athens; I will not make choice of slavery; be my winding-sheet the white one of liberty.

Sir actor, let me recall to you a fine passage from one of your tragedies[104]:

> *But even at the point of death*
> *She forethought took to fall in seemly wise.*

She was but a girl; and shall Demosthenes choose an unseemly life before a seemly death, and forget what Xenocrates and Plato have said of immortality? And then he was stirred to some bitter speech upon men puffed up by fortune. What remains to tell? At last, as I now besought and now threatened, mingling the stern and mild, 'Had I been Archias,' he said, 'I had yielded; but seeing that I am Demosthenes, your pardon, good sir, if my nature recoils from baseness.'

---

[104] Euripides, *Hecuba*. See *Polyxena* in Notes.

Then I was minded to hale him off by force. Which when he observed, I saw him smile and glance at the God. *Archias* (he said) *believes that there is no might, no refuge for the human soul, but arms and war-ships, walls and camps. He scorns that equipment of mine which is proof against Illyrians and Triballi and Macedonians, surer than that wooden wall*[105] *of old, which the God averred none should prevail against. Secure in this I ever took a fearless course; fearless I braved the might of Macedonia; little I cared for Euctemon or Aristogiton, for Pytheas and Callimedon, for Philip in the old days, for Archias to-day.*

And then, Lay no hand upon me. Be it not mine to bring   outrage upon the temple; I will but greet the God, and follow of my free will. And for me, I put reliance upon this, and when he lifted his hand to his mouth, I thought it was but to do obeisance.

Ant. And it was indeed--?

Ar. We put his servant to the question later, and learned from her that he had long had poison by him, to give him liberty by parting soul from body. He had not yet passed the holy threshold, when he fixed his eye on me and said:

'Take *this* to Antipater; Demosthenes you shall not take, no, by------' And methought he would have added, by the men that fell at Marathon.

And with that farewell he parted. So ends, O King, the   siege of Demosthenes.

Ant. Archias, that was Demosthenes. Hail to that unconquerable soul! how lofty the spirit, how republican the care, that would never be parted from their warrant of freedom! Enough; the man has gone his way, to live the life they tell of in the Isles of the heroic Blest, or to walk the paths that, if tales be true, the heaven-bound spirits tread; he shall attend, surely, on none but that Zeus who is named of Freedom. For his body, we will send it to Athens, a nobler offering to that land than the men that died at Marathon.

---

[105] Oracle in Herodotus vii. 141:
'A bulwark of wood at the last Zeus grants to the Trito-born goddess, Sole to remain unwasted.' *G. C. Macaulay.* Variously interpreted of the thorn hedge of the Acropolis, and of the Athenian fleet.

THE GODS IN COUNCIL

Zeus. Hermes. Momus

Zeus. Now, gentlemen, enough of that muttering and whispering in corners. You complain that our banquets are thrown open to a number of undesirable persons. Very well:

the Assembly has been convened for the purpose of dealing with this very point, and every one is at liberty to declare his sentiments openly, and bring what allegations he will.--Hermes, make formal proclamation to that effect

Her. All duly qualified divinities are hereby invited to address the Assembly on the subject of foreigners and immigrants. Mo. Have I your permission to speak, sir?

Zeus. It is not needed; you have heard the proclamation.

Mo. I desire, then, to protest against the insufferable vanity of some among us who, not content with their own promotion to godhead, would introduce their dependants and underlings here as our equals. Sir, I shall express myself on this subject with that blunt sincerity which is inseparable from my character. I am known to the world as one whose unfettered tongue cannot refrain from speech in the presence of wrong-doing; as one who probes matters to the bottom, and says what he thinks, without concealment, without fear, and without scruple. My frankness is burdensome to the generality of Gods, who mistake it for censoriousness; I have been termed by such the Accuser General. But I shall none the less avail myself of the freedom accorded to me by the proclamation--and by your permission, sir--to speak my mind without reserve.--There are, I repeat it, many persons who, despite their mixed origin, have been admitted to our feasts and councils upon terms of equality; and who, not satisfied with this, have brought hither their servants and satellites, and enrolled them among the Gods; and these menials now share in our rations and sacrifices without ever so much as paying the customary tax.

Zeus. These are riddles. Say what you mean in so many words, and let us have the names. Generalities of this kind can only give ground for random conjecture; they might apply to any one. You are a friend to sincerity:

speak on, then, without hesitation

Mo. This is really most gratifying. Such encouragement is precisely what I should have expected of a king of your exalted spirit; I will mention the name. I refer, in fact, to Dionysus. Although the mother of this truly estimable demi-god was not only a mortal, but a barbarian, and his maternal grandfather a tradesman in Phoenicia, one Cadmus, it was thought necessary to confer immortality upon him. With his own conduct since that time, I am not concerned; I shall have nothing to say on the subject of his snood, his inebriety, or his manner of walking. You may all see him for yourselves:

an effeminate, half-witted creature, reeking of strong liquor from the early hours of the day. But we are indebted to him for the presence of a whole tribe of his followers, whom he has introduced into our midst under the title of Gods. Such are Pan, Silenus, and the Satyrs; coarse persons, of frisky tendencies and eccentric appearance, drawn chiefly from the goat-herd class. The first-mentioned of these, besides being horned, has the hind-quarters of a goat, and his enormous beard is not unlike that of the same animal. Silenus is an old man with a bald head and a snub nose, who is generally to be seen riding on a donkey; he is of Lydian extraction. The Satyrs are Phrygians; they too are bald, and have pointed ears, and sprouting horns, like those of young kids. When I add that every one of these persons is provided with a tail, you will realize the extent of our obligation to Dionysus. And with these theological curiosities before their eyes, we wonder why it is that men think lightly of the Gods! I might have added that Dionysus has also brought us a couple of ladies:

Ariadne is one, his mistress, whose crown is now set among the host of stars; the other is farmer Icarius's daughter. And the cream of the jest is still to come:

the dog, Erigone's dog, must be translated too; the poor child would never be happy in Heaven without the sweet little pet! What can we call this but a drunken freak?

So much for Dionysus. I now proceed--

Zeus. Now, Momus, I see what you are coming to:

but you will kindly leave Asclepius and Heracles alone. Asclepius is a physician, and restores the sick; he is

More worth than many men.

And Heracles is my own son, and purchased his immortality with many toils. So not one word against either of them.

Mo. Very well, sir; as you wish, though I had something to say on that subject, too. You will excuse my remarking, at any rate, that they have something of a scorched appearance still. With reference to yourself, sir, a good deal might be said, if I could feel at liberty------

Zeus. Oh, as regards myself, you are,--perfectly at liberty. What, then, I am an interloper too, am I?

Mo. Worse than that, according to what they say in Crete:

your tomb is there on view. Not that I believe them, any more than I believe that Aegium story, about your being a changeling. But there is one thing that I think ought to be made clear. You yourself, sir, have set us the example in loose conduct of this kind; it is you we have to thank--you and your terrestrial gallantries and your transformations--for the present mixed state of society. We are quite uneasy about it. You will be caught, some day, and sacrificed as a bull; or some goldsmith will try his hand upon our gold-transmuted sire, and we shall have nothing to show for it but a bracelet, a necklace or a pair of earrings. The long and short of it is, that Heaven is simply *swarming* with these demi-gods of yours; there is no other word for it. It tickles a man considerably when he suddenly finds Heracles promoted to deity, and Eurystheus, his taskmaster, dead and buried, his tomb within easy distance of his slave's temple; or again when he observes in Thebes that Dionysus is a God, but that God's cousins, Pentheus, Actaeon, and Learchus, only mortals, and poor devils at that. You see, sir, ever since you gave the entrée to people of this sort, and turned your attention to the daughters of Earth, all the rest have followed suit; and the scandalous part of it is, that the Goddesses are just as bad as the Gods. Of the cases of Anchises, Tithonus, Endymion, Iasion, and others, I need say nothing; they are familiar to every one, and it would be tedious to expatiate further.

Zeus. Now I will have no reflections on Ganymede's antecedents; I shall be very angry with you, if you hurt the boy's feelings.

Mo. Ah; and out of consideration for him I suppose I must also abstain from any reference to the eagle, which is now a God like the rest of us, perches upon the royal sceptre, and may be expected at any moment to build his nest upon the head of Majesty?--Well, you must allow me Attis, Corybas, and Sabazius:

by what contrivance, now, did *they* get here? and that Mede there, Mithras, with the candys and tiara? why, the fellow cannot speak Greek; if you pledge him, he does not know what you mean. The consequence is, that Scythians and Goths, observing their success, snap their fingers at us, and distribute divinity and immortality right and left; that was how the slave Zamolxis's name slipped into our register. However, let that pass. But I should just like to ask that Egyptian there--the dog-faced gentleman in the linen suit[106]--who *he* is, and whether he proposes to establish his divinity by barking? And will the piebald bull yonder[107], from Memphis, explain what use he has for a temple, an oracle, or a priest? As for the ibises and monkeys and goats and worse absurdities that are bundled in upon us, goodness knows how, from Egypt, I am ashamed to speak of them; nor do I understand how you, gentlemen, can endure to see such creatures enjoying a prestige equal to or greater than your own.--And you yourself, sir, must surely find ram's horns a great inconvenience?

Zeus. Certainly, it is disgraceful the way these Egyptians go on. At the same time, Momus, there is an occult significance in most of these things; and it ill becomes you, who are not of the initiated, to ridicule them.

Mo. Oh, come now:

a God is one thing, and a person with a dog's head is another; I need no initiation to tell me that.

Zeus. Well, that will do for the Egyptians; time must be taken for the consideration of their case. Proceed to others.

---

[106] Anubis.
[107] Apis.

Mo. Trophonius and Amphilochus come next. The thought of the latter, in particular, causes my blood to boil:

the father[108] is a matricide and an outcast, and the son, if you please, sets up for a prophet in Cilicia, and retails information--usually incorrect--to a believing public at the rate of twopence an oracle. That is how Apollo here has fallen into disrepute:

it needs but a quack (and quacks are plentiful), a sprinkling of oil, and a garland or two, and an oracle may be had in these days wherever there is an altar or a stone pillar. Fever patients may now be cured either at Olympia by the statue of Polydamas the athlete, or in Thasos by that of Theagenes. Hector receives sacrifice at Troy:

Protesilaus just across the water on Chersonese. Ever since the number of Gods has thus multiplied, perjury and temple-robbery have been on the increase. In short, men do not care two straws about us; nor can I blame them.

That is all I have to say on the subject of bastards and new importations. But I have also observed with considerable amusement the introduction of various strange names, denoting persons who neither have nor could conceivably have any existence among us. Show me this Virtue of whom we hear so much; show me Nature, and Destiny, and Fortune, if they are anything more than unsubstantial names, the vain imaginings of some philosopher's empty head. Yet these flimsy personifications have so far gained upon the weak intelligences of mankind, that not a man will now sacrifice to us, knowing that though he should present us with a myriad of hecatombs, Fortune will none the less work out that destiny which has been appointed for each man from the beginning. I should take it kindly of you, sir, if you would tell me whether you have ever seen Virtue or Fortune or Destiny anywhere? I know that you must have heard of them often enough, from the philosophers, unless your ears are deaf enough to be proof against their bawlings.

Much more might be said:

but I forbear. I perceive that the public indignation has already risen to hissing point; especially in those quarters in which my plain truths have told home.

In conclusion, sir, I have drawn up a bill dealing with this   subject; which, with your permission, I shall now read.

Zeus. Very well; some of your points are reasonable enough. We must put a check on these abuses, or they will get worse.

Mo.

---

[108] Amphiaraus, the father of Amphilochus, neither slew his own mother, Hypermnestra, nor procured her death. He did, however, procure the death of his wife, Eriphyle, at the hand of her son Alcmaeon; and in this remote sense was a matricide. It must be confessed that a great deal of the peculiar guilt of matricide evaporates in the process of explanation. The reader may prefer to suppose simply that Lucian has made a slip.

On the seventh day of the month in the prytany of Zeus and the presidency of Posidon Apollo in the chair the following Bill introduced by Sleep was read by Momus son of Night before a true and lawful meeting of the Assembly whom Fortune direct.

Whereas *numerous persons both Greeks and barbarians being in no way entitled to the franchise have by means unknown procured their names to be enrolled on our register filling the Heavens with false Gods troubling our banquets with a tumultuous rout of miscellaneous polyglot humanity and causing a deficiency in the supplies of ambrosia and nectar whereby the price of the latter commodity owing to increased consumption has risen to four pounds the half-pint:*

And whereas *the said persons have presumptuously forced themselves into the places of genuine and old-established deities and in contravention of law and custom have further claimed precedence of the same deities upon the Earth:*

It has seemed good to the Senate and People that *an Assembly be convened upon Olympus at or about the time of the winter solstice for the purpose of electing a Commission of Inquiry the Commissioners to be duly-qualified Gods seven in number of whom three to be appointed from the most ancient Senate of Cronus and the remaining four from the twelve Gods of whom Zeus to be one and the said Commissioners shall before taking their seats swear by Styx according to the established form and Hermes shall summon by proclamation all such as claim admission to the Assembly to appear and bring with them sworn witnesses together with documentary proofs of their origin and all such persons shall successively appear before the Commissioners and the Commissioners after examination of their claims shall either declare them to be Gods or dismiss them to their own tombs and family vaults and if the Commissioners subsequently discover in Heaven any person so disqualified from entering such person shall be thrown into Tartarus and further each God shall follow his own profession and no other and it shall not be lawful either for Athene to heal the sick or for Asclepius to deliver oracles or for Apollo to practise three professions at once but only one either prophecy or music or medicine according as he shall select and instructions shall be issued to philosophers forbidding them either to invent meaningless names or to talk nonsense about matters of which they know nothing and if a temple and sacrificial honours have already been accorded to any disqualified person his statue shall be thrown down and that of Zeus or Hera or Athene or other God substituted in its place and his city shall provide him with a tomb and set up a pillar in lieu of his altar and against any person refusing to appear before the Commissioners in accordance with the proclamation judgement shall be given by default.*

That, gentlemen, is the Bill.

Zeus. And a very equitable one it is, Momus. All in favour of this Bill hold up their hands! Or no:

our opponents are sure to be in a majority. You may all go away now, and when Hermes makes the proclamation, every one must come, bringing with him complete particulars and proofs, with his father's and mother's names, his tribe and clan, and the reason and circumstances of his deification. And any of you who fail to produce your proofs will find it is no use having great temples on the Earth, or passing there for Gods; that will not help you with the Commissioners.

THE CYNIC

Lycinus. A Cynic

Ly. Give an account of yourself, my man. You wear a beard and let your hair grow; you eschew shirts; you exhibit your skin; your feet are bare; you choose a wandering, outcast, beastly life; unlike other people, you make your own body the object of your severities; you go from place to place sleeping on the hard ground where chance finds you, with the result that your old cloak, neither light nor soft nor gay to begin with, has a plentiful load of filth to carry about with it. Why is it all?

Cy. It meets my needs. It was easy to come by, and it gives its owner no trouble. It is the cloak for me.

Pray tell me, do you not call extravagance a vice? Ly. Oh, yes.

Cy. And economy a virtue?

Ly. Yes, again.

Cy. Then, if you find me living economically, and others extravagantly, why blame me instead of them?

Ly. I do not call your life more economical than other people's; I call it more destitute--destitution and want, that is what it is; you are no better than the poor who beg their daily bread.

Cy. That brings us to the questions, What is want, and what is sufficiency? Shall we try to find the answers? Ly. If you like, yes.

Cy. A man's sufficiency is that which meets his necessities; will that do?

Ly. I pass that.

Cy. And want occurs when the supply falls short of necessity--does not meet the need?

Ly. Yes.

Cy. Very well, then, I am not in want; nothing of mine fails to satisfy my need.

Ly. How do you make that out?

Cy. Well, consider the purpose of anything we require; the purpose of a house is protection?

Ly. Yes.

Cy. Clothing--what is that for? protection too, I think.

Ly. Yes.

Cy. But now, pray, what is the purpose of the protection, in turn? the better condition of the protected, I presume.

Ly. I agree.

Cy. Then do you think my feet are in worse condition than yours?

Ly. I cannot say.

Cy. Oh, yes; look at it this way; what have feet to do?

Ly. Walk.

Cy. And do you think my feet walk worse than yours, or than the average man's?

Ly. Oh, not that, I dare say.

Cy. Then they are not in worse condition, if they do their work as well.

Ly. That may be so.

Cy. So it appears that, as far as feet go, I am in no worse condition than other people.

Ly. No, I do not think you are.

Cy. Well, the rest of my body, then? If it is in worse condition, it must be weaker, strength being the virtue of the body. Is mine weaker?

Ly. Not that I see.

Cy. Consequently, neither my feet nor the rest of my body need protection, it seems; if they did, they would be in bad condition; for want is always an evil, and deteriorates the thing concerned. But again, there is no sign, either, of my, body's being nourished the worse for its nourishment's being of a common sort.

Ly. None whatever.

Cy. It would not be healthy, if it were badly nourished; for bad food injures the body.

Ly. That is true.

Cy. If so, it is for you to explain why you blame me and depreciate my life and call it miserable.

Ly. Easily explained. Nature (which you honour) and the Gods have given us the earth, and brought all sorts of good things out of it, providing us with abundance not merely for our necessities, but for our pleasures; and then you abstain from all or nearly all of it, and utilize these good things no more than the beasts. Your drink is water, just like theirs; you eat what you pick up, like a dog, and the dog's bed is as good as yours; straw is enough for either of you. Then your clothes are no more presentable than a beggar's. Now, if this sort of contentment is to pass for wisdom, God must have been all wrong in making sheep woolly, filling grapes with wine, and providing all our infinite variety of oil, honey, and the rest, that we might have food of every sort, pleasant drink, money, soft beds, fine houses, all the wonderful paraphernalia of civilization, in fact; for the productions of art are God's gifts to us too. To live without all these would be miserable enough even if one could not help it, as prisoners cannot, for instance; it is far more so if the abstention is forced upon a man by himself; it is then sheer madness.

Cy. You may be right. But take this case, now. A rich man, indulging genial kindly instincts, entertains at a banquet all sorts and conditions of men; some of them are sick, others sound, and the dishes provided are as various as the guests. There is one of these to whom nothing comes amiss; he has his finger in every dish, not only the ones within easy reach, but those some way off that were intended for the invalids; this though he is in rude health, has not

683

more than one stomach, requires little to nourish him, and is likely to be upset by a surfeit. What is your opinion of this gentleman? is he a man of sense?

Ly. Why, no.

Cy. Is he temperate?

Ly. No, nor that.

Cy. Well, then there is another guest at the same table; he seems unconscious of all that variety, fixes on some dish close by that suits his need, eats moderately of it and confines himself to it without a glance at the rest. You surely find him a more temperate and better man than the other?

Ly. Certainly.

Cy. Do you see, or must I explain?

Ly. What?

Cy. That the hospitable entertainer is God, who provides this variety of all kinds that each may have something to suit him; this is for the sound, that for the sick; this for the strong and that for the weak; it is not all for all of us; each is to take what is within reach, and of that only what he most needs.

Now you others are like the greedy unrestrained person who lays hands on everything; local productions will not do for you, the world must be your storehouse; your native land and its seas are quite insufficient; you purchase your pleasures from the ends of the earth, prefer the exotic to the home growth, the costly to the cheap, the rare to the common; in fact you would rather have troubles and complications than avoid them. Most of the precious instruments of happiness that you so pride yourselves upon are won only by vexation and worry. Give a moment's thought, if you will, to the gold you all pray for, to the silver, the costly houses, the elaborate dresses, and do not forget their conditions precedent, the trouble and toil and danger they cost-- nay, the blood and mortality and ruin; not only do numbers perish at sea on their account, or endure miseries in the acquisition or working of them; besides that, they have very likely to be fought for, or the desire of them makes friends plot against friends, children against parents, wives against husbands.

And how purposeless it all is! embroidered clothes have no more warmth in them than others, gilded houses keep out the rain no better, the drink is no sweeter out of a silver cup, or a gold one for that matter, an ivory bed makes sleep no softer; on the contrary, your fortunate man on his ivory bed between his delicate sheets constantly finds himself wooing sleep in vain. And as to the elaborate dressing of food, I need hardly say that instead of aiding nutrition it injures the body and breeds diseases in it.

As superfluous to mention the abuse of the sexual instinct, so easily managed if indulgence were not made an object. And if madness and corruption were limited to that--; but men must take nowadays to perverting the use of everything they have, turning it to unnatural purposes, like him who insists on making a carriage of a couch.

Ly. Is there such a person?

Cy. Why, he is you; you for whom men are beasts of burden, you who make them shoulder your couch-carriages, and loll up there yourselves in luxury, driving your men like so many asses and bidding them turn this way and not that; this is one of the outward and visible signs of your happiness.

Again, when people use edible things not for food but to get dye out of--the murex-dyers, for instance--are they not abusing God's gifts?

Ly. Certainly not; the flesh of the murex can provide a pigment as well as food.

Cy. Ah, but it was not made for that. So you can *force* a mixing-bowl to do the work of a saucepan; but that is not what it was made for. However, it is impossible to exhaust these people's wrong-headedness; it is endless. And because I will not join them, you reproach me. My life is that of the orderly man I described; I make merry on what comes to hand, use what is cheap, and have no yearning for the elaborate and exotic.

Moreover, if you think that because I need and use but few   things I live the life of a beast, that argument lands you in the conclusion that the Gods are yet lower than the beasts; for they' have no needs at all. But to clear your ideas on the comparative merits of great and small needs, you have only to reflect that children have more needs than adults, women than men, the sick than the well, and generally the inferior than the superior. Accordingly, the Gods have no needs, and those men the fewest who are nearest Gods.

Take Heracles, the best man that ever lived, a divine man, and rightly reckoned a God; was it wrong-headedness that made him go about in nothing but a lion's skin, insensible to all the needs you feel? No, he was not wrong-headed, who righted other people's wrongs; he was not poor, who was lord of land and sea. Wherever he went, he was master; he never met his superior or his equal as long as he lived. Do you suppose he could not get sheets and shoes, and therefore went as he did? absurd! he had self-control and fortitude; he wanted power, and not luxury.

And Theseus his disciple--king of all the Athenians, son of Posidon, says the legend, and best of his generation,--he too chose to go naked and unshod; it was his pleasure to let his hair and beard grow; and not *his* pleasure only, but all his contemporaries'; they were better men than you, and would no more have let you shave them than a lion would; soft smooth flesh was very well for women, they thought; as for them, they were men, and were content to look it; the beard was man's ornament, like the lion's, or the horse's mane; God had made certain beautiful and decorative additions to those creatures; and so he had to man, in the beard. Well, I admire those ancients and would fain be like them; I have not the smallest ' admiration for the present generation's wonderful felicity--tables! clothes! bodies artificially polished all over! not a hair to grow on any of the places where nature plants it!

My prayer would be that my feet might be just hoofs, like Chiron's in the story, that I might need bedclothes no more than the lion, and costly food no more than the dog. Let my sufficient bed be the whole earth, my house this

685

universe, and the food of my choice the easiest procurable. May I have no need, I nor any that I call friend, of gold and silver. For all human evils spring from the desire of these, seditions and wars, conspiracies and murders. The fountain of them all is the desire of more. Never be that desire mine; let me never wish for more than my share, but be content with less.

Such are our aspirations--considerably different from other people's. It is no wonder that our get-up is peculiar, since the peculiarity of our underlying principle is so marked. I cannot make out why you allow a harpist his proper robe and get-up--and so the flute-player has his, and the tragic actor his--, but will not be consistent and recognize any uniform for a good man; the good man must be like every one else, of course, regardless of the fact that every one else is all wrong. Well, if the good are to have a uniform of their own, there can be none better than that which the average sensual man will consider most improper, and reject with most decision for himself.

Now my uniform consists of a rough hairy skin, a threadbare cloak, long hair, and bare feet, whereas yours is for all the world that of some minister to vice; there is not a pin to choose between you--the gay colours, the soft texture, the number of garments you are swathed in, the shoes, the sleeked hair, the very scent of you; for the more blessed you are, the more do you exhale perfumes like his. What value can one attach to a man whom one's nose would identify for one of those minions? The consequence is, you are equal to no more work than they are, and to quite as much pleasure. You feed like them, you sleep like them, you walk like them--except so far as you avoid walking by getting yourselves conveyed like parcels by porters or animals; as for me, my feet take me anywhere that I want to go. I can put up with cold and heat and be content with the works of God--such a miserable wretch am I--, whereas you blessed ones are displeased with everything that happens and grumble without ceasing; what is is intolerable, what is not you pine for, in winter for summer, in summer for winter, in heat for cold, in cold for heat, as fastidious and peevish as so many invalids; only their reason is to be found in their illness, and yours in your characters.

And then, because we occasionally make mistakes in practice, you recommend us to change our plan and correct our principles, the fact being that you in your own affairs go quite at random, never acting on deliberation or reason, but always on habit and appetite. You are no better than people washed about by a flood; they drift with the current, you with your appetites. There is a story of a man on a vicious horse that just gives your case. The horse ran away with him, and at the pace it was going at he could not get off. A man in the way asked him where he was off to; 'wherever this beast chooses,' was the reply. So if one asked you where you were bound for, if you cared to tell the truth you would say either generally, wherever your appetites chose, or in particular, where pleasure chose to-day, where fancy chose to-morrow, and where avarice chose another day; or sometimes it is rage, sometimes fear, sometimes any other such feeling, that takes you whither it will. You ride not one horse, but many at different times, all vicious, and all out of control. They are carrying you straight for pits and cliffs; but you do not realize that you are bound for a fall till the fall comes.

The old cloak, the shaggy hair, the whole get-up that you ridicule, has this effect; it enables me to live a quiet life, doing as I will and keeping the company I want. No ignorant uneducated person will have anything to say to one dressed like this; and the soft livers turn the other way as soon as I am in sight. But the refined, the reasonable, the earnest, seek me out; they are the men who seek me, because they are the men I wish to see. At the doors of those whom the world counts happy I do not dance attendance; their gold crowns and their purple I call ostentation, and them I laugh to scorn.

These externals that you pour contempt upon, you may learn that they are seemly enough not merely for good men, but for Gods, if you will look at the Gods' statues; do those resemble you, or me? Do not confine your attention to Greece; take a tour round the foreign temples too, and see whether the Gods treat their hair and beards like me, or let the painters and sculptors shave them. Most of them, you will find, have no more shirt than I have, either. I hope you will not venture to describe again as mean an appearance that is accepted as godlike.

THE PURIST PURIZED

Lycinus. Purist

Ly. Are you the man whose scent is so keen for a blunder, and who is himself blunder-proof?

Pur. I think I may say so.

Ly. I suppose one must be blunder-proof, to detect the man who is not so?

Pur. Assuredly.

Ly. Do I understand that you are proof?

Pur. How could I call myself educated, if I made blunders at my age?

Ly. Well, shall you be able to detect a culprit, and convict him if he denies it?

Pur. Of course I shall.

Ly. Catch me out, then; I will make one just now.

Pur. Say on.

Ly. Why, the deed is done, and you have missed it.

Pur. You are joking, of course?

Ly. No, upon my honour. The blunder is made, and you none the wiser. Well, try again; but you are not infallible on these sort of things.

Pur. Well?

Ly. Again, the blunder made, and you unconscious.

Pur. How can that be, before you have opened your lips?

Ly. Oh yes, I opened them, and to a blunder; but you never see them. I quite doubt you seeing this one even.

Pur. Well, there is something very queer about it if I do not know a solecism when I hear it.

Ly. One begins to doubt, when a man has missed three.

Pur. Three? What do you mean?

Ly. A complete triolet of them.

Pur. You are certainly joking.

Ly. And you are as certainly a poor detective.

Pur. If you were to say something, one might have a chance.

Ly. Four chances you have had, and no result. It would have been a fine feather in your hat to have got them all.

Pur. Nothing fine about it; it is no more than I undertook.

Ly. Why, there you are again!

Pur. Again?

Ly. 'Feather in your hat'!

Pur. I don't know what you mean.

Ly. Precisely; you do not know. And now suppose you go first; you do not like following, that is what it is; you understand, if you chose.

Pur. Oh, I am willing enough; only you have not made any solecisms in the usual sense.

Ly. How about that last? Now watch me well, as you did not get me that time.

Pur. I cannot say I did.

Ly. Now for a rabbit, then; there, that 's him! Has he got by? There he is, that 's him, I tell you. Hims enough to fill a warren, if you don't wake up.

Pur. Oh, I am wide awake.

Ly. Well, they are gone.

Pur. Never!

Ly. The fact is, your too much learning renders you unconscious to solecisms; whatever case I take, it is always the same.

Pur. What you mean by that I am sure I don't know; but I have often caught people out in blunders.

Ly. Well, you will catch me about the time that you are a sucking child again. By the way, a babe laying in his cradle would hardly jar on your notions of grammar, if you have not yet got me.

Pur. Well, I am convinced.

Ly. Now, if we cannot detect blunders like these, we are not likely to know much about our own; you see, you have just missed another. Very well now, never again call yourself competent either to detect blunders or to avoid them.

This is my blunt way, you see. Socrates of Mopsus, with whom I was acquainted in Egypt, used to put his corrections more delicately, so as not to humiliate the offender. Here are some specimens:

What time do you set out on your travels?--What time? Oh, I see, you thought I started to-day.

The patrimonial income supplies me well enough.--Patrimonial? But your father is not dead?

So-and-so is a tribes-man of mine.--Oh, you are a savage, are you?

The fellow is a boozy.--Oh, Boozy was his mother's name, was it?

Worser luck I never knew.--Well, you need not make it worserer.

I always said he had a good 'eart.--Yes, quite an artist.

So glad to see you, old cock!--Come, allow me humanity.

Contemptuous fellow! I would not go near him.--If he were contemptible, it would not matter, I suppose.

He is the most unique of friends.--Good; one likes degrees in uniqueness.

How aggravating!--Indeed? what does it aggravate?

So I ascended up.--Ingenious man, doubling your speed like that.

I had to do it; I was in an engagement.--Like Xenophon's hoplites.

I got round him.--Comprehensive person.

They went to law, but were compounded.--You don't say they didn't get apart again?

He would apply the same delicate treatment to people unsound in their Attic.

'That's the truth of it,' said some one, 'between you and I.' Ah no, you will have to admit that you and me are wrong there.'

Another person giving a circumstantial account of a local legend said:

'So when she mingled with Heracles--' 'Without Heracles's mingling with her? '

He asked a man who told him that he must have a close crop, what his particular felony had been.

'There I quarrel,' said his opponent in an argument. 'it takes two to make a quarrel.'

When some one described his sick servant as undergoing torture, he asked, 'What for? what do they suppose they are going to get out of him?'

Some one was said to be going ahead in his studies. 'Let me see,' he said; 'it is Plato, I think, who calls that making progress.'

'Will we have a fine day?' 'If God shall.'

'Archaist, curse not thy friend' he retorted, to a man who called him curst instead of crusty.

A man once used the phrase, 'I was trying to save his face.' But is he in any danger of losing it?' asked Socrates.

'Chided,' said one man, 'chode,' another. He disclaimed all acquaintance with either form.

A person who volunteered 'but and if' was commended for his generosity.

Some one tried him with 'y-pleased'; 'no, no,' said he; 'that is too much of a good thing.'

'I expect him momently,' some one announced. 'A good phrase,' he said; 'so is "minutely"; we have excellent authority for "daily."'

'Look you!' said a man, meaning 'look' 'Yes, what am I to look you at?'

He took up a man who said, 'Yes, I can grapple with that,' meaning that he understood, with 'Oh, you are going to throw me, are you? how?'

'How shrill those fives are!' said some one. 'Oh, come now,' said Socrates; 'seditions and strives, but not drums and fives.'

'That man is heavily weighed,' one man observed. 'You are quite right; there is no such word as weighted.'

'He has thrived on it,' some one assured him. 'The people among whom he has thrived cannot be very particular.'

People were very fond of calling it at-one-ment. 'Yes, all right,' he would say; 'I know what it means.'

Mention being made of a black-hen, he supposed that would be the female of the grey-cock.

Some one said he had been eating sparrowgrass. 'You'll be trying groundsel next,' was his comment.

But enough of Socrates. Shall we have another match onthe old lines? I will give you nothing but first-rate ones. Have your eyes open. You will surely be able to do it now, after hearing such a list of them.

Pur. I am by no means so sure of that. Proceed, however.

Ly. Not sure? well, but here you have the door broad open.

Pur. Say on.

Ly. I have said.

Pur. Nothing that I observed.

Ly. What, not observed 'broad open'?

Pur. No.

Ly. Well, what is to happen, if you cannot follow now? Every man can crow on his own hay-cock, and I thought this was yours. Did you get that hay-cock? You don't seem to attend; look at the mutual help Socrates and I have just given you.

Pur. I am attending; but you are so sly with them.

Ly. Monstrous sly, is it not, to say 'mutual' instead of 'joint'? Well, that is settled up; but for your general ignorance, I defy any God short of Apollo to cure it. He gives council to all who ask it; but on you that council is thrown away.

Pur. Yes, I declare, so it was!

Ly. Perhaps one at a time are too few?

Pur. I think that must be it.

Ly. How did 'one are' get past you?

Pur Ah, I didn't see it, again.

Ly. By the way, do you know of any one who is on the look in for a wife?

Pur. What *are* you talking about?

Ly. Show me the man who is on the look in, and I will show you a solecist.

Pur. But what have I to do with solecists on the look in for wives?

Ly. Ah, if you knew that, you would be the man you pretend to be. So much for that. Now, if a man came to you and said that he had left his wife's home, would you stand that?

Pur. Of course I should, if he had provocation.

Ly. And if you caught him committing a solecism; would you stand it?

Pur. Certainly not.

Ly. Quite right too. We should never permit solecisms in a friend, but teach him better. Now, what are your feelings when you hear a man deprecating his own merits, and depreciating his friend's excessive gratitude?

Pur. Feelings? only that he shows a very proper feeling.

Ly. Then, as you cannot feel the difference between 'deprecate' and 'depreciate,' shall we conclude that you are an ignoramus?

Pur. Outrageous insolence!

Ly. Outrageous? I shall be, ere much, if I go on talking to you.--Now I should have said that 'ere much' was a blunder, but it does not strike you so.

Pur. Oh, stop, for goodness' sake! Look here, try this way; I want to get *my* profit out of it too.

Ly. Well?

Pur. Suppose you were to go through all the blunders you say I have missed, and tell me what is the right thing for each.

Ly. Good gracious, no; it would take us till midnight. No; you can look those out for yourself. Meanwhile, we had better take fresh ones, as we have only a quarter of an hour (by the way, never pronounce the 'h' in hour; that sounds dreadful). Then as to that outrage which you say I have committed upon you; if I were to speak of an outrage committed *against* you, that would be another thing.

Pur. Would it?

Ly. Yes; an outrage *upon* you must be committed upon you personally, in the shape of blows, interference with your liberty, or the like. An outrage *against* you is upon something that belongs to you; he who does an outrage upon your wife, child, friend, or slave, does it against you. This distinction, however, does not apply to inanimate things. An 'outrage against' is a legitimate phrase with them, as when Plato talks in the *Symposium* of an outrage against a proverb.

Pur. Ah, I see now.

Ly. Do you also see that the exchange of one for the other is a solecism?

Pur. Yes, I shall know that for the future.

Ly. And if a person were to use 'interchange' there instead of 'exchange,' what would you take him to mean?

Pur. Just the same.

Ly. Why, how can they be equivalent? Exchange is merely the substitution of one expression for another, the improper for the proper; whereas interchange involves a false statement[109].

---

[109] The words here represented by 'exchange' and 'interchange' are the Greek verbs from which are derived the grammarian's names for the (not very clearly distinguished) figures of speech, Hypallage and Enallage. We take it, however, that 'exchange' and 'interchange' give the distinction fairly in the present context, the former indicating a single, the latter a mutual substitution between two terms. For if one of the two differs from the other in being more comprehensive, as 'outrage against' is more comprehensive than 'outrage upon,' it is then true that the substitution of the more for the less comprehensive has no worse effect than making the statement lack precision, while the double substitution produces a false statement.

Let it be supposed that *A* kicks *B*'s dog. Four descriptions are conceivable:

--

Pur. I see now; exchange is the use of a loose instead of a precise expression, while interchange is the use of both expressions, each in the other's place.

Ly. These subtleties are not unpleasing. Similarly, when we are concerned with a person, it is in our own interest; but when we are concerned for him, it is in his It is true the phrases are sometimes confused, but there are those who observe the distinction; and it is as well to be on the safe side.

Pur. Quite true.

Ly. Now, can you tell me the difference between 'setting' and 'sitting,' or between 'be seated ' and 'sit'?

Pur. No; but I have heard you say that 'sit yourself ' is a barbarism.

Ly. Yes, quite so; but now I tell you that 'be seated ' is not the same as 'sit.'

Pur. Why, what may the difference be?

Ly. When a man is on his legs, you can only tell him to be seated; but if he is seated already, you can tell him to sit still:

Sit where thou art; we find us seats elsewhere.

It means 'remain sitting,' you see. Here again we have to say that it is a mistake to reverse the expressions. And as to 'set' and 'sit,' surely it is the whole difference between transitive and intransitive?

Pur. That is clear enough; go on; this is the way to teach.

Ly. Or the only way you can learn? Well, do you know what a historian is?

(*The explanation of this point appears to have dropped out of the MSS.-- Translators.*)

---

(1) It is an outrage upon the dog.

(2) It is an outrage against *B.*

(3) It is an outrage against the dog.

(q) It is an outrage upon *B.*

The first two can both be stated; each is true, and each is precise. (3) can also be stated; 'exchange' has taken place; the more comprehensive terns has been substituted; the statement is true, but not precise. But if (3) and (4) are both stated, 'interchange' has taken place; the less comprehensive has been substituted for the more, as well as *vice versa*; and (4) is not only not precise, it is false.

Pur. Oh, yes, I quite see, after your lucid explanation.

Ly. Now I daresay you think servility and servitude are the same; but I am aware of a considerable difference between them.

Pur. Namely--?

Ly. The first depends on yourself, the other on some one else.

Pur. Quite right.

Ly. Oh, you will pick up all sorts of information, if you give up thinking you know more than you do.

Pur. I give it up from this moment.

Ly. Then we will break off for the present, and take the rest another time.

NOTES EXPLANATORY OF

ALLUSIONS TO PERSONS, &c.

These notes are collected here instead of being put at the foot of pages in order to avoid repetition, and also that they may not be obtruded on those who do not need them. No connected account of the persons or things commented upon is to be looked for, the intention being merely to give the particular facts that will make Lucian's meaning clear. When a name is not given, it may be taken either that we are unable, or that we have considered it unnecessary, to add to the information contained in the text.

References in italics are to pieces in the translation, the number, if any, indicating the section. References in capitals are to articles in these Notes.

The Notes are intended to be used by the reader whenever he wishes for information upon a name. Reference is not made to them at the foot of pages in the text unless there would be a difficulty in knowing what name to consult.

ACADEMY. A grove or garden in the suburbs of Athens, in which Plato taught; afterwards used as a name for the school of philosophy that acknowledged him as its founder. For Plato's characteristic doctrines, see under PLATO. Lucian's references to the school are (1) as eristic or argumentative. The Socratic method of eliciting truth being by discussion, and the Academy being descended from Socrates through Plato, it might be regarded as especially argumentative. (2) as disputing the possibility of judgement, and urging suspension. The Academy is divided into the Old, Middle, and New; of which the Middle Academy neglected the positive teachings of Plato, and developed rather the destructive analytic method of Socrates. approaching nearly to the position of the Sceptics or followers of Pyrrho.

ACHILLES. Son of Peleus and the Goddess Thetis. When his mother gave him the choice between a glorious life and a long one, he chose the former; but, when interviewed by Odysseus on the occasion of the latter's visit to Hades, regretted his choice. Among the arms given him by Thetis was a shield on which Hephaestus had represented various scenes of peace and war.

ACTAEON. A huntsman who, having seen Artemis bathing, was punished by being torn to pieces by his own hounds.

ADONIS. A beautiful youth beloved by Aphrodite. Died of a wound received from a boar on Lebanon; but was allowed to spend half each year with Aphrodite on earth.

AEACUS. A son of Zeus, deified after death, and given authority in Hades.

AËDON. A woman who, having accidentally killed her own son, was compassionately changed by Zeus into a nightingale.

AEGIS. Zeus's goat's-skin shield, which he transferred to Athene, who attached to it the head of Medusa. *See* GORGONS.

AEGYPTUS. Brother of Danaus, who for fear of him fled with his fifty daughters from Libya to Argos.

AENIANES. An insignificant Greek tribe south of Thessaly.

AESCHINES (1). Born 389 B.C. The great rival of Demosthenes. Son of a humble elementary schoolmaster. Accused by Timarchus, retorted by convicting him of immorality. According to Demosthenes, was in the pay of Philip of Macedon, and a traitor to Athens.

AESCHINES (2). A philosopher, pupil of Socrates, and author of dialogues.

AËTION. A painter, probably contemporary with Lucian, and not to be identified with the Aëtion (flourished 350 B.C.) mentioned by Pliny.

AGAMEMNON. King of Mycenae and leader of the Greeks against Troy. After his return, was murdered by his wife Clytemnestra and her paramour Aegisthus. His son Orestes and daughter Electra, with Pylades, avenged him.

AGATHOBULUS. Unknown philosopher, teacher of Demonax and Peregrine.

AGATHON. Athenian tragic poet, friend of Euripides and Plato.

AGĒNOR. King of Phoenicia, son of Posidon, father of Cadmus and Europa.

AGLAÏA. 'The bright one,' one of the Graces, mother of Nireus.

AJAX (1). Son of Telamon, greatest Greek warrior next to Achilles. Claimed the latter's arms after his death, and when they were adjudged to Odysseus went mad, slew sheep in mistake for Greeks, and then committed suicide.

AJAX (2). Son of Oïleus, king of Locris. Slain by Posidon for defying his power when wrecked.

ALCAEUS. The wrestler mentioned in *The Way to write History* (9), probably lived about 40 A.D.

ALCAMENES. Athenian sculptor, 428 B.C.

ALCESTIS. Wife of Admetus. He was allowed by Apollo to find a substitute to die instead of him; she alone consented, died, and was brought back from the dead by Heracles.

ALCIBIADES. Son of Clinias, Athenian statesman, and chief instigator of the disastrous Sicilian expedition. Banished for sacrilege. Afterwards recalled with great rejoicings.

ALCINOÜS. King of Phaeacia. Entertained Odysseus on his way home from Troy, and heard the story of his adventures.

ALCMENA. Wife of Amphitryon, and mother, by Zeus, of Heracles.

ALEXANDER (1) of Macedon. Son of Philip and Olympias, but represented by legend as begotten by Ammon, the Libyan Zeus. Taught by Aristotle. Killed his best friend Clitus in his cups, carried about Callisthenes, suspected of plotting, in an iron cage. Overthrew the empire of Darius at Issus and Arbela, 333 and 331 B.C. Married the Bactrian Roxana among others. In India, defeated King Porus and took the virgin fortress Aornus. Died at Babylon, handing his ring to Perdiccas.

ALEXANDER (2) of Pherae. Tyrant. Murdered 357 B.C. by his wife Thebe.

ALEXANDER (3) of Abonutichus. 'The narrative of Lucian would appear to be a mere romance, were it not confirmed by some medals of Antoninus and M. Aurelius' (*Smith's Dictionary of Biography and Mythology*).

ALPHĒÜS. River in Arcadia and Elis, partly subterranean, which gave rise to the tale.

AMALTHĒA. A nymph who fed Zeus with goat's milk. The goat's horn, broken off by Zeus, became the cornucopia.

AMMON. *See* ZEUS.

AMPHĪON. When he played the lyre, the stones moved of their own accord to make the walls of Thebes.

AMPHITRITE. Wife of Posidon.

AMPHITRYON. Husband of Alcmena and putative father of Heracles.

ANACĒUM. Temple of Castor and Pollux.

ANACHARSIS. Scythian prince. Visited Athens about 594 B.C.

ANACREON. Lyric poet of Teos. Sang of love and wine. Died 478 B.C.

ANAXAGORAS. Philosopher accused of impiety at Athens 450 B.C. Saved by Pericles.

ANAXARCHUS. Philosopher, accompanied Alexander into Asia, 334 B.C.

ANDROMEDA Her mother Cassiopeia, queen of Ethiopia, 'set her beauty's praise above the sea-nymphs,' for which Andromeda had to be exposed to a sea-monster. She was rescued by Perseus.

ANTĒA. See BELLEROPHON.

ANTIOCHUS. King of Syria, 280-261 B.C. Called Soter after his victory over the Galatians. Son of Seleucus; fell in love with his step-mother Stratonice, whom his father ceded to him.

ANTIOPE. Mother by Zeus of Amphion and Zethus.

ANTIPATER. Macedonian general, left as regent by Alexander in Macedonia, of which he became king after Alexander's death.

ANTISTHENES. Athenian philosopher, about 400 B.C. Founder of the Cynics.

ANŪBIS. Dog-headed Egyptian God, identified by the Greeks with Hermes.

ANȲTUS. See under SOCRATES.

AORNUS. The word means unvisited by birds. See under ALEXANDER (1).

APHRODITE. Goddess of love, born of the sea foam, mother by Zeus of Eros, by Bacchus of Priapus, by Hermes of Hermaphrodites, and by the mortal Anchises of Aeneas. Her girdle or cestus conferred magic beauty on the wearer. Often called 'Golden' by Homer. Worshipped under the titles of Urania (heavenly) and Pandemus (common). Wife of Hephaestus.

APIS. Egyptian bull-God. Some details are given in *Sacrifice* (15).

APOLLO. Son of Zeus and Leto. Represented as youthful, beautiful, beardless, long-haired. Brother of Artemis and father of Asclepius by Coronis. Doctor, harpist, president of the Muses, archer, sender and averter of pestilence, giver of oracles at Delphi, &c. Lover of Daphne, who changed to a laurel to escape him, Hyacinth, whom he accidentally killed with a quoit, and Branchus, to whom he gave oracular power at Didyma, afterwards called Branchidae. When Zeus slew Asclepius with the thunderbolt, Apollo killed the Cyclopes who had forged it; he was punished by being compelled to serve as a mortal on earth, where he kept the flocks of Admetus, and built the wall of Troy for Laomedon. Called Lycean as slayer of wolves, and Pythian from Pytho or Delphi.

APOLLONIUS (1) Rhodius. An Alexandrine poet, 200 B.C., author of the *Argonautica.*

APOLLONIUS (2) of Tyana. Born 4 B.C. A Pythagorean who pretended to miraculous powers.

APOLLONIUS (3). Stoic philosopher, sent for by Antoninus Pius to instruct his adopted son M. Aurelius.

ARCHELAÜS, king of Macedonia, 453-399 B.C. A great patron of letters.

ARCHIAS. An actor employed by Antipater for political purposes.

ARCHILOCHUS. An iambic poet of Paros, 690 B.C.

AREOPAGUS. An ancient Athenian council and law-court.

ARES. God of war, son of Zeus and Hera. Intrigued with Aphrodite.

ARĒTE. Wife of Alcinous.

ARETHUSA. A nymph. Pursued by the river-god Alpheus, fled to Sicily, where she became a fountain.

ARGO. The ship that went on the quest of the Golden Fleece; built by Athene, who inserted a plank from the Dodonaean oak, which gave prophecies.

ARGUS. The hundred-eyed guard of Io.

ARIADNE. *See* THESEUS.

ARION. Famous harper, 625 B.C. For his story, see *Dialogues of Sea-Gods*, viii.

ARISTARCHUS. *See* HOMER.

ARISTIDES. Athenian statesman called 'the just.' Great rival of Themistocles. Died poor. Date of death, 468 B.C.

ARISTIPPUS. Philosopher of Cyrene, founder of the Cyrenaic school. *See* CYRENAICS. Disciple of Socrates. Spent some time at the court of Dionysius. Flourished 370 B.C.

ARISTOGĪTON (1). With Harmodius, slew Hipparchus, brother of the Athenian tyrant Hippias, 554 B.C. The tyranny fell shortly after, and the two friends had the credit of liberating Athens.

ARISTOGĪTON (2). Athenian orator and adversary of Demosthenes.

ARISTOPHANES. Athenian writer of comedy, 444-380 B.C. Socrates is ridiculed in his *Clouds*.

ARISTOTLE. Philosopher, 384-322 B.C. Founder of the Peripatetic school, which see. Taught Alexander of Macedon, and Demosthenes.

ARMENIA. The Parthian war waged by Lucius Verus, 162-165 A.D., was begun in consequence of a Roman legion's being cut to pieces in Armenia by Vologesus, king of Parthia.

ARRIAN. A Bithynian philosopher and historian, pupil of Epictetus. He was made a Roman citizen and attained the consulship. Wrote the *Anabasis Alexandri*, and the *Discourses* and *Enchiridion* of Epictetus.

ARTEMIS. Daughter of Leto and sister of Apollo. Virgin, huntress. Under the name Ilithyia, presides over childbirth. Worshipped at Tauri in Scythia with human sacrifice.

ARTEMISIUM. The scene of Athenian naval victories before Salamis over the Persians.

ASCLEPIUS. Son of Apollo and Coronis. The God of medicine and health. For restoring the dead to life was slain by Zeus with the thunderbolt. Afterwards admitted to Olympus as a God.

ASTYANAX. Infant son of Hector and Andromache. Flung from the walls of Troy by the Greeks.

ATHAMAS. By Hera's command married Nephele, by whom he had Phrixus and Helle. His begetting Learchus and Melicertes by the mortal Ino offended Hera, who drove him mad. Ino threw herself with Melicertes into the sea, and both became sea-gods, called Leucothea and Palaemon. Phrixus and Helle, saved by Nephele from Ino's persecution, had fled upon the Golden Ram, from which Helle falling gave her name to the Hellespont.

ATHENE. Sprang full-armed from the brain of Zeus. Remained a virgin. Carried Medusa's head on the aegis given to her by Zeus. Personification of power and wisdom. Gave breath to the men moulded of clay by Prometheus. Special patroness of Athens, where she was known as Polias, or city-goddess.

ATHENIANS. The Athenians thought themselves 'autochthones', produced from the very soil of Attica.

ATHOS. Mountain in Chalcidice, at the foot of which Xerxes cut a canal for his armada against Greece, to avoid the storms that prevailed there.

ATROPUS. *See* FATES.

ATTALUS II. King of Pergamum, poisoned by his son or nephew.

ATTHIS. A history of Attica, by Philochorus, about 300 B.C.

ATTIS. Phrygian shepherd, beloved by Rhea, who made him vow celibacy. Being driven mad by Rhea for violating this vow, he mutilated himself; and this became the custom among Rhea's priests, the Galli.

AUGEAS. *See* HERACLES.

AULIS. A port in Boeotia. *See* IPHIGENIA.

AURELIUS, M. Roman emperor, 161--180 A.D. Engaged in war with the Marcomanni and Quadi for almost the whole of his reign.

BACCHUS. *See* DIONYSUS.

BACIS. A prophet (or several prophets) to whom oracles were attributed.

BELLEROPHON. A Corinthian prince. Having slain a man, fled for purification to Proetus of Argos, whose wife Antea fell in love with him and, being repulsed, accused him to Proetus. Proetus sent him to the king of Lycia with a letter requesting his execution. To ensure his death, the king told him to kill the monster Chimera (goat, serpent, and lion),which the winged horse Pegasus, however, enabled him to do.

BENDIS. A Thracian Goddess, identified with the Greek Artemis.

BRANCHUS. *See* APOLLO.

BRASIDAS. The most distinguished Spartan in the first part of the Peloponnesian War. Trying to dislodge Demosthenes from Pylos, ran his galley ashore, and fainted from the wounds received.

BRIMO. 'Grim.' A name of Persephone.

BRISEÏS. Daughter of the Trojan Brises. Being captured, fell to Achilles's share, from whom she was taken by Agamemnon.

BULIS and SPERCHIS. Two Spartans, given up to Xerxes to atone for his heralds' having been slain; the king refused to retaliate.

BUSĪRIS. King of Egypt, who used to sacrifice all strangers to Zeus. When he attempted to offer Heracles, Heracles offered him.

CADMUS. Came from Tyre, once an island, to Greece, bringing with him the Phoenician alphabet. Told at Delphi to follow a certain cow, and build a town where she should lie down; built the Cadmea, citadel of Thebes. Having slain a dragon that guarded a well, was told to sow its teeth, from which sprang the Sparti, or sown men, afterwards Thebans. Married Harmonia, by whom he had Semele and other children.

CALAMIS. Sculptor, 440 B.C. For Sosandra see note on *Portrait-Study* (4).

CALĀNUS. Indian gymnosophist. Accompanied Alexander in India. Being ill at eighty-three, burnt himself.

CALISTO. Beloved by Zeus. Turned by the jealous Hera into a bear, and by Zeus into the constellation of that name.

CALLIMACHUS. Famous Alexandrine grammarian and poet. Wrote eight hundred works. 260 B.C.

CALLIMEDON. Athenian orator in the Macedonian interest.

CALLISTHENES. A philosopher, who, accompanying Alexander, offended him by rude criticism. The king had him carried about in chains, which caused his death by disease.

CALYPSO Nymph of Ogygia, where Odysseus was shipwrecked. Promised him immortality if he would remain; he refused, and the Gods compelled her to let him go.

CAMBYSES. Son of Cyrus the Great, and king of Persia, 529-522 B.C.

CASSIOPEIA. *See* ANDROMEDA.

CASTALIA. Fountain on Mount Parnassus, in which Apollo's priestess had to bathe before giving an oracle.

CASTOR and POLLUX. Also called Dioscuri, and Anaces. Sons of Zeus and Leda, one mortal, the other immortal; the mortal being killed, the two were allowed to divide the other's immortality, spending alternate days in the upper and lower worlds. Pollux a great boxer. Patrons of sailors, appearing in storms as flames, and guiding the ship to safety. Worshipped especially at Sparta, where they were born.

CEBES. Theban disciple of Socrates, wrote an allegorical 'Picture' of human life.

CECROPS. The first king of Athens.

CELSUS. An Epicurean to whom Lucian addresses the *Alexander*. Origen, in replying to a treatise against Christianity written by a Celsus, accuses him of being an Epicurean; and Origen's Celsus has accordingly been identified with Lucian's, but from Origen's own account of Celsus's position there is reason to doubt whether he could have been an Epicurean.

CERAMĪCUS. A quarter in the north-west of Athens, both within and without the walls, which were here passed by the Dipylon or Double Gate.

CERBERUS. The three-headed dog that guarded Hades. Allowed Orpheus to pass, being charmed by the sound of his lyre.

CERCŌPES. Droll and thievish gnomes, who robbed Heracles in his sleep.

CERCYON. King of Eleusis, wrestled with all strangers, killing those whom he overcame. Theseus threw and killed him.

CĒRȲCES. 'Heralds.' A priestly family at Athens.

CHAEREPHON. *See* SOCRATES.

CHAERONĒA. Here Philip defeated the Athenians and Boeotians, and ended the liberty of Greece, 338 B.C.

CHALDEANS. In general, Babylonians; in particular, wizards.

CHARES. Athenian general, one of the commanders at Chaeronea.

CHARMIDES. A favourite pupil of Socrates.

CHARON. The ferryman of Hades, who conducts the souls of the dead across Styx and Acheron.

CHARŎPUS. 'Bright-eyed,' father of the beautiful Nireus.

CHIMERA. *See* BELLEROPHON.

CHIRON. A wise centaur who taught Achilles.

CHRYSES. Trojan priest of Apollo, whose daughter Chryseis was taken by the Greeks and given to Agamemnon. When he asked her from Agamemnon and was refused, he appealed to Apollo.

CHRYSIPPUS. 280-207 B.C. Regarded as the chief of the Stoic school, which see, though Zeno was the actual founder. Chrys- = gold-. As to Lucian's thrice-repeated allusion to his helebore treatment, nothing seems to be known; it was a recognized cure for madness; perhaps he took it to cure himself of care for the ordinary human objects of pursuit.

CINYRAS. Son of Apollo, priest of Aphrodite, and father of Adonis.

CLEANTHES. Stoic philosopher. Lucian's account of his death in The Runaways seems incorrect. Having been told to abstain from food for two days to cure an ulcer, he said that as he had advanced so far towards death, it was a pity to have the trouble over again, and continued to abstain till he died.

CLEARCHUS. Spartan commander of the ten thousand Greek mercenaries employed by Cyrus the younger; their retreat under Xenophon is described in the Anabasis.

CLEON. A bellicose Athenian demagogue in the Peloponnesian war; also employed as a general.

CLĪNIAS. Father of Alcibiades.

CLITUS. *See* ALEXANDER (I).

CLOTHO. *See* FATES.

CLOUD-CUCKOO-LAND. A town built by the Birds, in Aristophanes's play of that name.

CLYMENE. Wife of Helius.

CLYTEMNESTRA. Wife and murderer of Agamemnon, slain in revenge by her own son Orestes.

COCYTUS. 'Wailing,' one of the rivers of Hades.

CODRUS. King of Athens. An oracle declared that Dorians invading Attica should succeed, if the Attic king was spared; Codrus disguising himself contrived to be slain in their camp.

COLOSSUS. Statue at Rhodes of the Sun-god Helius, 105 feet high.

CORYBANTES. Priests of Cybele or Rhea, sometimes called descendants of Corybas, the Goddess's son. Danced wildly with drum and cymbal.

COTYTTO. The Goddess of debauchery, whose festivals were celebrated during the night. Her priests were called Baptae.

CRANĒUM. An open place with a cypress-grove outside Corinth.

CRATES. 320 B.C. *See* CYNICS.

CREON. King of Thebes. A prominent figure in many tragedies.

CREUSA. A princess of Corinth. Jason was to marry her, having divorced Medea, who provided a poisoned robe, which Creusa putting on was burnt to death.

CRITIUS and NESIOTES. Sculptors slightly earlier than Phidias. Their group of the tyrannicides, set up 477 B.C., was famous. The passage in *The Rhetorician's Vade-mecum* is the chief authority for their style.

CROESUS. King of Lydia, 560-546 B.C. To test Apollo's oracle, he asked what he would be doing on a certain day. The answer was, 'boiling tortoise and lamb,' which was correct. Thus convinced, he gave great gifts to the oracle, including golden bricks, and, acting on another oracle, which said that he by crossing the Halys should destroy a mighty empire, attacked Cyrus, king of Persia, who subdued and deposed him. Thus was verified the warning given to him by Solon, in the famous conversation reported in the *Charon*. The story of his son Atys is given in *Zeus Cross-examined* (12). His other son was born deaf and dumb, but when his father was in danger from Cyrus's soldiers, was enabled to say:

 Do not kill the king. His name is a commonplace for wealth and vicissitudes.

CRONĬDES. 'Son of Cronus,' i.e. Zeus.

CRONOSOLON. Solon being known as a legislator, the name is meant to suggest 'Cronus legislating' through his mouthpiece the priest.

CRONUS. King of Heaven in the dynasty of the Titans, which preceded that of the Gods. Deprived his father Uranus of his virility and of his government. Fearing dethronement from his own sons, he devoured them as soon as born:

his wife Rhea, however, concealed from him Zeus, Posidon, and Pluto, the first of whom deposed him. The time of his reign was looked back to as the Golden Age of plenty, equality, and virtue. The Saturnalia, or feast of the Latin God Saturn, who was commonly identified with Cronus, was a symbolic revival of that golden age.

CTESIAS. Author of (1) a long history of Persia, probably a really valuable work, and (2) a treatise on India, the fables mixed up in which caused him to be looked upon as an author who deserved no credit. He was a Greek physician at the court of Artaxerxes Mnemon. Flourished about 401 B.C.

CYBELE. See RHEA.

CYCLŌPES. A one-eyed race of shepherds, or, according to another account, of smiths in the service of Hephaestus, in Etna. Polyphemus, the chief of them, was son of Posidon.

CYLLARABIS. A gymnasium in or near Argos, which would be unsuitable for cultivation.

CYNAEGĪRUS. Brother of Aeschylus. At Marathon, pursuing the defeated Persians, laid hold of one of their ships. His hand being cut off, substituted the other; that cut off, gripped it with his teeth.

CYNICS. A school of philosophers, so called either because Antisthenes the Athenian, their founder (born 444. B.C.), and a pupil of Socrates, taught in the gymnasium called the Cynosarges, or else because their mode of life was regarded as no better than that of a dog (cyn-). Diogenes, Crates, Menippus, and (in his own time) Demonax, are mentioned by Lucian as favourable specimens of the school. Their ideal may be said, to have been plain living and high thinking; virtue is the only good; the essence of virtue is self-control; pleasure is an evil if sought for itself. The dialogue called *The Cynic* gives a not unfair view of their asceticism. *The Peregrine* and *The Runaways* illustrate the abuses to which this philosophy was liable, owing to the small intellectual demand it made, and the pride it generated. The Cynics were cosmopolitan, individualist, and outspoken; their repulsive personal negligence, and their free use of their philosophic staves as offensive weapons, are often alluded to.

CYNURIA See OTHRYADES.

CYRENAICS. Aristippus, the founder of this school, was a disciple of Socrates, but developed only the practical side of his master's philosophy. Since the only things of which we can be absolutely certain are our sensations of pleasure and pain, all our actions should be calculated with a view to securing the one and avoiding the other. The principle is not so debased as it sounds, since there are higher and lower pleasures, present and future gratifications. Epicureanism and modern Utilitarianism are developments.

CYRUS. The Great. King of Persia, 559-529 B.C.

DAEDALUS. A famous artificer. He, with his son Icarus, fled from Minos, king of Crete, by means of wings fastened on with wax. He himself arrived safely in Italy; but Icarus flying too high, the wax melted, his wings dropped off, and he fell into the sea that was afterwards called after him.

DANAË. Daughter of Acrisius (upon whose name there is a jest in the *Demonax*), king of Argos. Her father, anxious that she should not have a child, confined her in a brazen tower:

but, Zeus visiting her in a shower of gold, she gave birth to Perseus. Mother and child were thrown into the sea in a chest, but were saved.

DANAÏDS. When the fifty sons of Aegyptus followed the daughters of Danaüs to Greece, and demanded them in marriage, Danaüs consented, but supplied each of them with a dagger to kill her husband on the bridal night. Their punishment was to pour water perpetually into a leaky cask.

DAPHNE. *See* APOLLO.

DAVUS. Stock name for a slave in Greek comedies.

DELPHI. On the Gulf of Corinth, below Mount Parnassus; an oracle of Apollo, the most famous in Greece.

DEMADES. An Athenian orator, in the Macedonian interest; but put to death by Antipater, 318 B.C.

DEME. An Athenian citizen was officially described by the addition of the names of his father, his deme, and his tribe, to his own. The demes were local divisions of Attica, like our parishes; the tribes were groupings, independent of locality, of these demes into ten divisions for administrative purposes.

DEMETER. Sister of Zeus, mother of Persephone, Goddess of the fruits of the earth (Earth-mother).

DEMETRIUS (1). Poliorcetes. King of Macedonia, 294-287 B.C.

DEMETRIUS (2). A Platonic philosopher about 85 B.C.

DEMETRIUS (3). A distinguished cynic philosopher, of Sunium, teacher of Demonax, and probably the hero of the story in the *Toxaris*.

DEMOCRITUS. A philosopher of Abdera, 460-361 B.C., famous as the author of the atomic theory, as the laughing philosopher, and for the wide extent of his knowledge.

DEMŌNAX. A cynic and eclectic philosopher, senior contemporary of Lucian, from whose 'Life' all that is known of him is gathered.

DEMOSTHENES (1). One of the most distinguished Athenian generals in the Peloponnesian war. *See* BRASIDAS. Put to death by the Syracusans on the failure of the Sicilian expedition.

DEMOSTHENES (2). The Athenian orator. His father was a rich manufacturer of arms. Being defrauded by his guardians, took to oratory first for the purpose of suing them. His self-training is famous; the allusions in the *Demosthenes* are thus explained:

he lived in a cave to study undisturbed, shaving half his head to keep him there, studied his gestures in a mirror and corrected a shrug by hanging a naked sword over his shoulders, improved his articulation and voice by holding pebbles in his mouth and shouting at the waves, took lessons from Satyrus the actor, copied out Thucydides eight times. The great object of his life was to keep Greece and especially Athens free from subjection to Macedon.

DEUCALION and PYRRHA. The two who survived, according to the Greek flood-legend, to repeople the earth.

DIASIA. Festival of Zeus at Athens.

DIOGENES. 412-323 B.C. His father was a banker of Sinope. He went to Athens and became a philosopher of the Cynic school, which see, as a disciple of Antisthenes. He is said to have lived in a tub.

DIOMEDE. One of the chief Greek heroes at the siege of Troy.

DION. A citizen of Syracuse under the two Dionysii; when Plato visited Dionysius I, Dion became his disciple; being afterwards banished by Dionysius II, he returned and expelled the tyrant.

DIONYSIA. There were four annual festivals in honour of Dionysus at Athens. The Great Dionysia was the chief occasion for the production of new tragedies and comedies.

DIONYSIUS I and II. Father and son, tyrants of Syracuse, 405-343 B.C. The elder was a great patron of literature, and himself wrote verses and tragedies.

DIONYSUS, or BACCHUS. Son of Zeus and the Theban Semele. For his birth see SEMELE. Travelled through Egypt, Asia, &c., introducing the vine and punishing all who slighted his power. His female worshippers were known as Bacchantes, who roamed the country with dishevelled locks, carrying the thyrsus and crying *evoe*.

DIOPĪTHES. An Athenian commander frequently employed against Philip of Macedon.

DIOSCŪRI. *See* CASTOR.

DIOTĪMA. A priestess at Mantinea, called by Socrates (in Plato's *Symposium*) his instructress in the art of love.

DODŌNA. Ancient oracle of Zeus in Epirus, where responses were given by the rustling leaves of the sacred trees.

DOSIADAS. Author of two enigmatic poems whose verses are so arranged as to present the profile of an altar.

DRACHMA. Greek coin worth tenpence.

DRACO. Ancient Athenian lawgiver, 621 B.C.

DROMO. Stock name for a slave.

ELECTRA. *See* AGAMEMNON.

ELEUSIS. A town a few miles from Athens, where the Mysteries were celebrated.

ELEVEN, THE. The board at Athens in charge of prisons and executions.

EMPEDOCLES. A Pythagorean philosopher, 444 B.C. His skill in medicine and natural knowledge caused him to be credited with supernatural powers. He fell or threw himself into the crater of Etna, as some say that by his sudden disappearance he might be believed to be a God; but his brazen sandal was thrown up and betrayed him.

EMPŪSA. A monstrous spectre believed to devour human beings, and capable of assuming different forms.

ENDYMION. A beautiful Carian youth with whom Selene fell in love.

ENĪPEUS. A river and river-god in Thessaly.

EPHIALTES and OTUS. The two giants who piled Ossa upon Olympus and Pelion upon Ossa to scale heaven.

EPICTETUS. A celebrated Stoic philosopher of the first century A.D. Expelled from Rome with the other philosophers by Domitian. His *Discourses* and *Enchiridion*, still much read, are the notes of his teaching collected by his pupil Arrian.

EPICUREANS. The school of philosophy instituted by Epicurus (342-270 B.C.). He combined the physics of Democritus with the ethics of Aristippus; adopting the atomic theory of the former, he deduced from it the indifference or non-existence of Gods; and he qualified Aristippus's exaltation of pleasure by preferring mental and permanent to bodily and immediate gratification. Their religious attitude caused them to be held in abhorrence by other schools.

EPIMENIDES. Poet and prophet of Crete. The *Rip van Winkle* of antiquity, but a historical character.

EPIMETHEUS, 'after-thought,' was the brother of Prometheus, 'forethought.'

ERECHTHEUS II. Ancient king of Athens. Posidon, offended by the slaying of his son Eumolpus, demanded the sacrifice of one of Erechtheus's daughters; one being drawn by lot, the other three would not survive her.

ERICHTHONIUS, or ERECHTHEUS I. King of Athens, and son of Hephaestus; his mother was not Athene, but Ge.

ERIDĂNUS. Greek name of the Po.

ERIGŎNE. See ICARUS.

ERINYES. Also called Furies, Eumenides, and Dread Goddesses, employed in punishing the wicked, whether in Hades or on earth, where they represent the pangs of conscience.

ERIS. The Goddess of discord; for her story, see *Dialogues of Sea-Gods*, V.

EROS. God of love, the Latin Cupid. Lucian plays with the two accounts of his birth and age. According to one, he was older than all the Olympian Gods; according to the other, son of Zeus and Aphrodite.

ETHIOPIANS. The Gods were in the habit of visiting the blameless Ethiopians ' and being feasted by them, according to Homer.

EUBŪLUS. The most influential statesman of the Athenian party opposed to Demosthenes and in favour of peace with Philip.

EUCTĒMON. An Athenian suborned by Demosthenes's enemy Midias to bring against Demosthenes a charge of deserting while on military service.

EUMOLPUS. A Thracian bard who joined the Eleusinians in an expedition against Athens, but was defeated and slain. He was regarded as the founder of the Eleusinian Mysteries, and his family, the Eumolpidae, continued to be the priests of Demeter there.

EUPHORBUS. *See* PYTHAGORAS.

EUPHORION. Epic poet of Chalcis, 276 B.C.

EUPOLIS. Among the most famous poets of the Old Comedy, with Aristophanes and Cratinus

EURIPIDES. The most philosophic of the Greek tragedians. Born 480 B.C., died 406 B.C. at the court of Archelaus, king of Macedonia, whither he had retired from Athens about 408 B.C.

EUROPA. Daughter of the Phoenician king Agenor, and sister of Cadmus; carried away by Zeus, who assumed the form of a white bull.

EURYBATUS. An Ephesian who betrayed Croesus to Cyrus, and became a byword for treachery.

EURYDICE. *See* ORPHEUS.

EURYSTHEUS. King of Tiryns. *See* HERACLES.

EURȲTUS. King of Oechalia; challenged Apollo to a match with the bow, and was killed for his presumption.

EUXINE. 'The hospitable' (εὔξεος); a euphemism for 'the inhospitable,' ἄξενος. The Black Sea.

EXADIUS. One of the Lapithae, who were assisted by Nestor in their fight against the Centaurs.

FATES. The Three Sisters to whose power even the Gods must submit, and who regulate every human life. Clotho holds the distaff, Lachesis spins, and Atropus cuts the thread of life. Lucian also gives them other functions.

FAVORĪNUS. A famous sophist, contemporary with Demonax, whose jests against him depend on the fact that he was supposed to be a eunuch.

GALATEA. The 'milk-white,' a Nereid, loved by Polyphemus.

GALLI. *See* ATTIS.

GANYMEDE. A beautiful Trojan youth, beloved by Zeus, and carried off by him to be the Gods' cupbearer.

GE. 'Earth,' wife of Uranus ('Heaven'), mother of Cronus, Rhea, and the other Titans.

GERȲON. A three-bodied Spanish giant. *See* HERACLES.

GIANTS. The brood that sprang from the blood of Uranus when mutilated. They made war on Heaven, armed with rocks and trees; but the Gods destroyed them and buried them under volcanoes.

GLAUCUS. A famous boxer.

GLYCERA. Stock name for a courtesan.

GODS. The XII were Zeus, Posidon, Apollo, Ares, Hephaestus, Hermes, Hera, Athene, Artemis, Aphrodite, Hestia, Demeter.

GORGIAS. Orator and sophist, of Leontini in Sicily, fifth century B.C. He is a character in one of Plato's dialogues.

GORGONS. Three sisters with snaky hair, brazen claws, wings, scales, &c. Medusa, the only mortal one, was slain by Perseus with Athene's help, to whom he gave the head (which had the power of petrifying all who looked upon it) after using it against the sea-monster.

GYGES. A Lydian who found a ring that being turned rendered him invisible. By its means he usurped the Lydian throne, which he held 716-678 B.C. His wealth was proverbial.

GYLIPPUS. The Spartan chiefly instrumental in defeating the Sicilian expedition of the Athenians.

HARMONIA. Daughter of Ares and Aphrodite, wife of Cadmus.

HARPIES. Monstrous birds with women's faces, sent by Zeus to torment Phineus by defiling and carrying off all food placed on his table.

HECATE. A deity attendant on Persephone in Hades. Goddess of cross-roads and much invoked by witches. For Hecate's supper, and 'dining with Hecate,' see note on *Dialogues of the Dead*, i.;

HECUBA. Wife of Priam; a character in many Greek tragedies.

HEGESIAS. Sculptor. *See* CRITIUS, the description of whom applies to him also.

HELEN. Most of her history will be found in *Dialogues of the Gods*, xx. Her abduction by Paris caused the Trojan war, after which she returned to Menelaus.

HĒLIUS. God of the sun; one of the Titans.

HELLE. *See* ATHAMAS

HELLEBORE. *See* CHRYSIPPUS.

HELLESPONT. *See* XERXES.

HEPHAESTION. A Macedonian, the special friend of Alexander, who caused divine honours to be paid him after his death, 325 B.C.

HEPHAESTUS. Son of Zeus and Hera; god of fire and of metal-working, having his forge in Etna.

HERA. Daughter of Cronus and Rhea, wife and sister of Zeus, queen of Heaven.

HERACLES. Son of Alcmena, who bore twins, the divine Heracles son of Zeus, and the mortal Iphicles son of her husband Amphitryon. Married Megara, but, driven mad by the jealous Hera, killed their children. To expiate the crime entered the service of Eurystheus for twelve years, and performed for him twelve labours, among which were:

Slaying of Hydra (as two heads sprang for each cut off, Iolaus assisted him by searing the stumps); Shooting of Stymphalian birds; Capture of Diomede's man-eating horses; Cleansing of the stables of Augeas; Slaying of Nemean lion (whose skin he always afterwards wore); Driving away of Geryon's oxen (on which expedition he erected the Pillars of Hercules at the straits of Gibraltar). Other incidents:

He went down to Hades to rescue Alcestis; founded and presided at the Olympic games; held up the heavens for Atlas; served with Omphale in woman's dress to atone for the murder, in a fit of madness, of his friend Iphitus; while drinking wine with Pholus, was attacked by the other centaurs and slew them. His last wife, Deianira, being jealous gave him a poisoned shirt; and in the resulting agony he caused Philoctetes to build a pyre and burn him on Mount Oeta, leaving his bow and arrows to the boy.

HERACLĪTUS. A physical philosopher of Ephesus, about 500 B.C. Conceived fire as the origin of all things, and continual movement as the necessary condition of existence Known as the weeping philosopher, in opposition to Democritus, the laughing.

HERMAGORAS. 'Hermes of the Market'; a statue of Hermes in the Athenian market-place.

HERMAPHRODITUS. *See* APHRODITE.

HERMES. Son of Zeus and Maia. Messenger, cupbearer, porter, crier, &c., of the Gods. God of windfalls, trade, thievery, music, and speech. He is represented with wings on his sandals and hat, and with the caduceus, a staff entwined with serpents. For his slaying of Argus, see *Dialogues of the Gods*, iii. He is charged with the conducting of the dead to Hades. Said to have been born on Mount Cyllene in Arcadia. Identified with the dog-headed Egyptian God Anubis.

HERMOCRATES The Syracusan most energetic in resisting the Sicilian expedition.

HERODES ATTICUS. Born about 104 A. D. The most famous rhetorician of his time. Used his great wealth in conferring benefits on the Greek towns, especially Athens; the aqueduct at Olympia is an instance. Mourned his wife Regilla and his favourite Pollux in the manner described in the *Demonax*.

HERODOTUS. Of Halicarnassus, born 484 B.C. Wrote in the Ionic dialect a history of the Graeco-Persian War, in nine books, to which the names of the Muses were given in recognition of their excellence.

HEROES. Used in two senses:

(1) of demi-gods, born of a mortal and an immortal parent; (2) of the chiefs of the Trojan war period.

HESIOD. Of Ascra in Boeotia, about 850 B.C. According to his own account he was originally a shepherd, who, tending his flocks on Helicon, received from the Muses a laurel-branch, and with it the gift of poetry. His chief poems are the *Works and Days*, a didactic agricultural poem, and the *Theogony*, a work on the genealogies of Gods and heroes. The passage on Virtue so often alluded to by Lucian runs as follows:

'Vice you may have in abundance with ease; smooth is the road to it, and very near it dwells. But this side of Virtue the immortal Gods have set much toil; long and steep is the track to it, and rough at its setting out:

but when a man has reached the top, then is its hardness turned to ease.'

HIMERAEUS. An Athenian orator, who opposed Macedonia after the death of Alexander, and fled to escape being surrendered to Antipater. Being caught by Archias, he was put to death.

HIPPIAS. A sophist of Elis, able but vain, contemporary of Socrates; a character in two of Plato's dialogues.

HIPPOCLĪDES. An Athenian of the sixth century B.C.; lost his chance of marrying the daughter of Clisthenes tyrant of Sicyon by dancing on his head, and remarked that 'Hippoclides did not care.'

HIPPOCRATES. A famous physician of Cos, 469-357 B.C.

HIPPOCRENE and OLMEUM. Fountains on Mount Helicon, sacred to the Muses.

HIPPOLYTA. *See* THESEUS.

HIPPOLYTUS. Son of Theseus and Hippolyta. His stepmother Phaedra fell in love with him, and being rejected accused him to his father. Theseus believed and asked Posidon to destroy him; he was thrown from his chariot and dragged to death by his horses, frightened at a monster sent by Posidon.

HIPPŌNAX. Greek iambic poet, 546-520 B.C.

HOMER. His poems formed the basis of Greek education and religion; Lucian perpetually quotes him, and refers to the questions of his birthplace and blindness. Famous ancient Homeric critics were Zoïlus (called Homeromastix), Zenodotus, and Aristarchus.

HYACINTH. *See* APOLLO.

HYDRA. *See* HERACLES.

HYLAS. Beautiful youth, beloved by Heracles, and carried off by the water-nymphs.

HYMENAEUS. The God of marriage.

HYMETTUS. Mountain of Attica, famous for marble and bees.

HYPERBOLUS. A disreputable Athenian demagogue, murdered 411 B.C.

HYPERBOREANS. A mythical people dwelling beyond the North wind in perpetual sunshine and happiness. Magical powers were attributed to them.

HYPERIDES. Athenian orator, generally acting with Demosthenes, though he accused him on one occasion. His tongue was cut out and he executed by Antipater.

IAMBŪLUS. A Greek writer on India, sufficiently characterized in *The True History* (3). 'Oceanica' is not an actual title.

IAPĔTUS. A Titan, brother of Cronus, and father of Prometheus.

ICARIUS. An Athenian who received Dionysus in Attica and learned from him the cultivation of the vine. Some peasants to whom he gave wine slew him in drunkenness. His daughter Erigone was led to his grave by his dog Maera, and hanged herself on the tree under which he lay. Dionysus placed the three in heaven as Arcturus, The Virgin, and Procyon (the lesser dog-star).

ICARUS. *See* DAEDALUS.

IDA. Mountain close to Troy.

ILISSUS. A small river at Athens.

ILITHYIA. Goddess of child-birth, generally identified with Artemis.

INO. *See* ATHAMAS.

IO. Daughter of Inachus, king of Argos. Zeus in love with her changed her to a heifer for concealment; Hera discovering it placed her under the care of Argus, who however was slain by Hermes at Zeus's command. Io swam to Egypt, conducted by Hermes, and there bore a son to Zeus.

IOLAÜS. Nephew of Heracles, and helped him against the hydra. Restored to youthful vigour by Hebe.

IPHIGENIA. Daughter of Agamemnon, was to be sacrificed to Artemis to secure the passage of the Greek fleet to Troy; but Artemis substituted a hart, and transported her to Tauri in Scythia, where as priestess she had to sacrifice all strangers. She saved her brother Orestes, on the point of being thus immolated, and fled with him to Greece.

IRIS. Goddess of the rainbow, sometimes charged with messages from heaven to earth.

IRUS. The beggar in the *Odyssey* who boxes with Odysseus.

ISIS. Egyptian Goddess, sometimes identified with Io.

ISMENUS. The river of Thebes.

ISOCRATES. 436-338 B.C. The greatest of Greek oratorical writers and teachers, but debarred from speaking by timidity and a weak voice.

IXĪON. King of the Lapithae, admitted by Zeus to the table of the Gods; his story will be found in *Dialogues of the Gods*, vi.

LABDACIDS. Laius, Oedipus, Eteocles and Polynices, Antigone and Ismene, the subjects of many Greek tragedies, were descended from Labdacus the Theban.

LAERTES. Father of Odysseus and king of Ithaca.

LAÏS. A famous courtesan of Corinth.

LAÏUS. King of Thebes and father of Oedipus, who slew him in ignorance of his identity, and so fulfilled an oracle.

LAOMEDON. *See* APOLLO.

LAPITHAE. A Thessalian people. When they invited the centaurs to the marriage feast of Pirithoüs, who was one of them, a quarrel and bloodshed arose.

LEDA. Wife of Tyndareus, king of Sparta, loved by Zeus, who took the form of a swan. She produced two eggs, from one of which came Pollux and Helen, children of Zeus, and from the other Castor and Clytemnestra, of Tyndareus.

LEMNIAN WOMEN. Having offended Aphrodite, were abandoned by their husbands, and in revenge murdered all their male relations.

LEONIDAS. The king of Sparta who held Thermopylae with a small force against all the host of Xerxes till nearly all his men were slain, 480 B.C.

LEOSTHENES Commander of the Greeks in the Lamian war, for emancipation after Alexander's death.

LETHE. One of the rivers of Hades, of which all must drink and forget their lives on earth. Lucian, however, like other writers, does not trouble himself about this forgetfulness when it is inconvenient. There is also a river of the name in Spain, to which perhaps Charon refers in the *Voyage to the Lower World*.

LETO. A Goddess loved by Zeus, and regarded with jealousy by Hera, who set the serpent Pytho to watch her, and induced the earth to refuse her a place in which to be delivered of her children. Posidon solved the difficulty by bringing up Delos from the depths of the sea and fixing it. Here Leto gave birth to Apollo and Artemis. Apollo afterwards slew Pytho. Leto was insulted by Niobe, daughter of Tantalus, proud of her seven sons and seven daughters; she was avenged by Apollo and Artemis, who shot all Niobe's children, and Niobe wept till she turned to stone.

LEUCOTHEA. See ATHAMAS.

LOTUS. The plant of which he who ate lost all wish of returning home.

LYCEUM. See PERIPATETICS.

LYCOPHRON Poet and grammarian 270 B.C. His poem *Alexandra* or *Cassandra* consists of supposed oracles of Cassandra, 'of no poetic value, but forms an inexhaustible mine of grammatical, historical, and mythological erudition.'

LYCURGUS (1). Ancient lawgiver at Sparta, who established the constitution and training that gave Sparta its military pre-eminence, 884 B.C.

LYCURGUS (2). Attic orator, a warm supporter of Demosthenes.

LYNCEUS. One of the Argonauts; could distinguish small objects at nine miles.

LYSIMACHUS. One of Alexander's generals, succeeded to Thrace on the division of the Macedonian empire. His wife Arsinoë made him believe that his son Agathocles was plotting against him, and he put him to death.

LYSIPPUS. A great sculptor, of Sicyon, in the time of Alexander.

MAEANDRIUS. Secretary to Polycrates, tyrant of Samos, to whose power he succeeded in 522 B.C.

MAGI. A priesthood among the Medes and Persians, founded by Zoroaster.

MAIA. Mother of Hermes.

MALTHACE. Stock name for a courtesan.

MANDROBŪLUS. Of Samos. He found a great treasure, his gratitude for which was expressed at the time with an offering of a golden sheep, on the first anniversary of the event with a silver one, on the second with a copper, and on the third with none at all

MARATHON. A village in Attica, the scene of a great victory of the Athenians over the Persians in 490 B.C.

MARGĪTES. Hero of a comic epic poem, formerly supposed to be Homer's. His name became proverbial for stupidity.

MARSYAS. A Phrygian Satyr, who challenged Apollo to a musical contest, and being defeated by him was flayed alive.

MAUSŌLUS. King of Caria, 377-353 B.C. His wife Artemisia raised a splendid monument to him after his death.

MEDEA. Daughter of Æetes king of Colchis, and famous for her skill in witchcraft. Falling in love with Jason when he came to Colchis for the Golden Fleece, she assisted him to obtain it, and followed him to Greece as his wife. When Jason afterwards deserted her for the daughter of Creon, she revenged herself by slaying her own children by him, and his second wife.

MELAMPUS. A seer, whose ears were cleansed by some young snakes that he had preserved from death, with the result that he was enabled to understand the language of birds.

MELEÄGER. Son of Oeneus, king of Calydon, and leader of the heroes who slew the boar that Artemis, offended at Oeneus's neglect in not asking her to a certain feast, had sent to ravage his country. Being in love with Atalanta, he gave her the boar's hide, and subsequently slew his mother's brothers for taking it from her. To avenge their death, his mother Althaea threw into the fire that fatal firebrand whose consumption, as she knew from the Fates, must be followed by his death.

MELĒTUS. An obscure tragic poet, one of the accusers of Socrates.

MĔLIA. A Nereid, mother of the river-god Ismenus.

MELICERTES. See ATHAMAS.

MENANDER. A distinguished Athenian poet of the New Comedy, 342-291 B.C.

MENELAUS. Brother of Agamemnon, and Helen's husband. The abduction of Helen by the Trojan Paris was the cause of the Trojan War.

MENIPPUS. A Cynic philosopher, originally a slave, of Gadara in Coele-Syria. His date is placed about 60 B.C. It is probable that Lucian was much indebted to the writings of Menippus, which are now lost, though an imitation of them is still preserved in the *Menippean Satires* of Varro. Among the titles of his works are *A Visit to the Shades*, *Wills*, and *Letters of the Gods*. He appears frequently as a character in Lucian's dialogues.

MENTOR. A famous silversmith, before 356 B.C.

METRODORUS. A distinguished Epicurean philosopher, 330-277 B.C.

MIDAS. A king of Phrygia, to whom Dionysus granted the power of changing all that he touched into gold. Being unable in consequence to obtain any nourishment, Midas was permitted to cancel this privilege by bathing in the Pactolus. Chosen as a judge in a musical contest between Pan and Apollo he decided against the latter, who changed his ears into those of an ass.

MIDIAS. A wealthy Athenian, and a bitter enemy of Demosthenes, whose speech against him is extant.

MILO. Of Croton, a famous athlete, of whom various feats of strength are recorded.

MILTIADES. Son of Cimon. Commanded the Athenians at Marathon. He afterwards used the power entrusted to him for his private purposes, and the charges brought against him were better justified than is implied in *Slander* (29).

MINA. A sum of money--£4 1*s.* 3*d.*

MINOS I. Son of Zeus and Europa, brother of Rhadamanthus. King and legislator of Crete and, after his death, a judge in Hades.

MINOS II. Grandson of Minos I, and king of Crete. Made war on the Athenians and compelled them to send to Crete an annual tribute of seven youths and seven maidens, to be devoured by the Minotaur, the monstrous offspring of Pasiphae and a bull. See THESEUS.

MINOTAUR. *See* MINOS II

MITHRAS. God of the sun among the Persians.

MOMUS. Son of Night, and God of criticism.

MORMO. A female spectre, used to frighten children with.

MUSAEUS. The supposed author of various poetical works. His origin is doubtful; he is sometimes called the son of Orpheus.

MUSES. The Goddesses of poetry, and of the arts and sciences. They were nine in number, and were the daughters of Zeus and Mnemosyne (Memory). Mount Helicon in Boeotia was their favourite haunt.

MUSONIUS RUFUS. A celebrated Stoic philosopher, banished by Nero in 66 A. D. on the pretext of conspiracy.

MYIA. Of this daughter of Pythagoras we have no certain information.

MYRON. A celebrated sculptor, born about 480 B.C.

MYSTERIES (Eleusinian). Eumolpus, Musaeus, and Demeter, are all mentioned as the founders of these Mysteries, in which were commemorated the rape of Persephone by Pluto, and the wanderings of Demeter in search of her. They were held annually, the Greater at Eleusis and Athens, the Lesser at Agrae. Persons initiated at the Lesser could only be admitted to the Greater after a year's interval. A part of the Greater Mysteries, to which those only were admitted who had been fully initiated, and had taken the oath of secrecy, consisted of a torchlight procession from Athens to the temple of Demeter at Eleusis, after which the initiated were purified, repeated the oath of secrecy, and were admitted to the inner sanctuary of the temple. Of the secret doctrines there divulged nothing is known.

NARCISSUS. A youth so beautiful that he fell in love with his image reflected in a pool.

NAUSICAA. The beautiful daughter of Alcinous and Arete, who received Odysseus with kindness when cast up by the sea.

NELEUS. Of Scepsis; he is known to have been in possession of the MSS. of Aristotle, and may therefore have been a patron of literature.

NEMESIS. 'Wrath,' the Goddess who avenges presumption.

NEOPTOLEMUS, also called Pyrrhus, son of Achilles, after whose death the seer declared that Troy could not be taken without the help of his son. He distinguished himself in the taking.

NEPHELE. *See* ATHAMAS. Changed to a cloud after his desertion of her.

NEREÏDS. The sea nymphs, daughters of Nereus, a sea-God.

NESIOTES. *See* CRITICS.

NESTOR. Oldest and wisest of the Greek chiefs at Troy. His cup was one that 'scarce could another move from the table when it was full, but old Nestor lifted it with ease.'

NICANDER. Grammarian, poet, and physician of Colophon, about 140 B.C. Wrote *Theriaca* and *Alexipharmaca*, works on poisons and antidotes.

NICIAS. The Athenian general in command of the Sicilian expedition, 415 B.C. Put to death by the Syracusans.

NICOSTRATUS. A wrestler and double Olympic victor, about 40 A. D.

NIOBE. *See* LETO.

NIREUS. A Greek at the siege of Troy, famous for beauty.

NUMA. Second king of Rome; his reign was marked by peace and the founding of religious institutions.

ODYSSEUS. Son of Laertes, king of Ithaca. To escape joining the Greeks against Troy, simulated madness by driving a plough for a chariot, with one ox and one horse. Palamedes exposed him by threatening Odysseus's son Telemachus with a sword, when he confessed. In revenge, he ruined Palamedes at Troy, convicting him by forged evidence of treacherous dealings with the enemy. When Agamemnon lost heart, and was for returning, Odysseus prevailed on the Greeks not to give up. Took ten years getting home, detained by Calypso, by Circe, and otherwise. Circe enabled him to visit Hades and consult Tiresias. Escaped the Sirens by stopping his crew's ears with wax, and having himself bound to the mast.

OENEUS. *See* MELEAGER.

OLYMPIA. In Ells; the Olympic games took place every four years, and, starting from 776 B.C., from which time a record of them was kept, were used for dating events, under the name of Olympiads. The games were the occasion of the largest gatherings of Greeks that took place.

OLYMPIAS. Wife of Philip of Macedon and mother of Alexander.

OLYMPIĒUM. A temple of Zeus at Athens, begun by the tyrant Pisistratus (560-527 B.C.), but not finished till the time of Hadrian (117-138 A. D.).

OLYMPUS (1). A mountain separating Macedonia and Thessaly, the summit of which was the residence of the Gods.

OLYMPUS (2). A celebrated flute-player of Phrygia.

OMPHALE. *See* HERACLES.

ORESTES. *See* AGAMEMNON.

ORION. A giant and hunter of Boeotia. Blinded by Oenopion for ill-treatment of his daughter Merope, he recovered his sight by the help of Cedalion, who directed his eyes towards the rising sun.

ORITHYIA. Daughter of Erechtheus, king of Athens. Carried off by Boreas.

ORPHEUS. A Thracian musician, son of the Muse Calliope. His music charmed wild beasts, trees, and rocks, and prevailed upon Pluto to restore his wife Eurydice, on condition that Orpheus should not look back to see that she was following him; this condition not being observed, Eurydice remained in Hades. Orpheus was afterwards torn in pieces by the Thracian women, and his head and lyre thrown into the Hebrus, and carried to Lesbos.

OSIRIS. An Egyptian king, deified after death, as the husband of Isis.

OSROËS. Son of Vologesus I. A king of Parthia, engaged in war with the Emperor Trajan.

OTHRYADES. The only survivor of the three hundred Spartans who fought with three hundred Argives for the possession of Thyrea in Cynuria. Being left for dead by the two Argive survivors, he raised a trophy on the field, with an inscription in his own blood, and thus secured the victory.

OTUS. *See* EPHIALTES.

PACTŌLUS. A Lydian river, whose sands were said to contain gold.

PAEAN. (1) A name of Apollo; (2) a song sung before or after a battle.

PALAMEDES. A Greek hero in the Trojan War. *See under* ODYSSEUS. Said to have added certain letters to the Greek alphabet.

PAN. A rustic God, son of Hermes and Penelope. Invented the Pan's pipe, and attended upon Dionysus. Represented with horns and goat's legs.

PANATHENAEA. Two festivals of this name were celebrated at Athens with games, sacrifices, &c.; the Lesser annually, the Greater every fourth year.

PANCRATIUM. A contest in the public games, in which both boxing and wrestling were employed.

PANGAEUS. A range of mountains in Macedonia, famous for gold and silver mines.

PANTHEA (1). Wife of Abradatas, king of Susa. Her spirit and loyalty are commended by Xenophon.

PANTHEA (2). Presumably the mistress of the Emperor Lucius Verus.

PARIS. Son of Priam king of Troy.

PARMENIO. An able lieutenant of Alexander.

PARTHENIUS. A Greek elegiac poet, about 30 B.C.

PARTHIANS. The successors in Asia of the Persian monarchy. The war between their king Vologesus III and Rome, 162-165 A. D., was conducted on the Roman side by the Emperor Lucius Verus. He brought it to a successful conclusion, more by the merits of his lieutenants, Cassius and Statius Priscus, than his own.

PARTHONĪCE. 'Conquest of the Parthians,' quoted as an affected poetical-sounding title.

PATROCLUS. Friend and follower of Achilles, who, when he sulked himself, lent him his armour, in which Patroclus won great renown; but Apollo struck him senseless, Euphorbus ran him through, and Hector gave him the last fatal blow.

PEGASUS. *See* BELLEROPHON.

721

PELASGICUM. A space under the Acropolis at Athens, unoccupied till the Spartan invasions in the Peloponnesian war brought the country Attics into the town.

PELEUS. Father of Achilles.

PĔLIAS. King of Iolcus, usurper of his nephew Jason's rights. When Medea restored Jason's father Aeson to youth by cutting him to pieces and boiling him, she persuaded the daughters of Pelias to try the same system with their father, which resulted in his death.

PELOPIDS. The descendants of Pelops, many of them, as Atreus and Thyestes, Agamemnon and Menelaus, Orestes, Electra and Iphigenia, famous in tragic story.

PENELOPE. Wife of Odysseus.

PENTHEUS. King of Thebes, resisted the introduction of Dionysus's rites; the God caused his Bacchantes, among them Pentheus's mother Agave, to tear him to pieces in their frenzy.

PERDICCAS. One of Alexander's generals, who, on the strength of the dying king's having handed him his ring, claimed the succession, but was defeated by the combination of Ptolemy, Antipater, and other generals, and finally assassinated.

PEREGRINE. Nothing can be added to Lucian's description of him in the *Death of Peregrine*, but that he is a historical character.

PERIANDER. Son of Cypselus, and tyrant of Corinth. A patron of literature, and one of the Seven Sages.

PERICLES. Greatest of Athenian statesmen. A pupil of Anaxagoras. He was nicknamed 'Olympian.' Lucian mentions his funeral speech, delivered in 435 B.C., and his intercourse with the famous Milesian courtesan Aspasia, by whom he had a son Pericles.

PERIPATETICS. Aristotle of Stagira (385-323 B.C.), the founder of this school of philosophers, studied for twenty years under Plato. In 335 B.C. he began teaching independently in the Lyceum, a public garden at Athens. The name Peripatetic refers to his habit of walking about while lecturing. Forty-six of his works remain, though perhaps only in the form of notes. They are remarkable for the rigidly systematic treatment applied to all subjects alike, to Ethics and Poetry, not less than to Zoology and Mechanics. Most notable of his doctrines is that which refers all definable things to four Causes, viz., Matter, the existence of which is Potentiality, and the Moving, Final, and Formal Causes, whose operation is included under the general term Energy; the combination of Potentiality and Energy resulting in the perfection of the completed thing. The *summum bonum*, according to Aristotle, is Eudaemonia (Happiness); and each virtue is the mean between the excess and defect of some quality. The virtuous mean between avarice and profuseness, or between luxury and asceticism, might perhaps involve that respect for money with which Lucian reproaches the Peripatetics. The ten Categories, or Predicaments, were an attempt to classify all existing things; among them were Substance, Quality, Quantity, Relation, Time, and Place.

PERSEPHONE. Daughter of Zeus and Demeter. Pluto, with the permission of Zeus, carried her down to Hades. Demeter, discovering the truth after a long search, left Heaven in anger, and took up her abode on earth. Zeus now ordered Pluto to restore Persephone:

as, however, she had partaken of food in the lower world, she was compelled to return thither for one-third of each year.

PERSEUS. His story is given under DANAE, GORGONS, and ANDROMEDA.

PHAEACIANS. A fabulous people described in the Odyssey as inhabiting Scheria. Alcinous was their king.

PHAEDRA. Daughter of Minos of Crete, and wife of Theseus. *See* HIPPOLYTUS.

PHAEDRUS. A character in two of the dialogues of Plato, whose friend he was.

PHAETHON. Son of Helius and Clymene. Being allowed on one occasion to drive the chariot of the sun, he lost control of the horses, and almost consumed the earth with fire. Zeus slew him with a thunderbolt, and cast him into the river Eridanus. His sisters, changed into poplars on its banks, wept tears of amber for his loss.

PHALARIS. Tyrant of Agrigentum in Sicily, 570-564 B.C. For the brazen bull in which he is said to have burnt many victims alive, see *Phalaris I.*

PHAON. An ugly old boatman at Mytilene, with whom Sappho is said to have fallen in love, after he had been made young and beautiful by Aphrodite as a reward for carrying her across the sea without payment.

PHARUS. A small island off the coast of Egypt, on which was a famous lighthouse, built by Ptolemy II.

PHĪDIAS. Famous Athenian sculptor, 490-432 B.C. The chryselephantine statue of Zeus at Olympia was his work.

PHILIP OF MACEDON. King, 359-336 B.C. Raised Macedon from an insignificant State to the mistress of Greece, and made possible the conquests of his son Alexander by his organization. Used diplomacy as much as arms to effect his ends, and systematically bribed persons in the states opposed to him, especially in Athens.

PHILIPPIDES. More usually called Phidippides.

PHILO. The person to whom Lucian addresses *The Way to write History* is unknown.

PHILOCRATES. Prominent Athenian, probably in the pay of Philip, into whose hands he constantly played.

PHILOCTĒTES. Armour-bearer of Heracles, inherited his bow. Left at Lemnos on the way to Troy, because a wound from a snake-bite rendered him offensive by its stench. Later, an oracle declaring the bow necessary for the capture of Troy, Odysseus went and induced him to come.

PHILOSOPHY. Lucian is fond of ridiculing the different schools of philosophy, some for their paradoxical choice of ends, some for their hypocrisy in practically disregarding their own precepts. The regulation philosophic garb and appearance also comes in for satire; it consisted of threadbare cloak, wallet, and staff, with long beard. A brief account of the chief schools will be found under ACADEMY, CYNICS, CYRENAICS, PERIPATETICS, STOICS, EPICUREANS, SCEPTICS, PLATO, PYTHAGORAS.

PHILOXENUS. A poet, who, for his severe criticism of a poem of Dionysius I, was imprisoned in the Syracusan quarries. The tyrant, having pardoned him and invited him to dinner, recited another poem he had composed. Asked his opinion of it, Philoxenus made no direct reply, but said, 'Take me back to the quarries.'

PHINEUS. King of Bithynia, blinded by Zeus for unjustly blinding his own children; and *see* HARPIES.

PHLEGETHON. 'Burning,' one of the infernal rivers.

PHOCION. Athenian statesman and general, died 318 B.C.; distinguished for virtue, moderation, and poverty.

PHOEBUS. *See* APOLLO.

PHOENIX (1). Son of Amyntor king of Argos. Blinded by his father, fled to Peleus, was cured by Chiron of his blindness, and became tutor to Achilles.

PHOENIX (2). An Indian bird which lived five hundred years and then cremated itself, another rising from its ashes.

PHOLUS. *See* HERACLES.

PHRIXUS. *See* ATHAMAS.

PHRYGIANS. Troy being in Phrygia, 'Phrygians' is often used for 'Trojans.'

PHRYNE. Famous Athenian courtesan, 328 B.C.

PHRYNON. Athenian politician in the Macedonian interest, associated by Demosthenes especially with Philocrates.

PIRAEUS. The port of Athens, about five miles off.

PISA. The town in Elis, near which the Olympic games were held.

PITCH-PLASTERS were employed by women and by effeminate men for removing the hair from the body.

PITYOCAMPTES. 'Pine-bender,' descriptive surname of the robber Sinis, who killed travellers by fastening them to the top of a pine bent down and then allowed to spring up. He was killed by Theseus in the same way.

PLATAEA. A town in Boeotia, near which the final battle of the Graeco-Persian war was fought, 478 B.C. The Persians were defeated.

PLATO. An Athenian philosopher (428-347 B.C.), and pupil of Socrates, whom in his dialogues he often makes the mouthpiece of his own doctrines. He studied in Africa, Egypt, Italy, and Sicily, and returned to Athens in 386 B.C. to lecture in the gymnasium of the Academy. He paid three visits to the Syracusan court of Dionysius I and II. The Platonic theory of Ideas is an attempt to secure accuracy of definition (which is the first step towards knowledge), by contemplation of those abstract types or Ideas of things, of which external objects are in every case only an imperfect manifestation, and which are perceptible to us by reason of our familiarity with them in a previous existence; for the soul is immortal, and what we call the acquisition of knowledge is in fact only recollection. In his *Republic* we have a sketch of a model state, in which philosophers are to be kings, and community of women is recommended as a means of securing scientific breeding.

PLUTO. 'Rich' in dead, according to Lucian's derivation; also called Hades. Drew lots with his brothers Zeus and Posidon, and received the Lower World for his share. His wife was Persephone.

PLUTUS. Son of Iasion and Demeter, and God of wealth. Blinded by Zeus.

PNYX. The place where the Athenian Assembly was held. It was cut out of the side of a small hill west of the Acropolis.

PODALIRIUS. Son of Asclepius, and brother of Machaon, with whom he led the Thessalians of Tricca against Troy. Both brothers inherited their father's medical skill.

POECĪLE. The 'Painted' Porch in. the Athenian marketplace, adorned with paintings of Polygnotus. Here Zeno, the founder of the Stoic philosophy, opened his school, which was accordingly often spoken of as 'The Porch.'

POENAE. 'Punishments.' Infernal spirits, akin to the Erinyes.

POLEMON. Athenian philosopher, head of the Academy, 315 B.C. Had been dissolute in youth, but was converted, as related in *The Double Indictment*, by Xenocrates.

POLIAS. *See* ATHENE.

POLLUX (I). *See* CASTOR.

POLLUX (2). *See* HERODES.

POLUS (I). A rhetorician of Agrigentum, pupil of Gorgias, with whom he is introduced by Plato in the *Gorgias*.

POLUS (2). A celebrated tragic actor.

POLYCLITUS. 452-412 B.C. A Sicyonian sculptor, reckoned the equal of Phidias. His 'canon' was a bronze statue in which he exemplified the principles that he had laid down in a book to which he gave the same name. The *Diadumenus*, or youth tying on a fillet, was one of his most famous works.

POLYCRATES. Powerful tyrant of Samos. Frightened by his excessive prosperity, tried to propitiate Nemesis by throwing into the sea a ring that he prized highly; but a fisherman found it in a fish, and returned it, a sign that his offering was rejected. He was lured to Asia by Oroetes, satrap of Sardis, and by him crucified, 522 B.C.

POLYDĂMAS. Olympic victor, 408 B.C. Marvellous stories are told of his strength.

POLYGNOTUS. Famous painter, of Thasos, 422 B.C.

POLYNĪCES. One of the sons of Oedipus, who killed each other.

POLYPHEMUS. *See* CYCLOPES. His story is given *Dialogues of the Sea-Gods*, i.

POLYXĔNA. Daughter of Priam and Hecuba, loved by Achilles, who after his death demanded that she should be sacrificed to his manes. She submitted willingly, and was slain by Neoptolemus at his father's tomb.

PORCH, THE. *See* POECILE and STOICS.

PORUS. *See* ALEXANDER (I).

POSIDON. Son of Cronus, brother of Zeus and Pluto, received the sea as his province. Assisted Apollo in building the walls of Troy for Laomedon.

PRAXITELES. Athenian sculptor, 364 B.C. With Scopas, headed the later Attic school, known less for sublimity than beauty. The Cnidian *Aphrodite* was his.

PRIĀPUS. Son of Dionysus and Aphrodite, worshipped especially at Lampsacus.

PRŎDĬCUS. Sophist of Ceos, often at Athens, where Socrates is said to have attended his lectures, about 430 B.C. Spoken of by Plato with more respect than most sophists, and famous for his apologue of *The Choice of Heracles*, between Pleasure and Virtue.

PROETUS. *See* BELLEROPHON.

PROMETHEUS. Son of Iapetus, and therefore first cousin of Zeus, who nailed him up on the Caucasus, and instructed an eagle to devour his liver, which grew again each night. The provocation had been threefold:

(1) Prometheus, forming clay figures, had persuaded Athene to breathe life into them, and thus created man; (2) he had stolen fire from Heaven for the use of man; (3) by dividing a slain animal into two portions, one consisting of bones wrapped up in fat, the other of the lean parts, and persuading Zeus to choose the former as his share, he had secured the more desirable portion of sacrificial animals for man. The confusion of the sexes alluded to in the *Literary Prometheus* (7) is perhaps drawn from Plato's account in the *Symposium* of the creation of double beings, who possessed the characteristics of both sexes, and referred by Lucian to Prometheus on his own responsibility; though in Phaedrus (Fables, iv. 54) Prometheus is charged with a confusion of the sexes in a different sense.

PROTESILAÜS. A Thessalian, son of Iphiclus, and the first Greek slain by the Trojans. Permitted to return to life for a few hours to see his wife Laodamia.

PROTEUS. The prophetic old man of the sea, from whom it was only possible to obtain information by seizing him; this was difficult, as he changed into many different shapes. Peregrine (whom see) took the name of Proteus.

PTOLEMY (1). Son of Lagus, surnamed Soter. A general of Alexander, and afterwards king of Egypt. Died 283 B.C.

PTOLEMY (2) Philadelphus, son of Ptolemy Soter. Married his sister Arsinoe, 309-247 B.C.

PTOLEMY (3) Dionysus. King of Egypt, 80-51 B.C.

PUZZLES. Lucian is never tired of ridiculing the verbal quibbles in which the philosophers of his time indulged. He attributes them especially to the Stoics, whose insistence on pure reason, as opposed to emotion, for the guide of life, resulted in much attention to logic, including its paradoxical forms. Among these logical puzzles are the following:

(1) Sorites, the heap trick. Suppose a heap of corn. Is it a heap? Yes. Take a grain away. Is it a heap? Yes. And so on, till only one grain is left. The drawing of the line is impossible. (2) The Horns. If you have not lost a thing, you still have it? Certainly. Have you lost your horns? No. Then you are horned. (3) The Crocodile. A child is caught by a crocodile; the father asks him to give it back. I will, says the crocodile, on condition that you tell me correctly whether I shall do so or not. The dilemma is obvious. (4) The Day and Night. This appears to be a proof that there is no such thing as night, through the ambiguity in 'Day being, Night cannot be,' which in Greek, though not in English, is equally natural in the sense of Since it is day, it cannot be night, and, If day exists, night cannot. (5) The Reaper. I will prove to you that you will not reap your corn, thus. If you reap it, you will not either-reap-or-not-reap, but reap. If you do not reap it, you will not either-reap-or-not-reap, but not reap. So in each case you will not either reap or not reap, that is, there will be no reaping. (6) The Rightful Owner. Unexplained; but *see* Epictetus, ii, xix. (7) and (8) The Electra, and The Man in the Hood, sufficiently explained in *Sale of Creeds* (22).

PYANEPSION. An Attic month.

PYLADES. Cousin and friend of Orestes.

PYRRHUS. Stock name for a slave. Used jestingly in Sale of Creeds instead of Pyrrho.

PYRRHO. Of Elis. About 300 B.C. Gave up painting to become a philosopher, and was the founder of the Sceptics.

PYRRHUS. King of Epirus, 295-272 B.C. The greatest general of his time, won several victories over the Romans.

PYTHAGORAS. Born at Samos, settled at Croton in Italy. 580-510 B.C. The early Ionic philosophers, as Thales and Heraclitus, had found the origin of all things in some one principle, as water, or fire. Pythagoras found it in number and proportion; hence the name Order (κόσμος), which he first gave to the universe; hence also the mystic importance attached to certain numbers, e. g. the Decad, called Tetractys (which we have translated 'quaternion') as made by the addition of the first four integers (1 + 2 + 3 + 4= 10), and the Pentagram, or figure resulting from the production of all the sides of a regular pentagon till they intersect. Pythagoras had travelled in Egypt, and perhaps brought thence his most famous doctrines of the immortality of the soul and transmigration; he is said to have retained the memory of his own previous existences, especially as Euphorbus the Trojan, whose shield he recognized; human knowledge, for him as for Plato, would be accounted for as recollection from earlier lives. He instituted a brotherhood of his disciples, with elaborate training and different degrees; and the Pythagorean 'Ipse dixit,' implying that what the master had said was not open to argument, marks the strict subordination; a novice had to observe silence for five years. Pythagoras left no writings, and this, combined with the mystic character of his speculations on number and his specially authoritative position, gave occasion to innumerable legends, misrepresentations, and extensions. The Pythagorean prohibition of beans as food has never been explained; *see* Mayor's note on Juv. xv. 174. The usual account is that he thought the souls of his parents might be in them. The story of his appearing at the Olympic games with a golden thigh is one of the later legends illustrative of his supposed assumption of superhuman qualities, which made him the model of impostors or half-impostors like Apollonius of Tyana, Alexander of Abonutichus, or Paracelsus.

PYTHEAS. An Athenian orator, of disreputable character; an enemy of Demosthenes.

PYTHON. An eloquent Byzantine orator in the pay of Philip of Macedon.

RHADAMANTHUS. Son of Zeus and Europa, and brother of Minos. After his death, a judge in Hades.

RHEA, or CYBELE. Daughter of Uranus and Ge, wife of Cronus, and mother of Zeus, Hera, Posidon, Pluto, Hestia, and Demeter. Her worship, celebrated by the Corybantes and the Galli, was of a wild and enthusiastic character. She is commonly represented as being drawn by lions. *See also under* ATTIS.

SABAZIUS. A Phrygian deity, of doubtful origin, commonly described as a son of Rhea.

SALAMIS. An island off the west coast of Attica, the scene of a great naval victory of the Athenians over the Persians in 480 B.C. It is to this victory that the oracle refers, quoted in the *Zeus Tragoedus*.

SALII. The dancing priests of Mars, said to have been instituted by Numa.

SALMŌNEUS. Son of Aeolus, and brother of Sisyphus. Zeus slew him with the thunderbolt, for claiming sacrifice, and imitating the thunder and lightning.

SAPPHO. A Lesbian poetess of the sixth century B.C. Taken as a type of elegance in the *Portrait-study*.

SARDANAPĀLUS. Last king of the Assyrian empire of Nineveh. Lucian's favourite type of luxury and effeminacy.

SARPĒDON. Son of Zeus and Laodamia, slain in the Trojan war by Patroclus.

SATURNALIA. The feast of the Latin God Saturn, held in the month of December. During the feast, all ranks devoted themselves to merriment, presents were exchanged, and public gambling was officially recognized. A mock king was also chosen, who could impose forfeits on his subjects. Lucian does not speak of the Saturnalia by that name, but only of the feast of Cronus, with whom Saturn was identified; and in some cases it is possible that he refers to a feast of Cronus himself.

SATYRS. Beings connected with the worship of Dionysus, and represented with snub noses, horns, and tails.

SCEPTICS. A school of philosophers founded by Pyrrho of Elis, who flourished 325 B.C. Abstention from definition, and suspension of judgement, were the guiding principles of the school.

SCHERIA. See PHAEACIANS.

SCIRON. A robber who infested the frontier of Attica and Megara, and compelled travellers to wash his feet upon the edge of the Scironian precipice, kicking them over into the sea during the operation. He was slain by Theseus.

SCŎPAS. A famous sculptor of Paros, flourished 400-350 B.C.

SELĒNE. Goddess of the moon. Fell in love with Endymion.

SELEUCUS. Surnamed Nicator. First king of Syria, 312280 B.C. For his wife Stratonice see ANTIOCHUS.

SEMELE. Daughter of Cadmus and Harmonia. Beloved by Zeus. Incited by the machinations of Hera, she prevailed upon Zeus against his will to appear to her in all his splendour. His lightnings consumed her; but the child Dionysus, with whom she was pregnant, was saved by Zeus, and matured within his thigh.

SEMIRĂMIS and her husband Ninus were the founders of the Assyrian empire of Nineveh. Her date is placed at about 2000 B.C. She built numerous cities.

SILĒNUS. A Satyr, son of Hermes or of Pan. Usually represented as drunk, and riding on an ass, in attendance on Dionysus.

SIMONIDES. Of Ceos; a famous lyric poet, 556-467 B.C. Said to have added four letters to the alphabet.

SISYPHUS. King of Corinth, fraudulent and avaricious. Punished in the lower world by having to roll a stone up hill, which as soon as he reached the top always fell to the bottom again

SOCRATES. Son of Sophroniscus and Phaenarete, 469-399 B.C.

He abandoned sculpture (his father's profession) for the study of philosophy, in which he was remarkable for the preference that he gave to ethics over physics, and for the method of dialectic, or logical conversation carried on by means of question and answer, for the purpose of eliciting accurate definition. He was frequently ridiculed on the comic stage by Aristophanes and other poets. In 399 B.C. a charge of impiety was brought against him by Anytus and Meletus, and he was condemned to drink hemlock. Socrates served with credit at the battle of Delium, 424 B.C. An oracle given to his disciple Chaerephon pronounced Socrates to be the wisest of men:

Socrates himself claimed to know one thing only--that he knew nothing. Lucian alludes to his favourite oaths, the dog and plane-tree. For the (Platonic) theory of Ideas, and the community of women, see PLATO.

SOLI. A city on the coast of Cilicia, proverbial for the bad Greek spoken there.

SOLON. A famous Athenian legislator, 594 B.C. Said to have visited Croesus of Lydia.

SOPHIST. At Athens this word denoted in particular a paid teacher of grammar, rhetoric, politics, mathematics, &c. Lucian sometimes uses it also for 'philosopher,' and perhaps sometimes in the modern sense of a quibbler.

SOPHRONISCUS. Father of Socrates.

SPARTANS. Among the means adopted to train the youths in fortitude were competitive scourgings at the altar of Artemis Orthia, which must be endured without sign of distress.

STESICHŎRUS. Lyric poet of Himera, 612 B.C. Lost his sight after lampooning Helen, and only recovered it by composing a retractation, 'palinode.'

STHENEBOEA. Another name for Antea; see BELLEROPHON.

STOICS School of philosophy, so called from the Stoa Poecile, or Painted Porch, at Athens, in which Zeno their founder taught. Zeno, Cleanthes, Chrysippus, were the first three heads, starting 310 B.C. Stoicism was a great influence among the Romans, as with the emperor M. Aurelius. Its aim was purely practical, to make man independent of his surroundings. The 'wise man,' who formed his views on pure reason, would recognize that virtue or duty was the only end, and that pleasure and pain, wealth, power, and everything else that did not depend on his own choice, were 'things indifferent.' He would ultimately attain to 'apathy,' and be completely unmoved by the ordinary objects of desire or aversion, being, in whatever external condition, the 'only king,' the 'only happy.' They paid great attention to logic, much reasoning being necessary to establish these paradoxes, whence their reputation for verbal quibbles, and their elaborate technical terms for the relations between sensation and the mental processes. Later Stoics relaxed the severity of the 'indifference ' doctrine by dividing *indifferentia* into *praeposita* and *rejecta*; e. g. health was to be preferred to sickness, though virtue was consistent with either. This would open the door to the preference of wealth, and account for Lucian's sneer at Stoic usurers. The Stoic physics was a materialistic pantheism.

STRATONICE. *See* ANTIOCHUS.

STYX. 'Loathing,' one of the infernal rivers. The oath by it was the only one that could bind the Immortals.

TAENĂRUM. Southern point of Greece, supposed way from earth to Hades.

TALENT. Sum of money, about £250.

TALOS (1). Nephew of Daedalus, famous artificer, worshipped as a hero at Athens.

TALOS (2). A brazen man made by Hephaestus, given to Minos, and employed as a sentinel to walk round Crete thrice daily.

TANĂGRA. Town in Boeotia, famous for a breed of fighting cocks.

TELLUS. See *Charon* (10).

TEREUS. Son of Ares and king of Thrace, committed bigamy with Procne and Philomela, daughters of Pandion. The two wives were changed at their own request to nightingale and swallow, and Tereus became a hoopoe.

TEUCER. Step-brother of Ajax Telamonius, and best archer among the Greeks at Troy.

THAÏS. A famous Athenian courtesan, accompanied Alexander.

THAMȲRIS. Thracian bard, blinded by the Muses for presuming to challenge them.

THEANO (1). Wife of Antenor and priestess of Athene at Troy.

THEANO (2). Female philosopher of Pythagoras's school, perhaps his wife

THEBE. A daughter of Prometheus, from whom Thebes had its name.

THEMISTOCLES. Saviour of Greece in the Persian war, 480-478 B.C.; he convinced the Athenians that the famous oracle meant by 'wooden walls,' and 'divine Salamis,' to promise a naval victory there if they trusted to their fleet.

THEOPHRASTUS. Head of the Peripatetic school after Aristotle.

THEOPOMPUS. Of Chios, historian, of the fourth century B.C.

THERICLES. A Corinthian potter, of uncertain date.

THERSĪTES. A Greek at Troy, deformed, impudent, and a demagogue.

THESEUS. Son of Aegeus, king of Athens. Destroyed Sciron, Pityocamptes, Cercyon, and other evil-doers. Slew the Minotaur (*see* Minos II) in the Cretan Labyrinth, and escaped thence by means of the clue given to him by Minos's daughter Ariadne, of whom he was enamoured, but whom he afterwards deserted in Naxos, where she was found and married by Dionysus. Made an expedition against the Amazons, and carried off their queen Antiope, whose sister Hippolyta afterwards invaded Attica, but was repelled by Theseus. By Antiope he had a son Hippolytus, with whom his second wife Phaedra fell in love. Assisted by his friend Pirithoüs, Theseus carried off Helen from Sparta, and kept her at Aphidnae.

THESMOPHORIA. Festival of Demeter at Athens.

THĔTIS. Mother of Achilles.

THYESTES. Son of Pelops and brother of Atreus. The latter, having been wronged by him, killed and served up to him his own sons.

THYRSUS. A wand of the narthex plant, carried by the bacchantes, with its head wreathed in vine or ivy, which concealed a steel point.

TIBIUS. Stock name for a slave.

TIMON. The Misanthrope, lived during the Peloponnesian war.

TIRĔSIAS. A Theban seer; was changed into a girl as the result of striking two serpents. Seven years later, he recovered his sex in the same way. Asked by Zeus and Hera to decide their dispute which sex was constituted with stronger passions, said, the woman. Hera, offended, blinded him; Zeus consoled him with the gift of prophecy. *See* ODYSSEUS also.

TITANS. The dynasty previous to that of the Olympian Gods, till Zeus deposed Cronus, and imprisoned him and the other children of Uranus and Ge in Tartarus.

TITHONUS. The husband of Eos (Aurora), who gave him immortality, but not immortal youth, whence the use of his name for a withered old man.

TITORMUS. An Aetolian shepherd of gigantic strength.

TITYUS. A giant punished by vultures in Hades for violence offered to Artemis.

TRIBE. *See* DEME.

TRIPTOLEMUS. Favourite of Demeter, who gave him a winged chariot and seeds of wheat, which he scattered as he drove over the earth.

TRITON. A Sea-God, son of Posidon and Amphitrite.

TRITONIA. A name for Athene, of doubtful explanation.

TROPHONIUS. A mortal worshipped as a hero after death. His oracle was consulted in a cave in Boeotia.

TYRO. For her story see *Dialogues of the Sea-Gods*, xiii. Lucian plays on the name elsewhere (*tyrus*, cheese).

URANUS. *See* CRONUS and GE.

VOLOGĔSUS III. *See* PARTHIANS

XENOCRATES. Distinguished philosopher of the Academy, friend of Plato and Aristotle.

XERXES. King of Persia, 485-465 B.C. Invader of Greece, 480 B.C. His bridge over the Hellespont and canal past Mount Athos were proverbially foolish exercises of power.

ZAMOLXIS. A Thracian who, having been a slave of Pythagoras in Samos, learned his doctrines, and communicated them to the Thracians after his escape. He was deified in Thrace after death.

ZENO. *See* STOICS.

ZENODOTUS. *See* HOMER.

ZEUS. Son of Cronus, and of Rhea, who saved him at birth in the manner described under CRONUS. With the help of the Cyclopes, who gave him the thunderbolt, and of the Giants, he overthrew Cronus and the other Titans, imprisoned them in Tartarus, and established himself as king of the Gods. The Giants afterwards revolted, but were crushed with the assistance of Hera. Zeus now became the father of Persephone by Demeter, of the Muses by Mnemosyne, of Apollo and Artemis by Leto, of Hebe, Ares, and Ilithyia by Hera, and of Athene, who was born from his head. He was the lover also of the mortals, Danae, Semele, Europa, Io, and many others, in various disguises. On one occasion Posidon, Hera, and Athene conspired against him, but were frustrated by Thetis and Briareus. Zeus in gratitude, at the request of Thetis, punished the Greeks for their ill-treatment of Achilles by persuading Agamemnon with a lying dream to make a premature attack upon Troy. His superiority to the other Gods is expressed in the boast alluded to in *Dialogues of the Gods*, xxi. Lucian also refers to the Cretan story, according to which Zeus lay buried in that island. His usual attributes are the sceptre, the eagle, and the thunderbolt. The famous statue of Zeus at Olympia was by Phidias. In Egypt he was identified with Ammon.

ZEUXIS. Celebrated painter of Heraclea, 424-400 B.C.

ZOÏLUS. *See* HOMER.

ZOPȲRUS. A Persian who mutilated himself horribly to gain entrance to Babylon and betray it to Darius.